PSYCHOLOGY IN ACTION
Basic Readings

PSYCHOLOGY IN ACTION

Basic Readings

Edited by

FRED McKINNEY

Professor of Psychology
University of Missouri

The Macmillan Company, New York
Collier-Macmillan Limited, London

Second Printing, 1967

Library of Congress catalog card number: 67–10479

THE MACMILLAN COMPANY,
NEW YORK
COLLIER-MACMILLAN CANADA, LTD.,
TORONTO, ONTARIO

PRINTED IN THE UNITED STATES OF AMERICA

PREFACE

Every instructor of the introductory course in psychology knows that many students are interested in the application of psychological fact and method to their milieu—the student world of jobs, marriage, politics, war, sports. But frequently this interest is received with conscious estrangement by instructors whose hope it is to entice the better student into more intensive and direct contact with the world of psychological theory and methodology. How to bring about a *rapprochement?*

In assembling these selections, it has been my goal to provide demonstrations and proofs that the psychologists' endeavors in the applied fields relate very closely to the considerations and concerns of students. The assumption has been made that students will glean from textbooks basic psychological knowledge. These articles can highlight and extend the introduction to psychology by showing how the psychologist uses essential fact and methodology to deal realistically with a remarkable and rich variety of problems common to the interests of both the student and the instructor.

The origins of these selections are varied, reaching from standard journal sources to popular publications. Articles are evenly distributed over the traditional survey of beginning contemporary psychology. Where complex passages have seemed irrelevant to student understanding and appreciation, they have been excised or footnoted.

Multiple suggestions for use of the book for brief reports or discussions, as well as a list of concepts covered to aid in a review of some of the basic ideas presented, are included. References to other research and writing that appear in the selected papers have been retained, for the most part, to increase the potential utility of the volume. These references appear in alphabetical order at the back of the book.

While I suspect that some of my views of psychology are readily apparent, I have not attempted primarily to support my favorite ideas, to solve or simplify any complexities of the subject itself, or to illustrate any single theoretical bias. I have departed from the prevailing convention for readings of this sort by favoring readability and briefer selections—many of which are excerpts from books, further lending a broader perspective to the collection.

Various important characteristics of each article should be apparent to the reader, for they are the germ and, I hope, the fruit of this volume. Beyond serving the function assigned to it, each article does put forth, it seems, strength and clarity and individuality. Each was chosen for its potential to evoke thought and discussion. A central criterion was, of course, representation of the wide interests, assumptions, and methodology of recognized contributors to psychology and to its sister behavioral sources.

Gathered from among many hundreds, these source articles do, it seems to me, faithfully represent various applications of basic psychological processes. They can add a significant dimension to student understanding of the beginning course and appreciation of the work of the psychologist.

I am indebted to many of my colleagues for assistance in the selection and processing of these writings. Dr. Melvin Marx assisted me in reaching the objective of the volume. Dr. Robert Daniel contributed advice from his experience in editing the introductory readings. Dr. Wayne Anderson examined the selections and reacted to them. Dr. M. Mike Nawas assisted in the choice of the title of the book. Mr. Don Muilenberg assisted in the preparation of the bibliography, and Mrs. Norma Hurley, Miss Doyne McKinney, and Mrs. Mary Ellen Keyes were helpful in the stenographic chores. As always, my wife Margery Mulkern McKinney gave daily advice from her editorial experience.

FRED MCKINNEY
University of Missouri

TO THE STUDENT

I have collected these articles mainly with you in mind. They are in response to your questions, your observed interests, and your searches for understanding of yourself and the world of today and tomorrow. May you and your instructors find in these selections a view of the broad activity of the modern psychologist. May they, in addition, stimulate thought about contemporary and future realistic problems with which you and your peers must cope.

The modern psychologist is empirically oriented. He bases his generalizations on responsible observations of human behavior and experience. I have, therefore, included studies from the laboratory and field studies that, we hope, will beckon you to further exploration. The studies in this collection are, however, largely concerned with practical problems.

The range of issues includes development of individual selfhood and emotional balance, personal learning and training, leadership, management and decision-making, communication, religion, creativeness, military defense and peace, and space exploration, as well as the less rational phases of man—dreams, hypnosis, neurotic self-defeating activity, psychoses, homosexuality, and alcoholism. You may observe that this source book pays more attention than your text does to subjective matters and human experience, and has a more humanistic emphasis—more difficult phenomena to study. Even though these studies arouse more human interest, they are given relatively less space in most academic texts. Though they may not be in the mainstream of psychological investigation, they are receiving more attention than previously. Since this book is primarily a supplement to a basic text, it is appropriate to include these phenomena.

You may note also that the selections are relatively brief. I have included not only writings by well-known psychologists but also selections by engaging writers, which have appeared in the current magazines and less technical journals. You may want to continue to read such readily accessible articles and think about them in the leisure time that our industrial society is making increasingly available to you. Not all selections are as simply and delightfully written as those of professional writers, but most of the selections should have meaning for *you*, the modern student, in your understanding of how the psychologist and his colleagues in related fields think and work.

After each article, there are questions and comments about the implications of the selection. Surely you will raise other questions. You may want to discuss the implications of the selections with your fellow students and your instructors in and out of class. I trust that the contents and format of this book will help reverse today's distressful tendency in college for knowledge to be imparted to students who are sitting passively in large lecture sections. I am suggesting that your instructors may find it convenient for you to divide into small groups on certain days to discuss these articles and their implications. For a further description of how this or other procedures might produce more overt reactions on your part to ideas and findings, see "Use of the Selections" at the back of the book.

Lastly, I have anticipated that you might, sometime during the course, raise questions about the entire volume, such as: What, generally, are the different authors saying? What are the general trends in man's behavior and experience? *What is man essentially?* How does the psychologist go about studying and understanding him, and how is this knowledge used? Are there some uniting trends aimed at this diversity? What are they?

And now I bid you enjoyable and enriching reading and discussion.

F. McK.

CONTENTS

Chapter I

PERSONAL LIFE

[1] MAN'S SEARCH FOR MEANING

The following excerpt is a good note on which to begin these selections. Man is a restless, striving, purposive creature, and in his self-conscious moments he attempts to find meanings for his life. Some psychologists are interested not only in a carefully scientific analysis of behavior but also in man as a personality, an individual.

There is a new trend in the thinking of some writers in psychology and related fields that has been called the *existential movement*. It is not a systematized school of thought. The writers reflecting this viewpoint differ in many particulars, but they have in common a certain manner of viewing man.

Very briefly, the existentially oriented psychologist places an emphasis on the total dynamic self-conscious individual, striving in the real world to find meanings for his life; coming to grips with his conflicts and anxieties; making concrete choices in everyday life—thereby enhancing his own values and making life more worth living.

The following excerpt gives you a glimpse of the existential posture. It shows how one looks at man if he assumes this stance. There will be other selections in this book that deal with an approach to an understanding of man which is antithetical to this one—more atomistic, analytical, and abstract.

Gordon W. Allport is impressed with the existential movement in behavioral science. He introduces the small volume *Man's Search for Meaning*, written by a psychiatrist who first called his book "From Death-Camp to Existentialism." First we see Allport's reaction to Frankl's experiences in a concentration camp and his system of psychotherapy. Then we dip into a part of this gripping book to observe how Frankl helped his fellow prisoners in the concentration camp during "a very low mood." Finally, we look into some of Frankl's basic concepts of logotherapy, his means of assisting a person to find meaning in his life.

Viktor E. Frankl

PREFACE (BY GORDON W. ALLPORT)

Dr. Frankl, author-psychiatrist, sometimes asks his patients who suffer from a multitude of torments great and small, "Why do you not commit suicide?" From their answers he can often find the guideline for his psychotherapy: in one life there is love for one's children to tie to; in another life, a talent to be used; in a third, perhaps only lingering memories worth preserving. To weave these slender threads of a broken life into a firm pattern of meaning and responsibility is the object and challenge of *logotherapy*, which is Dr. Frankl's own version of modern *existential analysis*.

In this book, Dr. Frankl explains the experience which led to the discovery of logotherapy. As a long-time prisoner in bestial concentration camps he found himself stripped to naked existence. His father, mother, brother, and his wife died in camps or were sent to the gas ovens, so that, excepting for his sister, his entire family perished in these camps. How could he—every possession lost, every value destroyed, suffering from hunger, cold and brutality, hourly expecting extermination—how could he find life worth preserving? A psychiatrist who personally has faced such extremity is a psychiatrist worth listening to. He, if anyone, should be able to view our human condition wisely and with compassion. Dr. Frankl's words have a profoundly honest ring, for they rest on experiences too deep for deception. What he has to say gains in prestige because of his present position on the Medical Faculty of the University of Vienna and because of the renown of the logotherapy clinics that today are springing up in many lands, patterned on his own famous Neurological Poliklinik in Vienna.

One cannot help but compare Viktor Frankl's approach to theory and therapy with the work of his predecessor, Sigmund Freud. Both physicians concern themselves primarily with the nature and cure of neuroses. Freud finds the root of these distressing disorders in the anxiety caused by conflicting and unconscious motives. Frankl distinguishes several forms of neurosis, and traces some of them (the noögenic neuroses) to the failure of the sufferer to *find meaning and a sense of responsibility in his existence.** Freud stresses frustration in the sexual life; Frankl, frustration in the *will-to-meaning*. In Europe today there is a marked turning away from Freud and a widespread embracing of existential analysis, which takes several related forms—the school of logotherapy being one. It is characteristic of Frankl's tolerant outlook that he does not repudiate Freud, but builds gladly on his contributions; nor does he quarrel with other forms of existential therapy, but welcomes kinship with them.

The present narrative, brief though it is, is artfully constructed and gripping. On two occasions I have read it through at a single sitting, unable to break away from its spell. Somewhere beyond the midpoint of the story Dr. Frankl introduces his own philosophy of logotherapy. He introduces it so gently into the continuing narrative that only after finishing the book does the reader realize that here is an essay of profound depth, and not just one more brutal tale of concentration camps.

From this autobiographical fragment the reader learns much. He learns what a human being does when he suddenly realizes he has "nothing to lose except his so ridiculously naked life." Frankl's description of the mixed flow of emotion and apathy is arresting. First to the rescue comes a cold detached curiosity concerning one's fate. Swiftly, too, come strategies to preserve the remnants of one's life, though the chances of surviving are slight. Hunger, humiliation, fear, and deep anger at injustice are rendered tolerable by closely guarded images of beloved persons, by religion, by a grim sense of humor, and even by glimpses of the healing beauties of nature—a tree or a sunset.

But these moments of comfort do not establish the will to live unless they help the prisoner make *larger sense out of his apparently senseless suffering.** It is here that we encounter the central theme of existentialism: *to live is to suffer, to survive is to find meaning in the suffering.** If there is a purpose in life at all, there must be a purpose in suffering and in dying. But no man can tell another what this purpose is. Each must find out for himself, and must accept the responsibility that his answer prescribes. If he succeeds, he will continue to grow in spite of all indignities. Frankl is fond of quoting Nietzsche, "He who has a *why* to live can bear with almost any *how*."

In the concentration camp, every circumstance conspires to make the prisoner lose his hold. All the familiar goals in life are snatched away. What alone remains is "the last of human freedoms"—the ability to "choose one's attitude in a given set of circumstances." This ultimate freedom, recognized by the ancient Stoics as well as by modern existentialists, takes on vivid significance in Frankl's story. The prisoners were only average men, but some, at least, by choosing to be "worthy of their suffering" proved man's capacity to rise above his outward fate.

As a psychotherapist, the author, of course, wants to know how men can

* Editor's italics.

be helped to achieve this distinctively human capacity. How can one awaken in a patient the feeling that he is responsible to life for something, however grim his circumstances may be? Frankl gives us a moving account of one collective therapeutic session he held with his fellow prisoners.

EXPERIENCES IN A CONCENTRATION CAMP

I remember an incident when there was occasion for psycho-therapeutic work on the inmates of a whole hut, due to an intensification of their receptiveness because of a certain external situation.

It had been a bad day. On parade, an announcement had been made about the many actions that would, from then on, be regarded as sabotage and therefore punishable by immediate death by hanging. Among these were crimes such as cutting small strips from our old blankets (in order to impro-vise ankle supports) and very minor "thefts." A few days previously a semi-starved prisoner had broken into the potato store to steal a few pounds of potatoes. The theft had been discovered and some prisoners had recognized the "burglar." When the camp authorities heard about it they ordered that the guilty man be given up to them or the whole camp would starve for a day. Naturally the 2,500 men preferred to fast.

On the evening of this day of fasting, we lay in our earthen huts—in a very low mood. Very little was said and every word sounded irritable. Then, to make matters even worse, the light went out. Tempers reached their low-est ebb. But our senior block warden was a wise man. He improvised a little talk about all that was on our minds at that moment. He talked about the many comrades who had died in the last few days, either of sickness or of suicide. But he also mentioned what may have been the real reason for their deaths: giving up hope. He maintained that there should be some way of preventing possible future victims from reaching this extreme state. And it was to me that the warden pointed to give this advice.

God knows, I was not in the mood to give psychological explanations or to preach any sermons—to offer my comrades a kind of medical care of their souls. I was cold and hungry, irritable and tired, but I had to make the effort and use this unique opportunity. Encouragement was now more necessary than ever.

So I began by mentioning the most trivial of comforts first. I said that even in this Europe in the sixth winter of the Second World War, our situation was not the most terrible we could think of. I said that each of us had to ask himself what irreplaceable losses he had suffered up to then. I speculated that for most of them these losses had really been few. Whoever was still alive had reason for hope. Health, family, happiness, professional abilities, fortune, position in society—all these were things that could be achieved again or restored. After all, we still had all our bones intact. Whatever we had gone through could still be an asset to us in the future. And I quoted from Nietzsche: *"Was mich nicht umbringt, macht mich stärker."* (That which does not kill me, makes me stronger.)

Then I spoke about the future. I said that to the impartial the future must seem hopeless. I agreed that each of us could guess for himself how small were his chances of survival. I told them that although there was still no typhus epidemic in the camp, I estimated my own chances at about one in twenty. But I also told them that, in spite of this, I had no intention of losing hope and giving up. For no man knew what the future would bring, much less the next hour. Even if we could not expect any sensational military events in the next few days, who knew better than we, with our experience of camps, how great chances sometimes opened up, quite suddenly, at least for the individual. For instance, one might be attached unexpectedly to a special group with exceptionally good working conditions—for this was the kind of thing which constituted the "luck" of the prisoner.

But I did not only talk of the future and the veil which was drawn over it. I also mentioned the past; all its joys, and how its light shone even in the present darkness. Again I quoted a poet—to avoid sounding like a preacher myself—who had written, *"Was Du erlebt, kann keine Macht der Welt Dir rauben."* (What you have experienced, no power on earth can take from you.) Not only our experiences, but all we have done, whatever great thoughts we may have had, and all we have suffered, all this is not lost, though it is past; we have brought it into being. Having been is also a kind of being, and perhaps the surest kind.

Then I spoke of the many opportunities of giving life a meaning. I told my comrades (who lay motionless, although occasionally a sigh could be heard) that human life, under any circumstances, never ceases to have a meaning, and that this infinite meaning of life includes suffering and dying, privation and death. I asked the poor creatures who listened to me attentively in the darkness of the hut to face up to the seriousness of our position. They must not lose hope but should keep their courage in the certainty that the hopelessness of our struggle did not detract from its dignity and its meaning. I said that someone looks down on each of us in difficult hours—a friend, a wife, somebody alive or dead, or a God—and he would not expect us to disappoint him. He would hope to find us suffering proudly—not miserably—knowing how to die.

And finally I spoke of our sacrifice, which had meaning in every case. It was in the nature of this sacrifice that it should appear to be pointless in the normal world, the world of material success. But in reality our sacrifice did have a meaning. Those of us who had any religious faith, I said frankly, could understand without difficulty. I told them of a comrade who on his arrival in camp had tried to make a pact with Heaven that his suffering and death should save the human being he loved from a painful end. For this man, suf-

fering and death were meaningful; his was a sacrifice of the deepest significance. He did not want to die for nothing. None of us wanted that.

The purpose of my words was to find a full meaning in our life, then and
there, in that hut and in that practically hopeless situation. I saw that my
efforts had been successful. When the electric bulb flared up again, I saw
the miserable figures of my friends limping toward me to thank me with
tears in their eyes. But I have to confess here that only too rarely had I the
inner strength to make contact with my companions in suffering and that I
must have missed many opportunities for doing so.

THE ESSENCE OF EXISTENCE

This emphasis on responsibleness is reflected in the categorical imperative
of logotherapy, which is: "So live as if you were living already for the second
time and as if you had acted the first time as wrongly as you are about to act
now!" It seems to me that there is nothing that would stimulate a man's
sense of responsibleness more than this maxim, which invites him to imagine
first that the present is past and, second, that the past may yet be changed
and amended. Such a precept confronts him with life's *finiteness* as well as
the *finality* of what he makes out of both his life and himself.

Logotherapy tries to make the patient fully aware of his own responsibleness; therefore it must leave to him the option for what, to what, or to whom
he understands himself to be responsible. That is why a logotherapist is the
least tempted of all psychotherapists to impose value judgments on the patient, for he will never permit the patient to pass on to the doctor the responsibility of judging.

It is, therefore, up to the patient to decide whether he should interpret
his life task as being responsible to society or to his own conscience. The majority, however, consider themselves accountable before God; they represent
those who do not interpret their own lives merely in terms of a task assigned
to them but also in terms of the taskmaster who has assigned it to them.

Logotherapy is neither teaching nor preaching. It is as far removed from
logical reasoning as it is from moral exhortation. To put it figuratively, the
role played by a logotherapist is rather that of an eye specialist than that of
a painter. A painter tries to convey to us a picture of the world as he sees it;
an ophthalmologist tries to enable us to see the world as it really is. The
logotherapist's role consists in widening and broadening the visual field of the
patient so that the whole spectrum of meaning and values becomes conscious
and visible to him. Logotherapy does not need to impose any judgments on
the patient, for, actually, truth imposes itself and needs no intervention.

By declaring that man is a responsible creature and must actualize the
potential meaning of his life, I wish to stress that the true meaning of life is
to be found in the world rather than within man or his own *psyche*, as though
it were a closed system. By the same token, the real aim of human existence

cannot be found in what is called self-actualization.* Human existence is essentially self-transcendence rather than self-actualization. Self-actualization is not a possible aim at all, for the simple reason that the more a man would strive for it, the more he would miss it. For only to the extent to which man commits himself to the fulfillment of his life's meaning, to this extent he also actualizes himself. In other words, self-actualization cannot be attained if it is made an end in itself, but only as a side effect of self-transcendence.

The world must not be regarded as a mere expression of one's self. Nor must the world be considered as a mere instrument, or as a means to the end of one's self-actualization. In both cases, the world view, or the *Weltanschauung*, turns into a *Weltentwertung*, i.e., a depreciation of the world.

Thus far we have shown that the meaning of life always changes, but that it never ceases to be. According to logotherapy, we can discover this meaning in life in three different ways: (1) by doing a deed; (2) by experiencing a value; and (3) by suffering. The first, the way of achievement or accomplishment, is quite obvious. The second and third need further elaboration.

The second way of finding a meaning in life is by experiencing something, such as a work of nature or culture; and also by experiencing someone, i.e., by love.

THE MEANING OF LOVE

Love is the only way to grasp another human being in the innermost core of his personality. No one can become fully aware of the very essence of another human being unless he loves him. By the spiritual act of love he is enabled to see the essential traits and features in the beloved person; and even more, he sees that which is potential in him, that which is not yet actualized but yet ought to be actualized. Furthermore, by his love, the loving person enables the beloved person to actualize these potentialities. By making him aware of what he can be and of what he should become, he makes these potentialities come true.

In logotherapy, love is not interpreted as a mere epiphenomenon [1] of sexual drives and instincts in the sense of a so-called sublimation. Love is as primary a phenomenon as sex. Normally, sex is a mode of expression for love. Sex is justified, even sanctified, as soon as, but only as long as, it is a vehicle of love. Thus love is not understood as a mere side effect of sex but sex as a way of expressing the experience of that ultimate togetherness that is called love.

A third way to find a meaning in life is by suffering.

---

* *Self-actualization:* refers to the need to become what one is capable of becoming.—Ed.
[1] A phenomenon that occurs as the result of a primary phenomenon.

IMPLICATIONS

What do the ideas expressed in this selection mean to you? Do these lines prompt you to express purpose and meaning in your life? If not, how have you best found your purposes?

One approach to finding the meaning of life is to ask oneself this question: "What would I be willing to die for?" What is your answer?

Which of these suggestions seems most feasible in finding greater life meaning: (1) doing a deed; (2) experiencing a value (including experiencing someone); (3) suffering?

Another approach we shall leave until later: How does Frankl's kind of directive therapy differ from the other attempts to help emotionally disturbed persons (which we discuss under mental health in Chapter X)?

REFERENCES

You can find further discussion of the existential movement in psychology in May (1961) and Maslow (1962). Allport has written a book, *Becoming* (1955), that may interest you.

[2] LAUGHTER: ITS FUNCTIONS

It has been said that he who laughs, lasts! Laughter is a a form of human behavior that has received written comment since as early as Sophocles in 450 B.C. In the United States today, one who can make another laugh is cherished and, moreover, handsomely rewarded if he makes jest his vocation. In fact, the nationally known comedians earn some of the highest personal incomes.

The recorded quotations on laughter from early times vary in their evaluation of this form of behavior. In Ecclesiastes we read, "A fool lifteth up his voice with laughter, and a wise man doth scarcely smile a little." This may be contrasted with Martial, who wrote in his epigrams in the year A.D. 86, "If you are wise, laugh." Literature is sprinkled with references to human laughter. We find it in folk sayings, in proverbs, in Shakespeare's plays, and in the writings of philosophers.

Now a modern psychologist appears on the scene to write from the studies, placing laughter in a more biological context. It has not yet been systematically subjected to experiment, but using the knowledge we do have, our contributor, Brian Foss of the University of London, wrote an interesting popular essay, pointing out that in fifty years we may have controlled experiments to give us more hard facts. What are the functions of laughter in a psychological context?

Brian Foss

Reprinted from Brian Foss, "The Functions of Laughter," *New Scientist*, No. 242, Vol. 11 (London: New Scientist, 1961), pp. 20–22, by permission of the author.

Laughter has many biological functions—for example, as an expression of joy in social situations, as an aggressive weapon in competitive situations, as a relief of tension. In convulsive laughter it appears that energy radiates from a "laughing center" in the brain to other parts of the nervous system.

Darwin thought that laughter was of no great biological use. He considered that laughing and crying were the results of a single mechanism working in opposite directions. In one direction the mechanism produced crying, which Darwin thought to be defensive and useful, and which justified the existence of the mechanism; but the laughter which resulted from its working in the opposite direction was thought to be a by-product of little biological importance. New ways of thinking, largely inspired by Darwin, suggest that he was wrong. Laughing has many important functions and many causes.

An American, P. T. Young, has made a list of occasions for laughter as recorded by American undergraduates. The records were made at the end of the day and are therefore of the more memorable occasions. The following are examples:

A pillow fight in the dormitory
A girl friend tore her dress
I fell during skating
A dog came in during a lecture
A mispronounced word in rhetoric class
Being teased about my corpulence
Lizzie trying to do a fairy dance

> My opponents in a bridge game bidding four spades when I held two aces
>   and the king, jack and five of spades
> An article by a priest on the sex life of H. G. Wells

The most commonly recalled occasions were ordinary conversations, jokes, puns, and wisecracks; then came humorous situations, incidents, actions, or antics of people. In 98 per cent of cases, laughter occurred in a social setting. In fact, it is very rare for a person to laugh if he knows he is entirely out of earshot. This applies even to laughing while reading, and it suggests that one of the more important functions of laughter is communication. The varieties of facial expression and noise produced by one person in laughter can constitute a language. There is no reason why the laugher need be aware of what he is communicating; nor need the listener and viewer be aware that he is interpreting (and sometimes misinterpreting) the signals and often acting on them. Some of this language can be easily classified, and fits with a biological view of behavior. The following are some of the easier examples.

1. The laugh that means "I'm happy." The expectation is that it will be answered by a similar laugh, or at least a smile, the absence of which can be very chilling.

2. The laugh, produced in a group of people, which means "I'm *persona grata* with this group. I'm in." This laugh makes for group cohesion, but it is also used as a ploy in gamesmanship. It is very "one up" to be seen in a group laughing heartily with the VIP of the party.

3. The laugh which is used to get attention. This is often obvious, especially in its gauche form (when it clearly derives from example 1), but it can be subtle. There is an allied laugh which means "I'm listening (still)."

4. A common use of spoken language is as a prod to force someone into reacting. Many conventional phrases (or just "hullo!") are used in this way. One function seems to be to sound the other person's attitude—for instance, to find out if "he's on my side." Laughs and smiles are used a great deal like this, often between complete strangers.

5. A rather unpleasant laugh is the "I'm all right, Jack" laugh. It is one example of competitive behavior, a jockeying for position, which is very obvious in children, and which is analogous to "dominance fighting" in animals.

If we look at these examples biologically, three basic principles can be seen.

1. Laughing may occur as an expression of joy. It appears in babies at about twenty weeks of age, and it may be instinctive. This laugh tends to make bystanders behave pleasantly to the child, and the child will therefore tend to repeat it. In psychological jargon, the laugh is reinforced and the probability of its occurrence increases as a result.

2. Laughing makes for group cohesion through homogeneity of feeling within the group. It is likely that this increases the viability of groups. Animal ethologists have pointed out that, in social animals, evolution has often favored characteristics which are important for homogeneous action of the group as a whole. For instance, many birds display their tail feathers at the approach of danger and this results in the whole flock taking to flight. Such "social releasers" increase the survival chances of the group. Also, when they involve movements or sounds, many members of the group may start producing them. There is a contagion analogous to that found when laughter spreads in a group of people. Nevertheless it seems far-fetched to suppose that this contagious laughter exists because it increases the probability of human survival. A child's first laughs are reinforced *only* in a social situation, so that when he grows up he will be *conditioned* to laughing in social situations.

3. Laughing can be used as a weapon in competitive situations. Competition is so common in the animal kingdom that one might expect any means of human communication to be used competitively. Animals achieve dominance by actual fighting, but also by less destructive methods such as threatening displays, loud noises, and birdsong. Such behavior has two main functions: the selecting and keeping of a mate and the defense of territories. The biological value of dominance fighting could be that the rearing of young is carried out more efficiently as a result; but it also has the effect that the more dominant animals are the more likely to propagate, and they are usually the largest and strongest. Hence the species benefits in the long run. Hierarchies emerge as the result of such fighting, and they are very clear in the monkey and ape groups, where there is usually a single male overlord. Human societies also have their hierarchies, but they are established through more subtle means than fighting, threatening or shouting (except perhaps in some juvenile gangs). Nevertheless there is a strong element of aggression in the methods used by man to achieve status, and this is true of laughing when it is used in this particular way.

There remain several kinds of laughter in which it is difficult to see a biological function. For example—laughing after a period of tension; laughing at jokes, antics, etc.; laughing at deformities and stuttering (frowned on, but common in children); laughing caused by tickling. Animal behavior can again throw light on the first of these.

When two herring gulls meet at the boundary of their territories, the tendencies to fight and to flee may be in balance, and the result is a conflict between these opposing tendencies. On these occasions gulls often indulge in what appears to be quite irrelevant behavior: they peck at bits of grass, twig, etc., and throw them sideways. This looks like part of their nest-building behavior appearing out of context and is known as "displacement activity." The ethologists have suggested that this is a "sparking over" of energy in the nervous system as a result of the blocking of the usual outlets. This sort of thing can be seen at a reflex level in humans when overstimulation occurs. For instance, a person coming into bright sunlight may sneeze; or if the semicircular canals of the inner ear are overstimulated through bodily motion, there may be a "sparking over" of energy to the nearby center in the brain which initiates vomiting, and travel sickness is the result.

Everyday observations suggest that laughter may result from a similar mechanism. Subjectively it feels as if tension builds up and is relieved by laughing. This can happen after the natural response to a situation has been inhibited (usually so that behavior will conform to what the group expects of one). If people have been frightened but have suppressed their overt reactions of fear, they will laugh readily when an opportunity occurs. Many jokes and comic situations rely on the building up of tension in a similar way.

Crying is the natural reaction of a small child who has fallen down. (Crying in some form is the instinctive reaction of many diverse animals in situations where it is necessary to attract the parent.) As the child gets older the attitude of parents and other children is that this is a "cry baby" reaction, and the child learns to suppress the crying, and gradually comes to relieve the pent-up tension by laughing instead. (Perhaps this transition is "easy" for the nervous system, since the two conditions have much in common, especially the diaphragm movements and the tears.) There are many situations in which society exerts pressure on the child to inhibit unpleasant emotional responses, and in most cases laughing may occur as a substitute. This is true for reactions to anything sudden and startling, to sinister objects, and for occasions when aggression or fleeing would be natural responses.

In adults, this transition period is long forgotten, but the substitute responses remain. We laugh, especially in company, at the mildly shocking, startling, sinister, frightening, aggression-provoking. Indeed, occasions for mirth can be found in any situations in which society has enforced an inhibition of primitive responses. This seems the most plausible explanation for the existence of sex and lavatory jokes, many of which overdetermine the laughter in that they involve a building up of tension, an unexpectedness of *dénouement*, and a use of socially disapproved subjects.

One of the puzzling things is that people laugh not only when mishaps occur to themselves but to others. One explanation of this is that the laugher "identifies" himself with the victim. But there is another possibility. Laughter is used a great deal as a weapon against people who do not conform to one's own group. Teen-agers laugh at "oldies"; old people laugh at the antics of jive; laymen laugh at the jargon of scientists. Christopher Fry's heroine, accused by the majority group of being a witch, sought a world of more reasonable people—"I have come to have the protection of your laughter." Laughter functions to withstand outside onslaughts on a group, and to preserve its mores. If a child fails to conform to his gang, he will be laughed at. If he fails to conform to that other gang, the adult world of his own society, he will also be laughed at. But once he has become a conformist, he will suppress his nonconformist behavior and replace it by laughter at those who are still outside. The American undergraduate who laughed at "a mispronounced word in rhetoric class" was showing that he was now a conformist, and that such mishaps no longer happened to him.

Is laughing at deformity and stuttering also of this kind? Possibly it may be even more primitive. It is well known that many animals will destroy or drive out a member of their species that is injured or deformed or otherwise unusual. This behavior seems to be instinctive. It suggests that human laughing at deformity might also have an instinctive basis (and hence not be susceptible to analysis by introspection).

It is often said that tickling is a social phenomenon—that one cannot tickle oneself. In fact, many people can tickle themselves, but they cannot so easily make themselves laugh by doing this. The laughter again seems to depend on a social situation. Tickling would normally be the result of a small live object on the skin, a potentially noxious body, and the natural response is avoidance. Horses are well endowed with an ability to twitch a small area of skin to ward off insects. We cannot do this and have to take grosser avoiding action. When tickling is done by another human being, avoidance is usually made difficult, and tension builds up so that intense body movements, and perhaps laughter, may follow. This response to such a small stimulus seems excessive, and some psychologists would have it that tickling originally has a quasi-sexual significance, the natural responses to which have become inhibited. Hence the great release of energy would result from the displacing of instinctive urges. It is certainly puzzling that a baby will smile, laugh, and gurgle when being tickled, in a way that seems completely devoid of the underlying displeasure of the adult's response.

Why is it that laughter has come to have so many functions? It may be because it is one of the more efficient ways of communicating. It is the most accurately recognized of all facial expressions. This is contrary to the general rule that the more primitive emotional expressions are the easiest to recognize, since laughing is generally judged to be a late development in evolution (though probably not as recent as smiling). Also contrary to the general rule is that anger is one of the most difficult to recognize. The most important clue in discriminating facial expressions is the conformation of the mouth, and the human face has evolved in such a way that it can express laughing and smiling in an exaggerated form, largely because of hairlessness and the mobility of the lips. In anger, the corners of the lips are raised so as to show the canine teeth, but this has become rather ineffective in man because of his small canines. Also a laugh can be heard as well as seen, and both sound and appearance can be modulated in a variety of ways, so making it possible to convey a wealth of information.

What happens in the brain during laughing? It was explained that travel sickness is thought to be due to a spread of excitation to the "vomiting center," a locus in the brain which, when stimulated, results in vomiting. Is there a similar center for laughing? The neurologist Sir Henry Head thought that there might be one in the thalamus, since lesions in this area often result in pathological laughter—laughter with no obvious cause and no appropriate feeling; but it is now known that lesions in many parts of the nervous system may have this result. However, it is true that electrical stimulation of part of the thalamus will produce laughing responses, at least in the chimpanzee.

Laughing in excess is usually accompanied by many other responses—gross body movements, foot stamping, hand clapping, and even convulsions. It is as though there were a building up of energy which radiates to the parts of the nervous system which control these movements. Professor D. O. Hebb, of McGill University, believes that the irradiation occurs in certain networks in the nervous system, which have come to be called "arousal systems," since they have the functions of increasing both sensations and movements, usually in a gross fashion, but sometimes favoring certain patterns of movement. Hebb suggests that one of these patterns might be the excessive movements seen in hearty laughter.

Any account of laughter cannot easily be put to the test. It would require experiments in which humans were submitted to exactly controlled conditions from birth onward—a quite impracticable and unethical requirement. In these circumstances it is impossible to be certain of any one explanation. It is necessary to argue largely by analogy, trying to produce an account which is not incompatible with scientific beliefs of the moment. An account in fifty years' time is likely to be very different.

IMPLICATIONS

What meanings of laughter that are mentioned in the selection have you noticed in your experience? Does laughter have any other meanings to you? What hypothesis might be advanced about the personality organization of the individual who rarely laughs? How do you evaluate now the humorous remark, "I am laughing to keep from crying"? What are some reasons why people do not laugh at a remark that is intended to be funny?

REFERENCES

The author refers to a study of laughter by Young (1937). See also Leuba (1941).

[3] A SENSE OF HUMOR

Rare is the individual who will confess that he lacks a sense of humor, yet relatively little has been written about this trait, even by psychologists. A sense of humor is closely akin to the capacity to laugh, but it is a human characteristic more subtle, more valuable, and associated with greater maturity.

This trait seems to be held universally in high esteem. Recently, humor has come to the forefront in psychological writings as the more humanistic psychologists have pointed to the neglect of the study of such human experiences and behavior as spontaneity, humor, naturalness, and courage. Moreover, some empirical studies of creativity have shown the more creative individuals to have, more often, a sense of humor.

The topic has interested the psychologist Gordon W. Allport in his attempt to answer the question: What is a mature personality? Here is Allport's brief discussion of the nature of a sense of humor and some suggestions as to where we might find it.

Gordon W. Allport

Reprinted from G. W. Allport, *Pattern and Growth in Personality* (New York: Holt, Rinehart and Winston, 1961), pp. 292–294, by permission of the publisher and the author.

HUMOR

Perhaps the most striking correlate of insight is the sense of humor. In one unpublished study where subjects rated one another on a large number of traits, the correlation between ratings on insight and humor turned out to be .88. Such a high coefficient means either that personalities with marked insight are also high in humor, or else that the raters were not able to distinguish between the two qualities. In either case the result is important.

The personality of Socrates shows the close association of the two traits. Legend tells how at a performance of Aristophanes' *Clouds* he stood up in order that the amused audience might better compare his face with the mask that was intended to ridicule him. Possessed of good insight, he was able to view the caricature in a detached way, and to aid the jest by laughing at himself.

What, then, is a sense of humor? The novelist Meredith says it is the ability to laugh at the things one loves (including, of course, oneself and all that pertains to oneself), and still to love them. The real humorist perceives behind some solemn event—himself, for instance—the contrast between pretension and performance.

The sense of humor must be distinguished sharply from the cruder sense of the comic. The latter is a common possession of almost all people, children as well as adults. What is ordinarily considered funny—on the stage, in comic strips, on TV—consists usually of absurdities, horse play, or puns. For the most part it consists in the degradation of some imagined opponent. The aggressive impulse is only slightly disguised. Aristotle, Hobbes, and many others have seen in this "sudden glory" of one's own ego the secret of all laughter. Related to aggressive wit (which derides the other fellow) is laughter at the risqué which seems due to the release of suppressions. Aggression and sex are at the basis of much that we call comic.

A young child has a keen sense of the comic, but seldom if ever laughs at himself. Even during adolescence the youth is more likely to view his failings with acute suffering than with laughter. There is evidence that people who are less intelligent, who have low aesthetic and theoretical values, prefer the comic and lack a sense of humor based on the real relationships in life. Landis & Ross (1933).

The reason why insight and humor march hand in hand is probably because at bottom they are a single phenomenon—the phenomenon of self-objectification. The man who has the most complete sense of proportion concerning his own qualities and cherished values is able to perceive their incongruities and absurdities in certain settings.

As with insight, almost everyone claims to have a rare sense of humor. The same students who evaluated their own insight in comparison with that of other people were asked to estimate their sense of humor. Ninety-four per cent replied that it was as good as or better than the average.

Stephen Leacock has observed the same conceit. In *My Discovery of England*, he writes: "A peculiar interest always attaches to humor. There is no quality of the human mind about which its possessor is more sensitive than the sense of humor. A man will freely confess that he has no ear for music, or no taste for fiction, or even no interest in religion. But I have yet to see the man who announces that he has no sense of humor. In point of fact, every man is apt to think himself possessed of an exceptional gift in this direction. . . ."

It is only fair to state that up to now psychologists have had very little success in measuring either insight or the sense of humor. We are dealing here with the subtler reaches of personality—a territory which we hope psychologists will explore with more success in the future than in the past.

IMPLICATIONS

Write out the specific questions you think Allport answered in his discussion. How many persons do you know with a sense of humor who also possess superior intelligence and aesthetic and theoretical values? How do you explain the finding that people who are more creative tend to have a better sense of humor?

Guilford takes a slightly different view than Allport. He takes note of findings by Andrews (1943)—who factorially analyzed humor into these forms: (1) derisive humor, (2) immoral humor, (3) insight humor, (4) pun humor, (5) risqué humor, and (6) incongruity humor —and suggests that when a person perceives another as having a sense of humor, he means that that person is strong in the form that he himself appreciates. This is a cautious scientific approach, and it raises a question about the existence of a unitary sense of humor. Reread the Allport excerpt and decide which of these views seems hypothetically most tenable until your further research helps you to answer this question more completely.

REFERENCES

For a discussion of humor in terms of factors, see Guilford (1959). Maslow (1950) offers a study of *self-actualizing persons* who seem to reach their potential in a balanced manner. A citation of the relationship between creativity and sense of humor can be found in Berelson and Steiner (1964). See also Andrews (1943).

[4] SEXUAL BEHAVIOR: REVIEWS OF THE KINSEY REPORTS

In early 1948, there appeared a thick volume filled with statistical tables and with what seemed to some curious purchasers, rather dull technical writing. The book *Sexual Behavior in the Human Male,* rapidly became the least-read best seller.

One reviewer of the book said that it contained more dynamite than any other scientific document since Darwin's *Origin of the Species.* Another reviewer, a distinguished psychologist, observed that "no one has ever obtained so much information from so many persons regarding the most secret phases of their sexual histories." The author's name, Kinsey, became widely known. More lines were written about the book than it contained. It elicited comment from practically all professional groups, and it was responsibly praised and criticized. Now, approximately two decades later, sex attitudes and, possibly, sex behavior in the Western world undoubtedly have been influenced by its publication.

It would be difficult to present the total findings reported in *Sexual Behavior in the Human Male* and in its companion volume, *Sexual Behavior in the Human Female,* by brief selections or even by summaries from the books themselves. Moreover, the critical reactions and evaluations of the reports are as important as the findings. Kinsey, as a scientist, was frankly interested in the relationship of various classifiable factors to *orgasm*—a somewhat restricted biological problem. However, the orgasm is the climax of a sexual adventure and experience and has wide ramifications in Western culture. It involves individual *self and social attitudes*, various ambivalent feelings, guilt, and the many responses motivated by these experiences. To give an introduction to Kinsey's revolutionary books, we are including three reviews by writers with different backgrounds who were writing for different audiences.

ABOUT ... THE HUMAN MALE

Reviewers of books like those by Alfred Kinsey and his co-workers, with so many reported findings, will differ in what impresses them. We see here the emphases of two reviewers of the same book, published in two different magazines.

Our first selection, by a physician and marriage counselor, lists the implications related to (1) the influence of early conditioning, (2) ages in relationship to frequency of sexual activity, (3) difference in sex behavior among different social levels, (4) intensity of drive and the age at which the individual becomes adolescent, (5) the moral and medical problems of premarital relations, and (6) the frequency of homosexual relationships.

Abraham Stone

Reprinted from a review by Abraham Stone, *Saturday Review* (New York: Saturday Review, 1948), pp. 17–18, by permission of the publisher and Charles Korn, Executor of Dr. Stone's Estate.

Kinsey has done for the present generation what Havelock Ellis did for the previous one. Ellis, with few valid statistical data but with deep insight and understanding, depicted the various manifestations of human sex behavior and opened man's mind to an appreciation of the varieties of human sex patterns. Kinsey and his co-workers, on the basis of a unique collection of sex histories obtained through personal interviews of some 5,000 men, have given us in the present volume a factual and provocative study of male sex behavior which will enrich human knowledge and which is bound to influence markedly man's thinking and attitudes.

The main theme of the Kinsey book is a study of the frequency of male sex experiences, and of the types of "sexual outlets" which lead to orgasm. These two manifestations are analyzed in great, often in minute, detail in accordance with several biological and social factors. They are correlated with the age of the individual, the age at which he becomes adolescent, his educational background, the occupational class to which he belongs, his rural or urban background, and the nature and strength of his religious affiliations.

The emphasis of the study is perhaps too exclusively upon the physical and mechanistic aspects of sex activity. Little attention is given to the psychological and emotional overtones of sex satisfaction—to affection and tenderness and human sentiment as influences in sex behavior. The word "love," for instance, is hardly mentioned and does not even appear in the index. But this is only the first volume and the subsequent ones will perhaps deal more fully with the more subtle aspects of human sex conduct.

At the beginning of the volume, Kinsey states that "each person who reads the report will want to make interpretations in accordance with his understanding of moral values and social significance; but that is not part of the scientific method, and indeed scientists have no special capacities for making such evaluations. Nevertheless, throughout the report, directly or indirectly, bluntly or subtly, in many ways, Kinsey does make interpretations and evaluations" of his findings. He does not, it is true, pass judgment on any form of sexual activity, but he does point out the social implications, and creates an "attitude" in his approach to these problems. . . .

The statistical data collected by Kinsey and his co-workers on the sexual behavior of the American male will be the source of a vast amount of comment, discussion, and debate. Some of the findings have been fairly well known before and will not cause much surprise to the informed reader. There are other data in the report, however, that had hitherto not been recognized that are of tremendous social significance. Many of them have a direct and immediate bearing upon the problems of sex education, marriage, and family living.

What are some of the implications of the Kinsey report?

1. Of basic importance is Kinsey's *emphasis on early conditioning* * as of paramount importance in determining the sex pattern of the individual. The attitudes engendered in childhood may determine a boy's sex pattern for life. This fact may have long been recognized by psychiatrists and child educators, but Kinsey reinforces this knowledge with impressive statistical data. This knowledge will have to filter down to the general public so that parents may re-evaluate their thinking, their attitudes, and their approach in child rearing and development.

2. Also of importance is the question of *age in relation to the frequency of sexual activity.* * A fact which had hitherto perhaps not been recognized is that maximum sexual activity occurs in the teens. Boys between sixteen and seventeen have more frequent sexual arousals leading to orgasms than they will have at any other period in their lives. With an increasing lag between the ages at which boys biologically mature and economic security is reached, there is a period of several years in the life of every boy when his sexual drive is apparently at its highest and for which no socially sanctioned outlet has yet been provided. The boy seeks his outlet in various fashions, in masturbation, in petting, in hetero- or homosexual relations—but all of these outlets still have the stamp of social disapproval and are therefore a source of much anxiety and conflict to the individual. What can be and should be done to alleviate the physical and psychological harm thus induced is a problem which the educator, social scientist, religious teacher, and physician will have to face frankly and squarely in the future.

3. The striking *differences in sex behavior among different social levels* * as revealed in the Kinsey report opens a new field for social thinking and social education. Throughout his life, the boy who is destined to have only a grade-school education will differ materially in the degree of his sex behavior and the source of outlets he will seek for his sexual satisfaction from the boy who will go to high school and to college. The psychiatrist and physician, the jurist and the minister who deal with sex problems and sex delinquencies will

* Editor's italics.

henceforth have to be much more aware of the educational and occupational background of those who come to them for counsel or before them for judgment.

4. The intensity of a boy's sexual drive is, according to the report, determined to a considerable degree by the *age at which he becomes adolescent.* * The earlier adolescence begins, the more sexually active the boy will be not only during his youth but even in later life. There may be some question about the accuracy of this particular inquiry so far as it depended upon men trying to reconstruct from memory the date of the onset of their adolescence, but if the data are accurate, they show that frequent sexual activity in youth does not impair the sexual capacities at a later age. This is contrary to some statements found in literature on sex behavior and should help to allay many fears and anxieties of young people who have believed that their energies are being "used up" in frequent sexual arousal and orgasm.

As the age at which a boy becomes adolescent depends to a considerable degree upon his constitutional characteristics and the level of his general metabolic processes, it would seem that the degree of a man's sexual capacity is genetically determined. How he will exercise his sexual functions, however, the outlets he will seek for his sexual needs, whether he will resort to masturbation, premarital relations, or other sexual experience—this, according to the Kinsey findings, will be determined by his social culture and other environmental influences.

5. The problem of *premarital relations* * confronts us with two aspects for consideration—the moral and the medical. From the latter point of view, the dangers inherent in promiscuous sex relations before marriage are the spread of venereal disease and the occurrence of unwanted pregnancies. The data show that at college level contraceptives are almost universally used and the incidence of both venereal disease and pregnancies is low. On the other hand, among the grade-school population contraceptives are rarely used, with a consequent high frequency of venereal infections and premarital pregnancies.

6. On the basis of the Kinsey report, the *frequency of homosexual relations* * is high. Kinsey's studies indicate that "at least 37 per cent of the male population has some homosexual experience between the beginning of adolescence and old age." It should be made very clear, however, that unless carefully read and interpreted the 37 per-cent figure may be misleading. It applies to men who have had any kind of homosexual experience in their lives, and in some instances this may have been but a single experience. It would be like assuming that anyone who had ever stolen a penny from his mother's pocketbook should be classed as a thief. Aside from this, however, the figures still show that 10 per cent of men between the ages of sixteen and sixty-five are homosexuals for at least three years and 4 per cent are exclusively homo-

* Editor's italics.

sexuals throughout their lives. This is very much higher than previously reported figures on the incidence of homosexuality in our culture.

How valid are the statistical data presented? ... A word of caution, however, is essential. The Kinsey data should not be regarded as final authority on questions of male sex behavior. Kinsey's findings will have to be more adequately supported by physical and psychological studies....

But whether the statistics in this first study are representative of the entire American population or not is really hardly of basic importance. The fact remains that Kinsey has successfully broken through an almost impenetrable wall of taboos, prohibitions, and inhibitions and has explored many "untrodden paths" of human sex behavior. These areas he has clearly marked and charted for those who have sight to read and the will to understand. His report will have immeasurable influence upon the sex mores of our time and our civilization.

MORE ABOUT ... THE HUMAN MALE

The second selection, part of a review by James R. Newman, puts an emphasis on the relationship of *social level* to American patterns of sex behavior. Here we get some suggestions as to the interrelationship between the *organic drive factors*, influenced by age and individual constitution, and the *social climate* of a subculture, operating through the family and the neighborhood. This review also discusses Kinsey's findings and the present sex laws. Finally, it includes Newman's discussion of Kinsey's methods of collecting the data.

James R. Newman

Reprinted from "The Proper Study of Mankind," *The New Republic*, © 1948, Harrison-Blaine of New Jersey, Inc.

CLASS AND SEX.   No general statement about the behavior of the American white male, as a class, is particularly revealing or useful. "There is no American pattern of sexual behavior, but scores of patterns, each of which is confined to a particular segment of our society."

For the purposes of this study, correlations and statistical breakdowns have been made for a number of factors; social level in particular has been measured by three "criteria": (1) educational level attained at termination of formal education; (2) occupational class; (3) occupational class of the person's parents.

The educational levels divide into three categories of duration: 0–8 years; 9–12 years; 13–plus years. Occupational class is broken into nine categories, ranging from laborers, skilled and unskilled, through professional men to the extremely wealthy. (Kinsey says his spectrum runs from "ne'er-do-wells to the Social Register," which may involve occasional circularity.) While the terms "upper" and "lower" social level are sometimes ambiguously used, I take it, in general, that "upper level" refers to persons with educational attainments of 13–plus (*i.e.*, at least one year of college), *or* to those in occupational class 7 (professional) or higher.

Kinsey shows no rosy embarrassment in the presence of the terms "upper class" and "lower class." "Social levels are hierarchies which are not supposed to exist in a democratic society, and many people would, therefore, deny their existence." But the fact is that "most persons do not in actuality move freely with those who belong to other levels"; social stratifications are real, and the various groups differ markedly in social custom and in many other areas of practice and belief. A gentleman jockey may, to be sure, not be a gentleman, but there are criteria, even beyond the economic, to distinguish him from a hard-working pickpocket.

The justification for differentiating by social level is strikingly demonstrated by the differences in sexual mores among the several groups. Differences in style of clothing, food habits, table manners, social courtesies, vocabulary, and so on are widely recognized, but Kinsey's findings of marked differences in sexual behavior comes, I think, as a surprise and is, in any case, a major contribution to a fresh appraisal of social problems related to sex.

In total sexual outlet, boys who will stop their education somewhere in grade school will average 20 to 30 per cent higher frequencies (number of orgasms per week) than boys who will ultimately go to college. Presumably these differences cannot be ascribed to formal schooling—since the same grade school holds both groups; thus either social or biologic factors, or both, may be responsible for these differing patterns of behavior.

Remark now one of Kinsey's most startling conclusions. The sexual behavior already discernible in grade school (and certainly fixed by age 16) in terms of both incidence (percentage of any particular group having experience with a particular outlet) and frequency of outlet is that which is usually adhered to with remarkable tenacity *for the balance of the person's life*. "The social-level picture for total outlet among married males is quite the same as for single males. The married males who have the highest total outlet are those who went into high school and not beyond.... What is true of populations in their teens usually holds true for those same populations at later ages, throughout the life span."

In the occupational classification the highest total outlet is among semiskilled laborers, and the next highest in the professional group. It is important here, as will appear immediately, to distinguish between total outlet and frequencies of particular outlets.

The highest incidence and the highest frequencies of masturbation among all single males, at all age levels, are on the college level. In the grade-school group of married males, only 1 to 3 per cent of total outlet comes from masturbation; among the married college group, the outlet from this source begins at 8.5 per cent during early years of marriage and rises to as much as 18 per cent in the later years.

It is in the attitudes on masturbation, premarital and extramarital intercourse, and prostitution that one may see the "most marked of all distinctions between social levels, and this is true whether the calculations are made by educational levels or by occupational classes."

Generally speaking, persons on the lower levels look upon masturbation as "unnatural" (and unnecessary), are less interested in kissing or petting, and find their highest outlet at almost all ages, single or married, in heterosexual intercourse, which they regard as a "natural, inevitable, and desirable thing" whether practiced with wives, companions, or prostitutes. "So nearly universal is premarital intercourse among grade-school groups that in two or three lower-level communities in which we have worked, we have been unable to find a solitary male who had not had sexual relations with girls by the time he was 16 or 17 years of age. In such a community, the occasional boy who has not had intercourse by that age is either physically incapacitated, mentally deficient, homosexual, or earmarked for moving out of his community and going to college."

The silhouette of upper-level behavior is in striking contrast as regards all these factors. The college male, as a result of social restraints, often chooses masturbation and petting as a substitute for intercourse with either companions or prostitutes. In the case of premarital intercourse, for example, the incidence figures are: grade-school level, 97 per cent; high-school level, 84 per cent; college level, 67 per cent. If frequencies are considered, the discrepancy is even more arresting, there being between seven and eight times as much premarital intercourse on the lower as on the higher levels. Again, 74 per cent of grade-school males, unmarried by 25, patronize prostitutes; the corresponding figure for college-bred males in the same class is 28 per cent.

A curious anomaly arises regarding marital intercourse. The college male, having adhered to the mores of his group before marriage, continues to conform afterward by finding 85 per cent of his total outlet in marital intercourse. The percentages for high-school and grade-school males are, corresponding to their mores, somewhat lower. But after a few years, the statistical curves of the lower- and upper-level married groups change direction and cross. By the time the college male is in his fifties, only 62 per cent of his total sexual outlet is in marital intercourse, while grade-school males of the same age find 88 per cent of their outlet in marriage.

"Some persons may interpret the data to mean that the lower level starts out by trying promiscuity and, as a result of that trial, finally decides that strict monogamy is a better policy; but it would be equally correct to say that the upper level starts out by trying monogamy and ultimately decides that variety is worth having."

The explanations, Kinsey admits, are not "quite correct," yet they undoubtedly embody elements of truth. To the extent that upper-level males diminishingly select marital intercourse as an outlet (for other than biologic reasons, such as age) they tend to revert to the premarital outlets of their class, notably masturbation. Kinsey offers the further explanation that the "coital adjustments of this group in marriage are frequently poor, particularly because of the low degree of erotic responsiveness which exists among many of the college-bred females."

For single males, homosexual relations occur most often among those who go to high school, but not beyond; least often in the group that goes to college. For both groups, however, the figures are amazingly high.

The accumulative incidence figure (total percentage of those who have had at least some homosexual contact resulting in orgasm) for single males of the high-school group is 32 per cent in the early adolescent years, 54 per cent of those not married by 30. The college-level percentages are 17 per cent by age 30 (all classes), although the number who ultimately have homosexual experience is 40 per cent of those not married by age 30. Ultimately, also 45 per cent of the grade-school group is involved.

Since many of the men in the army, navy, merchant marine, and similar organizations belong to the high-school educational level, the official announcement that less than one per cent of all American males applying for or inducted into war service were homosexual is not altogether convincing. On the other hand, one may not with wholly unimpaired sanity contemplate the judgment of those psychoanalysts who, as reported by Kinsey, estimate that no less (and, one may hope, no more) than 100 per cent of all males are homosexual.

Obviously, the difficulty of obtaining reliable data on this taboo-cursed activity is, as Kinsey repeatedly emphasizes, extreme. In general, the higher the social level the greater the urge to conceal the practice of "perversion." In regard to masturbation, however, what is "perverse" for a lower-level group may be accepted as a "lesser evil" and therefore scientifically rationalized by a higher-level group. As an example of the variations of cover-up, there is Kinsey's classic history of the army colonel who denied that he had ever had homosexual experience "unless it happened at night when he did not know anything about it." The only other person, according to Kinsey, who gave a similar explanation was a four-year-old boy.

Contrary to the fastidious pretensions of his level, the upper-level male responds much more readily than does his low-level counterpart to a variety of erotic stimuli, many of which would be classed as "vulgar." These would include pictures, burlesque shows, obscene stories, the sight of animals in coitus, love stories in moving pictures, and so on. There is no ready explanation for the difference—it is pointless to assert vaguely that the upper-level male has more imagination—although Kinsey suggests that since the lower-level male "comes nearer having as much coitus as he wants," he may well "look on such things as the use of pictures or literature to augment masturbatory fantasies as the strangest sort of perversion."

American attitudes on nudity are in a sense derived from the British, who, as Kinsey remarks, are the "most completely clothed people in the world." Group mores again account for a much higher acceptance of nudity at upper than at lower social levels. The act of undressing is so often looked upon, at the lower levels, as an affront to decency, even when executed in solitude, that many persons at this level "acquire a considerable knack of removing daytime clothing and of putting on night clothing, without ever exposing any part of the body." It goes almost without saying that the attitude toward nudity bears closely on many features of sexual practice.

What are the restraints on premarital intercourse at the various levels? One of Kinsey's excellent tables provides considerable enlightenment. At the upper level, more than 60 per cent are inhibited by moral considerations; the same suasion operates among only 20 to 25 per cent of those who have had, at most, only a high-school education. More than 20 per cent of college-bred males fear public opinion on their coital activities; at the lower levels the percentage is about 13 per cent. Fear of venereal disease, on the other hand, impresses 29 per cent of grade-school males, 25 per cent of high-school males and 24 per cent of the college males. Lack of opportunity keeps 35 per cent of lower-level males from this outlet, but operates in the case of 51 per cent of the upper level.

The item in the table, "Lack of interest in having more," is accompanied by percentages quite consistent with other data, indicating that at the lower levels the outlet of heterosexual intercourse is adopted much more frequently than at upper levels. Nineteen per cent of college men show this apathy, but more than 40 per cent of grade- and high-school men assert they are affected by indifference. The desire of the male "to marry a virgin" is strong at all levels, but slightly higher among college males. This of course cannot really be considered a restraint on intercourse, since there is the widespread distinction between "the kind of a girl one marries" and "the other kind."

Even in a practice so old and, as one might have judged, so uniform and so limited in variability of technique as kissing, there are great differences of practice depending on social level. What Kinsey calls the "deep kiss," which is apparently "a regular concomitant of coital activity among many of the vertebrates, and particularly among the mammals," is regularly experienced by nine out of ten males of the upper level. Its sanitary implications exercise no deterring influence on the better educated, even though the same group would for hygienic reasons disdain use of a common drinking glass. On the lower level, though a single drinking cup over the sink or in the water pail is often wholly acceptable, deep kissing is usually thought to be "dirty, filthy, and a source of disease." The arguments, at both levels, "have nothing to do with the real issues. They are rationalizations of mores which place taboos upon mouth contacts for reasons which only the student of custom can explain. Once again, it is the upper level which first reverted, through a considerable sophistication, to behavior which is biologically natural and basic."

This oral phase of sex play deserves particular attention for the light it may throw on the sometimes glib psychoanalytical generalizations respecting oral and anal eroticism.

"Most persons will be surprised to learn that positions in intercourse are as much a product of human cultures as languages and clothing, and that the common English-American position is rare in some other cultures. . . . The origin of our present custom is involved in early and later church history, and needs clarification before it can be presented with any authority. . . . What has been taken to be a question of biologic normality proves, once again, to be a matter of cultural development." Kinsey has abundant data to show that upper- and lower-level practices are widely divergent so far as coital positions are concerned.

The rationalizations of group behavior present a formidable obstacle to the improvement of understanding and forbearance in social attitudes and social action. It is difficult to make headway against deep-rooted customs at every level. Morality and sexual morality are approximately equivalent terms on the upper level; clean, fine, upright, honorable, etc., there "refer primarily to abstinence from socio-sexual relations"; masturbation, if not approved, is at least more readily condoned, and in any case is infinitely to be preferred to premarital intercourse; in the rare instances where unsanctioned coitus may be "forgiven," "love" is involved. At the lower levels, in all sexual behavior, even where moral issues play a part, by and large it is recognized that "nature will triumph over morals."

In studying social implications, assuming one credits Kinsey's findings, the world must be recognized as it is and not as one would want it to be. The sexual advice given by physicians, clinical psychologists, nurses, psychiatrists, marriage counselors, and others with similar responsibility is valuable, informed and enlightened only if it takes into serious account the sex attitudes and practices of the group from which each person stems. The bias of the upper levels is no less a bias because it comes from the upper levels or because it has the prestige and authority of church, state, and learning behind it. Both church and state have been known to err, and the theorems of the science of sex are not as persuasive as the theorem of Pythagoras.

Marriage counseling [writes Kinsey in a brilliant paragraph], as set up today, is based upon concepts of marriage, goals, and ideals which may appear right to the educational level from which the marriage counselors come, and from which most of the counselors' clients also come, but which mean something else in the communities from which a lower-level client may come. The sexual techniques which marriage counsels and marriage manuals recommend are designed to foster the sort of intellectual eroticism which the upper level esteems, and most of which would be anathema to a large portion of the population, and an outrage to their mores. Many marriage counselors would like to impose their own upper-level patterns on their clients, without regard to the complications which may develop when an individual is educated into something that puts him at discord with the mores of the society in which he was raised and in which he may still be living.

SEX AND THE LAW.   Our sex laws are a "codification of the sexual mores of the better educated portion of the population." Kinsey finds that the police often evince a better understanding of the vagaries of "delinquents" than do the college-bred judges. Only rarely will an arrest be made for violation of the laws against nonmarital intercourse, an illegal activity which the policeman most likely once practiced or is still practicing without any heavy sense of wrongdoing. "There are policemen who frankly state that they consider it one of their functions to keep the judge from knowing things that he simply does not understand."

While there are judges, from all levels, who have some understanding of the dimensions of the problem, most of them, like ourselves, do not. Considering the hideous taboos involved, the strict legal penalties, the periodic outbursts of the press to round up sex "fiends," and the small number of actual arrests, it would startle most of those (including judges) who assume the law is being enforced to learn that 85 per cent of the total male population has premarital intercourse, 59 per cent has experience in mouth-genital contacts, nearly 70 per cent has relations with prostitutes, between 35 and 40 per cent has extramarital intercourse, 37 per cent has homosexual experience, and 17 per cent of farm boys have animal intercourse—altogether a grand total of 95 per cent of the entire male population involved in illicit activities. The call for a "clean-up of the sex offenders in a community . . . is, in fine, a proposal that 5 per cent of the population should support the other 95 per cent in penal institutions."

THE DETECTIVE WORK.   Kinsey's entire work rests on the validity of his statistical data. If these are badly astray, his findings and conclusions are equally astray. Fully cognizant of this dependency, he has described his methods of investigation, including his interviewing technique, in some detail, setting forth the drawbacks and advantages of each step in the process with admirable candor.

If, then, there are misgivings with respect to his report, he deserves candor in return.

Specialists undoubtedly have grounds for complaint and criticism as well as much to be grateful for. There are not a few, as Kinsey has foreseen, who are sharpening their knives and heating the cauldron in anticipation of the feast at which Kinsey will be the main dish. But even from the standpoint of the general reader, there are understandable doubts as to the accuracy of many of Kinsey's results.

Each person interviewed was asked between 300 and 570 questions. These were asked at a rapid-fire rate in order (a) to cover the necessary ground in a feasible time, (b) to provide a "check" on fabrications. According to Kinsey, this staccato tempo is an effective check "as detectives and other law-enforcement officials well know."

This sounds to me a bit of precious nonsense bearing no relation, except by opposites, to sound scientific method. It may indeed have been necessary to ask that many questions, and to ask them rapidly in order to cover the ground, but there is no use pretending that the method was intrinsically desirable. Above all, Kinsey, who has dispelled so many vulgar errors, must realize by now that the phrase "as everybody well knows" is merely another way of saying "there is no shred of evidence to prove."

The answers given by the subjects were subsequently cross-checked, examined for internal consistency, correlated with findings of other studies, subjected to statistical tests, and in a number of cases there were "retakes." Other steps included a comparison of answers between spouses and a detailed comparison of the separate results obtained by each of the three principal interviewers.

RESERVATIONS. No one who has examined these correlations will doubt the impartiality and competence of the investigators; it remains that this is not the same thing as giving unqualified credence to the results of their work. Kinsey himself reminds us of this point repeatedly. Especially the data on total outlet and frequencies of particular sexual outlets must be scrutinized with the greatest care, periodically re-examined and correlated with fresh data. The age factor will in part determine what is and is not remembered, and at certain ages persons may exhibit peculiar attributes for recalling experiences which could not be recalled at another age.

Group attitudes may well have significant influence on the power of recall, although Kinsey, who deliberately omits any but brief references to psychological factors, scarcely examines the point. Surely the capacity for recalling, let alone uttering, descriptions of events involving sex behavior strongly disapproved by one's own group must differ from that of recalling events only mildly disapproved or fully accepted. If an individual, despite the attitude of his group, admits to an action strongly disapproved, the probability is high that he is speaking the truth. But what of the opposite case?

On balance, one should expect incidence, and perhaps frequency data, on such outlets as homosexuality and animal contacts to be low. Some males will boast, others will cover up; some of Kinsey's subjects were ready to talk to him (or to one of his associates) "in a few minutes" after being introduced, revealing their innermost intimacies at a headlong pace; others were extremely reluctant, and had to be coaxed, wined, dined, and socially stimulated before they would spout. The interviewing of children raised unusual obstacles, but the indefatigable interviewers were not to be discouraged. Kinsey's description of the interviewer "tussling" with a four-year-old boy while asking him whether he kissed neighborhood females of the same age, makes a memorable tableau in the history of science.

There are also some curious passages about the importance of looking people "square in the eye," a technique which will be regarded as an innovation in scientific method. At one point, in discussing the validity of his data, Kinsey claims no more than that the individual record is at least "not wholly specious." Elsewhere, in answer to the inquiry how an interviewer knows whether people are telling the truth, he asserts almost contemptuously, "As well ask a horse trader how he knows when to close a bargain"—a dangerous analogy.

FINAL ESTIMATE.   I must fall back on a trite phrase. None of the deficiencies to which I have alluded detracts seriously, in my opinion, from the great, solid virtues of the Kinsey report or fatally undermines the organic soundness of its foundations. It may well be, as Kinsey himself re-eamphasizes throughout, that few portions of the data are free of uncertainties, and that some of the statistics, while the best hitherto available, should be regarded with the most cautious skepticism. Yet the report as a whole in its major composites and correlations, in its silhouettes of group patterns and trends, constitutes a chart to which the social scientist must accord the most careful attention. To reject it on the ground that it is statistically unreliable would require, by parity of reasoning, the flat rejection of most of the social and medical sciences, since their statistical bricks have at least as much straw.

ABOUT ... THE HUMAN FEMALE: 5,940 WOMEN

The findings of the Kinsey team of investigators are just as startling for the female as for the male. The book, *Sexual Behavior in the Human Female*, corrects some common misimpressions about the sexual attitudes and behavior of women. Are the differences in sexual behavior found to exist between men and women the same as those perpetuated in the folklore? Certain relationship between *age and sex outlet* was found in the study of males. Does this exact relationship exist in the case of the female? How do women *differ* from men in what arouses and satisfies them sexually? These are a few of the questions answered by the study and reviewed in this magazine article, which was published shortly after the book appeared.

Staff of Time *Magazine*

Courtesy *Time*; copyright Time, Inc., 1953.

THE KEY FINDINGS. From what he has learned, within these limitations, Kinsey is convinced that a sexual revolution has taken place in the United States in the last thirty years, with women's behavior changed even more sharply than men's. His key findings about U.S. women:

They are by no means as frigid as they have been made out, and their sex lives often become more satisfactory with age.

Almost exactly 50 per cent have sexual intercourse before marriage (compared to 83 per cent of U.S. men, as reported in Kinsey's first volume).

About 26 per cent have extramarital relations (compared to 50 per cent of the males).

Ancient and modern myths which have pictured women as practicing fantastic secret perversions have little basis in fact. These aberrations are far commoner among the men, and the myths represent "the male's wishful thinking, a projection of his own desire . . ."

THE BIG CHANGE. The Gibson Girl of half a century ago, whaleboned into an hourglass shape, almost never heard the word "sex." It was a relatively new scientific term, to be distinguished from "love," which was too idealized, and "lust," which was too blunt.

Probably the Gibson Girl never heard of "petting" either, but if she was a late model (born in the 1890's and therefore included in Kinsey's sample), the chances are four out of five that she indulged in it under another name. Says Kinsey: "Many consider petting an invention of modern American youth—the by-product of an effete and morally degenerate . . . culture. It is taken by some to reflect the sort of moral bankruptcy which must lead to the collapse of any civilization. Older generations did, however, engage in flirting, flirtage, courting, bundling, spooning, mugging, smooching, larking, sparking . . ." But the late Gibson Girls rarely went further. If their testimony to Kinsey held back nothing, only one out of seven unmarried women born in the nineties had sexual intercourse by age 25, though the proportion jumped to two out of five by age 40.

Once married, there was a four-to-one chance that the girl who had been raised under Queen Victoria's long shadow would remain faithful to her husband, no matter how often he might be unfaithful to her. The double standard was still secure.

Then came the big change.

It happened, according to Kinsey's figures, around the end of World War I. The causes were various. Kinsey cites the writings of Havelock Ellis, one of the first scientists to combine psychology and biology, and Sigmund Freud, who put the spotlight on sex as a cause of human behavior. Of more immediate effect on the United States was the draft army, which threw together men from all walks of life and exposed 2,000,000 of them, overseas, to standards more sophisticated than their own. When they came home, they found U.S. women largely emancipated and close to winning the vote. There were other causes to which Kinsey pays little or no heed. One was Prohibition, which helped destroy respect for law and, indirectly, for all authority (and which also taught women to drink). Another was the widespread breakdown of formal religion. Perhaps at the root of all the causes was the inevitable reaction against the prim Victorian era, which itself was not nearly so safe and sound as it appeared. For beneath its placid surface, a social and intellectual revolution had long been rumbling, which enshrined science and progress as twin gods and established a view of man as a creature governed more by "environment" than by preordained morality.

By the mid-1920's, the new century seemed to be talking (and worrying) more about sex than previous ages. "Frankness" became a respectable pose for cocktail parties, parent-teachers' meetings, and literature. The novelists—Hemingway, D. H. Lawrence, and later Erskine Caldwell and Faulkner—were blatantly detailed, and behind them stood the anthropologists and psychoanalysts with their case histories. But the generation still had no Kinsey. It was left to him to clothe the subject in the sober, convincing, guaranteed-to-be-scientific garb of statistics.

FRIGIDITY.   When the Gibson Girls' daughters arrived on the scene, clochehatted flappers, short-skirted and prattling about repressions, this is what happened to the sex lives of U.S. women, according to Kinsey:

The number of women who went in for petting jumped to 91 per cent among those born in the first decade of the century, and to 99 per cent among their kid sisters and their daughters. The proportion of those who would carry petting, as Kinsey puts it, "to the point of orgasm" rose from one fourth to more than half.

Among women born in the early 1900's, intercourse before marriage was twice as frequent as among those born in the nineties. More than one out of three lost their virginity by age 25, and three out of five, if they were still unmarried at 40.

These more daring women of the restless generation enjoyed marriage more. Kinsey takes sharp issue with psychiatrists and a few gynecologists who have estimated that anywhere from one third to two thirds of U.S. women are frigid. Even during the first year of marriage, when the most drastic adjustments have to be made, three wives out of four reach complete fulfillment at least once. Between the ages of 21 and 40 they attain it from 84 per cent to 90 per cent of the time. In sum, says Kinsey, about three quarters of all sexual relations within marriage end in a satisfactory climax for the wife. However, he reports no case of a woman who attained climax 100 per cent of the time.

Most women born before 1900 had enjoyed no such fulfillment. Many of them, according to Kinsey, did not know that it was possible for a woman to have an orgasm, and if they did know, they thought it was "not nice." Now, says Kinsey, who puts great stock in quantitative analysis: "To have frigidity so reduced in the course of four decades is . . . a considerable achievement which may be credited, in part, to the franker attitudes and the freer discussion of sex which we have had in the U.S. during the past twenty years and to the increasing scientific and clinical understanding . . ."

FIDELITY. Among Kinsey's sample of women who had premarital intercourse, one third had relations with from two to five men, more than half with only one man—and 46 per cent only with the fiancé in the year or so before marriage. Are these women sorry? No. Whether they had later married or not, about three fourths said they had no regrets, and 12 to 13 per cent had only "minor" qualms. Among those who avoided intercourse before marriage, nine out of ten said they had done so primarily for moral reasons.

There have been other changes. A full third of the women born before 1900 told Kinsey that they wore night clothes during sexual intercourse. Now, more and more U.S. couples are having intercourse without covers or clothes (all but 8 per cent of today's newlyweds), and sleep "in the raw."

Most societies, remarks Kinsey in an anthropological aside, have a double standard about marital fidelity. A few, though they take a dim view of a woman who strays openly, covertly condone her actions if she is discreet and her husband does not become particularly disturbed. That, suggests Kinsey, is "the direction toward which American attitudes may be moving."

Among the 2,480 married women in his sample, one fourth eventually had relations outside marriage by age 40. The rate rose from 6 per cent in the late teens and 9 per cent in the twenties, to 26 per cent in the thirties and early forties. Women with different family and social backgrounds behave about the same, but the infidelity rate goes up with education: 31 per cent among those who have been to college, against 24 per cent of high-school graduates.

As for what Kinsey calls "other sexual outlets": 62 per cent of the women in his sample had masturbated at some time in their lives, but the activity was, for most, not continuous. (At some time, 92 per cent of men masturbate, and for most the activity is more continuous than for women.) Homosexual relationships are far less frequent among women than among men. The activity is virtually confined to unmarried women or those no longer married; a fifth of all Kinsey's subjects had had some such experience by age 40; one fourth of the unmarried, only 3 per cent while married. (Among unmarried men, half; of the married, 4.6 per cent.)

But unlike homosexual males, many of whom change partners frequently, half of these women had had only one partner, and one fifth had had only two.

AGE AND SEX.   Many who profess not to be shocked by Kinsey's findings dispute them on the coldly factual basis that Kinsey has only his subjects' word that they are telling the truth. To this, Kinsey can only reply that he does the best he can to insure accuracy by a kind of cross-reference questioning, so that a subject who has lied at the beginning of the interview will expose himself near the end. Beyond this, he has re-interviewed hundreds of subjects after lapses of two to ten years and they have told substantially the same story; this rules out carefree, offhand lying. However, Kinsey has found that males who have not gone beyond grade school are less reliable informants than the more highly educated, and probably they have exaggerated their juvenile conquests. Similarly, he concedes, women are likely to cover up, so that some of their indiscretions before or after marriage might not show up in his figures.

More important to Kinsey than mere tables of incidence are the underlying biological, physiological and psychological factors which determine sexual behavior. Kinsey believes that he has found out a lot about what men and women must know and do if they are to make a success of marriage.

The answers go back to puberty, and the popular fallacy that girls mature faster than boys. Kinsey notes that girls reach puberty a year earlier than boys, but this is only the beginning of adolescence and is no index to sexual maturity. Boys reach maturity (the height of their physical power for sexual activity) by their late teens, and are already on the downgrade in their early twenties. But the curve of a girl's growing need for sex (or the breaking down of her inhibitions) rises only slowly in her teens, keeps on rising slowly until she is 29 or 30. Even then there is no sharp peak: the curve levels off, leaving a smooth plateau until age 50 or 60. But the man's curve keeps on dropping, *i.e.*, his need for sexual activity generally declines while the woman's stays fairly high. This, says Kinsey, is one of the difficulties he has found in many marriages. It is heightened by the fact that in the early peak years of a man's activity, he resents his wife's seeming coldness. When her coldness has passed, so has his interest—"especially [if she] has previously objected to the frequency of his requests."

WHAT EVERY WOMAN WANTS.   Another common fallacy, says Kinsey, is the idea that the female is slower to respond sexually than the male. Not proved, he says. "Females appear to be capable of responding to the point of orgasm as quickly as males, and there are some females who respond more rapidly than any male." But there is a difference in responsiveness which may explain the common fallacy. It lies in women's psychology.

They are not as easily stimulated to sexual response as are men. Most of them get no reaction from seeing the male form in the nude, from "beef-cake" pictures of undraped athletes, or from erotic stories. What every woman wants, Kinsey has gathered from long hours of listening, is "a considerable amount of generalized emotional stimulation before there is any specific sexual contact." This is an ancient truth, known to scientists in the field and every successful husband, now confirmed by Kinsey's massive statistics.

IMPLICATIONS

You have read three reviews of the on-going studies by Kinsey and his co-workers on American sexual behavior. What impressed you most? What remarks in the reviews motivate you to read the original volumes for further facts and discussion?

To what extent can the findings about the sexual behavior of thousands of individuals, representing various backgrounds and personal organizations, have significance for *a single individual?* We really know nothing about the personality of the interviewed individual, of his thoughts, emotions, and the state of his physical or mental health. We are not told of his reactions to these sexual experiences or what motivational insecurities may have led to them. Some reviewers of these volumes, including the psychiatrist Karl Menninger, have reminded us that Kinsey has forced human sexual behavior into a zoological frame of reference and thereby neglected human psychology. It has been pointed out that the orgasm of a loving husband in the arms of his wife differs from that of a desperate homosexual trying to prove his masculinity. Why do you think Kinsey has regarded sex primarily as a biological reaction? What effect does this have on the interpretation of his findings?

Will these volumes, as the contents become known, reduce the widespread *guilt* felt from unconventional sex episodes? And how is guilt-lifting compatible with rational ethics and morality? Doubtless, sex is a strong biological urge in the years of youth, but so are the taboos and social consequences of impulsive sexual union. Would not a case study of the individual and the conditions that led up to his behavior and his entanglements, the guilt or scandal that resulted, give us a more realistic picture of the *total person* in his attempt to make an adjustment to his urges as well as to his self-respect and integrity?

REFENCES

Consult the Bibliography for reference to a thorough review by the veteran psychologist Terman (1948), an evaluation by the psychiatrist Menninger (1953), and the original volumes of Kinsey, Pomeroy, and Martin (1948), and Kinsey (1953).

[5] EGO STRENGTH AND THE POWER TO RALLY FROM SETBACK

Why is it that some individuals seem to be able to withstand crises better than others? The term *will power* was frequently used, long before systematic investigations were conducted on voluntary behavior. Usually, when this term was used, the speaker or writer inferred that those who lacked this capacity were morally culpable and that the development of will power was itself a completely voluntary matter. Thus, if one failed to have will power, it was one's own fault. Since then this capacity to make realistic decisions and sustain them has been examined in many clinical situations. The term *ego* has come into being; *ego functions* is probably a better substitute phrase. This concept refers to those processes concerned with decision-making, planning, and psychological defense.

Barron attempts to explore the idea of ego strength, a condition that varies with individuals and that explains to a large extent why some individuals can withstand trouble and misfortunes and even use such experiences for personal growth while others cannot. He has done this in a scientific manner, using terms in a well-explored inventory, the Minnesota Multiphastic Personality Inventory. Examples of the relevant items are given in this selection. Barron thus has been able to assess ego strength by comparing self-evaluating statements of those individuals who recover more readily from *emotional disturbance* with statements of those who do not.

Frank Barron

Reprinted from Frank Barron, *Creativity and Psychological Health*
(Princeton, N.J.: D. Van Nostrand Company, 1963), pp. 121–124,
132–134. Courtesy of D. Van Nostrand Company, Inc.

Everyone alive has troubles and problems, and as we learned from our
studies of especially "sound" individuals, the most important consideration
in determining personal effectiveness is not the amount of trouble or misfortune (within limits) a person encounters, but *how he responds* to the
vicissitudes and challenges of life. This capacity to meet problems without
being dismayed and overwhelmed, to endure suffering and face great loss without foundering, is an aspect of psychological strength and vitality that deserves special study.

In what follows, we shall first describe the development and cross-validation of a scale originally designed to predict the response of psychoneurotic
patients to psychotherapy. Consideration of the scale content and its correlates, however, has suggested that a somewhat broader psychological interpretation being placed upon it, making it useful as an assessment device in any
situation where some estimate of adaptability and personal resourcefulness is
wanted. It appears to measure the various aspects of effective personal functioning that are usually subsumed under the term "ego strength."

The scale consists of 68 items from the Minnesota Multiphasic Personality
Inventory, selected from a total MMPI pool of 550 items on the basis of significant correlation with rated improvement in our 33 psychoneurotic patients
who had been treated for six months in a clinic. The test responses of the
patients were obtained before psychotherapy began, so that the scale, so far
as logic of construction is concerned, is designed to predict whether or not
after about six months of therapy the patient will have improved.

The sample of 33 patients . . . was divided into two groups: 17 patients who
were judged to have clearly improved, and 16 patients who were judged to be
unimproved. And although the sample was small, the cases were intensively
studied, and the two skilled judges who had thoroughly acquainted themselves with the course of the therapy (although not themselves involved in it
otherwise) were in considerable agreement (r of .91 *) in their independent
ratings of degree of improvement. While one would not ordinarily base
scale development on a sample of this size, it was reasoned here that a small
number of well-studied cases who were classified with high reliability, and,
as collateral evidence indicated, with high accuracy as well, would serve

---

* These are standard measures of reliability or significance.

better than the practical alternative, which was to get a large sample in which the therapist's rating of outcome was accepted uncritically.

When the Improved and Unimproved groups were scored on this 68-item scale, the mean of the Improved group proved to be 52.7, that of the Unimproved group 29.1, a difference which is significant well beyond the .01 level (t of 10.3 *). The odd-even reliability of the scale in a clinic population of 126 patients is .76. Test-retest reliability after three months in a sample of 30 cases is .72.

The 68 items of the scale are presented below,† arranged in groups according to the kinds of psychological homogeneities that, in the judgment of the writer, are involved in the item content.

Physical functioning and physiological stability. 153. During the past few years I have been well most of the time (T). 51. I am in just as good physical health as most of my friends (T).

Psychasthenia and seclusiveness. 384. I feel unable to tell anyone all about myself (F). 489. I feel sympathetic toward people who tend to hang on to their griefs and troubles (F).

Attitudes toward religion. 95. I go to church almost every week (T). 488. I pray several times every week (F).

Moral posture. 410. I would certainly enjoy beating a crook at his own game (T). 181. When I get bored, I like to stir up some excitement (T).

Sense of reality. 33. I have had very peculiar and strange experiences (F). 349. I have strange and peculiar thoughts (F).

Personal adequacy, ability to cope. 389. My plans have frequently seemed so full of difficulties that I have had to give them up (F). 82. I am easily downed in an argument (F).

Phobias, infantile anxieties. 367. I am not afraid of fire (T). 525. I am made nervous by certain animals (F).

Miscellaneous. 221. I like science (T). 513. I think Lincoln was greater than Washington (T).

The pretherapy *characteristics of patients who improve in therapy, as compared with those who do not improve,*‡ might be summarized as follows:

Improved: (a) good physical functioning; (b) spontaneity, ability to share emotional experiences; (c) conventional church membership, but nonfundamentalist and undogmatic in religious beliefs; (d) permissive morality; (e) good contact with reality; (f) feelings of personal adequacy and vitality; (g) physical courage and lack of fear.

---

* These are standard measures of reliability or significance.

† Included here are only two sample items in each group. T or F indicates the favorable answer.

‡ Editor's italics.

Unimproved: (a) many and chronic physical ailments; (b) broodiness, inhibition, a strong need for emotional seclusion, worrisomeness; (c) intense religious experiences, belief in prayer, miracles, the Bible; (d) repressive and punitive morality; (e) dissociation and ego alienation; (f) confusion, submissiveness, chronic fatigue; (g) phobias and infantile anxieties.

...At this point, however, it may be useful to give a very brief résumé of the determinants and marks of ego strength as the term is here being used, drawing both upon these statistical findings and upon general observation of normal psychological functioning.

Ego strength is, first of all, a function simply of intelligence. Since comprehension of experience depends mostly on the degree of organization in the central nervous system, the scope of the ego will vary with the quality of the brain.

Scope does not depend solely upon cognition, however. Psychodynamics enter chiefly in relation to the mechanism of repression. Repression operates in the service of homeostasis, and so serves an economic function that is indispensable in maintaining the organism in an integral form in its environment. However, repression may be so extensive as to become a false economy; when broad areas of experience are lost to consciousness through repression, the ego may be said to be less strong (*i.e.*, less able to adapt) as a consequence. To state the matter positively, ego strength requires a flexible repression mechanism, so that the person may be said to be optimally open to experience, though capable of excluding phenomena that cannot be assimilated to the structure of the self.

Physiological stability and regularity of physical functioning is the biological matrix in which the ego thrives, or attains maximum strength. Generally speaking, the ego is at its strongest in the years of physical maturity, granting good bodily health. Ego strength is increasing as the organism grows toward maturity, levels off in the "prime of life," and declines thereafter with increasing age.

The crucial years in determining ego strength are the first five years of life. Severe ego dysfunction in those years is virtually irreversible. In the normal course of development, a regular sequence of ego crises and ego achievements may be discerned. The first achievement of the ego in relation to experience is the attainment of a stable and facile distinction between inner and outer sources of stimulation. This is the indispensable basis of the "sense of reality"; an inability to make this distinction is the primary mark of functional psychosis, in which introjection and projection no longer operate under the control of the ego. Paranoias and psychotic depressions and excitements are the diagnostic syndromes consequent upon such ego failure. A strong ego, on the other hand, consistently recognizes the independent and autonomous existence of objects other than itself, and also is able to take a reflective attitude toward its own existence and the laws of its being. Building upon this basic distinction of inner and outer sources of experience, the ego gradually attains mastery of bodily functions involving intake and output, which includes experiencing the erotic component in such functions. Such later character traits as the ability to get and to give good things, to hold on to what one wants and to let go when necessary, to be able to rise to the occasion, to make things go, to build and to conserve, to understand and to predict, all have their beginnings in the early years when the most important of ego crises occur. The later achievements of the normal ego involve primarily the synthesis of these earlier acquisitions of mastery; the most important outcomes have to do with personal identity in work and in love, and finally with the individual's participation in community experience, which would include some understanding of man in relation to nature, and of nature itself.

IMPLICATIONS

See if you can state in your own words what you understand ego strength to be. What are the specific indices of a strong versus a weak ego as described in this selection? Reread the items separating individuals who improve in therapy from those who do not. Can you also, in terms of these items, formulate some personal suggestions for more hygienic attitudes and habits? Try your skill at this. Would you venture to formulate some child-rearing advice that may help to develop healthier attitudes? To what extent does this selection give you some insight into yourself and those who know you best? Why do you think current thinkers like Barron have achieved greater clarity into ego functions than the earlier writers who discussed the matter in terms of will power?

REFERENCES

Is making an effective personal adjustment a matter of following rules? As previously implied, it is not. When young individuals who are judged to be stable, mature, and in reasonable control of their own lives are compared with persons of low emotional stability, the differences seem to be in terms of developmental background. Factors such as stable family setting with presence of both parents who are respected, establishment of independence from the family, and, later, enduring heterosexual relations are important. Several studies have shown this.

These studies reveal that the *psychological climate* in which the individual lives is important—a healthy one fosters the potentialities for personal growth and encourages development of those attitudes and traits characteristic of stable people. These characteristics are (1) capacity to deal with one's environment and an effective organization of effort toward goals, (2) a correct perception of oneself and the world, and (3) a unity of personality, an integrity which allows one to live satisfactorily with oneself and one's fellows (see Jahoda, 1958).

The emphasis is not only on understanding the forces of one's physical equipment and environment but on using one's individuality for responsible social growth. (See White, 1952; Shoben, 1957; McKinney, 1960; Symonds, 1951.) Those in the existential movement in psychological thinking emphasize particularly the achievement of a personally meaningful and responsible existence. (See Maslow, 1962; Frankl, 1963.)

[6] SELF-UNDERSTANDING IN THE PREDICTION OF BEHAVIOR

Have you ever considered the many factors that influence your behavior? Some of these major factors are heredity, physical condition, mental capacity and aptitudes, family environment, cultural background, social experience, educational experience, and self-insight. Which of these factors would you speculate are most important in the development of what you are today? How essential is self-insight in the control of one's behavior? Self-insight includes the individual's understanding and acceptance of himself and of the reality situations in which he finds himself.

Rogers and his associates show us in this study how these complex and sometimes elusive factors are rated and evaluated. They verbalize in specific terms how *extremely poor adjustment* differs from *excellent adjustment,* and how the individual with poor self-understanding and self-acceptance differs from the individual who has achieved this.

Carl R. Rogers, Bill L. Kell, and Helen McNeil

Reprinted from Carl R. Rogers, Bill L. Kell, and Helen McNeil, "The Role of Self-Understanding in the Prediction of Behavior," *Journal of Consulting Psychology*, Vol. 12 (Washington, D.C.: American Psychological Association, 1948), pp. 174–186, by permission of the publisher and the two senior authors.

A number of years ago, a study in prediction of the behavior and adjustment of delinquent adolescents was made by Kell (1942) under the supervision of the senior author. The major finding of the study was so striking and so unexpected that the completed research was laid aside until it might be confirmed or disproved by additional work. Later, Miss McNeil (1944) repeated the identical method of study on a new group of cases with results which confirmed, though less strikingly, the same findings. It now appears appropriate to present these two studies in somewhat condensed form, together with some of the implications which they seem to have for clinical practice and personality research.

THE HYPOTHESIS

The hypothesis was the same in both studies. It was that given sufficient information concerning the factors which presumably enter into the determination of an individual's behavior, it should be possible to make ratings of these factors which would predict with some degree of accuracy the individual's later adjustment. More specifically, given information regarding an *individual's heredity, physical condition, mental status, family environment, cultural background, social experience, educational experience, and self-insight,** it should be possible to rate these factors as to their favorableness for normal development, and on the basis of these ratings predict future adjustment. If behavior is caused by factors such as those listed, then an evaluation of such factors should provide a basis for estimating the type of behavioral adjustment which is likely to ensue.

THE PLAN OF THE STUDIES

The plan of both studies was identical and contained the following general elements.

1. To select a group of delinquent children for whom there was an ade-

* Editor's italics.

quate amount of diagnostic information, and follow-up reports of adjustment covering a period of approximately two years following the initial study.

2. To make ratings of the various factors which might determine behavior, by means of the so-called "Component Factor Method" (described below), these ratings to be entirely on the basis of information available at the time of the initial study, without any reference to the follow-up data.

3. To make independent ratings of the adjustment of the individual two years after the diagnostic study, these ratings to be made without reference to the information obtained in the diagnostic evaluation.

4. To analyze the material for possible correlations between each component factor and later adjustment, also for correlations between all the factors taken together and later adjustment. To consider whether the behavior of these delinquents might have been in any way predicted by this method, from the information available at the time of the initial study.

The way in which these steps were carried out is presented in some detail in the sections which follow.

THE SELECTION OF THE GROUPS

The cases which were used in this study were obtained from the files of the Bureau of Juvenile Research, Columbus, Ohio, and it was due to the wholehearted cooperation of this organization that the research was possible. The procedure was as follows. Mr. Kell went over a few cases to see whether the information contained in the case histories and in the follow-up files was adequate for the type of analysis which he wished to make. It appeared that in many cases the information was adequate for his purposes. None of these preliminary cases was used in the research. He then took 155 cases which had been studied by the BJR after June 1937, and on which there was reported to be follow-up information two to three years after the diagnostic study. Cases were selected at random except that there was some perusal of the follow-up reports to make sure that both failures and successes in adjustment were being included. This was the only contact with the follow-up reports prior to the specific study of the follow-up material reported later.

When the Component-Factor ratings were made on these 155 cases, it was found that the information was inadequate in 71 cases, and these were dropped. In making the ratings on follow-up adjustment, information was found to be inadequate in 9 additional cases, thus bringing the total number included in the research to 75. It does not appear that lack of information in the case record would be a selective factor related to the problems being studied in this research.

In the study made by Miss McNeil, 141 cases were initially selected, the criteria being similar, with the added item that they should all be new cases which had not been utilized in the Kell study. She found it necessary to drop out 65 cases because of inadequate information, thus leaving 76 individuals in her group. Thus in the two studies taken together, there are 151 individuals on whom the reported findings are based.

Certain general facts about the two groups are listed in Table 1.

TABLE 1

CHARACTERISTICS OF THE GROUPS INCLUDED IN THE KELL
AND McNEIL STUDIES

Characteristic	Kell's Group	McNeil's Group
Average age at time of diagnostic study	15–2	14–6
Range in age	8–9 to 17–11	7–9 to 18–1
Number of boys	57	59
Number of girls	18	17
Whites	65	66
Negroes	10	10
Average I.Q.	94	90
Range in I.Q.	45 to 136	41 to 140
From rural homes	unknown	9
From urban homes	unknown	67

In an analysis made by Miss McNeil's group, it was found that the behavior difficulties were those that we have come to regard as typical of a juvenile delinquent group—stealing, truancy from school and home, incorrigible behavior, untruthfulness, and sex misdemeanors heading the list of complaints. There were 27 of the group who had previously been in court. Broken and discordant homes were the rule, and more than half of the group had had some foster home or institutional experience away from their own home. In general it may be said that the adolescents included in the study appear to be typical of individuals coming to a juvenile court or behavior clinic.

THE RATING OF COMPONENT FACTORS

When the groups had been selected, the next step was to rate those factors in the child's background and experience which might presumably be related to future behavior and adjustment. For this purpose the component factor method of case analysis, devised by Rogers and the staff of the Rochester Guidance Center, and described in an earlier publication (Rogers, 1939) was used. Since the findings are in terms of the categories used in this device, some description of it is given here, though for a full account of its development or its use in other research (Kell, 1942; Bennett & Rogers, 1941b), the reader is referred elsewhere. The rationale behind this method of rating and analysis, and a brief description of the method, is given by Rogers in the following statement:

Behavior problems are due to the fact that a child of certain hereditary equipment is dealt with in a certain manner by members of his family environment and at the same time affected by certain broader cultural and social influences. If any one of these elements is altered, the behavior picture is also altered. To understand behavior we must view it as the complex result of all these component factors. Thus in the method under consideration, the forces which have operated in the child's experience are grouped under eight factors, defined so far as possible in terms which will have general understanding. Each of these factors . . . is rated in the case of the individual child on a seven-point scale, ranging from influences which are destructive to the child's welfare, to conditions and forces ideal for the child's adjustment. This rating scale is made more objective by means of sample ratings, with experimentally determined values, set up as guideposts (Rogers, 1939).

The eight factors which are to be rated on the basis of material in the case history are defined in specific terms. For each factor there are also a series of illustrative ratings, taken from cases, and showing the average scale value which was given to the material by six clinician judges. The definitions to be kept in mind by the rater are stated below as given in the original description by Rogers, and as used by Kell and McNeil in these studies. In the interests of brevity the illustrative ratings have been omitted, except for the family factor, the factor of social experience, and the factor of self-insight. These are included to show the type of guide which was available to the rater.

Rating on Hereditary Factor

Consider the child's strain of inheritance, as evidenced by parents, relatives, siblings; hereditary predisposition to disease; feeble-mindedness, epilepsy, or psychoses in the ancestry; evidence of neuroses or physical or emotional instability in the ancestry; marked social inadequacy in the ancestry as shown by chronic alcoholism, repeated jail terms. On the constructive side consider freedom from disease and taints and marked social adequacy.

Rating on Physical Factors

Consider the child's inherited physical and neurological constitution; his physical development, size, and weight in relation to norm; physical defects, inferiorities, or abnormalities; glandular dysfunction; physical instability, nervousness, hyperactivity; disease history, with special attention to long periods of illness, or diseases such as tuberculosis, epilepsy, encephalitis, venereal disease, chorea; defects of the special senses. On the constructive side consider freedom from illness or defects, superior physique.

Rating on Mentality Factor

Consider the child's mental capacities as shown by his development, intelligence test ratings, school achievement, vocational achievement. Consider special abilities and disabilities which have a bearing on his mental functioning. Consider the quality of his intelligence, alertness, persistence, ability to concentrate.

Rating on Family Influences

Consider the family circle within which the child has developed—the attitudes which have surrounded him. Consider the emotional atmosphere within the home —marital discord or harmony, sibling rivalries, attitudes of domination, oversolicitude, rejection, or normal parental love. Frictions or conflicts in regard to illegitimacy or other family irregularity. The child's reaction to the home is also to be considered—reactions toward parents and siblings, toward family standards and discipline. Degree of community of interests with other members of the family.

Rating on Economic and Cultural Influences

Consider the family income, status of father's occupation, social standing in the community, degree of comfort and educative influences within the home; consider the community type—whether delinquency area, residential area, rural area; consider the community standards of behavior and culture; the school, libraries, and recreational resources available.

Rating on the Social Factor

Consider range and extent of child's social experience; isolation or group contacts; the type of companions available; the social skills the child has achieved considered in relation to his age; experience in group membership and leadership; organizing ability and social initiative; status in the schoolroom group; friendships with own and opposite sex, considered in relation to age; social relationships with adults; social adjustment to the neighborhood and community; general social maturity or lack of it.

Rating on Education, Training, and Supervision

Consider the education, training, and supervision the child has had outside the home. Ordinarily this will mean primarily his school experience. Consider such things as the type of school which the child has attended; the changes of school; the continuity and consistency of school experience; consistency of discipline, both in school and between home and school; the degree of healthy stimulation, the extent to which tasks have been adapted to ability; the insight shown by teachers and school authorities; the behavior ideals actually inculcated; the cooperation and similarity of viewpoint between home and school.

Rating on Self-Insight

Consider in relation to the norm for his age, the degree to which the child has or lacks understanding of his own situation and problems; consider such things as defensiveness; inability to admit faults, or tendency to depreciate self and exaggerate faults. Consider not only intellectual understanding of problem but emotional acceptance of the reality situation. Consider child's planfulness and willingness to take responsibility for self; ability to be objectively self-critical. Consider stability of attitudes—whether erratic and changeable or cautious and settled.

In view of some of the findings to be presented later, it should be pointed out that in the development of this instrument, the factor of self-insight was added rather apologetically at the end of the list. Says Rogers, in introducing a discussion of this factor, "The seven factors which have been described would seem to be the basic elements which, coming together in complex fashion, determine the behavior of the individual. For the young child an evaluation of these factors should be sufficient to gain an understanding of the child's reactions. With the older child, however, the attitudes which he holds toward himself and his behavior are decidedly significant and worthy of evaluation. That these attitudes are formed by the interaction of the other factors in the child's experience is undoubtedly true, but they also operate as an important influence to shape his future behavior" (Rogers, 1939).

Using this component factor instrument as described, Kell and McNeil rated each of the eight factors for each of the subjects in their groups. The material on which the ratings were based was the initial diagnostic study of the child made while he was at the Bureau of Juvenile Research. This material included written case histories, psychometric examinations, interviews with the child by a psychologist or psychiatrist, or both, report of physical examination, and other similar information. The only materials which were not used in making the rating judgments were the over-all diagnostic report compiled by the Bureau, and the follow-up information. The former was excluded because it was felt the ratings should be made on the basis of the material itself, rather than on someone's interpretation of that material. The follow-up information was of course excluded because it was to be rated independently.

No measure of the reliability of the ratings in the present studies was made, but it has been shown by Rogers that the degree of reliability in the clinical use of these rating scales may be expressed by the statement that in rating specific items, the standard deviation of clinician's judgments ranges from .3 to .6 of a scale step, with heredity and mentality showing the highest reliability, and family and self-insight factors the lowest. When six clinicians rated five cases (rather than specific items from cases) on every factor, the reliability was somewhat lower, 66 per cent of the judgments being in agreement within two scale steps on the seven-point scale (Rogers, 1939).

THE RATING OF LATER ADJUSTMENT

In order to provide an objective measure of the individual's later adjustment, with which the initial ratings might be correlated, Kell devised a scale for rating the behavior of the individual during the two- or three-year period following the diagnostic study. This too was a seven-point scale, ranging from extremely poor adjustment to excellent adjustment. The typical characteristics which were set up for the different points on the scale are as follows:

Rating Scale of Follow-Up Adjustment
−3 Extremely poor adjustment. Individual in difficulties constantly. A confirmed delinquent or criminal. If institutionalized, makes an unsatisfactory adjustment

there—fights continuously against regulations, disliked by other inmates, etc. If in own home, continually disrupts the family, a constant behavior problem at home and in school. Insane or extremely neurotic. Finds few, if any, normal satisfactions. No satisfactory adjustment in any situation.

−2   Poor adjustment. Continues in some delinquent or criminal activities, but does not seem hopeless. In court a number of times. Gains most satisfactions in an antisocial manner. If institutionalized, makes a partial adjustment to the institution's routine and regulations. If in own home, continues as a behavior problem most of the time, in conflict with school and may drop out. Cannot hold a job or function satisfactorily at one. May adjust satisfactorily in a few situations. Seems quite neurotic. Cannot adjust in foster home.

−1   Near average adjustment. Continues in a few delinquent activities. May be in court once or twice. If institutionalized, makes a satisfactory adjustment and shows evidence of adjusting outside the institution. If in own home, continues as a problem, but not as a severe one. Continues as a school problem, but makes some progress. May be able to hold a job, but does not function too well at it. May exhibit some neurotic symptoms which have a slight effect on total adjustment. May have to be placed in several foster homes, but finally makes a fairly satisfactory adjustment. Adjusts in some situations and not in others.

 0   Average adjustment. In few, if any, delinquencies. May be in court once for minor delinquencies and then released. Neurotic tendencies mild and have little effect on total adjustment. Makes a satisfactory adjustment in the home —may have a few minor family difficulties. Makes average progress in school in relation to ability. Makes satisfactory adjustment in foster home. Is able to hold a job, but is not exceptional at it. Adjusts in most situations.

+1   Above average adjustment. Never in court again. Delinquent tendencies, if any, must be so mild that he is never in any serious difficulty. No evident neurotic symptoms. Very little aggressive, antisocial behavior. Makes a good adjustment to the family situation if returned home. Makes good progress in school. Does quite well on a job. Makes a good foster-home adjustment. Adjusts in nearly all situations.

+2   Very good adjustment. Seems to make the best of nearly every situation. No evidence of any delinquent tendencies. No antisocial behavior. Makes a good school adjustment. Does very well on a job. Never any evident conflict with family if returned home. Makes a very satisfactory foster-home adjustment.

+3   Excellent adjustment. Makes the best of every situation. Never any question of stability or antisocial trends. Seems to make best possible adjustment to family. Excellent adjustment in school, college indicated, etc. Makes excellent progress on a job. Foster-home adjustment the best possible (Kell, 1942).

Using this rating scale, Kell and McNeil turned to the follow-up report of the cases in their respective groups, and, without reference to the diagnostic study, evaluated the two to three years of behavior which were described in the follow-up material. This material was made up of reports from probation officers, social workers, and institution officials.

To illustrate the range of later adjustments which were found in the group, and the use of the rating scale on adjustments, Kell's notes abstracting the follow-up reports on three cases, and the ratings assigned to these cases, are given below:

−3 Ran away from foster home. Committed to Boys' Industrial School for stealing. Later released. Practiced sex perversion. Committed to Massillon State Hospital—ran away from there. Very poor present adjustment. Continuing sex perversion.

0 Girl made a fair adjustment in first foster home. Did not get along well in second and third foster homes. Later made a good adjustment in a fourth foster home. Now married. Apparently is doing well.

+2 Boy has graduated from high school with good marks. Now employed as a blueprint reader at $40.00 per week. Adjustment very good. Says, "BJR is the best thing that ever happened to me" (Kell, 1942).

A word is in order in regard to the experiences of these children during the follow-up period. It is fortunate for the purposes of this study (though not for the children) that very little in the way of intensive casework or psychotherapy was utilized in the treatment of these delinquents. We say that this is fortunate for the study, because obviously the aim of all treatment is to defeat the statistical probabilities involved in prediction. That is, the caseworker or therapist in working with a person is endeavoring to alter the behavior which would objectively be predicted for this individual, and thus is hoping to make the prediction an erroneous one. The only type of treatment recommendations which were apt to be carried out in the group under study were the recommendations that the child be placed on probation, or placed in a foster home or institution. There is no way of measuring or indicating the amount of treatment effort invested in these children. It may be said, however, that the amount was relatively small, and that if one grants any efficacy to treatment effort then in so far as this study is concerned, it would only act to reduce the accuracy of behavioral prediction. In other words, whatever predictive accuracy is achieved by the method used, it is safe to say that it would have been greater had no treatment of any kind been attempted.

FINDINGS

We are now ready to consider the analysis of the data collected. It should be clear that for each child in the two groups we have a rating on each of eight factors as to the extent to which those factors are likely to produce normal or well-adjusted behavior. These ratings were made on the basis of information available at the time the child came to the BJR. We have also independent ratings of the child's adjustment during the two-year period following the initial study. The major aspect of the analysis consists in the correlation of these predictive judgments with the evaluations of actual behavior.

The first finding of significance is that all the predictive factors which were rated showed a positive correlation with later adjustment. That is, the child with good heredity, or good health, or favorable family environment, etc., is more likely to display normal and well-adjusted behavior during the two-year period following the study than is the child who is less favored in any of these respects. This would tend to support the general hypothesis that behavior is the result of multiple causation, and that the factors which were selected for study are at least some of the effective elements which seem to determine adjustment or maladjustment.

TABLE 2
CORRELATION OF RATINGS ON COMPONENT FACTORS WITH RATINGS
OF LATER ADJUSTMENT

Factor	Correlations with adjustment	
	Kell study N = 75	McNeil study N = 76
Self-insight	.84**	.41**
Social experience	.55**	.36**
Mentality	.39**	.15
Hereditary	.37**	.23*
Family environment	.36**	.14
Economic and cultural	.28*	.07
Physical	.25*	.13
Education and training	.11	.20
Total averaged ratings	.66**	.27*

* These correlations are significant at the 5-per-cent level of confidence.
** These correlations are significant at the 1-per-cent level of confidence.

But the unexpected finding which gives quite a different meaning to this material is the predictive importance of the individual's understanding of himself. As will be seen from Table 2, the correlation between self-insight and later adjustment was .84, an unusually high relationship for material of this sort. It was this surprising finding which lead the investigators first to check the data for possible errors and finally to lay it aside until it could be thoroughly rechecked on a new group. In the McNeil study, all the correlations are consistently lower, a puzzling fact which we have been unable to explain, but self-insight again comes out as the best predictor of behavior, correlating .41 with outcome.

In both studies the factor which was second in predictive significance was the social experience and social adequacy of the child. The respective correlations were .55 and .36, both statistically significant. The relationship between the other factors and adjustment was positive, but lower than these two, with the McNeil study finding lower significance for the factors of mentality and economic-cultural influence, and somewhat higher weight for education and training, when her results are compared with those of Kell.

As would be expected, when the various ratings on the separate factors were averaged, they correlated positively with outcome, r's of .66 and .27 respectively being obtained in the two studies. This represents a questionable method of prediction, where the factors obviously have different weightings.

The material from Table 2 may be summarized by stating that in predicting the behavior of a problem adolescent, the *extent to which he faces and accepts himself, and has a realistic view of himself and reality,* provides, of the factors studied, the best estimate of his future adjustment. The second best predictor would be the *satisfactoriness of his social contacts, the adequacy of his social relationships.* These two are outstandingly better bases of prediction than any of the other factors studied, but positive correlation with later adjustments is found in ratings of the hereditary stock from which the individual has sprung; his mentality and mental functioning; the emotional climate of his family environment; his physical condition and health; and finally the economic, cultural, and educational influences to which he has been exposed. These factors would be of predictive significance roughly in the order named.

Further Analysis Related to Self-Insight

Since the factor which had most doubtfully been included in the Component Factor method proved to correlate most highly with outcome, special attention will be given to its analysis.

In the first place, the reader may wish to know the type of material upon which the ratings were based. Here are some of the summarized notes from the two investigators' records, indicating the material relating to self-insight which was found in the cases, and the rating based upon it.

—3 Refuses to discuss his delinquencies; will not or cannot discuss problems arising out of family conflicts; denies his share of responsibility even when confronted with the facts (McNeil, 1944).

—2 Quite frank and open in discussing her misbehavior, but stories are unreliable. Is proud of her misbehavior—does not feel responsible. Does not recognize that family situation is the cause of much of her trouble (Kell, 1942).

—1 Cautious, fairly truthful, correcting statements on own initiative. Feels some responsibility, realizing he is too easily influenced. Makes no complaints about the family but appears to understand somewhat its poor influence (McNeil, 1944).

+1 Understands his home situation fairly well, not clear about his relationship to it. Recognizes source of difficulties, but needs help in managing them. Admits his delinquencies truthfully with something similar to "They were not to blame. I was on the wrong track" (McNeil, 1944).

+2 Freely admits her delinquencies, recognizing and accepting the basis of parental antagonism and rejection. Planful and cooperative. Responsible when placed on her own. Tells facts frankly, recognizes and understands mother's instability and her own need for personal responsibility. Responsive and cooperative in behavior and in making future plans (McNeil, 1944).

* Editor's italics.

These examples may be sufficient to indicate the rather crude character of the material available for making this as well as the other ratings. If such significant correlations are achieved on the basis of general case material, the possibility is at least suggested that more refined ways of investigating the degree of self-understanding might give even more significant results.

Since both self-insight and the social factor gave high correlations with outcome, it was thought wise to investigate the degree of relationship between these two factors. In the Kell group, the correlation between the ratings on self-insight and the ratings on the social factor was .66, in the McNeil group, .63. This is a high degree of interrelationship which does not seem to be explainable on the basis of similarity of definitions of the two factors, or similarity of the material being rated. For example, the notes from three cases as to the social factor, with their respective ratings, are as follows:

−3 Does not get along well with sibs or school companions. Quarrelsome. Mistreats other children, and cruel to small children and animals. Not successful in trial social adjustment opportunities.

0 Somewhat of a leader among the older delinquent boys. Has a passable manner, likes sports, likes to impress the girls.

+2 Plays on a team. Friends are not delinquents. Good mixer, liked by others in the neighborhood and school. Has a good stamp collection. Has three very close friends (McNeil, 1944).

There would seem to be no obvious reason why ratings based on this type of data should correlate closely with ratings made on self-insight. It would seem that the relationship may be of a more underlying nature.

In another attempt to analyze the meaning of the high correlation of the self-insight factor with later adjustment, this correlation was separately computed for boys and girls, and for Negroes and whites. The differences were not striking, and some of the groups were small, but in both studies the correlation was higher for the girls than for the boys, and for the Negroes than for the whites.

Another line of investigation gave special consideration to those children who remained in their own homes during the follow-up period. It had been a surprise to the investigators that family environment had not correlated highly with outcome, and that self-understanding had correlated so highly. As the material was examined, it appeared possible that the fact that a sizable number of children from the poorest homes had been removed from their own families as a result of the diagnostic study might have influenced these results. Consequently both Kell and McNeil selected from their groups those children who had been returned to their own homes during the follow-up period. They also endeavored to determine whether the factor of self-insight was less operative when the home conditions were very unfavorable, by selecting out those with family factors rated −2 or −3, who had been returned to these very unfavorable homes.

TABLE 3

THE CORRELATION OF SELF-INSIGHT WITH ADJUSTMENT AMONG CHILDREN
RETURNED TO THEIR OWN HOMES

Group	Kell's study		McNeil's study	
	N	r	N	r
Children whose family environment was rated −2 or −3	28	.76*	28	.31
Children whose family environment was rated −1 or 0	15	.78*	12	.49
All children returned to their own homes	43	.79*	47	.43*

* Significant at the 1-per-cent level of confidence.

The results are shown in Table 3. It will be seen that the correlation between insight and later adjustment is relatively unchanged, even when the child comes from, and returns to, a very unfavorable home situation. It is still true that a much better prediction of adjustment can be based upon a consideration of the degree of self-understanding, than upon any analysis of the home environment. McNeil further checked this by correlating the family environment factor with later adjustment in the group of 47 children returned to their own homes. This r was .20. It is higher than the similar correlation for the group as a whole (.14 in her study), but much lower than the correlation of .43 between self-insight and later adjustment.

When the child is removed from his own home and placed in a foster home, the operation of self-insight as a predictor is enhanced. There were 10 children in Kell's group thus placed and 15 in McNeil's. The correlations between self-insight and later adjustment for these two small groups were .98 (!) and .54 respectively. Both of these correlations are significant, the first at the 1-per-cent level and the second at the 5-per-cent level, in spite of the small numbers involved.

Limitations of the Findings

Since some of the findings of these studies appear to have considerable significance if they are confirmed by other research, it should be mentioned that they were uncovered in investigations which have certain flaws and limitations. Those limitations which are evident to the investigators will be briefly stated.

It is unfortunate that there is no study of the reliability of the Component-Factor ratings in these two studies. Knowledge of the degree of reliability present in a previous study does not entirely compensate for this. There is no study of the reliability of the ratings on final adjustment.

A more serious flaw is the fact that the same judge rated both the initial factors and the final adjustment, even though these ratings were made independently and some time apart. The investigator made some 600 ratings of individual factors in the 75 cases; then, without reference to these or to the material upon which they were based, made the ratings on the follow-up material. It would certainly be preferable to have another judge make these judgments. It may be said, however, that if there was any unconscious bias operating in this situation, it could not account for the surprising showing of the self-insight factor, since whatever bias existed was in the direction of supposing that the emotional climate of the family was probably the most influential factor in the determination of behavior.

Another limitation of the studies as a whole is the fact that the rating scales for the eight factors and also for the later adjustment are crude instruments lacking in the degree of refinement which would be desirable in objective research. The information in the case folders was also often lacking in the specificity which would be desirable.

These limitations are real, yet their operation would for the most part tend to reduce correlations. There would seem to be nothing in the design or conduct of the study which would explain the degree of relationship which was found between self-insight and adjustment.

There is one other element in the studies which deserves critical consideration, and that is the sharp difference in the correlations found by the two investigators. It appears from an examination of the data that it is not due to any difference in the range of the ratings, or to any statistical artifact which can be discovered. Whether it is due to a difference in clinical discrimination in making the ratings, or to some other cause, is unknown. As long as it is unexplained, it would appear that it might cover some unrecognized source of error.

Summary of the Findings

To recapitulate the findings of the two investigations:

1. The ratings of the eight factors specified in the component-factor method all showed a positive correlation with ratings of the individual's later adjustment, in the group of 151 cases studied.

2. The size of these correlations as found in the two studies differed sharply in amount, but there was a high degree of correspondence in the relative significance of the factors.

3. The rating of the *individual's understanding and acceptance of himself and the reality situation* * was, in both studies, the best predictor of what his future adjustment would be.

4. In both studies the factor which was second in predictive capacity was the *social experience and social adequacy* * of the individual.

* Editor's italics.

5. In decreasing order, these factors were also found to have some capacity for prediction of future behavior: the heredity of the individual; his intellectual functioning; the emotional atmosphere which the child has experienced in the family; the economic and cultural conditions which have surrounded him; the quality and consistency of his educational environment.

6. A high degree of relationship was found between the rating on self-insight and the rating on social experience. This correlation does not appear to be explained on the basis of simple overlapping of materials rated, but may involve some deeper relationship between the two factors.

7. In the group of children who came from, and remained in, highly undesirable atmospheres, it was still true that the degree of *self-understanding* * was the best predictor of adjustment, much better than an evaluation of the home influence itself.

8. In children who are removed from highly undesirable home atmosphere and placed in foster homes, the degree of *self-understanding* * is a decidedly accurate predictor of future adjustment or maladjustment.

IMPLICATIONS OF THE FINDINGS

Only gradually, as the clinical experience of the authors has pointed in the same direction as the results of this research, has the full significance of the foregoing findings been recognized and appreciated. Only as work in psychotherapy has driven home the importance of the individual's concept of himself and his relation to reality, and the close relationship between these perceptions and his behavior, have the findings of this research been understood. (See reference 6 for an expression of this line of thought.) It is another experience to illustrate that objective facts have little meaning until they fit, in some recognizable way, into our frame of reference.

If the present studies are confirmed in their central findings by further research, then there are three broad implications which deserve consideration. The *first is the socially hopeful character of the findings.* * Studies in prediction based upon correlating isolated background facts with later adjustment seem uniformly depressing because they add up to the total conclusion that the more adverse the factors operating in the individual's life, the more hopeless he becomes from any social point of view. The present studies do not flatly contradict this conclusion. It is true that a poor heredity and the presence of destructive organic factors, and a culturally deprived background, all predispose, to some degree, toward a less adequate adjustment. But the significant fact is that the element which above all others should be the most subject to natural change or planned alteration, the individual's acceptance of himself and of reality, is also the most important determiner of his future behavior. Rather than feeling that a person is inevitably doomed by unalter-

* Editor's italics.

able forces which have shaped him, this study suggests that the most potent influence in his future behavior is one which is certainly alterable to some degree without any change in his physical or social heredity or in his present environment. The most powerful determinant would appear to lie in the attitudes of the person himself.

A *second implication* * which should be mentioned is that the results of these studies would point toward a *drastic revision of the methods of dealing with or treating individuals who exhibit delinquent or problem behavior.* * In the groups which were studied, and in other similar groups, practically all of the investment of money and effort is directed toward altering factors which appear to be only to a small degree determinative of behavior. Vast amounts are expended on foster homes and children's institutions in order to alter the child's whole environment, considerable amounts on probationary supervision which is little more than a checking up on the youngster, considerable sums on the alleviation of physical deficiencies, but practically nothing on any direct approach to the problem of revising the child's attitudes toward himself. Likewise only a small fraction of the total treatment effort goes to changing the child's social adjustment, which appears to be second only to self-insight in its significance.

If treatment effort was to be expended in most efficient form, in the light of the results of this study, then effective psychotherapy, either individual or group, aimed at *helping the child achieve a more realistic acceptance of his impulses and abilities, and a realistic appraisal of his situation,* * would be the major investment. Social experiences might need to be provided concurrently, or the psychotherapy might assist him in developing more constructively the social relationships which he has. In any event, it would not be the quantity of social contact, but the degree to which the individual built mature give-and-take relationships with others, which would be regarded as important. A distinctly lesser amount of effort might be expended in endeavoring to improve the family relationships and the economic status. Some effort to enrich the cultural stimulation of the child might also be justified. The primary aim throughout would be to provide the opportunities for emotional release, insightful acceptance of self, and positive reorientation of self, which every successful psychotherapy entails. Such opportunities might be offered through the clinic, through the classroom with a specially trained teacher, through special school counseling services, or through group therapy carried on in conjunction with a recreational group. The whole focus of effort would be almost the reverse of the accepted procedures at the present time.

The final implication carried by the results of this study is that if the individual's view of himself and reality is so important—the degree of his defensiveness, the degree of acceptance of himself, his realistic appraisal of reality, his degree of independence and planfulness, his ability to be objectively self-

* Editor's italics.

critical—then a great deal of research is needed in this area. Studies are needed to discover how healthy perceptions of this sort occur, and the circumstances which cause the individual to become defensive and lacking in insight. We need much deeper research into the way in which the individual views himself, and the fashion in which his internal view of experience influences his behavior. Finally we need penetrating investigations of the ways in which such views of experience may be altered in the direction of realism and self-acceptance. Such research would move us forward a great distance in our knowledge of how to deal with those with behavior disorders.

IMPLICATIONS

How would you now go about evaluating a child you may interview in respect to such factors as heredity, physique, mentality, family influences, and so on? What are the implications of the major findings that self-understanding and acceptance of oneself and reality are highly important in predicting later adjustment? Why do you think these factors are apparently so important? You may want to come back to a discussion of these findings after you have read the selections in Chapter XI on counseling and psychotherapy. Do these findings support one kind of therapy over another?

REFERENCES

Consult the Bibliography for references cited in the article.

Chapter II

CHILDHOOD, ADOLESCENCE, MATURITY

[7] THE NATURE OF LOVE

How have psychologists attempted to explain the development of love, which has long held, as Harlow points out, a vast interest and fascination for human beings? Is the expression of love learned? Is it a *secondary drive* or a *basic motive?* Can its bases and development be discovered by carefully controlled experiments? How does a psychologist manipulate the stimulus and response variables to discover the nature of love? Let us see what Harry Harlow has discovered in his studies of neonatal and infant monkeys. You will find this presented in a scientific but delightfully humorous manner.

Harry F. Harlow

Reprinted from Harry F. Harlow, "The Nature of Love," *American Psychologist*, Vol. 13 (Washington, D.C.: American Psychological Association, 1958), pp. 673–680, 683–685, by permission of the publisher and the author.

Love is a wondrous state, deep, tender, and rewarding. Because of its intimate and personal nature it is regarded by some as an improper topic for experimental research. But, whatever our personal feelings may be, our assigned mission as psychologists is to analyze all facets of human and animal behavior into their component variables. So far as love or affection is concerned, psychologists have failed in this mission. The little we know about love does not transcend simple observation, and the little we write about it has been written better by poets and novelists. But of greater concern is the fact that psychologists tend to give progressively less attention to a motive which pervades our entire lives. Psychologists, at least psychologists who write textbooks, not only show no interest in the origin and development of love or affection, but they seem to be unaware of its very existence.

The apparent repression of love * by modern psychologists stands in sharp contrast with the attitude taken by many famous and normal people. The word "love" has the highest reference frequency of any word cited in Bartlett's book of *Familiar Quotations*. It would appear that this emotion has long had a vast interest and fascination for human beings, regardless of the attitude taken by psychologists; but the quotations cited, even by famous and normal people, have a mundane redundancy. These authors and authorities have stolen love from the child and infant and made it the exclusive property of the adolescent and adult.

Thoughtful men, and probably all women, have speculated on the nature of love. From the developmental point of view, the general plan is quite clear: the initial love responses of the human being are those made by the infant to the mother or some mother surrogate. From this intimate attachment of the child to the mother, multiple learned and generalized affectional responses are formed.

Unfortunately, beyond these simple facts we know little about the fundamental variables underlying the formation of affectional responses and little about the mechanisms through which the love of the infant for the mother develops into the multifaceted response patterns characterizing love or affection in the adult. Because of the dearth of experimentation, theories about the fundamental nature of affection have evolved at the level of observation, intuition, and discerning guesswork, whether these have been proposed by psychologists, sociologists, anthropologists, physicians, or psychoanalysts.

The position commonly held by psychologists * and sociologists is quite clear: the basic motives are, for the most part, the primary drives—particularly hunger, thirst, elimination, pain, and sex—and all other motives, including love or affection, are derived or secondary drives. The mother is associated with the reduction of the primary drives—particularly hunger, thirst, and pain—and through learning, affection or love is derived.

It is entirely reasonable to believe that the mother through association with food may become a secondary-reinforcing agent, but this is an inadequate mechanism to account for the persistence of the infant-maternal ties. There is a spate of researches on the formation of secondary reinforcers to hunger and thirst reduction. There can be no question that almost any external stimulus can become a secondary reinforcer if properly associated with tissue-need reduction, but the fact remains that this redundant literature demonstrates unequivocally that such derived drives suffer relatively rapid experi-

* Editor's italics.

mental extinction. Contrariwise human affection does not extinguish when the mother ceases to have intimate association with the drives in question. Instead, the affectional ties to the mother show a lifelong, unrelenting persistence and, even more surprising, widely expanding generality.

Oddly enough, one of the few psychologists who took a position counter to modern psychological dogma was John B. Watson, who believed that love was an innate emotion elicited by cutaneous stimulation of the erogenous zones. But experimental psychologists, with their peculiar propensity to discover facts that are not true, brushed this theory aside by demonstrating that the human neonate had no differentiable emotions, and they established a fundamental psychological law that prophets are without honor in their own profession.

The psychoanalysts * have concerned themselves with the problem of the nature of the development of love in the neonate and infant, using ill and aging human beings as subjects. They have discovered the overwhelming importance of the breast and related this to the oral erotic tendencies developed at an age preceding their subjects' memories. Their theories range from a belief that the infant has an innate need to achieve and suckle at the breast to beliefs not unlike commonly accepted psychological theories. There are exceptions, as seen in the recent writings of John Bowlby, who attributes importance not only to food and thirst satisfaction, but also to "primary object-clinging," a need for intimate physical contact, which is initially associated with the mother.

As far as I know, there exists no *direct experimental analysis* * of the relative importance of the stimulus variables determining the affectional or love responses in the neonatal and infant primate. Unfortunately, the human neonate is a limited experimental subject for such researches because of his inadequate motor capabilities. By the time the human infant's motor responses can be precisely measured, the antecedent determining conditions cannot be defined, having been lost in a jumble and jungle of confounded variables.

Many of these difficulties can be resolved by the use of the neonatal and infant macaque monkey as the subject for the analysis of basic affectional variables. It is possible to make precise measurements in this primate beginning at two to ten days of age, depending upon the maturational status of the individual animal at birth. The macaque infant differs from the human infant in that the monkey is more mature at birth and grows more rapidly; but the basic responses relating to affection, including nursing, contact, clinging, and even visual and auditory exploration, exhibit no fundamental differences in the two species. Even the development of perception, fear, frustration, and learning capability follows very similar sequences in rhesus monkeys and human children.

* Editor's italics.

Three years' experimentation * before we started our studies on affection gave us experience with the neonatal monkey. We had separated more than sixty of these animals from their mothers six to twelve hours after birth and suckled them on tiny bottles. The infant mortality was only a small fraction of what would have obtained had we let the monkey mothers raise their infants. Our bottle-fed babies were healthier and heavier than monkey-mother-reared infants. We know that we are better monkey mothers than are real monkey mothers thanks to synthetic diets, vitamins, iron extracts, penicillin, chloromycetin, 5 per cent glucose, and constant, tender, loving care.

During the course of these studies, we noticed that the laboratory-raised babies showed strong attachment to the cloth pads (folded gauze diapers) which were used to cover the hardware-cloth floors of their cages. The infants clung to these pads and engaged in violent temper tantrums when the pads were removed and replaced for sanitary reasons. Such contact need or responsiveness had been reported previously by Gertrude van Wagenen for the monkey and by Thomas McCulloch and George Haslerud for the chimpanzee and is reminiscent of the devotion often exhibited by human infants to their pillows, blankets, and soft, cuddly stuffed toys. . . . The baby, human or monkey, if it is to survive, must clutch at more than a straw.

We had also discovered during some allied observational studies that a baby monkey raised on a bare wire-mesh cage floor survives with difficulty, if at all, during the first five days of life. If a wire-mesh cone is introduced, the baby does better; and, if the cone is covered with terry cloth, husky, healthy, happy babies evolve. It takes more than a baby and a box to make a normal monkey. We were impressed by the possibility that, above and beyond the bubbling fountain of breast or bottle, contact comfort might be a very important variable in the development of the infant's affection for the mother.

At this point we decided to study the development of affectional responses of neonatal and infant monkeys to an artificial, inanimate mother, and so we built a surrogate mother which we hoped and believed would be a good surrogate mother. In devising this surrogate mother, we were dependent neither upon the capriciousness of evolutionary processes nor upon mutations produced by chance radioactive fallout. Instead, we designed the mother surrogate in terms of modern human-engineering principles. We produced a perfectly proportioned, streamlined body stripped of unnecessary bulges and appendices. Redundancy in the surrogate mother's system was avoided by reducing the number of breasts from two to one and placing this unibreast in an upper-thoracic, sagittal position, thus maximizing the natural and known perceptual-motor capabilities of the infant operator. The surrogate was made from a block of wood, covered with sponge rubber, and sheathed in tan cotton terry cloth. A light bulb behind her radiated heat. The result was a mother, soft, warm, and tender, a mother with infinite patience, a mother

* Editor's italics.

Figure 1. Wire and cloth mother surrogates.

available twenty-four hours a day, a mother that never scolded her infant and never struck or bit her baby in anger. Furthermore, we designed a mother-machine with maximal maintenance efficiency since failure of any system or function could be resolved by the simple substitution of black boxes and new component parts. It is our opinion that we engineered a very

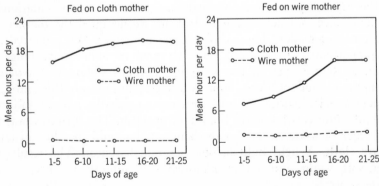

Figure 2. Time spent on cloth and wire mother surrogates.

superior monkey mother, although this position is not held universally by the monkey fathers.

Before beginning our initial experiment we also designed and constructed *a second mother surrogate,** a surrogate in which we deliberately built less than the maximal capability for contact comfort. This surrogate mother is illustrated in Figure 1. She is made of wire mesh, a substance entirely adequate to provide postural support and nursing capability, and she is warmed by radiant heat. Her body differs in no essential way from that of the cloth mother surrogate other than in the quality of the contact comfort which she can supply.

In our initial experiment, the dual mother-surrogate condition, a cloth mother and a wire mother were placed in different cubicles attached to the infant's living cage as shown in Figure 1. For four newborn monkeys the cloth mother lactated and the wire mother did not; and, for the other four, this condition was reversed. In either condition the infant received all its milk through the mother surrogate as soon as it was able to maintain itself in this way, a capability achieved within two or three days except in the case of very immature infants. Supplementary feedings were given until the milk intake from the mother surrogate was adequate. Thus, the experiment was designed as a test of the relative importance of the variables of contact comfort and nursing comfort. During the first 14 days of life, the monkey's cage floor was covered with a heating pad wrapped in a folded gauze diaper, and thereafter the cage floor was bare. The infants were always free to leave the heating pad or cage floor to contact either mother, and the time spent on the surrogate mothers was automatically recorded. Figure 2 shows the total time spent on the cloth and wire mothers under the two conditions of feeding. These data make it obvious that contact comfort is a variable of overwhelming importance in the development of affectional responses, whereas lactation is a variable of negligible importance. With age and opportunity to learn, subjects with the lactating wire mother showed decreasing responsiveness to her and increasing responsiveness to the nonlactating cloth mother, a finding completely contrary to any interpretation of derived drive in which the mother form becomes conditioned to hunger-thirst reduction. The persistence of these differential responses throughout 165 consecutive days of testing is evident in Figure 3.

One control group of neonatal monkeys was raised on a single wire mother, and a second control group was raised on a single cloth mother.* There were no differences between these two groups in amount of milk ingested or in weight gain. The only difference between the groups lay in the composition of the feces, the softer stools of the wire-mother infants suggesting psychosomatic involvement. The wire mother is biologically adequate but psychologically inept.

* Editor's italics.

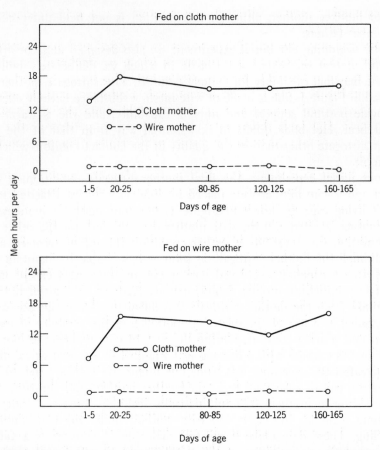

Figure 3. Long-term contact time on cloth and wire mother surrogates.

We were not surprised to discover that contact comfort was an important basic affectional or love variable, but we did not expect it to overshadow so completely the variable of nursing; indeed, the disparity is so great as to suggest that the primary function of nursing as an affectional variable is that of insuring frequent and intimate body contact of the infant with the mother. Certainly, man cannot live by milk alone. Love is an emotion that does not need to be bottle- or spoon-fed, and we may be sure that there is nothing to be gained by giving lip service to love.

A charming lady once heard me describe these experiments; and when I subsequently talked to her, her face brightened with sudden insight: "Now I know what's wrong with me," she said, "I'm just a wire mother." Perhaps she was lucky. She might have been a wire wife.

We believe that contact comfort has long served the animal kingdom as a motivating agent for affectional responses. Since at the present time we have no experimental data to substantiate this position, we supply information which must be accepted, if at all, on the basis of face validity. . . .

One function of the real mother, human or subhuman, and presumably of a mother surrogate, is to provide a haven of safety for the infant in times of fear and danger. The frightened or ailing child clings to its mother, not its father; and this selective responsiveness in times of distress, disturbance, or danger may be used as a measure of the strength of affectional bonds. We have tested this kind of differential responsiveness by presenting to the infants in their cages, in the presence of the two mothers, various fear-producing stimuli such as the moving toy bear. A typical response to a fear stimulus is shown in Figure 4, and the data on differential responsiveness are presented in Figure 5. It is apparent that the cloth mother is highly preferred over the wire one, and this differential selectivity is enhanced by age and experience. In this situation, the variable of nursing appears to be of absolutely no importance: the infant consistently seeks the soft mother surrogate regardless of nursing condition.

Similarly, the mother or mother surrogate provides its young with a source of security, and this role or function is seen with special clarity when mother and child are in a strange situation. At the present time we have completed tests for this relationship on four of our eight baby monkeys assigned to the dual mother-surrogate condition by introducing them for three minutes into the strange environment of a room measuring six feet by six feet by six feet (also called the "open-field test") and containing multiple stimuli known to elicit curiosity-manipulatory responses in baby monkeys. The subjects were placed in this situation twice a week for eight weeks with no mother surrogate present during alternate sessions and the cloth mother present during the others. A cloth diaper was always available as one of the stimuli throughout all sessions. After one or two adaptation sessions, the infants always rushed to the mother surrogate when she was present and clutched her, rubbed their bodies against her, and frequently manipulated her body and face. After a few additional sessions, the infants began to use the mother surrogate as a source of security, a base of operations. They would explore and manipulate a stimulus and then return to the mother before adventuring again into the strange new world. The behavior of these infants was quite different when the mother was absent from the room. Frequently they would freeze in a crouched position, as is illustrated in Figure 6. Emotionality indices such as vocalization, crouching, rocking, and sucking increased sharply. Total emotionality score was cut in half when the mother was present. In the absence of the mother, some of the experimental monkeys would rush to the center of the room where the mother was customarily placed and then run rapidly from object to object, screaming and crying all the while. Continuous, frantic clutching of their bodies was very common, even when not in the crouching position. These monkeys frequently contacted and clutched

FIGURE 4. Typical response to cloth mother surrogate in fear test.

the cloth diaper, but this action never pacified them. The same behavior occurred in the presence of the wire mother. No difference between the cloth-mother-fed and wire-mother-fed infants was demonstrated under either condition. . . .

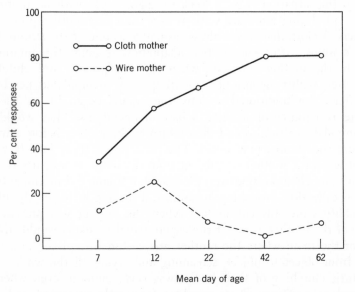

FIGURE 5. Differential responsiveness in fear tests.

FIGURE 6. Response in the open-field test in the absence of the mother surrogate.

We have already described the *group of four control infants that had never lived in the presence of any mother surrogate and had demonstrated no sign of affection or security in the presence of the cloth mothers* * introduced in test sessions. When these infants reached the age of 250 days, cubicles containing both a cloth mother and a wire mother were attached to their cages. There was no lactation in these mothers, for the monkeys were on a solid-food diet. The initial reaction of the monkeys to the alterations was one of extreme disturbance. All the infants screamed violently and made repeated attempts to escape the cage whenever the door was opened. They kept a maximum distance from the mother surrogates and exhibited a considerable amount of rocking and crouching behavior, indicative of emotionality. Our first thought was that the critical period for the development of maternally directed affection had passed and that these macaque children were doomed to live as affectional orphans. Fortunately, these behaviors continued for only 12 to 48 hours and then gradually ebbed, changing from indifference to active contact on, and exploration of, the surrogates. The home-cage behavior of these control monkeys slowly became similar to that of the animals raised with the mother surrogates from birth. Their manipu-

* Editor's italics.

lation and play on the cloth mother became progressively more vigorous to the point of actual mutilation, particularly during the morning after the cloth mother had been given her daily change of terry covering. The control subjects were now actively running to the cloth mother when frightened and had to be coaxed from her to be taken from the cage for formal testing.

Objective evidence of these changing behaviors is given in Figure 7, which plots the amount of time these infants spent on the mother surrogates. Within 10 days, mean contact time is approximately nine hours and this measure remains relatively constant throughout the next 30 days. Consistent with the results on the subjects reared from birth with dual mothers, these late-adopted infants spent less than one and one half hours per day in contact with the wire mothers, and this activity level was relatively constant throughout the test sessions. Although the maximum time that the control monkeys spent on the cloth mother was only about half that spent by the original dual mother-surrogate group, we cannot be sure that this discrepancy is a function of differential early experience. The control monkeys were about three months older when the mothers were attached to their cages than the experimental animals had been when their mothers were removed and the retention tests begun. Thus, we do not know what the amount of contact would be for a 250-day-old animal raised from birth with surrogate mothers. Nevertheless, the magnitude of the differences and the fact that the

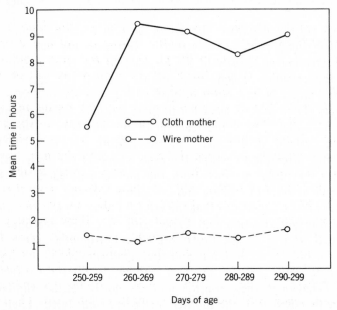

Figure 7. Differential time spent on cloth and wire mother surrogates by monkeys started at 250 days of age.

contact-time curves for the mothered-from-birth infants had remained constant for almost 150 days suggest that early experience with the mother is a variable of measurable importance. . . .

That the control monkeys develop affection or love for the cloth mother when she is introduced into the cage at 250 days of age cannot be questioned. There is every reason to believe, however, that this interval of delay depresses the intensity of the affectional response below that of the infant monkeys that were surrogate-mothered from birth onward. In interpreting these data, it is well to remember that the control monkeys had had continuous opportunity to observe and hear other monkeys housed in adjacent cages and that they had had limited opportunity to view and contact surrogate mothers in the test situations, even though they did not exploit the opportunities.

During the last two years, we have observed the behavior of two infants raised by their own mothers. Love for the real mother and love for the surrogate mother appear to be very similar. The baby macaque spends many hours a day clinging to its real mother. If away from the mother when frightened, it rushes to her and in her presence shows comfort and composure. As far as we can observe, the infant monkey's affection for the real mother is strong, but no stronger than that of the experimental monkey for the surrogate cloth mother, and the security that the infant gains from the presence of the real mother is no greater than the security it gains from a cloth surrogate. . . . But, whether the mother is real or a cloth surrogate, there does develop a deep and abiding bond between mother and child. In one case it may be the call of the wild and in the other the McCall of civilization, but in both cases there is "togetherness."

In spite of the importance of contact comfort, there is reason to believe that other variables of measurable importance will be discovered. Postural support may be such a variable, and it has been suggested that, when we build arms into the mother surrogate, 10 is the minimal number required to provide adequate child care. Rocking motion may be such a variable, and we are comparing rocking and stationary mother surrogates and inclined planes. The differential responsiveness to cloth mother and cloth-covered inclined plane suggests that clinging as well as contact is an affectional variable of importance. Sounds, particularly natural, maternal sounds, may operate as either unlearned or learned affectional variables. Visual responsiveness may be such a variable, and it is possible that some semblance of visual imprinting may develop in the neonatal monkey. There are indications that this becomes a variable of importance during the course of infancy through some maturational process. . . .

Since we can measure neonatal and infant affectional responses to mother surrogates, and since we know they are strong and persisting, we are in a position to assess the effects of feeding and contactual schedules; consistency and inconsistency in the mother surrogates; and early, intermediate, and late

maternal deprivation. Again, we have here a family of problems of fundamental interest and theoretical importance.

If the researches completed and proposed make a contribution, I shall be
grateful; but I have also given full thought to possible practical applications.
The socioeconomic demands of the present and the threatened socioeconomic demands of the future have led the American woman to displace, or
threaten to displace, the American man in science and industry. If this process
continues, the problem of proper child-rearing practices faces us with startling
clarity. It is cheering in view of this trend to realize that the American male
is physically endowed with all the really essential equipment to compete
with the American female on equal terms in one essential activity: the rearing of infants. We now know that women in the working classes are not needed
in the home because of their primary mammalian capabilities; and it is possible that in the foreseeable future neonatal nursing will not be regarded as
a necessity, but as a luxury—to use Veblen's term—a form of conspicuous
consumption limited perhaps to the upper classes. But whatever course history may take, it is comforting to know that we are now in contact with the
nature of love.

IMPLICATIONS

Which findings in this experiment had the greatest meaning for you?
What do you think are the implications of this study for early child care?
Read the paragraph under "References," which mentions other studies
that show the effect of inadequate mothering. What are the next studies
that you think need to be conducted in this area?

REFERENCES

Harlow and his associates have continued experiments on affectional
responses. The monkeys that were raised with cloth-surrogate mothers
showed inadequate sex behavior and became poor mothers when they
were finally impregnated and then bore young. In addition, the researchers found that monkeys separated from their mothers and raised in wire
cages that permitted them to see, hear, and call to other infants but not
to contact them became mute, stared fixedly into space, and appeared
indifferent to people and other monkeys. Some clutched their head in
their hands and rocked back and forth, others went into violent rages,
tearing at their own legs with such fury that they sometimes required
medical attention. These monkeys, obviously abnormal, also failed to

show normal sex behavior. Monkeys that have never known a real mother "become mothers—helpless, hopeless, heartless mothers, devoid, or almost devoid, of any maternal feelings." (See Harlow, 1962.)

[8] ANXIETY: CHILDREN'S FORM OF THE MANIFEST ANXIETY SCALE

Psychologists frequently use the term *anxiety* as an important concept in understanding emotional disturbance of varying degrees. The neurotic individual is often defined in terms of excessive anxiety. Anxiety has some of the physiological concomitants of fear, but it is an *objectless fear*, a vague fear; it usually is associated with *other people*, with their possible *punitive action*, and with ideas of *low self-worth*.

This selection presents a modification of a well-known and successfully used set of items that has distinguished between individuals judged high and those judged low in anxiety. These items show you what the psychologists mean by anxiety in terms of reportable experience and behavior. The writers tell us how they devised the children's form of the scale and how they report its reliability or consistency of measurement. In short, they illustrate some of the steps necessary to develop a personality scale. The selection gives you a detailed sample of one of the many verbal personality tests available today that are used frequently in the studies reported in chapters on personality.

Finding the anxious child is important. He is troubled, but he does not know why. Professional workers can help him by discovering the conditions producing the anxiety and in assisting him to cope with it. In some cases the workers use the motivation produced by the anxiety for the acquisition of skills that will enable the child to make a better adjustment.

Alfred Castaneda, Boyd R. McCandless, and David S. Palermo

Reprinted from Alfred Castaneda, Boyd R. McCandless, and David S. Palermo, "The Children's Form of the Manifest Anxiety Scale," *Child Development*, Vol. 27 (Chicago: The Society for Research in Child Development, 1956), pp. 318–319, by permission of the publisher and the authors. © Copyright 1956 by The Society for Research in Child Development, Inc.

An earlier version of the present scale was administered to approximately sixty subjects for the purposes of obtaining information regarding possible difficulties in the instructions for its administration and the comprehensibility of the items. A total of 42 anxiety items were selected and modified, and 11 additional items designed to provide an index of the subject's tendency to falsify his responses to the anxiety items were included in the present form of the test. A similar set of items was included by Taylor from the L scale of the MMPI for the same purpose, hence these 11 items will also be referred to as the L scale. All of these items were then submitted to two elementary school system officials for a final check on their comprehensibility for the population for which they were intended. The 42 anxiety items, constituting the anxiety scale of the present test, are reproduced in Table 1 with their appropriate ordinal numbers as they appear in the present form of the test. The index of the level of anxiety is obtained by summing the number of these items answered "yes."

TABLE 1

ANXIETY ITEMS INCLUDED IN THE ANXIETY SCALE AND NUMBERED AS THEY APPEAR IN THE PRESENT FORM OF THE TEST

1. It is hard for me to keep my mind on anything.
2. I get nervous when someone watches me work.
3. I feel I have to be best in everything.
4. I blush easily.
6. I notice my heart beats very fast sometimes.
7. At times I feel like shouting.
8. I wish I could be very far from here.
9. Others seem to do things easier than I can.
11. I am secretly afraid of a lot of things.
12. I feel that others do not like the way I do things.
13. I feel alone even when there are people around me.
14. I have trouble making up my mind.
15. I get nervous when things do not go the right way for me.
16. I worry most of the time.
18. I worry about what my parents will say to me.

19. Often I have trouble getting my breath.
20. I get angry easily.
22. My hands feel sweaty.
23. I have to go to the toilet more than most people.
24. Other children are happier than I.
25. I worry about what other people think about me.
26. I have trouble swallowing.
27. I have worried about things that did not really make any difference later.
28. My feelings get hurt easily.
29. I worry about doing the right things.
31. I worry about what is going to happen.
32. It is hard for me to go to sleep at night.
33. I worry about how well I am doing in school.
35. My feelings get hurt easily when I am scolded.
37. I often get lonesome when I am with people.
38. I feel someone will tell me I do things the wrong way.
39. I am afraid of the dark.
40. It is hard for me to keep my mind on my school work.
42. Often I feel sick in my stomach.
43. I worry when I go to bed at night.
44. I often do things I wish I had never done.
45. I get headaches.
46. I often worry about what could happen to my parents.
48. I get tired easily.
50. I have bad dreams.
51. I am nervous.
53. I often worry about something bad happening to me.

The 11 L scale items are reproduced in Table 2 with their appropriate ordinal numbers as they appear in the present form of the test. Items 10 and 49, if answered "no" contribute to the L scale score as do the remaining nine items if answered "yes." The index of the subject's tendency to *falsify his responses* * to the anxiety items, then, is the sum of these items answered in the designated manner.

TABLE 2

ITEMS INCLUDED IN THE L SCALE AND NUMBERED AS THEY APPEAR IN THE PRESENT FORM OF THE TEST

5. I like everyone I know.
10. I would rather win than lose in a game.
17. I am always kind.
21. I always have good manners.
30. I am always good.
34. I am always nice to everyone.
36. I tell the truth every single time.
41. I never get angry.
47. I never say things I shouldn't.
49. It is good to get high grades in school.
52. I never lie.

 * Editor's italics.

Copies of this test were distributed to the classroom teacher who administered it to her class on a group basis. The only instructions provided the teacher were those which appeared on the test itself and which she read to the class. The instructions were, "Read each question carefully. Put a circle around the word YES if you think it is true about you. Put a circle around the word NO if you think it is not true about you." Space was provided on the test sheet for the subject to identify himself by name, grade, sex and school. Approximately one week later the classroom teacher re-administered the test. A total of 15 classrooms from four different schools participated in the study. A total of 386 children participated in the first administration of the test. However, due primarily to absences, only 361 of these children were tested on the second administration. One week re-test reliabilities averaged at about .90 for the anxiety scale and at about .70 for the L scale.[1]

IMPLICATIONS

You might find it interesting to check these items yourself to discover the extent of your own manifest anxiety. In reading these items, you may discover that they were more descriptive of you (or someone you knew very well) earlier in life than at present. What events do you think brought about the change? Manifest anxiety consists of symptoms of a condition brought about to some extent by relationships with people in early life. What do you think are some of the interpersonal relationships that produce anxious people? (Selections 5 and 16 and your introductory textbook may help you to answer the last question.)

REFERENCES

The student who is interested in an experimental approach to anxiety and psychological stress will find in Mednick and Mednick (1963) a series of articles that are critical of the scale, including one by Taylor on manifest anxiety and another by Jessor and Hammond (1963).

[1] Intercorrelations between the anxiety scale and the L scale clustered around the zero value. Girls were found to score significantly higher than boys on both scales. Significant differences on the L scale were found to be associated with grade.

[9] THE CHILD'S INNER LIFE: INTERPRETATION OF PROJECTIVE DEVICES

What are some of the methods used by the psychologist to explore the inner life of the child? The clinical psychologist uses the child's responses to ambiguous pictures and figures as well as the child's own drawings to learn something of his needs and anxieties. These inner concerns influence the child's behavior even though he is not clearly aware of them. The techniques are known as *projective methods*.

A highly respected psychologist and her associates have reproduced children's drawings, which we include in this excerpt. The authors show us how the drawings have been used to obtain further understanding of the motivation and adjustment of the youngster.

You will notice that these drawings are interpreted with caution and responsibility and are supplementary to other data obtained on the child, his history, and observations of his behavior in important everyday situations. The qualified clinical psychologist advances hypotheses about the underlying motivation of his client to be substantiated or negated by the bulk of the observations made. In doing this, he exemplifies the scientific attitude.

Charlotte Buhler, Faith Smitter, Sybil Richardson, and Franklyn Bradshaw

From Charlotte Buhler, Faith Smitter, Sybil Richardson, and Franklyn Bradshaw, *Childhood Problems and the Teacher*, copyright 1952, Holt, Rinehart and Winston, Inc. Used by permission of the author and publisher. All rights reserved.

The main objection to projective techniques has been the difficulty of reliable interpretation of an individual's projections. Because of this difficulty there is danger of abusing projective methods.

People with empathy, intuition, and imagination often feel that they can interpret another's feelings and motives. Although they succeed often, their interpretations are far from reliable. Children's drawings, for instance, seem to offer an almost irresistible invitation to interpretation. For the alert and interested teacher, the temptation to think of the child who uses gay colors as gay, and to find clues to the child's personality in certain contents, is very great. But this should be done only with extreme caution unless the teacher has had clinical training. In order to interpret projective self-expression, the examiner must recognize that there are unique personal features in self-expression which exist only in this individual's "private world." Such features are understood only if one knows something about the individual's history. To the experienced worker, the detection of these unique features becomes an important clue to the discovery of emotionally traumatic experiences.

An interesting example is the little three-year-old girl who evidently had some problem in connection with the use of her hands. She went around the room touching things so that they fell down, but she never used her hands directly. She touched objects by pushing her doll's head toward the toys.
Later this same child built a stable for a toy cow and built it almost like a hand with blocks protruding like fingers. But there were six, not five blocks.
This child had been born with the anomaly of six fingers on one hand. Although operated on as a baby, she no doubt had heard about it and had also raised questions regarding the scar on her hand.
Another interesting example is the forty-one-year-old man who saw injured birds in the Rorschach ink blots in seven places in which most people saw quite different things. After the test, when the examiner asked whether he had any particular experience with birds, the subject was astonished by the question—he had not been conscious of seeing so many birds. Then he began to think and suddenly exclaimed that indeed as a boy of seven he had accidentally stepped on a little bird and crushed it. The incident bothered him for many years, after which he forgot it completely.

In addition to such unique experiences, projective techniques also show general human trends. These recurring content or form characteristics of projective productions have been submitted to standardizing procedures and can be interpreted generally as will be shown in the following.

SAMPLES OF PROJECTIVE MATERIAL

Drawings and Paintings

For the teacher, drawings and paintings, including finger paintings, are so much a part of her experience and interest that a sampling of this important material is given here.
A good example is *Vigdis* whose drawings (Figure 1) were reproduced with a short explanation of her problem. . . .
She is quite *conscious* of the fact that she loves her teacher more than her

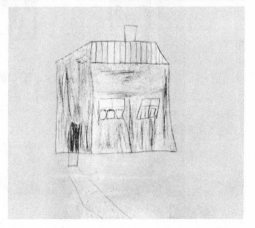

FIGURE 1. Vigdis, by the symbol of hand holding, indirectly expresses being close to the teacher and the husband but not to the grandparents.

grandparents; she wants her teacher to love her and to take her away from her grandparents into her own new home; Vigdis hopes to be welcome to the new husband also. She wants to be their child. She is *unconscious* of the fact that her drawings make a plea to the teacher to take her into her married life and into her new home as her child.

She gives a *direct* picture of herself with her grandparents and herself with the new couple. By the symbol of hand-holding she also *indirectly* expresses being close to the teacher and the husband but not to the grandparents.

In five-year-old *Tommy's* picture (Figure 2), there is an equally complex pattern of his conscious longing for the mother to be home, his unconscious fear and loneliness, his direct picture of the children at the windows, and his symbolic multiplication of many faces expressing the urgency he feels.

The deeper a child's problem, the more unconscious and unrealistic be-

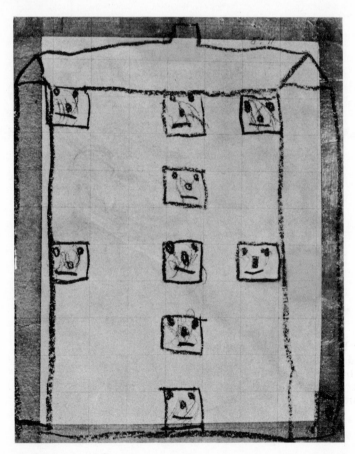

Figure 2. Tommy suggests longing for his mother to be home. The many faces in the windows express the urgency of his fear and loneliness.

comes the symbolism that expresses his disturbance. When *Frick* ... ties the house he draws to a tree, he forgets reality in which houses are never tied to trees. He just expresses his fear and his wish concerning his home's stability.

The relationship between *Leigh's* apple tree (Figure 3) and himself was even deeper. When Leigh came to therapy ... he was deeply disturbed by his soiling. The "ugly brown leaves" of the tree as well as the "dirty balls" of sand were semiconscious references to the soiling which shamed him. The leaves had to be burned; the balls to be buried. But the tree also had nice green leaves, and the tree must not burn. This was an unconscious reference to himself, to his good potentialities, and his wish that not Leigh but his shameful deeds be abolished.

This symbolic self-expression is deep because Leigh is not aware that his drawings and his sand formations relate to himself, or that he tells the therapist his problem by means of these products.

The therapist may or may not explain this symbolism to the child. Psychoanalysts formerly considered these interpretations to be essential. At present

FIGURE 3. Leigh's apple trees—the "ugly brown leaves" and "dirty balls" of sand were semiconscious references to the soiling that shamed him.

the prevailing tendency is to refrain from many interpretations, especially with younger children, and to achieve a certain amount of insight without making the child conscious of the way in which he revealed himself.

Leigh's apple tree is an *individual symbol* which refers to his private world. Leigh has been much interested in the burning of old leaves in his parents' back yard where grows this apple tree which he loves and climbs and which he identified with his home and himself. Other symbols are much more general and repetitious.

In spontaneous drawings of young children, the *house* appears most frequently. There seems to be a strong feeling about the protection that his home gives to the child. The strong identification of family and house is shown in one of the drawings that Wolff collected. At his instruction to "draw your family," a number of children drew the family beside their house.

In their drawings, many children surround their houses with fences, whether or not their own houses and yards have fences. The *fence* is another of the most frequently used symbols—to fence out potential aggressors or to imprison "bad" people.

Charlie, age eleven, makes a self-protective fence (Figure 4). So does nine-year-old *Henry* (Figure 5). *Henk*, an eight-year-old boy with severe anxieties caused by a very strict and punitive father, at first expresses his feelings that his house is a prison by painting barred windows. Then (Figure 6), probably becoming fearful that someone will guess how he feels, he covers the windows with paint, but ex-

FIGURE 4. Charles makes a self-protective fence.

presses his feeling about lack of freedom everywhere by enclosing every object in his world—the trees, the flowers, even the sun and garden. There is only one hope, the boat with which to escape outside.

The most unhappy feeling seems expressed in *Hallie's* drawing (Figure 7). The whole world is only fence and sky. It is empty of people, of things, of anything to have fun with—an empty prison.

The depth of feelings of imprisonment and the need for self-protection cannot be decided by looking at the drawings. The interpreter has to know more about the child, his background and history, his symptoms, and his ability or inability to project his feelings appropriately.

In remedial release work, children will quite frequently draw jails or witches. This need not always mean deep feelings of deprivation and hatred. Sometimes these drawings may express only acute anger and acute unhappiness. It is helpful, whenever possible, to have the child's comments on his drawings....

To the child, the *human figure* is as important as the *house*. The Good-

FIGURE 5. Henk has a strict and punitive father. He expresses his feelings of his house as a prison by painting barred windows.

FIGURE 6. Henk now covers windows to disguise his feelings; the boat is a hope to escape outside.

FIGURE 7. Hallie draws the whole world as fence and sky—empty of people and anything to have fun with.

enough "Draw-a-Man" test, originally devised for the purpose of testing intelligence, finds increasing application as a projective technique, because the attributes given to the human figure are often more expressive of the child's emotional responses than they are of his intellectual responses.

Children's self-portraits are also of great interest, revealing as they do children's attitudes toward their personalities and their moods. A frequent self-portrait is of the "lonely" child (Figure 8), done with unusually painstaking care.

Many of the examples we have used here show that *contents* as well as *formal* characteristics can be used for projection. This is as true of drawings as of other projective techniques, for example, the Rorschach and World tests. Protective fences, rigid schemation, confused disarrangements, over- or underemphasis of items, repetitions, worry over or disregard of detail—all are formal characteristics produced by an individual similarly in all these techniques. . . .

An unconscious formal symptom of importance is the child's worry over much detail and his overconscientious efforts to produce the most careful

FIGURE 8. Dagny's self-portrait of a lonely child done with unusual painstaking care.

detail. This is almost always a sign of excessive worry and of an emotionally disturbing perfectionism.

. . . *Paulinke's* flower garden (Figure 9), which is a happy content but, even so, not a release from worry, *Dagny's* detailed work on the girl in the snow (Figure 8), and *Henry's* detail on the garden fence (Figure 5) all belong in the same category.

A frequent content symbol used by little five- and six-year-old girls is the lonely child, as Dagny, age five, paints herself in the snow (Figure 8). "I want to stand all by myself," said another little girl who made such a drawing. Older lonely children paint "lonely" landscapes without people, sometimes without a sign of life, as *Ingrid* does in her second picture, "Road in the Sun" (Figure 10), or *Jerry* does in "The Desert" (Figure 11). Older children also sometimes express their distrust of people by choosing animals, particularly horses, as their friends.

It would be wrong to assume that all children's paintings refer to emotionally disturbing events. Six-year-old *Irma's* "Happy Birthday" (Figure 12) and ten-year-old Paulinke's "Flower Garden" (Figure 9) project happy feelings, and drawings such as "The Battle of Hastings" (Figure 13) by Douglas, age nine, represent intellectual and artistic interests.

Figure 9. Paulinke's flower garden—a happy content but not a release from worry.

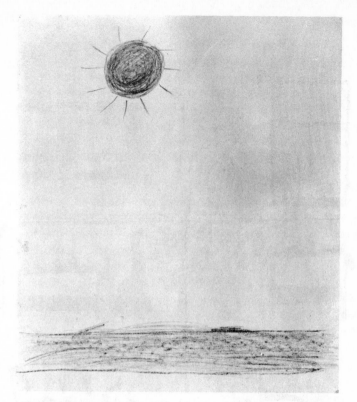

FIGURE 10. Ingrid's lonely landscape, "Road in the Sun."

FIGURE 11. Jerry's lonely landscape, "The Desert."

FIGURE 12. Irma's "Happy Birthday."

FIGURE 13. Douglas represents intellectual and artistic interests in his "The Battle of Hastings."

IMPLICATIONS

Which of the authors' interpretations of the drawings was clearest to you? If certain interpretations impressed you more than others, try to explain why. Did any ideas other than those stated by the authors occur to you as you observed the drawings? What differences do you note between those drawings that indicate emotional disturbance and those that do not? What cautions do you think psychologists should use in interpreting drawings?

REFERENCES

For further discussion of clinical application of projective drawings see Hammer (1958), Machover (1962) for personality projection in the drawing of a human figure, Allen (1958) for a review of drawing tests.

[10] PERSONALITY: ITS BIOLOGICAL FOUNDATIONS

Psychologists have been impressed by the pervasiveness of *learning* in human behavior. Almost every human act is and can be, with planning, greatly modified. This fact led some early behavioristic psychologists to assume that, with planning, a child could be molded into almost any kind of personality the parent or teacher desired. Much has been accomplished by *conditioning* and regimentation, but, as any experienced parent will attest, not all children can be taught the lessons that are carefully planned for them and, contrariwise, children learn and develop more as the result of basic talents and equipment than of external pressures.

Learning is important in human behavior; however, what is learned is not only a matter of environmental stimuli but also of inner motivations. Individuals differ greatly in physical and chemical structure, and the individual constitution determines, in relationship with the environment, what development will take place. Different people are different kinds of hosts to the environment they meet; some invite certain influences and repel others.

Roger J. Williams' selection shows the wide variation in biological equipment in the human being. At present there is not enough research on the complex *interrelationship between biological conditions and environmental influences* that together shape development in specific ways. However, the wide variation in anatomy and physiology presented in this selection can certainly be hypothesized to be related to the numerous individual differences found in personality, particularly as physiological function interacts with environment to motivate certain learned acts and not others.

Roger J. Williams

Reprinted from Roger J. Williams, "The Biological Approach to the Study of Personality" (Conference on Personality Development, May 5, 1960), by permission of the author and the Elizabeth McCormick Memorial Fund (The Chicago Community Trust).

... Pavlov (1941) found as a result of extensive study of many dogs that they often exhibited innate tendencies to react very differently to the same stimulus. He recognized in his dogs four basic types (1) excitable, (2) inhibitory, (3) equilibrated, and (4) active, as well as intermediate types. He recognized enormous differences in dogs with respect to their conditionability, and was by no means inclined to focus his attention solely upon the behavior of "*the* dog." Scott and others have in more recent times found ample justification for Pavlov's concern over the fundamental differences between dogs of different breeds and between individual dogs within each breed. These differences, which can be studied under controlled conditions in dogs vastly easier than in human beings, are *not* the result of training.

It is beyond dispute, of course, that dogs, cats, rats, and monkeys, for example, show species differences with respect to their patterns of conditionability. Stimuli which are highly effective for one species, may be of negligible importance for another. If hereditary factors make for interspecies differences, it is entirely reasonable to suppose that intraspecies differences would exist for the same reason. ...

It seems indefensible to assume that people are built in separate compartments, one anatomical, one physiological, one biochemical, one psychological, and that these compartments are unrelated or only distantly related to each other. Each human being possesses and exhibits unity. Certainly, anatomy is basic to physiology and biochemistry, and it may logically be presumed that it is also basic to psychology.

Let us look therefore in the *field of anatomy* * for facts which are pertinent to our problem.

Anatomists, partly for reasons of simplicity, have been prone in centuries past to concentrate on a single picture of the human body. Obvious concessions are made, when necessary, in considering the male and the female of the species, and always anatomists have been aware that within these two groups there are variations and anomalies. Only within the past decade (Anson, 1951), however, has comprehensive information been published which indicates how great these interindividual variations are and how widespread they are in the general population.

It makes no difference where we look, whether at the skeletal system, the *digestive tract,** the muscular system, the circulatory system, the respiratory system, the endocrine system, the nervous system, or even at the microscopic anatomy of the blood, we find tremendous morphological variations within the so-called normal range.

For example, normal stomachs vary greatly in shape, and about sixfold in size. Transverse colons vary widely in the positions at which they cross over in the abdomen, pelvic colon patterns vary widely. Arising from the aortic arch are two, three, four, and sometimes five and six branch arteries; the aorta itself varies greatly in size, and hearts differ morphologically and physiologically so that their pumping capacities in healthy young men vary widely. The size of arteries and the branching patterns are such that in each individual the various tissues and organs are supplied with blood unequally well, resulting in a distinctive pattern of blood supply for each.

Morphological differences in the *respiratory systems* * of normal people are basic to the fact that each person exhibits a distinctive breathing pattern as shown in the spirograms of different individuals made under comparable conditions.

Each *endocrine gland* * is subject to wide variation among "normal" individuals. Thyroid glands vary in weight about sixfold (Grollman, 1947), and the protein-bound iodine of the blood which measures the hormonal output varies to about the same degree (Williams, 1956). Parathyroid glands also vary about sixfold in total weight in so-called "normal" individuals, and the number of lobes vary from 2 to 12 (Grollman, 1947). The most prevalent number of lobes is 4, but some anatomists estimate that not over 50 per cent of the population have this number. The number of islets of Langerhans, which are responsible for insulin production, vary over a tenfold range in diabetes-free individuals (Pincus and Thimann, 1948). The thickness of the adrenal cortex where the critical adrenal hormones arise, is said to vary from 0.5 mm to 5 mm (tenfold) (Goldzieher, 1939).

* Editor's italics.

The morphology of the pituitary glands which produce about eight different hormones is so variable, when different healthy individuals are compared, as to allow for severalfold differences in the production of the individual hormones (Rasmussen, 1924, 1928). The male sex glands vary in weight from 10 to 45 grams (Grollman, 1947) in so-called "normal" males and much more than this if those with "subnormal" sex development are included. The female sex glands vary in weight over a fivefold range and the number of primordial ova present at the birth of "normal" female infants varies over a thirteenfold range (Grollman, 1947). It is evident that all individuals possess distinctive endocrine systems and that the individual hormonal activities may vary over a severalfold range in individuals who have no recognized hormonal difficulty.

The *nervous system* * is, of course, particularly interesting in connection with the personality problem, and the question arises whether substantial variations exist. The classification of the various kinds of sensory nerve endings, for example, is by no means complete nor satisfactory, and the precise functioning of many of the recognized types is unknown. Investigations involving "cold spots," "warm spots," and "pain spots" on the skin indicate that each individual exhibits a distinctive pattern of each. In a relatively recent study of pain spots in twenty-one healthy young adults, a high degree of variation was observed (Tindall and Kunkle, 1957). When subjected to carefully controlled test conditions, the right hand of one young man "A" showed 7 per cent of the area tested to be "highly sensitive," while in another, "B," the right hand showed 100 per cent "highly sensitive" areas. On A's hand, 49 per cent of the area registered "no pain" under standard pain producing test conditions. On B's hand, however, there was no area which registered "no pain."

It is evident that there is room for wide variations with respect to the numbers and distributions of sensory nerve endings in different individuals. That such differences exist is indicated by the extreme diversity in the reactions of individuals to many stimuli such as those involving seeing, hearing, and tasting. An entire lecture could easily be devoted to this subject alone.

The branching of the trunk nerves is as distinctive as that of the blood vessels. Anson (1951), for example, shows eight patterns of the branching of the facial nerve, each type representing, on the basis of examination of one hundred facial halves, from 5 to 22 per cent of the specimens. About 15 per cent of people do not have a direct pyramidal nerve tract in the spinal column; an unknown percentage have three splanchnic nerves as compared with the usual two; recurrent laryngeal nerves may be wholly unbranched or may have as many as six branches (Rustad, 1954); the termination of the spinal cord varies in different individuals over a range of three full vertebrae.

Variations in *brain anatomy* * have received little attention. Thirteen

* Editor's italics.

years ago, however, Lashley (1947) in a review wrote: "The brain is extremely variable in every character that has been subjected to measurement. Its diversities of structure within the species are of the same general character as are the differences between related species or even between orders of animals.... Even the limited evidence at hand, however, shows that individuals start life with brains differing enormously in structure; unlike in number, size, and arrangement of nerons as well as in grosser features."

Unfortunately, partly due to the complexity of the problem, there is no information whatever available as to how these enormous anatomical differences are related to the equally striking personality differences which are commonplace. Recently there has been published, primarily for the use of surgeons, an extensive study of differences in brain anatomy (Schattenbrand and Bailey, 1959). Up to the present in our discussion, we have paid attention only to certain facts of biology—those in the field of anatomy. Before we consider other areas—physiology, biochemistry, and psychology—it seems appropriate to note whether we have made any progress in uncovering facts that have important implications for personality development.

Consider the fact (I do regard it a fact and not a theory) that every individual person is endowed with a distinctive gastrointestinal tract, a distinctive circulatory system, a distinctive respiratory system, a distinctive endocrine system, a distinctive nervous system, and a morphologically distinctive brain; furthermore that the differences involved in this distinctiveness are never trifling and often are enormous. Can it be that this fact is inconsequential in relation to the problem of personality differences?

I am willing to take the position that this fact is of the *utmost* importance. The material in the area of anatomy alone is sufficient to convince anyone who comes upon the problem with an open mind that here is an obvious frontier which should yield many insights. Those who have accepted the Freudian idea that personality disorders arise from infantile conditioning will surely be led to see that, *in addition*, the distinctive bodily equipment of each individual infant is potentially important.

The failure of psychologists—and of biologists too—to deal seriously with innate individual differences in connection with many problems probably has deep roots.

McGill (1957) has said "Experimental psychologists ... ignore individual differences almost as an item of faith." The same statement holds, in the main, for physiological psychologists, physiologists, and biochemists. Anatomists have adopted in the past (and some do even at present) the same attitude. Generally speaking, individual differences are flies in the ointment which need to be removed and disregarded. Every subject becomes vastly simpler and more "scientific" when this is done.

If one is pursuing knowledge about personality, however, neglect of innate individual differences is fatal. All of biology and all of psychology have suffered, in my opinion, from at least a mild case of "universalitis," an over-ruling desire to generalize immediately—oftentimes long before sufficient facts are gathered to give the generalization validity. This desire to generalize is of itself laudable, but the willingness to do so without an adequate background of information is unscientific and has devastating effects in the area of personality study.

The most treacherous type of premature generalization is the one that is not stated, but is merely accepted as obvious or axiomatic. Such a generalization is hidden, for example, in the famous line of Alexander Pope, "The proper study of mankind is man." This common saying *assumes* the existence of a meaningful prototype, *man*, a universalized human being—an object of our primary concern. From the standpoint of the serious realistic study of personality, I object to this implied generalization. If we were to alter Pope's line to read "The proper study of mankind is men," we would have detracted from its poetic excellence, but we would have added immeasurably to its validity in the area of personality study.

"Universalitis" is probably born of fundamental egotism. If one can make sweeping generalizations, they are self-gratifying, they can be readily passed on to disciples, the atmosphere seems to clear, life becomes simple, and we approach being gods. It is more pleasant often to retain one's conceit than it is to be realistically humble and admit ignorance. "Universalitis" is thus a sign of immaturity. When personality study has grown up it will recognize realistically the tremendous diversity in personalities, the classification of which is extremely difficult and must be based upon far more data than we now have.

With these ideas as additional background for our thinking let us consider some of the other aspects of biology. *Physiologically and biochemically* * distinctiveness in gastrointestinal tracts is just as marked as is the distinctiveness in anatomy. The gastric juices of 5,000 individuals free from gastric disease were found to contain from 0 to 4300 units of pepsin (Osterberg, *et al.*, 1936). The range of hydrochloric acid in a smaller study of normal individuals was from 0.0 to 66.0 millequivalents per liter (Bernstein, 1952). No one can deny the probability that large variations also exist in the digestive juices which cannot be so readily investigated. Some "normal" hearts beat more than twice as fast as others (Heath, *et al.*, 1945), some have pumping capacities at least three times as large as others (King, *et al.*, 1952), and the blood of each individual is distinctive. The discovery of the existence of "blood groups" was just the beginning of our knowledge of the individuality of the blood. Enzyme levels in the blood, which are a reflection of fundamental biochemical differences, vary from one well individual to another over substantial ranges, sometimes tenfold or even thirtyfold or more (Williams, 1956).

* Editor's italics.

Our *neuromuscular systems* * are far from assembly-line products as can easily be demonstrated by a study of motor skills and by a large number of physiological tests. Our senses are by no means identical as has been made clear by taste tests for PTC and many other substances (Williams, 1956), by tests involving sense of smell (verbenas [Blakeslee, 1932], hydrocyanic acid [Kirk and Stenhouse, 1953], sense of sight (peripheral vision, foveal size, flicker fusion, and related phenomena, eighteen types of color "blindness"), sense of balance, pitch discriminations and hearing acuities at different frequencies, etc., etc. From the tremendous variation in the action of specific drugs and chemicals on different individuals, we gain further evidence of fundamental differences in physiology and biochemistry (Williams, 1956).

Thurstone's pioneering work on primary mental abilities called attention to the fact that human minds have different facets, and that some individuals may be relatively well endowed with respect to arithmetical facility, for example, while being relatively deficient in word familiarity or spatial imagery. Others may be strong in the area of word familiarity but weak in rote memory or arithmetic. Guilford has more recently suggested that there are at least forty facets to human minds, involving a group of memory factors, four groups of thinking factors, the latter involving abilities relating to discovering, evaluating and generating ideas (Guilford, 1955). All of this leaves room for a multitude of mental patterns (patterns of conditionability) which it seems reasonable to suppose must be related to the enormous variation in the anatomy of human brains. People, even when confronted with the same facts, do not think alike, and this appears to have a sound anatomical as well as psychological basis.

Those social anthropologists and other social scientists, who regard culture as the one factor which determines what an individual will be like, often say or imply that adult members of a society bear a very great resemblance to each other because of the similarities of their upbringing. In view of this common implication, it may be well to ask whether inborn differentness and distinctiveness fades out as a result of the adjustment of the individuals to the culture to which they are exposed. . . .

At the risk of being naive, it appears that the whole story we have been unfolding hangs together. Individual infants are endowed with far-reaching anatomical distinctiveness; each has a distinctive endocrine system, a highly distinctive nervous system, a highly distinctive brain. The same distinctiveness carries over into the sensory and biochemical realms, and into their individual psychologies. It is not surprising, therefore, that each individual upon reaching adulthood exhibits a distinctive patterns of likes and dislikes not only with respect to trivialities but also with respect to what may be regarded the most important things in life.

* Editor's italics.

That culture has a profound influence on our lives no one should deny. The serious question arises, however, as to the relative position that different factors occupy in producing distinctive personalities. To me it seems probable that one's distinctive endocrine system and one's distinctive brain morphology are more important factors than the toilet training one receives as an infant.

We cannot state as a demonstrated fact that differences in brain morphology or in endocrine systems have much to do with personality differences. On the other hand, we have no rigorous scientific proof that toilet training has any substantial effect on personality development. We can only surmise. In one sense, personality study is in its very early infancy.

Another pertinent question—simple but important—awaits a clear answer: Are patterns of *brain morphology inherited?* * On the basis of what is known about the inheritance of other morphological features, including fingerprints and the branching of blood vessels on the chest, etc., it may be *inferred* that specific morphological features in the brain are handed down by inheritance, but we do not have definitive proof.

A fact which makes the study of the inheritance of such morphological features difficult is that expressed by geneticists David and Snyder (1951) "...it has become more and more widely recognized that single-gene differences which produce readily distinguishable discontinuities in phenotype variation are completely nonrepresentative of the bulk of genetic variability in any species." Multiple gene effects are extremely common and in many cases, because of the complexity of the inheritance process, it is impossible to trace them in families or to know when and where such effects may be expected to arise. This complication is not the only one which exisits; there is also the possibility (and certainty in some species) of maternal influence (cytoplasmic) which does not follow the rules of gene-centered genetics, and can thus throw one's calculations off (Williams, 1960).

The complications of broad genetic study are so great that closely inbred animals which, according to the simpler concepts of genetics, should be nearly identical in body make-up, are often relatively far from it. Even within relatively closely inbred groups of animals each has a distinctive pattern of organ weights, a distinctive excretion pattern, and at the same time a distinctive pattern of behavioral responses....

Consideration of the available facts leads me to suppose, in the absence of completely definitive information, that differences in brain morphology, in endocrine patterns, in digestive, circulatory, muscular and nervous systems, etc., have important roots in heredity. It is difficult to see how such differences as exist could arise independent of heredity. The exact mechanisms whereby all these differences are inherited will probably be obscure many decades hence.

The recognition of hereditary factors does not by any means exclude from

* Editor's italics.

consideration the dynamic aspects of personality development. Potentialities and conditionabilities are inherited, not fixed characteristics. The widespread idea that personalities are developed from early childhood is fully in accord with an appreciation of the hereditary factors. Conditioning still takes place, but the recognition of innate biological differences calls attention to distinct make-up that each newborn baby possesses. Conditioning does not take place starting with assembly-line babies, each one, according to Watson, possessing exactly the same potentialities to develop into a "doctor, lawyer, artist, merchant, chief, and yes, even beggarman and thief." . . .

To tackle in one giant undertaking the problem of understanding, characterizing, and cataloguing all personalities from the biological or any other point of view seems hopeless. A strategy which seems far from hopeless, however, involves studying *one at a time* various personality characteristics to ascertain what biological roots they may have. The personality characteristics to be chosen for investigation should, obviously, be as definite as possible. They might include not only matters of temperament or emotion but also the ability to perform specified types of mental processes, or they might include personality problems of numerous types.

Studying even one particular personality characteristic to ascertain its biological roots is a large undertaking and might involve making scores, possibly hundreds, of measurements on every individual subjected to study. If one has some rational basis for selecting wisely the measurements to be made, the number of desirable measurements might be reduced. This fact would constitute an argument for selecting as the "personality problem" to be investigated, one for which the type of biological roots *might be* successfully guessed in advance. Such might include hyper- or hyposexuality, homosexuality, obesity, depressions, alcoholism, insomnia, accident proneness, etc. When one after another of personality disorders have been studied from this standpoint, it seems very likely that the whole picture will begin to clear and that the study of specific personality characteristics and problems will become successively easier the farther it progresses. What I am considering is obviously a relatively long-range proposal. . . .

Time will not permit a discussion of the numerous ways in which my own discipline, *biochemistry,** impinges on personality problems (Williams, 1956). The effects of various chemicals on personality behavior, the correlations between brain metabolism and behavior, the effects of various hormones on personality characteristics are all well recognized. What is not so well recognized is that each individual's body chemistry is distinctive and different, and that complex biochemical roots of personality characteristics are likely to be found when we look for them with due care and thoroughness.

Before I close this discussion, I want to stress a most important environ-

* Editor's italics.

mental factor which is capable of contributing enormously to healthy personality development.

The monumental work of Beadle and Tatum (1941) demonstrated for the first time the vital connection between genes and enzymes, and in effect, between heredity and biochemistry. Their work made clear the inevitable basis for individual body chemistry. As a direct consequence of this finding, it becomes inevitable that the nutritional needs of genetically distinctive individuals are quantitatively not the same. Carrying the idea still further, it becomes inescapable that the brain cells of individual people do not have quantitatively identical nutritional needs.

It has been amply demonstrated that malnutrition of various kinds can induce personality disorders. This was observed in the starvation studies of Keys and associates (1952), in thiamin deficiency studies (Wilder, 1952), in amino acid deficiency studies * and perhaps most notably in pellagra where unequivocal insanity may result from niacin deficiency and can be abolished promptly by administration of the missing vitamin. It has also been shown repeatedly that inadequacy of prenatal nutrition can cause all sorts of developmental difficulties and abnormalities in the growing fetus.

One of the most obvious environmental measures that can be taken to insure favorable personality development is to see, for example, that the nervous system of each distinctive individual, with his distinctive needs, receives prenatally and postnatally the best possible nourishment. Nourishment of brain cells like the nourishment of other cells throughout the body can be maintained at many levels of excellence, and, of course, achieving the best is no small order.

Serious attention to nutrition which must involve the utilization of substantial manpower and a great deal of human ingenuity and persistence can, I believe, make tremendous contributions to our knowledge of personality states and personality disorders, and to the alleviation and prevention of personality difficulties.

In *conclusion* † I would emphasize that the biological approach to personality, outstandingly important as I believe it to be, is not a substitute for all other valid approaches. Whatever we may know or may be able to accomplish by other approaches, if valid, is not lost. Consideration of the biological approach expands our horizon and gives us a much broader view. In my opinion, the insight we may gain from this approach will be most valuable and productive. I should reiterate also what I have said before, that personality study is in its early infancy.

---

* W. C. Rose, personal communication.
† Editor's italics.

IMPLICATIONS

In what anatomical and physiological areas shown to yield wide individual differences would you expect the greatest influence on behavior? In your own experience, have you thought that certain physical equipment might have influenced your development? Have you likewise suspected that certain physiological and biochemical processes have caused you—more than other children with whom you grew up—to tend to move toward or away from certain environmental situations?

REFERENCES

Consult the Bibliography for references cited in the article.

[11] WOMEN IN ROLE CONFLICT

Possibly you have read some of the popular discussions of the *feminine-identity* crisis in America. One book, entitled *The Feminine Mystique,* called attention to women who are puzzled by having so much materially and yet feeling empty, tired, nervous, and dissatisfied. These are symptoms; what are the causes? Are they the same for all women, or are they highly individual conflicts that impede growth toward wholeness and personal integration?

Nawas, a clinical psychologist, treats the problem here in terms of two major causative forces in American life: the *social and technological changes,* and the more subtle but ever so potent force of *cultural conditioning.* The co-ed will find this selection particularly meaningful, for she has undoubtedly experienced some of the strains discussed by Nawas; to the college man the selection offers a perspective that may help him to see members of the opposite sex as a little less puzzling and more predictable than they seem to be.

M. Mike Nawas

Excerpts from a paper by M. Mike Nawas, "Some Impediments to Growth and Adjustment in the Young Adult Years."

THE EFFECTS OF SOCIAL AND TECHNOLOGICAL CHANGES

That the modern woman is in a "dilemma" is one of the stock phrases in social science. Briefly stated, the points of view of various students of the problem are typically expressed along these lines. One of the outstanding changes in the past decades has been the emancipation of the woman. As a result of this, she has attained a large measure of equality with the male in the social, economic, political, and educational spheres; such equality has greatly improved her status as a citizen. On the other hand, the fact that this culture is traditionally "masculine" and that women attained their equal status at a very rapid pace impeded a thorough accommodation for these changes. As a result, the culture has not had enough time to make whole-hearted and consistent attempts to integrate these changes within its ethos. Furthermore, it is pointed out that the rapid social and technological changes, accompanied by a concomitant increase in the complexity of the social structure, created many new roles for women and removed some of the traditional ones. The role changes—which touch on every sphere of social life from leisure to professionalism—were too numerous and drastic.

These various factors—inconsistent values, role changes, and cultural contradictions—are said to have created many problems. Thus, there is said to be a large discrepancy between the concept of equality of the sexes and the core values of the culture. Moreover, the double standard still prevails in many areas of social activities. Frequently the goals set by each role are diametrically opposed to those set by other roles, resulting in contradictory expectations and inconsistent demands. Many of the roles which emerged in the past few decades are still in a fluid state and are too ambiguously defined. This situation, which is likely to generate conflicts and anxieties, makes it difficult for the parents to have a systematic "set" to guide them in preparing their daughters for their adult roles.

In her discussion of the "dilemma" of the modern woman, F. Kluckhohn (1953) focuses on the inconsistencies between the "core values" of the culture and the tenets of democracy and equality. She identifies three basic core values, whose expression is made very difficult for women: individualism, the cult of "doing" or the "doing personality," and future-centeredness or the bias for the future time dimension. Particularly through his occupational role, the male is given ample opportunity to fulfill these values; so far as women are concerned, individuality can be expressed only if it fits within her primary role as mother-wife, she is expected more to "be good" than to "do good," and though she is expected to look ahead, she lacks the freedom and cultural support to have autonomous and distant goals to strive for and fulfill. These incongruencies with the concept of democracy, Kluckhohn points out, create for the woman "a social problem of great magnitude," and render her role "badly defined, shot with contradictions, and in need of major alterations."

As an example of the contradictions, she draws attention to the fact that though the "mother-housewife" role is an inseparable unit, the former aspect of it is deified while the latter is derogated. The derogation is largely due to the influence of technology and mass media which make the role of the housewife look like a drudgery, providing few significant rewards and lacking the worth of accomplishment.

In his analysis of the modern conception of womanhood, Parsons (1949) is in agreement with Kluckhohn that the roles of the modern young woman are fraught with conflicts. His analysis of her emancipation leads him to believe that even the single role of "wife" is now fractionated, vacillating between "domestic," the "glamorous," and the "good companion" patterns. Each of these three types is said to be in conflict with the others, and, as he and Kluckhohn point out, each is incongruent with the dominant core values of the culture. Thus the unity inherent in the "mother-wife-housewife" roles, which are presumed to be the major life goals of the woman, is now shattered, and instead of internal consistency we have a cluster of discordant contradictions.

On a more concrete level, Hacker (1952) focuses her attention on the "double standard." Impressed by the pervasiveness of the "double standard" in this culture, she expresses the view that the situation of the modern female is such that it warrants classifying women as a "minority group." She points out that the inequalities within the alleged equality of the sexes permeate every aspect of the social structure, and in some respects exceed the ethnic and racial inequalities.

She says, for example, that even though more and more young women are going to college, their admission to professional schools, such as medicine and architecture, is blocked, and women's colleges are often inferior to colleges for men. In some states, women are barred from serving as jurors or holding political office; women's political activities are largely limited to the promotion of male candidates. In social life, freedom of expression and mobility are restricted. In the family setting, the boy is given priority over his sister in the enjoyment of such privileges as the use of the family car, taking trips, leaving home, or pursuing higher education. As a wife the woman is expected, and in some states required, to take the domicile of her husband. In cases of illegitimacy, the woman and not the man bears the scars of the stigma. Finally, women are not considered suited to hold high executive office or sit on the boards of directors of large corporations even though they own 80 per cent of the national wealth. With regard to wages, responsibility, promotion or supervisory activity, the woman usually takes a second seat to a male co-worker. In a number of states, women are discriminated against in some types of employment and are denied exclusive right to their earnings.

Of major concern to the psychologist are the conflicts which arise within the woman herself as a consequence of the assumed incompatibility between marriage and career, exemplified by the phrase "marriage versus career." Indeed, conflicts are said to arise whether the woman combines the two roles or happens to devote herself to one or the other.

On a very concrete level, an adequate performance of the two roles on the part of those who combine marriage and career places too many strains on the resources of energy of the woman. When the wife goes to work, she is still expected to take care of her household duties. Although some husbands do help their wives in the common household chores, an equitable division of labor between the two is not very common (*Bulletin of Women's Bureau,* 1947; Jahoda and Havel, 1955; La Follette, 1934).

Furthermore, if the woman's work is at a critical phase when a family member takes sick, she is faced with the dilemma of nursing the sick person or attending to her duties as a worker. It is not unlikely that the conflict between the working hours of the husband and those of his wife may lead to upsetting the routine of the household. These are only examples of the types of situations which, sooner or later, are likely to arise.

If it is true that the husband's occupation is the primary determiner of the family's "style of life" and status in the community (Parsons and Bayles, 1955), and that the institutional vestiges of male authority are still with us (Hacker, 1957; Kirkpatrick, 1936; Seward, 1946), one would expect that some men would feel slighted if their wives shared the occupational role with them. It is conceivable that at least some men—equalitarian as they may claim to be—may feel quite uneasy about the dissolution of the age-old division of labor which allocated to them the occupational arena. They may feel threatened that one of the very few remaining symbols of the husband's authority and status as the recognized "head" of the family is being threatened. Undoubtedly there are also some husbands who may feel that their wives' work does, in ways which they may not be able to verbalize, undermine their self-esteem and their perceptions of themselves as adequate providers. It is not unlikely that there are some husbands whose feelings of competitiveness might be aroused, particularly if the wife's income equals or exceeds their own. To avoid the disunity or disharmony in the family which such situations may create, the woman is likely to deprive herself of whatever satisfactions she derives from her work by quitting the job.

For the woman who fails to get married, a career is almost an inevitable alternative. Research on spinsters, or other single women, is conspicuously lacking, but the few sources available in the field (Davis, 1929; Dickinson and Beam, 1934; Harding, 1933; Hutton, 1935; Knopf, 1932) portray the single woman as a highly insecure, anxious, and maladjusted person. Apparently her occupational career, which is frequently successful, does little to protect her from the critical harassment of the social group which expects her to marry, or from her feelings of inferiority, emptiness, lack of purpose, and apprehensions of a lonely future.

The third category of women, those who stay home and restrict their roles to those of homemaking, are not free from problems in the work-marriage area either. In many cases, particularly where the family income is low, economic necessity compels the woman to seek work (*Bulletin of Women's Bureau*, 1948). This reality factor will be particularly distressing to those women who prefer to devote themselves exclusively to homemaking. Even if the economic necessity is not very pressing, the average woman would be attracted to doing some remunerative work, not because she particularly enjoys doing so but because she needs to acquire some luxury items which are becoming so valued in our society as to constitute a pressing social need.

Paradoxical as it may seem, these luxury items, particularly those which can be subsumed under "time-saving devices," seem according to some social scientists (Hacker, 1952; Kluckhohn, 1953; Linton, 1956; Lundberg and Farnham, 1947; Rose, 1952) to be a main source of conflict for the modern woman. They claim that the time-saving devices, food packaging, and the like, have become so numerous as to create a leisure problem for the woman. The leisure problem is further intensified by the fact that some of the functions of the family have been taken over by other socializing agencies.

Even where the time thus saved is absorbed in such ostensibly rewarding and culturally valued activities as increasing the attention to the affectional needs of the child and volunteering for community improvement ventures, social scientists discern that these outlets may be detrimental (Rose, 1952). Intensification of the mother-child bond, for example, could lead to symbiotic dependence; excessive social participation is a tantalizing mechanism of flight from family responsibility.

The conclusion from such observations is that many social scientists are inclined to believe that no matter what the modern woman does or does not do, she is "in trouble." This view is also shared by some educators who feel that higher education, as it now stands, generates more conflicts for the woman than it resolves.

Educators point out that college curriculums are for the most part oriented toward preparing the individual for a career. Although the marriage *versus* career dichotomy is increasingly giving way to the dual role of marriage *and* career (Empey, 1958; Mead, 1946; Mueller, 1959; Steinman, 1958), the issue is still very much alive, and education for career may serve to intensify rather than help dispel the incompatibility which the public mind assumes exists between marriage and career (Komarovsky, 1953; Taylor, 1956).

Difficulties also exist where the college curriculums are not oriented toward career preparation but are designed to foster the individual's general growth and to give the woman a "well-rounded" education. One educator points out that this culture has a deep-rooted conviction that higher education for women is really of no value (Tiedman, 1959). Since the young college woman is part of this culture, she is bound to echo this belief and question the wisdom of her pursuits. This conviction is perhaps based on the notion in the public mind that marriage as the primary goal of a woman is incompatible with higher education; self-realization for women is viewed as only possible through marriage (Frank, 1944; Komarovsky, 1953; Terman, 1938).

This notion may account, at least in part, for the observation that the college woman seems to face greater pressures for marriage—both from societal expectations and from within—than her noncollege sister does (Mueller, 1959). Komarovsky's (1953) discussion of the dilemma of the college woman substantiates this view. She states that in order to be accepted by and to appeal to the other sex, the young woman often assumes inferiority to the male even though by all standards she may be his intellectual superior.

Such questions as "Will I be able to marry?" "Should I play it dumb?" "Should I prepare for a career?" "If I graduate, would I accept a noncollege graduate as a husband?" and "Why am I seeking higher education anyway?" undoubtedly lay grounds for indulgence in self-doubt and anxious expectations which render the task of acquiring knowledge doubly difficult. With men and women now marrying at an increasingly earlier age, these questions are apt to be more disturbing than they were at a previous time.

THE EFFECTS OF CULTURAL CONDITIONING

The problems confronting the modern woman are not restricted to inconsistencies in our values or the double standard. There seems to be an equally serious inconsistency between the way we bring up our children during the pre-adult years and what we expect them to do as adults. Benedict (1955) referred to this phenomenon as the discontinuity of cultural conditioning. Discontinuity refers not only to a lack of continuity between the pre-adult and adult years but also to contradictions which place the individual in the difficult position of trying to behave in a way that is sometimes diametrically opposed to that which he has been conditioned to behave throughout the formative years from infancy onward. This is considered to be another area which contributes greatly toward role conflicts. Benedict believes that although there are cultural discontinuities in the lives of both males and females, they take a greater toll in the lives of girls than in the lives of boys.

Recent reviews of the subject of sex-role development document the fact that boys consistently prefer "masculine" activities, whereas girls, at least until their early teens, have a definite preference for the activities of boys to those of their own sex (Brown, 1958; Lynn, 1959). Various writers point out also that the culture is quite tolerant if the young girl engages in the activities of boys and that it exerts a great deal more pressure on the boy to restrict himself to "masculine" activities and behavior (Brown, 1958; Fauls, 1956; Goodenough, 1957). There is also agreement that boys, in contrast to girls, have a much clearer conception of their sex roles (Henry, 1947; Hurlock, 1953; Mead, 1949; Pabban, 1950; Seward, 1946).

As we turn now to some of the more specific areas of cultural conditioning, we find that the sexual sphere is perhaps one of the major dimensions of discontinuity. While the conflict in this area may be quite strong in adolescence (Kinsey, 1953; Mead, 1949), the major stress comes during marriage, where, as Ellis (1959) dramatically surmised, from a chaste, sexually inhibited person before marriage, the woman is expected to become a "prostitute for her husband," and to enjoy the role, too.

Another major dimension of cultural discontinuity of particular significance to young adulthood is in the area of autonomy. Experimental studies in perception amply demonstrate that in contrast to the male, the female, even as late as college age, is much more dependent on external sources of anchorage and that she is more susceptible to "temporary disorganization" when the visual field becomes less stable (Andrieux, 1955; Chaplin, 1955; Wapner and Witkin, 1950; Witkin, 1949). As a girl, the young woman has not been given much opportunity or encouragement to develop the capacity for autonomous action. She is said to be brought up in a more sheltered atmosphere than the boy (Komarovsky, 1953; Meltzer, 1943). If this sheltering is harmful now, it is likely to be a great deal more so in the future for, as Bronfenbrenner (1961) suggests, recent trends show that the woman's responsibilities in the area of child-rearing are multiplying still further inasmuch as she is now the primary disciplinarian of the children—thus experiencing a situation the reverse of her own overdependence on parents and other authority figures in pre-adulthood.

Related to this dimension is another important area of discontinuity which is said to be a source of much conflict for the young woman. It is contended that as she establishes her own family of procreation, the young woman will find it extremely difficult to shift her emotional attachment from the parents to the marital home. Many studies have demonstrated that girls have a stronger attachment and emotional bond to their parents as late as the adult years (Amatora, 1957; Burgess and Cottrell, 1939; Meltzer, 1943; Stagner, 1940; Terman, 1938; Williams, 1950; Winch, 1952). It is pointed out that as a mother the young woman is expected to be the main source of emotional support for her children, and unless she herself was emotionally emancipated, she will suffer great strain in having to serve as a haven for the child to lean on for emotional support and nurturance (Seward, 1946).

Undoubtedly many of the difficulties which the young adult female has to cope with arise in adolescence. However, it seems that whatever conflicts these difficulties may generate, they have very little impact before the individual begins to perform the roles of adulthood. The possibility also exists that even though the adolescent female may have some awareness of the problems she will have to face in the adult years, this awareness does not translate itself into actual conflict at the time. Rose (1952) goes even so far as to suggest complete lack of awareness on the part of the adolescent female of future problems. Rose addressed herself to the problem of finding out whether the role contradictions and ambiguities of adulthood are felt before marriage. In spite of the well-developed intellectual maturity and insight of her college women respondents, the investigator was appalled at the absence of conflict and the lack of awareness on the part of her subjects that the roles they would be enacting in a few years would be fraught with difficulties.

In an empirical investigation utilizing the Thematic Apperception Technique, the present writer found that the ego sufficiency and ego complexity of females decrease significantly from adolescence to young adulthood, a finding which attests to the extent of the strain which women are subjected to once they begin to perform the adult roles (Nawas, 1961). This was as true of adolescent females whose ego sufficiency and ego complexity scores in adolescence were high as it was for those whose scores were low.

IMPLICATIONS

If you are familiar with other interpretations of the feminine-identity crisis in America, do you find that Nawas' treatment of the problems differs from them? Try to describe how Nawas handles the problems. What does he look for? Does he make any recommendations—direct or indirect—for the solution of the problems? What impressed you most in Nawas' analysis of the causes of the problems? Why do you think women differ from men in their reactions to role conflicts?

REFERENCES

Consult the Bibliography for references cited in the article.

[12] AGE AND ACHIEVEMENT

Youth in America, as might be expected, does not seem to be greatly interested in the question of aging and in the factors related to it. It may be said that we—more than those in the Orient—place a premium on the youthful years and what is associated with them, without giving any serious thought to the rational bases of this position. College professors who spend a year or two teaching in another culture are sometimes surprised at the greater respect and prestige that their age gains for them, particularly in Asia and in the Middle East. What are the *roles* that youth and age play in an advancing culture?

In some areas of our culture, the value of youthfulness is clear. One of these areas is sports, and the advantage of the young over the older individual is obvious. But is the peak of achievement found in the early years in all sports? In activities other than sports, are productivity and creativity also associated with youth rather than with middle and old age? To what extent are the first few years after physical maturity the golden years of achievement in most fields of endeavor? What sort of achievement reaches its peak in later years?

Harvey C. Lehman has spent many years collecting data on this problem. The following selection, a concluding section in his book, answers these questions. He presents the ages of superior achievement in a number of fields: *science, music, literature, drama, art, movies,* and *sports,* as well as the peak ages for various positions of leadership. He then lists possible causes for manifestations of early maximum creativity and for the older age of leaders. What do the tables show?

Harvey C. Lehman

SUMMARY AND INTERPRETATION

By means of statistical distributions and graphs, the preceding chapters [of *Age and Achievement*], show the ages (1) at which outstanding thinkers have most frequently made (or first published) their momentous creative contributions, (2) at which leaders have most often attained important positions of leadership, and (3) at which high-salaried workers in several areas have most commonly received large annual incomes. A few data for professional athletes are included to show their similarity to the other findings.

The creative thinkers and the leaders whose lives were studied are mostly deceased persons. Because adequate data were not available for deceased recipients of large annual incomes and deceased athletes, living persons who fall in these two categories were studied. For all groups investigated, proper statistical allowance was made for the fact that young men are more numerous than older ones.

Because dates of first publication rather than dates of actual achievement were usually available, the only thing that can be asserted with certainty is the fact that, as regards their most profound insights, our creative workers attained their highest average rate of productivity *not later than* certain specified age levels.

The most notable *creative works of scientists and mathematicians* * were identified by experts in the various specialized fields of endeavor. For such fields as oil painting, education, philosophy, and literature, a consensus of the experts was obtained by a study of their published writings. In each field listed below the maximum average rate of highly superior production was found to occur not later than during the specified range of ages. For example, item 1 of this list, Chemistry, 26–30, is to be interpreted as follows: in proportion to the number of chemists that were alive at each successive age level, very superior contributions to the field of chemistry were made at the greatest average rate when the chemists were not more than 26–30. The remaining items here and those in the tabular lists that follow are to be interpreted in similar manner.

* Editor's italics.

Physical Sciences, Mathematics,
and Inventions
1. Chemistry, 26–30
2. Mathematics, 30–34
3. Physics, 30–34
4. Electronics, 30–34
5. Practical Inventions, 30–34
6. Surgical Techniques, 30–39
7. Geology, 35–39
8. Astronomy, 35–39

Biological Sciences
9. Botany, 30–34
10. Classical Descriptions of Disease, 30–34
11. Genetics, 30–39
12. Entomology, 30–39
13. Psychology, 30–39
14. Bacteriology, 35–39
15. Physiology, 35–39
16. Pathology, 35–39
17. Medical Discoveries, 35–39

In this, and in succeeding tabulations, very precise cross comparisons should not be attempted because the maximum ages vary somewhat both with the era during which the workers were born and also with the quality of the output under consideration, and it was not possible to equate all these different kinds of contributions upon both these bases.

For most types of superior *music,** the maximum average rate of good production is likely to occur in the thirties. Here are the maxima:

18. Instrumental Selections, 25–29
19. Vocal Solos, 30–34
20. Symphonies, 30–34
21. Chamber Music, 35–39

22. Orchestral Music, 35–39
23. Grand Opera, 35–39
24. Cantatas, 40–44
25. Light Opera and Musical Comedy, 40–44

For the study of *literary creativity,** fifty well-known histories of English literature were canvassed. The works most often cited by the fifty literary historians were assumed to be superior to those cited infrequently. Best-liked short stories were identified similarly by use of 102 source books, and "best books" were ascertained by study of a collation of fifty "best book" lists. As is revealed by the following tabulation, literary works that are good and permanently great are produced at the highest average rate by persons who are not over 45 years old. It is clear also that most types of poetry show maxima ten to fifteen years earlier than most prose writings other than short stories.

26. German Composers of Noteworthy Lyrics and Ballads, 22–26
27. Odes, 24–28
28. Elegies, 25–29
29. Pastoral Poetry, 25–29
30. Narrative Poetry, 25–29
31. Sonnets, 26–31
32. Lyric Poetry, 26–31
33. Satiric Poetry, 30–34
34. Short Stories, 30–34

35. Religious Poetry (Hymns), 32–36
36. Comedies, 32–36
37. Tragedies, 34–38
38. "Most Influential Books," 35–39
39. Hymns by Women, 36–38
40. Novels, 40–44
41. "Best Books," 40–44˙
42. Best Sellers, 40–44
43. Miscellaneous Prose Writings, 41–45

* Editor's italics.

Fifty histories of *philosophy*,* forty-nine histories of education, and twenty books dealing with the history of economics and political science were examined and the following maxima were obtained:

44. Logic, 35–39
45. Ethics, 35–39
46. Aesthetics, 35–39
47. "General" Philosophy, 35–39
48. Social Philosophy, 36–44

49. Metaphysics, 40–44
50. Contributions to Educational Theory and Practice, 35–39
51. Contributions to Economics and Political Science, 30–39

Although the maximum average rate of output of the most important philosophical books occurred at 35–39, the total range for best production extended from 22–80, and for mere quantity of output—good, bad, and indifferent—the production rate was almost constant from 30–70.

In the body of this book, mean ages, median ages, and modal ages are all set forth, but here in this summary, in order to save space, only modal ages are listed. Sixty books which contain lists of so-called "master paintings," one book on American sculpture, and one book on modern architecture yielded the following maxima:

52. Oil Paintings, 32–36
53. American Sculpture, 35–39

54. Modern Architecture, 40–44
55. Oil Paintings by Contemporary Artists, 40–44

Chapter 12 shows that a very large proportion of the most renowned men of science and the humanities *did their first important work before 25*,* and that in *general the earlier starters contributed better work and were more prolific* * than were the slow starters. In Chapters 12 and 13 more than one hundred examples of outstanding creative achievements by youths not over 21 are described briefly. To avoid giving the false impression that *only* the young can do great things (Goethe's remark to Eckermann), Chapter 14 cites numerous outstanding accomplishments at advanced ages.

For most types of creative work, the following generalizations have been derived. Within any given field of creative endeavor: (1) the maximum production rate for output of highest quality usually occurs at an earlier age than the maximum rate for less distinguished works by the same individuals; (2) the rate of good production usually does not change much in the middle years and the decline, when it comes, is gradual at all the other ages—much more gradual than its onset in the late teens or early twenties; (3) production of highest quality tends to fall off not only at an earlier age but also at a more rapid rate than does output of lesser merit; and because the statistical distributions of age for the highest quality of work are skewed toward the older age levels, both the mean and the median ages are higher than the modal values.

The first item in the following list of high-salaried workers shows that,

* Editor's italics.

when taken in relation to the total population alive at successive age levels, leading movie actors attain their greatest box-office popularity not later than 30–34.

56. Movie Actors who are "best-money makers," 30–34
57. Movie Actresses who are "best money-makers," 23–27
58. "Best" Movie Directors, 35–39

59. Receivers of "Earned" Annual Incomes of $50,000 or more, 60–64
60. Outstanding Commercial and Industrial Leaders, 65–69
61. Receivers of Annual Incomes of $1,000,000 or more, 80–89

Item 62 in the following tabulation shows that, in proportion to the number of men who were still alive at each successive age level, presidents of American colleges and universities have served most often at 50–54. The other items in this tabulation are to be interpreted similarly.

62. Presidents of American Colleges and Universities, 50–54
63. Presidents of the U.S. prior to Truman, 55–59
64. U.S. Ambassadors to Foreign Countries from 1875 to 1900, 60–64
65. U.S. Senators in 1925, 60–64

66. Men in Charge of the U.S. Army from 1925 to 1945, 60–64
67. Justices of the U.S. Supreme Court from 1900 to 1925, 70–74
68. Speakers of the U.S. House of Representatives from 1900 to 1940, 70–74
69. Popes, 82–92

An analysis of age data for the most highly successful *athletes* * reveals that their modal ages differ less from the norms for intellectual proficiency than is commonly supposed. The following comparisons are illustrative.

70. Professional Football Players, 22–26
71. Professional Prizefighters, 25–26
72. Professional Ice Hockey Players, 26
73. Professional Baseball Players, 27–28
74. Professional Tennis Players, 25–29
75. Automobile Racers, 26–30
76. Leading Contestants at Chess, 29–33

77. Professional Golfers, 31–36
78. Breakers of World Billiards Records, 31–36
79. Winners at Rifle and Pistol Shooting, 31–36
80. Winners of Important Bowling Championships, 31–36

To find out whether, with the passage of time, there has been any significant change in the modal ages at which important creative contributions have been made, data were isolated for noted achievers in such various fields as literature, practical invention, philosophy, geology, medicine, and the like. Two statistical distributions were then made for the workers in each field, one for those born prior to 1775, the other for those born between 1775 and 1850. In almost every instance the more recent workers exhibited their outstanding creative ingenuity at younger ages than did the workers of the earlier era.

In contrast with this age change for creative thinkers, the more recently

* Editor's italics.

born 50 per cent of most kinds of leaders were found to be significantly *older* than were their predecessors who held the same nominal positions—both in the United States and also in certain other countries. Thus, for each of the following groups of non-American leaders, the more recently born 50 per cent functioned at somewhat older ages than the earlier born 50 per cent: the popes of the Roman Catholic Church, the prime ministers of England, the archbishops of Canterbury, and hereditary rulers all over the world. The more recent leaders also were more nearly the same ages than were their predecessors.

When seven groups of earlier-born athletic champions were compared with seven groups of those more recently born, the field of sport being kept constant in each comparison, the later born were found to be older than the earlier born. The changes that have taken place in the modal ages of creative thinkers, leaders, and athletes all evidence the fact that these modal ages are not due solely to genetic factors. Whether the modal ages will continue to change and whether they can be subjected to some kind of human control are quite different questions.

A mere increase in man's longevity should not change greatly the modal ages at which man exhibits his greatest creative proficiency since, both for long-lived and for short-lived groups, the modal age occurs in the thirties. Although a part of the upward shift in the ages of leaders may be due to an increase in man's longevity, a possible alternative explanation is given in Chapter 17.

Possible Causes for the Early Maxima in Creativity

At present we are in no position to explain these curves of creativity that rise rapidly in early maturity and then decline slowly after attaining an earlier maximum. Undoubtedly, multiple causation operates in these complex behaviors and no discovered contributing condition is likely to be of itself a sufficient or necessary cause. Nevertheless, it is profitable here to list sixteen of the factors which have been suggested as contributing to these representative functions with their early maxima, for such factors indicate possible lines for further research. Here is the list:

1. A decline occurs prior to 40 in physical vigor, energy, and resistance to fatigue. This decline is probably far more important than such normal age changes as may occur in adult intelligence prior to outright senility.

2. A diminution in sensory capacity and motor precision also takes place with advance in age. For example, impaired vision and hearing handicap the older individual in many cumulative ways, and writing by hand also becomes more difficult with advance in age.

3. Serious illness, poor health, and various bodily infirmities more often influence adversely the production rates of older than of younger age groups.

4. Glandular changes continue throughout life. It is conceivable that hor-

mone research may some day reveal a partial explanation for the changes and especially for the early maxima.

5. In some instances unhappy marriages and maladjustment in the sex life, growing worse with advance in age, may have interfered with creative work.

6. The older age groups, more often than the younger, may have become indifferent toward creativity because of the death of a child, a mate, or some other dear one.

7. As compared with younger persons, older ones are apt to be more pre-occupied with the practical concerns of life, with earning a living, and with getting ahead.

8. Less favorable conditions for concentrated work sometimes come with success, promotion, enhanced prestige, and responsibility.

9. In some cases the youthful worker's primary ambition may not have been to discover the unknown or to create something new but to get renown. Having acquired prestige and recognition, such workers may try less hard for achievement.

10. Too easy, too great, or too early fame may conceivably breed complacency and induce one to rest on his previously won laurels before he has done his best possible creative work.

11. Some older persons may have become apathetic because they have experienced more often the deadening effect of nonrecognition and of destructive criticism.

12. As a result of negative transfer, the old generally are more inflexible than the young. This inflexibility may be a handicap to creative thinking, even though it is dependent on erudition.

13. Perhaps in part because of the foregoing factors, some older persons experience a decrease in motivation which leads to a weaker intellectual interest and curiosity.

14. Younger persons tend to have had a better formal education than their elders, they have grown to maturity in a more stimulating social and cultural milieu, and they have had less time to forget what they have learned.

15. In some few cases, outright psychosis has clouded what was previously a brilliant mind. Psychoses occur more often in the latter half of the normal life span.

16. In other extreme cases, the individual's normal productive powers may have been sapped by alcohol, narcotics, and other kinds of dissipation. Here, as elsewhere, it is difficult to separate cause from effect.

Possible Causes for the Older Ages of Leaders

The factors that make for the older ages of leaders are also multiple, complex, and variable. The mere age of a country or of a people is not the determining factor. For example, from 1907 to 1939 only 7 per cent of the service of Chinese cabinet members was rendered by men of 60 or above, whereas, for England, France, and the United States, the corresponding percentages were 41, 39, and 32 respectively. It is true also that from 1871 to 1918 the chancellors of the German empire had a median age more than ten years older than the median age of the German chancellors who served from 1918 to 1945. This latter age difference could not be due to greater longevity on the part of the German people during the *earlier* era. Data set forth in Chapters 11 and 17 of this book for some fifty other groups of leaders suggest that when a new group is being formed or when social unrest and dissatisfaction develop in a long-established organization, relatively youthful leaders are likely to emerge.

Consider next the possible contributory factors that cause leadership to occur usually at elderly ages. Examples of such factors are the following:

1. Normally, for most kinds of leaders, the attainment of their leadership depends largely upon what the leader's potential followers think of him and his prospective leadership, a relationship that is probably less usual for the creative thinker even though the latter must act more or less in harmony with his *Zeitgeist*.

2. Social institutions, like the church and the state, tend to be conservative; they are engaged primarily in the perpetuation of themselves and the existing cultural pattern. The leader is the instrument through which they act. Since older persons tend to be conservative more often than younger ones, the older are usually regarded as safer and saner leaders.

3. For most kinds of leaders the recognition received, the prestige attained, and the honor achieved are likely to be far greater than for those who do creative work. Thus, other things equal, members of the older age groups are likely to be more strongly motivated in seeking and exercising various kinds of leadership than they are in pursuing creative work.

4. The function of the leader differs from that of the creative thinker. Strictly speaking, leadership is less a personal attribute than a social relationship. An example of this is the fact that for many persons the leader serves as a father substitute, an important function which is, nevertheless, only one contributing factor, for there have been many young leaders.

5. Nominal leaders have sometimes remained in office for years after they became incapacitated by illness or by other bodily infirmities for the routine performance of their duties. Thus, and especially at the uppermost age levels, some years of nominal leadership may represent merely the ages at which certain individuals have drawn their salaries. Needless to say, my creativity data are not vitiated by any analogous factor.

Upon the basis of all these statistics what is one to *conclude?* * Whatever the causes of growth and decline, it remains clear that the genius does not

* Editor's italics.

function equally well throughout the years of adulthood. Superior creativity rises relatively rapidly to a maximum which ocurs usually in the thirties and then falls off slowly. Almost as soon as he becomes fully mature, man is confronted with a gerontic paradox that may be expressed in terms of positive and negative transfer. Old people probably have more transfer, both positive and negative, than do young ones. As a result of positive transfer, the old usually possess greater wisdom and erudition. These are invaluable assets. But when a situation requires a new way of looking at things, the acquisition of new techniques or even new vocabularies, the old seem stereotyped and rigid. To learn the new they often have to unlearn the old and that is twice as hard as learning without unlearning. But when a situation requires a store of past knowledge, then the old find their advantage over the young.

Possibly, every human behavior has its period of prime. No behavior can develop before the groundwork for it has been prepared; but in general, it appears that the conditions essential for creativity and originality, which can be displayed in private achievement, come earlier than those social skills which contribute to leadership and eminence and which inevitably must wait, not upon the insight of the leader himself but upon the insight of society about him.

IMPLICATIONS

Of the findings presented here on age and achievement, which data were contrary to your previous impressions? What would you say are the implications of this study for the college-age youth? How do you evaluate each of the various reasons Lehman gives for early maximum achievement and for the older age of leaders? In your opinion, what questions are not yet answered?

REFERENCES

You have probably noted that the author referred to various other chapters in his book. Consult the Bibliography for the reference to it. Lehman mentions some of the factors that slow down productivity with age. The increasing number of older people in the population has caused psychologists to turn their attention to the process of aging in the field of geriatrics. One of the problems of the older person is the relatively newer issue of *forced retirement* and the emotional disturbance it often engenders. Employment, despite undesirable features, generally provides certain human satisfactions. An individual usually receives emotional support from his work and from the people associated with it. When he retires, he can no longer engage in the role he has played for so many years; he must find a new identity. Partial retirement, tapering off over a period of years, or retiring into some meaningful adventure are some suggested adjustments to this difficulty. (See Breckinridge, 1953; Kleemeyer, 1961; Tuckman and Lorge, 1953.)

Women experience special problems when their children are grown and have left the home. The mother must find a new role. See Selection 11, which deals with women of various ages and their problem of identity. These are problems that some college students indirectly face as they leave the home and get some perspective on their parents and grandparents who are moving into the higher age groups.

[13] HAPPINESS IN MARRIAGE: PSYCHOLOGICAL FACTORS

Why are some individuals in our culture happier in marriage than others? This is an important question since there is about one divorce to every five marriages. American students are sometimes appalled when their Asian contemporaries on the campus seem satisfied with the vital role their parents play in choosing a spouse for them. The Asian students might point out that their marital customs have certain advantages when one considers the lack of maturity of many Westerners who marry. Moreover, they may argue that the outcome of the marriages in the two different parts of the world in terms of overt conflict in the families and divorce rates does not seem to favor the American freedom of choice. Of course, many issues are involved here besides the manner in which a spouse is chosen, but it raises questions about *readiness* and *compatibility* in marriage.

This selection is a classic; it is one of the early studies of marriage conducted by a distinguished pioneer in American psychology, Lewis M. Terman.

Lewis M. Terman

An examination of recent contributions to the literature on marriage reveals a great diversity of opinion about the factors most responsible for marital success or failure. On practically every aspect of the problem the pronouncements by leading authors are highly contradictory. The explanation of this situation lies partly in the bias of authors, partly in their willingness to generalize from inadequate data, and partly in the use of faulty techniques in the collection of information.

A study was accordingly planned which would investigate for a larger number of subjects the relationship between happiness scores and a great variety of possible factors, including not only personality factors but also background factors and factors having to do with sexual adjustments in the marriage. By the use of an improved technique for assuring anonymity of response, data were secured on these three sets of variables from 792 married couples who filled out the information schedules in the presence of a field assistant. The group studied represents a reasonably good sampling of the urban and semi-urban married population of California at the middle and upper-middle cultural levels, though the sampling appears to be somewhat biased in the direction of superior marital happiness.

THE MEASURE OF HAPPINESS USED

The marital-happiness score which was computed for each subject was based upon information regarding communality of interests, average amount of agreement or disagreement between spouses in ten different fields, customary methods of settling disagreements, regret of marriage, choice of spouse if life were to be lived over, contemplation of separation or divorce, subjective estimates of happiness, direct admission of unhappiness, and a complaint score based upon domestic grievances checked in a long list presented. Graded weights were assigned the various possible responses to these items on the basis of intercorrelations, and the total happiness score of a given subject was the sum of the weights corresponding to his individual responses. The resulting numeral score is a serviceable index of the degree of satisfaction that a subject has found in his marriage even though it cannot be regarded as a precise quantitative measure of such satisfaction.

The happiness scores ranged from practically zero to a maximum of 87 points, with a mean of 68.40 for husbands and 69.25 for wives. The respective standard deviations of the distributions were 17.35 and 18.75. The distributions for husbands and wives agreed closely throughout and were markedly skewed in the direction of high happiness. The scores of husbands and wives correlated to the extent of approximately .60, showing that the happiness of one spouse is to a surprising degree independent of the happiness of the other. This finding is new and perhaps rather significant. Its newness is probably explained by the fact that no previous investigation based upon a large group of subjects had secured its data by methods which prevented collaboration between husband and wife in filling out the information schedules. It is significant in the suggestion it carries that the degree of satisfaction which one finds in a marriage depends partly upon one's own characteristic attitudes and temperament and so need not closely parallel the happiness of one's marital partner.

PERSONALITY CORRELATES OF MARITAL HAPPINESS

The information schedule that was filled out by the subjects contained 233 personality test items dealing with interests, attitudes, likes and dislikes, habitual response patterns, and specific opinions as to what constitutes the ideal marriage. Of these, approximately 140 were found to show an appreciable degree of correlation with the happiness scores of either husbands or wives. The various possible responses to the valid items were then assigned score weights roughly in proportion to the extent to which they differentiated between subjects of high and low happiness scores. This made it possible to compute for each subject a "personality" score, which was merely the sum of the weights corresponding to the responses the subject had given. The personality score may be thought of as in some degree an index of the subject's temperamental predisposition to find happiness rather than unhappiness in the marital relationship. This index correlates approximately .46 with the marital-happiness scores of each spouse. Evidently the attitudes and emotional response patterns tapped by the personality items are by no means negligible as determiners of marital happiness.

By noting and classifying the individual items that differentiate between subjects of high and low happiness, it has been possible to piece together descriptive composite pictures of the happy and unhappy temperaments. For example, it is especially characteristic of unhappy subjects to be touchy or grouchy; to lose their tempers easily; to fight to get their own way; to be critical of others; to be careless of others' feelings; to chafe under discipline or to rebel against orders; to show any dislike that they may happen to feel; to be easily affected by praise or blame; to lack self-confidence; to be dominating in their relations with the opposite sex; to be little interested in old people, children, teaching, charity, or uplift activities; to be unconventional in their attitudes toward religion, drinking, and sexual ethics; to be bothered by useless thoughts; to be often in a state of excitement; and to alternate between happiness and sadness without apparent cause.

The above characterizations hold for the unhappy of both sexes. In many respects, however, the differences between the happy and unhappy follow a different pattern for husbands and wives.

The qualities of personality that predispose a person to happiness or unhappiness in his relations with others are of course far from being the sole cause of success or failure in marriage. Their importance, however, is so obvious from our data that the problem calls for further investigation, preferably by a combination of the statistical and clinical approaches.

BACKGROUND CORRELATES OF HAPPINESS

Background factors which in these marriages were totally uncorrelated with happiness scores, or for which the correlation was so small as to have almost no practical significance, include family income, occupation, presence or absence of children, amount of religious training, birth order, number of opposite-sex siblings, adolescent popularity, and spouse differences in age and schooling. Nearly all of the factors in this list have been regarded by one writer or another as highly important, especially presence or absence of children in the home and differences between husband and wife in age and schooling.

It is doubtlessly true that the presence of children often prevents the breaking up of a marriage, but the evidence indicates that it has little effect on the general level of marital happiness. Childless women past middle age do show a slight tendency to be less happy than the average, but childless men of this age tend to have happiness scores above the average. If there are individual marriages that are made more happy by the presence of children, these appear to be offset by other marriages that are made less happy.

From the vantage point of our data it appears that much nonsense has been written about the risks entailed by marrying on inadequate income or by marrying out of one's age or educational class. The correlation of income with happiness scores is zero. The happiest wives in our group are those who are from four to ten years older than their husbands; the happiest husbands are those who are twelve or more years older than their wives. Moreover, the spouses of these subjects rate as happy as the average for the entire population of subjects.

As for religious training, if this was ever a factor in marital happiness, it appears no longer to exert such an influence.

We may designate as of slight importance the factors that show a barely significant relationship to the happiness of one or both of the spouses. This list includes age at marriage, absolute amount of schooling, rated adequacy of sex instruction, sources of sex information, age of learning the origin of babies, number of siblings, circumstances of first meeting between the spouses, length of premarital acquaintance, length of engagement, attractiveness of opposite-sex parent, resemblance of subject's spouse to subject's opposite-sex parent, amount of adolescent "petting," and wife's experience of sex shock or her age at first menstruation. No factor in this list is sufficiently related to marital happiness to warrant a prediction weight of more than one point [1] for either husbands or wives. There has been a vast amount of exaggeration about the risks to marital happiness of early marriage, brief premarital acquaintance, inadequate sex instruction, adolescent "petting," and a history of sex shock on the part of the wife.

Expressed desire to be of the opposite sex tends to be associated with unhappiness in wives but not in husbands. A premarital attitude of disgust toward sex is unfavorable to happiness, and more so in men than in women. Frequent or severe punishment in childhood is reliably associated with unhappiness in both husbands and wives. The items mentioned in this paragraph carry a maximum prediction weight of two points for at least one of the spouses.

Next are five items carrying a maximum weight of three points for one spouse and two points for the other. They are: estimates on husbands and wives of their relative mental ability, parental attitudes toward the subject's early sex curiosity, amount of conflict with father, and amount of attachment to both father and mother.

As to relative mental ability, the most favorable situation is equality or near equality. Marked mental superiority of husband makes for happiness in the wife but for unhappiness in the husband; marked inferiority of husband makes the wife unhappy but does not greatly affect the husband.

Subjects whose parents rebuffed or punished them because of their early sex curiosity are definitely less happy than the average, this effect being somewhat more marked in husbands than in wives.

Strong attachment to either parent is markedly favorable to happiness, especially in the case of husbands. Conflict with the father is unfavorable to happiness, especially in the case of wives.

We come now to the four most important of the background items: happiness of parents, childhood happiness, conflict with mother, and type of home discipline. All of these carry a maximum weight of four or five points.

Happiness of parents rates highest, with a maximum weight of five points for husbands and four for wives. This item is more predictive of success or failure in marriage than a composite of half a dozen items such as income,

---

[1] The "prediction weights," ranging from one to five points, were based on the reliability of the differences between characteristics of two extreme groups (high and low happiness) of husbands and wives taken separately.

age at marriage, religious training, amount of adolescent "petting," or spouse difference in age or schooling.

Hardly less important is the rated happiness of respondent's childhood, with a maximum weight of four points for each spouse. Carrying the same weights is absence of conflict with mother. It appears that a record of conflict with mother constitutes a significantly greater threat to marital happiness than a record of conflict with father.

Childhood discipline that is firm, not harsh, is much more favorable to happiness than discipline that is lax, irregular, or excessively strict.

The ten background circumstances most predictive of marital happiness are (1) superior happiness of parents, (2) childhood happiness, (3) lack of conflict with mother, (4) home discipline that was firm, not harsh, (5) strong attachment to mother, (6) strong attachment to father, (7) lack of conflict with father, (8) parental frankness about matters of sex, (9) infrequency and mildness of childhood punishment, (10) premarital attitude toward sex that was free from disgust or aversion.

The subject who "passes" on all ten of these items is a distinctly better-than-average marital risk. Any one of the ten appears from the data of this study to be more important than virginity at marriage.

SEX FACTORS IN MARITAL HAPPINESS

Our study shows clearly that certain of the sex factors contribute materially to marital happiness or unhappiness. It shows no less clearly that others which have long been emphasized by sexologists as important are practically uncorrelated with happiness scores. The data, in fact, indicate that all of the sex factors combined are far from being the one major determinant of success in marriage.

Among the items yielding little or no correlation with happiness are both reported and preferred frequency of intercourse, estimated duration of intercourse, husband's ability to control ejaculation, methods of contraception used, distrust of contraceptives, fear of pregnancy, degree of pain experienced by wife at the first intercourse, wife's history of sex shock, rhythm in wife's sexual desire, ability of wife to experience multiple orgasms, and failure of the husband to be as dominant as the wife would like him to be in initiating or demanding intercourse.

The sex techniques that many writers regard as the primary key to happy marriage may be worth cultivating for their immediate sensual returns, but they exert no appreciable effect upon happiness scores. Their absence or imperfection is evidently not a major source of conflict or a major cause of separation, divorce, or regret of marriage. What is even more surprising, it appears that such techniques have no very marked effect on the wife's ability to experience the orgasm.

On the other hand, the wife's happiness score (though not her husband's) is reliably correlated with the amount of pleasure that she experienced at her first intercourse, and the husband's happiness is reliably correlated (negatively) with the wife's tendency to prudishness or excessive modesty.

Five of the six items that correlate quite markedly with the happiness scores are: number of sexual complaints checked, rated degree of satisfaction from intercourse with spouse, frequency with which intercourse is refused, reaction of the spouse who is refused, and frequency of desire for extramarital intercourse. The correlations, however, probably do not mean that the factors in question are to any great extent actual determiners of happiness or unhappiness. It is more likely that they are primarily symptoms. The discontented spouse rationalizes his (or her) unhappiness by finding fault with the sexual partner and at the same time develops longings for extramarital relationships.

Among the sex factors investigated are two that not only correlate markedly with happiness scores but are in all probability genuine determiners of them: viz., the wife's orgasm adequacy and husband-wife difference in strength of sex drive.

Two measures were available on relative strength of sex drive. One of these was the ratio (computed for each subject) between actual and preferred number of copulations per month; the other was based on husband's and wife's ratings of their relative passionateness. The two measures agree in showing that equality or near equality in sex drive is an important factor in happiness. As the disparity in drive increases to the point where one spouse is in a more or less chronic state of sex hunger and the other in a state of satiety, the happiness scores of both drop off significantly.

First in importance among the sex factors is the wife's orgasm adequacy, which correlates about .30 both with her own and with her husband's happiness score. It is of special interest that orgasm inadequacy of the wife affects her husband's happiness almost as unfavorably as her own. Between wives of the "never" group and wives of the "always" group, there is a difference of 16.3 points in mean happiness, and a difference of 13.0 points in the mean happiness scores of their husbands. Nevertheless, one finds every grade of happiness both in the "never" group and the "always" group. Adequacy of the wife in this respect favors happiness but does not guarantee it, while on the other hand a considerable minority among the inadequates have happiness scores above the general average.

THE RELATIVE IMPORTANCE OF SEXUAL AND PSYCHOLOGICAL COMPATIBILITY

Our data do not confirm the view so often heard that the key to happiness in marriage is nearly always to be found in sexual compatibility. They indicate, instead, that the influence of the sexual factors is at most no greater than that of the combined personality and background factors, and that it is probably less. The problem is complicated by the fact that the testimony of husband and wife regarding their sexual compatibility is influenced by their psychological compatibility. Couples who are psychologically well-mated are likely to show a surprising tolerance for the things that are not satisfactory in their sexual relationships. The psychologically ill-mated show no such tolerance but instead are prone to exaggeration in their reports on sexual maladjustments. The two sexual factors of genuine importance are wife's orgasm adequacy and relative strength of sex drive in the two spouses.

IMPLICATIONS

Most of us have an opportunity to observe the state of marriage because we are reared in families and live in neighborhoods of married people. From your experience, choose the marriages you know best and estimate whether the partners would have a high, low, or average happiness probability in terms of the items mentioned in the article. Now note the factors which you would surmise contributed most to happiness and unhappiness in these cases. What features in your life would tend to make for happiness or unhappiness in your own marriage?

REFERENCES

Other publications in this general area deserve mention: see Burgess and Cottrell (1939). Burgess and Wallin (1953) and Kelly (1939) are two studies on personality-background factors before and after marriage. These investigations seemed to show that some people are better marital risks than others.

An area of professional psychology shared with other behavioral descriptives has developed, which is known as *marriage counseling*. It assists the individual when he is having interpersonal difficulties in marriage. (See Kimber, 1961.)

Chapter III

TRAINING
AND EDUCATION

[14] DOES HIGHER EDUCATION
INFLUENCE STUDENT VALUES?

Does going to college for several years appreciably change the values of the student? How would you, in a line or two, describe what the average American student holds valuable? Should these values change during four years? Which aspects of the campus would you expect to bring about this change? You will find the following article (a summary of Jacob's book) much more interesting if you first write down your answers to these questions.

Philip E. Jacob

Reprinted from Philip E. Jacob, "Does Higher Education Influence Student Values?" *NEA Journal* (Washington, D.C.: National Education Association, 1958), pp. 35-38, by permission of the publisher and the author.

Colleges and universities must face a hard fact about their present accomplishment before they can plan realistically for their role in the not-too-distant future. For the most part, they seem to lack the capacity to influence students, or maybe today's students are incapable of being influenced by higher education.

In any case, a study of what happens to the values of American students of today shows that their college experience barely touches their standards of behavior, quality of judgment, sense of social responsibility, perspicacity of understanding, and guiding beliefs.

This means that if institutions of higher learning are expected to fulfill the historic humanistic mission of what we have called liberal education, they will have to learn how to do it. They are *not* doing it now with most of their students.

This conclusion stems from an analysis of three main types of data, which social scientists obtained from over one hundred institutions: studies of student attitudes conducted during the last fifteen years, recent evaluations of the outcomes of general education and other courses and of various methods of teaching, and a number of comprehensive self studies by particular institutions.[1]

Fortunately, not all evidence is negative. There are some institutions in which students' values seem to develop, some teachers whose influence penetrates and stays, and some educational techniques which help open the sensibilities as well as the intellectual perceptions of some students. But the prevailing situation concerning the influence of college on contemporary student values is as follows:

1. *The values of American college students are remarkably homogeneous, considering the variety of their backgrounds and their relatively unrestricted opportunities for freedom of thought and personal development.*

A dominant characteristic of the current student generation is that the students are gloriously contented both in regard to their present day-to-day activity and their outlook for the future.

The great majority of students appears unabashedly self-centered. They aspire to material gratifications for themselves and their families. They intend to look out for themselves first and expect others to do likewise.

Social harmony, with an easy tolerance of the dissident and the different, also pervades the student environment. Conformists themselves, the American students do not expect others to conform to the socially accepted standard. They are, for the most part, ready to live in a mobile society without racial, ethnic, or income barriers. But they do not intend to crusade for nondiscrimination, merely to accept it as it comes.

Although most students value the traditional code of moral virtues, they are not inclined to censure those who choose to depart from it. Nor do they feel personally bound to unvarying conformity to the code, especially when a lapse is socially sanctioned. For instance, systematic academic cheating is the custom at many major institutions.

Students normally express a need for religion and often attend church on Sundays, but their religion does not carry over into the secular world. The majority appear to believe that God's place is in church or home, not in business or community.

American students are also only dutifully responsive toward government.

[1] A detailed inventory and analysis of this material is available in a report prepared by Dr. Jacob for the Edward W. Hazen Foundation: *Changing Values in College.* Harper, 1957.

They expect to obey its laws and pay its taxes—without complaint but without enthusiasm. Except for voting, however, they are politically irresponsible and politically illiterate.

They have contradictory attitudes toward international affairs. They predict another major war within a dozen years, yet indicate that during the immediate future they expect to give little personal attention to international problems.

Students by and large set great stock by college in general and their own college in particular. Only a minority, however, seem to value their college education for its intellectual contribution or for its nurturing of personal character. Vocational preparation and skill and experience in social "adjustment" head the rewards which students expect from college.

The available data indicate that the profile just given may broadly characterize 75 or 80 per cent of the students. To the remainder, some or most of the generalizations are not applicable. Also, on some issues, such as how much government the country needs, students have no common mind. But the dominant impression is of a nation-wide norm of values pervading the campus.

2. *The main effect of higher education upon student values is to bring about general acceptance of a body of standards and attitude characteristics of college-bred men and women in America.*

There tends to be more homogeneity and greater consistency of values among college seniors than among freshmen, indicating that the senior has ironed out serious conflicts of values or at least achieved a workable compromise. Throughout college, changes are rarely drastic or sudden. Such changes as do occur tend to emerge on the periphery of the student's character rather than to affect his core of values.

The values of college graduates do differ in some ways from the rest of society. They are more concerned with status, achievement, and prestige. As a whole, they tend to be more self-important, more conservative, more tolerant, and less superstitious and prejudiced than those without college.

It seems reasonable to credit these differences to college, partly to its positive influence in bringing students' outlook into line with a "standard," partly to a subtle selective process which tends to eliminate those not sufficiently adaptive to acquire the value patterns of the college graduate.

But to call this process a liberalization of student values is to use a misnomer. The impact of college rather is to socialize the individual, to refine or shape up his values so that he can fit into his society more congenially.

3. *For the most part, students' values do not vary greatly whether they have pursued a conventional liberal-arts program, an integrated general-education curriculum, or a professional-vocational option.*

The more liberally educated students may take a somewhat more active interest in community responsibilities and keep better informed about public affairs. But the distinction is not striking, and it does not occur consistently. It does not justify the conclusion that a student acquires a greater maturity of judgment on issues of social policy or a more sensitive regard for human values because he has had more liberal education.

There is also no solid evidence of a delayed reaction. The college alumnus exhibits no unusual trademark identifying his undergraduate curriculum.

The same negative conclusion applies to the general effect of social-science courses. Although many students testify that such courses have increased their understanding of world affairs or interest in politics, the values actually expressed by social-science students—either verbally or in action—are little different from those of others. There is little evidence, for instance, that actual participation in public life has increased as a result of students' taking social science.

4. *Quality of teaching has little effect upon the value outcomes of students' general education.*

Students have demonstrated an uncanny capacity to evaluate the performance of instructors according to objective criteria. Yet, by and large, the impact of the teacher they consider good is indistinguishable from that of the poor one—at least in terms of his influence upon the students' values.

Some teachers, however, do exert a profound influence on *some* students, even to the point of causing particular individuals to adopt new and usually more socially responsible vocational goals. It is perhaps significant that faculty members having this power are likely to be those whose own value commitments are openly expressed and who are outgoing and warm in their student relationships.

5. *The method of instruction seems to have only a minor influence on students' value judgments.*

Under special circumstances, "student-centered" teaching reportedly has resulted in a more satisfactory student adjustment and a more congenial learning situation. But the weight of evidence gives little indication that different teaching methods—say, the lecture system versus recitation, conference, discussion, or tutorial methods—greatly alter students' beliefs or behavior.

However, individual students are often deeply affected by participation in experiences which vividly confront them with value issues, and possibly demand decisions on their part whose consequences they can witness.

But the practical difficulties of working such activities into the educational process are very great, especially in the general part of the curriculum in which large numbers of students are involved. For the essence of a potent laboratory practice in citizenship, a creative work camp, a meaningful experiment in international living, a stimulating work-study curriculum, or even a well conceived field study is this: each student personally engages in the action.

Vicarious experience does not deliver the same punch, even though role-playing techniques in the classroom and the analysis of challenging case studies and problem situations do arouse more interest.

6. *Similar as the patterns of student values appear on a mass view, the intellectual, cultural, or moral climate of some institutions stands out as having a peculiar potency.*

The response of students to education within these institutions is strikingly different from the national pattern.

Such colleges and universities do not fit any institutional type. However, they seem to have in common a high level of expectancy of their students. *What* is expected is not the same.

For instance, the institution may primarily stress intellectual initiative, profound respect for the worth of work, world-mindedness, or a dedication to humanitarian service. But everyone is conscious of the mission to which the institution stands dedicated, though this is not necessarily loudly trumpeted at every convocation, nor elaborated in the college or university bulletin.

In these colleges, students seem drawn to live up to the college standard, even if it means a wrench from their previous ways of thought.

With a distinctive quality of this kind, an institution evokes a deep loyalty from students, alumni, and staff. A community of values is created which persists long after graduation and often influences the choice of college by the next generation.

7. *Recent research has identified certain personality characteristics of students which filter their educational experiences.*

Some students have a set of mind so rigid, an outlook on human relations so stereotyped, and a reliance on authority so compulsive that they are incapable of understanding, much less accepting, new ideas. Such students quail in the presence of conflict and uncertainty. They crave "right answers," recoil from creative discussion.

Under most conditions of general education, where content and teaching method have been more or less standardized to suit the average student, the personalities just described become dead wood. A few institutions, however, are exploring special approaches to general education for this type of student, with promising results.

These students rarely achieve the autonomy of those whose personality is freer to start with. But they have shown striking gains in critical thinking and developed more responsible and sensitive social values when their general education in social science, for instance, has been tailored to their particular needs. Because the number of students with such personality characteristics is large and growing, this type of experimentation seems unusually important.

The points presented here imply that no specific curricular pattern of liberal education, no pedigree of instructor, and no wizardry of instructional method should be patented for its impact on students' values. Indeed, the impact of American higher education as a whole upon the value patterns of college youth as a whole seems negligible.

The values of some students do change in college. But even with these, the impetus to change does not come primarily from the formal educational process. It comes from the distinctive climate of a few institutions, the individual and personal magnetism of a sensitive teacher with strong values, or the value-laden personal experiences which students occasionally undergo during college.

In short, college can contribute to the growth of a student's values only when it penetrates the core of his life and confronts him with fresh and often disturbing implications, which are different from those which he and his society have taken for granted. This can hardly occur as a by-product of a curricular assembly line. It requires a highly personal relationship between the college community and the individual student—a relationship that is warm and considerate but at the same time mutually aggravating.

IMPLICATIONS

Jacob describes the student who is rigid and stereotyped in his thinking and who becomes discouraged in the presence of conflict and uncertainty. To what extent do you find these traits in yourself or your friends? Jacob's compilation was done on research that reflected students' attitudes prior to the 1960's. Is the majority of students different today? What forces on your campus seem to create a community of values that persists after graduation, which Jacob found in some colleges? Is the minority who has always sought to change the world for the better more prevalent today? Read the excerpt under "References" of a recent editorial in *Christianity and Crisis* which suggested this. Do you perceive your campus as this writer does?

REFERENCES

Jacob's book (1957), from which Selection 14 is taken, gives a good review of the studies on change of attitudes during the college years.

There are other books and studies on the college graduate that you may find rewarding to read. Pace (1941) sampled graduates and college dropouts of the twenties. He found—as did Jacob—that these former students were politically passive and that intellectual and aesthetic pursuits did not loom large in their post-college life. Havemann and West (1952) reported that alumni were satisfied with their college experience if not with the specific curriculum they chose. *Grades* tended to be related to college success in all fields but business. Higher grades also went along with greater college contentment, with their major and specialty. A more recent volume edited by the psychologist Sanford (1964) has chapters on the entering student, the teacher, dropouts, the college community, the college in society, and proposals for change.

The following is an excerpt from *Christianity and Crisis*, entitled "Ferment on the Campus." *

Commencement, 1965, brings the end of the most turbulent year on college campuses within recent memory. This has not been the year of giddy foolishness—of goldfish swallowing, panty raids, and competitions to stack improbable numbers of students in telephone booths. Instead, it has been a time of demonstrations, strikes, teach-ins, trips to Washington, and sit-downs to prevent trips to Washington. . . .

Many a student has taken a fresh look at our world. He has seen Vietnam, Latin America, poverty in the U.S., the pampering suburbs, and the decay of cities. He has seen the mediocrity of the affluent society. And what he has seen has not pleased him. On the most elite Ivy League campuses, students have been heard to envy the militant Negro youth who have found a cause worthy of their sacrifices.

[15] TEACHING MACHINES

Today, most college students have heard of teaching machines. Some students have used them knowingly; other students have found help in their courses by turning to a programed workbook, thereby using a booklike teaching machine and perhaps not realizing what it was or why they found it so valuable.

Industry, which long ago learned to appreciate machines, has found the teaching machine; so has the military establishment, which has included the teaching machine in the training program.

Why are the teaching machine and *programed learning* valuable? Basically, what do they consist of? What are the learning principles involved in constructing an efficient teaching machine? Skinner, an outstanding experimentalist and systematist in the psychology of learning, has worked with the teaching machine and in this selection answers some of these questions.

---

* Reprinted from *Christianity and Crisis*, Vol. XXV, 10 (June 14, 1965).

B. F. Skinner

Reprinted from B. F. Skinner, "Teaching Machines," *Science*, Vol. 128 (Washington, D.C.: American Association for the Advancement of Science, October 24, 1958), pp. 969–977, by permission of the publisher and the author.

There are more people in the world than ever before, and a far greater part of them want an education. The demand cannot be met simply by building more schools and training more teachers. Education must become more efficient. To this end, curricula must be revised and simplified, and textbooks and classroom techniques improved. In any other field, a demand for increased production would have led at once to the invention of labor-saving capital equipment. Education has reached this stage very late, possibly through a misconception of its task. Thanks to the advent of television, however, the so-called audio-visual aids are being re-examined. Film projectors, television sets, phonographs, and tape recorders are finding their way into American schools and colleges.

Audio-visual aids supplement and may even supplant lectures, demonstrations, and textbooks. In doing so they serve one function of the teacher: they present material to the student and, when successful, make it so clear and interesting that the student learns. There is another function to which they contribute little or nothing. It is best seen in the productive interchange between teacher and student in the small classroom or tutorial situation. Much of that interchange has already been sacrificed in American education in order to teach large numbers of students. There is a real danger that it will be wholly obscured if use of equipment designed simply to *present* material becomes widespread. The student is becoming more and more a mere passive receiver of instruction. . . .

If our current knowledge of the acquisition and maintenance of verbal behavior is to be applied to education, some sort of teaching machine is needed. Contingencies of reinforcement which change the behavior of lower organisms often cannot be arranged by hand; rather elaborate apparatus is needed. The human organism requires even more subtle instrumentation. An appropriate teaching machine will have several important features. The student must *compose* his response rather than select it from a set of alternatives, as in a multiple-choice self-rater. One reason for this is that we want him to recall rather than recognize—to make a response as well as see that it is right. Another reason is that effective multiple-choice material must contain plausible wrong responses, which are out of place in the delicate process of "shaping" behavior because they strengthen unwanted forms. Although it is much easier to build a machine to score multiple-choice answers than to evaluate a composed response, the technical advantage is outweighed by these and other considerations.

A second requirement of a minimal teaching machine also distinguishes it from earlier versions. In acquiring complex behavior, the student must pass through a carefully designed sequence of steps, often of considerable length. Each step must be so small that it can always be taken, yet in taking it the student moves somewhat closer to fully competent behavior. The machine must make sure that these steps are taken in a carefully prescribed order.

Several machines with the required characteristics have been built and tested. Sets of separate presentations or "frames" of visual material are stored on disks, cards, or tapes. One frame is presented at a time, adjacent frames being out of sight. In one type of machine, the student composes a response by moving printed figures or letters (Skinner, 1954). His setting is compared by the machine with a coded response. If the two correspond, the machine automatically presents the next frame. If they do not, the response is cleared, and another must be composed. The student cannot proceed to a second step until the first has been taken. A machine of this kind is being tested in teaching spelling, arithmetic, and other subjects in the lower grades.

For more advanced students—from junior high school, say, through college —a machine which senses an arrangement of letters or figures is unnecessarily rigid in specifying form of response. Fortunately, such students may be asked to compare their responses with printed material revealed by the machine. In the machine shown in Figure 1, material is printed in thirty radial frames on a 12-inch disk. The student inserts the disk and closes the machine. He cannot proceed until the machine has been locked, and, once he has begun, the machine cannot be unlocked. All but a corner of one frame is visible through a window. The student writes his response on a paper strip exposed through a second opening. By lifting a lever on the front of the machine, he moves what he has written under a transparent cover and uncovers the correct response in the remaining corner of the frame. If the two responses correspond, he moves the lever horizontally. This movement punches a hole in the paper opposite his response, recording the fact that he called it correct, and alters the machine so that the frame will not appear again when the student works around the disk a second time. Whether the response was correct or not, a second frame appears when the lever is returned to its starting position. The student proceeds in this way until he has responded to all frames. He then works around the disk a second time, but only those frames appear to which he has not correctly responded. When the disk revolves without stopping, the assignment is finished. (The student is asked to repeat each frame until a correct response is made to allow for the fact that, in telling him that a response is wrong, such a machine tells him what is right.)

The machine itself, of course, does not teach. It simply brings the student

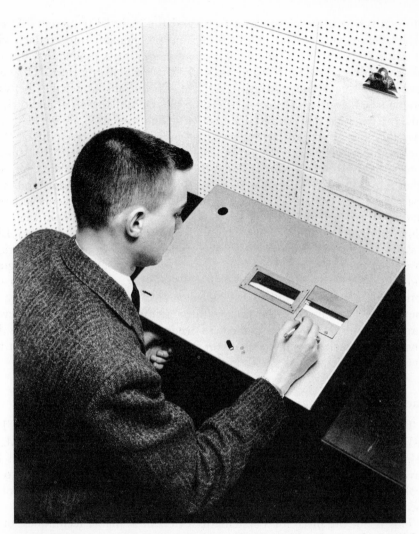

FIGURE 1. Student at work on a teaching machine. One frame of material is partly visible in the left-hand window. The student writes his response on a strip of paper exposed at the right. He then lifts a lever with his left hand, advancing his written response under a transparent cover and uncovering the correct response in the upper corner of the frame. If he is right, he moves the lever to the right, punching a hole alongside the response he has called right and altering the machine so that that frame will not appear again when he goes through the series a second time. A new frame appears when the lever is returned to its starting position.

into contact with the person who composed the material it presents. It is a labor-saving device because it can bring one programmer into contact with an indefinite number of students. This may suggest mass production, but the effect upon each student is surprisingly like that of a private tutor. The comparison holds in several respects. (1) There is a constant interchange between program and students. Unlike lectures, textbooks, and the usual audio-visual aids, the machine induces sustained activity. The student is always alert and busy. (2) Like a good tutor, the machine insists that a given point be thoroughly understood, either frame by frame or set by set, before the student moves on. Lectures, textbooks, and their mechanized equivalents, on the other hand, proceed without making sure that the student understands and easily leave him behind. (3) Like a good tutor the machine presents just that material for which the student is ready. It asks him to take only that step which he is at the moment best equipped and most likely to take. (4) Like a skillful tutor the machine helps the student to come up with the right answer. It does this in part through the orderly construction of the program and in part with techniques of hinting, prompting, suggesting, and so on, derived from an analysis of verbal behavior (Skinner, 1957). (5) Lastly, of course, the machine, like the private tutor, reinforces the student for every correct response, using this immediate feedback not only to shape his behavior most efficiently but to maintain it in strength in a manner which the layman would describe as "holding the student's interest."

PROGRAMING MATERIAL

The success of such a machine depends on the material used in it. The task of programing a given subject is at first sight rather formidable. Many helpful techniques can be derived from a general analysis of the relevant behavioral processes, verbal and nonverbal. Specific forms of behavior are to be evoked and, through differential reinforcement, brought under the control of specific stimuli.

This is not the place for a systematic review of available techniques, or of the kind of research which may be expected to discover others. However, the machines themselves cannot be adequately described without giving a few examples of programs. We may begin with a set of frames (see Table 1) designed to teach a third- or fourth-grade pupil to spell the word *manufacture*. The six frames are presented in the order shown, and the pupil moves sliders to expose letters in the open squares.

The word to be learned appears in boldface in frame 1, with an example and a simple definition. The pupil's first task is simply to copy it. When he does so correctly, frame 2 appears. He must now copy selectively: he must identify "fact" as the common part of "manufacture" and "factory." This helps him to spell the word and also to acquire a separable "atomic" verbal operant (Skinner, 1957). In frame 3 another root must be copied selectively from "manual." In frame 4 the pupil must for the first time insert letters without copying. Since he is asked to insert the same letter in two places, a wrong response will be doubly conspicuous, and the chance of failure is thereby minimized. The same principle governs frame 5. In frame 6 the pupil spells the word to complete the sentence used as an example in frame 1. Even a poor student is likely to do this correctly because he has just composed or completed the word five times, has made two important root-responses, and has learned that two letters occur in the word twice. He has probably learned to spell the word without having made a mistake.

TABLE 1

A set of frames designed to teach a third- or fourth-grade pupil to spell the word "manufacture"

1. Manufacture means to make or build. Chair factories manufacture chairs. Copy the word here:

    ☐ ☐ ☐ ☐ ☐ ☐ ☐ ☐ ☐ ☐ ☐

2. Part of the word is like part of the word <u>factory</u>. Both parts come from an old word meaning <u>make</u> or <u>build</u>.

    m a n u ☐ ☐ ☐ ☐ u r e

3. Part of the word is like part of the word <u>manual</u>. Both parts come from an old word for <u>hand</u>. Many things used to be made by hand.

    ☐ ☐ ☐ ☐ f a c t u r e

4. The same letter goes in both spaces:

    m ☐ n u f ☐ c t u r e

5. The same letter goes in both spaces:

    m a n ☐ f a c t ☐ r e

6. Chair factories ☐ ☐ ☐ ☐ ☐ ☐ ☐ ☐ ☐ ☐ chairs.

Teaching spelling is mainly a process of shaping complex forms of behavior. In other subjects—for example, arithmetic—responses must be brought under the control of appropriate stimuli. Unfortunately the material which has been prepared for teaching arithmetic [1] does not lend itself to excerpting. The numbers 0 through 9 are generated in relation to objects, quantities, and scales. The operations of addition, subtraction, multiplication, and division are thoroughly developed before the number 10 is reached. In the course of this the pupil composes equations and expressions in a great variety of alternative forms. He completes not only $5 + 4 = \square$, but $\square + 4 = 9$, $5 \square 4 = 9$, and

---

[1] This material was prepared with the assistance of Susan R. Meyer.

so on, aided in most cases by illustrative materials. No appeal is made to rote memorizing, even in the later acquisition of the tables. The student is expected to arrive at $9 \times 7 = 63$, not by memorizing it as he would memorize a line of poetry, but by putting into practice such principles as that nine times a number is the same as ten times the number minus the number (both of these being "obvious" or already well learned), that the digits in a multiple of nine add to nine, that in composing successive multiples of nine one counts backward (*nine, eight*een, twenty-*seven*, thirty-*six*, and so on), that nine times a single digit is a number beginning with one less than the digit (nine times *six* is *fifty* something), and possibly even that the product of two numbers separated by only one number is equal to the square of the separating number minus one (the square of eight already being familiar from a special series of frames concerned with squares).

Programs of this sort run to great length. At least five or six frames per word, four grades of spelling may require 20,000 or 25,000 frames, and three or four grades of arithmetic, as many again. If these figures seem large, it is only because we are thinking of the normal contact between teacher and pupil. Admittedly, a teacher cannot supervise 10,000 or 15,000 responses made by each pupil per year. But the pupil's time is not so limited. In any case, surprisingly little time is needed. Fifteen minutes per day on a machine should suffice for each of these programs, the machines being free for other students for the rest of each day. (It is probably because traditional methods are so inefficient that we have been led to suppose that education requires such a prodigious part of a young person's day.)

A simple technique used in programing material at the high-school or college level, by means of the machine shown in Figure 1, is exemplified in teaching a student to recite a poem. The first line is presented with several unimportant letters omitted. The student must read the line "meaningfully" and supply the missing letters. The second, third, and fourth frames present succeeding lines in the same way. In the fifth frame the first line reappears with other letters also missing. Since the student has recently read the line, he can complete it correctly. He does the same for the second, third, and fourth lines. Subsequent frames are increasingly incomplete, and eventually—say, after 20 or 24 frames—the student reproduces all four lines without external help, and quite possibly without having made a wrong response. The technique is similar to that used in teaching spelling: responses are first controlled by a text, but this is slowly reduced (colloquially, "vanished") until the responses can be emitted without a text, each member in a series of responses being now under the "intraverbal" control of other members.

"Vanishing" can be used in teaching other types of verbal behavior. When a student describes the geography of part of the world or the anatomy of part of the body, or names plants and animals from specimens or pictures, verbal responses are controlled by nonverbal stimuli. In setting up such behavior, the student is first asked to report features of a fully labeled map, picture, or object, and the labels are then vanished. In teaching a map, for example, the machine asks the student to describe spatial relations among cities, countries, rivers, and so on, as shown on a fully labeled map. He is then asked to do the same with a map in which the names are incomplete or, possibly, lacking. Eventually he is asked to report the same relations with no map at all. If the material has been well programed, he can do so correctly. Instruction is sometimes concerned not so much with imparting a new repertoire of verbal responses as with getting the student to describe something accurately in any available terms. The machine can "make sure the student understands" a graph, diagram, chart, or picture by asking him to identify and explain its features—correcting him, of course, whenever he is wrong.

In addition to charts, maps, graphs, models, and so on, the student may have access to auditory material. In learning to take dictation in a foreign language, for example, he selects a short passage on an indexing phonograph according to instructions given by the machine. He listens to the passage as often as necessary and then transcribes it. The machine then reveals the correct text. The student may listen to the passage again to discover the sources of any error. The indexing phonograph may also be used with the machine to teach other language skills, as well as telegraphic code, music, speech, parts of literary and dramatic appreciation, and other subjects.

A typical program combines many of these functions. The set of frames shown in Table 2 is designed to induce the student of high-school physics to talk intelligently, and to some extent technically, about the emission of light from an incandescent source. In using the machine the student will write a word or phrase to complete a given item and then uncover the corresponding word or phrase shown here in the column at the right. The reader who wishes to get the "feel" of the material should cover the right-hand column with a card, uncovering each line only after he has completed the corresponding item.

Several programing techniques are exemplified by the set of frames in Table 2. Technical terms are introduced slowly. For example, the familiar term "fine wire" in frame 2 is followed by a definition of the technical term "filament" in frame 4; "filament" is then asked for in the presence of the nonscientific synonym in frame 5 and without the synonym in frame 9. In the same way "glow," "give off light," and "send out light" in early frames are followed by a definition of "emit" with a synonym in frame 7. Various inflected forms of "emit" then follow, and "emit" itself is asked for with a synonym in frame 16. It is asked for without a synonym but in a helpful phrase in frame 30, and "emitted" and "emission" are asked for without help in frames 33 and 34. The relation between temperature and amount and color of light is developed in several frames before a formal statement using the word "temperature" is asked for in frame 12. "Incandescent" is defined and used in frame 13, is used again in frame 14, and is asked for in frame 15, the student receiving a thematic prompt from the recurring phrase "incandescent source of light." A formal prompt is supplied by "candle." In frame 25 the new response "energy" is easily evoked by the words "form of..." because the expression "form of energy" is used earlier in the frame. "Energy" appears again in the next two frames and is finally asked for, without aid, in frame 28. Frames 30 through 35 discuss the limiting temperatures of incandescent objects, while reviewing several kinds of sources. The figure 800 is used in three frames. Two intervening frames then permit some time to pass before the response "800" is asked for.

TABLE 2

PART OF A PROGRAM IN HIGH-SCHOOL PHYSICS. THE MACHINE PRESENTS ONE ITEM AT A TIME. THE STUDENT COMPLETES THE ITEM AND THEN UNCOVERS THE CORRESPONDING WORD OR PHRASE SHOWN AT THE RIGHT.

Sentence to be completed	Word to be supplied
1. The important parts of a flashlight are the battery and the bulb. When we "turn on" a flashlight, we close a switch which connects the battery with the _____.	bulb
2. When we turn on a flashlight, an electric current flows through the fine wire in the _____ and causes it to grow hot.	bulb
3. When the hot wire glows brightly, we say that it gives off or sends out heat and _____.	light
4. The fine wire in the bulb is called a filament. The bulb "lights up" when the filament is heated by the passage of a(n) _____ current.	electric
5. When a weak battery produces little current, the fine wire, or _____, does not get very hot.	filament
6. A filament which is *less* hot sends out or gives off _____ light.	less
7. "Emit" means "send out." The amount of light sent out, or "emitted," by a filament depends on how _____ the filament is.	hot
8. The higher the temperature of the filament the _____ the light emitted by it.	brighter, stronger filament
9. If a flashlight battery is weak, the _____ in the bulb may still glow, but with only a dull red color.	
10. The light from a very hot filament is colored yellow or white. The light from a filament which is not very hot is colored _____.	red
11. A blacksmith or other metal worker sometimes makes sure that a bar of iron is heated to a "cherry red" before hammering it into shape. He uses the _____ of the light emitted by the bar to tell how hot it is.	color

TABLE 2 (*Continued*)

Sentence to be completed	Word to be supplied
12. Both the color and the amount of light depend on the _____ of the emitting filament or bar.	temperature
13. An object which emits light because it is hot is called "incandescent." A flashlight bulb is an incandescent source of _____.	light
14. A neon tube emits light but remains cool. It is, therefore, not an incandescent _____ of light.	source
15. A candle flame is hot. It is a (n) _____ source of light.	incandescent
16. The hot wick of a candle gives off small pieces or particles of carbon which burn in the flame. Before or while burning, the hot particles send out, or _____, light.	emit
17. A long candlewick produces a flame in which oxygen does not reach all the carbon particles. Without oxygen the particles cannot burn. Particles which do not burn rise above the flame as _____.	smoke
18. We can show that there are particles of carbon in a candle flame, even when it is not smoking, by holding a piece of metal in the flame. The metal cools some of the particles before they burn, and the unburned carbon _____ collect on the metal as soot.	particles
19. The particles of carbon in soot or smoke no longer emit light because they are _____ than when they were in the flame.	cooler, colder
20. The reddish part of candle flame has the same color as the filament in a flashlight with a weak battery. We might guess that the yellow or white parts of a candle flame are _____ than the reddish part.	hotter
21. "Putting out" an incandescent electric light means turning off the current so that the filament grows too _____ to emit light.	cold, cool
22. Setting fire to the wick of an oil lamp is called _____ the lamp.	lighting
23. The sun is our principal _____ of light, as well as of heat.	source
24. The sun is not only very bright but very hot. It is a powerful _____ source of light.	incandescent
25. Light is a form of energy. In "emitting light" an object changes, or "converts," one form of _____ into another.	energy
26. The electrical energy supplied by the battery in a flashlight is converted to _____ and _____.	heat, light; light, heat
27. If we leave a flashlight on, all the energy stored in the battery will finally be changed or _____ into heat and light.	converted
28. The light from a candle flame comes from the _____ released by chemical changes as the candle burns.	energy

TABLE 2 (*Continued*)

Sentence to be completed	Word to be supplied
29. A nearly "dead" battery may make a flashlight bulb warm to the touch, but the filament may still not be enough to emit light—in other words, the filament will not be _____ at that temperature.	incandescent
30. Objects, such as a filament, carbon particles, or iron bars, become incandescent when heated to about 800 degrees Celsius. At that temperature they begin to _____ .	emit light
31. When raised to any temperature above 800 degrees Celsius, an object such as an iron bar will emit light. Although the bar may melt or vaporize, its particles will be _____ no matter how hot they get.	incandescent
32. About 800 degrees Celsius is the lower limit of the temperature at which particles emit light. There is no upper limit of the _____ at which emission of light occurs.	temperature
33. Sunlight is _____ by very hot gases near the surface of the sun.	emitted
34. Complex changes similar to an atomic explosion generate the great heat which explains the _____ of light by the sun.	emission
35. Below about _____ degrees Celsius an object is not an incandescent source of light.	800

Unwanted responses are eliminated with special techniques. If, for example, the second sentence in frame 24 were simply "It is a(n) _____ source of light," the two "very's" would frequently lead the student to fill the blank with "strong" or a synonym thereof. This is prevented by inserting the word "powerful" to make a synonym redundant. Similarly, in frame 3 the words "heat and" pre-empt the response "heat," which would otherwise correctly fill the blank.

The net effect of such material is more than the acquisition of facts and terms. Beginning with a largely unverbalized acquaintance with flashlights, candles, and so on, the student is induced to talk about familiar events, together with a few new facts, with a fairly technical vocabulary. He applies the same terms to facts which he may never before have seen to be similar. The emission of light from an incandescent source takes shape as a topic or field of inquiry. An understanding of the subject emerges which is often quite surprising in view of the fragmentation required in item building.

It is not easy to construct such a program. Where a confusing or elliptical passage in a textbook is forgivable because it can be clarified by the teacher, machine material must be self-contained and wholly adequate. There are other reasons why textbooks, lecture outlines, and film scripts are of little help in preparing a program. They are usually not logical or developmental arrangements of material but stratagems which the authors have found successful under existing classroom conditions. The examples they give are more often chosen to hold the student's interest than to clarify terms and principles. In composing material for the machine, the programmer may go directly to the point.

A first step is to define the field. A second is to collect technical terms, facts, laws, principles, and cases. These must then be arranged in a plausible developmental order—linear if possible, branching if necessary. A mechanical arrangement, such as a card filing system, helps. The material is distributed among the frames of a program to achieve an arbitrary density. In the final composition of an item, techniques for strengthening asked-for responses and for transferring control from one variable to another are chosen from a list according to a given schedule in order to prevent the establishment of irrelevant verbal tendencies appropriate to a single technique. When one set of frames has been composed, its terms and facts are seeded mechanically among succeeding sets, where they will again be referred to in composing later items to make sure that the earlier repertoire remains active. Thus, the technical terms, facts, and examples in Table 2 have been distributed for re-use in succeeding sets on reflection, absorption, and transmission, where they are incorporated into items dealing mainly with other matters. Sets of frames for explicit review can, of course, be constructed. Further research will presumably discover other, possibly more effective, techniques. Meanwhile, it must be admitted that a considerable measure of art is needed in composing a successful program.

Whether good programing is to remain an art or to become a scientific technology, it is reassuring to know that there is a final authority—the student. An unexpected advantage of machine instruction has proved to be the feedback to the *programmer*. In the elementary school machine, provision is made for discovering which frames commonly yield wrong responses, and in the high-school and college machine the paper strips bearing written answers are available for analysis. A trial run of the first version of a program quickly reveals frames which need to be altered, or sequences which need to be lengthened. One or two revisions in the light of a few dozen responses work a great improvement. No comparable feedback is available to the lecturer, textbook writer, or maker of films. Although one text or film may seem to be better than another, it is usually impossible to say, for example, that a given sentence on a given page or a particular sequence in a film is causing trouble.

Difficult as programing is, it has its compensations. It is a salutary thing to try to guarantee a right response at every step in the presentation of a subject matter. The programmer will usually find that he has been accustomed to leave much to the student—that he has frequently omitted essential steps and neglected to invoke relevant points. The responses made to his material may reveal surprising ambiguities. Unless he is lucky, he may find that he still has something to learn about his subject. He will almost certainly find that he needs to learn a great deal more about the behavioral changes he is trying to induce in the student. This effect of the machine in confronting the programmer with the full scope of his task may in itself produce a considerable improvement in education.

CONCLUSION

An analysis of education within the framework of a science of behavior has broad implications. Our schools, in particular our "progressive" schools, are often held responsible for many current problems, including juvenile delinquency and the threat of a more powerful foreign technology. One remedy frequently suggested is a return to older techniques, especially to a greater "discipline" in schools. Presumably this is to be obtained with some form of punishment, to be administered either with certain classical instruments of physical injury—the dried bullock's tail of the Greek teacher or the cane of the English schoolmaster—or as disapproval or failure, the frequency of which is to be increased by "raising standards." This is probably not a feasible solution. Not only education but Western culture as a whole is moving away from aversive practices. We cannot prepare young people for one kind of life in institutions organized on quite different principles. The discipline of the birch rod may facilitate learning, but we must remember that it also breeds followers of dictators and revolutionists.

In the light of our present knowledge, a school system must be called a failure if it cannot induce students to learn except by threatening them for not learning. That this has always been the standard pattern simply emphasizes the importance of modern techniques. John Dewey was speaking for his culture and his time when he attacked aversive educational practices and appealed to teachers to turn to positive and humane methods. What he threw out should have been thrown out. Unfortunately he had too little to put in its place. Progressive education has been a temporizing measure which can now be effectively supplemented. Aversive practices can not only be replaced, they can be replaced with far more powerful techniques. The possibilities should be thoroughly explored if we are to build an educational system which will meet the present demand without sacrificing democratic principles.

IMPLICATIONS

Have you ever used a teaching machine or a programed workbook? What is your impression of it? What did you appreciate or dislike about it? What are the learning principles highlighted in the use of the teaching machine? What implications does it make for traditional teaching? What advantages has traditional teaching over it? If you have not used a teaching machine or programed work book, you may be better able to evaluate the process by working the programed material in Table 2.

REFERENCES
Consult the Bibliography for references cited in the article.

[16] WHEN TEACHERS FACE THEMSELVES

We started this book on the note of the importance of meaningfulness in life's quest. Here we present an article that begins, "The search for meaning is essentially a search for self." It is addressed to teachers, but it may well have been addressed to you because at the college level you learn best what you teach yourself.

Meaningfulness in life is important to counteract the modern problems of *anxiety* and *emptiness* which too many people experience in our affluent society. How is meaningfulness achieved in the practical learning situation? The answer is through personal involvement—seeking self-implication in knowledge and in social interaction. Jersild, an outstanding educational psychologist best known for his classic volumes on child psychology, states here what the search for meaning in teaching and education involves. He discusses the role of self-acceptance in the educative process.

The importance of self-understanding in growth as a person was shown rather dramatically in two studies by Rogers, Kell, and McNeil, involving delinquent children on whom diagnostic follow-up data were available. Independent ratings of their adjustment two years after diagnosis were obtained. The ratings of the *individual's understanding and acceptance of himself and the reality situation* was found to be in both studies *the best predictor of what his future adjustment would be.* (See Selection 6.)

Now read a discussion of the relationship between the search for meaning and self-understanding.

Arthur T. Jersild

Reprinted from Arthur T. Jersild, *When Teachers Face Themselves* (New York: Teachers College Press, Columbia University, 1955), by permission of the publisher and the author.

The search for meaning is essentially a search for self. Meaning constitutes, in many respects, the substance of the self.

Where there is meaning, there is involvement. When something has meaning, one is committed to it. Where there is meaning, there is conviction. Such commitment and conviction is something different from conformity, or merely playing a part, or living as a cog in a machine, or losing one's individuality in what Kierkegaard has called the "featureless crowd." Where meaning is lacking in one's work as a teacher, the self is uninvolved. The substance is lacking, and teaching is just an empty formality.

The problem of meaninglessness overlaps in many ways the problems of anxiety and loneliness. It is largely by virtue of a lack of meaning—a kind of emotional emptiness that prevails when things don't matter—that the lonely person feels lonely. It is partly because of a lack of meaning or a distortion of meaning such as is found in pretenses and inner disharmonies that the anxious person is anxious.

About 60 per cent of the people responding to the Personal Issues Inventory [1] indicated that meaninglessness was a problem on which they would like *to have help in understanding themselves.** In expressing this problem, many said they were not sure what they wanted from life—what it was important to be or do or get from life; some said that what they were doing or what was happening didn't seem to mean much; some said they saw little or no meaning in many of the things they had to learn or teach. Some expressed meaninglessness by default, so to speak, indicating that they got involved in so many activities and responsibilities that they had little time for themselves.

The need for helping children and grown men and women to face and find something essentially meaningful glares at us from headlines telling of tensions in the world we live in. Man has made fabulous progress in exploring the external dimensions of his world and in controlling its physical properties

---

* Editor's italics.
[1] The reader will find a complete breakdown of this inventory in the original source of this article, pp. 149–163.

but this power has not been matched by a cultivation of his courage to draw upon other resources of his humanity. We are frightened lest he use his power to destroy himself. Modern man, for all his contrivances, is still as much in need of finding himself and facing the meaning of his existence as he was many eras ago. No invention in science or gimmick in education can obviate the necessity for this search.

The problem of meaninglessness—which Tillich has referred to as the anxiety of emptiness and the anxiety of meaninglessness—prevails not simply among teachers and their captive pupils. Meaninglessness is a common condition in college and graduate teaching. Much of what goes on in the name of learning is simply an academic enterprise. Even religion, as has been pointed out earlier, can be pursued in a meaningless way.

EDUCATION AND THE SEARCH FOR MEANING

The crucial test in the search for meaning in education is the *personal implication* of what we learn and teach. In some educational circles this will sound strange, for it often seems to be assumed that a body of information is in itself meaningful.

If we as educators are to face the problem of meaninglessness, we must make an effort to conduct education in depth—to move toward something that is personally significant beyond the façade of facts, subject matter, logic, and reason behind which human motives and a person's real struggles and strivings are often concealed. This does not mean the rejection of subject matter—far from it—but it does mean helping the learner to relate himself to what he is learning and to fit what he learns into the fabric of his life in a meaningful way.

Such an endeavor means an effort to overcome the prevailing tendency in education to encourage the learner to understand everything except himself.

It means an effort to achieve a *better integration of thinking and feeling* * on the part of both children and adults.

It means an effort to cut through the pretense of "interest" in learning, which children and adults so widely adopt in order to conform or to escape disapproval from their elders. It means also that the process of learning will not be used as a means of competing with others and gaining power over them.

Actually, each subject that is taught in elementary or high school or college could, in one way or another, for certain learners, be deeply charged with meaning. Each subject could, in one way or another, help some young person discover his skills and explore or use his resources.

The study of history, to give only one example, can be an intensely meaningful experience, for history is filled with the *substance of human hopes and*

* Editor's italics.

*fears: man's struggles, his pride, his shame, his courage, his joy.** Much of history—perhaps all—can be taught in such a way that there is a direct line of emotional and intellectual communication from historical characters and actions to the intimate personal lives of the learners.

The same is true with respect to literature and all other academic subjects. It is certainly true with respect to physical education and all the arts, skills, and crafts, for each of these enterprises can be undertaken in a manner that has a *direct and immediate personal implication.**

But, instead, much of what teachers have to learn, much of what they have to teach, and much of what the millions of pupils who attend our schools are compelled to study is not meaningful but meaningless, largely because we have assumed that knowledge has value apart from its meaning for the one who acquires it. When we consider the problem of meaninglessness, it is not extreme to say that one of the basic troubles in education is that as educators *we have not had the courage to face the personal implications of our calling.**

HELPING OTHERS THROUGH FACING ONESELF

To help a pupil to have meaningful experiences, a teacher must know the pupil as a person. This means . . . that the teacher must strive to know himself.

In the school there are countless opportunities for *helping the child in his search to find himself.** He can be helped to discover his aptitudes and abilities, to face some of his inner difficulties, and to realize his limits. What the teacher does strongly affects the pupil's attitudes regarding his worth as a person since, as has been noted, life at school is heavily invested with praise and blame, pride and shame, acceptance and rejection, success and failure. Everything in the relation between a teacher and a student has or might have a significant effect on *what a child thinks and feels about himself.**

To have insight into the child's strivings and the problems he faces, the teacher must strive to face the same problems within his own life. These problems are largely emotional in nature.

To be able to understand and sympathize with a child who is hostile (and all children are more or less), the teacher must face his own hostile tendencies and try to accept the implications of his anger as it occurs, say, in his annoyance with his pupils, in his impatience with himself, and in his feuds with other teachers.

He must seek to understand the devices he uses to avoid responsibility for himself by blaming others.

To appreciate another's fears, a person must try to examine his own fears.

* Editor's italics.

He must face them as they appear in his phobias, squeamishness, fear of misfortune, timidity, uncertainties, unwillingness to take a chance, worry concerning what others may think of him.

Unless a teacher can, at least to some extent, face his own anxiety, he will be uncomprehending when children helplessly express theirs. He may be harsh when children's anxieties break through in such signs as inability to learn, impertinence, inattentiveness, restlessness, irritability, and the like.

A teacher's understanding of others can be only as deep as the wisdom he possesses when he looks inward upon himself. The more genuinely he seeks to face the problems of his own life the more he will be able to realize his kinship with others, whether they are younger or older, like him or unlike him in education, wealth, religion, or professional rank.

How does one achieve understanding of self?

One broad principle is this: *To gain in knowledge of self, one must have the courage to seek it and the humility to accept what one may find.* If one has such courage and such humility, one can seek professional help and one can draw on many resources in everyday life.

One can learn from experience of life's joys and tragedies. One can profit from trying to catch the meaning of one's anger, joy, depression, fear, desire to inflict pain, and so forth.

A valuable help in self-examination, which may be mainly intellectual but may also strike at a deep emotional level, is the reading of books written by compassionate people who have made some progress in their own painful struggle to know themselves.

The method of "participant observation" offers one means of taking a look at oneself. One records what one hears and sees and what one's feelings are as one listens in on a discussion or visits a class. Then, with the help of others, one examines this record and compares it with records kept by other observers. This comparison may show how what one notices is determined by habits of thought that are taken for granted. What one perceives "objectively" is often a projection of one's own subjective state, and thus may tell more about oneself than about the people one observes.

This broad principle also holds: *Just as it is within an interpersonal setting that one acquires most of the attitudes involved in one's view of oneself, so it is likely that only in an interpersonal setting can a person be helped to come to grips with some of the meanings of these attitudes.*

A relationship that can promote knowledge of self prevails when one seeks private therapy or joins with others in a group therapy situation. It exists also, to some degree, *whenever one enters into relationship with people in any walk of life who can help one gain perspective on oneself.** In a group, a person may be helped to see his anger, fear, and protective devices as others see them. The way others express themselves or respond to him may help

* Editor's italics.

him perceive in a new and self-revealing light some of the evidences of shame, self-effacement, anxiety, vindictiveness, and other outcroppings of deep-seated attitudes of which ordinarily he is not aware. Similarly, to witness a mimicking of his conduct by a child or by a role-playing peer may throw some light on unrecognized conflicts.

Some of the richest possibilities for self-examination can be found in relationships with others from month to month and from year to year. In the teaching profession we have hardly begun to explore and to tap these resources for growth in self-knowledge, although some work is being done in this area. If people could encourage one another to come out from behind the curtain that commonly conceals their emotions from others and from themselves, these emotions might be faced in an insight-producing way.

In a larger sense, particular procedures that are used for growing in self-understanding are less important than the courage to face this need. Self-knowledge can be acquired in many ways. It is not something that is attained once and for all. Those who are blind to themselves have a little of it, and a capacity to acquire more; and an outstanding mark of those who have acquired the deepest knowledge is that they still are seeking. No one procedure alone will give the answer, since the search for selfhood, when genuine, is pursued through all channels of experience as long as a person lives.

Facing the Role of Feeling in Thinking

In the foregoing section the emphasis has been on the need for facing our own emotions if we are to make any progress in understanding the emotions of others. But there is a need for facing emotion also in dealing with what, on the surface, may seem to be the purely intellectual and academic aspects of the school's program. Much of what is called thinking is actually governed by undisclosed feelings. Logic is often ruled by desire; intellectual arguments are often the instruments of fear or anger. To the extent that this is true, the full meaning of what seems to be an intellectual discourse is not revealed or shared. To think straight, to communicate what we are thinking, and to think effectively about what someone else is trying to communicate, it is *important to know how we feel, and how feeling influences our thoughts and the thoughts of others.** It is necessary to take account of emotional factors in thinking if the intellect is to be given a chance to function freely.

We let our feelings govern the nature of our reasoning, without knowing that we are doing so, when we project our own bias onto a discussion of a historical issue, or a problem of discipline or scholarship, or a decision as to what courses a high school student *must* take to be allowed to go to college, etc., without once asking ourselves: Is this really pure reasoning, or am I perhaps projecting my own prejudices or yielding in meek but compulsive compliance to what others have demanded?

* Editor's italics.

During the presidential campaign of 1952, a forum was held whose avowed purpose was to try to inquire beneath the reasons people usually gave to others and to themselves for supporting one candidate or opposing another. The members of the forum were instructors and graduate students. It soon became apparent that it was very difficult for these people even to ask themselves: Is there *perhaps* an emotional reason, apart from the logical reasons I give, for my support of one candidate or bitter opposition to another? What, on an *emotional* level, does this campaign mean, and what do the candidates symbolize in my own emotional life? How do I *feel* toward the personalities, parties, and issues, as distinguished from what I believe I *think* about them? The venture was a failure. The hour was spent in a rehash of the hackneyed arguments used in the campaign materials of both parties.

Someone might say that to ask people in education even to consider that there might be an emotional bias in the reasoning they use to support a political candidate is simply asking too much of human nature. Maybe it is. But unless we at least try to understand the role of feeling in our thinking, we are simply going through the motions of thinking. We are not making full use of our capacity to reason.

FACING THE PERSONAL IMPLICATIONS OF IDEAS

One complaint often made by teachers in training is that they have to learn a lot of theory without being shown how to put the theory into practice. This is a problem, but it is probably not the basic problem. The problem may be that teachers are resisting the meaning of the theory as it applies to themselves. Any theory in education that has its roots in the realities of life has an immediate practical meaning to those who are willing to accept it.

Often, when teachers look for a practical application—a method, a gimmick, a prescription, a rule of thumb—they are trying not to grasp but to avoid the meaning a theory might have for them. Theory and practice are often out of gear in education because as teachers—like all other human beings—we like to externalize rather than internalize a theory. Our immediate response often is to become manipulative: to do something to someone else.

The writer has faced this problem repeatedly in his work with the concept underlying this book: that an essential function of education is to help the growing child understand himself and *develop healthy attitudes of self-acceptance.** In some classroom situations dealing with self-understanding which the writer has had an opportunity to observe, teachers have done almost everything except the one thing that is needful. They have gotten long check lists of children's interests. They have talked to parents about the pupils. They have gotten the young people to express by a vote what to them seemed to be their most urgent and important problems. They have sup-

* Editor's italics.

plied movies and exhibits and have used all kinds of paraphernalia. But in doing all this, they often seemed to leave out the one essential thing: their own direct, personal involvement.

IMPLICATIONS

How would you translate Jersild's general suggestions to teachers into concrete attitudes and actions that you, the student, might apply to make your subject more a part of your life? Compile a list in your own words and compare it with the lists of your fellow students. Discuss any differences you may find between their lists and yours. How does this selection relate to Selection 1, in which Frankl discusses meaningfulness in a crisis situation?

What, specifically, does self-acceptance involve? What are some of the aspects of self most difficult to accept? Why is this the case? Give an example from experience of how facing oneself enables one to help another more effectively.

REFERENCES

In a volume edited by Hamachek (1965), related to the *self* in growth, teaching, and learning, you may find the studies by Rogers, Kell, and McNeil and other studies and theoretical discussions of the role of the self in behavior and experience. (See Selection 6.)

Another book of readings, edited by Severin (1965), presents viewpoints of psychology by the humanistically oriented.

[17] LEARNING TO THINK

Are people born as thinkers and nonthinkers, or can one learn to be more of a thinker? Statements about the mental capacity of men of various races and of different animals are often based on the assumption that the capacity to solve problems is purely a function of the native equipment of the individual—that he either shows this higher mental capacity or he does not. Only recently are the strictures concerning who can learn what being loosened. For this reason the research reported by the Harlows in this selection, although not answering the problem definitely, opens the way for more research on facilitating higher-level learning and thinking—a great need in the day of upgrading jobs and performances for the electronic age.

Harry F. Harlow and Margaret Kuenne Harlow

How does an infant, born with only a few simple reactions, develop into an adult capable of rapid learning and the almost incredibly complex mental processes known as thinking? This is one of psychology's unsolved problems. Most modern explanations are not much more enlightening than those offered by eighteenth-century French and English philosophers, who suggested that the mind developed merely by the process of associating ideas or experiences with one another. Even the early philosophers realized that this was not a completely adequate explanation.

The speed and complexity of a human being's mental processes, and the intricacy of the nerve mechanisms that presumably underlie them, suggest that the brain is not simply a passive network of communications but develops some kind of organization that facilitates learning and thinking. Whether such organizing principles exist has been a matter of considerable dispute. At one extreme, some modern psychologists deny that they do and describe learning as a mere *trial-and-error process* *—a blind fumbling about until a solution accidentally appears. At the other extreme, there are psychologists who hold that people learn through an innate *insight* * that reveals relationships to them.

To investigate, and to *reconcile,** if possible, these seemingly antagonistic positions, a series of studies of the learning process has been carried out at the University of Wisconsin. Some of these have been made with young children, but most of the research has been on monkeys.

For two basic reasons animals are particularly good subjects for the investigation of learning at a fundamental level. One is that it is possible to control their entire learning history: the psychologist knows the problems

* Editor's italics.

to which they have been exposed, the amount of training they have had on each, and the record of their performance. The other reason is that the animals' adaptive processes are more simple than those of human beings, especially during the first stages of the attack on a problem. Often the animals' reactions throw into clear relief certain mechanisms that operate more obscurely in man. Of course, this is only a relative simplicity. All the higher mammals possess intricate nervous systems and can solve complex problems. Indeed, it is doubtful that man possesses any fundamental intellectual process, except true language, that is not also present in his more lowly biological brethren.

Tests of animal learning of the trial-and-error type have been made in innumerable laboratories. In the special tests devised for our experiments, we set out to determine whether monkeys could progress from trial-and-error learning to the ability to solve a problem immediately by insight.

One of the first experiments was a simple discrimination test. The monkeys were confronted with a small board on which lay two objects different in color, size, and shape. If a monkey picked up the correct object, it was rewarded by finding raisins or peanuts underneath. The position of the objects was shifted on the board in an irregular manner from trial to trial, and the trials were continued until the monkey learned to choose the correct object. The unusual feature of the experiment was that the test was repeated many times, with several hundred different pairs of objects. In other words, instead of training a monkey to solve a single problem, as had been done in most previous psychological work of this kind, *we trained the animal on many problems,** all of the same general type, but with varying kinds of objects.

When the monkeys first faced this test, they learned by the slow, laborious, fumble-and-find process. But as a monkey solved problem after problem of the same kind, its behavior changed in a most dramatic way. It learned each new problem with progressively greater efficiency, until eventually the monkey showed perfect insight when faced with this particular kind of situation—*it solved the problem in one trial.** If it chose the correct object on the first trial, it rarely made an error on subsequent trials. If it chose the incorrect object on the first trial, it immediately shifted to the correct object, and subsequently responded almost perfectly.

Thus the test appeared to demonstrate that *trial-and-error and insight are but two different phases of one long continuous process.** They are not different capacities, but merely represent the orderly development of a learning and thinking process.

A long series of these discrimination problems was also run on a group of nursery-school children two to five years of age. Young children were chosen because they have a minimum of previous experience. The conditions in the children's tests were only slightly different from those for the monkeys: they

* Editor's italics.

were rewarded by finding brightly colored macaroni beads instead of raisins and peanuts. Most of the children, like the monkeys, made many errors in the early stages of the tests and only gradually learned to solve a problem in one trial. As a group the children learned more rapidly than the monkeys, but they made the same types of errors. And the "smartest" monkeys learned faster than the "dullest" children.

We have called this process of progressive learning the formation of a "learning set." The subject learns an organized set of habits that enables him to meet effectively each new problem of this particular kind. A single set would provide only limited aid in enabling an animal to adapt to an ever-changing environment. But a host of different learning sets may supply the raw material for human thinking.

We have trained monkeys and children to solve problems much more complex than the ones thus far described. For instance, a deliberate attempt is made to confuse the subjects by reversing the conditions of the discrimination test. The previously correct object is no longer rewarded, and the previously incorrect object is always rewarded. When monkeys and children face this *switch-over* * for the first time, they make many errors, persistently choosing the objects they had previously been trained to choose. Gradually, from problem to problem, the number of such errors decreases until finally the first reversal trial is followed by perfect performance. A single failure becomes the cue to the subject to shift his choice from the object which has been rewarded many times to the object which has never been rewarded before. In this type of test, children learn much more rapidly than monkeys.

A group of monkeys that had formed the *discrimination-reversal* * learning set was later trained on a further refinement of the problem. This time the reward value of the objects was *reversed for only one trial,* * and was then shifted back to the original relationship. After many problems, the monkeys learned to ignore the single reversal and treated it as if the experimenter had made an error!

The problem was made more complicated, in another test, by offering the subjects a choice among *three objects instead of two.* * There is a tray containing three food wells. Two are covered by one kind of object, and the third is covered by another kind. The animal must choose the odd object. Suppose the objects are building blocks and funnels. In half the trials, there are two blocks and a funnel, and the correct object is the funnel. Then a switch is made to two funnels and one block. Now the correct object is the block. The animal must learn a subtle distinction here: it is not the shape of the object that is important, but its *relation* * to the other two. The meaning of a specific object may change from trial to trial. This problem is something like the one a child faces in trying to learn to use the words "I," "you," and "he" properly. The meaning of the words changes according to the speaker.

* Editor's italics.

When the child is speaking, "I" refers to himself, "you" to the person addressed, and "he" to some third person. When the child is addressed, the child is no longer "I" but "you." And when others speak of him, the terms shift again.

Monkeys and children were trained on a series of these oddity problems, 24 trials being allowed for the solution of each problem. At first they floundered, but they improved from problem to problem until they learned to respond to each new problem with perfect or nearly perfect scores. And on this complex type of problem, the monkeys did better than most of the children!

One of the most striking findings from these tests was that *once the monkeys have formed these learning sets, they retain them for long periods* * and can use them appropriately as the occasion demands. After a lapse of a year or more, a monkey regains top efficiency, in a few minutes or hours of practice, on a problem that it may have taken many weeks to master originally.

All our studies indicate that the ability to solve problems without fumbling is not inborn but is acquired gradually. So we must re-examine the evidence offered in support of the theory that animals possess some innate insight that has nothing to do with learning.

The cornerstone of this theory is the work of the famous Gestalt psychologist Wolfgang Köhler on the behavior of chimpanzees. In a series of brilliant studies, he clearly showed that these apes can use sticks to help them obtain bananas beyond their reach. They employed the sticks to knock the bananas down, to rake them in, to climb, and to vault. The animals sometimes assembled short sticks to make a pole long enough to reach the food, and even used sticks in combination with stacked boxes to knock down high-dangling bait. That the chimpanzees frequently solve these problems suddenly, as if by a flash of insight, impressed Köhler as evidence of an ability to reason independently of learning. He even suggested that this ability might differentiate apes and men from other animals.

Unfortunately, since Köhler's animals had been captured in the jungle, he had no record of their previous learning. Recent studies on chimpanzees born in captivity at the Yerkes Laboratory of Primate Biology at Orange Park, Fla., throw doubt on the validity of Köhler's interpretations. Herbert Birch of the Yerkes Laboratory reported that when he gave sticks to four-year-old chimps in their cages, they showed little sign at first of ability to use them as tools. Gradually, in the course of three days, they learned to use the sticks to touch objects beyond their reach. Later the animals solved very simple stick problems fairly well, but they had difficulty with more complex problems.

Extending Birch's investigations, the late Paul Schiller presented a series of stick tasks to a group of chimpanzees from two to over eight years of age.

* Editor's italics.

The younger the animal, the more slowly it mastered the problems. Some young subjects took hundreds of trials to perform efficiently on even the simplest problems, while old, experienced animals solved them with little practice. *None of the apes solved the tasks initially with sudden insight.**

Even at the human level there is no evidence that children possess any innate endowment that enables them to solve tool problems with insight. Augusta Alpert of Columbia University tried some of Köhler's simple chimpanzee tests on bright nursery-school children. The younger children typically went through a trial-and-error process before solving the problems. Some of them failed to solve the easiest problem in the series in five experimental sessions.

Eunice Mathieson presented more difficult Köhler-type tasks to a group of University of Minnesota nursery-school children. The results were even more overwhelmingly against the notion that tool problems are solved by flashes of natural insight. The children rarely solved a problem without making many mistakes.

This research, then, supports our findings. In all clear-cut tests—that is, whenever the animals' entire learning history is known—monkeys, apes, and children at *first solve problems by trial and error. Only gradually does such behavior give way to immediate solutions.**

We began by pointing out that psychologists have sought to find in the higher mental processes *some organizing mechanism or principle that would explain learning and thinking.** We can now suggest such a mechanism: the *learning set.** Suppose we picture mental activity as a continuous structure built up, step by step, by the solution of increasingly difficult problems, from the simplest problem in learning to the most complex one in thinking. At each level the individual tries out various responses to solve each given task. At the lowest level he selects from unlearned responses or previously learned habits. As his experience increases, habits that do not help in the solution drop out and useful habits become established. After solving many problems of a certain kind, he develops organized patterns of responses that meet the demands of this type of situation. These patterns, or learning sets, can also be applied to the solution of still more complex problems. Eventually the individual may *organize simple learning sets into more complex patterns of learning sets, which in turn are available for transfer as units to new situations.**

Thus the individual learns to cope with more and more difficult problems. At the highest stage in this progression, the intelligent human adult selects from innumerable, previously acquired learning sets the raw material for thinking. His many years of education in school and outside have been devoted to building up these complex learning sets, and he comes to manipu-

* Editor's italics.

154 Learning to Think

late them with such ease that he and his observers may easily lose sight of their origin and development.

The fundamental role that *language plays* * in the thinking process may be deduced easily from our experiments. They suggest that words are stimuli or signs that call forth the particular learning sets most appropriate for solving a given problem. If you listen to yourself "talk" while you are thinking, you will find that this is exactly what is happening. You review the different ways of solving a problem and decide which is the best. When you ask a friend for advice, you are asking him to give you a word stimulus which will tell you the appropriate learning set or sets for the solution of your problem.

This principle is particularly well illustrated by some of our monkey experiments. Though monkeys do not talk, they can learn to identify symbols with appropriate learning sets. We have trained our monkeys to respond to signs in the form of differently colored trays on which the test objects appear. In one test the monkeys were presented with three different objects—a red U-shaped block, a green U-shaped block and a red cross-shaped block. Thus two of the objects were alike in form and two alike in color. When the objects were shown on an orange tray, the monkeys had to choose the green block, that is, the object that was odd in color. When they were shown on a cream-colored tray, the animals had to choose the cross-shaped block, that is, the object odd in form. After the monkeys had formed these two learning sets, the color cue of the tray enabled them to make the proper choice, trial after trial, without error. In a sense, the *animals responded to a simple sign language.** The difficulty of this test may be judged by the fact that the German neurologist Kurt Goldstein, using similar tests for human beings, found that people with organic brain disorders could not solve such tasks efficiently.

At the Wisconsin laboratories, Benjamin Winsten devised an even more difficult test for the monkeys. This problem tested the animals' ability to recognize similarities and differences, a kind of task frequently used on children's intelligence tests. Nine objects were placed on a tray and the monkey was handed one of them as a sample. The animal's problem was to pick out all identical objects, leaving all the rest on the tray. In the most complicated form of this test, the monkey was given a sample which was not identical with the objects to be selected but was only a symbol for them. The animal was handed an unpainted triangle as a sign to pick out all red objects, and an unpainted circle as a sign to select all blue objects. One monkey learned to respond almost perfectly. Given a triangle, he would pick every object with any red on it; given a circle, he selected only the objects with blue on them.

All these data indicate that *animals, human and subhuman, must learn to think.** Thinking does not develop spontaneously as an expression of innate abilities; it is the end result of a long learning process. Years ago the British

* Editor's italics.

biologist, Thomas Henry Huxley, suggested that "the brain secretes thought as the liver secretes bile." Nothing could be further from the truth. The brain is essential to thought, but the untutored brain is not enough, no matter how good a brain it may be. An untrained brain is sufficient for trial-and-error, fumble-through behavior, but only training enables an individual to think in terms of ideas and concepts.

IMPLICATIONS

How would you state succinctly the findings and their implications presented in this selection? In a recent book, the psychologist Clark (1965) points out that underprivileged children treated as uneducable invariably become uneducable. He deals primarily with the academic inferiority of Negro students in ghetto schools. Do you see any relationship of the Harlow article to Clark's statement? What implications for learning in college does this selection have, if any?

REFERENCES

Psychologists in the United Kingdom are interested in the development of problem-solving ability; see Hunter (1961) for a review of relevant literature.

[18] HUMAN RELATIONS: A TECHNIQUE FOR TRAINING SUPERVISORS

Today in the United States, there is a general interest in understanding and influencing human relations. To influence the interactions between individuals in crucial everyday situations, however, we need more than understanding. Many people are interested in developing the *skills* involved in supervising men and conducting meetings in which conflict over ideas is inevitable. This article, written by psychologists with considerable experience in group relations, suggests one of the realistic methods of training individuals in human-relations skills through multiple role-playing.

It is suggested that you use this role-playing problem in your class. If this suggestion is followed, a decision should be made as to which students play which role before reading the part of the article entitled "Setting up the role-playing procedure."

Norman R. F. Maier and Lester F. Zerfoss

Reprinted from Norman R. F. Maier and Lester F. Zerfoss, "MRP: A Technique for Training Large Groups of Supervisors and Its Potential Use in Social Research," *Human Relations*, Vol. 5 (Ann Arbor: The University of Michigan, Research Center for Group Dynamics, 1952), pp. 177–186, by permission of the publisher and the senior author.

Human-relations skills are difficult to learn merely through reading or by hearing lectures. To be effective, training in the skills must be accompanied by attitude and feeling changes. A supervisor who does not respect his employees will have difficulty in practicing effective methods because his approaches will not hide his basic attitude. It is because skills and attitudes are so interdependent in personnel work that training methods must incorporate both.

One of the important approaches in the improvement of supervisors is that of increasing their employees' participation in the solving of some of the day-to-day job problems. Many employees are distrustful of changes in the job, and there frequently is a feeling that the supervisor plays favorites and discriminates against others. Techniques of selling employees on changes that affect them, and the usual procedures designed to develop fair practices, usually fail to solve these attitudinal problems (Coch and French, 1948; Lewin, 1947). It is exactly in these areas that employee participation seems to be most valuable and for which the group decision method (Bradford and Lippitt, 1945; Lewin, 1947; Lewin, *et al.*, 1939; Maier, 1948) (in which the supervisor shares his problem with his group) has been developed.

However, there is great deal of resistance on the part of supervisors to sharing work problems with their groups because they feel they are giving up something in the process (Maier, 1949). In order to overcome this resistance, new types of training methods are needed. These new methods require that the supervisors learn through participation because they, like rank and file employees, also shy away from changes that affect them.

Discussion meetings (Coch and French, 1948; Maier, 1948, 1949) and role-playing procedures (Bavelas, 1947; Bradford and Lippitt, 1945; Lippitt, *et al.*,

1947) are two of the best participation training methods. However, their nature is such as to limit their uses to training in small groups. In training large groups, it has been necessary to confine one's procedures to lectures, visual aids, movies, and demonstrations. None of these approaches permits active participation and practice. An audience-participation technique, recently developed by Donald Phillips (1948), has received a high degree of acceptance in industry. It is one of the first methods to permit small group discussions within the general framework of an audience situation. The procedure, often referred to as "Phillips 66," accomplishes general participation by dividing the audience into committees of six, each of which holds a discussion for six minutes on some specific question previously put to them. The major limitation of the Phillips 66 method is that the subject matter to be used for discussion is limited in scope, and it can only be adapted to certain types of situations.

Recently, we have tested a procedure at The Detroit Edison Company which combines the role-playing approach with Phillips 66, and which may be described as Multiple Role Playing (MRP). This method permits role-playing to be carried out in such manner that all members of a large audience can participate. The purpose of the technique is to give each member of an audience a first-hand experience in the group decision method. It permits the training of supervisors in skills of leading discussions and at the same time gives them an experience of the way things appear to employees, by finding themselves placed in the employee's position. Training supervisors to use group decision requires that they develop: (1) confidence in the way employees behave when given an opportunity to solve job problems, and (2) skill in putting a problem to the group. The MRP method serves in both of these capacities. The experiences obtained in these group discussions give the participants an opportunity to discover that the way employees behave depends greatly upon the kind of situation the supervisor creates. Thus, both the attitude of the supervisor and his skill in leading the discussion directly determine the outcome of the conference. Participants who function as employees see the errors that the supervisor makes and discover how their own reactions are influenced by the situation he creates. Participants who serve as supervisors can discover how conflicts in groups become resolved and find ways to help the process along. All can experience some of the emotional loadings that attach themselves to matters of prestige and fair play. The few participants who function as observers can discover how lifelike a role-playing process might become, and they can observe how the discussion process leads to attitude changes. As an observer, a person can have a disinterested attitude and objectively evaluate the process.

In repeating this method, different persons can function as observers, supervisors, and employees and thus gain a variety of experiences from these exchanges in function.

In order to make the group decision experience a success with untrained leaders, it is important that the problem be so structured that the leader is likely to do a good job and that the group will readily participate in the discussion. To accomplish good discussion leadership, the problem used for our demonstration was one for which the supervisor is unlikely to have a ready-made solution. In having no preferred solution himself, he is inclined to act permissively, and thus encourage free and frank discussion instead of imposing or selling his own views. To produce a lively discussion, the problem that is used must be one which creates a conflict in attitudes. In order to solve the problem, these attitudes have to become reconciled.

The work situation described in this article is based on an actual case in industry and raises the type of problem that a crew can solve more satisfactorily than a supervisor. As such, it readily lends itself to a group decision rather than an autocratic decision which is imposed on the crew by the supervisor. In the real-life situation, the foreman had a new truck to distribute. He realized that his decision would not meet with approval since each man would feel he had a claim. He therefore put the problem to the crew. The crew solved the problem in such a way that there was a general exchange of trucks so that each man got a different truck, and at the same time the poorest truck was discarded. Everyone was satisfied with the solution.

In setting up this problem for role-playing, we have given each participant a personal attitude so that a typical set of lifelike conflicts would be created. This is the usual procedure in role-playing. The deviation from the usual procedure is that the same roles are simultaneously played by many groups, each without the guidance of a trainer. This absence of specific guidance during the role-playing process makes standardization more essential and requires the use of clear-cut problems. However, we find that these limitations are not serious.

SETTING UP THE ROLE-PLAYING PROCEDURE

1. The first step in the procedure is for the trainer or the person in charge of the meeting to request the audience to divide itself into groups of six, with three persons in one row turning around to meet with three persons directly behind them. Assistants can be an aid to help persons in odd seats join others in making up these groups. By arranging the seating rows in multiples of three, the task of organizing the groups is simplified. (In our situation, the seats themselves could be turned around and thus made for more comfort.)

Since the number of persons required in a group is six, there may be a remainder of from one to five persons. Each of those extra persons is asked to join one of the discussion groups and serve as an observer.

2. When the audience has been divided into groups, the trainer announces that each group will receive a set of instructions. The persons who pass out the material will hand these instructions to one member of each group. This member will play the part of Walt Marshall, the foreman of a crew of repairmen. The other five members of the group will be repairmen who report to Walt Marshall. The foreman is to keep this material until instructed further. In the meantime, he may look over the top page, labeled "Walt Marshall—Foreman of the Repair Crew."

3. The trainer then asks the crew members of all groups to give their attention while he reads them their instructions.

General Instructions for Crew:

You are repairmen for a large company and drive to various locations in the city to do your work. Each of you drives a small truck, and you take pride in keeping it looking good. You have a possessive feeling about your trucks and like to keep them in good running order. Naturally, you like to have new trucks, too, because a new truck gives you a feeling of pride.

Here are some facts about the trucks and the men in the crew who report to Walt Marshall, the supervisor of repairs:

George—17 years with the company, has a 2-year-old Ford truck.
Bill—11 years with the company, has a 5-year-old Dodge truck.
John—10 years with the company, has a 4-year-old Ford truck.
Charlie—5 years with the company, has a 3-year-old Ford truck.
Hank—3 years with the company, has a 5-year-old Chevrolet truck.

Most of you do all of your driving in the city, but John and Charlie cover the jobs in the suburbs.

In acting your part in role-playing, accept the facts as given as well as assume the attitude supplied in your specific role. From this point on let your feelings develop in accordance with the events that transpire in the role-playing process. When facts or events arise which are not covered by the roles, make up things which are consistent with the way it might be in a real-life situation.

The names of the five men, years of service, age, and make of truck should then be placed on an easel chart or blackboard so that ready reference to them can be made.

4. The foreman is then asked to pass out the material he has been given, which consists of six sets of instructions, one for each person in the group. He should keep the top set for himself and pass out one set of instructions, beginning on his left, to each of his five crewmen. The sequence of the instructions should be George, Bill, John, Charlie, and Hank so that the seating order corresponds to the order of seniority as listed on the easel.

The content of the specific instructions for each member of the group is as follows:

Walt Marshall—Foreman of Repair Crew

You are the foreman of a crew of repairmen, each of whom drives a small service truck to and from his various jobs. Every so often you get a new truck to exchange for an old one, and you have the problem of deciding to which of your men you should give the new truck. Often there are hard feelings because each man seems to feel he is entitled to the new truck; so you have a tough time being fair. As a matter of fact, it usually turns out that whatever you decide, most of the men consider wrong. You now have to face the issue again because a new truck has just been allocated to you for distribution. The new truck is a Chevrolet.

Here are some brief facts about your situation:

George—17 years with the company, has a two-year-old Ford truck.

Bill—11 years with the company, has a five-year-old Dodge truck.

John—10 years with the company, has a four-year-old Ford truck.

Charlie—5 years with the company, has a three-year-old Ford truck.

Hank—3 years with the company, has a five-year-old Chevrolet truck.

All of the men do city driving, making fairly short trips, except for John and Charlie who cover the suburbs.

In order to handle this problem you have decided to put the decision up to the men themselves. You will tell them about the new truck and will put the problem in terms of what would be the most fair way to distribute the truck. Avoid taking a position yourself because you want to do what the men think is most fair.

George: When a new Chevrolet truck becomes available, you think you should get it because you have most seniority and don't like your present truck. Your own car is a Chevrolet, and you prefer a Chevrolet truck such as you drove before you got the Ford.

Bill: You feel you deserve a new truck. Your present truck is old, and since the senior man has a fairly new truck, you should get the next one. You have taken excellent care of your present Dodge and have kept it looking like new. A man deserves to be rewarded if he treats a company truck like his own.

John: You have to do more driving than most of the other men because you work in the suburbs. You have a fairly old truck and feel you should have a new one because you do so much driving.

Charlie: The heater in your present truck is inadequate. Since Hank backed into the door of your truck, it has never been repaired to fit right. The door lets in too much cold air, and you attribute your frequent colds to this. You want a warm truck since you have a good deal of driving to do. As long as it has good tires, brakes, and is comfortable you don't care about its make.

Hank: You have the poorest truck in the crew. It is five years old, and before you got it, it had been in a bad wreck. It has never been good, and you've put up with it for three years. It's about time you got a good truck to drive, and you feel the next one should be yours. You have a good accident record. The only accident you had was when you sprung the door of Charlie's truck when he opened it as you backed out of the garage. You hope the new truck is a Ford since you prefer to drive one.

Members are asked to study their roles until they have a feeling for them. It is perhaps necessary to caution them not to show their roles to each other, but to put them aside when they have finished with them.

5. When everyone is ready, the trainer gives the signal for the foreman to take the responsibility of starting their meetings. Each foreman should assume that he has called his men together and that he is seated with them to discuss a problem.

6. Less than half an hour is adequate for most groups to solve the prob-

lem. (If the leader and his assistants observe the groups, they can pretty well judge when most of the groups have reached a solution.) Before interrupting the discussion, it is desirable to announce from the floor that three more minutes will be allowed the groups to settle on some arrangement.

7. At the end of the three-minute period, the members are asked to break off their discussions and join in the analysis of the results.

ANALYZING THE RESULTS

The extent of the analysis need not be confined to the points discussed below, but the analysis should cover the following points:

1. Determination of the number of groups arriving at a solution. (In obtaining this figure, only the foreman should vote.)

2. Determination of the number of men who are satisfied with the solution. (In this case, only the repairmen of crews which reached a solution should raise their hands.) This figure is important because it indicates the degree of satisfaction obtained from the procedure. The chairman may ask how this degree of acceptance compares with what would have been obtained if the foreman had supplied the solution.

3. Determination of number of crews which discarded Hank's truck. (In this case only the foremen should raise their hands.) The proportion of the number of times that Hank's truck was discarded to the number of groups becomes a measure of the quality of the solution. The fear that men might fail to discard the poorest truck would constitute one of the reasons why a foreman might hesitate to put such a problem to them. If the proportion of crews discarding the poorest truck is very large, it indicates that the danger of not having the poorest truck discarded is more imagined than real.

4. Determination of the number of crews in which the new truck went to various members of the crew. (In this case only the foreman should vote on the five alternatives.) This analysis brings out the variety of solutions obtained and shows that the same problem with the same roles produces different solutions. Under such circumstances it becomes clear that a company could not work out a policy that would be satisfying to all crews.

This analysis might also be followed by questions such as, "In how many cases did George use his seniority and make a strong demand for the new truck?" "How often did he get it when he was that kind of a George?" "How often did George get the new truck when he did not throw his seniority around?" Such questions frequently reveal that George is more likely to get the new truck when he is a reasonable person and is considerate of men with less service than when he is demanding.

5. Determination of the number of crews in which
  (a) All men obtained a different truck.
  (b) Four men obtained a different truck.

    (c) Three men obtained a different truck.
    (d) Two men obtained a different truck.
    (e) No exchange in old trucks were made and only the man receiving the new truck benefited.

(Only the foreman should vote on these alternatives.) This analysis gives an idea of the extent to which all men were given consideration. If time is taken to analyze these data, it might be found that the foreman's conduct of the meeting determined the number of men who benefited by the addition of a new truck to the crew.

Following the analysis of the crews, the persons serving as observers should be asked to give their evaluations of the discussion meetings they observed. Their report may include: (a) the way the foreman put the problem, (b) the extent to which he hampered the discussion, (c) the extent to which he imposed his own ideas, and (d) evaluation of things he did which helped things along. These reports not only involve the observers in the procedure, but add supplementary material on the different approaches various foremen may have used.

Some Sample Results

We have tested the case in three audiences. In one of these, 17 groups were formed and in 14 of these, all persons were satisfied with the solution they had reached. A total of 5 individuals out of 102 were dissatisfied with the solutions of their groups. In the second group tested, 6 groups were used and 2 persons (in two different groups) out of 42 were dissatisfied. In the third audience, 19 out of 21 groups had time to reach a decision and only one person in each of two groups was dissatisfied. If we combine our groups, we find that 42 out of 44 groups reached a decision and only 9 out of 220 repairmen (4.1 per cent) were dissatisfied.

In each of three tests of the method, all persons participating readily agreed that anything approaching the degree of satisfaction shown could not have been obtained if supervisors had supplied the solution.

In 41 out of the 42 groups, Hank's truck (the poorest one) was eliminated. This result clearly shows that the group decisions were in accordance with the interests of good management. Thus the fear that group decisions might lead to poor-quality decisions was not supported.

The new truck went to George, the senior man, in 20 of the 42 groups. In 16 cases out of 28, he got it when he did not insist on it because of his seniority, and in 4 cases out of 10, he got it by defending his rank. Thus George gained most when he acted least in his own selfish interests.

A great variety of solutions developed in these groups. The new truck went to each of the individuals in one group or another; the frequency being in the order of George, John, Hank, Bill, and Charlie. In most instances there was a general exchange of trucks. All men got a different truck in 4 groups; 4 men got a different truck in 10 groups; 3 men in 16 groups; 2 in 8 groups; and only 1 got a different truck (the new one) in 4 groups.

From descriptions of the discussion process, there seemed to be a trend in which the general exchange of trucks was greatest when the leader was permissive. The first part of the discussion develops a conflict of interests, and if the leader is permissive at this stage, the idea of exchanging trucks develops. Many men who played the part of the supervisor were surprised at this development because most of them went into the discussion with the idea of getting the new truck assigned to some particular individual and getting the rest of the group to agree on who was most needy. It is this emphasis on the leader's part which prevents the general exchange which usually develops out of the free discussion. Thus the idea that all can profit when the crew gets a new truck emerges as a new idea, and it is a group product.

GENERAL EVALUATION

The technique of MRP has some distinct advantages over ordinary role-playing. When many groups of persons engage in role-playing at the same time, the process is facilitated since all of them enter into it without the embarrassment that comes from feeling that they are being observed. Thus groups which have never experienced role-playing quickly get the spirit of the procedure and go into the process in a natural and interested manner. The feeling that the situation is unreal and artificial, which nonparticipants frequently report, is eliminated because all become involved. Because this method reduces self-consciousness, it is particularly helpful for initiating role-playing techniques in supervisory training.

A second value that emerges is the fact that real-live data are obtained from the subsequent analysis. A single role-playing case raises questions which have to do with the fact that a certain individual determined the outcome and so the result may not be typical. In being able to draw upon various groups, one is able to make comparisons and generalizations which could not be made without a rich background of experience. The idea that solutions are tailored to fit a particular group of personalities is clearly brought home by the fact that solutions vary even when the problem and the roles are identical.

Thus we find that in the process of attempting to induce into a large group some of the benefits of small group discussion and role-playing, we not only succeeded in achieving some of these advantages, but captured some entirely new ones.

The MRP method can be used for all types of role-playing which are so effective for attitude change and the development of skills. One must however structure the roles so as to conform to the purpose of the training and the experience of the participants. Thus, if one wishes to emphasize (a) leadership skills in putting a problem to a group, (b) discussion-leading skills, (c) sensitivity to the feelings of others, (d) ways for dealing with hostile persons, (e) skills to upgrade the quality of decisions, and (f) methods to cause a group to feel responsible for reaching decisions acceptable to all, one must design role-playing situations which will highlight these performance areas.

Uses of MRP in Social Research

MRP also can be used as a tool to evaluate various kinds of leadership approaches, as well as to measure the effect of different kinds of participants on the outcome of a discussion. For example, the leaders of half of the groups may receive instructions which differ from those supplied by the other half. These differences may be as follows:

(a) Encourage disagreement in your group vs. discourage disagreement in your group;

(b) Suggest possible solutions to your group vs. be careful not to suggest any solutions yourself;

(c) Try to sell a particular solution that seems fair to you vs. be careful not to show any preference for any solution suggested; and,

(d) Have your group explore a variety of solutions before selling on any one idea vs. hurry the group along so that leisurely exploration of many ideas is discouraged.

The effect of different kinds of participants can be tested by making the roles slightly different for two sets of groups. For example, (a) George can be asked to insist on getting the truck in one set and asked to help out Hank's case in the other; (b) one set of groups might be so instructed that they form two cliques, whereas the other set of groups are not so instructed; and (c) one set of groups may have one member who is asked to play the part of a conciliatory individual, whereas in the other set of groups the same individual may be requested to play the part of a belligerent person.

By comparing the outcomes of two sets of groups with similarly instructed leaders and the differences obtained with differently instructed leaders working with similarly instructed groups, one can demonstrate the importance of the injected differences.

The use of the observer can also be expanded by having one or two such persons in each group. (The purpose of two observers is to see to what extent different persons vary in what they see in the same situation. With experience these differences rapidly decline.)

The observers' reports are of particular value in pointing up how each person's remarks has an effect on the behavior of others. Their comments would tend to sensitize participants to important details in the discussion process, and the reports of skilled observers would become a valuable training aid to participants. The use of observers would be of special value in the training of individuals who meet repeatedly in conferences.

IMPLICATIONS

Do you understand the Phillips 66 method well enough to use it in student groups? What application of it can you see in the college situation? What are its advantages over lectures, movies, and demonstrations? When is multiple role-playing more appropriate?

You and other members of your class may enjoy using the method suggested in this article for a role-playing situation. This will give you some experience in human relations and furnish you with examples of what happens when a decision has to be made as a result of human give and take. It was suggested that you read the article up to the section headed "Analyzing the Results"; then, together with six fellow students (each reading only materials on his role), set up the role-playing situation. After your group has come to some decision, the observer taking notes on the behavior of the group can report to the class what has happened. The experiences of the different groups then can be compared, including the participant's approach to the problem. You will then be in a position to analyze your results and to compare them with those reported in the article.

REFERENCES

Consult the Bibliography for references cited in the article.

Chapter IV

CAREERS
AND LEADERSHIP

[19] A CAREER IN PSYCHOLOGY

The following questions frequently arise among undergraduate psychology students: "What are the career opportunities in psychology?" "What does the preparation for a psychologist entail?" Not all students who ask these questions are qualified or motivated to take extensive graduate work, yet they are interested in what psychology can teach them in preparation for related applied fields, such as *personnel administration, market and public opinion surveys, advertising, public relations, public personnel administration,* and *social work* of various kinds. These related fields require a certain amount of academic work in undergraduate and graduate work as a supplement to professional instruction.

This selection is from a booklet distributed by the American Psychological Association. It deals primarily with preparation for academic and professional psychology, and it can assist the student in determining whether professional psychology or a related applied career is what he can best pursue. We have followed the lead of the writers, Ross and Lockman, and have introduced the selection with a statement from the Preamble of the *Ethical Standards of Psychologists*.

Sherman Ross and Robert F. Lockman

Reprinted from Sherman Ross and Robert F. Lockman, *A Career in Psychology* (Washington, D.C.: American Psychological Association, 1963), pp. 5–19, 23–24, by permission of the publisher and the authors.

The psychologist believes in the dignity and worth of the individual human being. He is committed to increasing man's understanding of himself and others. While pursuing this endeavor, he protects the welfare of any person who may seek his service or of any subject, human or animal, that may be the object of his study. He does not use his professional position or relationships, nor does he knowingly permit his own services to be used by others, for purposes inconsistent with these values. While demanding for himself freedom of inquiry and communication, he accepts the responsibility this freedom confers: for competence where he claims it, for objectivity in the report of his findings, and for consideration of the best interests of his colleagues and of society.*

> * Preamble, *Ethical Standards of Psychologists*,
> Adopted by the American Psychological Association
> Council of Representatives, September 1962.

INTRODUCTION

There are more than 25,000 psychologists in the United States today. Over 35 per cent work in colleges and universities. About 25 per cent of them work for federal, state, and municipal governments in hospitals, clinics, prisons, laboratories, and military settings. Over 20 per cent work for industry, business, and other private organizations. About 10 per cent work in public and private schools, while less than 10 per cent are self-employed.

Here are some of the basic and applied problems that psychologists work on:

1. How can astronauts be trained to perform effectively while confined in a capsule traveling at tremendous speeds through space?

2. What are the effects of new tranquilizers on the behavior of normal and disturbed people?

3. What are the roots of prejudice and strife between groups and nations and how can international tensions be reduced?

4. How can electronic systems be designed so that they can be better operated and maintained by humans?

5. How does a "conscience" develop in young children and under what conditions will it fail to develop?

6. How can the right people be selected for different jobs or educational programs?

7. What are the neurophysiological mechanisms related to perception, motivation, and learning?

8. What are the best methods for teaching different subjects and under what conditions?

9. How do different supervisory practices affect employees' morale?

10. What psychological changes occur in the aged, and how can knowledge of these be utilized to enrich the life of the ever increasing group of older citizens?

Psychologists are continually searching for answers to questions such as these in a world where technological progress has outdistanced the scientific understanding of people.

Although psychology includes a diversity of problems and attracts people with widely different interests, psychologists are unified by a common concern with the question: What makes people and other organisms tick? Or less colloquially: How do human beings and other organisms perceive, learn, think, develop, operate, and relate to one another? Psychology is still a relatively young science and profession, but it is expanding rapidly into different problem areas. Small wonder that many people are confused about the roles of psychologists. But by the same token, psychology is a tremendously exciting and significant field of study today.

WHAT IS PSYCHOLOGY?

Psychology has at least three major facets of interest to the modern student. First, it is an established, *scholarly discipline* represented in the study and work of colleges and universities. Second, it is a *science* of important standing which has been developing remarkably in its basic and applied aspects. Third, it is a growing *profession* with its own viewpoints and methods.

Because of its central concern with human and animal behavior, psychology has many relationships with other disciplines, sciences, and professions. The history of psychology is deeply rooted in philosophy and in the natural sciences. Psychology as a science has its origins in the biological and social sciences. Finally, in the application and utilization of knowledge, psychology is involved with other fields such as education, physics, engineering, medicine, law, religion, psychiatry, advertising, and social work.

Psychologists differ among themselves. They differ in the type and amount of training they have received. They differ in specific work experiences. They differ in the kinds of skills and competencies which they have. They differ in the wide variety of settings in which they work. On the other hand, one purpose [of this booklet] is to present some of the underlying characteristics that are common to psychologists.

As a group, psychologists are interested in contributions to knowledge about human and animal behavior, the communication of such information, and its application. There are several major functions in which psychologists are engaged, functions which are by no means mutually exclusive. Some psychologists devote themselves to the discovery of new knowledge. Others are college professors. Another large group is concerned with applying knowledge, information, and techniques to the solution of practical problems* of individuals and groups. Finally, some psychologists are administrators and managers.

Figure 1 views psychology from the standpoint of the various subfields it encompasses in order of their size.[1] These subfields represent a convenient way of identifying the kinds of psychological *subject matter* in which advanced degrees can be taken.

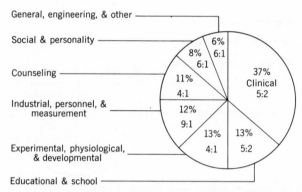

FIGURE 1. Subfields of psychology showing ratios of men to women.

WHAT DO PSYCHOLOGISTS DO?

As previously mentioned, psychology is a broad field with a wide range of functions, interests, and activities. A number of major subfields have been mentioned. Now it might be of value to outline the major work activities which psychologists frequently perform. Figure 2 depicts these work activities.

BEHAVIORAL MODIFICATION. In common with a number of other professional workers, many psychologists (particularly in the clinical and counseling areas) are concerned with the application and use of psychological principles and techniques, generally in face-to-face situations, to modify individual or group behavior in ways that can result in improved motivation, communication, adjustment, adaptation, performance, or vocational and educational attainment.

[1] Data for all figures in this brochure came from the 1960 National Register of Scientific and Technical Personnel.

TEACHING OR TRAINING.   Psychologists work as professors in colleges and universities. They also work on training programs in industry, business, hospitals, and the military services.

RESEARCH.   Psychologists perform basic and applied research on such topics as the development of behavior, differences among various groups and species, social interaction, and motivation and learning processes. Research involves the systematic study of human or animal behavior with experimental, statistical, clinical, and other research techniques. Its purpose is to collect useful information under controlled or known conditions in order to advance our knowledge about behavior by the solution of theoretical and practical problems. Psychologists are very much concerned with the interrelationships between physiological, environmental, social, and occupational factors as they relate to behavior.

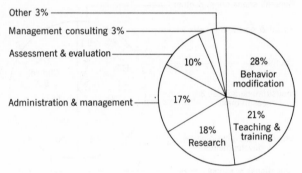

FIGURE 2. Major work activities of psychologists.

ADMINISTRATION.   Psychologists have frequently been drawn into administration in the organizations in which they work. Administration refers to the planning, developing, organizing, and executing of programs. Psychologists as executives are found in hospitals, clinics, research laboratories, educational institutions, government agencies, and business organizations.

ASSESSMENT AND EVALUATION.   These functions of psychologists involve the use of methods, instruments, and techniques for the purpose of measuring, understanding, or predicting behavior. Under this heading is included the administration and interpretation of measures of intelligence, achievement, aptitude, interests, personality, social interaction, and interpersonal relations. The instruments commonly used include tests, inventories, rating scales, interviews, personal histories, and direct observation.

CONSULTING.   Another role of psychologists is that of providing expert professional opinion or knowledge in the application and the use of psychological methods, theories, and techniques. As consulting experts, psychologists are involved in numerous socially important activities. They work with business and industry, federal and state agencies, educational and scientific groups.

WHERE DO PSYCHOLOGISTS WORK?

Psychologists can be found in many different organizations in large communities and in small ones. As in many other professions, however, most are concentrated in large metropolitan areas. Figure 3 provides some details about their employers.

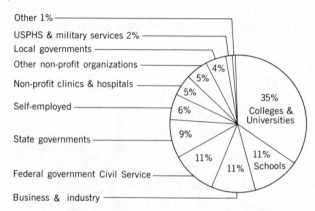

Other 1%
USPHS & military services 2%
Local governments
Other non-profit organizations — 4%
Non-profit clinics & hospitals — 5%
5%
Self-employed — 6%
35% Colleges & Universities
State governments — 9%
11%
11% 11% Schools
Federal government Civil Service
Business & industry

FIGURE 3. Employers of psychologists.

The largest single group of psychologists is employed by colleges and universities in such roles as professors, research scientists, and staff officers. Other psychologists in universities have major responsibility for student personnel work and may combine personal counseling and teaching activities.

The second largest group of psychologists is employed by various government agencies. There is a great demand in the federal service for psychologists with skill and experience in research methodology to work on problems concerned with personnel selection and training, the solution of military problems, and the study of physiological and social processes. Many psychologists in the government work in the diagnosis and treatment of people with emotional problems in general and specialized hospitals and in outpatient clinic settings. The agencies which employ most of the psychologists in the federal government are the Veterans Administration, the Department of Defense, the Department of Health, Education, and Welfare (including the Public Health Service and Office of Education), and the space and intelligence agencies. Psychologists in state and local government agencies occupy positions roughly parallel to those found in the federal government, but with more emphasis on clinical psychology and mental health activities.

Many psychologists are employed by public and private school systems, and by private organizations such as general and mental hospitals, clinics, and private philanthropic, charitable, and research foundations.

Psychologists who work in industry, business, and other private organizations may be employed by a particular company or may serve through a consulting organization. In either case, typical problems include the development of techniques for personnel selection and training, the application of human factors to equipment and systems design, the improvement of employee motivation and morale, and the enhancement of organizational effectiveness. Finally, a number of psychologists are self-employed as clinicians and consultants in private practice.

The geographic distribution of psychologists is depicted on the map of the United States in Figure 4.

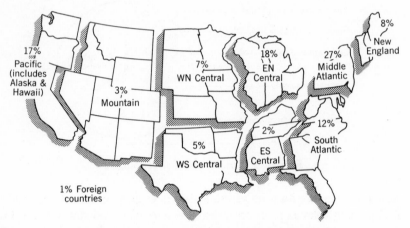

FIGURE 4. Geographic distribution of psychologists.

How Do I Become a Psychologist?

Psychology straddles the dividing line between the biological and social sciences. Some areas of psychology, and some psychologists, are oriented toward biology, as in physiological or comparative psychology. Other areas are much closer to the social sciences, such as social or personality psychology. Since people with different interests are attracted to psychology, following is a picture of the alternative pathways of becoming a psychologist.

The master's degree with a major in psychology is rapidly becoming the minimal educational requirement for professional employment as a psychologist, and less than 5 per cent of psychologists do not have graduate degrees. A Ph.D. degree is needed for many entrance positions, and over 60 per cent of psychologists have earned doctorates, as shown in Figure 5. Average salaries for doctorates range two to three thousand dollars a year higher than for nondoctoral degree holders. Psychologists with the doctorate are eligible for responsible teaching, research, and clinical and counseling positions. Psychologists with masters' degrees may qualify for jobs involving the administration and interpretation of psychological tests, collection and analysis of data, market research, and personnel and administrative duties. In addition, they may teach in some colleges and counsel students. Many serve as school psychologists in public and private schools.

The bachelor's degree is not considered sufficient background education for professional employment. However, some young people with this level of training may secure routine jobs in work related to psychology or in other fields where training in psychology may be useful.

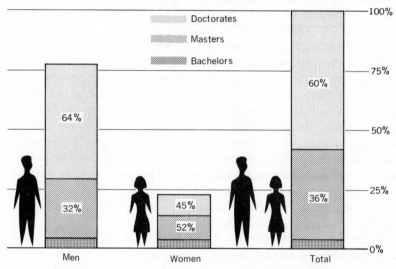

FIGURE 5. Highest academic degrees for psychologists.

Advanced training is most commonly obtained in graduate departments of psychology. At least one year of full-time graduate study is required to earn the master's degree, and sometimes it takes longer. For the Ph.D. degree, a total of four or five years of graduate work may be required, particularly if the student holds a part-time job such as graduate assistant. In clinical psychology, the requirements for the Ph.D. degree generally include the equivalent of one year of internship experience. In some universities, advanced training may be secured in departments other than psychology, often in schools of education and of medicine, occasionally in departments of sociology and of physiology.

HIGH SCHOOL. Many high schools offer elementary courses in psychology and the number is increasing. Annual "Science Fairs" for high school students also include psychology projects in their competitions.

COLLEGE WORK. Many individuals believe that an undergraduate program in psychology should first be a part of a liberal education and thus provide some general understanding of psychology as a way of studying human behavior. A second purpose of the undergraduate program is to provide a background for students going into graduate work in psychology, as well as into a variety of other professions in which an understanding of the principles of human behavior is important: medicine, law, religion, social work, personnel work, advertising, and engineering. Thus, the undergraduate psychology program does *not* provide *professional* training.

There are good reasons for this. In this century, psychology has undergone rapid development as a science and as a profession. With the growing complexity of psychological knowledge, employment opportunities in psychology for students with advanced degrees have greatly expanded, while opportunities for students with bachelors' degrees have become correspondingly limited. It is possible for persons without graduate degrees to find employment in some related capacity, such as workers with private welfare agencies, probation officers, and psychological technicians in government service. However, most employers require that their psychologist employees possess a graduate degree as an indication of professional competence. As a matter of fact, the trend seems to be that soon many jobs will be open only to psychologists with doctoral degrees. On the other hand, the great demand for psychological services may eventually result in a nondoctoral category for some psychological workers. An undergraduate degree in psychology can certainly be considered a useful and important background in the area. But, as the bachelor's degree of the premedical or prelaw student is not a professional degree, so the bachelor's degree in psychology does not provide the specialized training needed by a professional psychologist.

It should be pointed out that an undergraduate major in psychology is often found to be of real advantage in business or other professional careers, since graduates may be called upon to use their psychological background in conjunction with their work. And, as mentioned earlier, the undergraduate program is of great value for preprofessional students in various fields, providing a basic understanding of the psychological aspects of work in their respective fields.

GRADUATE STUDY. Graduate training is not just a matter of taking a set of courses or earning a number of credit hours. The graduate degrees represent the attainment of a high level of proficiency and individual scholarship. Therefore, they are not automatically granted after a given amount of classwork has been completed.

The content of the graduate program is worked out for each student, with a common set of courses early in the program and subsequent specialization, depending on his interests, in some area such as industrial, developmental, experimental, educational, counseling, clinical, or social psychology. Most programs require a foreign language reading ability as well as proficiency in research techniques such as measurements and statistics.

There are three major aspects in admission to graduate study: general academic ability and performance, college course background, and specific local requirements. Standards for admission to graduate programs in psychology are quite high. Most schools require at least a B average in undergraduate work. The selection committee may also check on whether or not you earned this average by taking a lot of easy courses. (Keep this in mind during your undergraduate years!)

Specific requirements for admission vary quite a bit among different graduate schools, regardless of the area of specialization taken by the graduate student. An undergraduate major in psychology may be required for enrollment in some schools. Other institutions prefer students with a broader educational background. Basic psychology courses, supplemented by work in the biological and physical sciences, statistics, mathematics, and the social sciences, are the most frequent requirements. Most universities have more applicants for graduate study in psychology, particularly for the Ph.D., than can be accepted.

Generally speaking, the major part of a psychologist's training takes place in the graduate program. Many departments prefer the applicant with a broad but solid background to the one with narrow specialization and a lot of technique courses. In addition, most programs give you the opportunity to make up for any deficiencies in your undergraduate education during the first year of graduate study.

Most graduate departments have rather early deadlines for applications for fall admission and assistantships, some as early as February. While you do not need to make up your mind about it as a college freshman, don't wait until graduation to decide. You may then find it is too late to get admitted for the fall term in the school of your choice. Talk to your adviser in plenty of time. Also, most schools require, in addition to your transcript, a test score on the Graduate Record Examination, Miller Analogies Test, or some other examination, and letters of recommendation from your psychology professors as evidence of your academic potential and interest. Therefore, you should try to show your teachers that you have the interest and ability to do graduate work. Some extra work, like participation in research, might help by providing you with an introduction to graduate work and by giving staff members a better chance to evaluate your potential for it. . . .

WHAT IS THE EMPLOYMENT FUTURE?

The need for fully trained psychologists far exceeds the number currently being trained. It is estimated that there are at least three positions available across all subfields of psychology for every qualified psychologist. In the field of clinical psychology, positions are available for every suitably trained person at the master's level, but opportunities for full professional employment are becoming more restricted in many specialties for persons holding masters' degrees, as indicated earlier.

Many factors point to the continued rapid expansion of psychology. Among them are the increasing recognition of the contributions of psychology by educational institutions, government agencies, private industry, and the public; the growing concern with the problems of mental health; the emergence of the federal government as a major sponsor of psychological research and psychological training; and the needs of universities and private industry. All come together to create a great demand for well-trained people.

A large growth is anticipated in the number of psychologists required by state agencies. Many mental hospitals are currently understaffed, and many mental health clinics and community clinics will require clinical, counseling, social, and other kinds of psychologists. Prisons, training schools, and other institutions are using psychologists more extensively. Growing public-school enrollments and an increased awareness of the needs for testing and counseling children are expected to increase the employment of psychologists in schools. The growing enrollments in colleges and universities will demand more psychologists as teachers, researchers, and counselors. The increasing use of psychological techniques by industry and business is creating new openings for experimental, industrial, personnel, social, and human factors psychologists. The Veterans Administration, Departments of Defense, of Health, Education, and Welfare, and other federal agencies, and the variety of state programs have increasing needs for psychologists who are specialists in clinical, counseling, experimental, human factors, physiological, social, and engineering psychology.

So the market for the skills and services of trained psychologists is an encouraging one. Average salaries range around $10,000 * a year and are comparable to those of other sciences. In addition to the monetary rewards involved, there are often sizable fringe benefits and personal satisfactions earned by many of those who participate in this diverse, energetic, and significant field of psychology.

IMPLICATIONS

This selection is meant for those students who think they want to become professional psychologists. Many students who at first consider psychology as a profession later decide they are more interested in the use of psychological findings in a more applied field such as those italicized in the introduction to this selection. What do you see as the major

* Note date of this article. The figure for salaries is changing yearly.—Ed.

emphasis in preparation for a career in psychology that may not be required for the fields of application mentioned in the introduction? What questions about a career in psychology are not answered in this selection? Try to describe what graduate work in psychology consists of generally.

REFERENCES

For more detailed background material of some of the issues raised in this selection consult the following sources: Raimy (1950) deals with clinical training; Roe, *et al.* (1959) describes graduate education; Webb (1962) discusses the profession as a whole; Wright (1959) gives an account of rehabilitation.

[20] WHO IS THE CREATIVE PERSON?

Is the individual who obtains a high score on an intelligence test and receives good school grades always the most creative person? If not, how can we locate the child or youth who has great promise of being a creative individual and who will in the future make original contributions to the arts, sciences, and technology?

What do we know at present about the personality, the motivations, hobbies, and upbringing of individuals who show creativity? Can we detect them by widely administering to groups tests of creative *abilities?* If not by ability tests alone, what aspects of personality should we seek to assess in order to locate creative persons?

Does the American educational system favor the development of creativity, or does it encourage conformist mentality? To what extent are creatively oriented children interesting to their teachers and peers?

We lack conclusive answers to all these questions, but we have data on many of them. Also, there is today a literature reporting attempts to investigate the distinctions between those who show originality in their personal productions and those who do not. Here is an article by P. E. Vernon, who discusses briefly some of the independent investigations in different places and presents a summary of many of the findings. He concludes with his own evaluations of some of the psychological means of investigating creativity as well as with a helpful list of references on these researches.

P. E. Vernon

Reprinted from P. E. Vernon, "Creativity and Intelligence," *Educational Research*, Vol. VI, No. 3 (Slough, Bucks, England: National Foundation for Educational Research), pp. 163–169, by permission of the publisher and the author.

INTRODUCTION

Creativity is the latest fashion in American educational psychology. In broad outline, such writers as Getzels and Jackson (1962), Torrance (1962), and Calvin Taylor (1962), hold that not only our current intelligence and attainment tests but also the whole educational system tend to favor the conformist mentality, the pupil or student who is good at amassing facts, accepting what his teachers and lecturers tell him, and thinking and writing along conventional lines; that truly creative ability is relatively independent of whatever is measured by intelligence tests or by school grades, and that we are therefore discouraging the production of creative individuals who will make future original contributions to the arts, sciences, and technologies.

THE WORK OF CALVIN TAYLOR

Calvin Taylor (1962) is the energetic organizer of a number of research conferences on creativity at the University of Utah. He has carried out various studies himself, or brought together the work of others, all tending to show that creative adults are not necessarily superior to less creative workers in scholastic achievement or in whatever is measured by intelligence tests. For example, industrial or air force scientists were assessed by their superiors for the productivity and originality of their work, and there was generally little relation to their previous educational achievement. Admittedly, they were pretty homogeneous, high-level groups, otherwise they could not have got their present jobs. But Taylor estimates—it is not quite clear on what evidence—that over the whole range of ability, the correlation of creativity with intelligence or other tests would not exceed .2 to .4. In another study the IQ's were available for air force recruits who submitted original suggestions in suggestion boxes, and the distribution of these was said to be no different from the distribution for recruits in general. Obviously, it is doubtful how far this can be regarded as a manifestation of creative talent. One of the main difficulties, Taylor admits, is that—with such groups as scientists—there is little consistency between different criteria. For example, number of publications, assessed worth of publications, ratings by superiors or peers on various aspects of creativeness tend to give quite low correlations with one another. It is not surprising that few if any ability tests give consistently worthwhile correlations with these somewhat conflicting criteria. There seems to be more promise in biographical inventory data. Here again the picture is far from clear, but more creative persons tend to claim more creative hobbies in their youth, to be rather solitary, independent people, nonconformists, with strong drives and motivation for distant goals.

TERMAN'S STUDIES

Terman's (1947) follow-up of high IQ children should also be mentioned. This group showed enormously greater productivity in the arts and sciences than would any group of average ability, though, at the same time, rather few reached the highest flights of creative talent, or could be called geniuses. This suggests that intelligence is of some relevance, and I would be inclined to give more weight to this evidence than to that of Taylor both because the IQ was tested in childhood, not concurrently, and because a good individual test— the Stanford-Binet—was used, rather than a conventional printed multiple-choice group test. Terman, in his survey with Cox (1926) of admitted geniuses from history, found quite a wide range of intelligence as estimated from recorded childhood achievements; but very few outstanding men in the arts and sciences fell below IQ 120. While rejecting the popular theory of the insanity of genius, Terman agreed that character and motivational factors were probably more important than purely intellectual ones—given a requisite (and high) level of general ability to begin with.

MACKINNON'S RESEARCHES AT THE CALIFORNIAN INSTITUTE

Anne Roe's (1952) studies of small groups of eminent scientists also throw some light on their personality make-up, their tendency to be lone wolves with an overriding sense of the worth of their own ideas. But the outstanding researches in this area are those of MacKinnon and his colleagues at the Californian Institute for Personality and Ability Research. They have taken immense trouble to collect large and representative groups of men who are accepted by their professions as among the most creative architects, scientists, engineers, writers, and inventors, to bring them—along with control groups of more pedestrian people in the same line—to the Institute for a few days and subject them to an intensive battery of personality and ability measures. The most accessible summary of MacKinnon's (1962) results is published in the Proceedings of the 1961, Copenhagen, International Applied Psychology

Congress—the volume on personality studies. He, too, tends to find all his subjects above average on ability tests and academic achievement—writers on verbal tests, scientists and engineers on nonverbal and spatial tests—though there was no strong differentiation between the more and the less creative; and he suggests that IQ is relatively unimportant beyond a certain minimum, probably around 120. About the only ability test that gave good differentiation was the Barron-Welsh Art test, where the creative individuals showed a greater liking for complex, asymmetrical as against conventional, abstract line drawings.

Some mean scores quoted in this table:

Artists	39
Highly creative architects	37
Writers	31½
Research scientists	30½
Architects generally	26
Low-creative scientists	19
Normal sample	18

Similarly on a word-association test, they tend to give unusual, but not highly unusual, associations.

Three tests in the personality area have consistently shown good differentiation—the Allport-Vernon-Lindzey Study of Values, where the creatives are characteristically high in artistic and theoretical, low in religious, economic and social values; secondly, the Strong Vocational Interest Blank, where they favor occupations like psychologist, architect, author as against banker, farmer, carpenter, salesman; and thirdly, the Myers-Briggs inventory, which tries to assess a person's Jungian type. Creatives are far more given to intuition- than to sensation-type thinking, and are more often introverted than extraverted. The Strong Blank also indicates a strong streak of femininity; creatives show a much greater willingness to accept and express their own feelings than is usual in the American male.

THE PERSONALITY OF CREATIVE INDIVIDUALS *

By interviews and questionnaires, a good deal was found about their personalities and upbringing which cannot be more than summarized briefly here. Though not emotionally unstable in the ordinary sense, they had often had *unhappy childhoods* † and school days and were *rebellious against school and college teachers;* † and, as previously suggested, they were characterized by a sense of *egoistic resoluteness, a belief in the value of their own work,*

* Editor's heading.
† Editor's italics.

*and strong motivation to achieve by independent thought and action. Their parents tended to encourage this autonomy and self-responsibility.** Of course, there is no single pattern, but this picture seems sufficiently general to justify the conclusion that *creative persons are distinguished more by interests, attitudes, and drives than by abilities,** and that, though schooling may contribute little but basic knowledge and skills, the truly creative individual survives poor teaching and even thrives on rebelling against it.

GUILFORD AND THE FACTORIAL APPROACH

We may now turn to the entirely different approach of the factor analyst and mental tester, whose aim is to measure creativeness and to show that it is a factor distinct from g or other accepted factors. J. P. Guilford (1955, 1956), at the University of Southern California, has carried out over the past twenty years an elaborate series of studies of high-grade adults, and claims to have isolated some sixty or more factors in the domains of cognition, memory, reasoning, planning, judgment and evaluation. In particular, he distinguishes, in the realm of thinking, what he calls convergent and divergent abilities—convergent when there is one right answer, predetermined by the tester, as happens in all multiple-choice tests, and divergent when the testee is encouraged to give as many different responses of his own as possible. The ordinary tests of fluency or speed and richness of association are examples of the latter, and factorists have distinguished several types of fluency, the chief ones being word fluency—for example, writing as many words ending in "–tion" as possible, regardless of meaning; and ideational fluency—writing as many names of animals, birds, or flowers, or as many descriptions of a parcel as possible, or giving inkblot associations, and so on.

Guilford claims at least three other factors in this area, originality, spontaneous flexibility, and adaptive flexibility. Originality is defined by tests involving unusual and clever responses. For example, the familiar consequences test—What would happen if everybody in the world suddenly doubled in size? Or writing down impossibilities; or making up anagrams from the letters contained in a long word. These can be scored for rarity or rated for cleverness. Spontaneous flexibility is freedom from inertia in giving a diversity of ideas. For example: Write down as many unusual uses as possible for a brick—say, murdering somebody, or using it as a paper weight; this is scored for the number of changes of category or type of response. Adaptive flexibility is measured by tricky problem tests where the solution involves ingenuity or thinking along unconventional lines.

Now one would certainly agree with Guilford that high-level intellectual abilities are much richer and more varied than what is measured by standard

* Editor's italics.

vocabulary, analogies, classification, reasoning, and similar tests. But psychometrists other than Guilford's own followers have not generally confirmed the enormous number of distinct factors that he claims. Almost certainly there is much overlapping, and a good deal of what is common to them could probably more simply be attributed to g,* or to such well-established group factors as verbal and spatial abilities, ideational fluency, and inductive reasoning. In a research at the London Institute of Education, Dr. Sultan (1962) tried out examples of most of Guilford's best creativity tests on second- and third-year English grammar-school pupils, along with reference tests of familiar factors. In his battery of forty variables, the factors with most variance were first the spatial, which covered also all the flexibility-of-closure and adaptive-flexibility tests; secondly, ideational fluency, which covered a large proportion of originality- and spontaneous-flexibility tests. Only one small factor appeared that could be named originality, and this was much better measured by a questionnaire test of creative vs. noncreative leisure-time interests and by teachers' art grades and Rorschach inkblots original responses than by Guilford's tests. Admittedly, these negative results could be attributed to Sultan's using much younger students, with less mature intellects than Guilford's, though in fact their scores were mostly fairly close to those of Guilford's adults. Or it may be that the English grammar school is apt to dampen creative talents, and that different results might be obtained at a more "progressive" type of school. But the conclusion I would draw is that factor analysis by itself cannot provide the answer. It is always possible to break down broader group factors into additional narrower ones by developing more and more detailed tests; but this does not prove that the additional factors correspond to important mental faculties. Just because a set of tests looks as though it involves creativity and gives lowish correlations with g, v, or k † tests does not mean that it measures what we recognize as creativity in daily life, unless we can show that they actually differentiate between adults or children known on other grounds to be creative and noncreative, and that they are consistently more valid for this purpose than g or other tests.

Now there is some validatory evidence of this type, but even Taylor admits that Guilford's tests are of doubtful practical value, and MacKinnon obtained entirely negative results on applying them to his creative groups. However, an interesting study by Barron (1955) did indicate some overlap with personality and attitude characteristics similar to those found among true creatives. Men who scored highly on originality, flexibility, or ideational fluency tests were apt to be more self-sufficient, radical, introverted, and nonconformist than low scorers.

* The letter *g* refers to a theoretical common *general* factor underlying all intellectual activities.—Ed.

† The *v* and *k* refer to broad group factors, *verbal* and *practical*, respectively, underlying intellectual activities.—Ed.

GETZELS AND JACKSON'S RESEARCH

This brings us to Getzels and Jackson's (1962) much publicized research, which was on very similar lines to Guilford's, but was carried out with younger high-school pupils. The main study consisted of a comparison of 26 pupils who were in the top 20 per cent of a battery of creativity tests, ingeniously adapted from Guilford's tests, but who were not outstanding in IQ, with another 28 who were in the top 20 per cent for IQ but not outstanding on creativity tests. The two groups were found to be about equally good in school attainment, and this appears to contradict the claim that creative individuals do not do as well in the conventional school system as conformists. But, as both groups happened to be very superior in IQ, the high-IQ group averaging 150, the high-creativity lower-IQ group averaging 127, the finding probably has no general significance. The high creatives did however do somewhat *better on tests of humor and wit,** and in breaking away from the stimulus in tests of free expression. They were *less conventional in their attitudes and aspirations.** On the whole, they *came from business classes rather than from professional-class families;* * professional parents would understandably be more apt to favor conformity to the school's intellectual ideals. Perhaps the most interesting finding was that the high-IQ group was rated superior on desirable personality traits by teachers, and that the sociometric status tended to be greater than that of the high-creativity group. This suggests a real possibility that, in Britain, some of the potentially most creative eighteen-year-olds may fail to get university places because they tend to be unpopular with their heads and are less good mixers. Conceivably this could also happen at 11+.

A GENERAL DISCUSSION AND SOME CRITICISMS

Now this seems to be rather weak evidence on which to base such far-reaching conclusions as Getzels does. The populations were too small and far too atypical of the normal range of ability to tell us anything worthwhile about the relative value of new and old tests. Moreover, the old tests consisted of various group intelligence tests which had been applied at various times in previous years so the scales were weighted against them. The correlations between IQ and creativity tests were around 0.3; or to put it in a more tendentious way as Getzels and Taylor do—had the pupils been selected by IQ, 70 per cent of those with high creativity would have been missed. Obviously, the correlation would have been very much higher with (a) a more representative range of ability, (b) a more up-to-date and reliable battery of g and v tests. Burt (1962) points out, moreover, that the correlations among

* Editor's italics.

the separate creativity tests were much about the same level as their correlations with the intelligence tests; in other words, there was even less evidence
for a factor of creativity distinct from g and v than there was in Guilford's investigations.[1] Had a well-balanced set of intelligence tests like the Stanford-
Binet been used, which includes divergent as well as convergent thinking
items, it might well have covered all that is measured by the creativity tests.
Indeed, Burt suggests that the creativity tests might be quite useful as component items in a new general intelligence scale.

Nevertheless, he agrees, as I do, that with a more adequately designed research, in which better g and v as well as creativity tests were applied to a
more typical population, it might be possible to distinguish one or more
small divergent-thinking group factors, though it is noteworthy that Sultan
obtained very little beyond ideational fluency at second-year-grammar-school
level; hence, it is even more doubtful whether at 11+ tests of a more creative
nature than the typical battery of verbal intelligence, English, and arithmetic would cover any fresh ground.

Another point which American workers have failed to consider is the long-
term reliability or predictive value of divergent-thinking tests. The situation
is likely to be quite similar to that with Thurstone's Primary Mental Abilities
tests. We know that it is fairly easy to measure verbal, spatial, inductive, and
other factors as partially distinguishable from g at age thirteen or earlier. But
it has been shown that such factor scores are far from stable; for example, the
correlation between induction at thirteen and induction at sixteen is scarcely
any higher than that between verbal ability at thirteen and induction at sixteen. I would suspect, then, that one might get at least as good, if not better,
predictions of performance on adult creativity tests from a reliable all-round
measure of g and v at thirteen or at 11+ than one could from Getzels' tests.

However, the most serious flaw is, of course, that Getzels, Guilford, and
others provide no real evidence for the assumption that their tests are valid
tests of creativity in general. They give us a few findings about the current
characteristics of the high scorers, but no follow-up data. True, it is interesting and suggestive that these high scorers appear to show some of the personality characteristics and attitudes which are consonant with the characteristics of the truly creative individuals studied by MacKinnon and Roe, but
the jump from creativity tests in the secondary school, or at 11+, to true
creativity at the university or later is far too great. Nor would one be justified
in trying to diagnose and select the potentially most creative at eleven or
eighteen on personality grounds, since there are lots of rebels, delinquents,

[1] E. P. Torrance has carried out several further researches on children and students in
which creativity tests likewise appeared to give very low correlations with standard intelligence tests. However, R. L. Thorndike, after examining Getzels', Guilford's, and Torrance's
evidence, concludes that divergent thinking tests still involve a fair amount of g, and that,
though a broad domain of creative thinking over and above g can be distinguished, it is
relatively "nebulous and loosely formed."

beatniks, introverts, CND's, idealists, and so forth with very much the same personality pattern who never create anything worthwhile. Leisure-time interests such as scientific hobbies and research, poetry writing and artistic talents, I would suggest, do begin to show themselves fairly definitely by sixteen, or even by twelve or ten, though these are obviously both difficult to evaluate and pretty unstable; they may or may not be diagnostic of future creative capacities. Burt makes the good point that we may be *barking up the wrong tree in thinking of, or trying to measure, creativity in general; it may be something highly specific to a particular field of interest.* Nevertheless, Terman's gifted pupils and his historical geniuses did appear to be characterized by great versatility; most of them might well have made their mark in a number of different fields.

CONCLUSIONS

I would not, of course, for a moment disparage further research in this country into possible diagnostic tests of the Getzels-Guilford type, although I have given, what seem to me, good reasons for doubting their reliability and validity. Incidentally, they are also exceedingly troublesome to score; it would be almost impossible to use them on any large scale in the same way as convergent tests like Moray House and National Foundation tests. The crucial difficulty in such research is, of course, to get a criterion without long-term follow-up over ten or twenty years. Assessments of creative talent by schools and even by universities are known to be far too heavily biased in favor of conventional academic attainment, though I would have thought that by 22 or so, good college tutors could give fairly useful judgments. But I would suggest that there is an even stronger case for research into the home and leisure and educational backgrounds of creative individuals. I strongly suspect that some schools do much more to stimulate and foster, or else to inhibit, creative talent than others. The fact that grammar-school work is so closely geared to G.C.E. may well be a highly adverse factor; though we have a slight advantage over the American high school in that our examinations are creative-response type instead of mostly multiple-choice; so that pupils who are lucky in being marked by examiners who welcome a spark of originality may stand more chance. I would suspect also that the influence of an inspiring teacher at school or university may be tremendously important. These then are the kind of topics which could, I believe, be more fruitfully investigated than the will-o'-the-wisp of selecting or not selecting potentially creative persons by creativity tests.

---

* Editor's italics.

IMPLICATIONS

Were there certain findings in this article that were surprising, perhaps even mildly shocking? To what extent do the statements support the popular view of the creative child? What are the implications for the education of the creative individual?

What has been your experience with the creative person? To what extent do you see creativity in yourself or in some persons whom you know well? What are the *problems* of the individual with creative proclivities?

REFERENCES

Consult the Bibliography for references cited in the article. See also Golann (1963), MacKinnon (1965), McNemar (1964), and Thorndike (1962).

[21] THE BUSINESS EXECUTIVE

What has been discovered about the psychodynamics of a successful business executive as compared with an unsuccessful one? What do the executives have in common? Is intellectual aptitude the major factor, or is it social relationships? What are the psychodynamics in the role the successful executive plays? What are the costs of being a successful executive? Why do some business executives not pay this price? Here is how Henry's research answers these questions. A brief description of the techniques used to obtain the data is given in footnote 1 of the selection.

William E. Henry

Reprinted from William E. Henry, "The Business Executive—the Psychodynamics of a Social Role," *The American Journal of Sociology*, Vol. 54, pp. 286–291, by permission of The University of Chicago Press. © Copyright 1949 by the University of Chicago.

The business executive is a central figure in the economic and social life of the United States. His direction of business enterprise and his participation in informal social groupings give him a place of significance in community life. In both its economic and social aspects, the role of the business executive is a highly visible one sociologically. It has clearly definable limits and characteristics known to the general public. These characteristics indicate the function of the business executive in the social structure, define the behavior expected of the individual executive, and serve as a guide to the selection of the novice.

Social pressure, plus the constant demands of the business organization of which he is a part, direct the behavior of the executive into the mold appropriate to the defined role. "Success" is the name applied to the wholehearted adoption of this role. It assumes that the individual behaves in the manner dictated by the society, and society rewards the individual with "success" if his behavior conforms to the role. It punishes him with "failure" should he deviate from it.

The participation in this role, however, is not a thing apart from the personality of the individual participant. It is not a game that the person is playing, it is the way of behaving and thinking that he knows best, that he finds rewarding, and in which he believes.

Thus the role as socially defined has its counterpart in the personality structure of the individuals who participate in it. To some extent the personality structure is reshaped to be in harmony with the social role. The extent to which such reshaping of the adult personality is possible, however, seems limited. An initial selection process occurs in order to reduce the amount of time involved in teaching the appropriate behavior. Those persons whose personality structure is most readily adaptable to this particular role tend to be selected to take this role. Whereas those whose personality is not already partially akin to this role are rejected.

This paper describes the personality communalities of a group of successful business executives. The research upon which it is based was undertaken to explore the general importance of personality structure in the selection of executive personnel. Many aptitude tests have been employed in the industry to decrease the risk involved in the hiring of untried personnel and to assist in their placement. These tests have been far less effective in the selection of high-level executive personnel than in the selection of clerical and other nonadministrating persons. Many business executives have found persons of unquestioned high intelligence often turn out to be ineffective when placed in positions of increased responsibility. The reasons for their failure lie in their social relationships. No really effective means has yet been found to clarify and predict this area of executive functioning. It is to this problem that our research [1] was directed.

---

[1] The research . . . involved the study of over 100 business executives in various types of business houses. The techniques employed were the Thematic Apperception Test, a short undirected interview, and a projective analysis of a number of traditional personality tests.

From the research it became clear that the "successful"[2] business executives studied had many personality characteristics in common. It was equally clear that an absence of these characteristics was coincident with "failure"[2] within the organization. This personality constellation might be thought of as the minimal requirement for "success" within our present business system and as the psychodynamic motivation of persons in this occupation. Individual uniqueness in personality was clearly present but despite these unique aspects, each executive had in common this personality pattern.

ACHIEVEMENT DESIRES.   All show high drive and achievement desire. They conceive of themselves as hard working and achieving people who must accomplish in order to be happy. The areas in which they do their work are clearly different, but each feels this drive for accomplishment. This should be distinguished from a type of pseudo-achievement drive in which the glory of the end product alone is stressed. The person with this latter type of drive, seldom found in the successful executives, looks to the future in terms of glory it provides him and the projects that he will have completed—as opposed to the achievement drive of the successful executive, which looks more to the sheer accomplishment of the work itself. The successful business leader gets much satisfaction from doing rather than merely from contemplating the completed product. To some extent this is the difference between the dreamer and the doer. It is not that the successful executives do not have an over-all goal in mind, nor that they do not derive satisfaction from the contemplation of future ease, nor that they do not gain pleasure from prestige. Far more real to them, however, is the continual stimulation that derives from the pleasure of immediate accomplishment.

The validity of our analyses, which were done "blind," rested upon the coincidence of identical conclusions from separately analyzed instruments, upon surveys of past job performance, and the anecdotal summary of present job behavior by the executive's superiors and associates. The writer wishes to express his thanks to these executives, to Dr. Burleigh Gardner of Social Research, Inc., under whose auspices the study was made, and to Carson McGuire, Robert F. Peck, Norman Martin and Harriett Bruce Moore of the University of Chicago for their assistance in the collection and analysis of data and clarification of conclusions.

[2] Success and failure as here used refer to the combined societal and business definition. All of our "successful" executives have a history of continuous promotion, are thought to be still "promotable" within the organization, are now in positions of major administrative responsibility, and are earning salaries within the upper ranges of current business salaries. Men in lower-level supervisory positions, men who are considered "failures" in executive positions, and men in clerical and laboring jobs show clear deviations from this pattern. This suggests, of course, that this pattern is specific for the successful business executive and that it serves to differentiate him from other groupings in industry. The majority of these executives come from distributive (rather than manufacturing) businesses of moderately loose organizational structure where cooperation and teamwork are valued and where relative independence of action is stressed within the framework of a clearly defined over-all company policy. In organizations in which far greater rigidity of structure is present or where outstanding independence of action is required, it is possible that there will be significant variations from the personality pattern presented here.

MOBILITY DRIVE. All the successful executives have strong mobility drives. They feel the necessity to move continually upward and to accumulate the rewards of increased accomplishment. For some the sense of successful mobility comes through the achievement of competence on the job. These men struggle for increased responsibility and derive a strong feeling of satisfaction from the completion of a task. Finished work and newly gained competence provide them with their sense of continued mobility.

A second group rely more upon the social prestige of increased status in their home communities or within the organizational hierarchy. To them the real objective is increased status. Competence in work is of value and at times crucial. But the satisfactions of the second group come from the social reputation, not from the personal feeling that necessary work has been well done. Both types of mobility drive are highly motivating. The zeal and energy put into the job is equal in both instances. The distinction appears in the kinds of work which the men find interesting. For the first group, the primary factor is the nature of the work itself—is it challenging, is it necessary, is it interesting? For the second group, the crucial factor is its relation to their goals of status mobility—is it a step in the direction of increased prestige, is it appropriate to my present problem, what would other people think of me if I did it?

THE IDEA OF AUTHORITY. The successful executive posits authority as a controlling but helpful relationship to superiors. He looks to his superiors as persons of more advanced training and experience whom he can consult on special problems and who issue to him certain guiding directives. He does not see the authority figures in his environment as destructive or prohibiting forces.

Those executives who view authority as a prohibiting and destructive force have difficulty relating themselves to superiors and resent their authority over them. They are either unable to work smoothly with their superiors, or indirectly and unconsciously do things to obstruct the work of their bosses or to assert their independence unnecessarily.

It is of interest that the dominant crystallization of attitudes about authority of these men is toward superior and toward subordinates, rather than toward Self. This implies that most crucial in their concept of authority is the view of being a part of a wider and more final authority system. In contrast, a few executives of the "Self-made," driving type characteristic of the past of business enterprise maintain a specific concept of authority with regard to Self. They are the men who most always forge their own frontiers, who are unable to operate within anyone else's framework, to whom cooperation and teamwork are foreign concepts. To these men, the ultimate authority is in themselves and their image does not include the surrounding area of shared or delegated power.

ORGANIZATION AND ITS IMPLICATIONS.   While executives who are successful vary considerably in their intelligence-test ratings, all of them have a high
degree of ability to organize unstructured situations and to see the implications of their organization. This implies that they have the ability to take
several seemingly isolated events or facts and to see relationships that exist
between them. Further, they are interested in looking into the future and are
concerned with predicting the outcome of their decisions and actions.

This ability to organize often results in a forced organization, however.
Even though some situations arise with which they feel unfamiliar and are
unable to cope, they still force an organization upon it. Thus they bring it
into the sphere of familiarity. This tendency operates partially as a mold, as a
pattern into which new or unfamiliar experiences are fit. This means, of
course, that there is a strong tendency to rely upon techniques that they know
will work and to resist situations which do not readily fit this mold.

DECISIVENESS.   Decisiveness is a further trait of this group. This does not
imply the popular idea of the executive making quick and final decisions in
rapid-fire succession, although this seems to be true of some of the executives.
More crucial, however, is an ability to come to a decision among several alternative courses of action—whether it be done on the spot or whether after
detailed consideration. Very seldom does this ability break down. While less
competent and well-organized individuals may become flustered and operate
inefficiently in certain spots, most of these men force their way to a conclusion. Nothing is too difficult for them to tackle at least and try to solve.
When poorly directed and not modified by proper judgment, this attitude
may be more of a handicap than a help. That is to say, this trait remains in
operation and results in decision-making action regardless of the reasonable-
ness of the decision or its reality in terms of related facts. The breakdown of
this trait (usually found only in cases where some more profound personality
change has also occurred) is one of the most disastrous for the executive. As
soon as this trait shows disturbance, the executive's superiors become apprehensive about him. This suggests an interesting relationship to the total
executive constellation. Whenever a junior executive loses this quality of decisiveness, he seems to pass out of the socially defined role. It is almost as
though the role demanded conviction and certainty as an integral aspect of
-it. The weakening of other aspects of the ideal executive constellation can
be readily reintegrated into the total constellation. The questioning of the
individual's certainty and decisiveness, however, results in a weakening of the
entire constellation and tends to be punished by superiors.

STRONG SELF-STRUCTURE.   One way of differentiating between people is in
the relative strength or weakness of their notions of self-identity, their self-
structure. Some persons lack definiteness and are easily influenced by outside
pressures. Some, such as these executives, are firm and well defined in their
sense of self-identity. They know what they are and what they want and have

well-developed techniques for getting what they want. The things they want and the techniques for getting them are of course quite different for each individual, but this strength and firmness is a common and necessary characteristic. It is, of course, true that too great firmness of sense of self-identity leads to rigidity and to inflexibility. And while some of these executives could genuinely be accused of this, in general they maintain considerable flexibility and adaptability *within the framework of their desires and within the often rather narrow possibilities of their own business organization.*

ACTIVITY AND AGGRESSION. The executive is essentially an active, striving, aggressive person. His underlying personality motivations are active and aggressive—although he is not necessarily aggressive and hostile overtly in his dealings with other people. This activity and aggressiveness are always well channelized into work or struggles for status and prestige. This implies a constant need to keep moving, to do something, to be active. This does not mean that they are always in bodily movement and moving physically from place to place (though this is often true), but rather that they are mentally and emotionally alert and active.

This constant motivator unfortunately cannot be shut off. It may be part of the reason why so many executives find themselves unable to take vacations leisurely or to stop worrying about already solved problems.

APPREHENSION AND THE FEAR OF FAILURE. If one is continually active and always trying to solve problems and arrive at decisions, any inability to do so successfully may well result in feelings of frustration. This seems to be true of the executives. In spite of their firmness of character and their drive to activity, they also harbor a rather pervasive feeling that they may not really succeed and be able to do the things they want. It is not implied that this sense of frustration comes only from their immediate business experience. It seems far more likely to be a feeling of long standing within the executives and to be only accentuated and reinforced by their present business experience.

This sense of the perpetually unattained is an integral part of this constellation and is part of its dilemma. It means that there is always some place to go, but no defined point at which to stop. It emphasizes the "self-propelled" nature of the dynamics of this role and highlights the inherent need to always keep moving and to see another goal always ahead. This also suggests that cessation of mobility and of struggling for new achievements will be accompanied by an inversion of this constant energy. The person whose mobility is blocked, either by his own limitations or by those of the social system, finds this energy diverted into other channels. Psychosomatic symptoms, the enlargement of interpersonal dissatisfactions, and the development of rationalized compulsive and/or paranoidlike defenses may reflect the redirection of this potent energy demand.

STRONG REALITY ORIENTATION.   The successful executives are strongly oriented to immediate realities and their implications. They are directly interested in the practical and the immediate and the direct. This is, of course, generally good for the immediate business situation, though an overdeveloped sense of reality may have secondary complications. If a man's sense of reality is too highly developed, he ceases to be a man of vision. For a man of vision must get above reality to plan and even dream about future possibilities. In addition, a too strong reality sense that does not find the realities in tune with the individual's ambitions may well leave a further sense of frustration and unpleasantness of reality. This happens to many executives who find progress and promotion too slow for their drives. The result is often a restlessness rather than activity, a fidgetiness rather than a well-channelized aggression, and a lack of ease that may well disrupt many of their usual interpersonal relations.

THE NATURE OF THEIR INTERPERSONAL RELATIONS.   In general, the mobile and successful executive looks to his superiors with a feeling of personal attachment and tends to identify with them. His superior represents for him a symbol of his own achievement and activity desires and he tends to identify himself with these traits in those who have achieved more. He is very responsive to his superiors—the nature of this responsiveness of course depending on his other feelings, his idea of authority, and the extent to which his sense of frustration is present.

On the other hand, he looks to his subordinates in a detached and impersonal way, seeing them as "doers of work" rather than as people. He treats them impersonally, with no real feeling of being akin to them or having deep interest in them as persons. It is almost as though he viewed his subordinates as representatives of things he has left behind, both factually and emotionally. Still uncertain of his next forward step, he cannot afford to become personally identified or emotionally involved with the past he has left behind. The only direction of his emotional energy that is real to him is upward and toward the symbols of that upward interest, his superiors.

This does not mean that he is cold and treats all subordinates casually. In fact, he tends to be generally sympathetic with many of them. This element of sympathy with subordinates is most apparent when the subordinate shows personality traits that are most like those of the superior. Thus the superior is able to take pride in certain successful young persons without at the same time feeling an equal interest in all subordinates.

THE ATTITUDE TOWARD HIS OWN PARENTS.   In a sense the successful executive is a "man who has left home." He feels and acts as though he were on his own, as though his emotional ties and obligations to his parents were severed. It seems to be most crucial that he has not retained resentment of his parents, but has rather simply broken their emotional hold on him and been left psychologically free to make his own decisions. We have found those who have not broken this tie to be either too dependent upon their superiors in the work situation, or to be resentful of their supervision (depending, of course, upon whether they have retained their dependency parental ties or rather they are still actively fighting against them).

In general, we find the relationship to the mother to have been the most clearly broken tie. The tie to the father remains positive in the sense that he views the father as a helpful but not restraining figure. Those men who still feel a strong emotional tie to the mother have systematically had difficulty in the business situation. The residual emotional tie seems contradictory to the necessary attitude of activity, progress, and channelized aggression. The tie to the father, however, must remain positive—as the emotional counterpart of the admired and more successful male figure. Without this image, struggle for success seems difficult.

THE NATURE OF DEPENDENCY FEELINGS AND CONCENTRATION UPON SELF. A special problem in differentiating the type of generally successful executive is the nature of his dependency feelings. It was pointed out above that the dependency upon the mother-image must be eliminated. For those executives who work within the framework of a large organization where cooperation and group-and-company loyalty are necessities, there must remain feelings of dependency upon the father-image and a need to operate within an established framework. This does not mean that the activity-aggression need cannot operate or that the individual is not decisive and self-directional. It means only that he is so within the framework of an already established set of over-all goals. For most executives, this over-all framework provides a needed guidance and allows them to concentrate upon their achievement and work demands with only minimal concern for policy making of the entire organization. For those executives who prefer complete independence and who are unable to work within a framework established by somebody else, the element of narcissism is much higher and their feelings of loyalty are only to themselves rather than to a father-image or its impersonal counterpart in company policy. These feelings differentiate the executives who can cooperate with others and who can promote the over-all policy of a company from those who must be the whole show themselves. Clearly, there are situations in which the person of high concentration upon self and low dependency-loyalty feelings is of great value. But he should be distinguished in advance and placed only in such situations where these traits are of value.

The successful executive represents a crystallization of many of the attitudes and values generally accepted by middle-class American society. The value of accumulaton and achievement, of self-directedness and independent thought and their rewards in prestige and status and property are found in this group. But they also pay the price of holding these values and by profiting from them. Uncertainty, constant activity, the continual fear of losing ground, the inability to be introspectively leisurely, the ever present fear of failure, and the artificial limitations put upon their emotionalized interpersonal relations —these are some of the costs of this role.

IMPLICATIONS

Have you known both types of executives mentioned in this article— those who have the psychodynamics that lead to success, and those who have different characteristics which do not lead to continual promotion and increased responsibility but to life satisfaction from other sources? How might an individual who is effective in working for a legislative or welfare-centered program, such as the Peace Corps, differ in personality pattern from the business executive? For example, would he have as strong a reality orientation, or have the same tie with his father, or represent as well middle-class America? Using the article as reference, you and your fellow students may find it interesting to choose several young friends and define their personality structure according to your own judgment. Remember, however, that success as an executive is only *one* kind of success in our complex society. And do not use this procedure to derogate any of your associates. To what extent do you see the twelve aspects of a common personality pattern mentioned in this selection as being compatible with each other?

REFERENCES

Fleishman (1961) has published a group of articles on leadership and supervision in industry containing a fairly large number of references. Bass (1965) has a chapter on supervisory behavior and another on psychological aspects of executive decision making. Likert (1961) discusses the executive use of employees in *decision making.*

[22] WHAT MAKES THE MIND SCIENTIFIC?

More and more we are impressed with the importance of the personal meaning of a vocation to the individual as a factor in leading him to a given field and motivating him to succeed in it. To those who are attracted to science, Roe's article becomes significant. We are living in an era and culture that is strongly colored by scientific advancements and by their importance for the course of our lives. The scientist alone, however, does not hold the key to the future. Values that dictate the use of science may be even more important; nevertheless, to use science for man and society, we must know something about the mind of the scientist, and this brief selection opens the door to Roe's valuable and prolific researches on scientists of various specialties.

Anne Roe

From Anne Roe, "What Makes the Mind Scientific?" *The New York Times Magazine* (1953). © 1965 by The New York Times Company. Reprinted by permission.

Man's accelerating progress in unlocking the doors to nature's mysteries has put a premium on scientific brains. As a discoverer of new horizons the scientist plays a crucial role in today's world. He and his works are in great demand.

Because so much depends on scientists and because the true scientist needs certain favorable conditions if he is to do his best work, it is important to examine the scientific mind and to know what are its characteristics. What qualities mark the scientific mind? How and to what extent does it differ from the minds of lawyers, writers, business men, and others? How does the scientist do his job? These questions are answered, at least in part, by a study made of sixty-four of our most eminent research scientists.

It should be noted at the start that there are no descriptive words that can be used about scientists that will apply to all scientists or will not also apply to some people who are not scientists. The same is true if you compare special kinds of scientists, such as physicists with anthropologists, or psychologists with chemists. This is natural enough, because scientists are also human beings. Nevertheless, there are some things which are more characteristic of scientists and of particular kinds of scientists than they are of other groups. The study, I should add, dealt primarily with the top, first-rate scientists whose creative efforts are largely in the field of pure research, rather than with those scientific workers whose jobs chiefly involve routines of applied research.

Consider, first, the scientist's attitude toward his work, for this furnishes a basic clue to the make-up of the scientific mind. There is a popular impression that outstanding scientists are likely to be absent-minded, rather shy geniuses who live in an abstruse world of their own, far removed from everyday realities. This is not necessarily so, yet there is an element of truth—and a very important one—in the picture. The element is the scientist's absorption in his work, which often seems to set him apart from other people.

CURIOSITY AND DEVOTION

The most distinctive thing about a first-class scientist is that he is completely wrapped up in science; he eats it and sleeps it. The chances are that he works nights and Sundays and goes on vacation only at his family's insistence. That is because he would rather be doing his work than anything else. He is not, it is true, unique in this respect; most men who go to the top in any field are devoted to their jobs. But the scientist, more than most, finds in his work the mental and emotional rewards which should and can produce the greatest results and the greatest personal satisfactions.

These satisfactions stem from two qualities of the scientific mind. One is curiosity. The other is an ability to work out solutions objectively and gain new knowledge independently and in the scientist's own way. Scientists, above all, are people who have retained a childlike curiosity, which many of us lose as we grow up. They have wanted very much to find out about things and have learned that within certain limits they can, little by little, discover what they want to know. Moreover, they have learned that they can find out things *for themselves*—not by asking someone else or by looking it up in a book (granting that it could be learned that way, which is often impossible) but instead thinking for themselves.

The research scientist, working in a university or research institute, selects his own problems and goes at them in his own way. No one tells him what to do or when. He must, and wants to, find out for himself. Even when he was in school, he preferred the teacher who stimulated him, or simply permitted him to work out the answers by himself, to the teacher who told him what to do each day. The need to become master of himself and his immediate environment is part of man's biological make-up. The scientist is one who has been fortunate enough to find a vocation which meets this need, for the gaining of knowledge is in itself a form of mastery, and deeply satisfying. Thus, the success of the scientist's work depends to an exceptional degree on his curiosity, love of the job, and personal initiative.

INTELLIGENCE

Scientists, as might be expected, are a very intelligent group of people, whether you judge by intelligence tests or by what they actually do. Mentally, they are all above the average, and some of them are very, very high in the scale indeed. In my opinion, it is necessary, if a person is to become a good scientist, to have an IQ of at least 120 or more, and, other things being equal, the higher the IQ the better the scientist if the intelligence is properly used.

I employed a special intelligence test in my study of eminent scientists (the usual ones are not difficult enough) which had separate parts for the different abilities we call verbal, spatial, and mathematical—that is, for understanding of words, for ability to imagine the manipulation of objects in space, and for ability to work out mathematical problems. I kept the tests separate because these abilities are not necessarily related; one may have very high verbal ability, yet not be very good at mathematics, or vice versa.

The average IQ's of this group approximated 165 for the verbal test, 135 for the spatial test, and 155 for the mathematical, and they ranged from around 125 to nearly 200, or just about as high as you can get. There are, of course, other people with high IQ's who do not become scientists. After all, the average IQ is 100, and about 10 per cent of our population have IQ's as high as 120 or more.

There were interesting differences among different kinds of scientists as to the sort of test they were best at. For example, experimental physicists are likely to be relatively better at manipulating objects in space than they were at understanding words. Theoretical physicists were terrific at both. (I did not give the physicists the mathematical test; I could not get one that would be difficult enough for them that the others could do at all.) Experimental psychologists, geneticists, and biochemists also tended to be better at the mathematical and spatial tests than at the verbal.

Botanists, anthropologists, and clinical and social psychologists, on the other hand, were likely to be better at the verbal test than at the others. For instance, there was an experimental physicist with a verbal-test result somewhat lower than the average of the total group, but with the highest of all in the spatial test. The biologist with the second highest score on the verbal test was below the group's average on both spatial and mathematical tests.

PERSONALITY

It was also possible to give these eminent scientists some personality tests. These showed that they tended to generalize more than the population at large and to look for unusual aspects of things. Again, there were differences among the different groups. The natural scientists seemed to show a very considerable independence of the need for close personal relations, but quite the contrary was true of the social scientists. In none of these groups are the individuals very aggressive, though the social scientists are the most likely to be. This, however, does not mean that the scientists can be pushed around. Far from it. They are, on the whole, a stubborn lot, but they are usually too busy with their own concerns to interfere with other people's affairs.

BACKGROUND

In their life histories, certain situations are common among them, but not unique to scientists. To judge by these samples, scientists tend to come from middle-class homes and to have fathers who were professional men, but particularly to come from homes in which learning is valued for its own sake as well as for the perquisites it may bring economically and socially. A large proportion of these first-rate scientists were first-born children, or at least oldest sons. The records indicate that the natural scientists as a group had tended to be somewhat isolated as boys, not to have been members of gangs and not to have had much social life. In contrast, the social scientists tended to have been leaders in student activities in college, interested in literature, and to have had active social lives from an early age.

Many had an early interest in the things that later became their vocations, though some did not. A number of the latter appear to have lacked this interest because when they were young, they did not realize the possibility of making a living at such things as theoretical physics or genetics or psychology, or if they had heard of such professions, it was without any suspicion that they themselves could enter them.

This assessment of the characteristics of the true scientist now brings us to the question: Under what circumstances does the scientific mind do its best work? It is evident that one of the most important elements in scientific work is the special freedom it gives its devotees to use their excellent minds to master knowledge in their own fashion. But if science offers this special freedom, it also requires special freedoms from and for the scientist.

No one can go far in science if he is not free to see things as they are. The man who is burdened by political or any other ideologies that restrict his thinking—whether they are accepted by him or imposed on him by society— is not free to examine the world to see if it is really in accordance with his beliefs. Men have not always and everywhere been free to become scientists. Creative productivity, not only in science but also in art and other fields, has varied greatly from culture to culture and from age to age in the same culture. From the periods and circumstances under which productivity has been high, it seems clear that an essential factor in any culture where creative activity flourishes is a high degree of independence and individual freedom.

A very few scientists work best under moderate pressure, a number work best under a little pressure (such as wanting to finish an experiment in time to report it at a particular scientific meeting), but most of them do their best work when pressures are at a minimum, and particularly when they are not emotionally disturbed by problems outside of their work. Moreover, they need time—often long periods of time—in which they may appear not to be working at all, for scientific progress requires a lot of almost unconscious thinking.

This is essential before most major advances, and it is the sort of thing that is difficult for nonscientists, such as some administrators, to understand and make provision for.

It would seem obvious that major advances in science are not made under the sort of working conditions that characterize the usual industry or government setup, with its precise assignment of duties and timing of them. In considering this, the distinction between science and technology—that is, between basic or pure science and applied science—must be kept clearly in mind. Most scientists working in industry or government are engaged primarily in the latter, which does not have the same requirements or the same satisfactions as pure science.

What happens when a research scientist tries to work "under orders" depends largely upon the working conditions and the man's real interest in the problem that falls to him. It is of course difficult for a trained research scientist who through his whole professional life has pursued the particular research that is of personal interest to him, and has done it in his own way, to alter his working habits suddenly and completely. This may eliminate the most important and satisfying aspect of his profession. Nevertheless, he may get along very well if he can become personally absorbed in the new problem and if the outside pressure is not too great.

But if he took on the job chiefly for the extra money or for some reason not important to him, it is likely that soon the lack of primary satisfactions will overbalance the immediate returns. Scientists and their families are not averse to having money, but usually other things are more important to them.

For the scientist, accustomed to talking and writing freely about his interests, government jobs with high secrecy requirements are especially difficult. Working conditions on some new government projects seem to have been specified by enemies, so perfectly are they designed to afford the maximum of frustration and minimum of emotional comfort to the scientist.

The wonder is that such extraordinary advances in pure science have been made under these conditions. The explanation probably is that the men at the top became thoroughly absorbed in the work or that they were sufficiently patriotic to drive themselves to do it even at considerable emotional cost.

Often the greater material freedom in the research itself has been a compensating factor; where no expense is spared for equipment and tools, the scientist can work on problems he could not possibly have touched before. But if he could not, even so, come to feel that they were his own problems, then research has faltered, or the man has quit or broken under the strain.

Given the qualities of the scientific mind—the driving curiosity, the personal approach to an enjoyment of the work, the high intelligence, the necessity for freedom—if the best creative faculties are to be used—it follows that management policies should be such as to cause a minimum of frustration to the scientific researcher. Enlightened management policies that give the scientist as much choice as possible in selecting his problem, that will make it possible for him to work in his own way and at his own time, and that are sensible in regard to security measures, would be a help.

Scientists do not regiment easily; they are stubborn and independent, and they have little patience with restrictions that seem to them unnecessary if not irrational. It is up to management and workers in other fields to realize these things about the scientific mind and make provision for them. In that way the nation can secure the best from its scientific brains.

IMPLICATIONS

To what extent do you find in yourself the attitudes, work habits, intellectual make-up, personality, and background of the scientist? You may find it interesting to use the factors and subfactors mentioned in the article, such as attitude toward a given kind of work, intelligence, personality, background, and so on, as an outline to assess your own inclinations toward some other vocation. Contrast the ideas presented here with those on creativity in Selection 20 and on the business executive in Selection 21.

REFERENCES

See Roe's book (1956) on the psychology of occupations.

Chapter V

PERSONNEL ISSUES

[23] THE GULLIBILITY OF PERSONNEL MANAGERS

For a long time, charlatans or psychological quacks have operated successfully, using untested and sometimes invalid personality-test devices and selling them to otherwise shrewd businessmen. Why are they successful? In his clever but bold study, Stagner gives us some insight into the reasons for their success.

Contrasted to the nostrums sold by the quacks are the selection-and-appraisal devices, bolstered by statistical tests, that are employed by well-trained and reputable psychologists. These instruments are accompanied by indication of *reliability* (consistency of measurement) and frank *validity* data (showing the extent to which the instrument measures that which it is proposed to measure). These more scientific devices are often more difficult to use and to understand. In terms of high-level predictability, they promise much less than fraudulent devices; but they are always considerably superior to chance or noncritical judgment. You might find it interesting to turn to Table 1 and answer the questions before reading the article.

Ross Stagner

Reprinted from Ross Stagner, "The Gullibility of Personnel Managers," *Personnel Psychology*, Vol. 11 (Cleveland: Personnel Psychology, 1958), pp. 347–352, by permission of the publisher and the author.

Psychological services are being offered for sale in all parts of the United States. Some of these are bona fide services by competent, well-trained people.

Others are marketing nothing but glittering generalities having no practical value.

In the field of engineering, chemistry, power sources, and raw materials supply, the average businessman has learned to think realistically and to demand quantitative evidence concerning the value of an item before buying it. In the novel field of psychological measurement, on the other hand, many executives are still amazingly gullible. They often purchase expensive "employee selection" programs with no scientific evidence that the service offered has any value whatever.

A common device of the high-pressure salesman who is dispensing a fake line of psychological "tests" runs something like this: "Statistics can be used to prove anything. Let me give you a real demonstration. You take this personality test yourself, and I'll give you the report based on your scores. If you don't agree that it is amazingly accurate, I won't even try to sell it to you." The gullible personnel manager takes the test, reads the report, is amazed by its accuracy, and spends a lot of his company's money for a device not worth the paper and printing.

Does this sound too extreme? Do you think the personnel manager is the best possible judge of a report on his own personality? Do you think this is the only sound basis for deciding about the validity of a test? Skeptics will be interested in the following report of a simple experiment conducted with a conference of personnel managers at the University of Illinois.

METHOD

The procedure involved giving the personnel managers a published personality inventory and collecting the blanks for scoring, assuring them that the reports would be returned within a few hours. The test was actually scored, according to the published key. However, *two* reports were prepared, one using a mimeographed profile sheet which showed each man exactly how he scored as compared with norm groups; this gave him a quantitative result which could be used practically. The other report was a "fake" personality analysis published by Forer (1949) with slight modifications to make it more plausible. The thirteen items shown in Table 1, which were collected by Forer from dream books and astrology charts, were interspersed with rather critical comments about the personality being tested. The person's name was written in red pencil at the top of the sheet, and the thirteen items listed were circled in red; thus, every man received an identical "personality analysis."

At the second meeting of the group, the fake report was distributed first. Everyone was asked to read only his own personality analysis, which was given by the items marked in red. Thus it appeared that each individual was

TABLE 1

EVALUATIONS OF ITEMS BY 68 PERSONNEL MANAGERS WHEN PRESENTED AS A "PERSONALITY ANALYSIS"

Item	Judgment as to accuracy of item Per cent * choosing				
	a†	b	c	d	e
1. You have a great need for other people to like and admire you.	39	46	13	1	1
4. You have a tendency to be critical of yourself.	46	36	15	3	0
5. You have a great deal of unused capacity which you have not turned to your advantage.	37	36	18	4	1
7. While you have some personality weaknesses, you are generally able to compensate for them.	34	55	9	0	0
9. Your sexual adjustment has presented problems for you.	15	16	16	33	19
10. Disciplined and self-controlled outside, you tend to be worrisome and insecure inside.	40	21	22	10	4
12. At times you have serious doubts as to whether you have made the right decision or done the right thing.	27	31	19	18	4
15. You prefer a certain amount of change and variety and become dissatisfied when hemmed in by restrictions and limitations.	63	28	7	1	1
16. You pride yourself as an independent thinker and do not accept others' statements without satisfactory proof.	49	31	12	4	4
18. You have found it unwise to be too frank in revealing yourself to others.	31	37	22	6	4
20. At times you are extroverted, affable, sociable, while at other times you are introverted, wary, reserved.	43	25	18	9	5
21. Some of your aspirations tend to be pretty unrealistic.	12	16	22	43	7
23. Security is one of your major goals in life.	40	31	15	9	5

* Not all percentages add to 100% because of omissions by an occasional subject.
† Definitions of scale steps as follows: a. amazingly accurate. b. rather good. c. about half and half. d. more wrong than right. e. almost entirely wrong.

getting a report designed for himself alone. (No such direct assertion was made by the speaker, but the illusion was effectively communicated.)

Each man was then asked to read over the items marked for him and decide how accurate he thought the description was. He was provided with a five-step scale, as follows: amazingly accurate; rather good; about half and half; more wrong than right; almost entirely wrong. He was asked to check this scale both for over-all impression and for each of the items marked in red.

After the "validity analysis" had been collected, the participants were asked to compare their personality reports. Upon discovering that all were identical, they set up a terrific noise, apparently compounded of resentment at being duped and amusement at themselves for being tricked.

After brief discussion, the genuine profile sheets were distributed and the difference between glittering generalities and a quantitative set of scores emphasized. The importance of statistical data on reliability and validity was also discussed at this point.

RESULTS

Perhaps the most important results were to be found in the insights reported by the participants, who quickly grasped the significance of the demonstration. However, numerical findings will be of some interest.

In terms of over-all evaluation of the "fake analysis," 50 per cent of a group of 68 personnel managers marked the description as amazingly accurate. Other judgments divided between "rather good" (40 per cent) and "about half and half" (10 per cent).

For comparison, we may cite results of two other groups. In a group of college students, 25 per cent considered this same "personality analysis" to be "amazingly accurate" and another 37 per cent judged it "rather good." In a class of industrial supervisors studying "human relations," the same personality analysis was considered "amazingly accurate" by 37 per cent, with 44 per cent rating it "rather good." Thus 62 per cent of the students and 81 per cent of the supervisors, as compared with 90 per cent of the personnel men, chose the first two steps on the validity scale defined in Table 1. The two industrial groups are not significantly different; the *greater skepticism of the students* * may have been due to their greater familiarity with test forms, and perhaps to some skepticism about the intent of the instructor.

The results for a group of 68 personnel managers on the eleven specific items are given in Table 1. It is clear from this table that any report using sentences such as those making up items 15, 16, 4, 20, 23, and 10 *will be popular with the recipient.** Even items 1, 5, 7, and 18 will get a good reception. Only items 9, 12, and 21 failed to get an enthusiastic approval from at least 30 per cent of the population.

Similar results were obtained from the group of supervisors, as well as from several classes of college students. It thus appears that the present finding need not be limited to personnel managers alone, although they merit special consideration because of their role in deciding upon employee selection devices.

* Editor's italics.

DISCUSSION

Industrial psychologists have some valuable wares to sell. But quacks and charlatans are always quick to move in on a new field and replace solid utility with glittering generalizations. The astonishing aspect of this demonstration to a professional psychologist is the credulity of the industrialist.

The sweeping character of the statements utilized in the fake personality analysis should be readily recognized. These propositions are so general that they can apply to anyone; as we note, 30 per cent to 50 per cent of a group of practicing personnel men accept most of them as "amazingly accurate" in an imputed self-description. Thus the shrewd salesman can easily dupe the personnel man *by appealing to his belief that his own judgment is better than statistics.** (Dozens of such demonstrations will be required to shake this belief in some industrialists' minds.) Seeing that the "test" elicits such remarkable insights into his own personality, the personnel manager concludes that it will do equally well with the applicants he wishes to analyze. It will, of course, do exactly as well; that is, it will spew out *glittering generalizations which apply to everyone and are distinctive for no one.** It will have no differential value for selection, placement, training, or any other personnel function.

It should be noted that these fake "personality reports" need not be phrased identically. The salesman need not use all thirteen of the items given in Table 1 for a given person, nor is he limited to these; there are many others, equally acceptable, some more flattering (these go to the higher executives). Thus the salesman can "test" several men in one organization without running out of nice generalizations. By judicious combinations of such items he can continue for quite a while without saying anything.

The present findings are not unique. Forer (1949) found that typical college students were easily taken in by his items. Sundberg (1955) reports that few people choose their own personality diagnosis, based on the Minnesota Multiphasic Personality Inventory, when it is matched with a set of vague generalizations like these. Dunnette (1957) comments, "It is an unfortunate fact that many otherwise hardheaded businessmen are today behaving in a rather gullible fashion" in regard to tests, and he credits Dr. Paul E. Meehl with coining the phrase, "the Barnum effect," to refer to the deceptive effect of these glittering generalities incorporated in testing reports.

These observations will not, it is hoped, decrease the interest of personnel men in professionally sound, scientifically evaluated personality measures. While most psychologists are cautious in recommending such devices, it seems certain that they can be utilized in certain industrial situations. Especial importance should be attached to the presence of quantitative data on

* Editor's italics.

reliability, on group norms, and on validation. Curiously enough, it seems that the third of these is least important. Validation needs to be repeated inside the establishment, with reference to criteria of performance appropriate to the position under study. But a test which does not elicit reliable individual differences, and a satisfactory spread of scores when applied to populations comparable to that in the establishment, cannot function as a personnel device. At best, it may make the employees think management is interested in them; at worst, it may result in erroneous placements, waste, and personnel disturbance.

The old Roman saying runs, *Caveat emptor*—let the buyer beware. This holds for personnel testing devices, especially as regards "personality tests." The personnel manager should avoid being seduced by the flattering report on his own fine qualities into purchasing a test which is worthless when evaluated scientifically.

IMPLICATIONS

You and your fellow students may find it interesting to discuss the implications of your own answers to the thirteen items in Table 1. How did your responses compare with those of the personnel managers? How do you explain the results? How would you proceed to convince business and personnel men of the superiority of reliable and valid measures produced by psychologists?

REFERENCES

Consult the Bibliography for references cited in the article.

[24] USING THE APPLICATION BLANK TO REDUCE OFFICE TURNOVER

Almost everyone has at one time or another filled out an application blank—for entrance to school or camp, for a job or some other appointment. The application asked for specific biographical data, and it may have seemed routine. If constructed well and completed by the applicant conscientiously, the application blank is a partial summary of the individual's history. Depending upon how it is used, it should have predictive value. Fleishman and Berniger describe how the ordinary application blank becomes a psychological instrument.

Other commonly used personnel procedures may be refined. The interview and the rating scale, if tested, revised, and employed by persons trained in their use, can be quite effective in personnel selection or other placement.

The following article is an example of how to use a simple application blank together with accumulated research on company records.

Edwin A. Fleishman and Joseph Berniger

Reprinted from Edwin A. Fleishman and Joseph Berniger, "One Way to Reduce Office Turnover," *Personnel Psychology*, Vol. 37 (Cleveland: Personnel Psychology, 1960), pp. 63–69, by permission of the publisher and the senior author.

Though the application blank, in one form or another, is omnipresent in business and industry, all too often it is used in a superficial and unsystematic manner. In many employment situations, for example, the personnel interviewer either merely scans the blank for items he considers pertinent or uses the information only as a point of departure for the employment interview. As a result, much of the wealth of information in the application blank is going to waste, or worse, is often improperly used. In actual fact, however, there is sufficient evidence to indicate that, properly validated and used, the application blank can markedly increase the efficiency of the company's selection procedures.

The rationale for using the application blank (though this is seldom verbalized explicitly) is that the applicant's personal history, such as his previous experience and interests, is predictive of his future success on the job. And, indeed, it does seem reasonable to assume that such data as previous employment history, specific skills, education, financial status, marital record, and so forth, reflect a person's motives, abilities, skills, level of aspiration, and adjustment to working situations.

A number of assumptions can be made from such information. For example, the fact that an applicant has held a similar job indicates the likelihood of his transferring some of his training to the new job. Similarly, what he has done successfully before is likely to reflect his basic abilities in that area, as well as his interest in and satisfaction derived from these activities.

Such personal history items as age, number of dependents, years of education, previous earnings, and amount of insurance have also been found to correlate with later proficiency on the job, earnings, length of tenure, or other criteria of job success. It should be emphasized, however, that the items found to be predictive of success in one job may not be the same for another, similar job —even in the same company. Furthermore, even for the same job, some items on the application blank may be more predictive of one particular aspect of job performance than of other aspects (for example, turnover, accidents, or earnings).

Hand in hand with this consideration is the fact that, in personnel selection, the application blank is usually reviewed as a whole by an employment interviewer, a procedure that obviously involves a great deal of subjective judgment on his part. Consequently, the success of the form in predicting job performance depends not only upon the accuracy of the job description used as a reference, but also upon the skill of the interviewer and, most importantly, on his knowledge of the validity of individual items in relation to certain jobs and criteria. Unfortunately, however, it is this last critical point that most organizations fail to check out with empirical data. In this article we shall endeavor to point out that such data are not difficult to obtain and may materially help the employment interviewer in arriving at better hiring decisions.

DESIGN OF THE STUDY

The study outlined here describes the way in which the potential value of the routine application blank used at Yale University was enhanced through appropriate research methods. The purpose of the study was to develop a way of scoring the application blank to select clerical and secretarial employees who were most likely to remain on the job. In other words, it was designed to explore the possibility of using the blank as part of a selection program aimed at reducing turnover.

The first step in the study was to find out which items in the application blank actually differentiated between short-tenure and long-tenure employees who had been hired at about the same time. For this purpose, 120 women office employees, all of whom had been hired between 1954 and 1956, were studied. Half of these, designated the "long tenure" group, were women whose tenure was from two to four years and who were still on the job. The other 60 employees had terminated within two years and accordingly were designated the short-tenure group. Of this group, 20 per cent had terminated within six months and 67 per cent within the first year. The sample excluded known "temporaries" and summer employees. The women studied had all been hired as "permanent" employees, and all who had left had done so voluntarily.

The application blank in question is similar to those used in most organizations. It takes up four pages and includes approximately forty items—personal data, work history, education, interests, office skills, and the like. The original application blanks of the employees in both the short- and long-tenure groups were examined and the responses to the individual items were then compared to determine which, if any, differentiated the employees who terminated from those who stayed and, if so, which items were the best predictors of tenure.

TABLE 1

HOW ITEM RESPONSES BY LONG- AND SHORT-TENURE
OFFICE EMPLOYEES COMPARED

Application Blank Items	Percentage of:		Weight Assigned to Response
	Short-tenure group	Long-tenure group	
Local address			
Within city	39	62	+2
Outlying suburbs	50	36	−2
Age			
Under 20	35	8	−3
21–25	38	32	−1
26–30	8	2	−1
31–35	7	10	0
35 and over	11	48	+3
Previous salary			
Under $2,000	31	30	0
$2,000–$3,000	41	38	0
$3,000–$4,000	13	12	0
Over $4,000	4	4	0
Age of children			
Preschool	12	4	−3
Public school	53	33	−3
High school or older	35	63	+3

A preliminary review suggested the ways in which to classify the answers to the various items. The next step was to tally the responses for each group and then convert them to percentages to facilitate comparisons. Some examples of items that did and did not differentiate between the two groups are shown in Table 1. As the table shows, local address, for instance, was a good differentiator, but previous salary was not. Certain responses to the question of age also distinguished between the two groups, as did "reason for leaving last employment," "occupation of husband," and "number of children."

WEIGHTING THE ITEMS

Since some items were found to be better predictors of tenure than others, it seemed reasonable to assign them more weight in the actual hiring procedure—the next step in our study. Thus, items that did not discriminate were weighted zero (*i.e.*, they were not counted). Others were weighted negatively (they counted against the applicant), and still others, positively (in favor of the applicant). For example, an address in the suburbs was more characteristic of short-tenure employees, and so this response was scored negatively. An address in the city, on the other hand, was scored positively. Similarly, "age over 35" received a positive weight, but "under 30" received a negative weight.

Next, the size of the weight was determined. Items that showed a bigger percentage difference between the long- and short-tenure groups were given a higher weight. For example, "age under 20" was weighted -3, whereas "age 26–30" was weighted only -1. (Though there are more precise methods for assigning weights [Stead and Shartle, 1940], we found that the simple but systematic procedure described above yielded comparable results.)

An applicant's total score is, of course, obtained by adding or subtracting the weights scored on each item on the application blank. In our first sample, we found that total scores ranged from -17 to 27, the average score for the short-tenure group being -2.3, while that for the long-tenure group was 8.9— a difference of 11.2, which is highly significant statistically. The correlation between the total scores made by these employees and their subsequent tenure was .77.

This correlation was, of course, misleading and spuriously high since we had calculated it from the very sample from which we had determined the weights for the individual items in the first place. To obtain an unbiased estimate of the validity of our scoring procedure, we had to try it out, therefore, on an independent sample of employees.

THE CROSS-VALIDATION STUDY

Accordingly, the application blanks of a second random sample of short- and long-tenure girls, hired during the same period, were drawn from the files. Again, the short-tenure group consisted of girls who had left within two years and the long-tenure group was composed of those who were still on the job after two years or more. The scoring system developed on the first sample was then applied to the application blanks of this second group (85 clerical and secretarial employees).

The range of scores for this sample was -10 to 21, and the correlation with subsequent tenure was .57. This confirmed that the weighted blank did possess a high degree of validity for predicting tenure. The average score for the short-tenure group was −0.7, while that of the long-tenure group was 6.3. Again, this was a statistically significant difference. A recheck was also made on the individual items, which showed, in general, that those items which differentiated in the first sample did so in the second sample as well.

We had, then, a selection instrument that indicated the probability of an applicant's staying with the organization or not, but the question of how to use it in reaching the actual hiring decision still remained. Of course, such factors as the relative importance of turnover in the organization, the number of available applicants during a hiring period, and other selection procedures in use have to be taken into account here. It is desirable, nonetheless, to set a score on the application blank that does the best job of differentiating between "long-" and "short-"tenure risks at the time of employment. In other words, what is needed is a cut-off score that will maximize correct hiring decisions; or—to put it another way—a score that will minimize both the number of people hired who will turn out to be short-tenure employees and the number rejected who would have actually remained on the job.

To establish our cut-off score, we used the method of "maximum differentiation." In other words, we tabulated the percentage of employees reaching or exceeding each score point in the range, −10 to 21. We then calculated the differences between the percentages obtained in the two groups at each score point to find the point of greatest differentiation.

The result is shown in Table 2, from which it will be seen that in our case the difference between the two groups reached its maximum at a score of +4. This told us that applicants scoring 4 points or more were most likely to stay on the job two years or more, whereas those scoring less than 4 could be considered potential short-tenure employees.

Figure 1 shows the degree of success that would have been achieved if this cutting score of +4 had been used on our second sample of 85 employees. The shaded areas represent the percentage of correct hiring decisions, and the unshaded areas, the percentage of incorrect hiring decisions. As may be seen, the personnel interviewer would have hired two out of three of the employees who stayed more than two years, and rejected approximately four out of five of those who had left before that time.

Finally, to facilitate routine scoring, we constructed a cardboard template for each page of the application blank (Wood, 1947). In the template are windows, which expose only the responses to be scored. The weights for each response are printed on the template next to the appropriate window.

An interesting offshoot of our study was the picture it yielded of the woman office worker most likely to be the best long-tenure risk at Yale University. We arrived at it by using the application blank items that differentiated between long- and short-tenure employees in both our original and our cross-validation

TABLE 2

OBTAINING A CUTTING SCORE BY USING "MAXIMUM DIFFERENTIATION"

| | Percentage of Subjects at or above a Given Score | | |
| | A | B | |
Total Score	Percentage of long-tenure employees	Percentage of short-tenure employees	Index of Differentiation (A Minus B)
21	4	0	4
20	4	0	4
19	4	0	4
18	12	0	12
17	16	0	16
16	20	0	20
15	20	0	20
14	24	0	24
13	24	3	21
12	28	3	25
11	32	5	27
10	36	8	28
9	40	10	30
8	40	14	26
7	44	15	29
6	48	17	31
5	60	20	40 *Point of*
4	68	22	46 *Greatest*
3	72	27	45 *Differ-*
2	72	32	40 *entiation*
1	72	39	13
0	80	42	18
−1	80	46	14
−2	80	54	16
−3	84	66	18
−4	92	68	24
−5	92	76	16
−6	92	85	7
−7	96	90	6
−8	96	94	2
−9	100	98	2
−10	100	100	0

Cutting Score is indicated at total score 4 / 3.

samples. Here is a profile of the typical long-tenure woman office employee at Yale:

She is 30 years old or over, has a local address rather than a suburban one, is married (but not to a student), or is a widow. Her husband is most likely to be an executive or a professional man. She may have one or two children, but if she

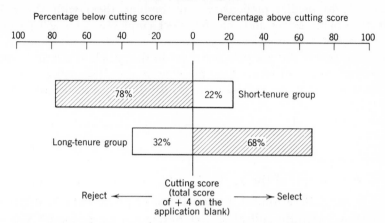

FIGURE 1. Percentages of correct hiring decisions that would have been obtained through using cutting score.

does, they are of high-school age or over. At least one member of her family has been employed at Yale. She herself is not employed at the time of application. She has had a business, secretarial school, or college education, and can often speak more than one language. If she can type, she does so at a speed of 50–60 words per minute. Usually, she cannot take shorthand—but if she does, it is at a relatively high rate of speed. She does not list more than one outside interest aside from work, and that one indicates that she is most interested in organizations and people. Finally, she spent at least two years at her last job.

The findings of our study bear out those obtained in previous studies at the Prudential Life Insurance Company (Kreidt and Gadel, 1953) and the Minnesota Mining and Manufacturing Company (Kirchner and Dunnette, 1957), both of which showed that a high degree of predictability of turnover among female office employees was achieved from a weighted application blank. Our study extends the generality of these findings from two diverse companies to a university organization. However, an examination of all three studies underscores the fact that the specific biographical items contributing to prediction of turnover vary from one organizational setting to the next. Thus, while the validity of the general technique for predicting turnover has been established for clerical employees, the weighted· application blank that will work best for a particular company must be tailor-made for that organization.

Another consideration worth mentioning, perhaps, is that though the biographical data used here have been found to be most useful in predicting turnover, other studies have indicated that such data are also of value in predicting accidents and proficiency. (They have been found especially useful in predicting proficiency in the sales field [The AI-4-48, 1951].) Of course, turnover and proficiency are not unrelated—it is well known that many girls leave because of low proficiency. However, the company that uses other selection instruments to predict proficiency can combine them with the weighted application blank scores and thereby select employees who will be the best risks in terms of both proficiency *and* tenure.

One final point: the research described in this article is relatively inexpensive. Indeed, most companies have file drawers literally bulging with application blank data that are well suited to the kind of analysis described here.

IMPLICATIONS

How did the use of the application blank in the selection differ from its use in most situations? Can you think of other ways to use personal information carefully collected and buttressed by research? What personal history items in addition to those used here would you suggest for use in classifying both successful and ineffective salesmen? Research workers?

REFERENCES

Consult the Bibliography for references cited in the article.

[25] HOW PEOPLE INTERACT IN CONFERENCES

Executives and leaders in business, government, education, and other areas spend considerable time in conferences that are usually called to deal with specific problems. Talk can be subjected to formal observation and analysis and we can learn what actually takes place during these conferences. How does the psychologist study the conference objectively? The average conference group has dual leaders —an "idea man" and a "best-liked man." In this selection, you will notice some trends in human behavior in a group situation. To know this has value in handling a group in conference.

Robert F. Bales

From "How People Interact in Conferences," *Scientific American,* Vol. 192, pp. 31–35. Reprinted with permission. Copyright © 1955 in the U.S. and Berne Convention countries by Scientific American, Inc. All rights reserved. Available separately @ 20¢ as offprint No. 451 from W. H. Freeman & Co., 600 Market St., San Francisco, Calif.

Social interaction is made up largely of the talking that people do when they get together. Talk is an elusive object of study, in spite of the fact that a good deal of it exists. It is also a rather sensitive subject. Even a friend might find it hard to put up with a dissection of the following kind: "I was just noticing how much you talk. In the last ten minutes I noticed that you made a total of 114 remarks, while I made a total of 86. According to my count, you gave about twice as many opinions as facts. Although I agreed with you fifteen times and didn't disagree at all, I noticed that you stammered once and blushed twice."

I first began to develop a systematic procedure for analyzing social inter-action when I became interested in trying to account for the success of Alco-holics Anonymous in helping apparently hopeless drinkers to stop drinking. Although I attended meetings and talked with many members, I did not feel free to ask all the questions I wished. Consequently I fell back on observation and began to develop crude methods for recording who did what, who spoke to whom, and how. Eventually even this quiet occupation began to appear sinister and the effort was abandoned. But by this time, my fascination with the process of social interaction had developed to the point of no return. I decided that I must pursue my studies in the more favorable conditions of a laboratory.

A number of laboratories for the study of social interaction within small groups and organizations have been started in the last ten years—in hospitals, clinics, special research centers, and military installations. The studies and experiments I shall describe were conducted in one of the earliest of these laboratories, established in 1947 at Harvard University.

The laboratory consists of a large, well-lighted room for the group under study and an adjoining room for observers, who listen and watch from behind windows with one-way vision. The subjects are told at the beginning that the room has been constructed for the special purpose of studying group discus-sion, that a complete sound recording will be made, and that there are ob-servers behind the one-way mirrors. The purpose of the separation is not to deceive the subjects but to minimize interaction between them and the observing team.

After much research, we developed a standardized task from which significant generalizations could be drawn. A group of persons (ranging from two to seven in number) is asked to discuss a complex human relations problem of the sort typically faced by an administrator. Each member of the group first reads a five-page presentation of facts about the case to be discussed, but each is left uncertain as to whether he has been given exactly the same range of facts as the others in the group. The members are not introduced to one another or coached in any way; they must develop their own organization and procedure. They are to consider the facts and report to an administrator, as if they were his staff, their joint conclusions concerning the problem and what should be done about it. They are allowed forty minutes for the discussion. The group is observed for four such sessions.

On the other side of the one-way screen, the observers systematically record every step of the interaction, not omitting such items as nods and frowns. Each observer has a small machine with a moving paper tape on which he writes in code a description of every act—an act being defined essentially as a single statement, question, or gesture. Acts ordinarily occur at the rate of fifteen to twenty per minute. The recorded information on each includes identification of the person speaking and the person spoken to and classification of the act according to predetermined categories. There are twelve categories, covering positive and negative reactions, questions and attempts to solve the problem by the offering of information, opinion or suggestions (see Figure 1).

As this table shows, on the average about half (56 per cent) of the acts during a group session fall into the categories of problem-solving attempts; the remaining 44 per cent are distributed among positive reactions, negative reactions, and questions. In other words, the process tends to be two-sided, with the reactions acting as a more or less constant feedback on the acceptability of the problem-solving attempts. The following is a typical example of the pattern of interchange:

Member 1: "I wonder if we have the same facts about the problem? [Asks for opinion.] Perhaps we should take some time in the beginning to find out." [Gives suggestion.]

Member 2: "Yes. [Agrees.] We may be able to fill in some gaps in our information. [Gives opinion.] Let's go around the table and each tell what the report said in his case." [Gives suggestion.]

This example illustrates that a speaker's first remark is likely to be a reaction, and if he continues speaking, the probability is very high that his second act will be a problem-solving attempt. Figure 2 sums up this finding statistically: about 50 per cent of the time a member's first remark in a series is a reaction, if he continues, about 80 per cent of the succeeding comments are opinions or other offerings classed as attempts to solve the problem.

When we examine the reactions, we find that positive reactions commonly outnumber negative ones about two to one during a session. It is as if after

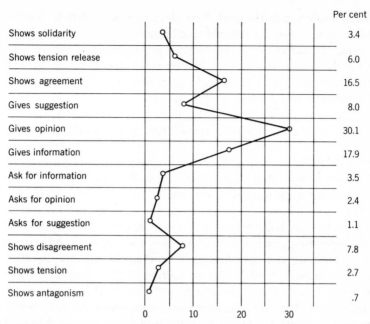

Per cent

Shows solidarity	3.4
Shows tension release	6.0
Shows agreement	16.5
Gives suggestion	8.0
Gives opinion	30.1
Gives information	17.9
Ask for information	3.5
Asks for opinion	2.4
Asks for suggestion	1.1
Shows disagreement	7.8
Shows tension	2.7
Shows antagonism	.7

0   10   20   30

Figure 1. Types of acts in social interaction may be classed in four main categories: positive reactions, problem-solving attempts, questions, and negative reactions. The averages for 96 group sessions show that 56 per cent of the acts fall into the problem-solving category.

every negative reaction, the members of the group feel they must make another problem-solving attempt which meets with a positive reaction "just to catch up," and net forward progress is felt to be sufficiently secure only when a repetition of the problem-solving attempt meets unopposed acceptance. It may be that members employ repetition, or near repetition, as an error-checking device to determine whether the others "really agree." Social interaction, in common with many other goal-seeking control mechanisms, seems to depend upon error and correction of error for guidance.

The process of attempting to arrive at a group decision through discussion is in many ways very like the operation of a large-scale communication and control system such as an air-defense network. I recently compared the two processes in collaboration with John Kennedy of the Systems Research Laboratory at the Rand Corporation.

In the military case, there are three functions to be performed: surveillance of the air by radar, identification of planes as friendly or unknown, and direction of fighters sent out to intercept unknown planes. These are something like the three problems confronting our groups in the standard interaction task: assembling the given information on the case, evaluating it and proceeding toward a solution as the goal. Now the stepwise operations involved in the air-defense system may be tolerably well described as an interlocking series of seven types of information-processing operations (see Figure 3). Here *x* stands for the path of a plane tracked by radar, and *O* represents the class of objects unknown. If no known flight plan of a friendly plane coincides with *x*—a fact represented by the symbol *y*—then *x* must belong to the class *O*. Since there is a general rule, *W*, that all unknown planes are to be intercepted, the conclusion is that a specific order, *w*, should be given to intercept *x*.

Such a decision, involving many groups and interlocking processes is obviously a very complicated affair, socially as well as technically. The job of the decision-making organization is essentially to build and maintain through means of communication and evaluation a sufficiently complex and commonly accepted symbolic structure to guide or control the stages of behavior of all the operating units. *Effective decision making is basically a continuous process of building and maintaining a structure of cultural objects which in their totality constitute the common culture of the organization affected.**

The seven types of acts, or stages, just described are very general: they apply quite as well to the interaction of five experimental subjects in the laboratory group, trying to decide in forty minutes what the administrator in their case should do about his problem, as to the large-scale operations of an air-defense network. Not all of the elements in the process are primarily logical in character. They involve elements of perception, memory, association, and perhaps inductive insight. All sorts of motivational and evaluative pressures affect the process. The steps make sense not as a formally perfect chain of logic but rather as a set of symbol transformations which help to guide, although in an imperfect way, a process of decision-making behavior. Error checking is an integral part of this fallible process.

The reason for calling attention to the seven-step structure of the process is that it may help to explain the unequal ratios of suggestions, opinions and information offered in the problem-solving attempts of the groups in our tests. As Figure 3 shows, of every seven problem-solving attempts, on the average, four are opinions, two are offers of information, and one is a suggestion. It seems significant that in the idealized seven-step outline of the air-defense operation two steps have the interaction form of giving information, four intermediate steps have the interaction form of giving opinion, and only one step, the final one, has the form of giving a suggestion.

From the transcription of a group discussion it is often possible to reconstruct complete seven-step chains leading to agreement on specific points and the final conclusion. In a general way there is even a *tendency for the steps to proceed in a regular order in time.** During a session the rates of *giving information* * *tend to be highest in the first third of the meeting* * and to decline

* Editor's italics.

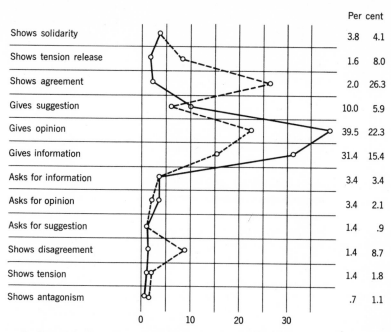

Per cent

	3.8	4.1
Shows solidarity		
Shows tension release	1.6	8.0
Shows agreement	2.0	26.3
Gives suggestion	10.0	5.9
Gives opinion	39.5	22.3
Gives information	31.4	15.4
Asks for information	3.4	3.4
Asks for opinion	3.4	2.1
Asks for suggestion	1.4	.9
Shows disagreement	1.4	8.7
Shows tension	1.4	1.8
Shows antagonism	.7	1.1

0   10   20   30

FIGURE 2. Pattern of action of individuals in a discussion is illustrated statistically. When a member takes the floor, his first remark (dashed curve) is likely to be a reaction to the preceding speaker. His next remarks (black curve) tend to be problem-solving attempts.

in the next two thirds (see Figure 4). Rates of *giving opinion are usually highest in the middle portion of the meeting.** Rates of *giving suggestion are generally low in the early period* * and reach their high point in the last third of the meeting.

Rates of both positive and negative reactions tend to rise from the first third of the meeting to the last third. These increases may be connected mainly with social and emotional problems of the group process itself. The ratio of negative to positive reactions tends to be higher in response to suggestions than in response to factual statements. The decision point is a critical bottleneck in the process. Once the decision point has been passed, however, the rates of negative reaction usually fall off and the rates of positive reaction rise sharply. Joking and laughter, indicating solidarity and tension release, become more frequent. With the problems of the task and common values stabilized for the time being by the decision, the interaction process apparently turns to restabilizing the emotional states of the individuals and their social relations to one another.

There is a good deal of evidence that the process of social interaction, like

* Editor's italics.

1. States primary observation: I observe a particular event, X.	(X)
2. Makes tentative induction: This particular event, X, may belong to the general class of objects, O.	...
3. Deduces conditional prediction: If this particular event, X, does belong to the general class, O, then it should be found associated with another particular event, Y.	...
4. States observation of check fact: I observe the predicated particular event, Y.	...
5. Identifies object as member of a class: I therefore identify X-Y as an object which is a member of the predicated general class of objects, O.	...
6. States major premise relating class of objects: All members of the general class of objects, O, should be treated by ways of the general class, W.	...
7. Proposes specific action: This particular object, X-Y, should therefore be treated in a particular way, W.	...

FIGURE 3. Process in reaching a group decision is analogous to the operation of a large-scale communication and control system such as the air-defense network. The steps consist of observing an object or event, comparing it with several possible identifications, considering the associated facts and, once its nature is understood, taking the appropriate action.

other processes involving feedback, tends to fall into oscillation as it "haunts" around a hypothetical steady state. Over a small time span the action tends to alternate every few acts between the problem-solving attempts of one person and the social-emotional reaction of some other. But this rapid oscillation is not quite rapid enough to keep all elements of the process in perfect balance. There is a drift toward inequality of participation, which in time has cumulative effects on the social relationships of the members. The reason for this drift may be seen fairly easily. When a person has completed one act, the chances are a little better than even that he will continue for another act. After each succeeding act, his probability of continuing drops, but never as far as if he simply flipped a coin at each point to determine whether to continue or to yield the floor. In fact, relatively speaking, he exceeds this chance probability by a larger and larger fraction with each succeeding act.

We have already noted that when a person continues several acts in succession, the probability is very high that he is giving information, opinion, or

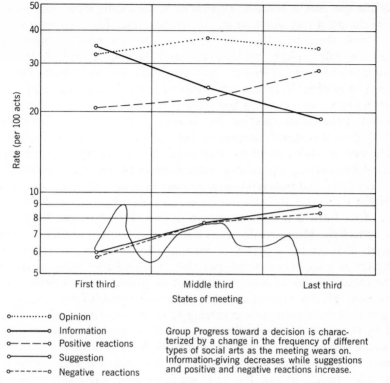

Group Progress toward a decision is characterized by a change in the frequency of different types of social acts as the meeting wears on. Information-giving decreases while suggestions and positive and negative reactions increase.

FIGURE 4. Group progress toward a decision is characterized by a change in the frequency of different types of social acts as the meeting wears on. Information giving decreases while suggestions and positive and negative reactions increase.

suggestion—in other words, specializing in problem-solving attempts. We may also infer from the seven-step theory of problem-solving attempts that the tendency to continue for several acts in succession is probably due in part to a felt need on the part of the speaker to provide inferences and check facts which will result in the acceptance of a more advanced step in the series, with an accepted suggestion as the goal.

This tendency toward inequality of participation over the short run has cumulative side effects on the social organization of the group. The man who gets his speech in first begins to build a reputation. Success in obtaining acceptance of problem-solving attempts seems to lead the successful person to do more of the same, with the result that eventually the members come to assume a rank order by task ability. In some groups the members reach a high degree of consensus on their ranking of "who had the best ideas." (The members are interviewed by questionnaire after each meeting.) Usually the persons so ranked also did the most talking and had higher-than-average rates of giving suggestions and opinion.

While one person becomes a specialist in advancing ideas, another is apt to be developing a specialization on the reactive side. The men most commonly rated "best liked" typically have higher-than-average rates of showing tension release (mainly smiling and laughing) and showing agreement. It is not impossible for the man ranked at the top in ideas also to be best liked, but apparently it is difficult. In one set of experiments, the top idea man had about an even chance of also being best liked at the end of the first meeting, but by the end of the fourth meeting, his chances were only about one in ten. The best-liked man is usually second or third in the participation hierarchy.

The task specialist seems to "lock onto" the person who is most responsive to what he is saying and address more remarks to him than to the others. In turn, the best-liked man talks more and agrees more with the top-ranking idea specialist than with any other member. The idea specialist and the best-liked man often form a mutually supporting pair. However, the best-liked man may attract the idea specialist even though they are not always in agreement. Indeed, in order for a person to become established in the minds of other members as a social-emotional specialist, it is probably more important that he be representative of their reactions, both positive and negative, than that he should ardently support everything the task specialist says. Apparently reactions that are emotionally gratifying to other members tend to be generalized by them into liking for the person who expresses the reactions.

Giving suggestions, necessary as it may be for accomplishment of the task, is more likely to arouse negative reactions than is giving information or opinions. This trends to put the task specialist in a vulnerable position. The group commonly develops a certain amount of negative feeling toward him. Not only is he likely to lose the status of being best liked, but he may lose his position as task leader unless he is sensitive to the problem and is well supported by other members. Even in a group which ends its first meeting with a high consensus on who has the best ideas, the second meeting is apt to see a challenge to his leadership, with a rise in rates of disagreement and antagonism and a precipitous drop in his popularity. But then, in a group where the original consensus was high, a peculiar thing seems to happen. Apparently as progress toward accomplishment of the task slows down, some members rally around the leader again and his popularity tends to rise. By the third meeting, the rates of disagreement and antagonism go down. The task leader may not retain all the liking that ·was transferred to him in his time of need, but the net effect of the hunting kind of oscillation that takes place is a tendency to maintain the original rank order of task ability.

In a group that starts with a low degree of consensus on who has the best ideas, the developments usually are more dismal. There tends to be a high turnover in the top ranks throughout the four meetings, with one would-be leader replacing another. In such a group the man ranked as having the best ideas is less apt to be best liked. Furthermore an additional specialist is likely to appear—a man who talks more than anybody else but is neither best liked nor most highly respected for his task ability.

It appears probable that whether the members will agree on who has the best ideas depends to a large degree on how well they agree on basic premises or norms—what we may call the "common culture." If such consensus is not present, at least implicitly, at the beginning, it may take a long time to build. While consensus on major values does not solve all the problems of arriving at a stable social organization, probably no stable organization is possible without this control factor. If it is lacking, the interaction process becomes primarily a means for the expression of individual emotional states.

Our studies have made clear that social stability is an extremely complex achievement: it takes time and patience to arrive at a common culture extensive enough and sensitive enough to regulate strong counter motives, to promote task accomplishment, to harmonize social relationships, and to rejuvenate itself whenever the conditions demand. A clear recognition of the complexity of cultural control of behavior should encourage us to believe that interminable series of meetings around the conference table, international and otherwise, are perhaps worth-while after all.

IMPLICATIONS

What impressed you most about the group behavior described in this article? How do you think you would behave in such a group? Which kind of interactor would you tend to become? Would you be either the best-liked person or the idea person?

You and your fellow students may find it interesting to form such a group, following the method used in this article. Some members of the group may be persuaded to act as volunteers, some as discussants, and some as observers. It might be good to have several observers, each attempting to record certain social behavior among the class performers and to ascertain whether trends similar to those in this article are evident.

REFERENCES

This study may be placed in the area of *group dynamics*. Selection 18 presents one of many applications of the techniques in this field. See also Cartwright and Zander (1960) and Shepherd (1964).

[26] BUDDY RATINGS: POPULARITY
CONTEST OR LEADERSHIP CRITERIA?

Buddy rating, used in military service, is a term for ratings by peers or co-workers who, by associating with a ratee during much of the day, have an opportunity to observe him in realistic situations. The following study describes the use of buddy ratings. The score is based on the number of fellow students who place the ratee among the five possessing most desirable personality traits and the number who place him among the five possessing least desirable traits. How do these buddy ratings, when analyzed, compare with supervisory ratings? Do they furnish a measure of effective performance in a complex social situation, other than the assessment of aptitude? How is a given procedure such as this tested for *reliability* or consistency and for *validity* or efficiency?

Robert J. Wherry and Douglas H. Fryer

Reprinted from Robert J. Wherry and Douglas H. Fryer, "Buddy Ratings: Popularity Contest or Leadership Criteria?" *Personnel Psychology*, Vol. 2 (Cleveland: Personnel Psychology, 1949),pp. 147–159, by permission of the publisher and the senior author.

In Brief [1]

The need for criteria against which to test predictors of leadership potential led some of the armed forces personnel research organizations to turn to "buddies," "peers" or co-workers for ratings in preference to evaluation by superiors. Industrial personnel research is also turning to this technique. There has been some criticism that "buddy ratings" are not criteria of leader-

---

[1] This study is based upon data collected in connection with Project No. 4071, Personnel Research Section, Adjutant General's Office, Department of the Army. The opinions expressed are those of the authors and do not necessarily express the official views of the Department of the Army.

ship, but rather mere popularity contests. This criticism deserves investigation. This study conducted on two officer candidate classes investigates the interrelationship of a dozen different criteria secured from several sources. These included ratings at various times throughout the six-month course by fellow students and by superiors as well as various course grades. Intensive statistical analysis of the results seem to justify the continued use of buddy ratings as leadership criteria. The buddy nominations (variable 1) measured as early as the first month of training the same factors which they measured three months later. Moreover, what they measured in the first month is the same as that rated by superiors, rating after four months' observation. The ratings by superiors measured something quite different in the first and fourth months. It was not until the fourth month that superiors' ratings reflected the leadership factor which fellow students identified in their first-month ratings.

THE SEARCH FOR CRITERIA

One problem is common to all groups engaged in personnel research. It is that of developing criteria of performance, efficiency, or behavior against which to test personnel devices, procedures, and methods. This problem is equally present in civilian and military research. In many situations, the only feasible measure consists of a rating of performance. But who can best do the rating—superiors, of whom there are at most one or two who know each worker; or co-worker, from whom a number of independent judgments can be secured?

When the war created an urgent need for research in almost every aspect of personnel, the workers in the field were faced with the need for developing criteria for numerous jobs. In many instances, selection programs were developed for training courses, and academic success could be used as a criterion for predictors in the aptitude areas. But most of the jobs for which selection was desired encompassed a great deal more than these aptitudes. Leadership, personality, and interest factors were at least as important as academic success. To secure criteria against which to test predictors in these areas, research workers were forced to fall back on ratings.

Well aware of the weaknesses of conventional rating methods, the personnel technicians sought to minimize them. To overcome the unreliability of individual ratings, they looked for situations in which a number of independent raters could be used. Even though a single rating may be unreliable, the average of a number of such ratings may provide a stable measure relatively free of bias and the idiosyncrasies of every single rater.

They recognized the fact that in any group it was easier to identify and rank the individuals who were extremely good and those who were extremely poor in the job than to rank the middle group. With only one or two raters for each man, this method identifies only extreme groups. However, with a sizable number of raters, it was possible to have each rater nominate the best four or five and the poorest four or five members of the group. Subtracting the number of "poor" from the number of "good" mentions and dividing the remainder by the number of possible mentions yielded a continuum usable for criterion purposes.

There was seldom if ever a situation in which the number of supervisors familiar with the efficiency of the worker was adequate to permit multiple nominations. For most jobs, on the other hand, there was a substantial number of co-workers in a position to observe the man's work if only they could, and would, evaluate it properly. The next natural step was to have the nominating of best and poorest workers done by the workers themselves. Many jobs lent themselves very well to this procedure. Groups in which the members worked close together, so that each worker knew the others, seemed so suited.

There were other aspects of peer or co-worker ratings that recommended this procedure to the personnel research worker. There are often aspects of a position which the co-worker is in a better position to evaluate than is the supervisor: *e.g.*, aspects of personality often carefully concealed from higher-ups.

Under the stimulus of this set of circumstances, evaluation by peers—"buddy ratings," if you will—increased in frequency in armed forces personnel research.

Like all criteria, they suffer from the need to accept them at face value. Standards against which to test them—criteria of criteria—do not usually exist. If there is available a yardstick against which to test a criterion, it would itself become the primary measure and the need for the criterion would at once vanish.

Thus, when the critics of buddy ratings objected and said they were no more than popularity contests, there was little evidence on which to refute the criticism. True, the critics offered no data in support of their contentions. Yet the burden of the proof rests with the advocates rather than with the critics of the procedure.

A RARE OPPORTUNITY

Usually the personnel research worker considers himself fortunate to be in a position to secure a single adequate criterion. In developing devices for the selection of enlisted men to attend Army Officer Candidate Schools, the staff of the Personnel Research Section found that it was in a position to collect *performance measures* * from a variety of sources. Further, it was possible to identify the situations in which several different kinds of raters were able to

* Editor's italics.

observe trainees. Finally, it was possible to observe a newly formed group that worked at a common task and whose members were in close association with each other.

THE GROUPS WE STUDIED

The studies were conducted at the Signal Corps Officer Candidate School at Fort Monmouth, N. J. The data were gathered in the summer of 1945. Two classes were studied. There were 82 officer candidates in the first class and 52 in the second.

THE VARIABLES

In addition to scores on a high-level intelligence test (Officer Candidate Test) and academic grades, *nine sets of ratings* * were collected by different methods, from different raters, and at different times. The ratings were collected from the first class (82 students) at the end of one, two, and four months in the school. In the case of the second class, ratings were collected only at the end of the first month of training. Table 1 describes the several criterion and predictor variables. . . .

In addition to the variables described in Table 1,† data were also available on the following:

Retention Beyond Two Months. Officer candidates were discharged at any time during the training period for academic inaptitude, disciplinary reasons, or failure to show promise of having the personality characteristics thought necessary in an officer. For purposes of study, each class was divided into two parts, those who were released prior to the end of the second month of work and those who were retained beyond that time.

Graduation. Failure (for any reason) to graduate from OCS and receive a commission represented a waste of time, money, and manpower. To determine the relationship between the various other variables and this personnel action, the classes were divided on the basis of whether or not each individual successfully completed the course.

Officer Candidate Test. This is a high-level pencil-and-paper test of general intelligence which had been administered to all applicants for OCS prior to their admission to the school.

Recommendation Blank. This is a standard form sent to civilian acquaintances of the applicant. The names are supplied by the candidate. It is primarily a checklist and rating form which is objectively scored.

OCS Interview. Prior to being selected to attend OCS, each candidate is interviewed by a board of officers. A standardized interview is employed and the members of the board rate the candidate on several traits observable in the interview and thought relevant to officer success. The forms are objectively scored.

Previous Performance. Ratings by noncommissioned officers under whom they had previously served were available for the officer candidates studied.

* Editor's italics.
† Condensed.

THE ANALYSIS

Four separate factorial analyses were computed. Three of the analyses were for the three sets of ratings collected in the first, second, and fourth month for class one. The fourth analysis was done for the variables collected on the second class at the end of the first month of training. Four factors were iden-

TABLE 1 *

THE CRITERION VARIABLES STUDIED

No.	Nature of Criterion
1.	*Anonymous Nominations by Students by Section:* Each student nominated 5 men in his section "who possess the personality traits least desirable in an Army officer." Score in this and other nominating criteria was: "most" mentions minus "least" mentions divided by possible mentions.
3.	*Average Leadership Ratings by Students by Section:* Every student rated each of the other students in his section for 10 leadership qualities on a school form. Each rating form was first averaged for the 10 ratings, and then all forms for a given student were in turn averaged.
5.	*Leadership Ranking by Senior Tactical Officer by Class:* The Senior Tactical Officer ranked the students in each class according to leadership. Position in the ranking was the student's score.
10.	*Average Academic Grades by Academic Instructors:* Based upon an average of daily and monthly objective examinations.

* Table 1 has been modified to describe samples of the criteria of conditions of each rating.—Ed.

tified by the analyses. The first three of these were common to all four analyses. The fourth was present only for the ratings collected from the first class in its fourth month.

Factor I. *Academic Standing.* Highest loadings for this factor are for academic grades (10),* leadership ratings by academic instructors (9), and for the Officer Candidate Test of Intelligence (11). Moderate to small, but always significant, loadings appear also on the Anonymous Nominations by Students (1) and for Average Leadership Ratings by Students (3), indicating that sectional standing among "buddies" was determined in part by the observed performance in the classroom. Student nominations by class (2) and all ratings by tactical officers (4, 5, 6, 7, 8) who were unacquainted with classroom performance showed insignificant loadings (with a slightly negative trend) on this factor. The factor is therefore identified as *Academic Standing.*

* These are the numbers of the criteria in the original Table I condensed above.—Ed.

Factor II. *Leadership*. High loadings on this factor occur for all student nominations and ratings by class or section (1, 2, 3) for all periods for both classes. While loadings are only moderate for early periods for ratings or ranking by tactical officers (4, 5), the loadings become equally high for ratings, rankings, and nominations by the tactical officers (4, 5, 6, 7, 8) after 4 months' acquaintanceship. Ratings by academic instructors (9) were low but significant, while those for grades (10) and the OCT (11) were not significant. The fact that both students and officers agree on this factor serves to identify it as *the leadership* factor which both were attempting to rate.

Factor III. *Tactical Standing*. This factor has loadings on all, and only on ratings, rankings, and nominations by tactical officers (4, 5, 6, 7, and 8). Loadings are about equally high for all periods. The lowest significant loading occurs on the officer efficiency report (8), where the nature of the forced-choice items in part controls the ratings. This factor is therefore identified as *standing in tactical performance*.

Factor IV. *Group Difference Correction*. This factor has moderate loadings on only the anonymous nominations *by class* of students (2) and tactical officers (7). The only other loading is a barely significant one for leadership ratings by junior tactical officers by class (4). This factor appears to be a *corrective element* based upon unequal range of leadership ability within the various sections.

RELIABILITY

To be at all useful, a criterion must naturally be reliable, *i.e.*, those who are rated high on the measure at one time should continue to be so rated after an elapse of time. This study permitted the comparison of a number of rating techniques on the first class after the passage of one month and again three months after the original ratings had been made. Table 2 shows these reliabilities. While student nominations and student leadership ratings were about equal in stability after the passage of one month, both were more reliable than ratings assigned by either the junior or senior tactical officers.

TABLE 2
REPEAT RELIABILITY OF SELECTED CRITERIA

Criterion	After 1 Month	After 4 Months
1. (Buddy Nominations)	.75	.58
3. (Buddy Ratings)	.76	.17
4. (Superiors' Ratings)	.42	.19
5. (Superiors' Ratings)	.58	.28

All of the reliability coefficients over a three-month period are smaller than over a one-month interval. The reliability of student nominations, however, remains at a level that may be considered useful. The reliability of the other three variables is such as to make doubtful their usefulness as criteria. In the case of the student's rating (as distinguished from nomination) and both junior and senior tactical officer ratings, it is clear that what they measure in the fourth month is something quite different than what they measure in the first month.

PREDICTABILITY

To the extent that criteria are collected for the purpose of using them as a basis for the testing and weighting of selection instruments, it is essential that they be predictable. The entire philosophy of personnel selection rests on the assumption that, to a degree at least, it is possible to predict in advance of selection which applicants for a job will be more and which less successful. If the measure of success criterion cannot be predicted even by itself, it is neither feasible nor worth-while to predict it by any battery of personnel instruments.

Table 3 compares the predictability of the nominating technique with that of academic grades for a number of possible selection instruments. Compari-

TABLE 3

PREDICTABILITY OF CRITERION 1 (BUDDY RATINGS) AND CRITERION 10 (ACADEMIC GRADES) BY VARIOUS KINDS OF PREDICTORS AFTER ONE MONTH (HIGHER COEFFICIENT IN EACH COMPARISON IS UNDERLINED)

	Buddy Ratings (Var. 1)		Academic Grades (Var. 10)	
	(1) Class (2)		(1) Class (2)	
Aptitude:				
Officer Candidate Test	.23	.29	.56	.80
Personality:				
Biographical Information Blank	.38	.43	.17	.34
Recommendation Blank	.41	.36	.12	.14
Interview	.18	.13	.05	−.04
Previous Performance:				
Ratings by Noncommissioned Officers	.19	.33	−.15	.15

sons are presented for both class one and class two. The Officer Candidate Test is the only selection instrument for which academic grade is more predictable than buddy nominations. This is gratifying, since the test was included to predict academic success. The other predictors were included to afford measures of the nonacademic aspects of leadership.

RELATION TO PERSONNEL ACTIONS

Personnel who fail the training course for a position (in this case those who do not graduate from Officer Candidate School) represent a waste of time and money. There is obviously no point in hiring employees who will never be put on the job for which they were employed or of sending men who will never become officers to Officer Candidate School. From this point of view, a desirable criterion should be fairly well related to retention in the school and to its successful completion. Table 4 compares buddy nominations and aca-

TABLE 4

CORRESPONDENCE OF CRITERION 1 (AN-S-S) AND CRITERION 10 (AAG-AI)
TO RETENTION (FOR AT LEAST 2 MONTHS) AND TO GRADUATION

	Buddy Ratings (AN-S-S)	Academic Grades (AAG-AI)
Retention (at least 2 months)	.70	.71
Graduation	.49	.50

demic grades with respect to their relationship to these personnel actions. Both criteria are equal in their relationship to separation and nongraduation. Thus it would appear that each is measuring an important aspect of success. Since the two criteria have low correlation, it is also clear that each is measuring a different aspect. In this situation, use of only one (and academic success is frequently used alone in such situations) would be doing only half the job. Obviously, ultimate success at Officer Candidate School depends as much on what buddy nominations measure as it does on what academic grades measure.

WHAT DOES IT ALL ADD UP TO?

The analysis of criteria has necessarily been predicated on what amounts to an examination of the internal relationships among the various ratings and other measures of success. The study has looked into the comparative predictability of buddy ratings and such other criteria as academic grades, attrition, and graduation. Moreover, the various available criterion measures have been shown to differ widely in their reliability.

From the analyses presented above, we may make the following tentative conclusions about the use of buddy nominations as criteria:

1. *From the factor analyses:*
   (a) Buddy ratings appear to be the purest measure of "leadership." Tactical officers are also able to rate this trait, but their ratings are quite heavily weighted by tactical standing. Academic instructor's ratings are practically useless for the evaluation of this trait.

(b) Co-workers are able, at the end of one month, to evaluate leadership to a degree equaled by instructors (tactical, not academic) only after four months of observation.

(c) Nominations (variable 1) which are more reliable than graphic ratings (variable 3) are equally good measures of leadership. They have the added advantage of being easier to secure.

(d) Nominations by class appear to be better measures of the leadership factor than any other variable. This would appear to indicate the advisability of predicting buddy ratings on the widest base upon which the acquaintanceship of the members of the group permits.

2. *From the reliability comparisons.* While both nominations and graphic ratings by co-workers show quite satisfactory reliability after one month, the reliability of nominations after four months is outstandingly higher than that of any of the other variables upon which the test was made. This is probably further evidence of the fact that the nominating technique has the property of early identification of the members of the group who constitute the two extremes of the leadership distribution.

3. *Predictability.* Except for prediction by the aptitude test, nominations were better predicted by all of the proposed selection devices than was the more commonly used academic grade criterion.

4. *Agreement with personnel action.* If ability to remain in the school at least two months is considered desirable, it may seem that nominations by buddies are as highly correlated as are academic grades, with this overall measure of success. Similarly, buddy ratings contribute as much as academic grades to the overall criterion of graduation.

IMPLICATIONS

We have here the application of psychological methodology to a complex work-a-day situation—a military training program. Observe how the psychologists have, without intrusion, found various criteria of merit in the performance of the trainees. In addition to nominations and ratings, such records as retention in training, graduation, test scores, scored recommendation blanks, and previous performance ratings were utilized and described. The authors arrived at these central variables: (1) academic standing, (2) leadership, and (3) tactical standing. Which ratings contributed most to each of these factors? To what extent can this sort of complex analysis apply to a situation in a large business enterprise? Do you have a situation in mind in which buddy ratings might contribute significantly to the evaluation of individuals?

REFERENCES

The nomination technique, utilizing peer ratings, has proved to be a promising technique for industry for a number of reasons: the number of ratees is large; the individual peer has had opportunity to observe the typical behavior of his colleagues; the opinions of group members influence an individual's actions. See Chapter IV in Anastasi (1964) for a discussion of the use of nomination and related techniques in *personal appraisal.* Weitz (1958) describes the use of peer ratings in predicting supervisory success.

[27] ULCERS IN "EXECUTIVE" MONKEYS

Fascinating experimental work introduces us to a topic that is gaining considerable popular interest—stress in the form of worry, fear, and conflict in everyday life, and its relationship to such gastrointestinal disorders as a "nervous stomach" and ulcers. The following selection relates how monkeys subjected to laboratory stress of a psychological nature developed observable gastrointestinal lesions. The study offers a good introduction to *psychosomatic diseases.*

Joseph V. Brady

Physicians and laymen alike have long recognized that emotional stress can produce bodily disease. Psychic disturbances can induce certain skin and respiratory disorders, can set off attacks of allergic asthma, and may even play a part in some forms of heart disease. Of all the body's systems, however, the gastrointestinal tract is perhaps the most vulnerable to emotional stress. The worries, fears, conflicts, and anxieties of daily life can produce gastrointestinal disorders ranging from the "nervous stomach," which most of us know at first hand, to the painful and often disabling ulcers which are the traditional occupational disease of business executives.

Emotional stress appears to produce ulcers by increasing the flow of the stomach's acid juices. The connection between emotional disturbance, stomach secretion, and ulcers is well documented. A recent study of 2,000 army

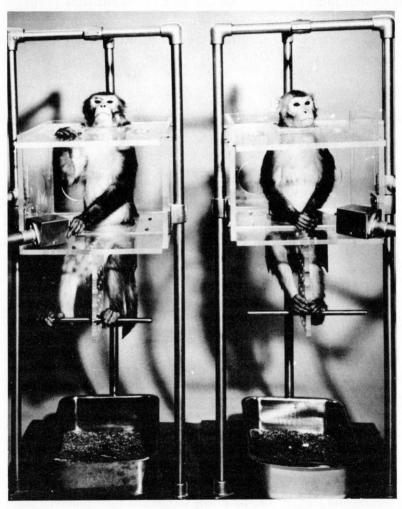

Conditioning experiment involves training monkeys in "restraining chairs." Both animals receive brief electric shocks at regular intervals. The "executive" monkey (*left*) has learned to press the lever in its left hand, which prevents shocks to both animals. The control monkey (*right*) has lost interest in its lever, which is a dummy. Only executive monkeys developed ulcers.

draftees, for example, found that those who showed emotional disturbance and excessive gastric secretion during their initial physical examination developed ulcers later on under the strains of military life.

But not every kind of emotional stress produces ulcers, and the same kind of stress will do so in one person and not in another. Experimental investigation of the problem is difficult. Animals obviously cannot provide wholly satisfactory experimental models of human mind-body interactions. They can, however, be studied under controlled conditions, and it is through animal experiments that we are finding leads to the cause of ulcers as well as to the effect of emotional stress on the organism in general.

Various investigators have succeeded in inducing ulcers in experimental animals by subjecting them to physical stress. But the role of the emotional processes in such experiments has been uncertain. Experiments on dogs by George F. Mahl of Yale University Medical School indicate that a "fear producing" situation lasting many hours increases the animals' gastric secretions, but these animals do not develop ulcers. William L. Sawrey and John D. Weisz of the University of Colorado produced ulcers in rats by subjecting them to a conflict situation: keeping them in a box where they could obtain food and water only by standing on a grid which gave them a mild electric shock. But this experiment, as Sawrey and Weisz themselves pointed out, did not prove conclusively that emotional stress was the crucial factor in producing the ulcers.

Our studies of ulcers in monkeys at the Walter Reed Army Institute of Research developed somewhat fortuitously. For several years, we had been investigating the emotional behavior of these animals. In some of our experiments, we had been keeping monkeys in "restraining chairs" (in which they could move their heads and limbs but not their bodies) while we conditioned them in various ways. Since these procedures seemed to impose considerable emotional stress on the animals, we decided that we ought to know something about their physiological reactions. Preliminary investigation showed that stress brought about dramatic alterations in the hormone content of the animals' blood, but a more extensive study of nineteen monkeys was brought to a halt when many of them died.

At first we considered this merely a stroke of bad luck, but the post-mortem findings showed that more than bad luck was involved. Many of the dead monkeys had developed ulcers as well as other extensive gastrointestinal damage. Such pathological conditions are normally rare in laboratory animals, and previous experiments with monkeys kept in restraining chairs up to six months convinced us that restraint alone did not produce the ulcers. Evidently the conditioning procedures were to blame.

One of the procedures which showed a high correlation with ulcers involved training the monkey to avoid an electric shock by pressing a lever. The animal received a brief shock on the feet at regular intervals, say, every twenty seconds. It could avoid the shock if it learned to press the lever at least once in every twenty-second interval. It does not take a monkey very long to master this problem; within a short time it is pressing the lever far oftener than once in twenty seconds. Only occasionally does it slow down enough to receive a shock as a reminder.

One possibility, of course, was that the monkeys which had developed ulcers under this procedure had done so not because of the psychological stress involved but rather as a cumulative result of the shocks. To test this possibility, we set up a controlled experiment, using two monkeys in "yoked chairs" in which both monkeys received shocks but only one monkey could prevent them. The experimental or "executive" monkey could prevent shocks to himself and his partner by pressing the lever; the control monkey's lever was a dummy. Thus both animals were subjected to the same physical stress (*i.e.*, both received the same number of shocks at the same time), but only the "executive" monkey was under the psychological stress of having to press the lever.

We placed the monkeys on a continuous schedule of alternate periods of shock avoidance and rest, arbitrarily choosing an interval of six hours for each period. As a cue for the executive monkey, we provided a red light which was turned on during the avoidance periods and turned off during the "off" hours. The animal soon learned to press its lever at a rate averaging between fifteen and twenty times a minute during the avoidance periods, and to stop pressing the lever when the red light was turned off. These responses showed no change throughout the experiment. The control monkey at first pressed the lever sporadically during both the avoidance and rest sessions, but lost interest in the lever within a few days.

After twenty-three days of a continuous six-hours-on, six-hours-off schedule the executive monkey died during one of the avoidance sessions. Our only advance warning had been the animal's failure to eat on the preceding day. It had lost no weight during the experiment, and it pressed the lever at an unflagging rate through the first two hours of its last avoidance session. Then it suddenly collapsed and had to be sacrificed. An autopsy revealed a large perforation in the wall of the duodenum—the upper part of the small intestine near its junction with the stomach, and a common site of ulcers in man. Microscopic analysis revealed both acute and chronic inflammation around this lesion. The control monkey, sacrificed in good health a few hours later, showed no gastrointestinal abnormalities. A second experiment using precisely the same procedure produced much the same results. This time the executive monkey developed ulcers in both the stomach and the duodenum; the control animal was again unaffected.

In a series of follow-up experiments . . . we have tried to isolate the physiological and psychological factors which produce the "laboratory ulcers." For example, one of our groups suggested that the "social" interaction between the two monkeys might be important. Certainly the most casual observation showed that considerable "communication" was going on between the two animals, who were seated within easy chattering distance of each other. We therefore studied several pairs of animals isolated from each other in sound-proof "telephone booths." Unfortunately, isolation failed to protect the executive monkeys, for they continued to develop ulcers.

More recently, however, we have found a factor or group of factors which does seem to be critical in producing ulcers. What we have learned seems to pivot on our chance selection of six hours as the interval for shock avoidance and for rest in the conditioning procedure. We made this discovery when we sought to improve on the results of our experiments. Though laboratory animals can rarely be made to develop ulcers, we had come upon a procedure that seemed to produce ulcers "to order." The only uncertainty was the length of exposure required. This varied greatly among individual monkeys; some came down with ulcers in eighteen days, others took as long as six weeks. If we could develop a technique guaranteed to produce ulcers in, say, ten days, we could stop the shock-avoidance sessions on the eighth or ninth day, apply various therapeutic measures, and study the monkey's response to them.

It seemed reasonable to assume that we might induce ulcers more rapidly and dependably by simply increasing the stress on the animals. We therefore put several monkeys on an eighteen-hours-on, six-hours-off schedule. After a few weeks, one of the animals died, but of tuberculosis, not ulcers. The rest continued to press their levers week after week with no apparent ill effects. Finally, when it began to seem as if we might have to wait for the animals to die of old age, we sacrificed them—and found no gastrointestinal abnormalities whatever!

We put another group on an even more strenuous schedule: thirty minutes on and thirty minutes off, with the shocks programed for every two seconds rather than every twenty. Again one of the animals died, this time of a generalized virus infection unrelated to ulcers. The others, after weeks of frantic lever-pressing, showed no gastrointestinal changes.

We had to conclude that *the crucial factor was not the degree or even the frequency of stress but was to be sought in the relationship between the length of the stress period and that of the rest period.** The six-hours-on, six-hours-off schedule had produced ulcers (and occasionally other somatic disorders) despite individual differences in monkeys, variations in diet, and maintenance routines and gross alterations in preliminary physiological tests. No other schedule we had tried produced ulcers at all.

This unexpected finding suggested that we should investigate what was going on in the monkeys' stomachs during the conditioning procedure. A standard technique for investigating gastric processes in experimental animals makes use of an artificial opening, or fistula, in the animal's abdominal and stomach walls through which the contents of its stomach can be sampled.

* Editor's italics.

Such fistulas have played an important role in expanding our knowledge of the gastrointestinal system. In the early nineteenth century, the famous U.S. Army surgeon William Beaumont made the first systematic study of the digestive process with the cooperation of a young Canadian who had a fistula due to an imperfectly healed gunshot wound. More than a century later, Stewart G. Wolf, Jr., and Harold G. Wolff at the Cornell University Medical College, with the help of a man who had a similar injury, conducted a pioneer investigation of the relationship between emotional stress and ulcers. They found that situations which produced feelings of anxiety or aggression in their subject stepped up his gastric secretions and engorged his stomach wall with blood. Physiological changes of this sort, they believed, are the precursors of ulcers.

Edwin Polish of our department of neuroendocrinology has been studying the stomach acidity of some of our executive monkeys by means of artificial fistulas. His measurements, though far from complete, seem to provide one possible explanation of the results of our experiments.

The stomach secretions of the executive monkeys do indeed become considerably more acid, but not (as one might expect) during the avoidance periods. When the animals are actually pressing the levers, the acidity of their stomachs rises little. The significant increase in acidity begins at the end of the avoidance session and reaches a peak several hours later, while the animal is presumably resting. This finding suggests a close relationship between the formation of ulcers and the cyclic character of the six-hours-on, six-hours-off procedure. *Emotional stress, it appears, must be intermittent—turning the animal's system on and off, so to speak—if it is to cause ulcers.** Continuous emotional stress seems to permit a stable adjustment (at least for a while) under which ulcers do not develop. It is tempting to consider the analogy of the vacuum tube or light bulb which seems to last much longer under conditions of continuous current than when it is subjected to frequent heating and cooling.

Like most analogies, this one limps badly and has its limitations. For example, our experiments show that periodic stress does not always bring on ulcers, and Polish's findings are consistent with this. His measurements indicate that the greatest increase in acidity occurs after a six-hour avoidance session. After a three-hour session, acidity rises, but less sharply; after a one-hour session, it does not rise at all. Periodic emotional stress apparently causes ulcers only if its period coincides with that of some natural rhythm of the gastrointestinal system.

Obviously our knowledge of the physiological and psychological processes which produce ulcers is far from complete. Our understanding of even the relatively well-controlled experiments I have described is just beginning to progress beyond the primitive level. We have yet to discover why emotional

* Editor's italics.

stress steps up the stomach's acidity later rather than immediately. We are still looking for a method of producing ulcers at will, in days rather than weeks. Eventually we hope to learn to detect an incipient ulcer before the animal collapses, by examining the subject's blood, urine, and other secretions, thus making post-mortem examinations unnecessary.

There are many other questions about the effects of emotional stress which we have not yet begun to investigate. Really thorough examination of the experimental animals might well show other types of damage of which we are at present unaware. The two monkeys which died of causes unrelated to ulcers, for example, may have succumbed because their resistance had been lowered in some way by psychological stress. It would be surprising to find physical processes wholly unimpaired in monkeys who have been on a thirty-minutes-on, thirty-minutes-off schedule for several weeks. The opportunity to bring psychosomatic relationships under experimental scrutiny in the laboratory seems to open broad horizons for research into the causes and alleviation of this poorly understood class of ills.

IMPLICATIONS

Briefly state what conditions did and did *not* produce ulcers in the animal. What conditions do you think might produce similar psychosomatic disorders in man? Can you conceive of some possible means of prevention, particularly for persons under pressure?

REFERENCES

See comments under "References" in the next selection, by Selye.

[28] THE STRESS OF LIFE

How does one deal with the stress of modern life—the *pressures, frustrations, conflicts,* and *anxieties* that take their toll in emotional, social, and psychosomatic disturbances? Selye, a well-respected scientist working on the psychological effects of stress on animals and men, summarizes these effects in his book, *The Stress of Life.*

Hans Selye

THE STRESS-QUOTIENT

These facts, which have been established by laboratory experiments on rats, also hold remarkably true when applied to the daily problems of man, including even his purely mental activities. In analyzing our stress-status, we must always think, not only of the total amount of stress in the body, but also of its proportionate distribution between various parts. To put this into the simplest terms, we might say that the stress-quotient to be watched is:

$$\frac{\text{local stress in any one part}}{\text{total stress in the body}}$$

If there is proportionately too much stress in any one part, you need diversion. If there is too much stress in the body as a whole, you must rest.

THE IMPORTANCE OF DEVIATION

Deviation is the act of turning something (for instance, a biologic mechanism) aside from its course. It is not necessarily a pleasant and relaxing diversion. We have seen, for instance, how severe shock (electroshock, drug shock) can—through its general stress effect upon all parts—deviate the body's somatic or psychic defense reactions from a habitual stereotyped course.

When the concentration of effort in any one part of our body or mind is not very intense and chronic, as we all know from experience, milder types of deviation are often quite effective (sports, dancing, music, reading, travel, whisky, chewing gum). These do not have to act primarily through the stress mechanism and the pituitary-adrenal axis, but they always cause a decentralization of our efforts, which often helps to restore a lopsided stress-quotient toward normal.

Deviation is particularly important in combating purely mental stress. Everyone knows how much harm can be caused by worry. The textbooks of psychosomatic medicine are full of case reports describing the production of gastric ulcers, hypertension, arthritis, and many other diseases by chronic worry about moral and economic problems. *Nothing is accomplished by telling such people not to worry.* They cannot help it. Here again, the best remedy is deviation, or general stress. By highlighting some other problem, through deviation, or by activating the whole body, by general stress, the source of worry automatically becomes less important in proportion.

This fact can be consciously used in practice. Of course, for a person who is to undergo a very dangerous surgical operation, or who finds himself on the verge of economic disaster, it is impossible to stop worrying just by deciding not to—especially if he is the worrying kind. *You must find something to put in the place of the worrying thoughts to chase them away.* This is deviation. If such a person undertakes some strenuous task which needs all his attention, he may still not forget his worries, but they will certainly fade. Nothing erases unpleasant thoughts more effectively than conscious concentration on pleasant ones. Many people do this subconsciously, but unless you know about the mechanism of diversion, it is difficult to do it well. Some neurotics compulsively concentrate on the most extraordinary and harmful things in the course of subconscious efforts to divert themselves from sexual frustrations. Psychoanalysts call this *sublimation,* which is defined as "the act of directing the energy of an impulse from its primitive aim to one that is culturally or ethically higher." I would not know about that; but it is deviation.

Incidentally, another practically important aspect of deviation is the development of a competition between memory and learning power. It seems that to some extent *newly learned facts occupy the place of previously learned or subsequently learnable ones.* Consequently there is a limit to how much you can burden your memory; and trying to remember too many things is certainly one of the major sources of psychologic stress. I make a conscious effort to forget immediately all that is unimportant and to jot down data of possible value (even at the price of having to prepare complex files). Thus I manage to keep my memory free for facts which are truly essential to me. I think this technique can help anyone to accomplish the greatest simplicity compatible with the degree of complexity of his intellectual life....

THE ULTIMATE AIM

As I see it, man's ultimate aim is *to express himself as fully as possible, according to his own lights.* Whether he seeks this by establishing harmony and communion with his Maker or with nature, he can do so only by finding that balance between long- and short-range aims, between sowing and harvesting, which best fits his own individuality.

The goal is certainly not to avoid stress. Stress is part of life. It is a natural by-product of all our activities; there is no more justification for avoiding stress than for shunning food, exercise, or love. But, in order to express yourself fully, you must first find your optimum stress level and then use your adaptation energy at a rate and in a direction adjusted to the innate structure of your mind and body.

The study of stress has shown that complete rest is not good, either for the body as a whole, or even for any organ within the body. Stress, applied in moderation, is necessary for life. Besides, enforced inactivity may be very harmful and cause more stress than normal activity.

I have always been against the advice of physicians who would send a high-strung, extremely active business executive to a long, enforced exile in some health resort, with the view of relieving him from stress by absolute inactivity. Naturally ambitious and active men often become much more tense when they feel frustrated by not being allowed to pursue their usual activities; if they cannot express themselves through actions, they spend the time worrying about what might be going on in their business during their absence.

At the risk of sounding facetious, let me present a little motto which I developed while analyzing stress in my experimental animals, in my colleagues, my friends, and myself. It may sound trivial and purely abstract, but it is based on solid biologic laws and—at least in my case—it works. Whatever happens during the day to threaten my equanimity or throw some doubt upon the value of my actions, I just think of this little jingle:

> Fight always for the highest attainable aim
> But never put up resistance in vain.

Everyone should *fight* for whatever seems really worthwhile to him. On the other hand, he should aim only for *things attainable* to him, for otherwise he will merely become frustrated. Finally, *resistance* should be put up whenever there is reasonable expectation of its succeeding, but never if we know it would be *in vain*.

It is not easy to live by this motto; it takes much practice and almost constant self-analysis. Any time during the day, in discussions, at work and at play, when I begin to feel keyed up, I consciously stop to analyze the situation. I ask myself: "Is this really the best thing I could do now, and is it worth the trouble of putting up resistance against counterarguments, boredom, or fatigue?" If the answer is no, I just stop; or whenever this cannot be done gracefully I simply "float" and let things go on as they will, with a minimum of active participation (*e.g.*, during most committee meetings, solemn academic ceremonies, and unavoidable interviews with crackpots).

Probably few people would be inclined to contest the soundness of this motto. The trick is to follow it! But that is where my assistance must stop. That is where you come in. This may sound like an anticlimactic ending, but it really should not. We all must live our own lives. No self-respecting person wants to go from cradle to grave sheepishly following the directives of another man.

IMPLICATIONS
Try to reword in meaningful terms the major ideas in the preceding excerpt from Selye. When do you feel stress? What situations offer you stress? What deviations are relaxing and satisfying in your ultimate aims to succeed in your vocation? How do you evaluate the author's advice about striving for the attainable? To what extent does Selye answer some of the questions Brady raised in the previous selection on ulcers in executive monkeys?

REFERENCES
You might find Selye's (1956) entire volume valuable. You should see some relationship between this article and the one by Barron, Selection 5. You might even relate the Selye selection to Jung and the associated comments in Selection 64.

[29] THE INDIVIDUAL AS A MEMBER OF MULTIPLE GROUPS

The term *organization man*, the title of a popular book of a few years ago, has become part of our vocabulary. William H. Whyte, an editor of *Fortune* Magazine, wrote about life under the protection of the big organization which promises security and a high standard of living. As a result of this organization life, Whyte maintains the American is turning from *ideals of hard work, thrift, and competitive struggle* to an ethic that emphasizes the *group* as a source of creativity, belief in *belonging* as the ultimate need, and use of science to achieve these ends. Further, he sees an inhibiting of individual initiative and imagination, an emphasis on techniques over content, stress upon the skills of attaining a goal isolated from the ultimate goal. Whyte, along with David Riesman (1950), and others, emphasizes the strength of conformity to external forces rather than to individual values.

To look into the question of the effect of groups on individuals, we might turn to a summary statement by Anne Anastasi in *Differential*

Psychology, an impressive volume on individual differences. She analyzes the nature of a variety of psychological groups and then succinctly discusses individuality in terms of group influences.

Anne Anastasi

Reprinted with permission of The Macmillan Company from *Differential Psychology* by Anne Anastasi. Third Edition © The Macmillan Company, 1958.

THE INDIVIDUAL AS A MEMBER OF MULTIPLE GROUPS

Psychologically the individual belongs to every group with which he shares behavior.[1] From this point of view, group membership is to be defined in terms of behavioral rather than biological categories. The effective grouping is not based upon the individual's race or sex or body build, but upon his experiential background. Thus if the individual is reared as a member of a certain national group with its own traditions and cultural background and its own peculiar complex of stimulating conditions, he will display the behavioral characteristics of that group regardless of his racial origin. It should be understood, of course, that mere physical presence does not constitute group membership in a psychological sense. If a Negro child were brought up in a community composed exclusively of whites, he would not necessarily receive the same social stimulation as a white child. Similarly, a boy who is brought up exclusively by female relatives will not develop the personality traits of a girl. A psychological group is based solely upon shared behavior and not upon geographical proximity or biological resemblance.

It follows from such a concept of group that any one individual is effectively a member of a large and varied set of groups. A *multiplicity of behavioral groups,* large and small, cut across each other in the individual's background.... The individual is born into a broad cultural division such as, for example, "Western civilization," with its characteristic sources of stimulation. He will develop certain aptitudes, emotional traits, attitudes, and beliefs as a result of his affiliation with this group. He is also a member of a given national group with its more specific traditional ways of acting.

If the individual displays certain physical characteristics, such as a particular skin color, facial conformation, and body build, he may be classified as a

---

[1] This criterion of a psychological group is essentially that formulated by Kantor (1929), who seems to have been the first to discuss social behavior in terms of *shared responses* to objects having common stimulus functions.

member of a given "racial" group which occupies a distinct position within the broader national division. Insofar as his racial background leads to certain social distinctions and culturally imposed differentiations of behavior, it will operate as an effective grouping. The same may be said of sex. If, within a given society, traditional beliefs in regard to sex differences exist so that the sexes are exposed to dissimilar psychological stimulation, then the individual's sex will in part determine his behavioral characteristics.

There are a number of other behavioral groupings which, although less frequently recognized and less clearly defined, may be equally influential in the individual's development. Thus it will be recalled that important psychological differences are usually found between the city-bred and country-bred child, as well as between different social classes. Similarly, the particular state, province, or other major division of a nation in which the individual is reared, and even the specific town and neighborhood in which he lives, will exert significant influences upon his intellectual and emotional development.

Other groups with which an individual identifies himself behaviorally include his occupational class, his religion, his political party, his club, his educational institution. That such groupings represent clear-cut cultural distinctions is readily illustrated by the stereotypes which have become attached to many of these groups. To people within our society, a distinct picture will be suggested by the mention of such designations as country doctor, businessman, Roman Catholic, Orthodox Jew, Republican, Rotarian, Harvard man. These groups influence the individual's behavior in two ways. First, they directly stimulate and foster certain ways of acting. Secondly, the reactions of other people to the individual are influenced by their knowledge of his group affiliation. The social attitudes and "social expectancy" which the individual encounters will in turn affect his behavior.

Family groupings, with their characteristic activities and traditions, constitute another important part of the individual's psychological environment. The degenerate Jukes and Kallikaks, eminent families such as the Huxleys and the Darwins, and many other striking examples testify to the cultural influence of family membership. Cutting across such family groupings are age distinctions. "Stages" are socially imposed upon the continuous life activities of the individual and he is treated more or less differently at each period. The individual may also look upon himself as belonging to a particular generation —he may be a member of the "older generation," the "young married set," the "teen-agers," and so forth. Even such apparently minor factors as one's hobbies and recreations will, in turn, affect the individual's subsequent behavior. Psychological membership in many new groups may result from a newly developed interest in bowling, stamp collecting, or early American pressed glass. The number of behavioral groupings could easily be multiplied. These examples will suffice to illustrate the nature of such groupings and their effect upon behavior development.

The individual may be regarded partly as a resultant of his multiple group memberships. To be sure, each individual also undergoes experiences that are absolutely unique to himself. Such experiences are probably less significant, however, in shaping the more basic aspects of his personality than is his shared behavior. The experiences that are common to a group of individuals have a certain degree of permanence in the sense that they will tend to be repeated more often and to be corroborated or re-enforced by other similar experiences. In general, the more highly organized the group, the more consistent and systematic will be the experiences its members undergo. This will tend to make the shared experiences on the whole more effective than the purely individual. Moreover, even the individual's idiosyncratic experiences will generally have certain cultural features which differentiate them from the idiosyncratic experiences of persons in other cultures. Thus an individual may compose a poem which is unique in its totality and to this extent unlike any poem ever written by any other person; but the fact that the poem is a political satire, that it is composed in the English language and in iambic pentameter, and that it is written with a ball-point pen are among the many distinctly cultural features of such an activity.

In view of the pronounced effect of such shared or common behavior upon the individual's development, it may appear surprising that individuals are no more alike in their behavior repertoire than we ordinarily find them to be. The extent of individual differences within any one group is extremely large. In fact, the variations among individuals have always proved to be more marked than the differences from one group to another. How can the "individuality" of each person be explained in terms of his shared experiential background?

The key to this problem seems to lie in the *multiplicity* of overlapping groups with which the individual may be behaviorally identified. The number of such groups is so great that the *specific combination* is unique for each individual. Not only does this furnish a stimulational basis for the existence of wide individual differences, but it also suggests a mechanism whereby the individual may "rise above" his group. There are many examples of individuals who have broken away from the customs and traditional ways of acting of their group. Through such situations, modifications of the group itself may also be effected.

In these cases the individual is not reacting contrary to his past experience, as might at first appear. This would be psychologically impossible. His behavior is the result of psychological membership in various *conflicting* groups. Many group memberships can exist side by side in a composite behavioral adjustment. But in certain cases two or more groups may foster different ways of reacting to the same situation. This enables the individual to become aware of the arbitrariness of the restrictions and tradition of each group, to evaluate them critically, and to regard them more "objectively." Membership in many diverse groups frees the individual from the intellectual and other limitations of each group and makes possible the fullest development of "individuality."

IMPLICATIONS

Does Anastasi have the same views as Whyte? If not, can you express the difference between their views? From Anastasi's analysis, how do you evaluate the force of individuality in a democracy like ours? To what extent do you think membership in multiple groups will free the individual from the *conformity forces* of the centralized mass media— advertising, television, radio, and magazines? To what overlapping cultural groups do you belong?

REFERENCES

Whyte's book (1956) is stimulating reading and Riesman's (1950) has become a classic.

Chapter VI

INDUSTRY
AND PUBLIC
RELATIONS

[30] THE PSYCHOLOGY OF LABOR-MANAGEMENT RELATIONS

How can the science of psychology serve a major modern industrial interaction—labor-management relationships? What roles can the psychologist play? What perspectives and techniques can he bring to the scene?

In the following outline, an excerpt from their book, *Psychology Applied to Industry*, Dunnette and Kirchner review the suggestions made by four psychologists. The outline alludes to services described in detail in other selections in this book. The clinical role is treated in Selection 56. Pertinent to the experimentalist's role are Selection 31, on safety, and Selection 49, on automation and human engineering. The role of the professional expert, analyzing interaction of people in conferences is shown well in Selection 25. Selection 39 deals with communication. The psychologist as a social scientist is reflected in Selection 36.

Treatment of the roles the psychologist can play has relevance for other areas of our social industrial America than that of labor-management relations, as evident in the references.

Marvin D. Dunnette and Wayne K. Kirchner

The Role of the Psychologist

... What can we say now about the proper role of the industrial psychologist in studying labor-management relations? There are at least four different roles that he may be called upon to play. These are

1. *Clinician.* Stagner (1963) sees the psychologist's role as one of helping to eliminate the childish and irrational components in the labor-management conflict. The major aim of the psychologist, in his role as a clinician, is to help parties in the conflict to achieve better understanding of themselves and of others. The psychologist's activities in selection, training, and policy planning can, of course, contribute to better understanding indirectly, but Stagner calls for a more direct approach focused on eliminating the misperceptions and personality problems detrimental to successful collective bargaining. Viewed in this way, the psychologist becomes primarily a communications link between labor and management, helping to interpret the union to management and vice versa.

2. *Experimentalist.* Barkin (1961), in discussing the generally negative view of psychology held by union members, sees the experimental or engineering psychologist as most capable of improving psychologists' image among union members. Anything done to make jobs safer and healthier is of obvious value; thus, the engineering psychologist's concern with the effects of equipment design and factors in the physical environment (heat, lighting, noise, etc.) on human endeavor fits him well for contributing to improved relations between labor and management. Barkin states that the findings of experimental and engineering psychologists need to be more broadly recognized and popularized.

3. *Professional expert.* Levenstein (1961) sees the psychologist in union-management relations as a professional expert, following in the footsteps of the industrial engineer and the lawyer who have preceded him. He points to a parallel between management's use of their services and those of psychologists. At first, unions distrusted both industrial engineers and lawyers, but soon they, too, began to seek aid from them in negotiations, handling of grievances, and arbitrations. Levenstein believes that the psychologist is in a similar position and that he is gaining more and more acceptance on both sides of the labor-management conflict. He believes that the industrial psychologist should be used as a professional expert, called in to gather facts

from which the negotiations may proceed. In other words, the role of the psychologist can be one of providing information to aid in reducing the areas of uncertainty between the two sides.

4. *Social scientist.* Shepard (1961) feels that the role of the psychologist in union-management relations should be to investigate experimentally the conditions under which real conflicts of interests are perceived and the manner in which they may be most easily resolved. In this role, the psychologist is primarily a researcher and a problem solving strategist. In promoting a problem-solving point of view, the psychologist would, therefore, help to dissipate the win-lose attitude so common now in collective bargaining, and he would help to create the conditions in which both sides would use their creative abilities in a joint effort to advance the interests of both.

Here then are four views of the psychologists involved in labor-management relations, clinician, social scientist, experimental psychologist, and professional expert. At present, unfortunately, it is rare for psychologists to have formally assigned responsibilities directly involving labor-management relations; however, it should be apparent from the above that the significance and diversity of his potential contributions are great. In fact, a psychologist simply by working in the industrial setting, can have a strong impact on the nature of union-management relations even if he is given no formal responsibility for them. Feinberg (1961) has pointed out that the industrial psychologist's concern with human behavior in industry automatically affects the fate of both union members and of the management team. The kinds of things the psychologist works with—employee selection, personnel training, human motivation, organizational form and structure—all have profound and presumably beneficial effects on the nature of employment relationships in industry. Thus, it is abundantly clear that the psychologist is in a central position from which to effect improved and more sensible labor-management relationships in the years ahead.

IMPLICATIONS

What do the other selections in this book illustrate concerning the four roles suggested for the psychologist? Mention is made in this article of employee selection, personnel training, human motivation, organizational form, and structure. What selections in this book refer to these topics? In what other situations requiring mediation may the psychologist lend a hand?

REFERENCES

Consult the Bibliography for references cited in the article.

[31] ACCIDENTS: CONTEMPORARY THEORIES OF SAFETY PSYCHOLOGY

You may have heard the phrase "accident proneness," a tendency for an individual to have repeated accidents in a given area of activity. How valid do you think this concept is? What are other psychological explanations of accidents? To what extent are unusual and distracting environmental stresses associated with accident frequencies? Will the frequency of accidents be reduced by the kind of environment that allows the worker freedom to set attainable goals and rewards him for being alert?

The following selection considers various explanations of accidents and summarizes interesting facts on accidents and their correlates.

Willard Kerr

Reprinted from Willard Kerr, "Contemporary Theories of Safety Psychology," *Journal of Social Psychology*, 45 (Provincetown: The Journal Press, 1957), pp. 3–9, with permission.

BACKGROUND

Probably the most universally ignored area of safety psychology is that pertaining to the psychological climate of the workplace. A devotion to safety gadgets on the one hand and concern for the alleged proneness factors within the accident repeater on the other hand 'has led to the almost total neglect of the situational factors which help shape work personality and help manufacture accident-free or accident-liable employees.

Many investigators (Van Zelst, 1954) have shown that becoming a safe worker is a typical learning function. The decline in accidents from date of employment in the typical job is a representative learning curve. But like other learning curves, the decline in error performance can be obstructed by a multitude of other factors. It now appears that *a chief obstruction to the rapid decline in error performance is defective psychological climate.* This

* Editor's italics.

conclusion, to be supported in this paper, stands in sharp contrast to past emphasis upon the accident proneness theory.

THE ACCIDENT PRONENESS THEORY

Before presenting the crucial evidence on this theory, the term "accident proneness" should be defined. *Accident proneness* is a constitutional (*i.e.*, permanent) tendency within the organism to engage in unsafe behavior within some stated field of vocational activity. A temporary tendency to have accidents is not proneness; it is liability. And proneness is not general; that is, its referrent to an activity field must be limited to be meaningful, for, obviously, *everyone* is "accident prone" in a general sense because there are potential tasks that no human being can perform without accident (*e.g.*, climb the outside walls of the Empire State Building to the top with one's bare hands).

Professors Mintz and Blum (1949) and Maritz (1950) have shown that the *accident proneness theory has been explaining entirely too much of the industrial accident rate.** The research of Cobb (1938–39), Johnson (1946) Whitlock and Crannell (1949), Forbes (1939), Farmer and Chambers (1929), and Harris (1949) point toward the same conclusion. Mintz and Blum showed that the frequency of "repeater" accidents approximates a pure chance (Poisson) distribution. Maritz then suggested that the final crucial test of variance in the industrial accident rate accounted for by proneness is the correlation between one's accidents experienced over two different periods of accident exposure—such as the last two years and the next two years. Ghiselli and Brown (1948) have collated eighteen such coefficients from the literature, and the present author has computed their median; it is .38. This typical value suggests that only about 15 per cent of the variance in individual accidents is accounted for by variance in individual accident proneness; furthermore, this even may be spuriously high because such coefficients are contaminated by the correlation of the worker's position hazard with the consistency of his accidents over split time periods. In fact, it is almost certain that much, if not most, of this 15 per cent of potential variance due to accident proneness actually is due to environmental factors (temperature differences, fumes, congestion-space-threat differences, etc.) left uncontrolled and hence correlated with each other in the eighteen coefficients cited.

Even allowing the unreasonable assumption that these eighteen coefficients were not influenced by fatigue and stress differences in different job locations, the 15 per cent of variance in accidents "accounted for" by proneness still leaves 85 per cent of the variance in accident rates unaccounted for.

It is interesting that an earlier study of automobile drivers by Forbes (1939) arrived independently at the similar conclusion that the accident *repeater contributes not more than three or four per cent to the accident prob-*

* Editor's italics.

*lem.** Both Johnson (1946) and Thorndike (1951) who later surveyed the entire research literature on automobile safety likewise found that such constitutional factors as basic aptitudes yielded negligible relationships with accident records. Relevant, also, is the fact that Hunt, Wittson, and Burton (1950) computed the psychiatric discharge rate at Naval induction stations and subsequently during World War II to vary between 4 and 9 per cent (such dischargees were, of course, those individuals regarded as "prone" to behavior unsafe to themselves and/or their country).

Two situational or climatic theories may explain the remaining non-chance variance.

THE GOALS-FREEDOM-ALERTNESS THEORY

Plainly, both management and union training activities, policies, and leaderships are responsible for some interference with the normal decline of error performance.

In stating this theory now, we hold that *great freedom to set reasonably attainable goals is accompanied typically by high quality work performance.* This theory regards an accident merely as a low-quality work behavior—a "scrappage" that happens to a person instead of to a thing. Raising the level of quality involves raising the level of alertness; such high alertness cannot be sustained except within a rewarding psychological climate. The more rich, therefore, the climate in diverse (economic and noneconomic) reward opportunities, the higher the level of alertness—and the higher the level of work quality. Obviously, the rewards system must be geared to support high-quality work behavior.

In business practice some training interferes by too much "telling what to do and what not to do" and too little encouragement to the new worker to do his own thinking and "stand on his own feet." Union leadership likewise often is guilty of too much propagandizing and not enough "asking" in relations with new workers. Such initial climate for the new worker is less conducive to alertness than to a relatively unmotivated, resigned, passive conformity to the apparently already structured total situation.

Accidents, of course, show that the total situation is *not* firmly structured and from them the worker gradually accepts more self responsibility in order to survive. But an accident is an expensive teaching device. Furthermore, if it occurs in a climate in which the employee is expected to supply his energy but not his opinions or ideas, the accident is misunderstood as a foreign intruder which does not belong in the scheme of events. In such circumstances, it rarely occurs to management, union, or worker that an accident is made necessary and inevitable in order to teach the employee his own individuality and essential personal dignity.

* Editor's italics.

Even the teaching efficiency of the accident itself is interfered with, however, if most aspects of the total psychological climate in effect deny that the individual's own mental content is important.

If the climate encourages the individual to set up long-term and short-term goals with reasonable probability of attainment, the *Gestalt* of the work situation seems less fixed and the worker feels himself to be a significant participant. Significant participation makes for habits of alertness, problem-raising, and problem-solving. The psychological work environment must *reward the worker emotionally for being alert,** for seeking to contribute constructive suggestions, for passing a tip to a co-worker on how best to do something or how not to get hurt, and for achievement out of the ordinary. The worker must feel free to exercise influence over his environment.

Considerable evidence supports this theory. Factory departments with more movement of personnel among departments, that is, intra-company transfer mobility, have fewer accidents (Kerr, 1950), the same is true of departments with greater promotion probability for the typical employee (*r* is $-.40$). Departments with the best suggestion records (rewarded) tend to have fewer accidents. Additional evidence of the influence of the stimulating individual climate on safety is found in the tendency toward fewer accidents in individual-type than in crew-type jobs at the International Harvester Works (Keenan, *et al.*, 1951). In individual-type work, the employee rarely is uncertain about his responsibility for consequences; he better knows his immediate work goals. Another interesting bit of evidence is that in two different studies (Keenan, *et al.*, 1951; Kerr, 1950) the factory departments with incentive pay systems, although problem departments in regards to monotony, lower job prestige, and lower promotion probability, still have no more accidents than departments without incentive pay systems. This seems in such defiance of expectations as to suggest that incentive pay systems restrict accidents by encouraging greater individual initiative and alertness.

Accidents are more frequent in jobs of lower-rated prestige (Keenan, *et al.*, 1951; Kerr, 1950); one interpretation of this finding is that climatically the job must seem worthy enough to the worker to sustain his euphoria level. This interpretation is supported by the finding of Hersey (1936) that out of 400 accidents which were studied clinically, more than half took place when the worker was in a worried, apprehensive, or some other low emotional state.

This individual goals-freedom-alertness theory suggests the climatic need for providing emotional reward opportunities for alertness—such as special economic incentives, prestige-building honors, extra privileges, machine and work space decoration contest participation, and representation on special committees and councils. These rewards held as attainable goals by workers in relatively "dead end" jobs should operate to raise the average level of alertness, not just to hazards but to everything.

* Editor's italics.

THE ADJUSTMENT STRESS THEORY

The individual goals-opportunity-alertness theory of safety seems to cover much of the variance not covered by the proneness theory, but some variance still remains and it appears necessary to verbalize a third theory. Probably almost all of the remaining variance can be explained by a third theory—*an adjustment stress theory. It holds that unusual, negative, distracting stress upon the organism increases its liability to accident or to other low-quality behavior.* This too is a climatic theory, because environment is internal as well as external, and this theory refers to distractive negative stresses imposed upon the individual organism either by internal environment (such as disease organisms, alcohol, or toxic items) or by external environment (such as temperature excesses, poor illumination, excessive noise level, excessive physical work strain). Its stresses are different from those experienced by the accident prone; their stresses result from a *constitutional* inadequacy. Ordinary adjustment stress is *not* the result of constitutional inadequacy but of temporary conditions.

What often appears at first to be constitutional accident proneness may be shown very clearly upon more careful examination to be the operation of *temporary* stress factors. The most sobering example of this is found in the curve of accident rates of successive age groups of industrial workers (Kerr, 1950). This curve shows high rates in the first ten years of the worklife and a secondary increase in rates between the ages of forty and fifty-five. These age periods also are the great stress periods in the typical worklife; this is suggested by the fact that the accident-rate curve and the turnover-rate curve superimpose almost perfectly upon each other when plotted through successive age groups of the industrial population. The alleged proneness within the young accident repeater is largely dissipated when one considers that most of the stress is environmental—and associated with adjustment to work discipline, attaining self-sufficiency away from parental ties, courtship, marriage, assumption of family economic responsibilities, and the struggle for a foothold on a vocational ladder that seems to lead somewhere worth-while. Another set of obvious stress explanations comes to mind to account for the "middle-age boom" in accident rate.

Temporary stress factors which already have been found significantly correlated with accident rates include employee age (Kerr, 1950), workplace temperature (Griffith, 1950), illumination (Vernon, *et al.*, 1931), mean rated comfort of the shop (r is $-.70$), degree of operational congestion, obvious danger factor threateningly present, manual effort involved in job (r is .47), weight of parts handled, frequency of parts handled (Keenan, *et al.*, 1951), alcohol consumption (Vernon, 1937), and influence of disease organisms (Newbold, 1919).

COMPLEMENTARY LIMITATIONS AND INTERPRETATIONS

It seems wise to emphasize that both of these new theories of safety complement each other as well as existing proneness theory. In the goals-freedom-alertness theory it must be recognized that (a) even under an optimal opportunity climate, individuals who lack the characteristics necessary for the work probably will continue to have accidents; (b) excessive physical stresses can cause accidents in any psychological climate; and (c) psychological stresses relative to adjustment to changing life aspirations, family and marital affairs, etc., still will carry over into the workplace psychological climate and cause accidents.

In the adjustment stress theory it must be admitted that individual differences do exist in ability to withstand what ordinarily would be stress-inducing situations. Yet, such individual differences account for less than one fifth of the variance in individual accident rates; therefore, the limitations on the accident proneness theory appear to be much more severe than those on the adjustment stress theory. The fact is that both employer judgment and job applicant judgment operate to prevent the operation of any great amount of accident proneness. While all of us are accident prone for one task or another, we don't ordinarily apply for or allow ourselves to be engaged in such tasks— and we probably couldn't get hired for such tasks if we tried.

On the basis of the evidence summarized and the author's own estimates, the variance in accident rates among industrial personnel probably distributes in terms of theoretical causation according to the following pattern:

Accident proneness	1% to 15%
Individual goals-opportunity-alertness	30% to 40%
Adjustment stress	45% to 60%
Total Variance	100%

Constructive thinking about the individual goals-opportunity-climate and about adjustment stresses should assist industry to escape the defeatism of the overly emphasized proneness theory and better understand and control accidents.

IMPLICATIONS

How many accidents—even minor ones that have caused slight injury or little destruction of property—have you had in your life? Have they occurred under similar conditions? If so, describe these conditions. Do your accidents seem to be due to a constitutional proneness, an *accident liability* (a temporary tendency), or can you relate them to the psychological climate at the time of the accident?

What do the theories supported by the data presented in this article suggest to you regarding the prevention of accidents in your daily life? Can you suggest specific conditions that should prevail to lower accident frequency or prevent accidents?

REFERENCES

Consult the Bibliography for references cited in the article. See also Greenwood and Woods (1919), Kitson (1922), and McGuire (1955).

[32] ACHIEVEMENT DRIVE AND ECONOMIC GROWTH

Do you realize that as an American youth you in all probability have strong achievement needs?

Here we have a selection by a psychologist who has developed methods for assessing differences in achievement motivation and has related this factor to effective business management and to the broader problems of achieving cultures or achieving societies. How does he assess individual achievement? What is the pattern of behavior found in the achieving personality?

David C. McClelland

Reprinted from David C. McClelland, "Business Drive and National Achievement," *Harvard Business Review,* July–August (Boston: Harvard University, 1962), pp. 99–112, by permission of the publisher and the author.

What accounts for the rise in civilization? Not external resources (*i.e.,* markets, minerals, trade routes, or factories), but the entrepreneurial spirit which exploits those resources—a spirit found most often among businessmen.

Who is ultimately responsible for the pace of economic growth in poor countries today? Not the economic planners or the politicians, but the executives whose drive (or lack of it) will determine whether the goals of the planners are fulfilled.

Why is Russia developing so rapidly that—if it continues its present rate of growth—it will catch up economically with the most advanced country in the world, the United States, in 25 or 30 years? Not, as the U.S.S.R. claims, because of the superiority of its Communist system, but because—by hook or by crook—it has managed to develop a strong spirit of entrepreneurship among its executives.

How can foreign aid be most efficiently used to help poor countries develop rapidly? Not by simply handing money over to their politicians or budget makers, but by using it in ways that will select, encourage, and develop those of their business executives who have a vigorous entrepreneurial spirit or a strong drive for achievement. In other words: *invest in a man, not just in a plan.*

What may be astonishing about some of these remarks is that they come from a college professor, and not from the National Association of Manufacturers. They are not the defensive drum rattlings of an embattled capitalist, but are my conclusions, based on nearly fifteen years of research, as a strictly academic psychologist, into the human motive that appears to be largely responsible for economic growth—research which has recently been summarized in my book, entitled *The Achieving Society* (McClelland, 1961).

Since I am an egghead from way back, nothing surprises me more than finding myself rescuing the businessman from the academic trash heap, dusting him off, and trying to give him the intellectual respectability that he has had a hard time maintaining for the last fifty years or so. For the fact is that the businessman has taken a beating, not just from the Marxists, who pictured him as a greedy capitalist, and the social critics, who held him responsible for the Great Depression of the 1930's, but even from himself, deep in his heart.

One of the queerest ironies of history, as John Kenneth Galbraith points out in *The Affluent Society*, is that in a sense Marx won his case with his sworn enemies, the capitalists. Marx loudly asserted that they were selfish and interested only in profits. In the end many agreed. They accepted the Marxist materialistic view of history. The modern businessman, says Galbraith, "suspects that the moral crusade of reformers, do-gooders, liberal politicians, and public servants, all their noble protestations notwithstanding, are based ultimately on self-interest. 'What,' he inquires, 'is their gimmick?'" (Galbraith, 1958).

If not only the Marxists, but Western economists, and even businessmen themselves, end up assuming that their main motive is self-interest and a quest for profit, it is small wonder that they have had a hard time holding their heads high in recent years.

But now the research I have done has come to the businessman's rescue by showing that everyone has been wrong, that it is *not* profit per se that makes the businessman tick but a strong desire for achievement, for doing a good job. Profit is simply one measure among several of how well the job has been done, but it is not necessarily the goal itself.

THE ACHIEVEMENT GOAL

But what exactly does the psychologist mean by the "desire for achievement"? How does he measure it in individuals or in nations? How does he know that it is so important for economic growth? Is it more important for businessmen to have this desire 'than it is for politicians, bishops, or generals? These are the kinds of questions which are answered at great length and with as much scientific precision as possible in my book. Here we must be content with the general outline of the argument, and develop it particularly as it applies to businessmen.

To begin with, psychologists try to find out what a man spends his time thinking and daydreaming about when he is not under pressure to think about anything in particular. What do his thoughts turn to when he is by himself or not engaged in a special job? Does he think about his family and friends, about relaxing and watching TV, about getting his superior off his back? Or does he spend his time thinking and planning how he can "sell" a particular customer, cut production costs, or invent a better steam trap or toothpaste tube?

If a man spends his time thinking about doing things better, the psychologist says he has a concern for achievement. In other words, he cares about achievement or he would not spend so much time thinking about it. If he spends his time thinking about family and friends, he has a concern for affiliation; if he speculates about who is boss, he has a concern for power, and so on. What differs in my approach from the one used by many psychologists is that my colleagues and I have not found it too helpful simply to *ask* a person about his motives, interests, and attitudes. Often he himself does not know very clearly what his basic concerns are—even more often he may be ashamed and cover some of them up. So what we do is to try and get a sample of his normal waking thoughts by asking him just to tell a few stories about some pictures.

Stories Within Stories

Let us take a look at some typical stories written by U.S. business executives. These men were asked to look briefly at a picture—in this case, a man at a worktable with a small family photograph at one side—and to spend about five minutes writing out a story suggested by the picture. Here is a very characteristic story:

The engineer is at work on Saturday when it is quiet and he has taken time to do a little daydreaming. He is the father of the two children in the picture—the husband of the woman shown. He has a happy home life and is dreaming about some pleasant outing they have had. He is also looking forward to a repeat of the incident which is now giving him pleasure to think about. He plans on the following day, Sunday, to use the afternoon to take his family for a short trip.

Obviously, no achievement-related thoughts have come to the author's mind as he thinks about the scene in the picture. Instead, it suggests spending time pleasantly with his family. His thoughts run along *affiliative* lines. He thinks readily about interpersonal relationship and having fun with other people. This, as a matter of fact, is the most characteristic reaction to this particular picture. But now consider another story:

A successful industrial designer is at his "work bench" toying with a new idea. He is "talking it out" with his f ..ily in the picture. Someone in the family dropped a comment about a shortcoming in a household gadget, and the designer has just "seen" a commercial use of the idea. He has picked up ideas from his family before—he is "telling" his family what a good idea it is, and "confidentially" he is going to take them on a big vacation because "their" idea was so good. The idea will be successful, and family pride and mutual admiration will be strengthened.

The author of this story maintains a strong interest in the family and in affiliative relationships, but has added an achievement theme. The family actually has helped him innovate—get a new idea that will be successful and obviously help him get ahead. Stories which contain references to good new ideas, such as a new product, an invention, or a unique accomplishment of any sort, are scored as reflecting a concern for achievement in the person who writes them. In sum, this man's mind tends to run most easily along the lines of accomplishing something or other. Finally, consider a third story:

The man is an engineer at a drafting board. The picture is of his family. He has a problem and is concentrating on it. It is merely an everyday occurrence—a problem which requires thought. How can he get that bridge to take the stress of possible high winds? He wants to arrive at a good solution of the problem by himself. He will discuss the problem with a few other engineers and make a decision which will be a correct one—he has the earmarks of competence.

The man who wrote this story—an assistant to a vice president, as a matter of fact—notices the family photograph, but that is all. His thoughts tend to focus on the problem that the engineer has to solve. In the scant five minutes allowed, he even thinks of a precise problem—how to build a bridge that will take the stress of possible high winds. He notes that the engineer wants to find a good solution by himself, that he goes and gets help from other experts and finally makes a correct decision. These all represent different aspects of a complete achievement sequence—defining the problem, wanting to solve it, thinking of means of solving it, thinking of difficulties that get in the way of solving it (either in one's self or in the environment), thinking of people who might help in solving it, and anticipating what would happen if one succeeded or failed.

Each of these different ideas about achievement gets a score of +1 in our scoring system so that the man in the last incident gets a score of +4 on the scale of concern or need for achievement (conventionally abbreviated to *n* Achievement). Similarly, the first man gets a score of −1 for his story since it is completely unrelated to achievement, and the second man a score of +2 because there are two ideas in it which are scorable as related to achievement.

Each man usually writes six such stories and gets a score for the whole test. The coding of the stories for "achievement imagery" is so objective that two expert scorers working independently rarely disagree. In fact, it has recently been programed for a high-speed computer that does the scoring rapidly, with complete objectivity, and fairly high accuracy. What the score for an individual represents is the frequency with which he tends to think spontaneously in achievement terms when that is not clearly expected of him (since the instructions for the test urge him to relax and to think freely and rapidly).

Thinking Makes It So

What are people good for who think like this all the time? It doesn't take much imagination to guess that they might make particularly good business executives. People who spend a lot of their time thinking about getting ahead, inventing new gadgets, defining problems that need to be solved, considering alternative means of solving them, and calling in experts for help should also be people who in real life *do* a lot of these things or at the very best are readier to do them when the occasion arises.

I recognize, of course, that this is an assumption that requires proof. But, as matters turned out, our research produced strong factual support. Look, for instance, at Exhibit I. It shows that in three countries representing different levels and types of economic development, managers or executives scored considerably higher on the average in achievement thinking than did professionals or specialists of comparable education and background. Take the two democratic countries shown there:

In the United States the comparison was between matched pairs of unit managers and specialists of the same position level, age, educational background, and length of service in an electric appliance company. The managers spent more of their time in the test writing about achievement than the specialists did.

The same was true of middle-level executives from various companies in Italy when contrasted with students of law, medicine, and theology who were roughly of the same intelligence level and social background.

In other words it takes a concern for achievement to be a manager in a

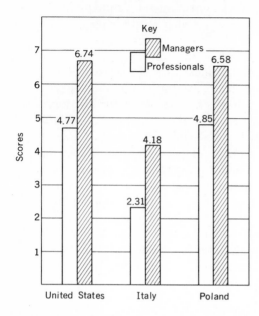

Exhibit I. Average *n* Achievement scores of managers and professionals in three countries.

foreign country like Italy, for instance, just as it does in the United States. It is worth noting in passing, however, that the level of achievement thinking among Italian managers is significantly lower than it is among American managers—which, as will be shown later, quite probably has something to do with the lower level and rate of economic development in Italy.

What about a Communist country? The figures for Poland are interesting because (1) the level of concern for achievement is about what it is in the United States, and (2) even in businesses owned and operated by the state, as in Poland, managers tend to have a higher concern for achievement than do other professionals.

Another even more striking result, not shown in Exhibit I, is the fact that there is *no real difference* between the average *n* Achievement score of managers working for the U.S. government (9.3) and those in U.S. private business generally (8.90). Apparently, a manager working for the Bureau of Ships in the Department of the Navy spends as much time thinking about achievement as his counterpart in Ford or Sears, Roebuck; government service does not weaken his entrepreneurial spirit. Whether he is able to be as effective as he might be in private business is another matter, not touched on here.

Careful quantitative studies of the prevalance of achievement concern among various types of executives also yield results in line with what one would expect. Thus, sales managers score higher than other types of managers do.

In general, more successful managers tend to score higher than do less successful managers (except in government service where promotion depends more on seniority). The picture is clear in small companies, where the president tends to score higher than his associates. In large companies, the picture is a little more complicated. Men in the lowest salary brackets (earning less than $20,000 a year) definitely have the lowest average n Achievement scores, while those in the next bracket up ($20,000 to $25,000 a year) have the highest average n Achievement level. Apparently an achievement concern helps one get out of the ranks of the lowest paid into a higher income bracket. But from there on, the trend fades. Men in the highest income brackets have a somewhat lower average concern for achievement, and apparently turn their thoughts to less achievement-oriented concerns. Possibly, these men are doing well enough to relax a little.

BUSINESSMEN AND ACHIEVEMENT

Businessmen usually raise either one of two questions at this point:

(1) "Where can I get this test for n Achievement? It sounds like a good way of picking young executives!"

(2) "Why is this concern for achievement specific to being a success as a business manager? What about other types of achievement? Why isn't the entrepreneurial spirit necessary for success as an opera star, a preacher, a great teacher, or a great scientist?"

The answer to the first question, unfortunately, is simple: no practicable, marketable test for assessing achievement concern exists as yet. The method of measurement we have been using is too sensitive, too easily influenced by the social atmosphere surrounding the people who take the test, to give reliable individual results. Under carefully controlled conditions, it works adequately to distinguish large groups of people like managers versus professionals, but it is not yet useful for individual selection. What we have here is a theoretical, scientific "breakthrough," not a practicable working device.

The second question is harder to answer but it takes us further in the direction of understanding exactly what kind of a person it is who spends a lot of his time thinking about achievement. To begin with, the facts are clear: many important types of professionals (doctors, lawyers, priests, or research scientists) fail to score on the average as high as business executives, yet, clearly their work is in every sense as much of an achievement as the businessman's. How come?

Let us consider a particular case for a moment—that of the research scientist. Certainly his work represents an important achievement, for he is the one who often makes the breakthrough on which new technological and economic advances depend. Shouldn't he be thinking about defining a problem, doing a good job of solving it, getting help from experts, etc.?

Yet, when we tested a number of such scientists—including several outstanding Nobel prize winners—we found, somewhat to our surprise, that they were not unusually high in *n* Achievement but rather tended to be average. Then it occurred to us that having a very high concern for achievement might make a person unsuitable for being a research scientist. Why? Simply because in research a man must often work for what may become very long periods of time without any knowledge of how well he is doing. He may not even know if he is on the right track for as much as five or ten years. But a man with a high need for achievement likes to know quickly whether he is accomplishing anything and quite possibly would become frustrated by the lack of feedback in basic science as to whether he is getting anywhere. He would then more likely move into an area such as management where results are more tangible. On the other hand, the research scientist obviously needs *some* achievement concern, or he is not likely to want to engage in his occupation at all.

Characteristics of Achievers

Considerations like these focus attention on what there is about the job of being a business entrepreneur or executive that should make such a job peculiarly appropriate for a man with a high concern for achievement. Or, to put it the other way around, a person with high *n* Achievement has certain characteristics which enable him to work best in certain types of situations that are to his liking. An entrepreneurial job simply provides him with more opportunities for making use of his talents than do other jobs. Through careful empirical research, we know a great deal by now about the man with high *n* Achievement, and his characteristics do seem to fit him unusually well for being a business executive. Specifically:

1. *To begin with, he likes situations in which he takes personal responsibility for finding solutions to problems.* The reason is obvious. Otherwise, he could get little personal achievement satisfaction from the successful outcome. No gambler, he does not relish situations where the outcome depends not on his abilities and efforts but on chance or other factors beyond his control. For example:

Some business-school students in one study played a game in which they had to choose between two options, in each of which they had only one chance in three of succeeding. For one option they rolled a die and if it came up, say, a 1 or a 3 (out of six possibilities), they won. For the other option they had to work on a difficult business problem which they knew only one out of three people had been able to solve in the time allotted.

Under these conditions, the men with high *n* Achievement regularly chose to work on the business problem, even though they knew the odds of success were statistically the same as for rolling the die.

To men strong in achievement concern, the idea of winning by chance simply does not produce the same achievement satisfaction as winning by their own personal efforts. Obviously, such a concern for taking personal responsibility is useful in a business executive. He may not be faced very often with the alternative of rolling dice to determine the outcome of a decision, but there are many other ways open to avoid personal responsibility, such as passing the buck, or trying to get someone else (or a committee) to take the responsibility for getting something done.

The famed self-confidence of a good executive (which actually is related to high achievement motivation) is also involved here. He thinks it can be done if *he* takes responsibility, and very often he is right because he has spent so much time thinking about how to do it that he does it better.

2. *Another characteristic of a man with a strong achievement concern is his tendency to set moderate achievement goals and to take "calculated risks."* Again his strategy is well suited to his needs, for only by taking on moderately difficult tasks is he likely to get the achievement satisfaction he wants. If he takes on an easy or routine problem, he will succeed but get very little satisfaction out of his success. If he takes on an extremely difficult problem, he is unlikely to get any satisfaction because he will not succeed. In between these two extremes, he stands the best chance of maximizing his sense of personal achievement.

The point can be made with the children's game of ring toss, some variant of which we have tried out at all ages to see how a person with high *n* Achievement approaches it. To illustrate:

The child is told that he scores when he succeeds in throwing a ring over a peg on the floor, but that he can stand anywhere he pleases. Obviously, if he stands next to the peg, he can score a ringer every time; but if he stands a long distance away, he will hardly ever get a ringer.

The curious fact is that the children with high concern for achievement quite consistently stand at moderate distances from the peg where they are most apt to get achievement satisfaction (or, to be more precise, where the decreasing probability-of-success curve crosses the increasing satisfaction-from-success curve). The ones with low *n* Achievement, on the other hand, distribute their choices of where to stand quite randomly over the entire distance. In other words, people with high *n* Achievement prefer a situation where there is a challenge, where there is some real risk of not succeeding, but not so great a risk that they might not overcome it by their own efforts.

Again, such a characteristic would seem to suit men unusually well for the role of business entrepreneur. The businessman is always in a position of taking calculated risks, of deciding how difficult a given decision will be to carry out. If he is too safe and conservative, and refuses to innovate, to invest enough in research or product development or advertising, he is likely to lose out to a more aggressive competitor. On the other hand, if he invests too much or overextends himself, he is also likely to lose out. Clearly, then, the business executive should be a man with a high concern for achievement who is used to setting moderate goals for himself and calculating carefully how much he can do successfully.

Therefore, we waste our time feeling sorry for the entrepreneur whose constant complaints are that he is overworking, that he has more problems than he knows how to deal with, that he is doomed to ulcers because of overwork, and so on. The bald truth is that if he has high *n* Achievement, he loves all those challenges he complains about. In fact, a careful study might well show that he creates most of them for himself. He may talk about quitting business and living on his investments, but if he did, he might then *really* get ulcers. The state of mind of being a little overextended is precisely the one he seeks, since overcoming difficulties gives him achievement satisfaction. His real problem is that of keeping the difficulties from getting *too* big for him, which explains in part why he talks so much about them because it is a nagging problem for him to keep them at a level he can handle.

3. *The man who has a strong concern for achievement also wants concrete feedback as to how well he is doing.* Otherwise, how could he get any satisfaction out of what he had done? And business is almost unique in the amount of feedback it provides in the forms of sales, cost, production, and profit figures. It is really no accident that the symbol of the businessman in popular cartoons is a wall chart with a line on it going up or down. The businessman sooner or later knows how well he is doing; salesmen will often know their success from day to day. Furthermore, there is a concreteness in the knowledge of results which is missing from the kind of feedback professionals get.

Take, for example, the teacher as a representative professional. His job is to transmit certain attitudes and certain kinds of information to his students. He does get some degree of feedback as to how well he has done his job, but results are fairly imprecise and hardly concrete. His students, colleagues, and even his college's administration may indicate that they like his teaching, but he still has no real evidence that his students have *learned* anything from him. Many of his students do well on examinations, but he knows from past experience that they will forget most of that in a year or two. ·If he has high *n* Achievement and is really concerned about whether he has done his job well, he must be satisfied with sketchy, occasional evidence that his former pupils did absorb some of his ideas and attitudes. More likely, however, he is not a person with high *n* Achievement and is quite satisfied with the affection and recognition that he gets for his work which gratify other needs that he has.

The case of the true entrepreneur is different. Suppose he is a book publisher. He gets a manuscript and together with his editors decides that it is worth publication. At time of issuance, everyone is satisfied that he is launching a worth-while product. But then something devastatingly concrete happens—something far more definite than ever happens to a teacher—namely, those monthly sales figures.

Obviously not everyone likes to work in situations where the feedback is so concrete. It can prove him right, but it also can prove him wrong. Oddly enough, the person with high *n* Achievement has a compelling interest to know whether he was right or wrong. He thrives and is happier in this type of situation than he is in the professional situation.

Two further examples from our research may make the point clearer. Boys with high *n* Achievement tend to be good with their hands, to like working in a shop or with mechanical or electrical gadgets. What characterizes such play again is the concrete feedback it provides as to how well a person is doing. If he wires up an electric circuit and then throws the switch, the light either goes on or it does not. Knowledge of results is direct, immediate, and concrete. Boys with high *n* Achievement like this kind of situation, and while some may go on to become engineers, others often go into business where they can continue getting this kind of concrete feedback.

IMPLICATIONS

How strong do you estimate your motivations toward achievement to be, judging from the descriptions in this selection? What is your estimation of the strength of your motivation toward affiliation, your motivation toward some creative venture? In what respect is this selection like and unlike Selection 21, on the business executive?

REFERENCES

More studies of the achievement need and of other needs will be found in Atkinson (1958).

[33] PERSONALITY STUDIES OF CONSUMERS AND PRODUCT IMAGE

You purchase many commodities every month. Why do you spend your money for some things rather than for others? The studies reviewed in the following selection attempt to explore this kind of question.

Psychologists have been active with laboratory studies in the field of advertising since the early part of the twentieth century., Contemporary activity in this field has broadened to include not only a study of the consumer and the effect of advertising on him but also a consideration of his wants and preferences in the design or packaging of the product. The methods used in consumer psychology are applicable to the study of public opinion. What questions about consumers would you expect psychologists to investigate? Have you ever thought of certain products as having an "image" or a "feeling" attributed to them by the buyer? How is this "image" objectively discovered or manipulated by the advertiser?

This selection will introduce you to a modern book by a highly competent writer who covers in *Fields of Applied Psychology* all areas of application in which the psychologist has been engaged.

Anne Anastasi

PERSONALITY STUDIES OF CONSUMERS

Knowledge about the characteristics of various consumer publics has been one of the objectives of consumer research from its earliest beginnings. Media research provides information on demographic characteristics of the audience reached by specific newspapers, magazines, and radio or television programs. Armed with this information, the advertiser can choose the medium most suitable for his product and can adapt the appeal, wording, and other features of his ad to the particular audience. Thus food ads will be more successful if placed in a magazine read by housewives. Ads for a single product, such as cigarettes, may be very differently expressed for a college paper, a trade journal, or a general family magazine. Within one medium, placing book ads on the book review page not only selects the persons interested in books but reaches them at a time when they are specifically oriented toward books.

To choose his medium effectively, as well as to prepare a successful ad, the advertiser needs to know as much as possible about the consumers who use his product. Beginning with such simple demographic variables as sex, age, and socioeconomic level, consumer studies have been extended to include personality characteristics. Motivation researchers have used depth interviewing and projective tests to find out how users of a product or brand differ from nonusers (Dichter, 1947). Other investigators have employed personality inventories for the same purpose. Personality factors have been studied in relation to such consumer variables as motion-picture preferences (Scott, 1957), amount of cigarette smoking (Eysenck, *et al.*, 1960), being overweight and hence a potential buyer of reducing products (Kotkof, 1952), and listening to soap operas (Herzog, 1944).

An exploratory study of magazine readership used a special adaptation of the Allport-Vernon-Lindzey (A-V-L) Study of Values designed to fit the vocabulary and general information level of readers of mass circulation magazines. The test was administered to 300 men and women in six cities. When subjects were classified according to their expressed interests in different types of fiction and nonfiction articles, many significant differences in A-V-L score patterns were found.* In another study (Tucker and Painter, 1961), 133 male business-college students were given the Gordon Personal Profile and a disguised questionnaire containing questions on the use of various products, such as headache remedies, cigarettes, chewing gum, and deodorants. A number of low but significant relations were found between product use and personality test scores. For example, the use of headache remedies correlated negatively with ascendancy and emotional stability; the acceptance of new fashions correlated positively with ascendancy and sociability.

An unusually extensive and well-controlled study of consumer personality was conducted with the nation-wide, representative consumer panel of the J. Walter Thompson Company (Koponen, 1958, 1960). The Edwards Personal Preference Schedule (EPPS) was administered to 8,963 adult men and women who were classified as heads of households. The EPPS is designed to measure the relative strength of fifteen needs, such as achievement, affiliation, dominance, or change. In this study, significant mean differences in several needs were found among subgroups classified according to such demographic variables as age, sex, annual income, city size, and United States region. Such findings provide the advertiser with useful information about consumers in different markets.

A major part of the analysis consisted in the comparison of EPPS scores of consumer subgroups classified according to reported purchase of various commodities, such as cars, cigarettes, cosmetics, and paper towels. Subscribers to different magazines were similarly compared. Illustrative results obtained with male cigarette smokers and nonsmokers are given in Figure 1. The EPPS scores are expressed as percentiles based on adult male norms. The five scales listed on the graph yielded mean differences between nonsmokers and heavy smokers that were significant at the .01 level. The heavy smokers scored

---

* This is a printed inventory revealing the individual relative preference for certain values such as esthetic, economic, social, political and so on. See Engstrom and Powers (1959).

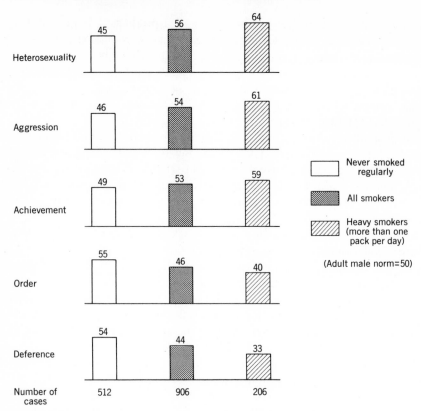

FIGURE 1. Mean scores on Edwards Personal Preference Schedule obtained by male cigarette smokers and nonsmokers. (*Adapted* from Koponen, 26, p. 9.)

higher in expressed needs for sex, aggression, and achievement, while the non-smokers scored higher in the needs for order and deference, or compliance. Further breakdown of results showed that smokers of filter cigarettes scored significantly higher than nonfilter smokers on dominance, change, and achievement; the nonfilter smokers scored significantly higher on aggression and autonomy, or the need for independence.

In still another part of the same project, mail order purchases made in response to different appeals were checked against EPPS scores. In each case, two groups were chosen from persons who scored at opposite ends of the distribution in the need under investigation but who were matched in such variables as age, income, and city size. A sales promotion piece was deliberately written to appeal to individuals high in that particular need. These advertisements were mailed to the members of both groups, and the resulting sales in the two groups were compared. A mail order ad written around the appeal for change, for example, brought in over twice as many returns from the group scoring high on the need for change as from the group scoring low in this need. In general, these validation studies revealed significant but low relationships between EPPS scores and buying behavior. Other factors, such as price, product characteristics, and nature of the offer proved to be more important in determining frequency of returns. To be sure, the influence of personality factors on buying behavior may vary with the product. But the data so far available suggest that this influence is generally small.

PRODUCT IMAGE

The terms "product image" and "product personality" refer to the composite of feeling tones and ideas associated with a product. Tea, for instance, was traditionally associated with old ladies, invalids, delicate china, and the affectations of the "tea shoppe." In the effort to change this image and to appeal to a wider public, advertisers began to feature pictures of young people and of rugged-looking men drinking tea for relaxation after work or sports (see Figure 2). For the same reason, such terms as "brisk," "robust," and "hearty" have been used more and more to describe tea in advertising copy.

Product image may also refer to a specific brand. Marlboro cigarettes were originally considered elegant and somewhat feminine. In the effort to alter this brand image, the company undertook an advertising campaign in which ranchers, hunters, and other sturdy outdoor types were shown smoking Marlboros and invariably displaying a tattoo mark. The previously cited British study indicated that different brands of gasoline have characteristic brand personalities. One was associated predominantly with young and sporty types, another with solid, respectable citizens.

Brand names and trademarks are often chosen so as to strengthen the desired brand image. The Campbell soup kids, Aunt Jemima, and Elsie the Borden cow are familiar examples. Of particular interests is the story of Green Giant peas (Crawford, 1960). A small company in Minnesota—The Minnesota Valley Canning Company—began to market canned peas grown from a seed that produced extra large peas. The company chose the brand name Green Giant and displayed a picture of a smiling green giant on the cans and in all advertisements of this product. Soon the green giant began to appear also on other canned goods prepared by this company, such as corn, and some of the other brand names were changed accordingly. Recognizing the popularity and effectiveness of this symbol, the company itself eventually changed its name to the Green Giant Company.

The Green Giant story illustrates a deliberate effort to transform a successful brand image into a corporate image. The reverse process is more common. In a well-established company, the strength of the corporate image increases public acceptance of each of its products. In some situations, however, it is

Why Willy Schaeffler's ski champs drink tea, the hot refresher

"At Denver University, ski teams drink hot tea for the same reason Olympic skiers drink it. I know Olympic skiers who actually make 'pit stops' to get a cup of hot tea," says Willy Schaeffler. "It refreshes you, helps you feel your best, helps you do your best. That's why we drink two, three or four cups of it every day."

Willy Schaeffler and his Denver University ski teams are only a few of the

thousands of coaches and athletes who know that tea, the hot refresher, brings out the best in a man.

Why don't you get the good of tea, too? Make it your hot refresher for a week or so and see how good you feel about it. Lively, satisfying taste...clean, fresh feeling in your mouth . . . and the "just great" glow you have when you're relaxed but on your toes and ready for action. *Take Tea—You'll See.*

Denver University has won NCAA skiing championships five of the six years Willy Schaeffler has coached them. Shown at left checking equipment for a goodwill tour to South America, Schaeffler says, "Tea gives you extra zip. But you don't need a skier to prove that. People all over the world have known it for centuries."

TEA COUNCIL OF THE U. S. A., INC., A NON-PROFIT ORGANIZATION

TEA
THE HOT
REFRESHER

FIGURE 2. Use of advertising to modify a product image. (Courtesy of Tea Council of the U.S.A., Inc.)

better not to identify all products with a single corporate image. If a company makes both breakfast food and fertilizer, it would undoubtedly be desirable to have different brand names for the two lines and to keep the brand images distinct.

Even when two very similar products are involved, the use of a single brand name may be undesirable when the products are designed for different consumer publics or when some of their characteristics might conflict. This is illustrated by what may be regarded as a postscript to the Green Giant story recounted above. The same company is now marketing a type of canned peas whose principal feature is that they are *small*. Typical advertising copy for these peas asserts that "Their small size tells you, the minute you open the can, that these are not ordinary peas.... They have a subtle sweetness ... that rivals the famed petits pois of France." * Under these conditions, it is understandable that the Green Giant company chose a *different* trade name for these peas.

Much of what was formerly described under the headings of "public relations" and "good will" has now been brought together under the concept of "corporate image" or "corporate personality" (Bristol, 1960). Institutional advertising ... is one of the recognized methods of building good will and developing a favorable corporate image. But to be effective, a corporate image needs to be much more than merely favorable—it must be specifically related to company objectives. A corporate image might, for example, suggest scientific advancement, old-fashioned goodness and dependability, elegance and distinction, or sturdiness and vigor. To combine or exchange these images might prove disastrous. A corporation cannot be all things to all people. It needs to formulate its objectives clearly and then set about developing a corporate image that fits these objectives. Conflicting and contradictory impressions tend only to confuse and weaken the corporate image.

To be sure, a corporation will be somewhat differently perceived by its different publics, including stockholders, employees, suppliers, distributors, customers, government officials, the press, and the communities in which it operates. Although recognizably different, these various corporate images will have a common core and will tend to influence each other. If a company's plants spread soot over the townspeople's homes or pollute their streams, these actions become a part of its corporate image. Advertising cannot do the whole job. The corporate image is affected by every aspect of a company's operation, from the quality of its products and the nature of its employee relations to the appearance of its buildings and grounds and the printing type used on its letterheads.

---

* Le Sueur advertisement, *The New Yorker*, Feb. 10, 1962, p. 88.

IMPLICATIONS

Think of several purchases you have made in the last few weeks. What personal needs—those mentioned in the selection, or others you may have—were satisfied by these purchases?

What car appeals to you most? What feeling do you have as you think of owning this car? Does it seem to have a certain "image" or personality as a product?

Why do you think men are more readily using fragrant after-shave lotions or colognes today when these were taboo for men only a few years ago?

After reading these brief descriptions of studies conducted on consumers and their buying behavior, you may find it interesting to state some questions about *advertising, public relations,* or *buying habits* that you would like to see answered by an empirical study.

REFERENCES

Consult the Bibliography for references cited in the article.

Chapter VII

SOCIAL ISSUES

[34] PREJUDICE IN CHILDREN

We all know that prejudice exists in America. Most thoughtful and realistic persons understand its threat to a democratic way of life. The questions the psychologist can bring to the problem are, How can the extent of prejudice in an individual be assessed or quantified? Is prejudice consistent from day to day and from situation to situation? Does it tend to be specific, that is, related to a single factor or group of experiences, or is it a trait or a result of personality structure? If prejudice is a developed phenomenon, what were the conditions that fostered its development, and what other behavior tendencies are related to it?

The following classic selection by a pioneer in the field answers most of these questions. This relatively early work has led to a field of psychology concerned with *ethnocentricism* (a clinically descriptive term for prejudice). It raises questions about that kind of personality development which leads to rigidity of perception and thought and an inability to deal effectively with the ambiguous situations that are so numerous in complex civilization. It has produced the hypothetical *authoritarian personality* and has stimulated research to discover just what persons so classified are like in terms of their reaction tendencies.

Else Frenkel-Brunswik tells how she went about classifying children as ethnocentric or flexible and what she learned about their contrasting attitudes toward people they considered "weak" or "different," toward members of the opposite sex, toward power and money, toward parents and teachers.

Else Frenkel-Brunswik

Reprinted from Else Frenkel-Brunswik, "Prejudice in Children," *Human Relations*, Vol. 1 (Ann Arbor: The University of Michigan, Research Center for Group Dynamics, 1948), pp. 295–306, by permission of the publisher.

A RESEARCH PROJECT ON ETHNIC PREJUDICE IN CHILDREN AND ADOLESCENTS

...A research project designed to throw light on the determinants of susceptibility to racial or ethnic prejudice and allied forms of undemocratic opinions and attitudes in children is being conducted at the Institute of Child Welfare of the University of California in Berkeley.

The age levels studied range from eleven to sixteen. The source of our present report includes attitude and personality tests as well as interviews with children and their parents. A total of about 1,500 boys and girls of varied socioeconomic background were studied, and 120 of those found extremely prejudiced or unprejudiced were interviewed according to a schedule prepared in advance. The parents of the children interviewed were visted and likewise interviewed.

In general, the results indicate that already at these age levels children's reactions to statements about men and society as well as their spontaneous formulations about these topics form a more or less consistent pattern. This pattern, in turn, seems to be related to certain personality features of the child. Though there can be little doubt about the existence of these relationships, there is evidence that they are not as consistent and rigid as those found with adults in an earlier, similarly conceived Public Opinion Study, also conducted in Berkeley.

We shall point out the *differences in the personalities of the ethnically prejudiced and unprejudiced child.** It will turn out that such prejudice is but *one aspect of a broader pattern of attitudes.** At the same time, we shall try *to discover areas of possible modifiability* * in the personality structure of the prejudiced child. As a first step, a description will be given of the social and political beliefs of such children. Next, we shall present a composite picture of their personality structure. An attempt will be made to study their social opinions and attitudes in relation to their basic personality needs.

* Editor's italics.

ESTABLISHMENT AND TESTING OF OPPOSITE EXTREMES

The initial classification of subjects was made on the basis of responses to a series of about fifty slogans of racial prejudice or tolerance as well as statements pertaining to more general social attitudes. A prejudice scale was thus constructed with items regarding the attitude of children toward five minority groups: Jews, Negroes, Japanese, Mexicans, and "out-groups" in general. It proceeds along established lines in that it covers such situations as eating in the same restaurant, living in the same neighborhood, participating at the same social affairs, letting in or keeping people out of the country, and stereotypical accusations of minority members such as cruelty of the Japanese, laziness of the Negroes, or radicalism and money-mindedness of the Jews.

It was found that some of the children *tend to reveal a stereotyped and rigid glorification of their own group and an aggressive rejection of out-groups and foreign countries.** The scale yielded split-half correlations of from .82 to .90 (uncorrected for length of test), indicating that ethnic prejudice is a *consistent and firmly established pattern* * not later than at the earliest of the age levels studied. In the present paper, the term "unprejudiced" (or "liberal") refers to those 25 per cent of the children who were found to be in greatest agreement with tolerant statements, whereas those in the opposite extreme quartile will be called "prejudiced" or "ethnocentric." The last two terms especially are to be understood to refer not only to racial or ethnic prejudice in the narrower sense of the word, but to a certain extent also to include its usual accompaniments, such as clannishness or national chauvinism and even glorification of family and self, in correspondence with the varying scope of what is being experienced as "in-group" in any given context.

The disjunctive statements made in this paper concerning other attitudes or personality traits found predominantly in one or other of the two extreme groups are all based on quantitative material gained from other tests or from the interviews. The tests involved were constructed on the basis of initial clinical data gathered from children with extreme standing on the prejudice scale. Aside from a separate scale for more general social attitudes, there was a personality test containing about 150 items. The interviews were evaluated in terms of a system of categories which had proved themselves to be especially relevant in this context. Statistical significance (often at as high a level as 1 per cent or better) is established for all differences referred to in this paper between the two extreme groups, with respect to test items and in most cases also with respect to over-all interview ratings. Quotations of answers to interview questions are added informally by way of illustration. It must also be kept in mind that the results presented here are limited to extremes only. Furthermore, they may well be less pronounced in cultures or subcultures in

* Editor's italics.

which the choice between alternative ideologies of the type involved here is less clear-cut.

In addition to revealing prejudice toward specific ethnic groups, the children classified as ethnocentric are in marked disagreement with such more general statements, also included in the defining scale, as the following:

> Different races and religions would get along better if they visited each other and shared things.
> America is a lot better off because of the foreign races that live here.

The liberal children endorse most of such statements with a considerable approximation to unanimity.

GENERAL SOCIAL ATTITUDES OF PREJUDICED AND UNPREJUDICED CHILDREN

Along similar lines are the children's spontaneous reactions in the interviews to the question: "What is America's biggest problem today?" The liberal children can more readily remove themselves from their immediate needs and think in terms of a far-reaching social good. Examples of the problems they list are

> "... the starving people in Europe, because the people in our country won't think of them and they should," or,
> "The atom bomb; how to do things about the atom bomb to keep peace in the world."

Ethnocentric children, on the other hand, are more concerned with things that affect their immediate welfare. They tend to give greatest prominence to such problems as

> "Taxes on everything, and the cost of living."

The question "How would you change America?" is answered similarly. Ethnocentric children tend to mention external things:

> "Clean up the streets—all that garbage lying around! See that everything is in order."

Liberal children, on the other hand, tend to mention such things as

> "So the Negroes wouldn't be beaten up like they are down South," or,
> "We should have a world police so that there would be no more wars."

We turn now to the test intended to ascertain even broader social attitudes. In this scale, as well as in the personality scales to be discussed next, differentiations are much more clear-cut at the later age levels studied. Study of the interviews suggests that this is in part due to a comprehension factor, but that there is also a genuine absence of the relationship in the younger children.

The following statements in this scale differentiate to a particularly significant degree between the prejudiced and unprejudiced children, with the prejudiced more often endorsing them:

If we keep on having labor troubles, we may have to turn the government over to a dictator who will prevent any more strikes.
It is better to have our government run by business men rather than by college professors.
The government is interfering too much with private business.

Paralleling the rejection of the out-group is a naive and selfish acceptance of the in-group. Thus, above age eleven approximately two fifths of the prejudiced extreme but only a scattered few of the opposite extreme group subscribe to the following two statements:

People who do not believe that we have the best kind of government in the world should be kicked out of the country.
Refugees should be thrown out of this country so that their jobs can be given to veterans.

A particularly narrow form of ethnocentrism is revealed in the tendency, prominent in the prejudiced child, to agree with the following statement:

Only people who are like myself have a right to be happy.

The selfish orientation toward their own country and the indifference and hostility against other countries is furthermore expressed in the agreement of almost half of the ethnocentric children with the following statement:

We should not send any of our food to foreign countries, but should think of America first.

The rejection of foreign countries by the ethnocentric child, and the projection of his own hostility onto them, may be considered to contribute to his affinity toward war. Thus, our ethnocentric children subscribe almost twice as often as the liberal to the statement:·

Most of the other countries of the world are really against us, but are afraid to show it.

There is, furthermore, the conviction—apparently deep-rooted in the personality structure of the prejudiced child—that wars are inevitable. Comparatively often he tends to endorse the following statement:

There will always be war, it is part of human nature.

In the interviews, where the children are able to express their opinions spontaneously, the ethnocentric children make remarks such as the following about war:

"One happens in every generation," or,
"The Bible says there will always be wars," or,
"Sure, we will have another war. Wars never end."

ANTI-WEAKNESS ATTITUDE OF THE PREJUDICED CHILD

The aggression of the ethnocentric children is not limited to minority groups and other countries but is part of a much more generalized rejection of all that is weak or different. Statements from additional scales help to assess such more general personality traits. Thus, the prejudiced child agrees more often than the unprejudiced with the statement:

The world would be perfect if we put on a desert island all of the weak, crooked, and feeble-minded people.

It is especially the prejudiced girl who tends to disagree with the following statement:

It is interesting to be friends with someone who thinks or feels differently from the way you do.

The in-group feeling is clearly expressed by her tendency to endorse the following statement:

Play fair with your own gang, and let the other kids look out for themselves.

DICHOTOMY OF SEX ROLES

Ethnocentric children tend to conceive of the other sex as out-group, and tend toward segregation from, and resentment against, the other sex. Associations of masculinity vs. femininity with strength vs. weakness need no further elaboration.

Around adolescence, the prejudiced of both sexes tend to agree with the statement:

Girls should only learn things that are useful around the house.

On the whole, ethnocentric children tend toward a rigid, dichotomizing conception of sex roles, being intolerant of passive or feminine manifestations in boys and masculine or tomboyish manifestations in girls. Thus, an ethnocentric girl, asked how girls should act around boys, answers:

"Act like a lady, not like a bunch of hoodlums. Girls should not ask boys to date. It is not ladylike."

Two of the liberal boys reply to the same questions as follows:

"It depends on their age; the girls should not be so afraid of the boys and not be shy," and,
"Talk about the things you like to talk about, about the same as another boy would."

Asked what is the worst occupation for a woman, one of the ethnocentric boys answers

"To earn her own living, usually the man does that."

On the other hand, a boy low on ethnocentrism answers to the same question

"What she doesn't like to do."

The intolerance the ethnocentric child tends to show toward manifestations of the opposite sex in himself or in others makes for bad heterosexual adjustment, as was also found in the study of adults. The rigid and exaggerated conception of masculinity and femininity further tends to lead to a strained relation to one's own sex role. Thus, the few children who, in reaction to some indirect questions, show envy of the role of the other sex are ethnocentric.

The liberal child, on the other hand, tends, as does the liberal adult, to have a more flexible conception of the sex roles as well as to face conflicts in this direction more openly. Boys in this group show less repression of feminine, girls less repression of masculine trends. At the same time, there is on the whole a better heterosexual development and less rejection of the opposite sex. Tolerance toward the other sex and the equalitarian relationship between the two sexes seems to be an important basis for tolerance in general and thus should be fostered by coeducational measures. This is one of the places where thinking in dichotomies has to be broken down.

POWER AND MONEY

The contempt the ethnocentric child has for the weak is related to his admiration of the strong, tough, and powerful, *per se*. He tends to disagree with the statement:

> Weak people deserve consideration; the world should not belong to the strong only.

And he relatively often agrees with the statements:

> Might makes right; the strong win out in the end.
> A person who wants to be a man should seek power.

The latter statement shows the ideal aspired to by the typical ethnocentric boy and demanded in men by the typical ethnocentric girl. This pseudo-masculine ideal often prevents a humanitarian outlook which is sometimes considered as soft and "sissified." The fear of weakness is expressed in the tendency of the ethnocentric boy to agree with a statement like

> If a person does not watch out, somebody will make a sucker out of him.

In the same context belongs the orientation toward money as a means of obtaining power, material benefits, and sometimes even friends. In the interviews of prejudiced children appear such statements as the following:

> "It means something if you want to buy a house or a car or a fur coat for your wife. No dollar, no friend; have a dollar, got a friend."

The over-libidinization of money leads not only to an exaggeration of its importance but also to an unrealistic fear of it as something evil. The following is typical of the statements made by some of the ethnocentric children:

> "It helps make enemies. Money is the root of all evil, they say."

Ambivalent Submission to Parents and Teachers

The admiration the ethnocentric child tends to have for success, power, and prestige may be assumed to result from submission to authority based on his fear of punishment and retaliation. The originally forced submission to parental authority apparently leads to a continued demand for autocratic leadership, strict discipline and punishment, as exercised not only by parents but also by parent substitutes. Thus, ethnocentric children, especially girls, tend to agree more often than liberal ones with the statements:

> Teachers should tell children what to do and not try to find out what the children want.
> It would be better if teachers would be more strict.

This attitude is also mirrored in their spontaneous statements made in the interviews while talking about parents and teachers. They tend to refer to the authoritarian aspects of the parent-child relationship whereas liberal children tend to emphasize the cooperative aspects of this relationship.

Though there tends to be a surface submission ,to authority in the ethnocentric, there is often, at the same time, an underlying resentment against authority. Apparently, this resentment is repressed for two reasons: first, because of a fear of retaliation for any open expression of resentment; and second, because of a fear of being deprived of the material benefits which persons in authority can give, and upon which the typical prejudiced child seems especially dependent. For the ethnocentric more than for the liberal, parents and other adults are conceived of as the deliverers of goods.

The following quotations illustrate the attitude of the ethnocentric child toward the parents as well as toward teachers. Asked to describe the perfect father, one of the boys in this group says:

"Does not give you everything you want, isn't very strict with you, doesn't let you do the outrageous things that you sometimes want to."

Typical of these children is the use of the negative in the characterization of the perfect parent and the references to the punitive and restrictive aspects. Others of these boys say about the perfect father:

"He spanks you when you are bad and doesn't give you too much money," or, "When you ask for something he ought not to give it to you right away. Not soft on you, strict."

Similar is the description of the perfect teacher by another ethnocentric boy:

"She is strict, treats all children the same, won't take any nonsense of them, keeps them organized in the playground, in class, in lines."

About teachers who are not liked an ethnocentric boy says:

"Those who tell you in a nice way instead of being strict and they don't make you mind."

The same group of children when asked how they would like to change their father sometimes reveal resentment and feelings of being deprived and victimized. One of the ethnocentric boys says:

"He wouldn't smoke a pipe, would not eat too much, wouldn't take all the food away from his son."

Along the same lines is the answer of an ethnocentric boy to the question, "For what should the hardest punishment be administered?"

"Should be for talking back to parents, it should be a whipping."

One of the girls in this group says:

"Naturally for murder, the next is for not paying attention to her mother and father. She should be sent to a juvenile home for not paying attention to her parents."

Another ethnocentric boy asks for punishment, too:

"Talking back, not minding, for example, if you are supposed to saw a certain amount of wood in one hour and don't do it, you should be punished for it."

Methodical clinical ratings of the interviews confirm the impressions gained from these quotations. The ethnocentric children tend to think in the category of *strictness and harshness* * when telling about their fathers, the liberal children tend to think primarily in terms of *companionship*.* The ratings also seem to indicate that ethnocentric children tend to complain more about neglect by their fathers. The interview ratings bear out the fearful submission to harsh punishment on the part of the typical ethnocentric child and the ability of the typical liberal child to assimilate punishment which is explained to them and for which their understanding is thus assured. Fear and dependency not only seem to prevent the ethnocentric child from any conscious criticism of the parents but even lead to an acceptance of punishment and to an "identification with the aggressor." The fact that the negative feelings against the parents have to be excluded from consciousness may be considered as contributing to the general lack of insight, rigidity of defense, and "narrowness of the ego." Since the unprejudiced child as a rule does not seem to have had to submit to stern authority in childhood (according to the interviews at least), he can afford in his later life not to long for strong authority, nor does he need to assert his strength against those who are weaker. The "anti-weakness" attitude referred to above seems thus to be directly related to the fearful submission to authority.

PARENTS' CONCERN WITH SOCIAL STATUS.
RIGID RULES AND DISCIPLINE

The hypothesis may be offered that it is *this repressed resentment toward authority which is displaced upon socially inferior and foreign groups*.* As may be seen from the interviews with the parents, the liberal child, in contrast

* Editor's italics.

to the ethnocentric child, is more likely to be treated as an equal and to be given the opportunity to express feelings of rebellion or disagreement. He thus learns at home the equalitarian and individualized approach to people, as the ethnocentric child learns the authoritarian and hierarchical way of thinking. Interviews with parents of ethnocentric children show an exaggerated social status concern. This may well be assumed to be the basis of a rigid and externalized set of values. What is socially accepted and what is helpful in the climbing of the social ladder is considered good, and what deviates, what is different and what is socially inferior is considered bad.

The parents of the ethnocentric children are often socially marginal. The less they can accept their marginality, the more urgent becomes the wish to belong to the privileged groups. This leads to the development of a kind of collective ego which is very different from genuine group identification and which must be assumed to contribute to ethnocentrism. With this narrow and steep path in mind, such parents are likely to be intolerant of any manifestation on the part of the children which seems to deter from, or to oppose the goal decided upon. The more urgent the social needs of the parents, the more they are apt to view the child's behavior in terms of their own instead of the child's needs. Since the values of the parents are outside the children's scope, yet are rigorously enforced, only a superficial identification with the parents and society can be achieved. The suppressed instinctive and hostile tendencies are apt to become diffuse and depersonalized and to lead an independent, autonomous life. In line with this, the over-all clinical ratings seem to indicate the more diffuse and explosive nature of the aggression of ethnocentric children, as compared with milder and more ego-acceptable forms of aggression in the typical liberal child. Thus, fascism and war must have a special appeal to ethnocentric children and adults, who expect liberation of their instincts in combination with approval by authorities.

MORALISM AND CONFORMITY

The influence of the parents must be considered at least a contributing factor to the tendency, observed in the ethnocentric child, to be more concerned with status values than are liberal children. He expects—and gives—social approval on the basis of external moral values, including cleanliness, politeness, and the like. He condemns others for their nonconformity to such values, conformity being an all-or-none affair. The functioning of his superego is mainly directed toward punishment, condemnation, and exclusion of others, mirroring thus the type of discipline to which he was exposed. Interview ratings show a tendency toward more moralistic condemnation on the part of the prejudiced child and greater permissiveness toward people in general on the part of the unprejudiced.

The trend to conformity of the ethnocentric child is expressed in his greater readiness to agree with the following statements:

There is only one right way to do anything.
Appearances are usually the best test.
One should avoid doing things in public which seem wrong to others even though one knows that these things are really all right.

Politeness, cleanliness, good manners appear again and again among the requirements of prejudiced children, especially the girls, for a perfect boy or perfect girl. Interview ratings indicate that ethnocentric children tend to mention in this connection purity, cleanliness, and what corresponds to a conventional conception of good personality, whereas the liberal children tend to mention companionship and fun.

In the light of what has been said before about the attitude of the typical ethnocentric child toward parents, we may assume that the conformity to approved social values is based on fear of retaliation by society for disobedience rather than on a real incorporation of those values. In order to conform, he demands a set of inflexible rules which he can follow, and he is most at ease when he can categorize and make value judgments in terms of good or bad.

INTOLERANCE OF AMBIGUITIES

Analysis of the interviews indicates that this *inflexibility of the ethnocentric child is part of a broader texture of rigidity and incapacity to face ambiguous situations.** Intolerance of ambiguity has been found above in his conception of the parent-child relationship and in his conception of the sex roles. It is also present in the organization of the perceptual and cognitive field.

That this rigidity represents a more generalized approach to the solving of problems even in fields where there is no social or emotional involvement has been experimentally demonstrated by Rokeach. In solving arithmetic problems, ethnocentric children show greater resistance to changing a given set which interferes with the direct and simple solution of a new task. Thus, even in children rigidity tends to be a pervasive trait. It must be added that it is rigidity in thinking that is related to ethnocentrism and not intelligence, *per se*; the IQ was found to be only very slightly (negatively) correlated with ethnocentrism.

Our interpretation then could be that ideas and tendencies which are nonconforming and which do not agree with rigid, simple, and prescribed solutions (such as submission to the strong) have to be repressed and displaced. When displaced into the social sphere, this is expressed in an overly moraliz-

* Editor's italics.

ing, authoritarian or generally destructive manner, and it is here that the ethnocentric child becomes a potential fascist. The choice of simple solutions apparently helps to reduce some of the repressed anxieties. These anxieties are often more directly expressed in the liberal child, since he does not tend as much to deny possible weakness or shortcomings in himself and his group as does the ethnocentric child.

CATASTROPHIC CONCEPTION OF THE WORLD

The anxieties and insecurities of the ethnocentric child are expressed more indirectly, *e.g.*, in a greater readiness to conceive of dangers and catastrophes in the outside world, to feel helplessly exposed to external powers and to subscribe to bizarre and superstitious statements. Thus, the ethnocentric child (as also in this instance the ethnocentric adult) relatively often tends to answer in the affirmative to the following three statements:

Some day a flood or earthquake will destroy everybody in the whole world.
There are more contagious diseases nowadays than ever before.
If everything would change, this world would be much better.

The tendency to wish for a diffuse and all-out change rather than for definite progress indicates how relatively poorly rooted the typical ethnocentric child is in the daily task of living and in his object relationships. Behind a rigid façade of conformity there seems to be an underlying fascination by the thought of chaos and destruction. A leader will thus be welcome who gives permission to this type of license. The ideal solution for this type of child and adult is to release what is dammed up, and thus remains unintegrated, under the protection of a leader representing the externalized superego.

We find dependency not only upon external authority but also upon inanimate external forces. Thus, ethnocentric children subscribe significantly more often to such superstitious statements as:

The position of the stars at the time of your birth tells your character and personality.
It is really true that a black cat crossing your path will bring bad luck.
You can protect yourself from bad luck by carrying a charm or good-luck piece.

It seems to be important for the typical ethnocentric child to use devices by which he can get evil dangerous forces to join him on his side as a substitute for an undeveloped self-reliance. In general, his attitudes tend to be less scientifically oriented and rational than that of the liberal child and he is likely to explain events for which he has no ready understanding in terms of chance factors.

COMPARATIVE FLEXIBILITY OF ETHNOCENTRISM IN CHILDREN

As indicated above, the personality structure of the ethnocentric child is similar to that of the ethnocentric adult. But while this personality pattern seems quite firmly established in the adult, it appears in the child as incipient, or as a potential direction for development. This is indicated by correlations which are all-round lower than the analogous ones in adults. For instance, we often find in ethnocentric adults a highly opportunistic, exploitative and manipulative attitude toward other people. The ethnocentric child, however, in spite of showing tendencies in the same direction, still generally seeks more primary satisfaction of his psychological needs. Thus, not only liberal minded children, but to a great extent children in general, tend to choose their friends from the standpoint of good companionship and "fun," whereas the ethnocentric adult tends to be more exclusively oriented toward status in his choice of friends. Furthermore, the ethnocentric child is more accessible to experience and reality than the ethnocentric adult who has rigidly structured his world according to his interests and desires. Finally, the child's position as a comparative underdog constitutes a possible resource for expanding the experimental basis for his sympathy for other underdogs.

In spite of all the differences between the ethnocentric and liberal child, it must be pointed out that with respect to many of the features mentioned above such as superstition or conformity, children in general have more of a touch of the ethnocentric than of the liberal adult. In turn, the ethnocentric adult may be considered as more infantile than is the liberal adult with respect to these variables. The older the children become, the greater the differences between the ethnocentric and the liberal child. All this seems to indicate that some of the trends which are connected with ethnocentrism are natural stages of development which have to be overcome if maturity is to be reached.

OVER-ALL PICTURE AND CONCLUSIONS

Let us review once more the personality structure and the background of the ethnocentric child and compare this with that of the liberal child. As mentioned before, the parents of the *ethnocentric child* * are highly *concerned with status.** They use more *harsh and rigid forms of discipline* * which the child generally submits to rather than accepts or understands. Parents are seen simultaneously as the providers of one's physical needs and as capricious arbiters of punishment. On the surface, the ethnocentric child tends, especially in his more general statements, to idealize his parents. There are, however, indications that the parent-child relationship is *lacking in genu-*

* Editor's italics.

*ine affection.** In many ethnocentric children, underlying feelings of being victimized are revealed by specific episodes, told by the children, of neglect, rejection and unjust punishment. The *pressure to conform** to parental authority and its externalized social values makes it impossible for the child to integrate or to express his instinctual and hostile tendencies. This lack of integration makes for a *narrow and rigid personality.** Thus instinctual tendencies cannot be utilized for constructive purposes, such as genuine ability for love or creative activities, for which both more permissiveness and more guidance on the part of the adult would be needed. Since the ethnocentric child often gets neither of these, he presents the dual aspects of being too inhibited, on the one hand, and of having the tendency to join wild and rough games on the other. The gang-oriented child may later conform to an "adult gang" without having acquired an internalized conscience which would control the direct and indirect expressions of aggression. When the inhibition is more pronounced, we have to do with the conventional pattern of ethnocentrism. Whenever disinhibition dominates the picture, we have to do with the delinquent variety of the ethnocentric. Since, however, delinquency also often looms behind the surface of rigid conventionality, the affinity of the two patterns should not be overlooked.

By contrast, the *liberal child** is more oriented toward *love and less toward power** than is the ethnocentric child. He is more *capable of giving affection** since he has received more real affection. He tends to *judge people more on the basis of their intrinsic worth** than does the ethnocentric child who places more emphasis on conformity to social mores. The liberal child, on the other hand, takes internal values and principles more seriously. Since he fears punishment and retaliation less than does the ethnocentric child, he is more able really to incorporate the values of society imposed upon him. The liberal child employs the help of adults in working out his problems of sex and aggression and thus can more easily withstand hateful propaganda both in the forms of defamation of minorities and of glorification of war. By virtue of the *greater integration of his instinctual life** he becomes a more creative and sublimated individual. He is thus more flexible and less likely to form stereotyped opinions about others. The interview ratings point toward a better developed, more integrated, and more internalized superego. The unprejudiced child seems to be able to express disagreement with, and resentment against, the parents more openly, resulting in a much greater degree of independence from the parents and from authorities in general. At the same time there is love-oriented dependence on parents and people in general which constitutes an important source of gratification.

This is not to say that the liberal child is necessarily always socially or personally better adjusted. He has more open anxieties, more directly faced insecurities, more conflicts. For the reduction of these conflicts, he does not

* Editor's italics.

as a rule use the simple though, in the last analysis, inappropriate and destructive methods characteristic of the ethnocentric child. It may be precisely this lack of displacement and projectivity which enables the liberal
child and adult to evaluate social and political events in a more realistic and
adequate fashion. This makes it less likely that the paradoxical attitudes of
depersonalizing human relationships and personally tinting political and social
events will be developed. Glorification of the in-group and vilification of the
out-group in the ethnocentric child recurs in the dimensions of power-weak-
ness, cleanliness-dirtiness, morality-immorality, conformance-difference, fair-
ness-unfairness, etc., thus mirroring some of the basic dimensions of their
outlook and personality dynamics. Above and beyond this, stereotypes provide
the individual enough latitude to project onto outgroups his specific problems, such as aggression, underlying weakness, or preoccupation with sex.
Different minority groups thereby seem to lend themselves to different types
of accusations.

From the point of view of society as a whole, the most important problem
therefore seems to be the *child's attitude toward authority.** Forced submission to authority produces only surface conformity countermanded by violent
underlying destructiveness, dangerous to the very society to which there seems
to be conformity. Only a frightened and frustrated child will tend to gain
safety and security by oversimplified black-white schematizations and categori-
zations on the basis of crude, external characteristics. Deliberately planned
democratic participation in school and family, individualized approach to the
child, and the right proportion of permissiveness and guidance may be instrumental in bringing about the attitude necessary for a genuine identification
with society and thus for international understanding.

IMPLICATIONS

How does the patterned behavior of the *ethnocentric* and the *flexible*
children compare with your observations of people who are highly
prejudiced and those who are relatively free of prejudice? Do any of
your observations about persons in either group fail to conform to
Frenkel-Brunswik's observations? Did this article make you aware of
your own intolerances? To what extent do you find it possible to tolerate
ambiguities? To what extent does this toleration depend on the area of
life in which the ambiguous situation occurs? What suggestions from
the article may help to deal with this serious social problem of prejudice?

* Editor's italics.

REFERENCES
You may be interested in looking over the continuation of this research leading to the concept of *authoritarian personality*—a syndrome or pattern of personality which may underlie the espousal of fascistic ideas and government. Many of the aspects of this syndrome are discussed in Adorno, Frenkel-Brunswik, *et al.* (1950). For a more critical approach to the concept of authoritarian personality as a widespread syndrome, see Christie and Jahoda (1954). For a discussion of rigidity of thinking, see Rokeach (1960).

[35] PSYCHOLOGICAL ALTERNATIVES TO WAR

One of the big problems we face as a civilization is the possibility of a nuclear war. Why, at this stage of our cultural progress, should war be a possibility? What do psychologists and other behavioral scientists know about present-day man and his social *milieu* that may enable us to understand his potentialities for war or peace?

In the following selection, Deutsch first raises the question of the inevitability of war. He points out the human misunderstandings that lead to war, and presents some psychological alternatives. He cites as an example of an important achievement in complex human understanding that between management and union. Deutsch employs such interesting psychological concepts as the *pressure for self-consistency*, which leads to oversimplified views; the *mote-beam mechanism*, which fosters misunderstanding in human relations; and *distorted perception*. He treats a complex problem simply, and abstract ideas are carefully illustrated.

Morton Deutsch

Reprinted from Morton Deutsch, "Psychological Alternatives to War," *Journal of Social Issues*, XVII, Vol. 2 (Washington, D.C.: The Society for the Psychological Study of Social Issues, 1962), pp. 97–119, by permission of the publisher and the author.

I shall assume the truth of the following propositions:

1. A large-scale nuclear war would achieve a result that no sane man could desire.

2. When a small war occurs, there is a risk that it may turn into a large war; this risk would be considerably enhanced by the use of nuclear weapons. In the course of many small wars, the probability of a great war would become almost a certainty.

3. The knowledge and capacity to make nuclear and other weapons of mass destruction cannot be destroyed; they will exist as long as mankind exists.

4. Any war in which a nuclear power is faced with the possibility of major defeat or a despairing outcome is likely to turn into a large-scale nuclear war even if nuclear disarmament had previously occurred.

5. A hostile peace will not long endure. From these propositions it follows that, if mankind is to avoid utter disaster, we must see to it that irrational men are not in a position to initiate nuclear war, we must find alternatives to war for resolving international conflicts and we must develop the conditions which will lead conflicting nations to select one or another of these alternatives rather than resort to war.

My discussion in this paper centers primarily on the question of: How do we take the hostility out of the hostile peace? This question proliferates into other, related questions: How do we prevent the misperceptions and misunderstandings in international relations which foster and perpetuate hostility? How do we move from a delicately balanced peace of mutual terror to a sturdy peace of mutual trust? How do we move in the direction of a world community in which law, institutions, obligations, and simple human decencies will enable mankind to enjoy a more amiable life? These are the central questions which must be answered if the world is to avoid disaster. The world will never again be in a position where it cannot destroy itself.

It is well for me to emphasize that opposition to war as a means of conflict resolution does *not* connote an opposition to controversy among nations. Controversy is as desirable as it is inevitable. It prevents stagnation, it is the medium through which problems can be aired and solutions arrived at; it is the heart of social change. Our objective is not to create a world in which controversy is suppressed but rather a world in which controversy is civilized; in which it is lively rather than deadly.

I do not pretend to have answers to the difficult questions I have raised. I raise them because I have something relevant to say and because I believe it is important to confront the fundamental questions. Too often we are distracted from them by short-run urgencies. You may well ask what can a psychologist say that is relevant? A wide reading, however, of acknowledged authorities in the study of war and international relations has convinced me that the dominant conceptions of international relations are psychological in nature. Such psychological concepts as "perception," "intention," "value," "hostility," "confidence," "trust," and "suspicion" recur repeatedly in discussions of war and peace.[1]

I wish to make it clear that what I have to say in this paper is *not* based upon well-established, scientifically verified, psychological knowledge. As psychologists, we have only meager, fragmentary knowledge of how to prevent or overcome distortions in social perceptions, of how to move from a situation of mutual suspicion to a situation of mutual trust, of how to establish cooperative relationships despite intense competitive orientations, of how to prevent bargaining deadlocks. I take it for granted that we need more and better research before we may claim to speak authoritatively on these matters. However, my intent here is not to outline the research which is needed but rather to discuss these urgent matters as wisely as I can. In so doing, I shall necessarily go beyond the facts to draw upon the insights and orientations which I have developed in a research career devoted to the understanding of the conditions affecting cooperation and in a psychoanalytic practice devoted to helping people overcome their self-defeating attitudes and their interpersonal distortions. The proposals which I make in this paper flow from these personal insights and orientations. They are, I believe, consistent with the meager knowledge that we have; but it is apparent that much more research-grounded knowledge is necessary if we are ever to get beyond the stage of "informed hunches." Although my "informed hunches" are offered with personal conviction, I hope that you will understand that my research continues and that I do not plan to leave these hunches untested.

Is War Inevitable?

Is it possible that war is inevitable, that the psychological nature of man is such that war is an indispensable outlet for his destructive urges? True, there have been wars throughout human history and men have found outlets for

---

[1] Perhaps there has been too much psychologizing about these matters; there are, after all, critical differences between persons and nations. Not the least of these is the fact that in a deadly quarrel between people it is the quarrelers who are most apt to be killed while, in a deadly quarrel among nations, the decision-makers are rarely the ones who have the highest probability of dying. Be that as it may, I shall assume that there is some merit in viewing nations, like persons, as behaving units in an environment and to conceive of international relations in terms somewhat analogous to those of interpersonal relations.

psychological drives of all kinds in war—sadistic, masochistic, creative, heroic, altruistic, adventurous, etc. Yet, as Jerome Frank . . . has pointed out, the historical prevalence of a behavior pattern is not proof of its inevitability. Human sacrifice in religious rites, slavery, sorcery, certain forms of child labor, etc., have largely disappeared in modern, industrialized nations although such practices have existed throughout human history.

William James, in his classic paper, "The Moral Equivalent of War" (1911), recognized that war and the military spirit produced certain virtues which are necessary to the survival of any society. However, he went on to point out that militarism and war is not the only means for achieving the virtues of self-discipline and social cohesiveness, that it is possible to find alternative means for achieving the same psychological ends. (It is of interest to note that James's suggestion for a moral equivalent to war was a "Peace Corps" of youth enlisted in an army against Nature.) The view that alternative means for satisfying psychological motives can always be found is, of course, a basic concept in modern psychology. Egon Brunswick (1952) went so far as to elevate "vicarious functioning" (*i.e.*, the equivalence and mutual intersubstitutability of different behaviors in relation to goal achievement) to the defining criterion of the subject matter of psychology.

Man's make-up may always contain the psychological characteristics which have found an outlet in militarism and war. There is no reason, however, to doubt that these characteristics can find satisfactory outlets in peaceful pursuits. Aggressiveness, adventurousness, idealism, and bravery will take a peaceful or destructive outlet depending upon the social, cultural, and political conditioning of the individual and upon the behavioral possibilities which exist within his social environment. Some may assert that war provides a more natural, spontaneous, or direct outlet for hostility and aggressiveness than any peaceful alternatives. Such an assertion is based upon a fundamental misconception of war: war is a highly complex, organized social activity in which personal outlets for aggression and hostility are primarily vicarious, symbolic, indirect, and infrequent for most of the participants. This is especially true for the highly mechanized warfare of modern times which largely eliminates the direct physical contact between the aggressor and his victim.[2] Moreover, it is evident that no matter what his psychological make-up an individual, *per se*, cannot make war. War-making requires the existence of complex social institutions necessary to organize and maintain a "war machine." This is not to say that a war machine cannot be activated by the decision of strategically placed individuals. Obviously, one of the great dangers of our era is that a

[2] War is vastly overrated as an outlet for direct aggressiveness; it does not compare with the directness of reckless automobile driving, a boxing match, or a football game. War is defined to be such a good outlet *only* because of our cultural conditioning: the military toys children are given to play with, the identification of heroism and bravery with war in so many novels, TV dramas, and films that we all are exposed to; the definition of patriotism in military terms in so many of our public ceremonials and holidays, etc.

small group of men have the power to create a nuclear holocaust. Even a strategically placed individual can only activate a war machine if it exists; the mass of people, not being strategically placed, cannot directly activate a war no matter what their psychological predispositions are. It is relevant to note here that research by T. Abel [3] indicates that warlike attitudes in the populace tend to follow rather than precede the outbreak of war.

The impersonal character of modern war, as Erich Fromm (1960) has pointed out, makes it difficult for an individual to comprehend fully the meaning of his actions as he kills. It is easier for most people to kill faceless symbols of human beings at a distance, than to kill people with one's bare hands. Thus, if the airmen of our Strategic Air Command were suddenly ordered to fly to the Soviet Union or China (or if Soviet airmen were ordered to fly to the United States) to drop nuclear weapons, most of them would comply. They would, I assume, be distressed by the thought, but they would comply. Would they comply if the killings were personal—if they had to burn, mutilate, or suffocate the victims one by one? The psychological danger of modern impersonal war is not that it is a good outlet for aggression but rather, to the contrary, that it does not permit the button-pusher to appreciate fully the destructive nature of his actions. Were he to do so, his destructive actions might be inhibited rather than encouraged.

MISPERCEPTIONS WHICH LEAD TO WAR

Neither war nor peace is psychologically inevitable. Exaggeration of the inevitability of war contributes to a self-fulfilling prophecy: it makes war more likely. Exaggeration of the inevitability of peace does not stimulate the intense effort necessary to create the conditions for a durable peace: a stable peace has to be invented and constructed. There is nothing inevitable about it.

A fundamental theorem of the psychological and social sciences is that man's behavior is determined by the world he perceives. Perception is not, however, always veridical to the world which is being perceived. There are a number of reasons why perceptions may be distorted. I would like to consider with you five common causes of misperception, to illustrate the operation of each in international relations, and to indicate how these misperceptions can be counteracted or prevented.

1. *The perception of any act is determined both by our perception of the act itself and by our perception of the context in which the act occurs.* Thus, the statement "You did that extremely well" will be perceived rather differently if a captain is saying it to a private than if a private is saying it to a captain. A common source of distorted social perception results from miscon-

---

[3] T. Abel is cited in Jessie Bernard (1957).

ceptions or false perceptions of context. The contexts of socials acts are often not immediately given in perception and often they are not obvious. When the context is not obvious, we tend to assume a familiar context—*i.e.*, the context which is most likely in terms of our own experience. Since both the present situations and past experiences of the actor and the perceiver may be rather different, it is not surprising that they will supply different contexts and interpret the same act quite differently. Misunderstandings of this sort, of course, are very likely when the actor and the perceiver come from rather different cultural backgrounds and they are not fully aware of these differences. The stock conversation of returning tourists consists of amusing or embarrassing anecdotes based upon misunderstandings of this sort.

Urie Bronfenbrenner's first-hand observations (1961) lead him to conclude that the Soviets and Americans have a similar view of one another; each says more or less the same things about the other. For example, each states: "*They* are the aggressors"; "*their* government exploits and deludes the people"; "the mass of *their* people is not really sympathetic to the regime"; "*they* cannot be trusted;" "*their* policy verges on madness"; etc.

It is my contention that mutual distortions such as those described above arise, in part, because of an inadequate understanding of the other's context. Take, for instance, the Soviet Union's reluctance to conclude any disarmament agreement which contains adequate provisions for international inspection and control. We view this as a device to prevent an agreement or to subvert any agreement on disarmament which might be worked out. However, as Joseph Nogee has pointed out in his monograph on "The Diplomacy of Disarmament" (1960, p. 275): "Under present circumstances, any international control group reflecting the realities of political power would inevitably include a majority of non-Communist nations. Decisions involving actual and potential interests vital to the USSR would have to be made continuously by a control board, the majority of whose members would represent social and economic systems the USSR considers inherently hostile. Any conflicts would ultimately have to be resolved by representatives of governments, and it is assumed that on all major decisions the capitalist nations would vote as a bloc.... Thus, for the Soviet Union, representation on a control board along the lines proposed by the West would be inherently inequitable...."

I may assert that one can subjectively test the creditability of the Soviet position by imagining our own reactions if the Soviet bloc could consistently outvote us at the UN or on an international disarmament control board. Under such conditions, in the present world situation, would we conclude an agreement which did not give us the security of a veto? I doubt it. Similarly, one can test the creditability of the American position by imagining that the Soviet Union had experienced a Pearl Harbor in a recent war and that it had no open access to information concerning the military preparations of the United States. Under such circumstances, in the present world situation, would it be less concerned about inspection and control than we are? I doubt it. . . .

How can we prevent and overcome distortions and misunderstandings of this sort? Obviously, more communication, a great increase in interchanges of scholars, artists, politicians, tourists, and the like might be helpful. However, I think we should take cognizance of the findings of the vast body of research on intergroup contact: casual contact of limited duration is more likely to support deeply rooted distortions than remove them. To have any important effect, contact must be prolonged, functional, and intimate.

I suggest that the most important principle to follow in international communication on issues where there is controversy is one suggested by Anatol Rapoport. . . . He advocates that each side be required to state the position of the other side to the other side's complete satisfaction before either side advocates its own position. Certainly the procedure would not eliminate all conflict, but it would eliminate those conflicts based upon misunderstanding. It forces one to place the other's action in a context which is acceptable to the other and, as a consequence, prevents one from arbitrarily rejecting the other's position as unreasonable or badly motivated. This is the strategy followed by the good psychotherapist.* By communicating to the patient his full understanding of the patient's behavior and by demonstrating the appropriateness of the patient's assumptions to the patient's behavior and past experiences, he creates the conditions under which the current validity of the patient's assumptions can be examined. The attempt to challenge or change the patient's behavior without mutual understanding of its assumptions usually produces only a defensive adherence to the challenged behavior.

2. *Our perceptions of the external world are often determined indirectly by the information we receive from others rather than by our direct experiences.* Human communication, like perception itself, is always selective. The perception of an event is usually less detailed, more abstract, and less complex than the event which is perceived; the communication about an event is also likely to be less detailed and less complex than its perception. The more human links there are in the communication of information about any event, the more simplified and distorted will be the representation of the event. Distortion in communication tends to take characteristic form: on the one hand, there is a tendency to accentuate the unusual, bizarre, controversial, deviant, violent, and unexpected; on the other hand, there is a tendency for communicators who are communicating to their superiors to communicate only that information which fits in with the preconceptions of their superiors.

If we examine our sources of information about international affairs, we see that they are particularly vulnerable to distorting influences. There are only a small number of American reporters in any country; they do not necessarily

* See Selection 56.—Ed.

work independently of one another. They are under subtle pressure to report items which will catch the reader's interest and conform to their publisher's viewpoint. In a period of hostility between nations, these conditions are not conducive to getting a clear understanding of how events are perceived by the other side or a clear understanding of the other's frame of reference.

I suggest that we should recognize the dangers inherent in not perceiving the other side's point of view regularly. Recognizing these dangers, shouldn't we offer to make arrangements with the Soviet Union whereby we would each be enabled to present our own point of view over the other's radio and TV and in their leading newspapers? Suppose the Soviet leaders are afraid to participate on a reciprocating basis, should we make the offer anyway? My answer is in the form of a question: Do we have anything to lose by understanding their viewpoint as well as we can; wouldn't "truth squads" adequately protect us from deliberate attempts to mislead us?

3. *Our perceptions of the world are often very much influenced by the need to conform to and agree with the perceptions of other people.* Thus, in some communities it would be difficult for an individual to survive if he perceived Negroes as his social equals or if he perceived Communist China as having legitimate grievances against the United States. If he acted upon his perceptions, he would be ostracized socially; if he conformed to the perceptions of other people without changing his own perceptions, so that they were similar to those prevalent in his community, he might feel little self-respect.

It is my impression that most social and political scientists, most specialists in international relations, most intellectuals who have thought about it, and many of our political leaders personally favor the admission of Communist China into the UN and favor our taking the initiative in attempting to normalize our relations with Communist China. Yet, conformity pressures keep silent most of us who favor such a change in policy. The strength of these conformity pressures in the United States on this issue is so great that it is difficult to think of Communist China or to talk about it in any terms except those which connote absolute, incorrigible evil. I believe this is an extremely dangerous situation, because without a fundamental change in United States-Chinese relations the world may be blown up shortly after China has acquired a stockpile of hydrogen bombs; this may take less than a decade.

How can we break through the veil of conformity and its distorting influences? Asch's (1956) insightful studies of conformity pressures point the way. His studies reveal that when the monolithic social front of conformity is broken by even one dissenter, other potential dissenters feel freer to break with the majority. The lesson is clear: those who dissent must express their opinions so that they are heard by others. If they do so, they may find more agreement than they anticipate.

4. *A considerable body of psychological research* [4] *indicates that an indi-*

---

[4] Much of this research is summarized in various articles in Katz (1960).

vidual attempts to perceive his environment in such a way that it is consistent with his self-perception. If an individual feels afraid, he tends to perceive his world as frightening; if he feels hostile, he is likely to see it as frustrating or unjust; if he feels weak and vulnerable, he is apt to see it as exploitative and powerful; if he is torn by self-doubt and self-conflict, he will tend to see it as at odds with him. Not only does an individual tend to see the external world in such a way as to justify his feelings and beliefs but also so as to justify his behavior. If an individual is a heavy smoker, he is apt to perceive cigarette smoking as less injurious to health than a nonsmoker; if he drives a car and injures a pedestrian, he is likely to blame the pedestrian; if he invests in something (*e.g.,* a munitions industry), he will attempt to justify and protect his investment. Moreover, there is much evidence that an individual tends to perceive the different parts of his world as consistent with one another. Thus, if somebody likes you, you expect him to dislike someone who dislikes you. If somebody disagrees with you, you are likely to expect him to agree with someone who disagrees with you.

The danger of the pressure for consistency is that it often leads to an oversimplified black-white view of the world. Take, for instance, the notions that since the interests of the United States and the Soviet Union are opposed in some respects, we must be opposed to or suspicious of anything that the Communists favor and must regard any nation that desires friendly relations with the Soviet Union as opposed to the United States. If the Soviet Union is against colonialism in Africa, must we be for it? If nations in Latin America wish to establish friendly, commercial relations with the Communist nations, must we feel threatened? If Canada helps Communist China by exporting food to it, must we suspect its loyalty to us? Are nations which are not for us necessarily for the Communists? The notions expressed in affirmative answers to these questions are consistent with the view that the conflict between the United States and the Soviet Union can only be ended by total defeat for one or the other. But is it not possible that the conflict can be resolved so that both sides are better off than they are now? Recognition of this latter possibility may suggest that what benefits the Soviet Union does not necessarily harm us, and that nations with amicable relations with both the United States and the Soviet Union may be an important asset in resolving the cold war before it turns into a hot one.

The pressure for self-consistency often leads to rigid, inflexible positions because it may be difficult to change a position that one has committed oneself to publicly without fear of loss of face. To some extent, I believe this is our situation vis-à-vis the admission of Communist China to the United Nations and with regard to our policies toward Cuba. We are frozen into positions which are unresponsive to changing circumstances because a change in our positions would seem to us to be admission of mistaken judgment which could lead to a loss of face.

What can we do to avoid the "consistency of little minds" and the rigidities of false pride? These dangers to accurate perception are most likely when an individual feels under threat, when his self-esteem is at stake. I think in such circumstances it is prudent to seek the advice and counsel of trusted friends who are not so emotionally involved in the issues. Thus, I think it would be wise to consult with such nations as Brazil, France, and Great Britain on our policy toward Cuba and Communist China precisely because they do not have as deep an involvement with these countries as we do. Similarly, consultation with more or less neutral nations such as India, Sweden, Austria, and Nigeria might prevent us from developing an oversimplified view of the nature of our relations with the Soviet Union.

5. Ichheiser (1949) has described a mechanism, similar to that of projection, which leads to misunderstandings in human relations: the *mote-beam mechanism*. It consists in perceiving certain characteristics in others which we do not perceive in ourselves. Thus, the characteristics are perceived as though they were peculiar traits of the others and, hence, the differences between the others and ourselves are accentuated. Since the traits we are unable or unwilling to recognize in others are usually traits we consider to be undesirable, the mote-beam mechanism results in a view of the other as peculiarly shameful or evil. Thus, although many of us who live here in the North easily recognize the shameful racial discrimination and segregation in the South, we avoid a clear awareness of the pervasive racial discrimination in our own communities.

Similarly, in international relations it is easy to recognize the lack of political liberties in the Soviet Union, their domination of the nations in Eastern Europe, their obstructiveness in the United Nations, etc., but it is difficult for us to recognize similar defects in the United States: *e.g.*, the disenfranchisement of most Negro voters in many states, our domination of Latin America, our unfair treatment of the American Indian, our stubbornness in the UN in pretending that the representative from Taiwan is the representative of Mainland China. Since the mote-beam mechanism, obviously, works on both sides, there is a tendency for each side to view the other as peculiarly immoral and for the views to mirror one another.

What can be done to make the mote-beam mechanism ineffective? The proposals I have made to counteract the effects of the other type of perceptual distortions are all relevant here. In addition, I would suggest that the mote-beam mechanism breeds on a moral-evaluative approach to behavior, on a readiness to condemn defects rather than to understand the circumstances which produced them. Psychoanalytic work suggests that the capacity to understand rather than to condemn is largely determined by the individual's sense of self-esteem, by his ability to cope with the external problem confronting him, and by his sense of resoluteness in overcoming his own defects. By analogy, I would suggest that we in the United States will have less need to overlook our own shortcomings or to be fascinated with the defects of others to the extent that we have a thriving society which is resolutely overcoming its own problems of racial prejudice, economic stagnation, and lack of dedication to common public purposes.

While distortions in perception are very common for the reasons I have outlined above, it is also true that, in many instances, everyday experience provides a corrective to the distortions. When reality is sufficiently compelling and when the contact with reality occurs with sufficient frequency, the distortions will be challenged and may yield. However, there are circumstances which tend to perpetuate and rigidify distortions. Let me briefly describe three major reasons for the perpetuation of distortions:

1. *A major psychological investment has been made in the distortion.* As a consequence, the individual may anticipate that giving up the investment will require drastic personal reorganization which might result in personal instability and the loss of social face and might precipitate unknown dangers. Anyone who has done psychoanalytic therapy with neurotic patients knows that no matter how costly and painful it is, a distorted but familiar mode of adjustment is hard to give up until the patient has sufficient self-confidence or confidence in his analyst to venture into unfamiliar terrain.

With regard to international relations, I think we have to consider that a disarmed world, a world without external tensions to justify internal political policies, a world without violence as a means of bringing about changes in the status quo would be an unfamiliar world: a world in which some would feel that their vested interests might be destroyed. For example, I am sure that many military men, scientists, industrialists, workers, and investors fear a disarmed world because they anticipate that their skills and knowledge will become obsolete, or they will lose social status, or they will lose financially. These fears have to be dealt with constructively or else they may produce defensive adherence to the views which justify a hostile, armed world. I suggest that we must carefully plan to anticipate the psychological difficulties in the transition to a peaceful, disarmed world. As a basic strategy to overcome some of these difficulties, I would recommened that we consider a policy of *overcompensating* those who might be adversely affected by the change: we want to change the nature of their psychological investment from an investment in military pursuits to one in peaceful pursuits.

2. *Certain distorted perceptions perpetuate themselves because they lead the individual to avoid contact or meaningful communication with the object or person being perceived.* This is especially true when the distortions lead to aversion or hostility toward the object being perceived. For example, for reasons which go back to my childhood and about which I am not clear, I have a strong aversion to coffee, becoming nauseated at the thought of drinking it. As a consequence, I avoid coffee and my aversion is perpetuated. Newcomb (1947) has described a similar process of *autistic hostility* in interpersonal

relations in which a hostile impulse may give rise to barriers to communication behind which a persistent attitude is protected. Similarly, in international relations, hostile attitudes between the United States and Communist China produce barriers to communication which eliminate the possibility of a change in attitudes. Here, the best antidote would seem to be communication which followed the rules of procedure suggested by Anatol Rapoport.

3. Merton, in his classic paper on *The Self-fulfilling Prophecy* (1957), has pointed out that distortions are often perpetuated because they may evoke new behavior which makes the originally *false* conception come true. The specious validity of the self-fulfilling prophecy perpetuates a reign of error. The prophet will cite the actual course of events as proof that he was right from the very beginning. The dynamics of the self-fulfilling prophecy help to explain individual pathology—e.g., the anxious student who, afraid he might fail, worries so much that he cannot study, with the consequence that he does fail. It also contributes to our understanding of social pathology—e.g., how prejudice and discrimination against the Negro keeps him in a position which seems to justify the prejudice and discrimination. So, too, in international relations. If the representatives of East and West believe that war is likely and either side attempts to increase its military security vis-à-vis the other, the other side's response will justify the initial move. The dynamics of an arms race has the inherent quality of a "folie à deux," wherein the self-fulfilling prophecies mutually reinforce one another.

PSYCHOLOGICAL ALTERNATIVES TO WAR

In the preceding section, I have attempted to indicate some of the sources of misperception in international relations and some of the conditions which tend to perpetuate the distortions or make them come true. Our present international situation suggests that the distortions have come true. The East and the West are in an arms race and in the throes of an ideological conflict in which each side, in reality, threatens and feels threatened by the other. How can we reverse this hostile spiral which is likely to result in mutual annihilation?

As I present some specific proposal, I will indicate the psychological assumptions underlying them: assumptions which come from theoretical and experimental research I have been doing on interpersonal trust and suspicion and interpersonal bargaining (Deutsch, 1949, 1958, 1960a, 1960b, 1961; Deutsch & Krauss, 1960).

1. *There are social situations which do not allow the possibility of "rational" behavior so long as the conditions for mutual trust do not exist.* Let me illustrate with a two-person game that I have used in my experimental work on trust and suspicion. In this game, each player has to choose between pressing a red button and a green button: if both players press the red but-

ton each loses $1.00; if both players press the green button, each wins $1.00; if Player A presses the green button and Player B presses the red button, A loses $2.00 and B gains $2.00; and if Player B presses the green button and Player A presses the red button, B loses $2.00 and A gains $2.00. A superficial rational calculation of self-interest would lead each player to press his red button since he either wins as much as he can or loses as little as he can this way. But, if both players consider only their self-interest and press their red buttons, each of them will lose. Players oriented toward defeating the other player or toward their self-interest only, when matched with similarly oriented players, do in fact choose the red button and do end up losing consistently.

I believe our current international situation is in some respects similar to the game I have described. A characteristic symptom of such "nonrational situations" is that any attempt on the part of any individual or nation to increase its own welfare or security (without regard to the security or welfare of the others) is self-defeating. In such situations the only way that an individual or nation can avoid being trapped in a mutually reinforcing, self-defeating cycle is to attempt to change the situation so that a basis of mutual trust can develop.

Comprehension of the basic nature of the situation we are in suggests that *mutual security* rather than national security should be our objective. The basic military axiom for both the East and West should be that *military actions should only be taken which increase the military security of both sides; military actions which give a military superiority to one side or the other should be avoided.* The military forces of both sides should be viewed as having the *common* primary aim of preventing either side (one's own or the other) from starting a deliberate or accidental war. Awareness of this common aim could be implemented by regular meetings of military leaders from East and West; the establishment of a continuing joint technical group of experts to work together to formulate disarmament and inspection plans; the establishment of mixed military units on each other's territory (see Kelman . . .), etc. The key point we must recognize is that if military inferiority is dangerous, so is military "superiority"; it is dangerous for either side to feel *tempted* or *frightened* into military action.

2. *Our research indicates that mutual trust is most likely to occur when people are positively oriented to each other's welfare—*i.e., *when each has a stake in the other's doing well rather than poorly.* Unfortunately, the East and West, at present, appear to have a greater stake in each other's defects and difficulties than in each other's welfare. Thus, the Communists gloat over our racial problems and our unemployment and we do likewise over their agricultural failures and their lack of political liberties.

We should, I believe, do everything possible to reverse this unfortunate state of affairs. First of all, we might start by accepting each other's existence as *legitimate* and by rejecting the view that the existence of the other, *per se,* is a threat to our own existence. As Talcott Parsons . . . has pointed out, there is considerable merit in viewing the ideological battle between East and West in the world community as somewhat akin to our own two-party system at the national level. An ideological conflict presupposes a common frame of reference in terms of which the ideological differences make sense. The ideologies of East and West do share many values in common: technological advance, economic development, universal education, encouragement of science, cultural progress, health advances, peace, national autonomy, etc. We must accept the possibility that one side or the other will obtain an advantage on particular issues when there is a conflict about the procedures for attaining these objectives. But this is not catastrophic unless each side views the conflict as an all-or-none conflict of survival.

To establish a basis for mutual trust we, of course, have to go beyond the recognition of each other's legitimacy to a relationship which promotes co-operative bonds. This would be facilitated by recognition of the profound human similarities which link all mankind together. The human situation no longer makes it feasible to view the world in terms of "we" or "they"; in the modern era, our destinies are linked objectively; the realistic attitude is is "we" *and* "they." More specifically, I think our situation would be improved rather than worsened if the people in the various Communist nations had a high standard of living, were well educated, and were reaping the fruits of the scientific revolution. Similarly, I think we would be better off rather than worse off if the political leaders of the Communist nations felt they were able to provide their citizenry with sufficient current gratifications and signs of progress to have their support; and if they were sufficiently confident of their own society not to fear intensive contacts with different points of view.

The implication of the above calls for a fundamental reorientation of our foreign policy toward the Communist nations. We must initiate cooperative trade policies, cooperative research programs, cooperative cultural exchanges, cooperative loan programs, cooperative agricultural programs, etc., and we must not be concerned if, at first, they appear to benefit more than we. We are, after all, more affluent than the Communist nations. Our objective should be simply to promote the values of economic well-being, educational attainment, scientific and industrial development which we share in common and which we believe are necessary to a stable, peaceful world. Let me emphasize here that I think this is especially important to do in our relations with Communist China. (It amazes me constantly that so little public attention is given to the extraordinary dangers involved in allowing our current relations with Communist China to continue in their present form.) The Communist nations (especially China) are likely to be suspicious of our motives, may even rebuff our initial attempts to establish cooperative relationships, and will undoubtedly not feel grateful for any assistance they may receive. These reactions are all to be expected because of the present context of international relations. Our policy of cooperation must be a *sustained* policy of *massive reconciliation* which does not reciprocate hostility and which always leaves open the possibility of mutual cooperation despite prior rebuff. In my view, we must sustain a cooperative initiative until it succeeds; in the long run, the alternative to mutual cooperation is mutual doom.

My rationale here is very simple. We have no realistic alternative but to coexist with the Soviet Union and Communist China. Coexistence among nations will be considerably less dangerous if we each recognize that poverty, illiteracy, economic difficulties, internal strain and crisis in a nation are likely to produce reckless, belligerent international policies rather than peaceful ones. After all, the delinquents and criminals in our local communities rarely come from those segments of our populace that are successfully dealing with their own internal problems or that are well integrated into and accepted by the broader community.

3. *To induce a cooperative orientation in another and to develop adherence to a set of rules or social norms for regulating interaction and for resolving disputes, it is necessary: (a) to demonstrate that one's own orientation to the other is cooperative; (b) to articulate fair rules which do not systematically disadvantage the other; (c) to demonstrate one's adherence to these rules; (d) to demonstrate to the other that he has more to gain (or less to lose) in the short and long run by adherence to the rules than by violation of them; and (e) to recognize that misunderstandings and disputes about compliance will inevitably occur and hence are not necessarily tokens of bad faith.*

The importance of a cooperative orientation to the development of mutual trust has been discussed above; it is reiterated here to emphasize the significance of a cooperative orientation in the development of any workable system of rules to regulate international relations. In discussion and negotiations concerning arms control and disarmament, there has been much emphasis on developing rules and procedures for inspection and control which do not rely upon cooperative orientations; surveillance of the other's actions is to replace trust in the other's intent. I think it is reasonable to assert that no social order can exist for long without a minimum basis in mutual trust; surveillance cannot do the trick by itself. This is not to deny the necessity of surveillance to buttress trust, to enable one's trustworthiness to be confirmed and one's suspicions to be rejected. However, I would question the view which seems to characterize our approach to arms control negotiations: namely, the less trust, the more surveillance. A more reasonable view might state that when there is little trust the only kinds of agreements which are feasible are ones which allow for simple, uncomplicated but highly reliable techniques of surveillance. Lack of trust between equals, paradoxically, calls for but also limits surveillance when the negotiations are not part of an effective community.

How can the formulation of fair rules be facilitated? A suggestion by Bertrand Russell . . . is pertinent here. He proposes the formation of a conciliation committee composed of the best minds from the East and West, with some of the leading thinkers from neutral nations also included. Such a committee, meeting together in quiet, unpublicized deliberation, might be given the responsibility of formulating rules which would be acceptable to both sides. The hope is that, with sufficient time, intelligent men of good will whose perspectives reach beyond the cold war may be able to formulate rules that are fair to all mankind.

Fair rules for certain matters, of course, do already exist. Some of these rules are written in the Charter of the United Nations, some in the decisions of the International Court of Justice at the Hague, some in the legal traditions which have governed various aspects of international relations through the centuries (*e.g.*, the international postal system, international trade, "freedom of the seas," ambassadorial rights). As Arthur Larson . . . has pointed out, there is much need for legal research to make the existing body of international rules accessible and up-to-date and establish a legal machinery which is also accessible and adapted to settling the kinds of disputes that today's world produces. In addition, there is a need to induce acceptance of the body of law and legal machinery by the persons affected.

4. *Mutual trust can occur even under circumstances where the parties involved are unconcerned with each other's welfare providing their relations to an outside, third party are such that this trust in him can substitute for their trust in one another.* This indirect or mediated trust is, of course, a most common form of trust in interpersonal relations. Since we exist in a community in which various types of third parties—the law, the police public opinion, mutual friends, etc.—can be mobilized to buttress an agreement, we can afford to be trusting even with a stranger in most circumstances. Unfortunately, in a bipolar world community, which does not contain powerful "third parties," it is difficult to substitute mediated trust for direct trust.

There are two policy implications of this fact which I would like to stress. The first is the importance of encouraging the development of several strong, neutral groups of nations and the development of a strong, neutral United Nations that might mediate in conflicts between East and West. We have, of course, to be aware of the dangers of a *tertius gaudens*, in which a third party would attempt to play East and West off against one another to its own advantage. However, what I am suggesting is not a third bloc but rather a group of diverse, independent nations with criss-crossing interests that have the common objective of developing and maintaining an orderly world. In a neutral United Nations, with a large group of independent voters, we would sometimes find ourselves on the losing side. But can we afford a United Nations in which the other side has little chance of ever winning a dispute with us?

The second implication follows from the realization that strong, responsible, independent nations and a strong, neutral United Nations do not yet exist and will take time to develop. Where no strong external community exists, it is important to recognize that bargaining—*i.e.*, the attempt to find a mutually satisfactory agreement in circumstances where there is a conflict of interest—cannot afford to be guided by a Machiavellian or "outwitting the other" attitude. Where no external community exists to compel agreement, the critical problem in bargaining is to establish sufficient community between the bargainers that a mutually satisfactory agreement becomes possible: the question of who obtains the minor advantages or disadvantages in a negotiation is trivial in comparison to the question of whether an agreement can be reached which leaves both parties better off than a lack of agreement. I stress this point because some political scientists and economists, misled by the fact that bargaining within a strong community can often fruitfully be conducted with a Machiavellian attitude, unwittingly assume that the same would be true where no real community exists.

In concluding this section, let me quote from a monograph on the *Causes of Industrial Peace* (National Planning Association, 1953, p. 92) which lists the conditions that have led to peaceful settlement of disputes under collective bargaining:*

1. There is full acceptance by management of the collective bargaining process and of unionism as an institution. The company considers a strong union an asset to management.

2. The union fully accepts private ownership and operation of the industry; it recognizes that the welfare of its members depends upon the successful operation of the business.

3. The union is strong, responsible, and democratic.

4. The company stays out of the union's internal affairs; it does not seek to alienate the workers' allegiance to their union.

5. Mutual trust and confidence exist between the parties. There have been no serious ideological incompatibilities.

6. Neither party to bargaining has adopted a legalistic approach to the solution of problems in the relationship.

7. Negotiations are "problem-centered"—more time is spent on day-to-day problems than on defining abstract principles.

8. There is widespread union-management consultation and highly developed information-sharing.

* See Selection 30.—Ed.

9. Grievances are settled promptly, in the local plant whenever possible. There is flexibility and informality within the procedure.

This is in accord with our discussion of the basic conditions for world peace: namely, the necessity of developing attitudes which consciously stress mutual acceptance, mutual welfare, mutual strength, mutual interest, and mutual trust and the necessity of developing approaches to disputes which consistently emphasize full communication, willingness to negotiate, and the specific issues in dispute rather than the ideological frame of reference of the parties in dispute.

IMPLICATIONS

This substantial selection on a crucial current problem deserves careful reading, a search for understanding, and detailed discussion. Which of Deutsch's ideas do you heartily endorse? Of which are you skeptical? Consider the psychological assumptions underlying his proposals and react to them.

You and your peers may find it interesting and profitable to use the content of this selection for a debate among several students who react differently to it.

Deutsch mentions a game experiment which may be duplicated by several members of your group. You can, by playing this experimental game, demonstrate the self-defeating nature of extreme self-interest.

REFERENCES

Consult the Bibliography for references cited in the article.

Many other outstanding members of the profession have been concerned with the psychological aspects of national and international affairs, as shown in Murphy (1953), Osgood (1961), Nielson (1962), Russell (1961), Janis and Katz (1959), Katz (1961), and Jacobson and Schachter (1954).

[36] SOCIETY AS THE PATIENT

Most of us adhere to the idea that the individual has complete control of his behavior and that he alone is responsible for his deviations from the norms of society. Astute writers today are challenging this idea as extreme and untenable. They hypothesize that a social order, too, might be sick and in need of treatment. We are at times willing to admit that Nazi Germany and Stalinist Russia were abnormal cultures. A resident of predominantly white northern United States might judge the southern small town as representative of a society that is not completely "well"; similarly, a southerner might point to New York City with its publicized *violence, drug addiction, prostitution, graft,* and *homosexuality* as an unwholesome society. But what about other communities?

Lawrence Frank, a wise and long-time observer of both the individual and the social scene, raises some disquieting questions. He discusses advantages of the concept of the sick society in viewing our present social problems.

Lawrence K. Frank

Reprinted from *American Journal of Sociology*, Vol. 42, by Lawrence K. Frank by permission of The University of Chicago Press.

There is a growing realization among thoughtful persons that our culture is sick, mentally disordered, and in need of treatment. This belief finds expression in many different forms and from a variety of professions. We have had, for example, *The Sickness of an Acquisitive Society,* by Tawney, and *Modern Education* by Rank, wherein society, not merely the individual, is portrayed as the patient.

Anyone who reflects upon the present situation in which our Western European culture finds itself cannot fail to see that we have passed from the condition in which deviations from a social norm were to be regarded as *ab*normal. Today we have so many deviations and maladjustments that the term "normal" has lost almost all significance. Indeed, we see efforts being made to erect many of the previously considered abnormalities into cultural patterns for general social adoption.

The disintegration of our traditional culture, with the decay of those ideas, conceptions, and beliefs upon which our social and individual lives were organized, brings us face to face with the problem of treating society, since individual therapy or punishment no longer has any value beyond mere alleviation of our symptoms. No one can complain that we in America lack self-appointed physicians who are ready, nay eager, to doctor our own society; and abroad we can see various treatments in progress which we are being invited to emulate.

The conception of a sick society in need of treatment has many advantages for diagnosis of our individual and social difficulties and for constructive therapy, although we may find it necessary to prescribe a long period of preparation before the patient will be ready for the remedies indicated. Perhaps the most immediate gain from adopting this conception is the simplification it brings. Instead of thinking in terms of a multiplicity of so-called social problems, each demanding special attention and a different remedy, we can view all of them as different symptoms of the same disease (Frank, 1925). That would be a real gain even if we cannot entirely agree upon the exact nature of the disease. If, for example, we could regard crime, mental disorders, family disorganization, juvenile delinquency, prostitution and sex offenses, and much that now passes as the result of pathological processes (*e.g.*, gastric ulcer) (Dunbar, 1935) as evidence, not of individual wickedness, incompetence, perversity, or pathology, but as human reactions to cultural disintegration, a forward step would be taken. At present we cherish a belief in a normal, intact society against which we see these criminals, these psychopaths, these warring husbands and wives, these recalcitrant adolescents, these shameless prostitutes and vicious sex offenders, as so many rebels who threaten society and so must be punished, disciplined, or otherwise individually treated. This assumption of individual depravity or perversity gives us a comfortable feeling that all is well socially, but that certain individuals are outrageously violating the laws and customs that all decent people uphold.

It is, indeed, interesting to see how this conception of a social norm, with individuals as violators and frustrators of normality, runs through so much of our thinking. In political life we cherish a fond belief in the essential soundness and efficacy of representative government. The cumulative evidence of social injustice, of corruption in office, of legislative "deals" and intrigues—the whole slimy trail of graft and misfeasance is treated as the vicious practices of dishonest politicians. We save our belief in democracy and in our representative political organization by imputing all their faults and shortcomings to individual malefactors. The remedy for political chicane is then viewed as investigation and prosecution: "Turn the rascals out. "

In our economic affairs we follow a similar practice. Rugged individualism, free enterprise, the money and credit economy, the price system with its supposed free play of economic forces and the law of supply and demand—all these are considered as naturally sound, effective economic practices based upon the very nature of society; if perverse and selfish individuals did not interfere with these natural forces, frustrate competition, and break these laws, we should have no economic troubles. When our industry and banking and commerce are crippled or paralyzed, we begin to look for the guilty persons who have interfered with normality. Some blame the stifling of competition, others the excess of competition, while others aim their accusations against this or that individual or organized group of individuals whose conduct is deemed to be uneconomic and therefore responsible for our troubles. The confusion over the nature and the perpetrators of these economic misdeeds provides occasion for vivacious, sometimes vituperative, argument, but we generally agree that the trouble comes from individual misdeeds that must be curbed by more laws, more regulation, and more severe punishment.

Likewise, in family life, difficulties are similarly treated in terms of individual wickedness and guilt, to be corrected by severe moral instruction and legal adjudication on a semicriminal basis, as in divorce. Similarly, the admitted inadequacy of the courts, both civil and criminal, is blamed upon individuals, corrupt judges, unprincipled shysters, and unethical practitioners, whose disloyalty to their high duty has stained the bright garments of Justice and prevented honest administration of the laws.

In every department and aspect of our social life, we find the same pattern of thought about our society: that our social ills come from individual misconduct that must be corrected and punished so that these supposed underlying social forces and social laws can operate without hindrance, thereby solving our social problems. Nor is this point of view confined merely to the man in the street and the unscrupulous manipulator who has learned to utilize these social myths for his own purposes. Our social scientists, with few exceptions, are strong believers in these supposed social forces and laws and underlying natural processes that, if left unhindered, would operate smoothly. Much of our social research is a persistent search for these underlying social, political, and economic systems, the discovery of which will, it is expected, bring social progress, just as physical science revealed the underlying physical-chemical processes that gave us our modern industry and technology. Indeed, these conceptions of normality and inherent order in society have dominated both lay and professional thinking for many generations (Frank, 1924, 1932).

If, then, we abandon this social mythology, as a growing number of individuals are urging, for another view of the situation, what have we as an alternative? The term "society as the patient" is a good analogy for discussion, but we need something more than a clever phrase as a basis for reconsidering our social theory and revising our social objectives. The conception of culture and personality, emphasizing the patterned behavior of man toward his group and toward other individuals, offers some promise of help, for it indicates at once that our society is only one of numerous ways of patterning and organizing human life and that what individuals do, for good or evil, is in response to the cultural demands and opportunities offered them (Mead, 1935).

This cultural conception reveals human conduct, not as whimsical or volitionally controlled, but as the way the individual takes over the ideas, beliefs, and practices of the traditional group life and, under their guidance, carries out his life processes (Sapir, 1934). In a secluded group where, over a long period of time, men have worked out a unified culture with appropriate sanctions and beliefs, the individual ordinarily finds the pattern of his life prepared for him and, within the permissions and restrictions it offers, he can achieve his life and fulfill his social responsibility. His culture dictates what he will be aware of, how he will respond to it and explain it, and what he can and must do with his organic needs and functions (Frank, 1928). In homogeneous cultures, individuals of aberrant temperaments are less likely to find it difficult to conform to the patterns laid down by their culture; when forced to do so, they can adapt themselves with a minimum of strain because their culture does not offer conflicting choices. In some cultures, it is the practice even to give specific exemptions to an individual whose temperament makes it difficult for him to conform to the patterns that are recognized as socially normal; such exemption saves the individual deviant from anxiety or guilt.

When we regard Western European culture that has emerged from an almost incredible background of conflict and confusion and mixture of peoples, and see that for centuries it has not been unified either in ideas and beliefs or in socially approved practices, we can begin to understand the etiology of the sickness of our society. Our culture has no unanimity of individual or social aims, no generally accepted sanctions, and no common patterns of ideas or conduct. All our basic ideas, conceptions, and beliefs have been in process of revision for the last three hundred years or more, beginning with the displacement of the older notions of the universe and man's place therein and going on now to the supersedure of the traditional animistic, voluntaristic conceptions of human nature and conduct and man's relation to his society. The American scene, moreover, has been successively invaded by representatives of widely different nationalities, who have accelerated the decay of the early American tradition that our changing industry has made inevitable. The picture is sufficiently familiar and has been adequately described so that no prolonged description is needed here.

If we bear in mind this culture disintegration, then our so-called social problems and the seeming perversity of individuals become intelligible. They are to be viewed as arising from the frantic efforts of individuals, lacking any sure direction and sanctions or guiding conception of life, to find some way of protecting themselves or of merely existing on any terms they can manage in a society being remade by technology. Having no strong loyalties and no consistent values or realizable ideals to cherish, the individual's conduct is naturally conflicting, confused, neurotic, and antisocial, if that term has any meaning in the absence of an established community purpose and ideal. The more skilful contrive to profit from the social confusion and their own lack of scruples, while others evade or break laws, become mentally disordered or diseased, or otherwise violate the older codes of conduct, damaging themselves and those whose lives they touch. No one is happy, it is apparent; the successful are driven as relentlessly as the failures by their sense of guilt, their compulsions, and their frustrations.

We see, then, that continued faith in the myths regarding an underlying social system comes from a need to cling to something that offers some sense and meaning in the social confusion and keeps alive the hope that things may be better. Cynicism is, of course, the refuge of the majority of successful men, especially professional men, who shrug their shoulders, acknowledge the decay of their professional scruples, but go on "getting theirs." There is, apparently, no profession or occupation that has not succumbed to the current practice of racketeering, which means that the traditional ethics and sense of responsibility are breaking down, leaving each one to pursue his own personal ends. It is neither fair nor useful to upbraid the individual who cannot singly maintain the old standards, even if they were workable, or withstand the competitive pressure to adopt the unscrupulous practices of the others. Campaigns for social reforms are unavailing since there are no new patterns or sanctions to which we can give allegiance, and we cannot return to the old since they offer no meaningful answers to our present perplexities. The only common faith we share at present is this social mythology which we cling to with increasing difficulty as the absurdity of such beliefs and the futility of our efforts to restore normality become more evident.

Where, then, does the cultural view help beyond providing another apt theory of social confusion which is useful as a point of vantage from which the intellectual can contemplate the vulgar scene? It transfers the focus of attention from the seemingly recalcitrant or perverse individual to the cultural patterns and sanctions. This revision of our thinking will modify the doctrine of individual responsibility and guilt that is not only an active factor in the growing criminality and insanity, but also a complete block to any understanding of the problem or any attempt at modification. If we accept the conception of society as the patient, absolve the individual from guilt, and regard these various social problems as symptoms of progressive cultural change, we can at least relieve some of our anxiety since we then have a definite and possibly manageable problem (Rank, 1935).

Here we must pause to take note of the chorus of objections this point of view always elicits. From many sides, but especially from religious and ethical groups and lawyers, vehement protest is made against any tampering with the concept of human volition, human autonomy, and individual responsibility. These ideas and beliefs have been of extraordinary value in the history of culture, since they made possible the devolution of social responsibility upon the individual and helped to create that belief in conscience which has so largely dominated conduct. To those who cherish this tradition and the moral gains it has brought, the undermining of the concept of individual responsibility appears as the greatest impiety and the beginning of social collapse. Is man to be viewed as a passive instrument of culture, deprived not only of volition and responsibility but also of self-determination? Is free will to be abandoned? But it must be recognized that the individual's conscience, his conception of right and wrong, his feeling of moral responsibility, are but the reflections of his culture. What we are learning to call the superego, that stern and implacable censor of our conduct and unrelenting director of our lives (the conscience of our moral tradition), is the culture that has been incorporated into the very personality of the individual. When the culture no longer provides for a superego that is integrated and wholesome, but by its many conflicts and ambiguities makes the superego socially ineffective, if not self-destructive, we must recognize the necessity of revising our ethical and moral ideas. Here we get a clue to the present situation wherein the lack of any clear, unambiguous patterns of conduct is producing distorted personalities who are not only wrecking themselves but ruining all others.

*It is curious how fondly we cherish this belief in free will, volition, and individual responsibility, along with the social myths, of implacable social forces that move with cosmic power.** The two beliefs are, in truth, complementary, representing the two conceptions under which cultural conformity and individual variability have been expressed and given sanctions of extra-human cogency (Frank, 1924). It is one thing to impute the inadequacy and breakdowns of our industrial, money economy to impersonal, social forces; it is quite a different matter to regard our economic perplexities as a product of the cultural traditions that might be changed. Again, it is obvious that the idea of human volition, of the power of choice and the responsibility for consequences, provides one framework of individual and group life, while the concept of individual variability within a cultural setting, that may be and often is individually disastrous, shifts the whole orientation of our thinking and forces us to consider how culture can be revised to avoid or mitigate these individual disturbances.

Instead of clinging to the traditional conceptions of individual autonomy and moral responsibility that were dependent upon a coherent culture for their effective operation, we must begin to think in terms of individuals caught in social confusion wherein individual conduct and ethics are no longer socially tolerable. The individual, instead of seeking his own personal salvation and security, must recognize his almost complete dependence upon the group life and see his only hope in and through cultural reorganization. The tradition of individual striving that was ushered in by the Renaissance has been the very process of this cultural disintegration, for the individual, in striving to be an individual, has broken down the inherited culture of common, shared beliefs and activities. Now that this necessary cultural disintegra-

* Editor's italics.

tion has been accomplished, almost to the point of unbearable confusion, we must face the task of constructing a new culture, with new goals, new beliefs, new patterns and sanctions, but predicated upon the enduring human values that must be continually restated and given renewed expression.

It is to be noted that in this need for redirecting individual lives toward a feeling of responsibility for the culture, helping the individual to realize that his personal fulfillment will come through and in the social life, we are in a very real sense completing a cycle. In the early period of Western European culture, especially Anglo-Saxon culture, the group was responsible for the individual and he, in turn, shared the common responsibilities, even legal guilt for the misconduct of other members of the group. Then, slowly and haltingly, came the emergence of the legal doctrine of individual responsibility and guilt for violating the social requirements and prohibitions and the replacement of status by contract. Today, we are moving toward a reinstatement of the ancient doctrine of group responsibility and a recognized status for the individual, with increasing individual subordination and allegiance to the group. The truly perplexing problem this trend presents is to prevent the stifling of individual ideas and experimentation by enforced conformity to the group patterns; but the current practices of repression and enforced conformity may be regarded as reactions of neurotic, if not psychotic, individuals against the present cultural disorder that produced their own distortions.

We are, indeed, asked to *give up these time-honored beliefs in human volition and responsibility,** but only to replace them with a larger and humanly more valuable belief in cultural self-determination, social volition, and group responsibility. This idea that man can remake his culture is, in that form at least, relatively novel, although it has many antecedents in the utopias that have been proposed in the past. It repudiates the concept of purely individual responsibility and of personal salvation, regardless of the ruin of others, for the larger concept of social responsibility that directs attention to the creation of a culture to serve human needs and values—a culture with a "vital sensibility" (Gasset, 1933).

Just as the emergence of the doctrine of individual responsibility brought an enormous gain to the individual and to society, so the doctrine of cultural determination will bring another great step forward in human life. It will give us both the courage and the faith to undertake the remaking of our culture, and it will provide the criteria for the new patterns and sanctions for the human needs of individuals who vary in capacities and skills but are basically alike in their physiological, psychological, and social requirements, and especially in their need of a common faith (Frank, 1934).

The process of remaking our culture is under way. The new social orders abroad have initiated the program, each with different goals and values, but

* Editor's italics.

316 Society As the Patient

agreeing in their repudiation of many of the older social theories and myths that forbade social change and in their relinquishment of the idea of human volition and an individualistic freedom with little or no social responsibility. Their specific aims and the frequently ruthless execution of these programs affront our sensibilities, but we must acknowledge that they are experimenting with cultural reorganization—the task which we must also undertake, peacefully and more humanly, we hope, and with real respect for individual differences.

In the history of ideas and social development it is not improbable that this discovery of the plasticity of culture may rank as one of the greatest of man's achievements since, from the beginning of history, he has been at the mercy of supposed necessities—the divine right of kings, the power of the church, and all the other forms of sovereignty and their justification by social and religious theorists, with the continual sacrifice of the individual life to the most aggressive or unscrupulous.

Today we must face the task of reconstructing our culture and creating our own design for living, in which the age-old cruelties, frustrations, and deprivations may, we must hope, be mitigated, if not eliminated. For that task we have need of more understanding of personality and culture and, above all, of faith in the value of human life which the new culture must serve. Until the culture makes the conservation of human values the dominant theme, the individual cannot, or will not, find his fulfillment.

IMPLICATIONS

As Frank states, there are those who vehemently protest any tampering with the concepts of human volition, autonomy, and individual responsibility. How do you think such a person would argue his position? You or one of your classmates may hold this view, and it should be interesting to debate the issue with one who supports Frank's position; namely, that we must replace individual volition and responsibility with a humanly more valuable belief in cultural self-determination, social volition, and group responsibility.

REFERENCES

Consult the Bibliography for references cited in the article.

[37] PREDICTING DELINQUENCY
IN THE CHILD

With what accuracy can we predict the occurrence of
delinquency in a child, knowing something about his family relations
and background? Are such factors as discipline and affection important?

Horwitz, a former Welfare Department investigator and now a successful writer, tells how the New York City Youth Board used a delinquency prediction table from the research of the Gluecks (1959). On
the basis of five intimate *factors in the child's environment,* considered
before the child showed signs of delinquency, the Youth Board predicted whether or not the child would become a delinquent. Horwitz
tells the story of several of these children and describes the results of
such predictions.

Julius Horwitz

From Julius Horwitz, "The Arithmetic of Delinquency," *The New
York Times Magazine* (1965). © 1965 by The New York Times
Company. Reprinted by permission.

In 1952, the New York City Youth Board decided to test the Social
Prediction Table developed by the Gluecks, who made an exhaustive study of
500 delinquent and 500 nondelinquent boys in the Boston area. Their findings were published in 1950 in their book, *Unraveling Juvenile Delinquency.*
The Glueck study stated that it would be possible to determine at the age of
five or six if a child would become delinquent or nondelinquent, by considering five factors in the environment of the child. *The factors were: discipline
of the boy by the father, supervision of the boy by the mother, affection of
the father for the boy, affection of the mother for the boy, the cohesion of the
home.** The Gluecks had worked from the records of boys who were already
delinquent. It was apparent that it would be necessary to follow the lives

* Editor's italics.

of a substantial number of boys for at least ten years in order to determine the accuracy of the Social Prediction Table. In New York State, a delinquent is a person at least seven years old and less than sixteen years of age who does an act which, if committed by an adult, would be a crime.

Last December the Youth Board issued a report based on a ten-year study of the Glueck table. The board followed the lives of 301 boys for a period of ten years and reported the following results: of 33 boys predicted as delinquent, 28 became delinquent, an 84.8 per cent accuracy in predicting delinquency. Of the 243 cases predicted as nondelinquents, 236, or 97.1 per cent, were nondelinquent. Of the 25 boys who were predicted as having an almost even chance of becoming delinquent or remaining nondelinquent, nine were delinquent and 16 remained nondelinquent. The findings were published in a booklet, A *Manual of Procedures for Application of the Glueck Prediction Table.* The price of the manual is $1 and the Youth Board said that the demand was so great that it is the first publication in the board's history that will show a profit.

The Youth Board selected a "high delinquency neighborhood"—a slum. A slum is a neighborhood where people infect one another with the virus of failure, and where children are infected long before the virus is detected.

The Bronx is a borough of 1,425,000 people and the South Bronx is one of its ugliest stretches. It was in this neighborhood that the Youth Board, with the cooperation of the Board of Education, selected for study all of the boys entering first grade in two public schools. The total number of boys was 303, 130 of them white, 131 Negro, 42 Puerto Rican. The Youth Board sent skilled case workers into the homes of all the boys to gather social data for rating the boys on the Glueck table.

The case workers gained entry into all 303 homes and prepared case records for each family. Over 50 per cent of the families were receiving public assistance and 89 per cent of the families eventually became known to the Department of Welfare.

The completed case records were rated according to the five factors isolated by the Gluecks. Each factor was given a numerical weight. The weights were added together and a score was entered for each child, representing his probable chance of becoming delinquent before his sixteenth birthday.

This is how the table worked for Dennis James, aged six. (The name, as with other case histories reported here, is fictitious.) Dennis was given no chance for surviving the social factors that molded the first six years of his life.

His first year of school started with a prophetic boom, for nothing in his existence had prepared him to accept school, to feel that school was important. This is his teacher's observation in the first grade: Dennis's behavior is impossible. He is a terrible fighter. He does not work. He can't sit with the rest of the class. He can't be put in line with another child. He seems to resent being told what to do. He just looks at his teacher with a blank stare.

Why should a six-year-old boy look at his teacher with a blank stare in the wonder world of polished desks, books, a green-tinted blackboard, chalk, crayons, a record player, the scrubbed faces of other children?

This is what the case workers reported: Dennis never saw his father. He vanished before he was born. Dennis never asked about his father. He doesn't know what a father is. The mother works. Dennis is supervised by a sixty-seven-year-old woman in the South Bronx. The mother works in a bakery. Dennis is more affectionate toward his mother than she is to him. What is the cohesion in the home? There appears to be no yelling or screaming. What marks did Dennis get on the Social Prediction Table? Supervision by mother 57.5, discipline by mother 82.9, cohesion of the family 61.3, total 201.7 or an *89.2 probability of becoming delinquent.**

Why is there no rating for the father? After preparing its original ratings based on the five-factor table the Youth Board realized it had penetrated into a world where there is no father. The welfare world of New York is a fatherless world. The father is an impregnator. He vanishes after he has planted his seed. He is frightened of the bloom. He will not buy his child a Golden Book, a pair of roller skates, a kite, a Good Humor ice cream, take him to a movie, or for a walk in the park. How can you rate a father if he doesn't exist? The Youth Board dropped its ratings for the affection shown by the father, the discipline shown by the father to his son, in deference to reality.

What did the teacher say in the second grade? Dennis won't listen. He won't behave without constant supervision. He can't count above three. He can't read. He can't write his name. He recognizes the number 1, and is delighted when he is called upon to identify the number 1 for the class. He brought a knife to school. He claims he needs it for protection.

Class C.R.M.D. 2. Dennis is identified as mentally retarded and is assigned to a class with this designation, which stands for Children with Retarded Mental Development. He is already a victim. A victim of the impact of a disadvantaged environment on learning, resulting in nonorganic mental retardation. Dennis has no organic pathology. His retardation is man-made and he is not alone. The President's Panel on Mental Retardation reports that out of 5½ million retarded persons in the United States, 4½ million of the retarded have no organic pathology and are retarded because of exposure to an environment that destroys the learning capacity of an otherwise normal child.

What happens later, in C.R.M.D. 7? Dennis's behavior is bad. He knocks down chairs. He does not appear to be vicious but he does hit other children. He is now reading on a first-grade level. On a Bronx subway, Dennis tries to steal a package. His first contact is made with the police.

* Editor's italics.

In junior high school, Dennis is still reading first-grade primer books. He talks in class about traveling in the subway late at night, going long distances underground. He speaks with no emotion, no sense that he is doing anything wrong. A psychiatrist is asked for an evaluation: Boy could be helped with a sympathetic, understanding adult, but the adult must be constantly with him to channel his energies. It is questionable if he can get through life on his own. The diagnosis: moderate mental retardation with sociopathic features.

What happened to Dennis before his sixteenth birthday? How did his prediction come through? Dennis knocked down an old lady on a Bronx street and kept kicking her in the face until he was grabbed by a police officer.

Here is Charles Burns with a fifty-fifty chance of delinquency. At six years of age he entered the first grade. His mother is on welfare. His father deserted before he was born, and never supported the family. Three of his brothers and sisters were born out of wedlock. His mother has been hospitalized twice at Central Islip State Hospital. Each time the mother is released from the hospital the father appears from out of the street, impregnates her and vanishes before he can see the face of his child.

One night the mother is found naked on a Brooklyn street, carrying her infant baby, sobbing for help. The mother is sent to Rockland State Hospital and comes out again to have another child. Charles is looked after by his grandmother. The grandmother runs the family. She reads the Bible to the children and hopes that God will listen.

What happens in 1-4, the first grade? Charles tells his teacher that his father beat up his mother, that his father is in jail. The teacher isn't sure that this is true and thinks it may be a fantasy.

In 2-1, the teacher reports: Charles has no idea of what he is doing.

In 3-1, the teacher reports that Charles is a "creep." But the teacher is aware that Charles comes up to her after class, that he tells her little things, little stories; he wants her to listen to him and she is candid enough to report that she doesn't like to listen to him.

In 5-6, the teacher reports: Charles just exists. Doesn't extend himself. Nothing seems to reach him.

In 6-2, Charles is reading on a second-grade level. Charles is bitten by a rat. His mother is in Bellevue. A welfare investigator reports that the children are dirty, the house dirty, the children piled up in one filthy room, sleeping four in a bed. The mother comes out of Bellevue, has a new man in her bed and is pregnant again. The children are placed with the grandmother.

And the grandmother saved Charles—at least at the point the study was concluded. He did not come into contact with the police, the courts, he did not commit serious and persistent acts, which if committed by an adult would be a crime.

The Youth Board followed the lives of 301 boys for a period of ten years, a remarkable achievement in the history of social research. Only one boy was lost to the researchers and one boy could not be rated. Out of the 301 boys, 44 became delinquent and 257 did not become delinquent. *The board had 100 per cent accuracy in predicting nondelinquency in the white group, 97 per cent accuracy for the Puerto Ricans and 93.8 per cent accuracy for the Negroes.**

In 54 of the families the boys lived only with their mothers, and no fathers or males were present; 32 of these families were Negro. In 68.5 per cent of the families, the homes were broken before the rated child was six years old. The study revealed a total of 124 broken homes. A "broken home" means there is no father, either in presence or in substance.

Illegitimacy was found in 80 per cent of the families of the boys who became delinquent and in 25 per cent of the families of nondelinquent boys. The white families had a 14.6 per cent rate of illegitimacy, the Puerto Rican families 22 per cent and the Negro families 47.7. The average number of people in a household was 4.5. In the delinquent families, 84.1 per cent received welfare and altogether 51.8 per cent of the total families were known to a bewildering array of social agencies. The 44 delinquents had 238 social-agency contacts.

Of the 301 families, 96 had one or more members who had a criminal record or a court record and 75 per cent of the 44 delinquent families had one or more members who were also delinquent.

Of the 44 delinquent boys, 18.2 per cent were mentally retarded and not one was rated by his teachers as possessing above average or superior intelligence. Of the 301 boys, 159 were behavior problems to their teachers, and 145 of the 159 were behavior problems in the first to third grades.

The police had contact with 108 of the boys, and the 44 delinquents had 169 contacts with the police. Fourteen of the 44 delinquents were serious and persistent delinquents before the age of ten, and ten of the boys became delinquent between the ages of eleven and twelve. Only five of the delinquent boys were known to be members of organized street gangs.

Most shocking, 39 of the 44 delinquents were classified as recidivists, which means the courts, the psychologists, the teachers, the guidance counselors, the training schools, couldn't put Humpty Dumpty together again.

What does this sickening array of statistics tell us? Are they news? Did you skip over them? Go back again. Each unit of the statistic is a human being, a child entering the first grade, in the richest city in the world, with the most elaborate network of social organizations in modern history.

The critics of the Youth Board study told me that the prediction tables, if used in the schools or by large government organizations, will stigmatize and label children and will repeat the disastrous impact of the IQ tests on slum children, which resulted in the teachers creating an expectancy of

* Editor's italics.

failure in the children because their IQs already doomed them to failure. The Youth Board states that the Social Prediction Table is a reasonable diagnostic tool for the early identification of boys who are likely to be a problem. The board does not say the table can prevent delinquency the table can only point to the need for intervention, for prevention.

What is to be done?

I asked Pedro Ramos. Pedro is twenty-six. He grew up in East Harlem. He was a member of a street gang until he moved to Oregon at the age of fourteen. He has just returned to New York with his own family. He remembers East Harlem from the 1950's, when it was impossible to walk down a street without protection and when the gangs ruled the sidewalk.

"It was bad, then, bad. The Dragons were killers. The Viceroys just liked to beat you up. . . . It was like war. But there was no dope then. I think I got out just in time. . . . One of my brothers got shot by the police. Guys were killed that you never read about in the newspapers. I've been thinking about those days. Why didn't I wind up in Otisville or Elmira? I think it was my mother. She saw to it that I always had a job, that I was always busy with school. I used to sweep out the market on East 116th Street when I was eight years old. I always had a job. But most of the guys didn't. They were just like nothing. They had nothing to say. Nothing to do. I'm going to see that my kids make it. . . ."

"Do you remember the old gang members?"

"Sure."

"Can you remember thinking about them, in the house, with your brothers, talking about which ones would make it, the ones that would wind up in jail?"

"We used to do that. Predicting."

"Let's go down the list. Do you remember any names?"

"Emanuel. I said he would wind up dead. He didn't. He killed a guy on East 114th Street and he's doing twenty years."

"Who else?"

"Ralph had a mother and father who were drunks. I thought he wouldn't make it. But he wound up a priest. There was Eddie. He once pointed a shotgun at a kid's head but the gun didn't go off. He didn't make it. He's a bum now. He's on drugs. . . ."

"What about your kids? You're living now in East Harlem. Everything around you is supposed to be bad for the kids. How do you feel about it, I mean raising the kids?" Pedro has three children. The oldest boy is four.

"I keep my kids in, off the streets. If you want to see the kids who won't make it look at their mothers. You don't have too many fathers around. There's a woman here on the top floor. There's no father. She has nine kids. They run around naked even in the winter. She doesn't give a damn about them. They hit the street in the morning and stay there. They don't think this is a house they live in. They throw garbage, they make it in the hallways, they scream, fight, they're wild. Kids like somebody to tell them what to do. They need authority. You can't frighten kids. How in the hell does a kid of five, six, seven, know what to do?"

What is to be done? Obviously, as Pedro Ramos told me after I explained the Social Prediction Table to him, somebody has to interfere, quick, with know-how.

We need to undo what we are now doing. We need to redeploy the existing social welfare world to meet the needs of children in trouble. The emphasis must begin before the child is in trouble. The social agencies cannot wait for the child in trouble to come to them, nor can the government agencies wait. If the Youth Board study, despite the intense criticism surrounding it, does anything, it will help create the need for a social body to take the responsibility for meeting the needs of children before they become delinquent, before they are unreachable.

The professional social world needs to listen to itself. Not one of the professions through its own efforts can meet the problem of working with delinquent children. Each profession has a contribution to make. Today there is no one to direct the individual professions toward the goal of preventing delinquency. As fantastic as it sounds, there is no project director. Imagine trying to send up a space capsule without a project director.

A Youth Department is required to take the responsibility of directing the professional social welfare world in services to children and their families, simply because no such responsibility now exists either in the social welfare world, or more profoundly, in the homes of tens of thousands of children, who have their link to the South Bronx.

We need to penetrate into the home, as though a plague were raging, all the adults dead and the children moaning in their cribs for help. The "unavailable mother"—unwed, indigent or surviving on welfare payments, socially deprived, economically deprived, intellectually deprived, often friendless, depressed, mentally disturbed, lonely, frightened, unable to supply the needs of a newborn child, already burdened with children she has rejected—the unavailable mother produces the unreachable child. This is the woman who needs the attention of the social welfare world.

I would recommend, as the first step in a preventive delinquency program, the establishment of a Mothers' Aid Agency, to meet the needs of the unavailable mother. It would be a bold step in the prevention of delinquency and dependency problems if every indigent woman, either wed or unwed, who leaves a hospital with a child, would be visited by a Mother's Aid, a woman trained to overcome the gap between the lonely destructive world of a slum-based environment and the natural endowment of a bawling healthy infant.

IMPLICATIONS

In this very brief journalistic report we get an idea of some of the psychological aspects of delinquency as well as some conception of the complexity of this social problem and its remedies. It will be noted that as these five psychological and environmental needs went unmet, the probability of delinquency increased. What do you see as central to these five factors? When these five needs are not met, what other influences do you think affect the child to make him commit an act considered criminal in an adult? In the case of Dennis, we are not told whether or not he knocked down the old lady for her purse, but we are told he continued to kick her in the face. Would you speculate as to why he showed such aggression and whether the fact that his victim was an old lady increased his violence?

REFERENCES

This selection explains the complexity of individual social problems. It shows why teams of behavioral scientists need to work together to ascertain causes and then, by manipulating the environment and the individual, they salvage some of the potential delinquents. It presents in concrete terms what a poverty program must involve in terms of professional activity.

The psychologist today can also be found in penal institutions and training schools working with individual prisoners as well as with law enforcement officers. See Dudycha (1955), Corsini and Miller (1954), Skelley (1954), and Klebanoff in Webb (1962).

[38] BRAINWASHING—SOCIAL PSYCHOLOGICAL FACTORS

Can we explain why some Americans during the Korean conflict collaborated with the enemy? Schein, a psychiatrist who extensively interviewed repatriates returning to the United States, presents in this selection the *social psychological factors* in brainwashing. He discusses its social aspects, since the Chinese seemed to emphasize control over groups rather than individuals.

Edgar H. Schein

Reprinted from Edgar H. Schein, "Reaction Patterns to Severe, Chronic Stress in American Army Prisoners of War of the Chinese," *Journal of Social Issues*, Vol. 13 (Washington, D.C.: The Society for the Study of Social Issues, 1957), pp. 21–30, by permission of the publisher.

In this paper I will outline some of the constellations of stress which prisoners of war faced during the Korean conflict, and describe some of the reaction patterns to these stresses. Rather than presenting a complete catalogue of their experiences (Schein, 1956), I have selected those aspects which seem to me to throw some light on the problem of collaboration with the enemy. I will give particular emphasis to the *social* psychological factors, because the Chinese approach to treatment of prisoners seemed to emphasize control over groups, rather than individuals.

My material is based on a variety of sources. I was in Korea during the repatriation, and had the opportunity to interview extensively twenty unselected repatriates. This basic material was supplemented by the information gathered by three psychiatrists, Drs. Harvey Strassman, Patrick Israel, and Clinton Tempereau, who together had seen some 300 men. On board ship returning to the United States, I also had the opportunity to sit in on bull sessions among repatriates in which many of the prison experiences were discussed. Additional details were obtained from the army dossiers on the men.

The typical experience of the prisoner of war must be divided into two broad phases. The first phase lasted anywhere from one to six months, beginning with capture, followed by exhausting marches to the north of Korea and severe privation in inadequately equipped temporary camps, terminating in assignment to a permanent prisoner of war camp.

The second phase, lasting two or more years, was marked by chronic pressures to collaborate and to give up existing group loyalties in favor of new ones. Thus, while physical stresses had been outstanding in the first six months, psychological stresses were outstanding in this second period.

The reactions of the men toward capture were influenced by their *over-all attitude toward the Korean situation.** Many of them felt inadequately prepared, both physically and psychologically. The physical training, equipment, and rotation system all came in for retrospective criticism, though this response might have been merely a rationalization for being captured. When the Chinese entered the war, they penetrated into rear areas, where they captured many men who were taken completely by surprise. The men felt that

* Editor's italics.

when positions were overrun, *their leadership was often less than adequate.** Thus, many men were disposed to blame the UN command for the unfortunate event of being captured.

On the psychological side, the men were not clearly aware of what they were fighting for or what kind of enemy they were opposing. In addition, the reports of the atrocities committed by the North Koreans led most men to expect death, torture, or nonrepatriation if captured.

It was in such a context that the soldier found his Chinese captor extending his hand in a friendly gesture and saying "Welcome" or "Congratulations, you've been *liberated.*" This Chinese tactic was part of their "lenient policy" which was explained to groups of prisoners shortly after capture in these terms: because the UN had entered the war illegally and was an aggressor, all UN military personnel were in fact war criminals, and *could* be shot summarily. But the average soldier was, after all, only carrying out orders for his leaders who were the real criminals. Therefore, the Chinese soldier would consider the POW a "student," and would teach him the "truth" about the war. Anyone who did not cooperate by going to school and by learning voluntarily could be reverted to his "war criminal" status and shot, particularly if a confession of "criminal" deeds could be obtained from him.

In the weeks following capture, the men were collected in large groups and marched north. From a physical point of view, *the stresses during these marches were very severe:* * there was no medicine for the wounded, the food was unpalatable and insufficient, especially by our standards, clothing was scarce in the face of severe winter weather, and shelter was inadequate and overcrowded. The Chinese set a severe pace and showed little consideration for weariness that was the product of wounds, diarrhea, and frostbite. Men who were not able to keep up were abandoned unless they were helped by their fellows. The men marched only at night and were kept under cover during the day, ostensibly as protection against strafing by our own planes.

From a psychological point of view, this situation is best described as *a recurring cycle of fear, relief, and new fear.** The men were afraid that they might die, that they might never be repatriated, that they might never again have a chance to communicate with the outside, and that no one even knew they were alive. The Chinese, on the other hand, were reassuring and promised that the men would be repatriated soon, that conditions would improve, and that they would soon be permitted to communicate with the outside.

One of the chief problems for the men was the *disorganization within the group itself.** It was difficult to maintain close group ties if one was competing with others for the essentials of life, and if one spent one's resting time in overcrowded huts among others who had severe diarrhea and were occasionally incontinent. Lines of authority often broke down, and with this, group cohe-

* Editor's italics.

sion and morale suffered. A few men attempted to escape, but they were usually recaptured in a short time and returned to the group. The Chinese also fostered low morale and the feeling of being abandoned by systematically reporting false news about United Nations defeats and losses.

In this situation, goals became increasingly short-run. As long as the men were marching, they had something to do and could look forward to relief from the harsh conditions of the march. However, arrival at a temporary camp was usually a severe disappointment. Not only were physical conditions as bad as ever, but the sedentary life in overcrowded quarters produced more disease and still lower morale.

What happened to the men under these conditions? During the one- to two-week marches, they became increasingly apathetic.[1] They developed a slow, plodding gait, called by one man a "prisoners' shuffle." Uppermost in their minds were fantasies of food: men remembered all the good meals they had ever had, or planned detailed menus for years into the future. To a lesser extent, they thought of loved ones at home, and about cars which seemed to them to symbolize freedom and the return home.

In the temporary camps, disease and exposure took a heavy toll in lives. But it was the feeling of many men, including some of the doctors who survived the experience, that some of these deaths were not warranted by a man's physical condition. Instead, what appeared to happen was that some *men became so apathetic that they ceased to care about their bodily needs.** They retreated further into themselves, refused to eat even what little food was available, refused to get any exercise, and eventually lay down as if waiting to die. The reports were emphatic concerning the lucidity and sanity of these men. They seemed willing to accept the prospect of death rather than to continue fighting a severely frustrating and depriving environment.

Two things seemed to save a man who was close to such "apathy" death: *getting him on his feet and doing something,** no matter how trivial, or getting him angry or concerned about some present or future problem. Usually it was the effort of a friend who maternally and insistently motivated the individual toward realistic goals which snapped him out of such a state of resignation. In one case such "therapy" consisted of kicking the man until he was mad enough to get up and fight.

Throughout this time, *the Chinese played the role of the benevolent but handicapped captor.** Prisoners were always reminded that it was their own air force bombing which was responsible for the inadequate supplies. Furthermore, they were reminded that they were getting treatment which was just as good as that which the average Chinese was getting. One important effect of this was that a man could never give *full* vent to his hostility toward the Chi-

---

* Editor's italics.
[1] A more detailed discussion of the apathy reaction may be found in Strassman, Thaler, and Schein (1956).

nese, even in fantasy. In their *manner* and *words* they were usually solicitous and sympathetic. The Chinese also implied that conditions could be better for a prisoner if he would take a more "cooperative" attitude, if he would support their propaganda for peace. Thus a man was made to feel that he was himself responsible for his traumatic circumstances.

Arrival at a permanent camp usually brought relief from many of these physical hardships. Food, shelter, and medicine, while not plentiful, appeared to be sufficient for the maintenance of life and some degree of health. However, the Chinese now increased sharply their efforts to *involve prisoners in their own propaganda program, and to undermine loyalties to their country.** This marks the beginning of the second phase of the imprisonment experience.

The Chinese program of subversion and indoctrination was thoroughly integrated into the entire camp routine and involved the manipulation of the entire social milieu of the prison camp. Its aims appeared to be to manage a large group of prisoners with a minimum staff of guards, to indoctrinate them with the Communist political ideology, to interrogate them to obtain intelligence information and confessions for propaganda purposes, and to develop a corps of collaborators within the prisoner group. What success the Chinese had stemmed from their *total* control of the environment, not from the application of any one technique.

The most significant feature of Chinese prisoner camp control was the systematic *destruction of the prisoners' formal and informal group structure.** Soon after arrival at a camp, the men were segregated by race, nationality, and rank. The Chinese put their own men in charge of the platoons and companies, and made arbitrary selections of POW squad leaders to remind the prisoners that their old rank system no longer had any validity. In addition, the Chinese attempted to undermine *informal* group structure by prohibiting any kind of group meeting, and by systematically fomenting mutual distrust by playing men off against one another. The most effective device to this end was the practice of obtaining from informers or Chinese spies detailed information about someone's activities, no matter how trivial, then calling him in to interrogate him about it. Such detailed surveillance of the men's activities made them feel that *their own ranks were so infiltrated by spies and informers that it was not safe to trust anyone.**

A similar device was used to obtain information during interrogation. After a man had resisted giving information for hours or days, he would be shown a signed statement by one of his fellow prisoners giving that same information. Still another device was to make prisoners who had not collaborated look like collaborators, by bestowing special favors upon them.

A particularly successful Chinese technique was their use of testimonials from other prisoners, such as the false germ-warfare confessions, and appeals

* Editor's italics.

based on familiar contexts, such as peace appeals. Confessions by prisoners or propaganda lectures given by collaborators had a particularly demoralizing effect, because only if resistance had been *unanimous* could a man solidly believe that his values were correct, even if he could not defend them logically.

If the men, in spite of their state of social disorganization, did manage to organize any kind of group activity, the Chinese would quickly break up the group by removing its leaders or key members and assigning them to another camp.

Loyalties to home and country were undermined by the systematic manipulation of mail. Usually only mail which carried bad news was delivered. If a man received no mail at all, the Chinese suggested that his loved ones had abandoned him.

Feelings of *social isolation* * were increased by the complete *information control* * maintained in the camps. Only the Communist press, radio, magazines, and movies were allowed.

The weakening of the prisoner group's social structure is particularly significant because we depend to such an extent on consensual validation in judging ourselves and others. The prisoners lost their most important sources of information and support concerning standards of behavior and beliefs. Often men who attempted to resist the Chinese by means other than *outright* obstruction or aggression failed to obtain the active support of others, often earning their suspicion instead.

At the same time, the Chinese did create a situation in which meaningful social relationships could be had through common political activity, such as the "peace" committees which served as propaganda organs. The Chinese interrogators or instructors sometimes lived with prisoners for long periods of time in order to establish close personal relationships with them.

The Communist doctrines were presented through compulsory lectures followed by compulsory group discussions, for the purpose of justifying the conclusions given at the end of the lectures. On the whole, this phase of indoctrination was ineffective because of the crudeness of the propaganda material used in the lectures. However, its constant repetition seemed eventually to influence those men who did not have well-formed political opinions to start with, particularly because no counterarguments could be heard. The group discussions were effective only if their monitor was someone who could keep control over the group and keep it on the topic of discussion. Attempts by the Chinese to use "progressive" POW's in the role of monitors were seldom successful because they aroused too much hostility in the men.

The Chinese also attempted to get prisoners to use mutual criticism and self-criticism in the fashion in which it is used within China.[2] Whenever a

* Editor's italics.
[2] See the paper by Robert J. Lifton (1957).

POW was caught breaking one of the innumerable camp rules, he was required to give an elaborate confession and *self-criticism,** no matter how trivial the offense. In general, the POW's were able to use this opportunity to ridicule the Chinese by taking advantage of their lack of understanding of slang and American idiom. They would emphasize the wrong parts of sentences or insert words and phrases which made it apparent to other prisoners that the joke was on the Chinese. Often men were required to make these confessions in front of large groups of other prisoners. If the man could successfully *communicate by a linguistic device his lack of sincerity, this ritual could backfire* * on the Chinese by giving the men an opportunity to express their solidarity (by sharing a communication which could not be understood by the Chinese). However, in other instances, prisoners who viewed such public confessions felt contempt for the confessor and felt their own group was being undermined still further by such public humiliation.

Various tales of how prisoners resisted the pressures put on them have been widely circulated in the press. For example, a number of prisoners ridiculed the Chinese by playing baseball with a basketball, yet telling the Chinese this was the correct way to play the game. Such stories suggest that morale and group solidarity was actually quite high in the camps. Our interviews with the men suggest that morale climbed sharply during the last *six* to *nine months* of imprisonment when the armistice talks were underway, when the compulsory indoctrination program had been put on a voluntary basis, and when the Chinese were improving camp conditions in anticipation of the repatriation. However, we heard practically no stories of successful group resistance or high morale from the first year or so in the camps when the indoctrination program was seriously pursued by the Chinese. (At that time the men had neither the time nor the opportunity to play any kind of games because all their time was spent on indoctrination activities or exhausting labor.)

Throughout, the Chinese created an environment in which *rewards* * such as extra food, medicine, special privileges, and status were given for cooperation and collaboration, while *threats* * of death, nonrepatriation, reprisal against family, torture, decreases in food and medicine, and imprisonment served to keep men from offering much resistance. Only imprisonment was consistently used as an actual punishment. *Chronic* resistance was usually handled by transferring the prisoner to a so-called "reactionary" camp.

Whatever behavior the Chinese attempted to elicit, they always *paced* their demands very carefully, they always required some level of *participation* from the prisoner, no matter how trivial, and they *repeated* endlessly.

To what extent did these pressures produce either changes in beliefs and attitudes, or collaboration? Close observation of the repatriates and the reports of the men themselves suggest that the Chinese did not have much

* Editor's italics.

success in changing beliefs and attitudes. Doubt and confusion were created in many prisoners as a result of having to examine so closely their own way of thinking, but very few changes, if any, occurred that resembled actual *conversion* to Communism. The type of prisoner who was most likely to become *sympathetic* toward Communism was the one who had chronically occupied a low status position in this society, and for whom the democratic principles were not very salient or meaningful.

*In producing collaboration, however, the Chinese were far more effective.** By collaboration I mean such activities as giving lectures for the Communists, writing and broadcasting propaganda, giving false confessions, writing and signing petitions, informing on fellow POW's, and so on; none of these activities required a personal change of belief. Some 10 to 15 per cent of the men chronically collaborated, but the dynamics of this response are very complex. By far the greatest determinant was the amount of pressure the Chinese put on a particular prisoner. Beyond this, the reports of the men permit one to isolate several sets of motives that operated, though it is impossible to tell how many cases of each type there may have been.

1. Some men collaborated for outright opportunistic reasons; these men lacked any kind of stable group identification, and exploited the situation for its material benefits without any regard for the consequences to themselves, their fellow prisoners, or their country.

2. Some men collaborated because their egos were too weak to withstand the physical and psychological rigors; these men were primarily motivated by fear, though they often rationalized their behavior; they were unable to resist any kind of authority figure, and could be blackmailed by the Chinese once they had begun to collaborate.

3. Some men collaborated with the firm conviction that they were infiltrating the Chinese ranks and obtaining intelligence information which would be useful to the UN forces. This was a convenient rationalization for anyone who could not withstand the pressures. Many of these men were initially tricked into collaboration or were motivated by a desire to communicate with the outside world. None of these men became ideologically confused; what Communist beliefs they might have professed were for the benefit of the Chinese only.

4. The prisoner who was vulnerable to the ideological appeal because of his low status in this society often collaborated with the conviction that he was doing the right thing in supporting the Communist peace movement. This group included the younger and less intelligent men from backward or rural areas, the malcontents, and members of various minority groups. These men often viewed themselves as failures in our society, and felt that society had never given them a chance. They were positively attracted by the immediate

* Editor's italics.

status and privileges which went with being a "progressive," and by the promise of important roles which they could presumably play in the peace movement of the future.

Perhaps the most important thing to note about collaboration is the manner in which the social disorganization contributed to it. A man might make a slanted radio broadcast in order to communicate with the outside, he might start reading Communist literature out of sheer boredom, he might give information which he knew the Chinese already had, and so on. Once this happened, however, the Chinese rewarded him, increased pressure on him to collaborate, and blackmailed him by threatening exposure. At the same time, in most cases, his fellow prisoners forced him into further collaboration by mistrusting him and ostracizing him. Thus a man had to stand entirely on his own judgment and strength, and both of these often failed. One of the most common failures was a man's lack of awareness concerning the effects of his own actions on the other prisoners, and the value of these actions for the Chinese propaganda effort. The man who confessed to germ warfare, thinking he could repudiate such a confession later, did not realize its immediate propaganda value to the Communists.

A certain percentage of men, though the exact number is difficult to estimate, exhibited chronic resistance and obstructionism toward Chinese indoctrination efforts. Many of these men were *well integrated with secure, stable group identifications who could withstand the social isolation and still exercise good judgment.** Others were chronic obstructionists whose histories showed recurring resistance to any form of authority. Still others were idealists or martyrs to religious and ethical principles, and still others were anxious, guilt-ridden individuals who could only cope with their own strong impulses to collaborate by denying them and over-reacting in the other direction.

By far the largest group of prisoners, however, established a complex compromise between the demands of the Chinese and their own value system. This adjustment, called by the men "playing it cool," consisted primarily of a physical and emotional withdrawal from the whole environment. These men learned to suspend their feelings and to adopt an attitude of watching and waiting, rather than hoping and planning. This reaction, though passive, was not as severe as the apathy described earlier. It was a difficult adjustment to maintain because some concessions had to be made to the Chinese in the form of trivial or well-timed collaborative acts, and in the form of a feigned interest in the indoctrination program. At the same time, each man had to be prepared to deal with the hostility of his buddies if he made an error in judgment.

* Editor's italics.

Discussion

This paper has placed particular emphasis on the social psychological factors involved in "brainwashing" because it is my opinion that the process is primarily concerned with social forces, not with the strengths and weaknesses of individual minds. It has often been asserted that drugs, hypnotic techniques, refined "mental tortures" and, more recently, implanted electrodes can make the task of the "brainwasher" much easier by rendering the human mind submissive with a minimum of effort. There is little question that such techniques can be used to elicit confessions or signatures on documents prepared by the captor; but so can withdrawal of food, water, or air produce the same results. The point is that the Chinese Communists do not appear to be interested in obtaining merely a confession or *transient* submission. Instead, they appear to be interested in producing changes in men which will be lasting and self-sustaining. A germ-warfare confession alone was not enough—the POW had to "testify" before an international commission explaining in detail how the bombs had been dropped, and had to tell his story in other prison camps to his fellow POW's.

There is little evidence that drugs, post-hypnotic suggestion, or implanted electrodes can now or ever will be able to produce the kind of behavior exhibited by many prisoners who collaborated and made false confessions. On the other hand, there is increasing evidence (Hinkle and Wolff, 1956; Lifton, 1956) that Russian and Chinese interrogation and indoctrination techniques *involve the destruction of the person's social ties and identifications, and the partial destruction of his ego.** If this is successfully accomplished, the person is *offered a new identity for himself and given the opportunity to identify with new groups.** What physical torture and deprivation are involved in this process may be either a calculated attempt to degrade and humiliate a man to destroy his image of himself as a dignified human being, or the product of fortuitous circumstances, *i.e.*, failure of supply lines to the prison, loss of temper on the part of the interrogator, an attempt to inspire fear in other prisoners by torturing one of them, and so on. We do not have sufficient evidence to determine which of these alternatives represents Communist intentions; possibly all of them are involved in the actual prison situation.

Ultimately that which sustains humans is their *personality integration born out of secure and stable group identifications.** One may be able to produce temporary submission by direct intervention in cortical processes, but only by destroying a man's self-image and his group supports can one produce any lasting changes in his beliefs and attitudes. By concerning ourselves with the problem of artificially creating submission in man, we run the real risk of overlooking the fact that we are in a genuine struggle of ideas with other

* Editor's italics.

portions of the world and that man often submits himself directly to ideas and principles.

To understand and combat "brainwashing," we must look at those social conditions which make people ready to accept new ideas from anyone who states them clearly and forcefully, and those social conditions which give people the sense of integrity which will sustain them when their immediate social and emotional supports are stripped away.

IMPLICATIONS

Of all the various techniques used by the Chinese in the Korean conflict, which are most understandable to you? Do you find it difficult to understand why certain techniques were effective? Which techniques? Why do you think the emphasis here is on social forces and not on the strengths and weaknesses of the individual persons? A group of psychologists—Farber, Harlow, and West (1957)—point out three aspects of the usual kind of brainwashing: *debility, dependency,* and *dread,* or *DDD.* They point out that resistance to suggestions given by the enemy can be broken down by intense and simultaneous application of these conditions. Are these three conditions the primary factors in Schein's article? In discussing (1) loss of customary social supports, (2) disturbance of the individual's identity with, and roles in, his social system, and (3) the substitution of new group identity, does Schein add any new factors to debility, dependency, and dread? How is the identification with a new group accomplished when it occurs?

REFERENCES

Consult the Bibliography for references cited in the article.

[39] COMMUNICATION: BARRIERS AND GATEWAYS

Has it occurred to you that many of our contemporary human problems are in part a breakdown in communication? Marriages about to end in divorce, labor-management disagreements leading to *strikes, international conflicts* escalating toward major wars, and parent-child misunderstandings reflected in *youth crises* are a few examples of situations in which there is not clear mutual understanding of the views of the adversaries. We find in these cases accusations and counteraccusations, aggressive and defensive statements, but little attempt to understand each other's views and to deal with them in an effective, mutually satisfying way. Probably today, more than at any other time in man's recorded history, there is greater effort expended toward accommodation of differing viewpoints—a realization that in order to live, we must let live.

Rogers and Roethlisberger, pioneers in the use of counseling and psychotherapy for adjustment to human problems, are qualified to suggest an attitude of mind as well as a *modus operandi* for dealing with human conflict. You probably will find a new use of the term *communication*—namely, communication with ourselves, within our personality—referring to understanding those aspects of our experience which we deny to awareness and which are not available to the managing part of ourselves but influence our behavior nonetheless.

Carl R. Rogers and F. J. Roethlisberger

Reprinted from Carl R. Rogers and F. J. Roethlisberger, "Barriers and Gateways to Communication," *Harvard Business Review*, Vol. 30 (Boston: Harvard University, 1952), pp. 46–52, by permission of the publisher and the authors.

It may seem curious that a person like myself, whose whole professional effort is devoted to psychotherapy, should be interested in problems of communication. What relationship is there between obstacles to communication and providing therapeutic help to individuals with emotional maladjustments?

Actually the relationship is very close indeed. The whole task of psychotherapy is the task of dealing with a failure in communication. The emotionally maladjusted person, the "neurotic," is in difficulty, first, because communication within himself has broken down and, secondly, because as a result of this his communication with others has been damaged. To put it another way, in the "neurotic" individual parts of himself which have been termed unconscious, or repressed, or denied to awareness, become blocked off so that they no longer communicate themselves to the conscious or managing part of himself; as long as this is true, there are distortions in the way he communicates himself to others, and so he suffers both within himself and in his interpersonal relations.

The task of psychotherapy is to help the person achieve, through a special relationship with a therapist, good communication within himself. Once this is achieved, he can communicate more freely and more effectively with others. We may say then that psychotherapy is good communication, within and between men. We may also turn that statement around and it will still be true. Good communication, free communication, within or between men, is always therapeutic.

It is, then, from a background of experience with communication in counseling and psychotherapy that I want to present two ideas: (1) I wish to state what I believe is one of the major factors in blocking or impeding communication, and then (2) I wish to present what in our experience has proved to be a very important way of improving or facilitating communication.

BARRIER: THE TENDENCY TO EVALUATE

I should like to propose, as a hypothesis for consideration, that the major barrier to mutual interpersonal communication is our very natural tendency to judge, to evaluate, to approve (or disapprove) the statement of the other person or the other group. Let me illustrate my meaning with some very simple examples. Suppose someone, commenting on this discussion, makes the statement, "I didn't like what that man said." What will you respond? Almost invariably your reply will be either approval or disapproval of the attitude expressed. Either you respond, "I didn't either; I thought it was terrible," or else you tend to reply, "Oh, I thought it was really good." In other words, your primary reaction is to evaluate it from *your* point of view, your own frame of reference.

Or take another example. Suppose I say with some feeling, "I think the Republicans are behaving in ways that show a lot of good, sound sense these days." What is the response that arises in your mind? The overwhelming likelihood is that it will be evaluative. In other words, you will find yourself agreeing, or disagreeing, or making some judgment about me such as "He must be a conservative," or "He seems solid in his thinking." Or let us take an illustration from the international scene. Russia says vehemently, "The treaty with Japan is a war plot on the part of the United States." We rise as one person to say, "That's a lie!"

This last illustration brings in another element connected with my hypothesis. Although the tendency to make evaluations is common in almost all interchange of language, it is very much heightened in those situations where feelings and emotions are deeply involved. So the stronger our feelings, the more likely it is that there will be no mutual element in the communication. There will be just two ideas, two feelings, two judgments, missing each other in psychological space.

I am sure you recognize this from your own experience. When you have not been emotionally involved yourself and have listened to a heated discussion, you often go away thinking, "Well, they actually weren't talking about the same thing." And they were not. Each was making a judgment, an evaluation, from his own frame of reference. There was really nothing which could be called communication in any genuine sense. This tendency to react to any emotionally meaningful statement by forming an evaluation of it from our own point of view is, I repeat, the major barrier to interpersonal communication.

GATEWAY: LISTENING WITH UNDERSTANDING

Is there any way of solving this problem, of avoiding this barrier? I feel that we are making exciting progress toward this goal, and I should like to present it as simply as I can. Real communication occurs, and this evaluative tendency is avoided, when we listen with understanding. What does that mean? It means to see the expressed idea and attitude from the other person's point of view, to sense how it feels to him, to achieve his frame of reference in regard to the thing he is talking about.

Stated so briefly, this may sound absurdly simple, but it is not. It is an approach which we have found extremely potent in the field of psychotherapy. It is the most effective agent we know for altering the basic personality structure of an individual and for improving his relationships and his communications with others. If I can listen to what he can tell me, if I can understand how it seems to him, if I can see its personal meaning for him, if I can sense the emotional flavor which it has for him, then I will be releasing potent forces of change in him.

Again, if I can really understand how he hates his father, or hates the company, or hates Communists—if I can catch the flavor of his fear of insanity, or his fear of atom bombs, or of Russia—it will be of the greatest help to him in altering those hatreds and fears and in establishing realistic and harmonious relationships with the very people and situations toward which he has felt hatred and fear. We know from our research that such empathic understanding—understanding *with* a person, not *about* him—is such an effective approach that it can bring about major changes in personality.

Some of you may be feeling that you listen well to people and yet you have never seen such results. The chances are great indeed that your listening has not been of the type I have described. Fortunately, I can suggest a little laboratory experiment which you can try to test the quality of your understanding. The next time you get into an argument with your wife, or your friend, or with a small group of friends, just stop the discussion for a moment and, for an experiment, institute this rule: "Each person can speak up for himself only *after* he has first restated the ideas and feelings of the previous speaker accurately and to that speaker's satisfaction."

You see what this would mean. It would simply mean that before presenting your own point of view, it would be necessary for you to achieve the other speaker's frame of reference—to understand his thoughts and feelings so well that you could summarize them for him. Sounds simple, doesn't it? But if you try it, you will discover that it is one of the most difficult things you have ever tried to do. However, once you have been able to see the other's point of view, your own comments will have to be drastically revised. You will also find the emotion going out of the discussion, the differences being reduced, and those differences which remain being of a rational and understandable sort. . . .

If, then, this way of approach is an effective avenue to good communication and good relationships, as I am quite sure you will agree if you try the experiment I have mentioned, why is it not more widely tried and used? I will try to list the difficulties which keep it from being utilized.

NEED FOR COURAGE.   In the first place it takes courage, a quality which is not too widespread. I am indebted to Dr. S. I. Hayakawa, the semanticist, for pointing out that to carry on psychotherapy in this fashion is to take a very real risk, and that courage is required. If you really understand another person in this way, if you are willing to enter his private world and see the way life appears to him, without any attempt to make evaluative judgments, you run the risk of being changed yourself. You might see it his way; you might find yourself influenced in your attitudes or your personality.

This risk of being changed is one of the most frightening prospects many of us can face. If I enter, as fully as I am able, into the private world of a neurotic or psychotic individual, isn't there a risk that I might become lost in that world? Most of us are afraid to take that risk. Or if we were listening to a Russian Communist . . . how many of us would dare to try to see the world from his point of view? The great majority of us could not *listen*; we would find ourselves compelled to *evaluate*, because listening would seem too dangerous. So the first requirement is courage, and we do not always have it.

HEIGHTENED EMOTIONS.   But there is a second obstacle. It is just when emotions are strongest that it is most difficult to achieve the frame of reference of the other person or group. Yet it is then that the attitude is most needed if communication is to be established. We have not found this to be an insuperable obstacle in our experience in psychotherapy. A third party, who is able to lay aside his own feelings and evaluations, can assist greatly by listening with understanding to each person or group and clarifying the views and attitudes each holds.

We have found this effective in small groups in which contradictory or antagonistic attitudes exist. When the parties to a dispute realize that they are being understood, that someone sees how the situation seems to them, the statements grow less exaggerated and less defensive, and it is no longer necessary to maintain the attitude, "I am 100 per cent right and you are 100 per cent wrong." The influence of such an understanding catalyst in the group permits the members to come closer and closer to the objective truth involved in the relationship. In this way mutual communication is established, and some type of agreement becomes much more possible.

So we may say that though heightened emotions make it much more difficult to understand *with* an opponent, our experience makes it clear that a neutral, understanding, catalyst type of leader or therapist can overcome this obstacle in a small group.

SIZE OF GROUP. That last phrase, however, suggests another obstacle to utilizing the approach I have described. Thus far all our experience has been with small face-to-face groups—groups exhibiting industrial tensions, religious tensions, racial tensions, and therapy groups in which many personal tensions are present. In these small groups our experience, confirmed by a limited amount of research, shows that this basic approach leads to improved communication, to greater acceptance of others and by others, and to attitudes which are more positive and more problem-solving in nature. There is a decrease in defensiveness, in exaggerated statements, in evaluative and critical behavior.

But these findings are from small groups. What about trying to achieve understanding between larger groups that are geographically remote, or between face-to-face groups that are not speaking for themselves but simply as representatives of others, like the delegates at Kaesong? Frankly we do not know the answers to these questions. I believe the situation might be put this way: As social scientists we have a tentative test-tube solution of the problem of breakdown in communication. But to confirm the validity of this test-tube solution and to adapt it to the enormous problems of communication breakdown between classes, groups, and nations would involve additional funds, much more research, and creative thinking of a high order.

Yet with our present limited knowledge we can see some steps which might be taken even in large groups to increase the amount of listening *with* and decrease the amount of evaluation *about*. To be imaginative for a moment, let us suppose that a therapeutically oriented international group went to the Russian leaders and said, "We want to achieve a genuine understanding of your views and, even more important, of your attitudes and feelings toward the United States. We will summarize and resummarize these views and feelings if necessary, until you agree that our description represents the situation as it seems to you."

Then suppose they did the same thing with the leaders in our own country. If they then gave the widest possible distribution to these two views, with the feelings clearly described but not expressed in name-calling, might not the effect be very great? It would not guarantee the type of understanding I have been describing, but it would make it much more possible. We can understand the feelings of a person who hates us much more readily when his attitudes are accurately described to us by a neutral third party than we can when he is shaking his fist at us. . . .

SUMMARY

In closing, I should like to summarize this small-scale solution to the problem of barriers in communication, and to point out certain of its characteristics.

I have said that our research and experience to date would make it appear that breakdowns in communication, and the evaluative tendency which is the major barrier to communication, can be avoided. The solution is provided by creating a situation in which each of the different parties comes to understand the other from the *other's* point of view. This has been achieved, in practice, even when feelings run high, by the influence of a person who is willing to understand each point of view empathically, and who thus acts as a catalyst to precipitate further understanding.

This procedure has important characteristics. It can be initiated by one party, without waiting for the other to be ready. It can even be initiated by a neutral third person, provided he can gain a minimum of cooperation from one of the parties.

This procedure can deal with the insincerities, the defensive exaggerations, the lies, the "false fronts" which characterize almost every failure in communication. These defensive distortions drop away with astonishing speed as people find that the only intent is to understand, not to judge.

This approach leads steadily and rapidly toward the discovery of the truth, toward a realistic appraisal of the objective barriers to communication. The dropping of some defensiveness by one party leads to further dropping of defensiveness by the other party, and truth is thus approached.

This procedure gradually achieves mutual communication. Mutual communication tends to be pointed toward solving a problem rather than toward attacking a person or group. It leads to a situation in which I see how the problem appears to you as well as to me, and you see how it appears to me as well as to you. Thus accurately and realistically defined, the problem is almost certain to yield to intelligent attack; or if it is in part insoluble, it will be comfortably accepted as such.

This then appears to be a test-tube solution to the breakdown of communication as it occurs in small groups. Can we take this small-scale answer, investigate it further, refine it, develop it, and apply it to the tragic and well-nigh fatal failures of communication which threaten the very existence of our modern world? It seems to me that this is a possibility and a challenge which we should explore.

IMPLICATIONS

Can you recall some examples of Rogers' statement that the stronger our feelings, the more likely it is that there will be no mutual element in the communication, that individuals will be expressing two different ideas of feelings and missing each other in psychological space? There is the suggestion here that *we cannot communicate effectively with others in critical areas if we cannot communicate within ourselves.* See to what extent you regard these suggestions as practicable for more effective communication with others.

You and your fellow students should find it interesting to stage a demonstration in small groups in which two individuals who are poles apart on an issue first debate the issue, then after a time put into practice the suggestion Rogers and Roethlisberger made in the article. In the latter case, *each individual can speak for himself only after he has restated the ideas and feelings of the previous speaker accurately and to that speaker's satisfaction.* In doing this, note whether there is a decrease in defensive and exaggerated statements and in evaluation and critical behavior, and on the other hand, an increase in positive and problem-solving activity.

REFERENCES

You doubtless have noted that Rogers and Roethlisberger have related the issues of communications to psychotherapy. Rogers' view on psychotherapy is mentioned briefly in Selection 55. One of his basic books is *Counseling and Psychotherapy* (1951).

Chapter VIII

RELIGION, LITERATURE, LAW

[40] RELIGION: A PSYCHOLOGIST VIEWS IT

Traditionally, college students have seemed to favor religion as a good topic for bull sessions. Empirically oriented psychologists, however, have not concerned themselves greatly with the topic of religion. Allport is an exception. Beginning with facts from studies, he and an associate conducted a questionnaire investigation on the religious attitudes and practices of the college student, the results of which are summarized in the following article.

Later, Allport explored the role of religion in the adult personality. In considering the criteria of a *mature personality*, he names "a unifying philosophy of life" as highly important. He then inferentially asks if personal religion or the religious sentiment is always a unifying philosophy of life. What is his answer?

Included here are excerpts from two of Allport's books, *The Individual and His Religion* and *Pattern and Growth in Personality*, to show how some psychologists interested in the total personality relate religion to individual behavior and experience.

Gordon W. Allport

Reprinted from Gordon W. Allport, *The Individual and His Religion* (New York: The Macmillan Company, 1950), pp. 44–45, by permission of the publisher.

THE RELIGION OF YOUTH

May we sum up by saying that (1) most students feel the need of including a religious sentiment somewhere within their maturing personalities; (2) for the most part they *believe in a God*,* though their view is not usually of the traditional theistic variety; (3) a bare quarter are in *essential matters orthodox* * and historically faithful to theological dogma; (4) the majority maintain some of the forms of traditional religious practices including prayer; (5) but the majority are clearly dissatisfied with institutional religion as it exists, so much so that 40 per cent of those who feel a religious need yet repudiate the church in which they were reared. If we take the entire student population who have had a religious upbringing, including those who feel no religious need and those who do, we find that 56 per cent reject the church in which they were trained.

It would be wrong to imply that these findings are peculiar to the present college generation. We know that for years the trends here described have been under way. A study (Katz and Allport, 1931) conducted at the University of Syracuse in 1926, for example, revealed that half the students at that time felt that, while they needed religion in their own lives, the current practices of the church were unsatisfactory. Only about one third felt that on the whole these practices were satisfactory—an estimate much like that obtained in the present study. Further, in respect to attitudes toward the deity, actually fewer of the Syracuse students in 1926 endorsed the extreme theistic position, although at the same time a smaller percentage endorsed agnosticism or atheism. Whereas at Syracuse only about 10 per cent abstained altogether from church attendance and devotional practices, our figure is nearer to one third. We must, of course, remember that not only a difference of time is here involved but also a different type of college population.

One additional comparison in time is of interest. A certain question included in our survey was identical with a question asked of 3,000 students at the University of Wisconsin in 1930. It had to do with attitudes toward the church. Very few in either institution subscribed to the position that the "Church is one sure and infallible foundation of civilized life"—6 per cent at Cambridge and 4 per cent at Wisconsin. But the second most favorable

* Editor's italics.

answer showed a significant difference. "On the whole," the statement reads, "the Church stands for the best in human life, although certain minor shortcomings and errors are necessarily apparent in it, as in all human institutions." To this proposition, 37 per cent of Harvard and Radcliffe students in 1946 gave assent, but only 24 per cent of Wisconsin students of both sexes in 1930. Correspondingly, statements markedly unfavourable to the church received much more endorsement sixteen years ago than today (Sheldon, 1942).

Such trend studies as are available, therefore, show that the disaffection of modern youth is probably no greater today than it was fifteen or twenty years ago. The problem is perennial, probably has been so for the last hundred years, perhaps longer.

THE RELIGIOUS SENTIMENT.* When we speak of a person's "unifying philosophy of life" we are likely to think first of his religion. (Spranger, we saw, regarded it as the most comprehensive and integrative of all value orientations.)

But here an immediate distinction must be drawn. The religious sentiments of many people—perhaps of most people—are decidedly immature. Often they are holdovers from childhood. They are self-centered constructions in which a deity is adopted who favors the immediate interests of the individual, like a Santa Claus or an overindulgent father. Or the sentiment may be of a tribal sort: "My church is better than your church. God prefers my people to your people." In cases of this sort, religion merely serves self-esteem. It is utilitarian and incidental in the life. It is a defense mechanism (often an escape mechanism) and does not embrace and guide the life as a whole. It is an "extrinsic" value in the sense that the person finds it "useful" in serving his immediate ends.

Studies show that ethnic prejudice is more common among churchgoers than among nonchurchgoers (Allport, 1954). This fact alone shows that religion is often devisive rather than unifying. Extrinsic religion lends support to exclusions, prejudices, hatreds that negate all our criteria of maturity. The self is not extended; there is no warm relating of self to others, no emotional security, no realistic perception, no self-insight or humor.

In short, we certainly cannot say that the religious sentiment is always a unifying philosophy of life.

At the same time, the religious sentiment may be of such an order that it does provide an inclusive solution to life's puzzles in the light of an intellegible theory. *It can do so if the religious quest is regarded as an end in itself,*† as the value underlying all things and desirable for its own sake. By

---

* Reprinted from G. W. Allport, *Pattern and Growth in Personality* (New York: Holt, Rinehart and Winston, 1961), pp. 300–303, by permission of the publisher and the author.
† Editor's italics.

surrendering himself to this purpose (not by "using" it), religion becomes an "intrinsic" value for the individual, and as such is comprehensive and integrative and motivational (Allport, 1950).

It may help to understand the religious sentiment thus defined if we *compare it with humor.** In one respect only are they alike. Both set a worrisome event in a new frame of reference, smashing, as it were, the context of literal-mindedness. Both humor and religion shed new light on life's troubles by taking them out of the routine frame. To view our problems humorously is to see them as of little consequence; to view them religiously is to see them in a serious scheme of changed meaning. In either case a new perspective results.

In all other respects they are different. Humor depends on seeing incongruity in events; religion sees an ultimate congruity. Since experiences cannot possibly be regarded at any one time as of great moment and as trivial, it follows that we cannot be simultaneously both reverent and jesting. We may joke and pray about the same disturbing events in life, but never at the same time.

What keeps the religious person from becoming a cynic—as thoroughgoing humorists must be—is the conviction that at bottom something is more important than laughter, namely, the fact that he, the laugher, as well as the laughter itself, has a place in the scheme of things. When this important issue is decided, there is still plenty of room for jesting. In fact, a case might be made for the superior sense of humor of the religious person who has settled once and for all what things are sacred and of ultimate value, for nothing else in the world then needs to be taken seriously. He can see that hosts of happenings are ludicrous, that men and women, including himself, are given to amusing vanities, actors upon a stage. To him nothing in their coming and going is of consequence unless it happens to touch the matter of their ultimate value in the scheme of things.

It is only the core and aim of a religious outlook that are beyond the reach of humor. Human foibles related to the religious intention are possible sources of amusement, examples being incongruous episodes that occur in church. But such incongruity does not affect the priority of the "ultimate concern."

Religion always involves more than a man's cognitive processes; nevertheless, being a response of the total self, rational thought is not excluded. All faith—whether religious or not—is an affirmation where knowledge, though made use of, is not the decisive factor. It is a truism that all men live by faith, for no one has knowledge that his values are worth-while; he only has faith that they are. Religious faith differs from other faith chiefly in its comprehensive character. It holds that, if knowledge were present, one would find that the universe as a whole, the facts of existence, the puzzling clash of good and evil, all make coherent sense. As for the content of one's religious

* Editor's italics.

faith, one takes what to him is the best and most rational "fit." *Mature* (*intrinsic*) *religion* * is a completely embracing theory of life but it is not a theory that can be proved in all detail.

Here we must reject the view that all religious impulses in a life are infantile, regressive, or escapist. That such "extrinsic" religion exists there is no doubt. Nor can we accept the view that institutional and orthodox religion is always a childish submission to authority and therefore immature. Plenty of thoughtful people find historic and traditional forms of religion the "best fit" to their own groping in terms of meaning and comprehensiveness. And so even orthodox religion may reflect more than childish awe and habit; it may reflect a carefully chosen, mature, and productive philosophy of life.

But we must not make the reciprocal error and assume that religion is the only unifying sentiment. Logically perhaps, since it aims to encompass all that lies within experience and all that lies beyond, it is ideally designed to confer unity. But the fact remains that many people find a high degree of unification in other directions.

W. H. Clark obtained judgments from approximately three hundred well-educated persons, nearly half of whom were listed in *Who's Who*. When they were asked to rate the constructive factors leading to creativity in their lives, the chief factor turned out to be "interest and satisfaction in work for its own sake," followed by a "desire to know and understand." Third came the desire to aid society. On the average, "religious motivation" came lower on the list, about equal to the "desire to create beauty." But an important fact is that people differ greatly in their ratings of the importance of religion. They tend to give it a high place or a very low place. The fairly low average ranking is due to the fact that the majority of cases studied did not consider it as their chief source of motivation (Clark, 1955).

Thus we cannot say for certain how common is the comprehensive religious sentiment as a unifying philosophy of life. There is evidence, however, that college alumni, when they are a decade or two out of college, are more religious than they were in college (Nelson, 1956; Kelley, 1955; Bender, 1958). The search for religious meaning seems to grow with advancing years.

[We can best conclude this discussion with the following excerpt, the final paragraphs in Allport's *The Individual and His Religion* in which he summarizes his theme.]

The Solitary Way †

My theme has been the diversity of form that subjective religion assumes. Many different desires may initiate the religious quest, desires as contrasting as

---

* Editor's italics.

† Reprinted from Gordon W. Allport, *The Individual and His Religion* (New York: The Macmillan Company, 1950), pp. 141–142, by permission of the publisher.

fear and curiosity, gratitude and conformity. Men show a varying capacity to outgrow their childhood religion, and to evolve a well-differentiated mature religious sentiment. There are many degrees in the comprehensiveness of this sentiment and in its power to integrate the life. There are different styles of doubting, different apperceptions of symbols, contrasting types of content that vary both with the culture and with the temperament and capacity of the believer. There are innumerable types of specific religious intentions. How the individual justifies his faith is a variable matter, and the certitude he achieves is his alone.

From its early beginnings to the end of the road, the religious quest of the individual is solitary. Though he is socially interdependent with others in a thousand ways, yet no one else is able to provide him with the faith he evolves, nor prescribe for him his pact with the cosmos.

Often the religious sentiment is merely rudimentary in the personality, but often, too, it is a pervasive structure marked by the deepest sincerity. It is the portion of personality that arises at the core of the life and is directed toward the infinite. It is the region of mental life that has the longest-range intentions, and for this reason is capable of conferring marked integration upon personality, engendering meaning and peace in the face of the tragedy and confusion of life.

A man's religion is the audacious bid he makes to bind himself to creation and to the Creator. It is his ultimate attempt to enlarge and to complete his own personality by finding the supreme context in which he rightly belongs.

IMPLICATIONS

Did the findings of the study on student attitudes surprise you, or do you think they are representative of the students you know? Do you agree with the author that a religious sentiment or some other unifying philosophy of life is essential to the well-integrated personality? In your experience, how many people did you encounter who have a *mature religious sentiment* as described by Allport? How would you test a religious orientation to determine whether it is a mature one or a holdover from childhood? Evaluate the paragraphs under "The Solitary Way" both objectively, as a critical student of psychology, and subjectively, as a person with a certain attitude toward religion.

REFERENCES

Early in the history of psychology, James (1902) wrote a book on religious experiences. Consult also the Bibliography for references cited in the article.

[41] PSYCHOLOGY IN RELATION TO LITERATURE

Psychology as a science is just a little over eighty years years old, but literature and scholarly writings have concerned themselves with human behavior, experiences, and motivation throughout the ages.

What is the *relationship between psychology and literature?* Several behavioral scientists have sought to explore this question.

Levitas (1963) has devoted two volumes to a collection of writings by philosophers, novelists, poets, mystics, and theologists on issues central to psychology. She regards the psychology-literature relationship as intimate: psychology helps to clarify some literary problems, and literature presents insights to psychology. Freud, for example, is acknowledged as one who made us aware of the role of the unconscious in literature and showed us that art transforms "fearsome visions of our dreams into an aesthetically satisfying and emotionally reassuring form."

Not all American psychologists will regard *intimate* as the best description of the relationship between their subject matter and literature, although there is greater realization of some relationship today than in the recent past. Allport (1937) took serious account of the importance of the role of literature in the study of personality and explained certain differences between the approaches of psychology and literature. Mainly, the latter is more ideographic, allows artistic accentuations, aims at entertainment, and ascribes causes and assigns correlates at random. He concluded that "psychology will not supplant literature nor will the hauteur of the artist hinder the growth of psychology" (p. 63).

Johnson (1961), in an excellent and more recent discussion of the relationship, admits that the two fields have a common serious concern with human nature, but holds their approaches to be now so different that this joint concern is hard to see. He grants, without compromising psychology's unique contribution as a science of human behavior, "that some psychological realities are too large for their scientific forceps to grasp, at best now, and others are too delicate" (p. 4). Hilgard (1962) felt a need to tell his introductory psychology audience of the importance of a better understanding between biological psychology and the humanistic disciplines and explains the distance between the two in terms of psychology's eagerness to "establish itself as a science and its still too recent divorce from philosophy." He states, however, that psychologists have committed themselves to the study of esthetics, language, values, and meanings.

Cohen, a British psychologist, devotes one of the chapters in *Humanistic Psychology* to psychology in relation to literature and gives examples of the relationship. The selection is a reproduction of most of that chapter.

John Cohen

Reprinted from John Cohen, *Humanistic Psychology* (London: George Allen & Unwin, 1958), pp. 189–194, by permission of the publisher and the author.

"If you render Voltaire less sensitive to criticism," said Diderot, "he will no longer be able to penetrate the soul of Mérope." This sentence sums up a volume which might be written on the way a writer's temperament affects his understanding of the characters he creates or subjects to critical analysis. Like many another novelist or poet, Balzac foreshadowed a great deal that was to be written by the psychologist on unconscious mental activity. He was most explicit perhaps when he declared, fifty years before Freud, that "some devotees of the more remote sciences may discover that the intellectual organization is but a kind of internal man who works out schemes and makes plans no less than the external man, and that the struggle between these two (invisible to our frail sight) is no less mortal than the war with the fate to which we subject our weak bodies."

These examples show that an intuitive mind may discover a whole realm of psychological theory later to be mapped out in detail by the patient investigator. On the other hand, in a variety of ways, a psychological approach has opened new avenues to the study of literature. Analysis of the content of the imagery of different poets showed, for example, that Shelley preferred to use images of smell, Keats images of taste and touch, Blake images of organic sensation, Swinburne images of movement, and Edgar Allen Poe and Schiller auditory images. Both Shakespeare and Goethe are rich in all forms of imagery, especially visual.

There have also been studies of some certain elements which enter into the appreciation of literature, for instance, how metaphors are understood by children of different ages. The results are sometimes rather striking. A boy of thirteen explained that Shakespeare's line "A tiger's heart wrapp'd in a woman's hide" meant that "women are harmless if left alone." Another boy understood "All the world's a stage" to mean that "it has daily turns." Schiller's line "hunger makes the world go round" was interpreted as meaning "if you are hungry, you feel dizzy," and the saying "there is poison in standing water" was said to mean "always drink from a tap."

A new orientation to literary criticism was made possible by Freudian theory. This was directed toward an understanding of the nature of creative writing, the choice of themes, the elaboration and resolution of plots, and, in particular, to the far-reaching influence of experiences in the author's infancy and childhood on his mature work.

Freud took the view that the writer is rather like a child at play. He creates a world of fantasy which he himself takes very seriously. He disguises it so that its self-centeredness is not apparent, and hence enables the reader to enjoy his own fantasy without guilt, reproach, or shame. The writer thus enlists the reader almost as an accomplice in releasing impulses which would otherwise find no outlet.

Freud further suggested that the recurrent themes of great novels and drama are often the expression of fundamental human conflict which is reflected unconsciously in the author's mind. The Oedipus theme of Sophocles is perhaps the most celebrated example. The manner in which this idea is applied to literary criticism is illustrated by Ernest Jones's penetrating analysis of *Hamlet*. The difficulty in understanding Hamlet's hesitancy has baffled countless critics. Ernest Jones argued that it can be resolved if we assume that Hamlet was unconsciously motivated by the same wish that led his uncle to kill his brother and marry Hamlet's mother.

Here, too, I should mention the mechanisms of projection and introjection which enable us to understand how identification with the characters in a story or play takes place by the author, on the one hand, and by the reader or theater audience on the other. Flaubert's remark: "Madame Bovary, c'est moi" is perhaps typical of what an author could say with reference to any of his characters.

A different branch of psychological theory suggests parallelisms with the representation of the human personality in literature. I refer to topological psychology which owes its origin to the late Kurt Lewin. In contrast to psychoanalysis which examines the life *history* of a person or the social *history* of a group, topological psychology analyzes the life *space* of the individual or group. Both systems, however, regard the mind as consisting of a number of interrelated functional systems which become more and more sharply divided with increasing age. Both lend themselves to spatial representation.

The novelist, poet, and dramatist are believed to be gifted with special insight into human life. They express this insight not in general concepts or in the form of hypotheses which can be put to the test, but in terms of individual persons. Now a mode of representing personality which could conceptualize the novelist's individual descriptions would have two distinct advantages. It would preserve the "person as a whole" without fragmentation and, second, little would be lost in passing from descriptions of individuals to descriptions of general characteristics in terms of which any single person might be described. Topological psychology claims to have these advantages. Its analysis is at once specific, for it relates to a *particular* person or group, and at the same time it is expressed in *general* terms. It exposes a "horizontal" section of personality at a given point of time, just as Freudian analysis exposes a "vertical" section by following a particular sequence of events over a period of years. It studies the factors operating *now*, not those in the past which led to or produced the *now*.

The point I wish to bring home is this: it seems that the kind of representation of the human personality made by topological psychology—in terms of *regions, paths, movement, barriers, boundaries,* and *tensions*—is one that comes naturally to many writers, and not only to writers of fiction. If so, the spontaneous insight and imagery of the writer would be in accord with the theoretical schemes of the psychologist. And we could assume that the psychologist's manner of conceiving and representing the personality is supported by the intuitive representations made by novelists, dramatists, and other creative writers.

Let me now give some instances from literature of representing human experience in topological imagery.

I begin with a quotation from Sherwood Anderson's short story *Seeds* (Anderson, 1921).

There is a note that comes into the human voice by which you may know real weariness. It comes when one has been trying with all his heart and soul to think his way along some difficult road of thought. *Of a sudden he finds himself unable to go on. Something within him stops. A tiny explosion takes place.* He bursts into words and talks, perhaps foolishly. Little side currents of his nature he didn't know were there run out and get themselves expressed. It is at such times that a man boasts, uses big words, and makes a fool of himself in general.

In this passage a difficult intellectual task is represented as a form of movement within a region. This movement continues until the boundary of the region is reached. Tension is then aroused, and the result is that a transformation takes place in neighboring regions of the personality.

The same effect is produced by Mauriac in the following passage from his story "The End of the Night" in *Thérèse*.

Yet it was borne in on her with complete certainty that *she had reached some sort of limit*—as when a tramp realises that *the path he is on leads nowhere* and loses itself in the sand.

We recollect that Dante begins the *Inferno* with a metaphor of this kind:

In the middle of the journey of our life, I came to myself in a dark wood where the straight way was lost. Ah! how hard a thing it is to tell what a wild, and rough, and stubborn wood this was ...

Stefan Zweig (1921), in his life of Romain Rolland, employs similar imagery: "He [Rolland] *halted on a road which he had recognized to be impassable,* but he did not forget his aim 'to defend greatness on earth.' "

I have come across two very similar examples of a very striking analogy between emotional experience, on the one hand, and physical movement and constraint, on the other hand. One is from Flaubert's *Sentimental Education* (1926) and the other again from Mauriac's *Thérèse.* Flaubert wrote:

He kept moving restlessly within the confines of his passion just as a prisoner keeps moving about in his dungeon.

Here passion is represented as a region with definite boundaries which cannot be crossed. Psychologically, from the point of view of restricted mobility, a man in the grip of a passion closely resembles a prisoner in a cell. In the one case, the zone of free movement and its boundaries are emotional; in the other case, they are made of bricks and mortar.

There is another point of particular psychological interest in relation to Flaubert that I ought to mention at this point. The conception of a *life space* for each individual implies that each person has his own characteristic and distinctive way of perceiving his surroundings, though physically and geographically they are the same surroundings of other people. Now, Maupassant attributes a remark to Flaubert that embodies this very idea. Flaubert said, "There is no truth except . . . in the fashion that we perceive the objects." This is a different way of saying that the manner in which the external world is perceived by us is determined by the structure of our individual minds. Maupassant added:

To Gustave Flaubert, a fact in itself signified nothing . . . instead of displaying the psychology of his personages in explanatory dissertations, he simply made it appear by their acts. The inward was thus unveiled by the outward, and without any psychological argument. . . .

This all too brief sketch has tried to convey the suggestion that the creative writer's intuitions about the structure of personality and the patterns of experience are paralleled and given a systematic form in the theoretical representations of topological psychology.[1] Marcel Proust was the great artist of the life history. Topological psychology may one day inspire another creative mind to express in the language of space what Proust achieved in the language of time.

---

[1] A remarkable example of the topological conception of mind which has come to my attention occurs in Shelley's recently discovered notebooks, particularly Shelley's drawing of a mental labyrinth. (See Neville Rogers' *Shelley at Work,* London: Oxford University Press, 1956.)

IMPLICATIONS

Of the various positions concerning the relationship of literature and psychology that are taken in the introduction to this selection, which do you favor: intimate, supplementary, or different? What can literature do that psychology cannot do in describing human behavior and experiences? What unique contribution does contemporary psychology make to the study of human behavior? Are experimentation and measurement psychology's only unique contributions? Would you care to supplement Cohen's discussion with examples from your own favorite literary selections?

REFERENCES

Consult the Bibliography for references cited in the article.

[42] EMOTIONAL EXPRESSION IN CHINESE LITERATURE

The American college today is cosmopolitan. Almost every dormitory has students from widely different cultures. As the American student of today comes to know contemporaries from abroad, he soon discovers superficial and profound cultural similarities and differences. He may have been told by his Oriental acquaintance that the relative value of human relationships and property differs between the East and the West. He may learn how much the Oriental cherishes friendship. And as the Oriental describes the nature of this friendship, the American collegian may realize that such interdependency, a possible deterrent to social mobility and the ideal of independency, is rare in contemporary United States.

To what extent, then, is it true that "East is East and West is West, and never the twain shall meet" or, contrariwise, that "human nature is the same all over the world"? The social scientists have always been interested in cultural differences and interactions; but the psychologist until recently has had only occasional tangential concern with various cultures. Klineberg is an exception. He has made significant contributions to the study of differences in test intelligence of various cultures, and his essay presents similarities and differences in Eastern and Western emotional expression as well as the suggestion that psychologists might use literature to study the behavioral expressions in different cultures.

Otto Klineberg

Reprinted from Otto Klineberg, "Emotional Expression in Chinese Literature," *Journal of Abnormal and Social Psychology*, Vol. 33 (Washington, D.C.: American Psychological Association, 1938), pp. 517–520, by permission of the publisher and the author.

The fact that the expression of the emotions is at least to some extent patterned by social factors is probably known to all psychologists. Even in our own society there is considerable evidence that this is so. When we turn to the descriptions of other cultures, instances of this patterning occur frequently. One of the most striking examples is the copious shedding of tears by the Andaman Islanders and the Maori of New Zealand when friends meet after an absence, or when two warring parties make peace. Another is the smile with which the Japanese responds to the scolding of his superior, or which accompanies his announcement of the death of his favorite son.

This paper represents part of a more extensive study of emotional expression among the Chinese, an investigation made possible by a Guggenheim Fellowship and a supplementary grant from the Social Science Research Council. Among the various techniques employed, it seemed valuable in the case of a civilization as articulate as the Chinese to examine at least a portion of the Chinese literature for the light it might throw on this problem. There is not much precedent for the reading of novels as a technique of psychological investigation, but in this case it seemed warranted at least as an introduction to more objective methods.

Before turning to the question of the kind of expression involved, a word should be said as to the related question of the amount of expression which the culture permits. There are, for example, many admonitions—especially to the young girl—not to show emotion too readily. In *Required Studies for Women* we find such warnings as the following: "Do not show your unhappiness easily and do not smile easily"; also, "Do not let your teeth be seen when you smile," that is, your smile must be so circumspect that the teeth do not show. On the other hand, there are many occasions on which the emotion of grief has to be displayed. One piece of advice from the same volume reads, "If your father or mother is sick, do not be far from his or her bed. Do not even take off your girdle. Taste all the medicine yourself. Pray your god for his or her health. If anything unfortunate happens, cry bitterly."

The alleged inscrutability of the Chinese, which as a matter of fact has been greatly exaggerated, completely breaks down in the case of grief. Not only is grief expressed, but there is an elaborate set of rules and regulations which insure that it shall be properly expressed. One of the Chinese classics is *The Book of Rites,* a considerable portion of which is devoted to the technique of the mourning ceremonial, with elaborate instructions as to just what procedure should be followed in order that the expression of the grief may be socially acceptable.

The most extreme degree of patterning of emotional expression is found on the Chinese stage, and is illustrated by the following examples from a Chinese *Treatise on Acting.* There is an occasional pattern which does conform closely to our own; for example, "taking the left sleeve with the right hand and raising it to the eyes as if to wipe the tears" is clearly an expression of sorrow. There are others, however, that are not so clear. To "draw one leg up and stand on one foot" means surprise. To "raise one hand as high as the face and fan the face with the sleeve" means anger, as does also to "blow the beard to make it fly up." Joy or satisfaction is represented by stretching "the left arm flatly to the left and the right arm to the right." To "move one hand around in front of the middle of the beard and touch your head with the fingers of the other hand" means sorrow, while to "put the middle part of the beard into the mouth with both hands and bite firmly" indicates that one has come to a decision. To "raise both hands above the head with the palms turned outward and the fingers pointing up, let the sleeves hang down behind the hands, then walk toward the other person, shake the sleeves over, and let the hands fall" means love.

There were two long novels which were read for this study; one, *The Dream of the Red Chamber,* was read in Chinese, with considerable help from Miss Wu T'ien Min, a graduate student at Yenching University, and the other, *All Men Are Brothers,* in Pearl Buck's English translation. These represent two of the three famous Chinese novels, the third being *The Romance of the Three Kingdoms. The Dream of the Red Chamber* is a love story; *All Men Are Brothers* is a tale of swashbuckling adventure dealing with the so-called "bandits" who are among the most picturesque figures of Chinese legend and history. Besides these, several modern stories were also consulted.

In some cases the descriptions of emotional expression correspond closely to our own. When we read (D.R.C.), for example, that "everyone trembled with a face the color of clay," there can be little doubt that fear is meant. The same holds for the statement that "every one of his hairs stood on end, and the pimples came out on the skin all over his body" (from "Married Life Awakening the World"). Other descriptions of fear (A.M.B.) are the following: "A cold sweat broke forth on his whole body, and he trembled without ceasing"; "it was as though her two feet were nailed to the ground and she would fain have shrieked but her mouth was like a mute's"; "they stood like death with mouths ajar"; "they were so frightened that their waters and wastes burst out of them." In general, it may be said that fear is expressed in very much the same way in the Chinese literature as in our own. As far as other emotions are concerned, in the sentence, "He gnashed his teeth until they were all but ground to dust," we recognize anger; "He was listless and silent" suggests sorrow; "His face was red and he went creeping alone outside the village" clearly indicates shame. There is no doubt of the frequent similarity between Chinese and Western forms of expression.

There are also differences, however. When we read "They stretched out their tongues" (D.R.C.), most of us would not recognize this description as meaning surprise, except for the context. This phrase as an expression of surprise occurs with great frequency, and it would be easy to give many examples. The sentence "Her eyes grew round and opened wide," would probably suggest to most of us surprise or fear; to the Chinese it usually means anger. This expression, with slight variations, also occurs very often. In the form "He made his two eyes round and stared at him" (A.M.B.), it can mean nothing but anger. "He would fain have swallowed him at a gulp" (A.M.B.) implies hatred; our own "I could eat you up!" has a somewhat different significance. "He scratched his ears and cheeks" would probably suggest embarrassment to us, but in *The Dream of the Red Chamber* it means happiness. "He clapped his hands" (D.R.C.) is likely to mean worry or disappointment.

The case of anger appears to be particularly interesting. We have already noted the expressions connected with "round eyes," "eyes wide open," "staring," etc. We find in addition descriptions like these: "He laughed a great ho-ho," and "He smiled a chill smile," and "He looked at them and he smiled and cursed them" (A.M.B.). Both the laugh and the smile of anger or contempt occur in our own culture, but apparently not nearly so frequently as in China and the Chinese literature. More curious still is the phrase "He was so angry that several times he fainted from his anger" (A.M.B.). This expression occurs frequently. When I showed wonder as to why this should be, Chinese friends said that they in turn could never understand why European women fainted so frequently in the mid-Victorian literature with which they were acquainted. Certainly the delicately nurtured young women of not so long ago did faint with astonishing ease and regularity; there were even etiquette books which taught them how to faint elegantly. Such a custom is certainly no less surprising than that the Chinese should faint in anger. The conclusion seems clear that fainting, like tears, may be conditioned by social custom to appear on widely varying occasions.

Most striking of all, perhaps, is the indication in the literature that people may die of anger. "His anger has risen so that he is ill of it and lies upon his bed, and his life cannot be long assured." " 'Today am I killed by anger' ...

and when he had finished speaking he let his soul go free" (A.M.B.). This phenomenon, incidentally, mysterious though it may sound, is reported as still occurring, and I saw one patient in a hospital in Peiping whose father was said to have died of anger after losing a lawsuit. It is important to note that a death of this kind cannot be explained as due to anything like an apoplectic stroke; it does not occur suddenly as a stroke would. When someone is very angry but is forced to suppress his anger because there is nothing he can do about it, he may become ill, faint many times, and take to his bed; death may follow after the lapse of some days or weeks. The only explanation is in terms of suggestion; the belief that people die of anger when they can do nothing about it may succeed in actually bringing on the death of an impressionable person. There is the parallel case of the Polynesian native who inadvertently eats the tabooed food of the chief, remains perfectly well as long as he does not know it, but may die when he learns what he has done.

These examples indicate that, although there are many similarities between the literary descriptions of the emotions in China and in the West, there are also important differences which must be recognized if Chinese literature is to be read intelligently. When the literary pattern is such that the expression alone is described but not labeled, real misunderstandings may arise. When I first read, for instance, "They stretched out their tongues," I did not know that surprise was meant. Our own literature is, of course, also rich in these unlabeled expressions. We read, "His jaw dropped"; "He gnashed his teeth"; "His lip curled"; "His eyes almost popped out of his head"; "He clenched his fists," etc., and in each case we know at once what emotion is indicated. These expressions are a part of language and must be learned in order to be understood.

The question arises as to the degree to which these Chinese literary expressions are related to expression in real life. Caution must certainly be exercised in inferring from one to the other. A Chinese reader of our literature, for instance, might conclude that laughter was dangerous to Westerners, in view of the frequency with which he read the expression "I nearly died laughing." I think I may say, however, on the basis of information obtained by methods other than the reading of novels, that the Chinese patterns which I have described do appear not only in the literature but also in real life. I may add that photographs illustrating these literary expressions are judged more easily by Chinese than by American subjects.

It seems to me to be worth-while to extend this literary approach to other cultures. In the writings of India, Japan, and other peoples of the Near and Far East, material must certainly be available which would further illustrate the extent and the nature of the cultural patterning of emotional expression.

IMPLICATIONS

To what extent did this selection recall behavioral differences you may have noted in persons from other cultures? Did it prompt you to realize that you failed to comprehend completely the behavior of an acquaintance of another land?

Is there anything in this study of emotional expression to suggest that emotions of human beings other than learned responses are essentially similar the world over? Why must we exert caution in drawing conclusions from the literature of a country as to the modal behavior of that culture?

Would it be profitable to engage in small group discussions with fellow students reared in a different social milieu to learn similarities and differences in values, motivation, and social customs in order to give greater perspective both to them and to you?

REFERENCES

Klineberg (1933) has written a book on race differences. Anastasi (1958) has a chapter on the same topic. Selection 32 discusses achievement in various societies in the world. See also Minturn and Rambert (1964), and Hsu (1961).

[43] LANGUAGE: A HOME-RAISED CHIMPANZEE

How important is language as it passes knowledge and the cultural achievements of man to the child in his development? What are the major differences between man and the chimpanzee that is reared in a typically human environment? Can the hypothetical genetic difference in brain structure of the chimp and man be overcome by exploiting the natural motor abilities of the animal in teaching him a language more appropriate to his native equipment?

We introduce this problem through an interesting account by Keith and Catherine Hayes of their experience in rearing a chimpanzee in their home. They suggest brain structure as the cause for the chimp's inability to learn human language. Today, psychologists, together with scholars in the field of language, are planning new approaches to this problem, and we provide under "References" notes on a proposed study by Premack and Schwartz that uses the chimp as subject.

Keith J. Hayes and Catherine Hayes

Reprinted from Keith J. and Catherine Hayes, "The Intellectual Development of a Home-Raised Chimpanzee," *American Philosophical Society*, Vol. 95 (Philadelphia: American Philosophical Society, 1951), pp. 105–109, by permission of the publisher and the senior author.

The anthropoid apes are of special interest to psychology because of their nearness to man on the phylogenetic scale. The degree of their similarity to man psychologically is rather uncertain, however, largely because the great majority of studies have utilized animals with very restricted backgrounds of experience. There is an ever-increasing body of evidence which indicates that the intellectual capacity of any animal—human or otherwise—depends not only on its hereditary endowment, but also, and to a considerable extent, on its psychological history. In view of such evidence, it seems unreasonable to suppose that an ape who has spent his whole life in a small, bare laboratory cage could perform at his maximum potential level on intellectual tasks.

In the present investigation, we are attempting to make a more satisfactory estimate of anthropoid intelligence by studying a young chimpanzee *whose background of experience is very much like that of a human child.** This type of project was suggested by Witmer forty-one years ago, and has been undertaken several times since then, the best-known investigation being that of Kellogg and Kellogg (1933). We hope, in the present study, to avoid various shortcomings such as brief duration, unsystematic observation, insufficient reporting, and inadequate objective records, which have detracted from the value of earlier efforts.

In addition to the obvious relevance of such a study to general problems of evolution, and comparative and physiological psychology, it may clarify certain features of human psychology by presenting them in different perspective. Language-using ability is one such feature which we shall discuss in detail, later. Another example is the problem known as the nature-nurture controversy: does a child primarily *mature* to a certain intellectual level by a genetically controlled process of physical growth; or is his intelligence *acquired*, more as the result of a gradual accumulation of knowledge from his con-

* Editor's italics.

tinued experience in a physical and social environment? This problem has been studied within the human species, but such studies are burdened with a number of difficulties: both variables tend to be restricted in range, and they tend to be correlated. In the present study, we hope to get more·clear-cut results by dealing with a greater range of the variables, and by keeping them unrelated. A chimpanzee raised as a child in a human home can be compared with normal human children, thus providing a large difference in heredity with constant environment. On the other hand, this same chimpanzee can be compared with its relatives who are raised in laboratory cages—constant heredity here being combined with a greater difference in environment than can be found within the human population.

Our subject, Viki, was adopted a few days after birth, and has now spent the first three years of her life in our home. She has been treated as nearly as possible like a human child, with a few exceptions. Our purpose necessitates a great many tests and experiments, to which most children are not subjected. When Viki appears to be markedly inferior in some respect, special training is usually given to determine whether the deficiency can be overcome. During much of her life, such training was given at mealtime, so that she worked for most of her food.

An extensive diary record is kept of her activities; she is compared with human children and laboratory chimpanzees in a variety of formal experiments; and photographic and motion picture records are made of the more significant features of her behavior.

In terms of results, this must be considered a progress report—the investigation is by no means completed, and if it were to be terminated at this point, our conclusions would have to be very tentative. Our subject is only three years old; it cannot be assumed that she has completed a greater proportion of her intellectual development than a human child has at this age; and the child is a very incomplete person at three. The typical three-year-old cannot count, draw, lace his shoes, play catch with a ball, or copy a simple construction of building blocks. Nevertheless, we have established a number of points which seem unlikely to be contradicted by our later results.

In general, *Viki's development has closely paralleled that of a normal human child,** her interests and abilities having appeared in roughly the same sequence, and at about the same rate. Her social behavior is that of an extrovert: she seeks the company and attention of people and is very friendly, though somewhat aggressive with those who allow her to dominate them.

Viki, like human children, spends most of her time in play—an activity which merits considerable attention because of the purpose it serves. Although play behavior is self-rewarding, and does not serve directly to satisfy any immediate biological need, it does provide experience which may later be useful in satisfying such needs.

* Editor's italics.

Viki's play is much more athletic than a child's—she spends a larger part of the day running, climbing, and jumping, and is constantly developing new and different ways of accomplishing the ostensibly, simple business of getting from one place to another. Her greater innate drive toward such activities appears to make a major contribution to her greater athletic skill—which is much more important to her semiarboreal species than it is to the terrestrial human.

On the other hand, she is *less vocal* *: while the human child commonly keeps up an almost continuous stream of chatter—with or without meaning, Viki is silent. She babbled a little during her first year, and at present she occasionally devotes a few minutes to rather stereotyped vocal play; but she gets only a small fraction of the practice which provides background for the human child's most distinctive accomplishment—language.

One of the more characteristic aspects of human play is the *use of various mechanical gadgets* *—that class of objects which are toys to the child, and tools to the adult. Viki does not appear to be seriously retarded here, either in interest or ability. She scribbles, cuts with shears, builds with blocks and tinker-toys, throws and catches balls, operates light switches and door latches, with about the same skill and enthusiasm as most three-year-old humans. One of her favorite toys at present is the telephone, which she holds to her ear while dialing a few numbers—at random.

She seems to have as much *preference for social play* * as people do. She leads us about by the hand, coaxes us to tickle her, begs for pickaback rides, brings us toys which are used in social games, and enlists our aid in exploiting new gadgets by firmly placing our hands at the appropriate spot. When new acquaintances are available, she usually plays with them, rather than with members of the family.

An especially interesting feature of human social play is *imitation* *; and here again, Viki shows no great difference. Just as a human child copies its parents' routine chores, so Viki dusts; washes dishes; sharpens pencils; saws, hammers, and sandpapers furniture; paints woodwork; and presses photographs in books.

Although such spontaneous imitation is often very striking, a more rigorous experimental analysis seemed desirable. Six problems were therefore prepared and presented to Viki and to four human children of about the same age. Four of these problems were also presented to a laboratory chimpanzee nine months older.

These *imitation problems* * involved obtaining a toy or piece of candy in various ways: by throwing a ball at it to knock it down; or by pushing it out of a long tunnel with a rod; or by operating a light switch on the wall, which released the prize magnetically from the ceiling. In some problems, the door of a box containing the prize was opened by using a stick to strike a distant

* Editor's italics.

FIGURE 1. Building a tower of blocks, at eighteen months.

string; or by burning a nearby string with a candle flame; or by pulling three levers in a certain sequence. The subject was allowed to attempt a solution first, to insure that it could not be done readily by insight or trial and error. The experimenter then demonstrated the proper procedure and allowed the subject to try again; if she was unsuccessful, additional demonstrations were given.

There was little difference between Viki and the children—they usually solved these problems within a few trials. The laboratory chimpanzee solved only one, however; his failure on the others appeared to be due, at least in part, to his lack of skill in manipulating the apparatus.

Viki can also *imitate in response to the command* * "do this," by copying the action we demonstrate, a procedure which is useful in helping her to learn new skills.

We have, of course, been interested in the evaluation of Viki's IQ, as measured by the intelligence tests designed for use with human children. Such tests are of doubtful validity, however, when applied to the children of psychologists who know in advance what items of behavior will be tested at various ages. Validity may also suffer somewhat from frequent retesting. Our

* Editor's italics.

results in this field must not, therefore, be taken too seriously. They appear to indicate, however, that Viki's *general intelligence has developed at about the same rate as that of a human child,** and is now at about the normal three-year-old level. She performs with appropriate skill on such test items as form boards, peg boards, picture puzzles, block piling, and buttoning. However, most intelligence tests include a large number of items which depend on the child's ability to use language—either directly, as in a question-and-answer situation, or indirectly, as where materials must be manipulated in accordance with relatively complicated verbal instructions. Viki fails completely on most such tests of *verbal* intelligence.

Language is,* in fact, the one field of behavior in which we have thus far been able to find a *large, clear-cut, and important superiority of man over chimpanzee.** Although Viki has learned to say a few words, the significance of this fact lies not in her learning to say them, but rather in the great difficulty with which she learned, and in the particular nature of this difficulty.

As an infant, Viki babbled much less than human babies do, and even this disappeared by five months of age. However, the variety of sounds observed in her babbling, and in her vocal expressions of emotion, left no doubt that her vocal mechanisms were adequate for producing satisfactory approximations of most of the elements of human speech.

Since it appeared unlikely that Viki would speak spontaneously, we began a speech training program when she was five months old. The first step was aimed at teaching her merely to vocalize on command, in order to obtain a reward. No specific sound was insisted upon at this stage. The task was surprisingly difficult. Although she seemed to learn what was required quickly, she had serious trouble with the motor skill of voluntary vocalization. It took her five months to learn to produce a hoarse, staccato grunt, quite unlike her normal spontaneous sounds. She could do this quickly and dependably, when told to "speak," but only with much grimacing and straining. This phase of the training was also given to several laboratory chimpanzees, with similar results.

By manipulating Viki's lips as she vocalized, we were able to make her say "mama." She soon learned to make the proper mouth movements herself, and could then say "mama" unaided—softly, and hoarsely, but quite acceptably.

Viki's *later words were learned more easily* * and by a different procedure. Like many other chimpanzees, she has developed a type of play which is superficially similar to babbling. It differs in that the sounds are produced entirely by mouth vibrations, without use of the larynx. Some of these sounds are roughly similar to certain human consonants, and since Viki readily imitates our production of them, we attempted to teach her to use them in words. By the time she was two-and-one-half years old, she had

* Editor's italics.

learned to pronounce satisfactory approximations of the whispered words "papa" and "cup." We did not manipulate her mouth in teaching these words, but simply insisted that she copy our example of a certain combination of play sounds.

She *did not use her three words meaningfully at first* *; but when we required her to employ them appropriately, she soon learned to address the proper experimenter as "mama" or "papa," and to say "cup" when she wanted something to drink. She sometimes confuses them, however—especially when we urge her to speak, or when she wants something very badly.

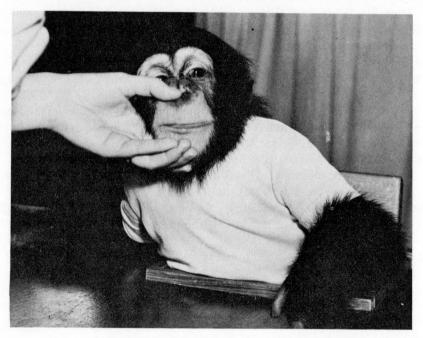

FIGURE 2. We help her to say "mama," at fourteen months.

When Viki is compared with various human individuals who display a similar degree of language deficiency, we find that she *bears little resemblance to those whose trouble is caused by feeble-mindedness or by abnormality of the speech organs; but she does quite closely resemble those cases, know as aphasics,* * whose deficiency is caused by abnormal brain structure, congenital or acquired. Like many aphasics, Viki is deficient in language comprehension, as well as in speech, though here the deficit is less striking.

The *conclusions* * to be drawn from this investigation must be considered very tentative. We are home-raising only one chimpanzee, who may or may

* Editor's italics.

not be typical of her species. She is only three years old, and cannot, therefore, be compared with man of the adult level.

If we assume, however, that Viki's mental development will continue to parallel that of man to maturity—as it appears to have done for the first three years—then our results strongly suggest that the two species are much more alike, psychologically, than has heretofore been supposed. They suggest, in fact, that man's superior ability to use language may be his only important *genetic* advantage. This one genetic advantage makes further advantages possible, however, since language is a means of sharing knowledge. Intelligence

Figure 3. The phone is a favorite plaything at age three, though she seldom says anything into it.

depends on three factors: the individual's innate capacity, his personal experience, and the experience he acquires second-hand, through communication with others. This last factor, while unimportant to most species, makes man less dependent on individual abilities, by providing him with a more effective "group intelligence."

We suspect that the importance of this *cultural factor** in determining the abilities of man has been seriously underestimated—an understandable error since men as we know them always have culture, giving us no opportunity to observe the effect of its absence. If an individual man could grow up in complete isolation from culture, and with only such knowledge as he could

* Editor's italics.

gain directly from his environment, we suspect that his behavior would be very different from that of the men we know, and would probably be quite apelike. We doubt that such a man could survive, in competition with the physically hardier anthropoids.

We suspect that the *species chimpanzee closely resembles our hypothetical, cultureless man,* with much the same individual capacities—except for language ability, the tool which man uses to build and maintain culture.

IMPLICATIONS

What do the conclusions drawn by Keith and Catherine Hayes mean to you, as man? Read the paragraphs under "References" about Premack's and Schwartz's proposed experiments. What are the basic differences between their proposal and the Hayes's experiment? Do you think Premack's and Schwartz's method will teach the animal a language? Why?

REFERENCES

For another study of a similar nature consult Kellogg and Kellogg (1933). Premack and Schwartz (1966) note the chimp's tendencies to imitate, particularly in the motor realm, and have devised a piece of apparatus (a vertical lever capable of swiveling in all directions and tilting to any degree) that the animal can learn to manipulate. The movements of the lever produce sounds that vary in frequency, amplitude, and duration. The experimenters are cognizant of the basic nature of language, and two laboratory assistants are teaching the young chimps a language, using sounds that are imitated by the chimps.

Presumably, the chimps can readily learn to manipulate the lever and associate attending sounds to various events. Both functional and non-meaningful sounds will be employed. This experiment (1) keeps language auditory, (2) supplies the animal with a more adequate motor expression, (3) reduces the cognitive task by simplifying language (a most important question at present is whether there are simple and complex languages), and (4) exploits the play, exploratory, and curiosity tendencies so prevalent in the chimp and in man. The experiment is at present at the pilot stage.

* Editor's italics.

[44] THE USE OF PSYCHOLOGISTS
IN LEGAL PRACTICE

What specific contributions can the contemporary practicing or academic psychologist make to the legal profession? Psychologist Redmount is a member of the Connecticut Bar and is well acquainted with the scientific activities and professional background of a
clinical and consultant psychologist. He has written the following article
in a popular vein for his fellow lawyers, and in it he brings up the kinds
of cases that they frequently encounter. He suggests how lawyers may
use the resources of a psychologist to add to their cases reliable facts
about individual behavior. Redmount is probably more enthusiastic
about the value of psychological knowledge and techniques than some
psychologists are; but he is intimately acquainted with the support that
the expert's data and opinions lend to a lawyer and his client. He cites
precedents for the use of certain procedures, and he presents the controversy and the court's decision on whether psychologists are independent experts in the area of mental disorder.

Robert S. Redmount

Reproduced with the permission of *The Practical Lawyer*, 101
North 33rd Street, Philadelphia, Pa. 19104. Subscription Rates:
$10 a year, $2.00 a single issue. Dr. Robert S. Redmount's article
appeared in the February 1965 issue, Vol. 11, No. 2, pp. 23–38.

The creative practice of law is a sensitive and resourceful blend that combines prudence in its reliance upon tested and established rules and procedures, and enterprise in its use of newer views and procedures that may prove
attractive and highly effective. In the practice of law, one gauges the promise
of newer methods and techniques in terms of their probable or proven ability
to protect and conserve the interests of clients, to create advantage for a client
because of the appeal of their added skill and reliability, and to clarify and

afford more reliability on matters of notable uncertainty. They may demonstrate their value to the attorney in counseling with his client in the law office or to the court in its consideration of some litigable issue.

The increasing range of systematic skills, techniques, and information about human behavior held by the psychologist, some well established and recognized and others experimental in character, affords a fertile resource to be tapped by the creative attorney in his practice of law. Following are some possibilities, both tried and untried, that may benefit an attorney in his office practice and in the conduct of litigation.

DRAFTING WILLS

Mr. Elder Crotchety, a client of strong passion and conviction, wishes to draft a will containing substantial devises and legacies that are highly partisan and unexpected. He knows that his designing sons will not approve and can be expected to contest the will on grounds of mental incompetence or undue influence. He wants his attorney to make the will, and the issue of competency or capacity, as ironclad as possible against destruction in court. He advises his attorney to leave no stone unturned in the exercise of effective preventive law procedures.

Attorney Sharp knows that mental incompetence and undue influence are legal concepts but that they assume some factual basis in judgments of human conduct. An attack on competency and capacity seeks to show poor operative intelligence and judgment, perhaps a lack of emotional stability verging on the abnormal, and possibly some distorted thinking and ideas.

Certification of Mental Competency

Gauged by professional standards and practices, among the most widely recognized and accepted individual psychological measures of intelligence (including within it denominators of alertness, comprehension, mental control, and social judgment) is the Wechsler Adult Intelligence Scale. The Rorschach Technique is a measure widely used to gauge emotional stability, and this, as well as the Thematic Apperception Test, is broadly used to assess distortion in, and the character of, thinking and ideas.

These assessment techniques have a history of decades of use in measuring mental and emotional capacities and dispositions in educational, military, medical, and other settings. Thousands of persons have been evaluated by these assessment techniques, which may be highly skillful and informative when they are utilized by competent and experienced psychologists.

Attorney Sharp might suggest to his client that, by taking a standard psychological examination in conjunction with the execution of his will, he may seek to certify his competency. Expert opinion may be offered and supported by measured facts and standards. The competence, relevancy, and probity of this timely expert certification may be strongly argued on the facts in a pro-gressive court, albeit there is as yet a dearth of legal precedent and litigation on the procedure.

This evidence should be viewed as more probative than the later reconstruction and retroactive judgments of competency that are now utilized. The cost in time and expense is negligible where an estate has any substantial value.

DAMAGES IN ACCIDENT CASES

Mrs. Fairly Hirt was recently involved in an automobile accident involving the negligence of another driver. Mrs. Hirt claims that her head was injured in the accident, that she had headaches that have now subsided, but that she has suffered permanent brain injury affecting her capacity to work. She has memory lapses and has confusion and difficulty with mental control (e.g., in arithmetic problems) such as did not previously exist. She also claims that she wrenched her back and now has severe, intermittent low back pains and, as a consequence of the accident and injury, she suffers a perpetual nervous condition.

The defendant claims and seeks to prove that Mrs. Hirt was always an emotionally unstable person and given to passing aches and pains of minor intensity. Defendant also claims Mrs. Hirt simply has a poor memory and is poor in arithmetic. The defendant's position is that there is no brain injury.

Attorney Tortle, for the plaintiff, seeks to prove not only brain damage and resultant consequences because of the accident and injury, but also an increase in anxiety and emotional disturbance. He also wishes to establish a degree of pain such as would indicate the need for very substantial compensation on the matter of pain, as well as upon the issues of mental and emotional injury.

Examinations for Brain Injury

Attorney Tortle observed, during a period of military hospitalization when on wartime duty, that psychologists were used to assess whether cortical functions had been impaired in a manner that had come to be recognized as characteristic of brain-injured persons. Psychological examinations, consisting of standardized and clinical tests of intellectual functioning, memory, perceptual-motor skills, and the like, were utilized as supportive evidence. The same or similar psychological examinations were used—and now, with the benefit of extensive clinical experience, continue to be used regularly—to suggest whether there might be evidence indicative of brain injury and to verify or anticipate the findings of neurologists on this issue.

Examinations for Emotional Disorder

It is also well-established practice for psychologists to conduct standard psychological examinations of emotional disturbance and disorder, either as a part of, or independently from, psychiatric examinations on the matter. The Rorschach and Thematic Apperception Test techniques, along with other techniques and measures, are widely used to give evidence of emotional instability and of the patterns of conduct that may result, and evidence of changes in emotional status and the like.

Measurement of Pain

The measurement of pain is a somewhat more uncertain, and consequently not a standard, psychological procedure. However, techniques that have been subjected to experimental verification have been developed and have been used by psychologists for this purpose. Generally, the psychologist's clinical examinations of a person require perhaps the greater part of a day, and then some additional hours are needed to evaluate the data and to prepare a report.

Competence of Psychologist to Testify

Attorney Tortle also has the benefit of favorable legal precedent to use the qualified psychologist and his proper examinations, not yet so much to assess pain, but more particularly to assess mental and emotional disturbance and abnormality. Psychologists in increasing numbers of cases have testified on such matters. The issue of the psychologist's competence to do so has been litigated in recent years consistently in the psychologist's favor.

The issue of the psychologist's competence and qualification to render expert testimony in the field of mental disturbances and disorders was thoroughly litigated in *Jenkins* v. *United States*, 307 F.2d 637 (D.C. Cir. 1962). The court sat en banc to consider the issue raised by virtue of the fact that the psychologist's professional opinions were excluded in the case by the trial court on grounds that the psychologist was incompetent to testify as an expert in the matter.

A brief as amicus curiae was submitted by the American Psychological Association. It argued that psychology, a learned profession with a considerable history and tradition, provides systematic training and occupational experience in the assessment of behavior and behavior disorders, that the profession of psychology is controlled and guided by ethical standards and certification practices, and that properly qualified psychologists are, indeed, expert in the field of mental disorder.

A brief as amicus curiae was also submitted by the American Psychiatric Association in opposition to this argument. This brief argued that mental disturbances and disorders are exclusively within the medical province, that psychiatrists are the only established medical experts on the matter, that psychological examinations and results are a part of the psychiatric examination to be evaluated by psychiatrists, but that they do not have independent standing and psychologists are not independent experts on the matter of mental disorder.

The court, in a 7–2 opinion, upheld the view that psychologists are independent experts in matters relating to the existence and effects of mental disorder and that the failure to allow the opinion of qualified psychologists on this issue is reversible error.

This holding is in line with the strong preponderance of decisions on the matter. See *Hidden* v. *Mutual Life Ins. Co.,* 217 F.2d 818, 821 (4th Cir. 1954); *Watson* v. *State,* 273 S.W.2d 879 (Tex. Crim. 1954); *Carter* v. *Oklahoma,* 376 P.2d 351 (Okla. Crim. 1962); *People* v. *Hawthorne,* 293 Mich. 15, 291 N.W. 205 (1940) (dictum); *State* v. *Padilla,* 66 N.M. 289, 347 P.2d 312 (1959) (dictum).

While these holdings have mostly to do with criminal matters, where mental disturbance or disorder comes up in connection with the issue of insanity, the psychological issues and evaluations in mental disturbance or disorder in tort matters are very similar and sometimes identical.

TESTIMONIAL RELIABILITY

Attorney H. E. Wonders is interviewing a prospective witness in his office, on behalf of a client. The witness, Pete Soshur, asserts unequivocally that he saw Mr. Panicki, and no other, behind the wheel of the car that brushed the plaintiff, knocked him down, and then sped off. If true, then Attorney Wonders feels he has an airtight case against Mr. Panicki on the matter of accident liability.

But, what if Mr. Soshur is not accurate in his identification and ultimately is proved to be lacking in credibility? Attorney Wonders' interview with Mr. Soshur is not entirely reassuring on this matter. He feels, too, that, since the matter of liability may well rest on Mr. Soshur's credibility, the judge, as the only trier in the case, is going to be strongly influenced by impressions and evidence relating to Soshur's ability to make accurate identification.

Testing Ability to Identify or Estimate

The ability to make correct identifications and estimations of physical reality (as in gauging distance, speed, color, and size) is measurable by psychologists using precise scientific procedures. While there are few widely used, standardized tests for these purposes, a psychologist can use brief, objective laboratory procedures to judge the reliability or consistency of a person's identification or estimation abilities, and he may compare one person's performance to that of others so as to get some judgment of relative capability.

Admittedly, at this point, this would require some creative interest and skill on the part of a psychologist, but these procedures can be developed for forensic purposes. The value of this kind of evidence is likely to be in the objective, scientific judgment procedure, with probative value in the findings. There is little or no tradition for the legal use of such evidence, but it may well appeal to an attorney or a court as having value, at least as a check upon impressionistic judgments of credibility. It may appeal as an addition to courtroom examination techniques and findings that determine credibility mostly by inference from logical inconsistencies or from approximately related observational oversight.

The laboratory procedures involved, particularly once they are developed, can be brief and inexpensive. In such circumstances, Attorney Wonders might feel the expenditure involved would be well worth-while if he had some greater assurance about witness Soshur's capabilities to make identification and, in addition, could present some objective evidence on this matter in court. The psychologist, being well-trained in precise experimental methods and in the assessment of behavior, would be quite competent to develop examining procedures and to make such appraisals.

TRADEMARK CASES

The Pepsicoke Bottling Company has fixed itself in public consciousness with its famous trademark "Pepsicoke 8" and the distinctive sign "P" enveloped by an 8.

A new competitor, the Pepticole Bottlers, Inc., has recently entered the market with its product. "Pepticole ∞" and the distinctive sign "P" enveloped by the sideways 8.

Pepsicoke, fearing the damage to its markets and public name, claims a trademark infringement and brings action against Pepticole Bottlers. The attorney for Pepsicoke seeks to establish, as an important element in his case, that the trademarks "Pepsicoke 8" and "Pepticole ∞" are confused by the public, and that the public assumes that "Pepticole ∞" is really "Pepsicoke 8."

Measurement of Associations

The psychologist, as a trained experimenter on matters of human conduct, can develop brief, simple, timed-exposure association experiments and carefully designed inquiries to compare reactions to "Pepsicoke 8" and "Pepticole ∞." This scientific evidence, based on a substantial and representative consumer sample, is likely to be of considerable probative value and may create a strong impression.

Such scientific experimentation, though brief for individual subjects, may involve some time and cost because of the desirability of having a good sample of consumer reactions. However, sampling may vary in scope, depending upon how virtually conclusive one requires or desires the experimental evidence to be. If the damages sought and the prospect of winning (with good evidence) are substantial, the time and expenditure for carefully conducted experiments relating to trademark infringements may be well spent.

Precedent has existed for the use of psychologists and their skills in trademark litigation since the case of *Coca-Cola Co.* v. *Chero-Cola Co.*, 273 Fed. 755 (D.C. Cir. 1921). In this case, psychological tests and experiments were used and testimony regarding these was received, but the testimony was not placed in issue or commented upon.

DOMESTIC RELATIONS PROBLEMS

Cyrus D. Kingman, an old friend and client of Attorney Foster Corplaw, is involved in a domestic dispute with his wife, and they have decided to seek a divorce. Attorney Corplaw, who has been asked to handle the matter, feels rather uncomfortable about it. His law firm does not handle divorce cases as a general rule, but he would like to help his old friend, Cyrus Kingman. He has known Cyrus and Beth Kingman for a long time and would like to see them stay together.

He wonders if divorce is necessary and if there are possibilities for reconciliation. On the other hand, he does not want to advise the Kingmans to seek reconciliation if this is likely to prove a rather involved and fruitless process. He wonders, too, how to advise them concerning custody of their two children if they should seek a divorce. He does not want to be unjust or insensitive to either spouse or to the needs of the children. He has some ideas of his own about the problems but knows that he does not have the degree of expert skill and knowledge that would be most penetrating in assessing the situation.

Advice on Marital Problems

Problems of family relations and child development have long been a familiar area of study for psychologists. In recent years, an increasing number of clinically trained psychologists have provided services as family relations and child development specialists. Some psychologists provide services as marriage counselors. Their functions are diagnostic, providing assessments and recommendations. They are also corrective, providing counseling and therapeutic services.

Attorney Corplaw might enlist the brief consultation of a psychologist who has special skills and sensitivities for marital problems. Such a person might meet with the Kingmans and, in the process of interview and examination, develop reliable judgment about the problems of the marriage, the prospects for conciliation, and desirable adjustments in the event of divorce. The Kingmans' involvement with a psychologist for this purpose would be brief and comparatively inexpensive. Attorney Corplaw would have a firmer basis from which to make further recommendations and to take further action with the Kingmans.

FAMILY AFFAIRS

Jeremiah Harwork and his wife Jenny are thinking of retiring. Through industry and frugality over thirty-five years, they have built up a prosperous business and a tidy nest egg. Jeremiah would like to perpetuate the Harwork Company in the Harwork family, but he is not sure how to go about it.

He would like to turn the business over to his son, Buzzy, but he doubts that Buzzy has the stability and the wisdom to oversee the business properly. He also has a daughter, Dolores, who appears to be rather unstable. He is not sure whether he should make provision for her care and guardianship in any disposition he makes, or whether he can count on her to be self-sustaining and a source of strength in protecting and preserving the Harwork interests.

Mr. and Mrs. Harwork differ in their view of the problem. Mr. Harwork feels some sort of a trust arrangement is desirable or that the interests should be assigned to other reliable management within the Harwork family. Mrs. Harwork wishes to make an outright assignment of the interests to the children, since she is confident they are perfectly capable of managing their affairs prudently. The Harworks have never agreed in their assessment of their children.

Furthermore, Mrs. Harwork is fearful that her husband really intends to convey the Harwork Company to a favorite brother of his, with the brother to offer assurances of a place for Buzzy and Dolores in the organization. Mrs. Harwork does not have confidence that her husband's brother would, as a practical matter, abide by any such understanding.

The Harworks have decided to place the matter in the hands of their trusted advisor, Attorney Solomon Pater, and they seek his advice as to the best course of action.

Attorney Pater, from his familiarity with the Harworks, is convinced that neither will be satisfied unless each can feel that the attorney is on his side and will be partial to his point of view. They both seek vindication, notably concerning their disparate views of the children, as much as they seek a solution. Neither is inclined toward a compromise or an experimental approach, since each is adamant in his need for full approval of his viewpoint.

Advice on Family Relationships

Attorney Pater is faced with a delicate situation involving many psychological factors. There is obviously hostility and suspicion between the Harworks where their children are concerned. It is perhaps desirable or necessary that the Harworks deal, at least briefly, with the psychological problem of their mutual feelings and their individual relationship with their children as a basis for better understanding and agreement.

From an astute professional point of view, it would also be important to know how deep-seated and sustaining are Buzzy's limitations. How unstable and perhaps mentally ill is the daughter, Dolores? In fact, a clinically trained and experienced psychologist can be called upon to deal with such problems, to offer tactful assistance and clarification through conferences with the Harworks and evaluation of their children.

This becomes an instrument for the clarification of problems as an adjunct to effective legal consultation and services. The discharge of tensions and uncertainties of a psychological nature might well be worth-while to the Harworks. Attorney Pater would be in a position to develop a legal solution to the Harworks' family-business problems that would be acceptable.

STANDARDS OF CONDUCT

In a suit against T-Am Airlines and Jason Service, Mrs. Dora Fright alleges that she was assaulted in flight by Mr. Service, acting in his capacity as a steward for the airline, and that T-Am was negligent in hiring Service for a position as steward. She claims that she suffered physical and mental anguish when she was assaulted by Mr. Service, that she is now permanently fearful of flying and this seriously handicaps her because of the travel requirements in her business, and that she suffers, in consequence of the assault, a permanent nervous condition.

The stipulated facts are that Mrs. Fright was enplaned along with other passengers on a T-Am flight from Chicago to San Francisco. At a certain point in the flight, passengers were cautioned that they were about to experience a good deal of bumpiness and discomfort.

During this period of fairly severe bumpiness, Mrs. Fright became hysterical. She began to cry and to moan. Then she became more upset and started to shriek and threatened to run up the aisle. She panicked, shouted that the plane was going to crash and that she was going to die, and she threatened to jump out of the plane.

Mr. Service, the steward, observing Mrs. Fright was hysterical and in a state of panic, and that, on this account, other passengers were becoming more upset and fearful, slapped Mrs. Fright in the face and told her very sternly to be quiet. Mrs. Fright, who was on the edge of her seat at the time, fell back into her seat sharply but without apparent injury, and her panic subsided. Shortly thereafter, the plane emerged from the area of turbulence, and the flight was continued and completed without further event.

Mr. Service and T-Am claim that Mr. Service's conduct was reasonable and proper under the circumstances, that he was rendering first aid, and that no assault is involved. Mrs. Fright argues that it was unnecessary for Mr. Service to strike her and this constituted a wanton act, that, had she been left alone, her momentary fears would have subsided, and that it was known and announced that the period of air turbulence would be brief.

A principal point in the litigation is whether Mr. Service did, in fact, act in the manner of a reasonable man and properly as a steward under the circumstances. The defendants risk considerable loss, in reputation and in monetary damages, should Mrs. Fright win her case or should there be a substantial settlement in her favor.

Attitude and Behavior Sampling

In view of the circumstances, Attorney Dilgent, for the defendants, desires to make the reasonable-man issue as airtight in his clients' favor as he possibly can. The services of a psychologist would be helpful in properly framing the issue and in conducting a brief systematic survey of opinion of a comparatively small, select sample of psychologists and psychiatrists familiar with hysterical conduct, of lay or random or average persons, and of stewards of T-Am and other airlines.

Courts and jury are still free to infer as they will about the proper expectation of a reasonable man, but carefully developed, systematic information on the matter, scientifically acquired by experts such as psychologists, is at least strong evidence.

The problem of legal admissibility of survey evidence would appear to rest more on the issue of proper and careful sample selection and sampling techniques (probity) than on the objection that evidence of this kind is hearsay (competency). It does not appear that survey techniques and information have been used as evidence relating to conduct of the reasonable man. They have been offered in evidence, however, on matters relating to trade practices. Some of the issues regarding the admissibility of survey evidence have been raised and litigated in *United States* v. *Aluminum Co. of America*, 35 F. Supp. 820 (S.D. N.Y. 1940) and *United States* v. *E. I. duPont de Nemours & Co.*, 177 F. Supp 1 (N.D. Ill. 1959).

Since this assessment is brief in scope and does not entail large or broad sample surveying, the expense in the acquisition of this information is not likely to be excessive or prohibitive for use in litigation. The positions of T-Am and Mr. Service may be substantially supported by such evidence.

COMPETENCY HEARINGS AND INSANITY PLEAS

The parents of Johnnie Malhom have retained Attorney David Goliath to defend their son against a charge of homicide. Johnnie, an excitable and sometimes morose young man, has killed his girl friend's father in a fit of rage.

Clinical Examination of Mental Status

Attorney Goliath has decided upon insanity as his best line of defense. He already has a psychiatric expert witness who will testify to the insanity of his client. He may well be able to fortify his case if he also utilizes a clinical psychologist and the specialized examination conducted by this expert as further, independent evidence.

Clinical psychologists conduct standard psychological examinations, consisting of the Rorschach, Thematic Apperception Test, and other techniques to determine the nature and extent of mental and emotional disorders in individuals. Substantial precedent exists for the acceptance and use of such testimony where the issue of insanity arises in criminal litigation. The psychologist's role as an expert witness on this matter has been upheld against challenge. See *Jenkins* v. *United States*, 307 F.2d 637 (D.C. Cir. 1962); *Carter* v. *Oklahoma*, 376 P.2d 351 (Okla. Crim. 1962); *Watson* v. *State*, 273 S.W.2d 879 (Tex. Crim. 1954); *People* v. *Hawthorne*, 293 Mich. 15, 291 N.W. 205 (1940) (dictum); *State* v. *Padilla*, 66 N.M. 289, 347 P.2d 312 (1959) (dictum).

Attorney Goliath might create a stronger impression in behalf of his client if he were to utilize a range of expert opinion, perhaps consisting of the testimony of a psychiatrist, or two psychiatrists, and a clinical psychologist.

BEHAVIOR TENDENCIES

Mrs. Ruth Iluck has brought suit against the Double Stamp Department Store, claiming serious injury as a result of the defendant's negligence in permitting obstructions in passageways. Mrs. Iluck's attorney, Louis Dessein, expects the defendant to make a strong argument of the facts that Mrs. Iluck had a slight accident in the same store a year before, that she had an automobile accident three years previously, and that she had had other occasional accidental injuries. Defendants seek to avoid liability in part by establishing that Mrs. Iluck is accident prone.

The existence or clear nonexistence of specific behavior tendencies and character dispositions are difficult matters to measure. At best, they are inferred, usually from a heuristic combination of prior acts and behavior that seem to be encompassed by a certain kind of notion or judgment, e.g., that John Doe has the character disposition to be dishonest.

Assessment of Accident Proneness

Psychologists, in their research use of a variety of personality measures, have sought to establish by psychological criteria the syndrome of accident proneness. Though findings are not conclusive as to the existence or measurement of such a syndrome, there is psychological evidence and opinion on the matter.

Attorney Dessein may effectively counter the Department Store's line of defense by presenting a psychologist as an expert witness to give evidence as to the scientific status, or lack of status, of the concept of accident proneness. He may have his client take a pertinent psychological examination of personality and, from expert testimony as to the results, perhaps establish that his client is not accident prone according to the best criteria available from scientific studies of the matter.

This evidence may be admissible, if only because it is based on systematic study of the issue and, to state the matter conservatively, is at least as valuable as the highly impressionistic data and judgments about behavior tendencies that are now permitted in testimony.

PERSONALITY INJURY IN PERSONAL RIGHTS AND CUSTODY CASES

Mrs. Adolph Prusse seeks to protect her daughter, eight-year-old Penny, from the influence of her ex-husband. She alleges his conduct is detrimental to the welfare of the child. She has petitioned to have visitation rights denied Penny's father on the ground that his sustained efforts to provide the child with sex education are immoral, unhealthy, and can cause permanent damage to her personality.

Mr. Prusse has made it a practice during Penny's authorized visits to him to show her pictures of nudes and to explain sexual relations to her. He has encouraged her nudity and has made it a point to have her see him nude when they arise in the morning and when he is in the bathroom. Mr. Prusse is adamant in his belief that such conduct is desirable and necessary so that Penny will have a full and accurate understanding of sex early in life. He argues that, as a result, she will benefit in that she will not be confused, hurt, or offended by sexual contact and experience when she becomes older.

Studies of Personality Development

Attorney Wright, counsel for Mrs. Prusse, is aware of a considerable body of psychological findings, knowledge, and opinion resulting from clinical and experimental investigations of child development. To support his client's position, he may call upon a qualified psychologist to provide expert testimony on professional information and opinion about the effects of different sex information practices, rendered at different ages, upon the personality development of a child.

Attorney Justin, representing Mr. Prusse in opposition to the petition, seeks to probe another factual issue in the case. To offset the effects of expert testimony, however limited, in favor of Mrs. Prusse, he might introduce psychological expert testimony of another sort. From a knowledgeable analysis of the existing body of psychological findings and opinion, he can present evidence showing the effect upon personality development when a child loses or is denied contact with a male parent.

Expert knowledge and testimony is unlikely to be conclusive. However, it may be sought and valued by the trial court as another and substantial course of information to aid in arriving at a diffcult decision on a complicated and not altogether familiar matter.

BUSINESS ORGANIZATION AND MANAGEMENT

Mr. J. Small Tycoon, a man in his early sixties, has decided to retire from active management of his corporate business. At the same time, he wishes to retain substantial control and to be assured that the enterprise will continue to be well managed and profitable. His stock holdings in the corporation represent a very substantial part of his wealth and he does not wish to see their value jeopardized. Mr. Tycoon meets with his attorney, Learned Wise, to seek his advice on some workable arrangements for the transfer of management and the granting of some minority control in the corporation to others who would carry on an active interest.

One possibility that has occurred to Mr. Tycoon is that he could vest some interest in, and give over managerial control to, some of his trusted long-time lieutenants. Mr. J. T. Figures, the comptroller, has an excellent grasp of the financial end of the business. He, perhaps, could be the new president, but he is a mild-mannered person who may have difficulty in being strong enough in the position to assert effective authority. Mr. Jonas Kitteridge is a whiz at technical development and knows how to get new products into production, but he lacks the breadth of knowledge or interest for over-all company direction. Swifton Rockett, the marketing manager, is a dynamo at marketing, but he is likely to run a loose, one-man show.

Mr. Tycoon has kept a firm hand on the corporate wheel, enabling these and other rather different personalities to jell as a unit. He is afraid that if he transferred to each of the aforenamed managers a 10-per-cent interest in the corporation and gave each top managerial responsibility, with one as the over-all leader, much bickering, rivalry, and inefficiency would develop.

He wonders if there is some way to organize management so as to capitalize on the strengths of his men and, at the same time, contain their liabilities. Mr. Tycoon feels that, since Attorney Wise is not only corporate counsel but also secretary to the corporation, he might have some valuable suggestions as to how to combine the legal and business solutions to his client's retirement problem.

Mr. Tycoon has also been informally negotiating for the purchase of a successful smaller company in the same line of business. This company is run by a very capable energetic younger man, Sylvester Bright, who appears to have the talent for making a success of corporate ventures. Mr. Tycoon is also considering Mr. Bright as the new president of the Tycoon Corporation, and this enters into his mind as he negotiates with Mr. Bright. However, he wonders if Mr. Bright would work well with Tycoon's trusted top lieutenants, whom he would like to retain. The question also arises of the kind of stock split that would be most desirable under such a management arrangement.

It is also possible that Mr. Bright's company could be merged with Mr. Tycoon's organization, or it could be retained as a wholly owned but independently managed subsidiary. Which arrangement would be most feasible would depend in part on the kind of personnel organization and working relationships that could be developed between the key personnel of the two companies.

Personnel Appraisal

A function that is well-established and widely recognized for some psychologists is the psychological assessment of personnel and the resolution of management organization problems using professional evaluation techniques and insights. Mr. Wise might be particularly helpful to his client, Mr. Tycoon, if he were to suggest personnel appraisal and consultation with a competent psychologist on the complex human relations problems presented in Mr. Tycoon's alternatives for arranging his personal retirement. The expert information and assessment is an adjunct to the legal consultation. It can be both helpful and reassuring to client Tycoon and attorney Wise as a basis for designing and executing the specific legal arrangements that would best carry out Mr. Tycoon's intent.

STATISTICAL PROBABILITIES IN BEHAVIOR

Mr. Frank Devoir, a defendant in a serious automobile accident involving large damage claims, is accused of wantonly reckless driving, which appears as the initial cause of the accident. It is alleged that this defendant, traveling at a high rate of speed, flagrantly and with wanton disregard ignored a stop sign and improperly entered a highway intersection. In consequence, the plaintiff, who had the right-of-way but was a short distance from the intersection, applied his brakes quickly, came to a sudden halt, and was severely damaged and permanently injured by another car that did not or could not stop and hit him from the rear.

Mr. Devoir seeks to mitigate, if not completely to avoid liability, by proving that it was virtually impossible for him to see the stop sign under the circumstances. Firstly, there was a black car some distance ahead consistently traveling in his lane and directly toward him, and this occupied his attention. Secondly, his attention was also drawn to the cars, including the plaintiff's, coming up quickly from the left, and he assumed they would slow down for him. Thirdly, he was traveling into a setting sun with a yellowish glow and could not readily see the yellow stop sign with this background and other distractions. Fourthly, he was initially traveling fast, but not at an improper rate of speed, and this gave him less than five seconds in which to see all the relevant elements, including the stop sign, and come to a stop.

PERCEPTUAL CAPABILITY. The defendant's argument here rests on a number of psychological assumptions and on the probabilities of certain behavior occurrences given certain circumstances. For instance, if a large background (sun and horizon) and a small object in front of it (stop sign) are of nearly the same (yellow) color, how many seconds will it take to see the small object from some distance away, with or without distractions? If a large moving object is directly in front, at what distance and in what length of time can an observer note a small stationary object (stop sign) in front of him? If a person is given five seconds to notice several objects varying in movement, color, and position, and perhaps importance, which will he observe and which will he omit? Since there is some variation among the reactions of different persons, the answers to each of these questions, pertinent to the defendant's case, may be expressed in terms of the statistical probability that a person would or would not perceive or act in a certain way.

The defendant's attorney might help his cause if he called a qualified psychologist to advise, and perhaps testify, as to the relevant scientific information in psychology that would throw light upon or answer the questions concerning the statistical probabilities or possibilities in personal conduct. Perception and perceptual capability is, and has been, a major area of experimentation for psychologists for many years. Many findings have been accumulated, and some may be relevant to the problems and issues presented in the defendant's case.

THE PROFESSIONAL QUALIFICATIONS AND CHOICE OF A PSYCHOLOGIST

Psychology, though an older science, is an emergent profession. There are over 20,000 members of the American Psychological Association, an organization founded in 1892 and the only national organization representing the discipline of psychology.

Today, every state has a state psychological organization affiliated with the American Psychological Association. Fifty-three per cent of the states have certification or licensing laws relating to the practice of psychology before the public. Thirty-nine per cent of the states have nonstatutory regulatory bodies, usually associated with the state psychological organization.

Qualified psychologists may be distinguished not only by certification but also by their specialized interests and competences. The national organization has some twenty different divisions. Among professional practitioners there are, notably, clinical psychologists, industrial psychologists, experimental psychologists, marriage counselors and child development specialists, educational and school psychologists, counseling psychologists, and social psychologists.

Some psychologists can develop and are proficient in varying combination of skills and problems and are equipped to deal with a variety of the problems with which an attorney is concerned.

CONCLUSION

Psychologists, for the most part, have little practical experience with attorneys and with the legal context. Some have served as expert witnesses, and others may have been approached or consulted more informally by attorneys. There are differences in training, interest, attitude, and temperament among psychologists, as there are among attorneys. Likely, factors of personal adjustment, involving matters of attitude and temperament, between a particular attorney and psychologist will determine whether natural professional barriers and biases can be overcome, and whether the psychologist, his skills and his knowledge, can be successfully utilized by the attorney.

IMPLICATIONS

What bodies of psychological knowledge and techniques mentioned by lawyer-psychologist Redmount are unknown to you? Did any ideas of how other psychological facts and methods might be used occur to you as you read this article? The psychologist who has a scientific orientation is likely to be extremely cautious about generalizations and is reluctant to indulge in dogmatic statements. Do you anticipate that his orientation may vary somewhat from that of the attorney who usually feels that he must have an airtight case and looks for clear-cut distinctions, such as sane or insane, competent or incompetent, innocent or guilty, rather than for the continuous gradations and indistinct lines between various increments of human behavior?

REFERENCES

For a modern, thorough review of suggestions concerning the psychologist and the law, see Anastasi (1964). The interest of psychologists in this area of conduct is long-standing. In 1908, Munsterberg published a book entitled *On the Witness Stand*. In the 1930's, there appeared volumes by Burtt (1931), and Robinson (1935); currently there are entire books devoted to psychological aspects of the law: Dudycha (1955) and Toch (1961). In addition, there are journal articles by Schofield (1956), McCary (1960), and Hoch and Darley (1962).

Chapter IX

MILITARY, SPACE, HUMAN ENGINEERING

[45] SEEING IN THE DARK

Many students in the introductory course in psychology regard the topic of sensation as dull and of little practical use. However, many of the findings from the psychological laboratory that at first glance seem technical and of little significance can be related to real-life situations with value.

During World War II, *Psychology of the Fighting Man* was compiled for the man in uniform. Approximately one third of its useful advice pertained to the psychology of sensation and perception. The following selection is a chapter from that book. Facts about vision in the dark, technically known as *rod vision*, are presented simply and interestingly and are followed by practical rules for seeing in the dark.

Edwin G. Boring and Marion Van de Water

Reprinted from Edwin G. Boring and Marion Van de Water, "Seeing in the Dark," *Psychology of the Fighting Man* (Washington, D.C.: National Academy of Sciences National Research Council), pp. 60–75, by permission of the publisher and the senior author.

Modern war is often war at night. That means that men must learn to see in the dark and to use their eyes in new and unfamiliar ways.

So the fighting man needs to know how to make the best use of his eyes at night—whether his job puts him in an airplane or a tank, on a ship, driving a truck, or just getting about on his own feet.

You can't make a man into an owl or a cat, but you can let him have rules and aids that will give him just enough edge on the enemy so that he can get in the first shot.

Everyone knows that when you go into a dark room from a bright one it is hard to see until your eyes have become used to the gloom. At a movie it takes a minute or two to see the vacant seat. It may take a couple of minutes more before you can recognize a friend. During these minutes your eyes are steadily becoming more sensitive to the faint light.

There are two ways in which your eyes adjust for seeing in the dark. They can open up to let in more light, and they can shift over to a more sensitive set of light detectors. They do both.

It's the pupil of the eye that opens up in the dark to let more light in— and closes down in bright light to a pinhead opening so as to keep out too much light. The pupil works like the diaphragm in a camera, which you open wide for taking pictures in dim light.

But the important change is this shift to the more sensitive set of detectors.

The retinas of your eyes (Fig. 1) have two batteries of light detectors called *cones* and *rods*. The nerve fibers run from them to the brain. The cones do the seeing in bright light, the rods at night. In twilight and bright moonlight both are working together.

The cones—there are millions of them in each eye—are packed together most closely in the very center of the retina, the part that does the most accurate seeing in daylight. That's why in daylight you always have to look directly at something in order to see it best. The cones also see colors.

The rods—and there are millions of them, too—are color-blind. That is why "all cats look gray at night." Cats really do—and so do trees and flowers, provided the night is dark enough. But a red or green signal light is seen as colored at night because it is bright enough to get the cones working.

The rods are packed most closely together at the outside edges of your retinas, and there aren't any rods at all in the very center. The part of your eye that is most sensitive in daylight is actually blind at night. So don't look directly at a thing to see it in the dark. Look alongside of it. That faint object out there in the dark, it caught your attention because it moved a little. What is it? It disappears when you look at it closely, but it's there again when you look to one side. Keep looking to one side or the other and you may be able to tell whether it's a man, or simply a bush that moved in the wind.

Both the rods and the cones are differently sensitive to different colors of light. The cones are most sensitive to yellow light. That's why yellows in daylight are brighter than reds, greens, and blues. The rods are most sensitive to yellow-green light, but they differ most from the cones in seeing blue light. To blue light they are one thousand times as sensitive as the cones.

So don't use blue lights in black outs. The enemy's eyes, like your own, can see blues easily in the dark. Use red lights instead, for the rods see pure red light as black. But don't use intense ordinary red light, because that is not pure and will affect the rods.

Night-eyes lack the sharp vision for detail that your day-eyes have. You can't read, or study an instrument dial, or examine a map, a road sign, or

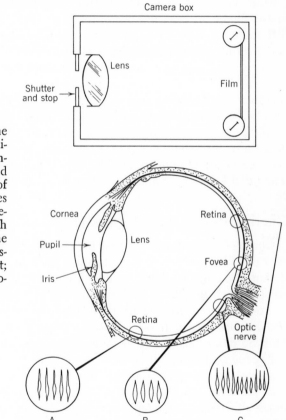

FIGURE 1. The eye and the camera in this much simplified diagram show the principal parts of a camera and the corresponding parts of the eye. The three circles beneath the eye are enlargements of the spots at which rods and cones appear on the retina. (A) Only rods present; (B) only cones present; and (C) rods and cones together.

your watch, by using your rods. For that you must put your cones to work by having more light, of course, shielding it carefully from the enemy if he is not to know where you are.

But night-eyes are extraordinarily sensitive to faint light. An ordinary candle flame or a lighted match could be seen ten miles away if the night were completely black, if there were no haze at all in the air. Even with haze and starlight, a match can be seen for many miles. So don't strike matches in a blackout or when the enemy may be watching.

It takes time—half an hour or more—for the rods to get completely into action after you have been in the light. When you first go from a brightly lighted room into a blacked-out night, you are at first completely blind. Neither the cones nor the rods work.

Then three things happen. First the pupils of your eyes dilate, letting more light into your eyes. That helps a little.

Next the cones get more sensitive. They divide up the blacks into blacks, dark grays and light grays. That takes about five minutes.

More slowly the rods get adjusted. You begin to see shapes and outlines in the gloom where there were not even vague bulking shadows when you first came in. This is due to a slow chemical change, which is rapid at first but not fully completed for half an hour.

The soldier who at a command or an alert signal leaves a lighted room to run on duty without having prepared his eyes is completely at the mercy of the enemy as far as his vision is concerned. By the time he gains the use of his night-eyes, the emergency may be all over.

And even when your eyes are adapted to the dark, flashing on a light, though only for a short time, may ruin your night vision for another half hour. You can lose by a few minutes of light all you gained by a half hour in the dark. The brighter the light and the longer you look at it, the more you lose.

GETTING READY TO SEE IN THE DARK

Complete darkness is the best preparation for night fighting. Protect your eyes from light before you start and while you are out. If you can't stay in darkness, keep the lights around you as low as possible and never look straight at them. And if you have to look at a lighted object, be quick about it. Looking at an instrument dial lighted only by radium paint can cut down the distance at which you can see a friendly or an enemy plane by 50 per cent. So don't look at the dial any longer than you must.

Experienced gun pointers and spotters know that they must not watch the flashes of their own guns as they fire. The flash of a six-inch gun can dull the eyes for more than a minute. Under continuous fire at dawn or dusk it is impossible to aim some rapid-fire guns accurately at a target when the gunners let themselves watch the flash. At night the effect is even greater. Luckily the flashes of rifles and small-caliber guns have much less effect on the eyes.

There are several ways in which you can become adapted to the dark even though you must work in fairly bright light. Each way is suitable only for certain kinds of jobs.

Ship pilots and bridge officers have long known a clever but simple trick. When they have to work their way among dark islands with the beacons unlit, or to move in company with other blacked-out ships, these men often have to go back and forth from a lookout post to a lighted bridge or chartroom.

When they go into the light, they cover one eye and use the other.

Then, when they come out into the night, they uncover this eye and use it.

To cover the eye, an ordinary black eye patch is sometimes used. This trick should not be used, however, to prepare for night duty except in an emergency. Experienced men know they must stay out of the light for fifteen minutes to half an hour before they go on night duty. With the patch over but one eye, only that eye becomes prepared, and two eyes are always better than one.

A better way to get the eyes dark-adapted is to work in deep *red light*. Remember that pure red has almost no effect on the rod cells of your night-eyes. So, if deep red light is available, you can read or work—if you have to—and still be dark-adapting your night-eyes so that you will be ready for nearly instant action in the dark. If you can't get bulbs of deep red, you may get by with a red cellophane covering for a light or an instrument. But the red cellophane is pretty poor because it lets through some orange and some white light that tend to desensitize your rods. Even the red bulb is not perfect and it ought not to be any brighter than is absolutely necessary.

The very best arrangement is tight-fitting *goggles* with red filters in them. They can be made so that only red light gets through, so that the rods are not affected at all. Put them on half an hour before your night duty begins. And take them off, of course, when you are outside in the dark or you will be quite blind.

The trouble with the use of red light and the goggles is that they keep you from distinguishing colors properly. Red lines on a white chart disappear in red light. Red and white signal lights look alike. All red objects become white or gray or some other color. Be careful about color if you have red goggles on.

It isn't enough to get your night-eyes working at full capacity by staying in the dark or using red light, red goggles, or patches. You have to learn to use night-eyes after you get them.

First try an experiment to show you how your eyes work in the dark. You must have a room that can be completely blacked out into which you can let just a little light, shutting the light out gradually. If the windows are dark, you can close the door slowly.

Take a sheet of typewriter paper. Cut it in two. Then cut one half in two, then one of these quarters in two, and keep on until you have a piece not more than a quarter of an inch across. You now have almost a dozen pieces of white paper ranging in size from a tiny scrap up to a piece about 8 by 5 inches. Lay them out on a black table or other dark surface.

Now shut the door and let your eyes get used to the dark. Wait ten minutes at the least—half an hour if you can spare the time.

Now open the door a crack until you can just see the smallest piece. The bigger pieces will be brighter than the smaller. The biggest piece will almost glow. The more light a piece reflects, the brighter it appears.

Now watch the big piece. You are seeing it with your cones. Gradually it will fade out until you cannot see it at all. That is the cones getting fatigued.

Now pay attention to the other pieces while trying to keep your eyes fixed on the place where the big piece disappeared. They are still visible—to the rods. In fact, viewed this way, out of the corner of your eye, they seem to glow as though phosphorescent.

If you look directly at one though, it disappears—because there are no rods in the center of the retina. Move your eyes away, however, and the little piece that disappeared pops back again into view. You can make them come and go. A piece is there when you don't look at it, gone when you fix your eyes on the spot where it was.

That's one alarming thing about being in a strange area in the dark. The object that might possibly be a sniper isn't there when you look at it, comes back when it thinks you aren't noticing.

You may not· in the dark be able to spot an airplane if you look directly at it. Yet you can pick it up again out of the corner of your eye if you will look away. It disappears again if you look straight at it. The same thing is true if you try to see a distant ship, an unlighted car or tank, or even a faint star.

Always remember, therefore, that you must look a little to one side in order to see best on a very dark night. Learn to pay attention to things which are just a little off the center of your field of vision. Learn to keep from looking directly at any object in the dark. As you feel your eyes drawn almost irresistibly toward what you want to see, just let them slide on over to the other side of it and look again with the tail of your eye. It takes practice to learn to do this without fail, but it is worth the trouble to learn the trick.

And don't keep looking steadily to the same side of the object, because then it will disappear too. Use first one side and then the other.

Try this out.

When you are in a darkened room or outdoors on a dark night, hold up your finger and look steadily at it. It will disappear. Look a little to one side and make it appear again. Keep staring and it will go again. Then look to the other side of it and let it come back.

This means that in searching the sea or sky for a dark object, you must look first at one area and then at another. When you think you have spotted something, look first to one side of it and then to the other—then above it, below it.

But don't ever try sweeping your eyes over the sky or horizon. You can't see well when the eyes are moving. Scan the sky, don't sweep it. Look here, then there, then at the next place.

Night-eyes are slow in responding except to bright objects and moving objects. You may have to look several times before you can be sure you have spotted something. But don't stare. Keep looking again and again, always just alongside of the dark, still object.

Small objects are much harder to see at night than in daytime. The average airplane becomes too small to be seen beyond 1000 feet on a clear starry night. But the plane is smaller when seen on edge from ahead, behind, or at the side. Then you may not spot it more than 400 or 500 feet away. So, if you are pursuing a plane, try to keep above or below it until you are close in.

The same thing should be done in chasing a boat. Keep off to one side when far away, if you can, so that the boat will be seen more nearly broadside on.

Night glasses are useful because they magnify an object without much loss of light. Binoculars magnify too, but they cut down the light so much that a very faint object disappears. The night glasses do not give so clear a view as the binoculars, but your night-eyes cannot see sharp outlines anyhow.

Darkness may make things look smaller. A tree in the dark in winter looks smaller because you cannot see the twigs and the ends of the branches at all. A plane at night seems to get larger when a searchlight falls upon it, because the light brings out so many details that could not be seen before.

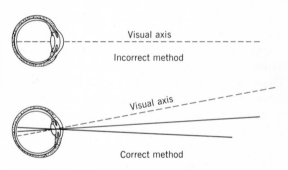

Figure 2. Technique for visual acuracy at night. Practice the use of the "corners of the eyes." Night targets are better seen by not looking directly at them. This is because the edges of the retina are more sensitive to dim light than is the very center of the retina.

The best you can do at night is to see dark fuzzy silhouettes of objects. That makes it hard to recognize objects, but you can learn recognition.

Even in daytime, *recognition* is largely a matter of jumping to conclusions from slight hints. You can recognize a friend long before you can see the color of his eyes, even before you can tell whether he has his nose on this morning. His general shape or his style of walk may be enough.

At night the clues are still fewer, and so it pays to study the silhouettes of ships and planes, to study them at all possible angles and positions. Then you may learn to tell one plane from another, one ship from another, even though you never do know just what clues you are using.

A lookout or scout at night can't afford to wait to be sure just what he has seen before reporting it or taking cover. Follow your hunches. Trust vague impressions. Those are the best rules for night seeing. The cautious man who waits to be sure may not live that long.

Sometimes you may be able to detect a moving airplane in the sky by its motion alone, or by what you don't see, more than by what you do see. If a star blinks out and then on again, something may have passed between you and it.

CONTRAST

Contrast helps vision. If the thing observed is much lighter or darker than its background, it is much more easily seen. Even at night the sky is so much lighter than the ground or the water that the chances of seeing an airplane from below against the sky are ever so much better than of seeing it from above against the ground—especially if it is painted dark on top to match the ground. A ship is easily seen against a dimly lighted sky. It is very clear against a coast not properly dimmed out. It may be invisible against the dark sea, or to an airplane flying over it.

But, if the white underside of a plane is illuminated by moonlight reflected from clouds beneath the plane, then the plane as seen from below may almost match the moonlit haze of the sky and disappear. That's in moonlight. You can't get the shaded underside of a plane light enough in daylight to match the daytime sky.

But contrast helps vision only when outlines are clear. For this reason the windshields of night fighters must be kept clear and free of scratches or fog. These scatter the light, make contours fuzzy, and reduce contrast. Careless night fighters have been known to tolerate enough dirt on their windshields to double the time it takes them to see a plane moving along nearby. And sailors on ships sometimes let the salt from the spray pile up in blotches on the glass. That is courting death.

For the same reason, it is important to keep down the light on your own side of the windshield. It produces glare, spoils outlines, reduces contrast, makes faint objects invisible. That is why you push up close to the window when you try to look out at night. By coming up close, you shade part of the glass and reduce the glare. If there has to be any light on your side of the glass, screen it from the glass.

GOOD FOOD AND GOOD HEALTH

There has been a great deal of talk about the effect of shortages of vitamins A and C on ability to see at night. These are the vitamins in fresh vegetables, cheese, and fruit. People who don't get anough of these vitamins do become poor in night vision, but the regular army and navy rations supply plenty of them. Occasionally, when ships are on long trips or when fighting lasts until fresh foods are all gone, a shortage of vitamins may occur. Then medical officers supply men who are likely to be on night duty with vitamin capsules. Extra vitamins don't improve night vision when your diet and your night vision are already normal.

Night vision is affected by fatigue. Anything that reduces your physical well-being has a greater effect on night vision that on day vision. Hangovers, slight illnesses, or excessive fatigue may double or even triple the amount of light needed to see a faint object in the dark.

So the night fighter must train for his job as a boxer trains for the big match. The boxer who is not at the peak of training is likely to be knocked out. The night fighter whose eyes are not at the peak of efficiency is likely to be killed.

RULES FOR SEEING IN THE DARK

1. *Protect your eyes from light* before you go on night duty and while you are out.

2. *Stay in the dark* beforehand, or use *red light* or red goggles. The goggles are best, when you can get them.

3. *Never look directly at any light,* nor at any illuminated object except in red light. If you must break this rule, be quick with your looking.

4. *Use the corners of your eyes* when you are out on duty. Keep looking alongside of what you think is there, until you have made up your mind about it.

5. *Keep your eyes moving.* Look and move, look and move. Don't sweep them over large regions, and don't stare continuously at one spot.

6. *Keep your windshield spotless,* free of dirt, salt, fog, and scratches.

7. *Keep down the light on your own side of the windshield,* and screen it from the windshield.

8. *Keep yourself wide awake and on the alert.* Don't break training. Use good sense about eating, drinking, and smoking. Keep rested, if you can.

9. *Practice recognition.* Learn by experience to recognize from slight clues the objects you need to recognize.

10. *Practice all the rules* for seeing at night until they become second nature to you. And use every possible device to aid you.

It is the night fighter with the best eyes who wins his part of the war.

IMPLICATIONS

Do the suggestions ending the article have any value in civilian life as, for example, for safety in night-driving? Almost all of the topics in discussion of sensation and perception in introductory psychology can be converted into practical information concerning the use of your senses in work or play situations. In fact, in a book from which this excerpt is taken, there are chapters on sight as a weapon, color and camouflage, hearing as a tool in warfare, smell as a sentry, the sense of position, and the sense of direction. You may find it interesting to see how many practical suggestions on sensation you can derive from other excerpts from your textbook material, and how these suggestions may be as simply stated as those given in the article.

REFERENCES

For other examples of applied psychology based in part on the psychology of sensation and perception, see Anastasi (1964), especially the chapters on working environment and equipment design.

Space technology, for one, is making use of findings in the field of sensation and perception, as indicated in Selection 47.

[46] UNDERSTIMULATION: DECREASED VARIATION IN THE SENSORY ENVIRONMENT

Have you ever been in a situation that required you to remain in the same place for a long period of time, during which there was nothing to occupy your attention? You would doubtless report at least boredom. One vivacious student in answer to the above question said, "I've been in a few situations like that, and if I had to stay there longer, I would have gone nuts!" The student in jest didn't know how close to the truth he came, as you will note in reading the effects of understimulation in the selection that follows.

W. Harold Bexton, Woodburn Heron, and Thomas H. Scott

Reprinted from W. Harold Bexton, Woodburn Heron, and Thomas H. Scott, "Effects of Decreased Variation in the Environment," *Canadian Journal of Psychology*, Vol. 8 (Hamilton, Ontario: The Canadian Psychological Association, 1954), pp. 70–76, by permission of the two senior authors.

This study began with a practical problem: the lapses of attention that may occur when a man must give close and prolonged attention to some aspect of an environment in which nothing is happening, or in which the changes are very regular. Watching a radar screen hour after hour is a prime example. As Mackworth (1950) and others have shown, when at last something *does* happen in such circumstances, the watcher may fail to respond. Such monotonous conditions exist in civilian occupations as well as in military ones (marine pilotage by radar, piloting aircraft on long flights), and here, too, lapses of attention may have extremely serious consequences. For example, such lapses may explain some otherwise inexplicable railroad and highway accidents.

Besides its practical significance, this problem has theoretical implications of great interest. There is much evidence from recent neurophysiological studies to indicate that the normal functioning of the waking brain depends on its being constantly exposed to sensory bombardment, which produces a continuing "arousal reaction." Work ... by S. K. Sharpless at McGill indicates, further, that when stimulation does not change, it rapidly loses its power to cause the arousal reaction. Thus, although one function of a stimulus is to evoke or guide a specific bit of behavior, it also has a nonspecific function, that of maintaining "arousal," probably through the brain-stem reticular formation.

In other words, the maintenance of normal, intelligent, adaptive behavior probably requires a continually varied sensory input. The brain is not like a calculating machine operated by an electric motor which is able to respond at once to specific cues after lying idle indefinitely. Instead, it is like one that must be kept warmed up and working. It seemed, therefore, worth-while to examine cognitive functioning during prolonged perceptual isolation, as far as this was practicable. Bremer (1953) has achieved such isolation by cutting the brain stem; college students, however, are reluctant to undergo brain operations for experimental purposes, so we had to be satisfied with less extreme isolation from the environment.

PROCEDURE

The subjects, 22 male college students, were paid to lie on a comfortable bed in a lighted cubicle 24 hours a day, with time out for eating and going to the toilet. During the whole experimental period, they wore translucent goggles which transmitted diffuse light but prevented pattern vision. Except when eating or at the toilet, the subject wore gloves and cardboard cuffs, the latter extending from below the elbow to beyond the fingertips. These permitted free joint movement but limited tactual perception. Communication between the subject and experimenters was provided by a small speaker system, and was kept to a minimum. Auditory stimulation was limited by the partially soundproof cubicle and by a U-shaped foam-rubber pillow in which the subject kept his head while in the cubicle. Moreover, the continuous hum provided by fans, air conditioner, and the amplifier leading to earphones in the pillow produced fairly efficient masking noise.

GENERAL EFFECTS

As might be expected from the evidence reviewed by Kleitman (1939) for onset of sleep following reduced stimulation in man and other animals, the subjects tended to spend the earlier part of the experimental session in sleep. Later they slept less, became bored, and appeared eager for stimulation. They would sing, whistle, talk to themselves, tap the cuffs together, or explore the cubicle with them. This boredom seemed to be partly due to deterioration in the capacity to think systematically and productively—an effect described below. The subjects also became very restless, displaying constant random movement, and they described the restlessness as unpleasant. Hence it was difficult to keep subjects for more than two or three days, despite the fact that the pay ($20 for a 24-hour day) was more than double what they could normally earn. Some subjects, in fact, left before testing could be completed.

There seemed to be unusual emotional liability during the experimental period. When doing tests, for instance, the subjects would seem very pleased when they did well, and upset if they had difficulty. They commented more freely about test items than when they were tested outside. While many reported that they felt elated during the first part of their stay in the cubicle, there was a marked increase in irritability toward the end of the experimental period.

On coming out of the cubicle after the experimental session, when goggles, cuffs, and gloves had been removed, the subjects seemed at first dazed. There also appeared to be some disturbance in visual perception, usually lasting no longer than one or two minutes. Subjects reported difficulty in focusing; objects appeared fuzzy and did not stand out from their backgrounds. There was a tendency for the environment to appear two-dimensional and colors seemed more saturated than usual. The subjects also reported feelings of confusion, headaches, a mild nausea, and fatigue; these conditions persisted in some cases for 24 hours after the session.

EFFECTS ON COGNITIVE PROCESSES

Our present concern is primarily with cognitive disturbances during the period of isolation and immediately afterward. The subjects reported that they were unable to concentrate on any topic for long while in the cubicle. Those who tried to review their studies or solve self-initiated intellectual problems found it difficult to do so. As a result, they lapsed into daydreaming, abandoned attempts at organized thinking, and let their thoughts wander. There were also reports of "blank periods," during which they seemed unable to think of anything at all.

In an attempt to measure some of the effects of cognitive processes, various

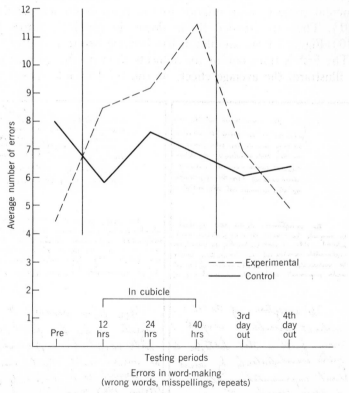

FIGURE 1. Mean error score for experimental and control subjects, before, during, and after the isolation period.

tests were given to the subjects before, during and after the period of isolation.

First, the tests given during isolation. Twelve subjects were given the following types of problem to do in their heads: multiplying two- and three-digit numbers; arithmetical problems (such as "how many times greater is twice 2½ than one half 2½?"); completion of number series; making a word from jumbled letters; making as many words as possible from the letters of a given word. Each subject was tested on problems of this type before going into the cubicle, after he had been in for 12, 24, and 48 hours, and three days after coming out of the cubicle. Twelve control subjects were given the same series of tasks at the same intervals. The average performance of the experimental subjects was inferior to that of the controls on all tests performed during the cubicle session. With our present small number of subjects, the differences are significant only for the error scores on the second anagram task ($p = .01$, see Figure 1). The groups are now being enlarged.

Secondly, tests given before entering the cubicle and immediately after leaving it. On the Kohs Block Test and the Wechsler Digit Symbol Test, the experimental subjects were inferior to the controls on leaving the cubicle ($p = .01$). They also tended to be slower in copying a prose paragraph ($p = .10$). Figure 2 gives samples of handwriting before and after the experiment. The first is from one of the subjects showing the greatest effect, the second illustrates the average effect. As the third sample shows, some sub-

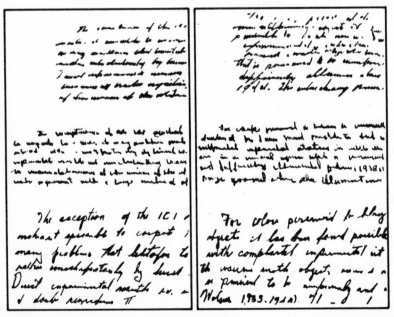

Figure 2. Specimens of handwriting before and after the isolation period.

jects were not affected. This disturbance in handwriting, though perhaps due to some sensori-motor disturbance, might also reflect cognitive or motivational changes.

HALLUCINATORY ACTIVITY

Finally, there were the hallucinations reported by the subjects while in the experimental apparatus. Among our early subjects there were several references, rather puzzling at first, to what one of them called "having a dream while awake." Then one of us, while serving as a subject, observed the phenomenon and realized its peculiarity and extent.

The visual phenomena were actually quite similar to what have been described for mescal intoxication, and to what Grey Walter (1953) has recently produced by exposure to flickering light. There have also been rare cases of hallucinations in aged persons without psychosis (Bartlet, 1951), which, like ours, involved no special chemical or visual stimulation. As we did not ask our first subjects specifically about these phenomena, we do not know the frequency among them. The last 14 subjects, however, were asked to report any "visual imagery" they observed, and our report is based on them. In general, where more "formed" (*i.e.*, more complex) hallucinations occurred, they were usually preceded by simpler forms of the phenomenon. Levels of complexity could be differentiated as follows: In the simplest form the visual field, with the eyes closed, changed from dark to light color; next in complexity were dots of light, lines, or simple geometrical patterns. All fourteen subjects reported such imagery, and said it was a new experience to them. Still more complex forms consisted in "wallpaper patterns," reported by eleven subjects, and isolated figures or objects, without background (*e.g.*, a row of little yellow men with black caps on and their mouths open; a German helmet), reported by seven subjects. Finally, there were integrated scenes (*e.g.*, a procession of squirrels with sacks over their shoulders marching "purposefully" across a snow field and out of the field of "vision"; prehistoric animals walking about in a jungle). Three of the fourteen subjects reported such scenes, frequently including dreamlike distortions, with the figures often being described as "like cartoons." One curious fact is that some of the hallucinations were reported as being inverted or tilted at an angle.

In general, the subjects were first surprised by these phenomena, and then amused or interested, waiting for what they would see next. Later, some subjects found them irritating, and complained that their vividness interfered with sleep. There was some control over content; by "trying," the subject might see certain objects suggested by the experimenter, but not always as he intended. Thus, one subject, trying to "get" a pen, saw first an inkblot, then a pencil, a green horse, and finally a pen; trying to "get" a shoe, he saw first a ski boot, then a moccasin. The imagery usually disappeared when the subject was doing a complex task, such as multiplying three-place numbers in his head, but not if he did physical exercises, or talked to the experimenter.

There were also reports of hallucinations involving other senses. One subject could hear the people speaking in his visual hallucinations, and another repeatedly heard the playing of a music box. Four subjects described kinesthetic and somesthetic phenomena. One reported seeing a miniature rocket ship discharging pellets that kept striking his arm, and one reported reaching out to touch a doorknob he saw before him and feeling an electric shock. The other two subjects reported a phenomenon which they found difficult to describe. They said it was as if there were two bodies side by side in the cubicle; in one case the two bodies overlapped, partly occupying the same space. Figure 3 shows this subject's subsequent drawing, made in an attempt to show what he meant.

Figure 3. Drawing made by a subject to show how he felt at one period in the cubicle. He reported that it was as if "there were two of me," and was momentarily unable to decide whether he was (A) or (B).

In addition, there were reports of feelings of "otherness" and bodily "strangeness" in which it was hard to know exactly what the subject meant. One subject said, "my mind seemed to be a ball of cotton-wool floating above my body"; another reported that his head felt detached from his body. These are familiar phenomena in certain cases of migraine, as described recently by Lippman (1952), and earlier by Lewis Carroll in *Alice in Wonderland*. As Lippman points out, Lewis Carroll was a sufferer from migraine, and it was suggested that Alice's bodily distortions are actually descriptions of Carroll's (*i.e.*, Charles Dodgson's) own experiences.

In summary, both the changes in intelligence-test performance and the hallucinatory activity, induced merely by limiting the variability of sensory input, provide direct evidence of a kind of dependence on the environment that has not been previously recognized. Further experimental study will be needed to elucidate the details of this relationship.

IMPLICATIONS

At the beginning of the article, the authors suggest the significance of experimental findings for certain vocations, such as that of the pilot and the radar operator. Do you think the findings reported in the selection have implications as to the ill effects of prolonged understimulation in prisoners, hospitalized patients, watchmen? What is the theoretical significance of these findings? What do they suggest concerning the nature of man's normal functioning? Can you think of other situations in which understimulation is deleterious or harmful?

REFERENCES

Other studies have been published since this one. See Heron, Doane, and Scott (1956); Doane, Mahatoo, Heron, and Scott (1959).

[47] PSYCHOLOGY AND THE SPACE FRONTIER

What contributions have psychologists made to the field of space flight, and what sort of role will they play in this venture in the future? Grether, technical director of the Behavioral Sciences Laboratory at USAF's Aerospace Medical Research Laboratories in Wright-Patterson Air Force Base, Ohio, is a pioneer in this new field. In this article, he reviews briefly the many problems that have been attacked by psychologists, including (1) the selection of astronauts, (2) the determination of their capabilities, (3) the design of the work stations to match capabilities, and (4) the design of training equipment and methods. Grether then outlines some of the jobs for future astronauts and indicates how the psychologist will contribute to the solution of inevitable problems.

Walter F. Grether

Reprinted from Walter F. Grether, "Psychology and the Space Frontier," *American Psychologist*, Vol. 17 (Washington, D.C.: American Psychological Association, 1962), pp. 92–101, by permission of the publisher and the author.

In the history of our world, few, if any, previous events have had an impact on science equal to the successful launching of vehicles into space. For many centuries, people have looked up at the heavenly bodies and dreamed of the time when men could leave the earth and explore the universe. While, as yet, only the most simple beginnings have been made in terms of manned trips into space, the gravitational ice has been broken; manned flights to the moon and the planets now appear within man's grasp. The achievement of this age-old dream of flight into space had to wait until our technology, particularly the physical and engineering sciences, had prepared the necessary foundation of scientific knowledge. Many further advances in science and technology must be made before the major objectives of manned space flight become possible. So dependent is space flight on science that the people of all nations around our globe measure the scientific capability of our country and the USSR by our successes in space. That this is a valid measure we, as psychologists, might disagree, but it is used nevertheless.

While the impact of space flight on many areas of physical science and engineering are quite obvious, what has been the effect on psychology and how has psychology been contributing to the national space flight efforts?

My purpose in this paper is to examine some of the activities of psychologists who have been most directly involved in space flight work, to see what the nature of their contribution has been, and to look at some of the future problems that space flight poses for psychology.

In a program as complex as that of Project Mercury, combining the efforts of many thousands of individuals, it is difficult to isolate the contributions of particular scientists. There are, however, quite a number of psychologists who have made important direct contributions to the Mercury Program and many more who contributed in ways which are less apparent, but, nevertheless, important. I will try to show some of the significant psychological contributions which I can identify.

No discussion of psychological contributions to Project Mercury would be complete without some mention of the selection program whereby the seven astronauts were chosen. Quite a large number of psychological tests were used in this selection program. Besides Robert Voas, the psychologists who played important roles in planning and carrying out the selection program were

David Trites, of the Air Force Personnel Laboratory, and William O'Connor, of the Naval School of Aviation Medicine. Since the Mercury astronaut selection program has already been well publicized, I will not go into it further here, but go on to discuss some of the vehicle design, training, and human performance aspects.

In the early planning of Project Mercury, it was generally thought that the extreme environmental stresses and the compressed time scale at the high speeds would make the pilot quite useless as a controller. Thus, it was thought that all vehicle functions must be automatically controlled just as in an un-manned satellite. The role of the astronaut was considered to be that of a passive passenger or a biological specimen with little, if any, control of the vehicle entrusted to him.

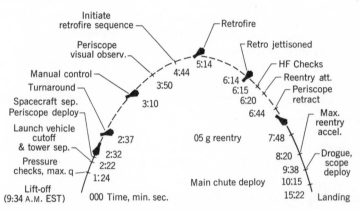

FIGURE 1. Major events during Mercury MR-3 flight. (From Shepard, 1961.)

As the Mercury Program advanced, the planned role of the astronaut became more and more like that of an aircraft pilot with some of the direct control of the vehicle in his hands. For many other functions that were automatically pro-gramed and controlled, the astronaut was provided with emergency controls as back-ups to the automatic systems. Thus, the astronaut could contribute much to the potential success of the mission and to his own safety.

Before reviewing the specific contributions of psychology to Project Mercury, let us first look at some of the pertinent data (Shepard, 1961; Voas, Van Bockel, Zedekar, and Backer, 1961).

Figure 1 shows the major events in the first Mercury (MR-3) flight by Alan Shepard on May 5, 1961. Along the outside of the parabolic curve, represent-ing the ballistic flight path, the major flight events are indicated. Under the curve is shown the time of the event in minutes after launch. Of particular interest to us here is that part of the flight from booster separation to the beginning of re-entry. This constituted the weightless portion of the flight.

But, more important, I think, is the fact that during most of this period Shepard had manual control of the attitude of his capsule.

... Shepard was engaged in communication with the ground. Of particular interest is the time during which he actually controlled attitude of the vehicle.

From the motion picture records obtained during the flight, Voas and his staff were able to plot the eye movements in terms of the area of the capsule being observed. ... The time period covered Shepherd's first attempts to control attitude. ... The attitude indicator, the periscope, the clock, and the manual fuel handles were occupying most of his attention.

Probably the most interesting psychological data from Shepard's flight is that relating to his *manual control* * of vehicle attitude. The control of attitude was a rather difficult tracking task. Control was accomplished with pairs of small rocket jets for each rotational axis. Thus it constituted an acceleration tracking task, about three axes. This task had been thoroughly practiced by Shepard and the other astronauts on various training simulators. One of these was a so-called procedures trainer, resembling a fixed-base aircraft flight simulator. Separate records for attitude control in pitch, yaw, and roll were made. ... They show that performance in actual flight was equal to that on the trainer. Certainly there is no evidence that the performance was degraded by weightlessness.

In obtaining these data on astronaut performance as well as in guiding the training of the Mercury pilots, Voas played a dominant role as a member of the Project Mercury team. I would like to cover briefly the work of several other psychologists who worked closely with Project Mercury and made significant contributions to the program.

As one of the major subcontractors to the McDonnell Aircraft Corporation, the Minneapolis-Honeywell Regulator Company developed much of the complex control equipment in the Mercury vehicle. At the initiation of this development, there were important questions about *how much control a human pilot could be expected to exercise under the stresses and speeds of space flight,* * and how to design the control system and related equipment to be used by the pilot. John Senders and his associates at Minneapolis-Honeywell made a thorough analysis of pilot's work load during Mercury flights, assuming different modes of operation and possible flight emergencies. This analysis used several engineering psychology techniques, including task simulation using analog computers, human transfer function analysis, and work-load (or task) analysis. This analysis demonstrated that the probable work load would be manageable by the pilot and that the pilot could manually control attitude of the vehicle during most phases of the Mercury mission.

One of the more specific inputs to the Mercury vehicle by John Senders

* Editor's italics.

and the group at Minneapolis-Honeywell relates to the attitude indicator. The attitude indicator is quite different from conventional aircraft attitude indicators in that the pitch and bank indications are on separate dials. Also novel is the manner of showing rate information at the center of the instrument. It appears to me that this novel integration of attitude and attitude rate information is excellently suited to the Mercury vehicle and mission. Without wishing to detract from the accomplishment of the Minneapolis-Honeywell group, it is of interest that earlier versions of this instrument have been studied for possible aircraft use both at our laboratory and in England.

Other major contributions to the design of the Mercury vehicle were made by Edward Jones and his associates at the McDonnell Aircraft Corporation where the Mercury capsule was designed and built. To use Jones' own term, we can describe the work of his group as "man's integration into the Mercury capsule." In other words, they did the human engineering of the system. One of the more interesting activities of the McDonnell group was their Failure Task Analysis. This consisted of an analysis of possible equipment failures that could occur during flight, a determination of the symptoms which the pilot or ground crew would have of the failure, the appropriate actions to take, and the consequences to be expected. It is easy to see the value of such a failure analysis for making improvements in the design, and for crew training. Much of the astronauts' training was based on this failure analysis. Although some type of failure analysis in design of complex systems is not new, I believe the McDonnell analysis was considerably more complete and detailed than any previously done, in terms of the cues to the pilot and the actions he could take. I fully expect that this technique will set a pattern for human engineering of future manned space vehicles.

Other important efforts of Jones and his group dealt with the visual problems of the astronaut, both inside and outside the Mercury capsule, and with the design of the procedures trainer (or simulator) to which I have already referred. In commenting on the training for his flight, Astronaut Shepard (1961) attached high value to two training devices, one of which was this procedures trainer.

The other trainer that Shepard felt was of great value was the *Navy human centrifuge* * at Johnsville, Pennsylvania. On this centrifuge, operating through a computer, the astronauts were able to experience the accelerations of flight as well as effects of their own control of the capsule. In the work with the Johnsville centrifuge, we again find psychologists playing an important role, in this case working very closely with navy physiologists and medical personnel. John L. Brown (1960) and, more recently, Randall Chambers have obtained performance measures of X-15 pilots and Mercury astronauts on the Johnsville centrifuge. Their experiments demonstrated that with properly designed hand controls the pilots could maintain quite good track-

* Editor's italics.

ing performance while exposed to high acceleration forces. Their experiments included the type of accelerations required to place a manned satellite into an earth orbit and bring it back into the atmosphere. These studies, plus the training which the astronauts obtained on the Johnsville centrifuge, contributed greatly to the Mercury Program.

Besides the problem of high accelerative forces during launch and re-entry, there has been the long-standing question of how men will be affected by the weightlessness that becomes the normal state of affairs in space. For psychologists, the primary question has been, how will the pilot or astronaut's work performance be affected by lack of gravitational force? The only satisfactory way of producing weightlessness without actually going out into space has been by flying an aircraft in a parabolic path so that gravity is exactly counterbalanced by centrifugal force. The first significant experiments on human performance as affected by weightlessness were done by Gerathewohl, Strughold, and Stallings (1957) in fighter-type aircraft at the Air Force School of Aviation Medicine. Later, experiments were conducted by Brown and others at our laboratory with subjects tied down as well as free floating in a cargo-type airplane. These experiments (Loftus and Hammer, 1961) proved that human performance would not be disrupted or even significantly affected for subjects strapped in their seats, as planned for Project Mercury. Thus another of the potential obstacles to space flight had been dispelled.

Just as kings of old protected themselves against the hazards of eating by having food tasters precede them, so the modern astronaut likes to have animals precede him to sample the hazards of space flight. Before Shepard's Mercury flight on May 5, 1961, a *chimpanzee, Ham,** was put through an approximate duplicate of the flight on January 31, 1961. Ham's successful return to earth verified not only the physiological safety of such a flight, but it also verified that voluntary manual performance could be carried out during the stresses and strains of a rocket launching, weightlessness, and re-entry. The credit for Ham's performance goes to two psychologists, Fred Rohles and Marvin Grunzke, at the Air Force Aeromedical Field Laboratory at Holloman Air Force Base. They had trained Ham to operate a lever in response to a light signal to avoid an electric shock. Ham had been trained to continue his task even while exposed to some of the environmental stresses of space flight. During his pioneering flight in a Mercury capsule, Ham continued faithfully at his task with only a few lapses during the most stressful periods.

From the foregoing samples, we can see that psychology and psychologists have made important contributions, along with many other sciences and scientists, in the early phases of our nation's space efforts. *These contributions have been generally in the selection of astronauts, the determination of astronaut capabilities and design of the work station to match these, and the*

* Editor's italics.

design of training equipment and methods for astronaut training.* These are the traditional areas of psychological contribution to personnel selection, human engineering, and training.

What has already been accomplished is only a small beginning by comparison with the work needed to meet the challenges of the future. Looking ahead a decade or two, let us examine some of the activities we can reasonably expect human beings to perform, or attempt to perfom, in space.

The following are some of the jobs now foreseen for future astronauts:

1. Work and live in a relatively small space vehicle for weeks or months.
2. Rendezvous and join up with another space vehicle in an earth orbit.
3. Move about the interior and exterior of a space vehicle and transfer from one vehicle to another.
4. Assemble or construct space platforms in an earth orbit.
5. Land a space vehicle on the moon, explore the surrounding surface, and return to earth.

All of these activities, of course, must be carried out under the handicap of an extremely hostile environment, including weightlessness (except on the moon), lack of atmosphere, extremes of temperature, and radiation. Even a superficial analysis tells us that here are many challenging problems for psychological research. Let us review a few of the problems and see how some psychologists are already subjecting them to vigorous attack. To keep it within manageable proportions, I have chosen to restrict this review to work either carried out or sponsored by our Behavioral Sciences Laboratory at Wright-Patterson Air Force Base.

In discussing contributions to Project Mercury, I have already mentioned research studies on human performance under weightless conditions, as obtained for brief periods in aircraft. From these aircraft studies and the brief flights of Shepard and Grissom, we are assured that the performance of a man strapped in his seat will not be impaired significantly by weightlessness.

The situation is quite different, however, if the man must move about and do work inside or outside his vehicle. For him the lack of gravity is a great inconvenience. Fiction writers have long ago solved the weightless man's problems by giving him magnetic shoes with which to walk on the walls and ceilings and a personal rocket gun with which to propel himself from place to place. These ideas of the fiction writers have been tested in our zero-g airplane by Brown, Simons, Gardner, and others (Loftus and Hammer, 1961; Simons, 1959; Simons and Gardner, 1960). Unfortunately, the problems are not so easily overcome as thought by the fiction writers.

For purposes of walking, magnetic shoes, suction cups, and other means of gluing the feet to a surface, have so far proved to be unsatisfactory substitutes for gravity. They hold only when touching the surface and lose their hold or

* Editor's italics.

pull when separated from the walking surface. Whereas the magnetic shoes and other adhesion methods fail to replace gravity for purposes of walking, they seem to be a good gravity substitute for human perception of the vertical. For all of our subjects who have tried the magnetic shoes, the ceiling of the airplane has immediately become the floor, or downward direction. Evidently, for the standing man under weightless conditions, down is always the direction where his feet are attached.

The fiction writer's personal rocket gun, for the weightless astronaut to use in moving from place to place, also turns out to have many weaknesses. Unless this thrust can be directed precisely at the center of mass, the subject's body will be thrown into a spin instead of being propelled in the desired direction. Unfortunately, men are not endowed with a sense organ to tell them the location of the center of mass. To make the personal rocket gun useful, therefore, will require some elaborations and improvements on the basic idea. Several of these are now being studied.

That men will ever propel themselves in open space with hand-held rocket guns seems somewhat doubtful. It is more likely that they will move from one vehicle to another within a small capsule with suitable rocket propulsion. Certainly, we can expect men to be guiding a spaceship so as to *rendezvous with another ship* * in approximately the same orbit. But the execution of such a rendezvous presents rather formidable problems in guidance and control. Any change in velocity of an orbiting object will cause it to seek a new orbit. Suppose a man in an orbiting capsule were to increase his speed to rendezvous with another satellite ahead of him in the same orbit. Because of the increased speed, his capsule would move out to an orbit of greater radius, but with a longer time per orbit. Thus, his capsule would move above and then drop behind the target satellite. Similarly, if the man were to decrease the speed of his capsule, it would drop to a lower but faster orbit. For executing a rendezvous, therefore, we truly have a case where the shortest distance is not a straight line, but an arc. This arc will end at the target satellite only if the amount and direction of thrust have been properly chosen.

Besides having complex control problems in executing a rendezvous with another spaceship, an astronaut faces rather difficult *problems of visual perception.** Usually his visual target, the other ship, will be seen against a background of black sky, punctuated only by stars. Usually part of the other vehicle will be brightly illuminated by direct sunlight, part of it by earth reflection, and part of it will be completely dark. The earth may or may not be visible. Thus, orientation cues for direction may be lacking. Here is a fertile field for visual perceptual research, which Baker and Steedman, in our laboratory, have begun to explore in a specially prepared dark room. Their research has been directed toward obtaining thresholds for the kind of target movements which an astronaut would be required to judge in visually con-

* Editor's italics.

trolling a rendezvous in space. . . . Thresholds were determined for target motion toward and away from the observer, using targets of different angular sizes. Note that for the largest target size the direction of movement can be judged correctly (90 per cent threshold) in less than 5 per cent of the observer-to-target distance. The curves have a break at about twelven minutes of visual angle. At the smaller visual angles, it appears that the target motion is judged not by size change but by a change in brightness much as in Ricco's Law. At the larger visual angles, the subject judges the target motion by the change in stimulus area.

A study of the human problems of performing assembly and construction operations in space has led several people in our laboratory to return to a traditional psychophysical technique that is almost as old as experimental psychology. This is the measurement of thresholds for lifted weights, but with a space-age twist. In space, objects have no weight, but their mass remains unchanged. Thus, it is of interest to know how the thresholds for mass alone compare with the thresholds for both weight and mass. Furthermore, we expect that in space many operations will have to be performed by remote manipulators such as those used in nuclear laboratories. . . . The thresholds for mass alone were obtained on a frictionless (air-bearing) table. Some measurements were also made under true weightless conditions in our zero-g airplane, which verified the validity of the results obtained on the frictionless table.

A final human problem of space flight which I will discuss is the problem of *long-term work and confinement in a very small vehicle.** Once placed in orbit, an earth satellite can keep going almost indefinitely without the application of additional thrust. If such a vehicle is manned, the limiting time that it can remain aloft is most likely to be the tolerance or endurance of the human crew. If the flight time exceeds about 24 hours, we must provide additional men for crew relief. Thus, we have the problems of how large a relief crew must be added and how the duty and rest periods should be scheduled. The situation is somewhat similar to that on a submarine that may remain submerged for weeks or months, except for, at least, one important difference. Unlike the submarine, the spaceship has a severe weight problem. To place each pound in orbit requires several hundred pounds of rocket thrust. Thus, to save weight, it is of the utmost importance that the total number of crew members be an absolute minimum; and these crew members must live and work in a very confined space.

Research on the problems of long-term confinement and work-rest cycles has been conducted for our laboratory by Adams and his colleagues at the Lockheed Aircraft Corporation at Marietta, Georgia. Chiles has monitored this program for our laboratory. The Lockheed research has been conducted in a crew station mockup with duty stations for up to five crew members and

* Editor's italics.

a small additional area for sleeping and eating. At each duty station is a work panel providing the subjects with the following tasks: probability monitoring, auditory vigilance, reaction time to warnings, and arithmetic computation. On all of these tasks, performance is continually recorded and there is provision for some recording of physiological measures.

A major experiment (Adams and Chiles, in preparation) conducted in the Lockheed mockup used two B-52 crews supplied by the Strategic Air Command. Each crew spent 15 days in the mockup on a work-rest cycle of 4 hours work and 2 hours rest for the entire 15 days. . . . Through the 15-day period there is only a moderate decline in performance in spite of the rather severe work-rest cycle of 4 hours work and 2 hours rest. The other significant finding is the diurnal cycle in the performance level with the low point during the morning of each day. This cycle persisted throughout the 15-day period in spite of the subjects having been removed from the usual day-night routine and environmental changes. . . . All of the performance tests showed evidence of a diurnal cycle and only a moderate decline in performance during the 15 days. On the pattern discrimination, task performance improved during the confinement period, almost certainly because of learning effects. The daily cycle appeared also in the physiological measurements taken during the fifteen-day study. . . .

From the results just shown, added to the verbal reports of the subjects in the 15-day study, we believe that well-motivated men can be expected to live and work in a confined space or other vehicle for up to 15 days on a schedule of 4 hours work and 2 hours rest. This means, of course, that the number of crew members over and above the duty stations to be manned need be only 50 per cent. Or, put another way, only three men could operate two duty stations on a continuous basis provided the three men are cross-trained on both duty stations.

There is, of course, much additional work by which psychologists are contributing to our nation's current and future space efforts that I have not attempted to cover in this review. There is, for example, the important and interesting work of Brant Clark and others at the Navy School of Aviation Medicine on the effects of slow rotation on human performance. Such rotation of a space vehicle offers a substitute for gravity in space. There have been many studies involving water immersion, isolation, and other techniques for simulating some of the changes in the sensory and social environment of space. Also, there are many psychologists working in government laboratories and in the guarded interiors of our major aircraft and other corporations, helping to shape the designs of our spaceships of the future.

In *concluding this review* * of psychology and the space frontier, I would like to restate several points made earlier:

* Editor's italics.

1. Psychology as a science has a vital role to play in the conquest of space.

2. Psychologists have responded with vigor and imagination to the challenging problems of space flight.

3. The space flight challenge brings with it the stimulation of new ideas and opens opportunities for new types of research on human behavior.

4. Psychology has much to gain in the form of new knowledge, and, also, in status as a science, from its participation in the push into space.

IMPLICATIONS

This review of the psychologists' contribution to our nation's space effort shows the importance of psychologists working as a team. Many separate human problems were the object of studies, the results of which all contributed to the final task of space flight. Which of the problems interested you most, and what, in brief, were the findings in respect to them? Can you think of an aspect of general psychology, such as motivation, perception, learning, emotion, adjustment, and individual differences, that was not involved in the studies reviewed here?

REFERENCES

Consult the Bibliography for references cited in the article.

[48] DELAYED VISUAL FEEDBACK AND BEHAVIOR

We normally take for granted sensory feedback from our behavior and fail to realize how much we depend upon it for the skillful performance of our daily skills. The effective public speaker depends upon interested response of the audience. The experienced skaters, skiers, and other athletes can perform well because they are constantly receiving sensory feedback from their muscles. We could extend our discussion of the importance of sensory feedback to all human skills and performances. Art, music, and public relations are just a few fields in which sensory feedback is necessary for efficient performance. Only recently have laboratory studies been performed on the disturbance of feedback on human functioning. This selection shows graphically what happens in the visual area.

William M. Smith, John W. McCrary, and Karl U. Smith

Reprinted from William M. Smith, John W. McCrary, and Karl U. Smith, "Delayed Visual Feedback and Behavior," *Science*, Vol. 132 (Washington, D.C.: American Association for the Advancement of Science, October 14, 1960), pp. 1013–1014, by permission of the publisher and the authors. Copyright 1960 by the American Association for the Advancement of science.

In the same way that the sound of a subject's voice can be stored momentarily on magnetic tape and played back during the course of speech (Lee, 1950) it is possible, through the use of newly developed video-tape recording and reproducing equipment, to store and play back the visual representation of a subject's performance field in such a way that the subject observes a televised display of his behavior shortly after the behavior has occurred. In this report we describe the results of some preliminary observations concerning the effects of such visual delay on a sample of visual-motor tasks.

The RCA laboratory magnetic tape video recording and reproducing system was used to produce delayed vision.* The subject sat in front of a television monitor (21-inch screen) which received the output of a second playback unit. A delay of approximately 520 msec. was provided. In order to prevent the subject from seeing the task area directly, a pair of special goggles was used. An RCA miniature television camera was located at eye level and next to the subject's head to minimize angular distortion of the televised performance field. Magnification of the performance field was approximately 1.5.

The subject carried out various tasks on the electronic handwriting analyzer, a device described by Smith and Bloom (1956), which permits the measurement of both manipulative and travel components of writing or similar motions. The subject observed on the television screen a portion of the writing surface of this device, together with his hand with the pencil in it and a part of his forearm.

The nine different tasks listed in Table 1 were performed by two subjects

* *Speech and Hearing Research*, Vol. 1, 12 (1958). We are grateful to the Acoustical and Electromechanical Laboratory of the RCA Laboratories of the Radio Corporation of America at Princeton, N.J., for providing the special television equipment and facilities used in obtaining these observations. In particular, we wish to acknowledge the technical assistance of W. D. Houghton of the above-mentioned laboratory.

under three conditions of observation; television-delay, television-no delay, normal (ordinary observation). Tasks, as well as sequences of words and syllables, were randomly assigned to each subject. Comparisons among the three conditions suffer from the lack of control for practice, in that the observations with delay were obtained two weeks prior to those obtained under the no-delay conditions, but in view of the magnitude and nature of the observed differences and the nature of the tasks themselves, not much significance is attached to the possible effects of practice from condition to condition. Instructions in all three cases were to perform the task as accurately and as rapidly as possible (and as neatly as possible in the case of writing tasks).

The first thing to be said about the effect on behavior of delayed visual feedback as revealed in these observations is that performance becomes inordinately difficult and frustrating. It is nearly impossible to perform the simplest of tasks, such as placing a dot in the center of a circle, with any reasonable degree of accuracy. Any localizing movement, in fact, demands great effort, and little accuracy is obtained. What normally would be fast, smooth, placing motions become erratic and oscillatory movements which assume a characteristic jerkiness. Handwriting, even of very familiar material, becomes severely degraded and in some cases completely illegible. In Figure 1 are reproduced some of the original records showing samples of star tracings, drawings of simple geometrical figures, maze tracings, and handwriting. Specimens from the records of the two no-delay conditions are given for purposes of comparison.

An error analysis of the writing material reveals that, in addition to the obvious degradation of legibility, particular kinds of errors occur. The most frequent kind of error in a total of 64 errors was letter duplication (40.6 per cent), examples of which can be seen in Figure 1, D and E. The predominance of this type of error parallels the findings of the Bergeijk and David study (1959) and agrees with the results on articulatory errors found in delayed auditory feedback.

Most frequent kind of error found in our observations was error of insertion—that is, the occurrence within a word of letters or part letters which did not belong there (26.6 per cent). There were a few errors of omission (7.8 per cent), one error of substitution, and a variety of miscellaneous errors (23.4 per cent). The relatively frequent occurrence of errors of duplication and insertion might be considered "graphic stammering and stuttering," analogous to the articulatory effects in speech due to delayed auditory feedback.

Evaluation of the accuracy of performance of the nonwriting tasks shows more dramatically the effects of delayed vision. In the star- and maze-tracing tasks, some of the records were so bad that they were literally unscorable. The star record in Figure 1 is the best example of this extreme degree of degraded performance. There was, however, an obvious improvement in these two

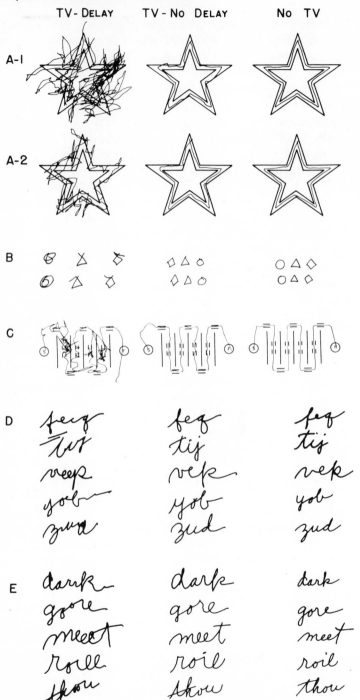

FIGURE 1. Sample records for some of the tasks performed under delayed visual feedback.

tasks over the few trials performed by each subject. An interesting question for future investigation is the degree of improvement obtainable in such tasks with extended practice.

In addition to the low quality and low accuracy of performance produced by the delayed visual feedback, very marked effects on temporal characteristics of performance were found. Table 1 summarizes the time data for the two subjects on all tasks for the three different conditions. The measures in this table represent the contact or manipulative time (the actual time the subject had the metal pencil touching the writing surface) expressed as means. As the table shows, some tasks required a tenfold or greater increase in time for

TABLE 1

Subject	TV delay	TV no-delay	Normal
		Time (sec)	
	Writing letters of alphabet		
A	2.0	0.6	0.6
B	1.2	0.7	0.5
	Star-tracing		
A	86.2	13.8	5.9
B	49.6	16.0	6.3
	Drawing 3 geometric figures		
A	6.1	3.5	3.5
B	5.0	6.4	4.7
	Writing 4-letter nonsense syllables		
A	4.8	4.1	2.0
B	6.4	2.4	1.9
	Writing 4-letter words		
A	4.3	1.7	1.5
B		2.6	1.6
	Maze-tracing		
A	102.8	18.0	7.2
B	107.6	23.9	7.6
	Writing Bergeijk-David words		
A	5.9	2.5	2.2
B	5.5	3.1	2.4
	Writing 3-letter nonsense syllables		
A	5.1	1.7	1.4
B		2.2	1.6
	Placing dots in 6 circles		
A	27.8	2.8	2.5
B	12.7	4.0	1.7

Manipulation or contact time for the various visual-motor tasks for each subject under the three conditions of observation. All values are means in seconds. Data on two tasks under the television-delay condition were not obtained for subject B.

completion, in comparison to the normal or television no-delay condition. Although not shown in the table, the separate measures of travel time (time the metal pencil was off the writing surface during the execution of writing movements, dotting circles, and so forth) provide similar results—namely consistent and marked increases in time for the delayed condition in comparison to the other two.

These results clearly emphasize the critical importance of the temporal aspects of visual feedback in the control and regulation of human performance. They are, in addition, in general agreement with the results of an unpublished study on simulated delayed visual feedback (Lee, 1950), with the results of the investigation of delayed handwriting by Bergeijk and David (1959), and with studies on the effect of delayed auditory feedback on speech, tapping and other motor performances (Chase, *et al.*, 1959). Delayed auditory or visual feedback seriously degrades performance, introduces characteristic redundant motions, increases performance time by marked amounts, and imposes upon the subject very difficult and frustrating conditions.

We believe that the technical achievement of video-tape recording places in the hands of investigators a very significant technique for the future study of human perception and motion.

ABSTRACT. By means of video-tape recording the visual presentation of a person's behavior, as he carries out some task, can be delayed in such a way that the individual sees what he is doing a short time after he has done it. The effects of this delay of visual feedback on a variety of simple visual-motor tasks are found to be both marked and deleterious, and in some respects similar to the effects of delayed auditory feedback on speech and motor tasks.

IMPLICATIONS

A veteran college lecturer began giving lectures on television and found himself experiencing more anxiety than he had felt since his high school public-speaking ventures. The unexpected nature of the anxiety added to his confusion and emotional disturbance. He attributed part of his difficulty to the absence of the typical visual and auditory feedback he had been receiving in "live" lectures. He was now experiencing in the studio irrelevant feedback from technicians who were actively doing their jobs but ignoring his presentation. His feedback was inattention, which signified lack of communication in the usual satisfactory manner. Can you recall from your experience events in which you were markedly disturbed by a variation in the habitual sensory feedback upon which you had unknowingly depended? Possibly you can now better understand some situation in which you were conscious of a sense of inefficiency or deterioration of performance.

Feedback is also an integral part of social communication. People communicate well in part because feedback reinforces understanding. See if you can relate Selection 39 to this issue.

REFERENCES
Consult the Bibliography for references cited in the article.

[49] AUTOMATION, HUMAN ENGINEERING, AND PSYCHOLOGY

What exactly is *automation,* and why is it of interest to the psychologist? How can psychology contribute to the problem of "trouble shooting" in maintenance? What is the new field of human engineering and the new concept of the man-machine system? What are examples of the human factors' problems encountered in modern industry?

These and other questions are answered in the following selection. Warren puts the issues in the historical perspective of seventy-five years and shows the present status of operation training in this pioneer area.

Neil D. Warren

Reprinted from Neil D. Warren, "Automation, Human Engineering and Psychology," *American Psychologist,* Vol. 11 (Washington, D.C.: American Psychological Association, 1956), pp. 531–536, by permission of the publisher and the author.

Automation simply defined as the replacement of man by machine or the use of machines to control machines is as old as machines themselves. For centuries the machine has been nibbling at the responsibilities—and privileges—of man, with the use of such devices as governors, thermostats, autopilots and other servo-controls. Now, with the advent of the continuous-process factory the machine is taking large parts of the areas of human responsibility which remain. To quote Drucker (1955):

> The Automation Revolution is here, and it is proceeding at high speed. But it will be many years before it permeates the entire economy. Most businesses will not convert to automation overnight but will go at it piecemeal, which will not be easy.... But the mental strain will be less. Fewer people will have to "relearn" fewer things; and they will have more time to do it in. While it is a major revolution, automation is therefore not likely to be dramatic; there will be no point when one can say: "This is the year when the American economy went into automation."
>
> But only the speed of automation is uncertain. There can be little doubt that the direction of our progress is toward it. There can be little doubt that it means a tremendous upgrading of the labor force in terms of skill, employment security, standard of living, and opportunity.

How far will this change go? In a previous consideration of this question (Warren, 1953), I was forced to the somewhat reluctant conclusion that there is no limit to the ingenuity of the inventor. It is unjustified complacency to believe that memory, reasoning, and judgment can never be the characteristics of machines—indeed they already exist.

In Volume I of the *American Journal of Psychology*, C. S. Pierce (1887) commented that the logical machine is inherently "destitute of all originality, all initiative. It cannot find its own problems." In 1955, I doubt that anyone can be sure that even this is not imminent. Pierce made this further observation: This lack of initiative "however, is no defect in a machine; we do not want it to do its own business, but ours. We no more want an original machine than a housebuilder would want an original journeyman, or an American board of college trustees would hire an original professor." In this comment lies a suggestion of the answer to the question of the ultimate goal of automation. The engineer will go just as far as society will permit. Ultimately, society must decide where to call a halt to the development of the machine.

We can expect industry to make use of automatic controls whenever it is economically advantageous to do so. In most industries this will mean considerable, but not complete, automation very soon. In others almost complete automation will be developed rapidly. I recently visited a large factory in which a new unit was being built. In it, I was told, the entire manufacturing process from the carloads of raw materials to the carload of finished product would be continuous and automatic. To some degree this is occurring throughout industry.

I wish to consider two of the many possible implications of this trend for the science and profession of psychology. First, there is increased need for both basic and applied research in the area of problem solving. Second, the application of information about human behavior to the design of man-machine systems is a rapidly expanding field. This is in the area often called human engineering.

Problem Solving

Besides the socioeconomic problems which industry must face, automation is causing a rapid shift in emphasis from operation to maintenance. The more complex the machine, the more difficult it is to keep it working properly. If our mechanized society is not to be throttled by its own machines, if it is not to suffer the fate of Bierce's inventor, maintenance must be successful. This will require a shift in manpower from operation. In one factory, which is changing to automatic controls, the ratio of maintenance personnel to operators has been approximately one to five. It is now nearer one to three and it is expected to reach one to one in the near future. It is probable that in a completely automatic factory the proportion of maintenance effort would greatly exceed that of operation. In one kind of military equipment, which is extremely complex, it is now estimated that for each hour of operation, forty man-hours of maintenance are required.

What is the relation of this trend to problem solving? The key ability of the mechanic who maintains complex machinery is not skill in repair or replacement of parts, but ability to determine what part is to be repaired or replaced. Anyone can replace a tube in a radio or television set. The skill required to replace other parts is not very great—but it takes something of an expert to determine which tube, capacitor, resistor, or what-not is defective. This skill in diagnosing the cause of a malfunction is like the diagnostic skill of the physician. For very complex machines the problem for the maintenance man is scarcely less difficult than that of the physician. In the machine, the process of diagnosis is called trouble shooting. In certain situations trouble-shooting experts are employed. Their job is diagnosis only and repair is left to other mechanics.

Trouble shooting is a form of problem solving, and the principles which apply to other kinds of problem solving will apply as well to it. The procedures may range from trial and error to logic.

It is of interest to note that there has been a considerable increase in study of the problem-solving process in the last five years. As evidence of this, the number of references in the *Psychological Abstracts* dealing with human problem solving has greatly increased on both absolute and relative bases. That this is in part due to a recognition of the importance of the subject for maintenance of machines is indicated by the fact that a considerable amount of the research reported has been sponsored by the air force and the navy. Also, in the 1954 *Abstracts* there appears, for the first time, a number of references specifically to the topic of trouble shooting. These will not be the last, since final answers to the questions of how to select, train, and use trouble-shooting experts are still to be secured. The need becomes greater daily. The production of automobiles, airplanes, home appliances, factory equipment, and so on, of ever-increasing complexity may soon overload our capacity to keep these machines operating.

As one example of research in this area, I may describe briefly a study we have undertaken under contract with the air force.[1] The purpose of the project has been to develop a procedure for training mechanics to do a better job of trouble shooting for a highly complex piece of electronic equipment.

The hypotheses were developed that there is a limited number of general principles in logical trouble shooting and that these principles can be learned as abstractions unrelated to any specific device.

The procedure involved recording complete protocols of the diagnostic steps of experts together with their verbalized reasons for each step. This was followed by an analysis of each protocol and a record of each abstracted principle in symbolic form. With an adequate sample of such protocols from a number of different experts, it appeared possible to establish a complete list of principles.

The learnability of such principles is to be tested by the use of a specially devised trainer in which each general principle can be demonstrated with any desired degree of complexity. The first year of effort has verified our first hypothesis: that there are general trouble-shooting principles; and the next year will establish whether or not they can be taught using the trainer and procedures devised for that purpose.

HUMAN ENGINEERING

The term "human engineering" is obnoxious to some members of the engineering profession. For that reason I have some reluctance to use it. However, it appears in the *Engineering Index* and in the *Industrial Arts Index* as well as in many articles and publications, so I believe it is here to stay. However, the *Industrial Arts Index* makes it clear that the term is a designation of a topic —and not of a profession. I think it can be demonstrated that this distinction is a valid one at present although it may not continue to be so.

Broadly defined, human engineering is a phase of engineering which applies knowledge of human factors to design of machines—or of products. It is broader than, and includes the fields of engineering psychology, biomechanics, applied experimental psychology, and others.

The first use of the term "human engineering" was as a title for processes of selection and placement of personnel in industry, and of the choice of a vocation for an individual. In industry this was a process of adapting man to the machine. Psychologists have worked in this area for many years.

When machines are relatively simple, selection and training achieve the

[1] Contract AF 18(600)–1206.

purpose of supplying adequate operators. As machines become increasingly complex and the demands upon the operator's skill and knowledge become greater, a point is reached where selection and training can no longer meet the needs.

This point has already been reached in some areas. A notable example is that of aviation. The complex pattern of instruments and controls in modern airplanes taxes the capacities of even the most expert airmen. Poorly designed instruments produce errors and confusion. The necessity of integrating the readings of several instruments to determine a single course of action dangerously delays the pilot's responses. The unsatisfactory design and location of controls result in mistakes which may be disastrous.

The solution requires designing the man-machine system in such a way as to take full advantage of man's assets and to avoid imposing on his limitations.

Another term of equal breadth which is intended to cover much of the area defined by human engineering is "ergonomics"—the study of man at work. One author has pointed out that ergonomics "is concerned with the study of human behavior in response to external stress, with particular reference to the stress-strain problems of man at work" (Hatch, 1955). Changes in design and in work methods can be expected to result from such study.

It is well to point out that consideration of human factors in design is not new—nor were professional psychologists pioneers in the field. It may be said, in all seriousness, that primitive man was a human engineer when he shaped the handle of his ax or club to fit his hand. Certainly engineering designers have taken the human factor into account to some degree for centuries. Even in the application of the sciences of physiology and psychology to design, engineers have pioneered, as Hatch has pointed out, "ahead of the specialists in those fields."

On the other hand, psychologists have not been entirely unaware of the possible applications of their science to such practical problems. In Volume II of the *American Journal of Psychology*, the first article is by E. C. Sanford, and is entitled "Personal Equation" (1889). In it is told the well-known incident which led to research on individual differences in reaction time. It is of interest that on page 653 of the same volume there is a report of a device to take into account human limitations in the observation of sudden phenomena.

Primarily as a result of the pressures of military needs during and following World War II, psychologists and others have become increasingly involved in human engineering. Some psychologists have adopted the title of "human engineer" to describe their own function. Seldom, however, can one individual—or one profession—provide the human factors knowledge required by the designer.

Consider, for example, this list of human factor problems encountered in one aircraft factory. This is a sample. Seventy-two were listed last spring and undoubtedly more have been added:

What is a comfortable finger pressure for knobs?
How much force should be required for a wheel control?
What is the volume occupied by a man?
What are the hourly rates of wash-water use?
What are the angles of vision from a prone position?
How far away can a pilot see another airplane?
What is the weight of the human head and brain?
What should be the height of a "no smoking" sign?
What are the effects of drugs on the human body in flight?
How much work space is required for a bartender in a cocktail lounge?

And so on.

Clearly, cooperative effort is called for. As in other areas, the psychologist can serve most effectively as part of a team in which each expert contributes his own special knowledge and skill to the solution of common problems. The trend in industry appears to be in this direction. Although the composition and organization of the team vary widely, there is usually a position for the psychologist.

Brigadier General Don Flickinger (1955), of the Air Force's Research and Development Command, has described a five-man "human factors team." The team captain is a flight surgeon, a specialist in aviation medicine. The other members are an anthropologist, a biophysicist, a physiologist, and a psychologist. The responsibilities of the psychologist include work-space layout, performance criteria, training requirements, component design and mission activities.

Teams of somewhat this make-up have been established in several aircraft factories and there is a trend extending to other industries as well. To consider and to evaluate this trend, it has been proposed that the American Society of Mechanical Engineers establish a working committee (Hatch, 1955), including engineers representing industrial engineering, time-and-motion study, machine tool design, plant layout and building design, and health and safety engineering, together with invited specialists in anatomy, physical anthropology, biomechanics, applied physiology, and applied psychology. This is another indication that psychologists will be part of the team approach to design problems.

What can the science and profession of psychology contribute to this important field?

General Flickinger has pointed out that, while there is no lack of interest in or appreciation of human factors, there are three reasons why they have not been fully taken into consideration. First, "lack of fundamental data in the human factors field" in a form usable by the engineers. As regards the first part of this "lack," psychologists can point to the consideraable body of fundamental data about human behavior. The experimental psychologists are investigating many specific problems and have formulated a few general principles which are pertinent to the human engineering field. The *Handbook of Human Engineering Data* (1952) first published in 1949 by the Tufts College Institute for Applied Experimental Psychology is, in its latest edition, a very imposing volume. Many psychologists stand ready to tell the designer the facts of psychology.

Are these data in a form usuable by engineers? Very probably they are not. We are accused of generalities. Industrialists and engineers distrust generalities. The data most frequently are derived from the aseptic conditions of the laboratory and are not "practical." Or, perhaps, we are not able to convey to the practical designer the significance of our findings.

A research engineer for an aircraft factory recently put it this way: When the design engineer realized that he was building aircraft which taxed the limitations of the human, he turned to those specialists, physiologists and psychologists who he assumed could tell him what he must do to alleviate these conditions. In all fairness, he admits they probably did, but he couldn't understand a single word of it.

I am reminded of Robert O. Carlson's (1953) comment about similar criticism from another applied area. He says,

Of course we . . . recognize that these criticisms are pure nonsense. Ask any (psychologist) and he may point out that such accusations are undoubtedly the manifestation of a fundamentally dichotomous role-status position in which the out-group . . . project their ambivalent affectual status vis-à-vis their significant-other group, . . . in such a manner so that their primordial unconscious aggression stemming from a latent role identification with an authority symbol, perhaps the outgrowth of a suppressed Oedipus complex, takes the form of a semantic-oriented aggressive syndrome against superordinate members of a prestige structure which seems to threaten their affect and basic ego constellation.

Carlson thinks such jargon is on its way out, and perhaps it doesn't exist in the engineering psychology field—but I'm not so sure. Psychologists often seem to find it necessary to express even simple ideas in words of many syllables. At one meeting I listened to a paper in which it was reported that the psychologist working as human engineer had caused to be installed—I quote—"a detachable inclement weather protective device." This, I suspect, bore considerable resemblance to an umbrella.

This problem is being worked on. *The Human Engineering Guide to Equipment Design* being prepared by a joint committee of the military services will be practical, direct, and understandable, even to a nonpsychologist. And if all the textbooks in engineering psychology, and human engineering, which are being written, are as good as their authors are capable of making them, there will soon be no room for the engineers to complain.

General Flickinger's (1955) second suggestion is that there is need for "a comprehensive plan for data collection, accumulation, validation, and dissemination to working groups, both scientists and engineers."

There have been many serious attempts to plan research in the human factors area. Anyone who begins trying to apply present knowledge to the man-machine problem will recognize the large, and often crucial areas, in which information is inadequate. Many psychologists have expressed disdain for the applied or "program" research. However, it is here that the opportunity is greatest; and this is the area in which the industrial psychologist can star on the human engineering team. Validation of procedures, evaluation of devices, and establishment of norms are tasks for which he is especially prepared. Moreover, just as industrialists have learned that basic research in the physical sciences is profitable, they will inevitably find it desirable to support basic research in psychology and other biological and social sciences. The Bell Telephone Laboratories has provided an example of this effort for many years.

The third lack is that of "training programs directed toward . . . greater integration of . . . knowledge and skills required by life (scientists) and engineering scientists alike which would prepare them for work in this highly complex field. . . ."

What is the situation with regard to courses designed to meet this need? Some part of the answer can be found in the results of a questionnaire survey of courses in the area of human factors in engineering design. The questionnaire was brief and simple but, even so, the number of responses was amazingly large and seems to indicate a considerable amount of interest in this field. The questions were addressed to 116 departments of industrial or mechanical engineering in the list accredited by the Engineers' Council for Professional Development. We received 104 replies.

Of the 104 answers, 67 indicated that no course in the area of human factors in design was offered.

Sixteen other departments reported that they did not have a course specifically covering the topic but that it was treated in part in other existing courses, such as *Motion and Time Study, Industrial Psychology, Industrial Management, Engineering Design*, etc. It is quite probable that many of the 67 reporting "No course" have similar partial coverage but did not report it since this question was not specifically asked.

The remaining 20 departments have one or more courses in the area. The titles are varied. . . .

Obviously, a course or two will not make human factors experts of these engineers. Perhaps they help to meet the need expressed by Professor T. F. Hatch (1955), of the American Society of Mechanical Engineers, that engineers "must acquire a deeper understanding of man" which they must "incorporate into their regular thinking and practice."

If the psychologist is to make an effective contribution to the human engineering field he must acquire a deeper understanding of the machine to incorporate into his thinking and practice. Courses in psychology for engineers and in engineering for psychologists are essential, if only to bridge the semantic chasm between the two disciplines.

At a more fundamental level, an interesting trend is developing which academic psychology must note. This is a combination of engineering training, through the undergraduate degree, and of graduate work in psychology through the Ph.D. degree. In this trend or in some modification of it there may develop a truly new professional who may legitimately call himself a human engineer. At the University of Southern California we have already given one Ph.D. with this combination of backgrounds, and there are five other students at various levels of graduate work in the Psychology Department. Other departments are experiencing the same trend. Since job opportunities in this field are great we mȧy expect the pressure to increase. We must give serious consideration to the kind of program.

The Age of Automation confronts not only the industrial psychologist but the entire profession with changes in research and training. It will undoubtedly add to the trend toward an increasing proportion of applied psychologists in the APA. But the experimental psychologist, if he cares, can be assured of the usefulness of his research in the areas of problem solving and learning, of perception, of motor skills, or for that matter of any other aspect of human behavior. Moreover, the experimental psychologist is discovering a fruitful approach to an understanding of human behavior as a result of examination of the behavior of machines.

Let the engineer learn more about man—and the psychologist more about the machine. Together, with other human factor experts, they will help industry to supply all of us products of greater efficiency, comfort and safety. We can expect greater value from the things we look at, manipulate, sit on, ride in, work with, or play with. More and more they will be designed to fit us. More and more they will reflect an acceptance of the statement of the philosopher Protagoras twenty-four centuries ago that "man is the measure of all things."

IMPLICATIONS

How would you paraphrase Warren's definition of automation? What are the implications of the automation trends for science and for the profession of psychology? What do you understand human engineering to be, and what is the psychologist's role in it? Can you think of some examples of a machine or gadget so designed as to take full advantage of the attributes of the man who uses it? From the information in this article, what is your answer to the question, "Will automation necessarily lead to more unemployment?"

REFERENCES

Additional readings in human factors research and team work both in industry and space technology may be found in Chapanis (1959), McCormick (1957), Flaherty (1961), Sells and Berry (1961), and Fleishman (1961).

Chapter X

ABNORMALITY AND MENTAL HEALTH

[50] AN AUTOBIOGRAPHY OF A SCHIZOPHRENIC EXPERIENCE

You probably know of *psychosis* as a form of serious mental illness and have heard of *schizophrenia*, a functional psychosis and the most common disorder among hospitalized mental patients. Few college students, however, have had any direct contact with a person with schizophrenia, often described as a lack of harmony or a "split" in personality functioning—particularly between emotions and conduct.

There are several forms of schizophrenia, with different kinds of symptoms. The woman who writes about her experience in the following selection is afflicted with catatonic schizophrenia, characterized by symptoms of unusual postures, repetitive movements, and speech. This patient was not completely in contact with the real world but rather had withdrawn into a world of her own. She reported awareness of some of the events in her environment, but she had no desire to communicate with reality. She talked extensively with imaginary companions, and reported visions and delusions. Although we lack an observer's description of this patient, the patient herself gives us an indication of her behavior as others might see it as well as a vivid description of her own thoughts and feelings.

Anonymous

Reprinted from an anonymous article, "Case Report: An Autobiography of a Schizophrenic Experience," *Journal of Abnormal and Social Psychology*, Vol. 51 (Washington, D.C.: American Psychological Association, 1953), pp. 677–689, by permission of the publisher.

Most of what follows is based on an unpublished autobiography written in the spring of 1951, shortly after I had returned home from the second of the three episodes of my schizophrenic experience. My disorder was diagnosed as catatonic schizophrenia.[1] The three episodes occurred over a four-year period. I am concentrating here chiefly on a description of the first episode. This occurred after I had received a year and a half of psychotherapy consisting of weekly contacts with a psychiatric social worker at a child guidance clinic. I had gone for this help when I had come to feel unable to deal with the problems that had arisen in my relations with my children. The disorder was coincidental with processes of personality change which had started some time before I went to the child guidance clinic for help and which continued after recovery from the acute illness.

BACKGROUND

SOCIAL POSITION.   When I first went to the child guidance clinic, I was, in terms of our social structure, the wife of a professional man and I had come from a professional, middle-class background. I had myself been trained as a social caseworker after I completed college.

I was married when I was twenty-one years old. During the following ten years, I had three children. At the time I experienced the first schizophrenic episode, I was thirty-six years old.

Ever since my college days, I had been an active member in groups interested in political and social reform and world peace. I had done organizational work and publicity for the C.I.O. union, to which I belonged, and later for the women's auxiliary. I became active for a time in a cooperative

---

[1] The writer was confined at Sheppard Pratt Hospital from November 1948 through April 1949. The diagnosis was catatonic schizophrenia. Remission occurred after three weeks under sodium amytal. The second confinement was at the same hospital from November 1949 through January 1950. Remission was spontaneous. The third confinement was at St. Elizabeths Hospital, and again the diagnosis was catatonic schizophrenia. It lasted from July 1951 through September 1952. Remission occurred after a series of seven electric shock treatments which were administered in July of 1952.

nursery school which my youngest child attended, and during the year before my illness had served as president of the organization. I had also been a collector for the Community Chest in my neighborhood. As a family we lived in our own home and were stable and settled in a particular locality.

In my personal relations I had always had an adequate number of friends and had never had any difficulty in making close friends. I had, however, been under the strain of steadily increasing anxiety at the time I consulted the clinic, and had also reached an impasse in which I felt incompetent as a mother. One of the chief problems I presented was my feeling that I lacked sufficient warmth in my relations to my two oldest children. My relation to my youngest child was secure and satisfying.

MARITAL AND SEXUAL ADJUSTMENT. I was faced during the period of psychotherapy with a crisis in my marital relationship and just before illness had decided upon divorce, which I finally obtained several years later after recovery from the schizophrenic disorder. Most of the clinical work was focused at first on the difficulties I had about asserting myself in personal relationships, and as I obtained emotional support from the therapist I began to be more self-confident. I began to use a greater amount of independent initiative and judgment in my daily life, and my relations to the children began to improve. The need for greater decisiveness and assertiveness in my relation with my children made it impossible for me to continue long-established relations of overdependency and overidentification which I had maintained in relation to my mother and my husband. There was a simultaneous break with both identifications. My long-suppressed negative reactions to certain aspects of my husband's personality finally came to the forefront. I had previously related to my husband both in a semimaternal and managerial as well as a submissive way. Hostility had been breaking through openly in dreams before I went for help, but generally I had been able to keep hostility and derogatory feelings out of consciousness so that I was able to maintain an adequate amount of warmth and tenderness in the relationship. The final break with my husband therefore constituted a severe emotional deprivation for me. It deprived me of physical and emotional closeness to which I had been accustomed for many years.

I sought compensations for this increasing isolation. I became involved in an intense love affair which aroused a feeling of semicompulsive dependency on this relationship. I seemed to be torn from my moorings and alienated from my former self because I had temporarily lost my normal investment in other interests. Intense feelings about childhood frustrations and disappointments in relation to my father were stirred up at this time and I seemed to feel these early deprivations more keenly in retrospect than I had during my childhood.

My dependency needs were acute at this time but an overinvestment in the extramarital relationship was causing me to lose powers of moral control and to disregard the interests of my children. I made desperate efforts to break the overattachment, and thought finally that I had succeeded. I found the best corrective was writing poetry and intellectual work which enabled me to fight off feelings of incipient depression. Creative activity was intensified but finally became compulsive and overabsorbing. I was not able to maintain a normal extraverted relation to my children, or to switch my attention at will to practical details of living. I experienced a sudden feeling of creative release before my illness, was convinced that I was rapidly attaining the height of my intellectual powers, and that for the first time in my life, I would be able to function up to the level of my ability in this direction.

During my entire married life I had been semifrigid, *i.e.*, I had been unable to attain orgasm except occasionally during sleep. I had, however, enjoyed sexual relationships, found them relaxing and emotionally renewing, and had seldom been bothered by residual tension. Capacity for sexual response increased gradually during the years of marriage but I remained semifrigid even in the extramarital relation described above. Divorce was finally necessary because I no longer felt attracted to my husband sexually after the emotional break was made.

I attained adequate capacity for vaginal orgasm during the recovery phase after the third episode of illness. The increase in sexuality that was associated with loss of inhibition had a terrifying impact during the early phases of psychosis and was expressed symbolically in the experience of "hell-fire" described below and in other ways. During the recovery phases, increased sexuality posed severe problems of control. The situation was aggravated at times by my isolation and by intense religious emotions which stimulated the entire body and increased the need for sex. For a while, casual relations with men were both intensely pleasurable and emotionally satisfying, since they were associated with a mystical and religious type of nonpersonal love and acceptance of other people. This phase wore off gradually and I returned to my usual needs for personal intimacy and personal love, lack of which increased my frustration and unhappiness in casual relations.

CHANGES IN SELF-PERCEPTION.   The new self-confidence I was obtaining from the relation with my therapist enabled me to see more clearly certain aspects of myself which I had seen before only dimly, outside of full awareness. To these aspects of my personality I had a strong negative reaction. My new perceptions disturbed the picture I had long held of myself as being primarily a highly social person, interested in community problems, and in the welfare of others. Later, during some periods of illness, I saw myself also as cold, indifferent to others, withdrawn, and at times as impulsively cruel. I became aware of the strength of my competitive ambitious feelings which had, however, largely been kept in check by my actual preoccupation with more highly social interests. I had expressed feelings of social distance and status by maintaining subdued but occasionally conscious attitudes of impatience and contempt for other people who did not seem to be as quick or competent as myself.

I also felt just before illness that I had failed to give an adequate amount of love to my two older children, and that I had not had full interest in their development as individuals after they had outgrown the stage of early childhood. The extramarital affair intensified insight and self-rejection because I felt that there were limiting and egotistical elements in my love, that I was giving no more than I was receiving, and that I still had an insufficient degree of love for my children.

LOSS OF EGO SUPPORT. Throughout most of the period of therapy I had a desire to impress my therapist and to win her approval. I went out of my way to take pains with my dress and personal appearance when I saw her. Later on, I began to feel that my point of view was changing, that my values were different from hers, and that there was no longer as much common ground for discussion. I also felt I knew myself better than she knew me. I was failing to communicate a good many of my half-formed thoughts about myself, partly because of limitations of time, and partly because these thoughts were not fully clear even to myself. At this point I was no longer able to obtain emotional support from the transference relationship.

In addition to increased loneliness caused by my marital problem, I was also conscious of an increasing intellectual isolation. I was losing a previously established sense of close group identification with organizations to which I had formerly belonged as I became aware that my views were beginning to differ from those of others which I had once accepted. I had previously had a sense of "we-ness" both in regard to family and other group associations. This was being replaced by a sense of personal separateness.

THE ILLNESS

THE ONSET STAGE. A few weeks before my illness I began to regress into success daydreams somewhat similar to, though not quite as naive and grandiose, as those I had had during early adolescence. I was puzzled by this tendency, though not greatly alarmed because it hardly seemed that my daydreaming self was a part of my adult ethical self. At the onset of panic, I was suddenly confronted with an overwhelming conviction that I had discovered the secrets of the universe, which were being rapidly made plain with incredible lucidity. The truths discovered seemed to be known immediately and directly, with absolute certainty. I had no sense of doubt or awareness of the possibility of doubt. In spite of former atheism and strong antireligious sentiments, I was suddenly convinced that it was possible to prove rationally the existence of God. I remember at the time trying to write an essay on cognition. I began to write compulsively and at the same time was aware that I was developing schizophrenia. I found later among the disorganized notes which I had carefully hidden away a number of passages that were quite lucid as well as others that were incoherent and full of symbolic sexual content. I also felt that I was embarking on a great Promethean adventure. I was filled with an audacious and unconquerable spirit. As panic mounted, I grew afraid of being alone, had an intense desire to communicate. I had for a short time a sense of exclusive mission but was able to struggle consciously against messianic delusions. These tendencies were replaced by a sense of burdensome and exclusive responsibility, which continued throughout the entire several years of illness.

SOME SPECIAL CHARACTERISTICS OF THE FIRST EPISODE.   During the first episode I was hyperactive and extremely tense. Feelings of guilt and self-rejection which I had started to have before onset were in evidence during the acute phase of illness only to a very minor degree and were expressed symbolically and nonrationally. It was only later on, during more rational and integrated periods of disturbance, that I developed an intense guilt consciousness and conscious self-repudiation. These guilt feelings were finally resolved and dissipated during periods of comparative rationality. I shall not discuss here the emotional functions of the guilt experience.

I did not feel especially isolated or actively lonely during the projective, fear-ridden first episode. I had little or no desire to communicate with real people, although I talked extensively with an imaginary companion. I felt painfully lonely during later phases of disturbance when I was more rational and in relatively normal contact with other people.

THE WORLD DISASTER EXPERIENCE.   Shortly after I was taken to the hospital for the first time in a rigid catatonic condition, I was plunged into the horror of a world catastrophe. I was being caught up in a cataclysm and totally dislocated. I myself had been responsible for setting the destructive forces into motion, although I had acted with no intent to harm, and defended myself with healthy indignation against the accusations of others. If I had done something wrong, I certainly was suffering the consequences along with everyone else. Part of the time I was exploring a new planet (a marvelous and breath-taking adventure) but it was too lonely, I could persuade no one to settle there, and I had to get back to the earth somehow. The earth, however, had been devastated by atomic bombs and most of its inhabitants killed. Only a few people—myself and the dimly perceived nursing staff—had escaped. At other times, I felt totally alone on the new planet.

The issue of world salvation was of predominant importance and I was trying to tell people how to go back to the abandoned earth. All personal matters relating to my family were forgotten. At times when the universe was collapsing, I was not sure that things would turn out all right. I thought I might have to stay in the endless hell-fire of atomic destruction. The chief horror consisted in the fact that I would never be able to die. I thought I would either have to figure out some form of suicide or else get a lobotomy.

During some of the time that I was dislocated in interplanetary space, I was also having vivid fantasies in connection with water, and these afforded me considerable relief. Water represented conservation of life, in contrast to its destruction by fire.

Water fantasies had started one or two days after admission to the hospital. I suddenly felt I had been plunged into a sea, was drowning and struggling for breath. At that point I realized that I was in a sedative tub. I saw that I was strapped in such a way that I was in no danger of drowning. I knew that as long as I was awake I would not need the straps because I would be careful not to drown, but I continued to feel terrified.

Water fantasies returned at times when I was given wet-pack treatments. I clearly remember reciting to myself some lines of Swinburne. I recalled only the first stanza of the poem and falsely interpolated at the end a line belonging to the second, thus skipping all parts in which the poet expressed a longing for death:

> I will go back to the great sweet mother
> Mother and lover of men, the sea.
> I will go down to her, I and none other,
> Close with her, kiss her, and mix her with me;
> Cling to her, strive with her, hold her fast;
> O fair white mother, in days long past
> Born without sister, born without brother,
> Wrought without hand in a world without stain.

It was not I who wanted to go back to the sea, because I myself was the sea, or maternal principle. The haunting recollection of this poem was followed by a vivid pleasurable hallucination of rape, by which I became pregnant. The entire illness after that was emotionally identified with childbirth, that is, with productive suffering. The baby had been too difficult to deliver, there had been a Caesarian operation, but vaguely in some way, the symbolic child could be saved though there was no actual child.

It was only at times when I was plunged directly into hell-fire that I felt there was no effort I could make except in the direction of death. At other times, though I seemed to be almost pulled apart in a disintegrating universe, I felt there must be some way I could hold things together. I was somehow an indispensable link in preventing total collapse. I was unable to think coherently or plan any action, but I had to use my poetic imagination instead, for poetry could be counted on not to lead me astray. As soon as I struggled into a little more coherence, I tried to think of other things I must do. What about "know thyself"? This did not seem to be helpful. Then I hit upon Polonius' lines:

> This above all: to thine own self be true,
> And it must follow as the night the day,
> Thou canst not then be false to any man.

After I remembered this, I was also able to feel that I was involved in the struggle for world peace and progress. The universe stopped whirling about so drastically and I felt more like my old self.

Quite frequently, during the following months, I kept coming back to Shakespeare's advice, which gave me some reassurance. I had, however, seen Laurence Olivier's *Hamlet* a few weeks before becoming sick, and had thought at the time that the statement would only apply to persons who had trustworthy social selves to begin with. This was my problem in a nutshell. There was a part of myself that had not been trustworthy, attributes which I had not liked, and which had to be eradicated. I was by no means rejecting myself completely, for incorporated into that self were all the values I cherished most. My feeling for nature, art, and science, and my general love of life seemed to be entirely in harmony with my value system and inseparable from it. I became aware during my first illness of the tremendous debt which I owed to the past.

During the first three weeks of hospitalization, I saw visions at various times. The capacity to see visions did not return after this period. These visions could be divided into two categories. The first type had no relation to and was not suggested by surrounding objects in the material environment, but were entirely projections of inner states of consciousness and appeared before my eyes in the same way that a motion picture is presented to the eye of the observer. The second type did not constitute true visions, but could rather be called visual hallucinations and distortions, sometimes suggested by the play of light and shadow, etc., acting upon an overwrought imagination. The true visions had definite but rather complex content and my attention was focused on grasping their meaning.

Occasionally during subsequent periods of disturbance, there was some distortion of vision and some degree of hallucination. On several occasions my eyes became markedly oversensitive to light. Ordinary colors appeared to be much too bright, and sunlight seemed dazzling in intensity. When this happened, ordinary reading was impossible, and print seemed excessively black.

THE FORMATION OF THE DELUSIONAL SYSTEM.   After the first few weeks of extreme disorganization, I began to acquire some relatively stable paranoid delusions. These delusions were accompanied by fear, and were based in part on erroneous perceptions and hallucinations, as well as on erroneous inferences from accurate perception. I also had a sense of discovery, creative excitement, and intense, at times mystical, inspiration in intervals when there was relief from fear.

During the paranoid period I thought I was being persecuted for my beliefs, that my enemies were actively trying to interfere with my activities, were trying to harm me, and at times even to kill me. I was primarily a citizen of the larger community. I was trying to persuade people who did not agree with me, but whom I felt could be won over, of the correctness of my beliefs. The only trouble was that it was difficult to get people to listen to me.

The picture of myself which I had at this time was much the same as that which I had always carried around with me during most of my adult life before I had become ethically self-conscious. I was a worthy citizen and was not afflicted with a sense of failure as a mother. I had regained a sense of inner control. I was once more a mature competent adult with great reserves of strength, and this was how I had almost always felt. I did, however, feel different from normal to the extent that I was in the midst of a bewildering and terrifying situation unlike anything I had ever encountered before. I was being compelled to focus attention on a new set of facts. Because of the continuously unpredictable nature of the delusional occurrences in the ward, the sense of routine and habit was almost entirely absent, I was dealing with novelty, consciousness was much more narrowly and sharply focused than normally, and a large mass of my previous memories and life reactions were inaccessible to me.

At no time during the first episode did I entirely lose feelings of personal guilt, and I retained some capacity for ethical awareness. In this situation, however, too great a preoccupation with problems of self-valuation would have impeded the fulfillment of my social mission. For the most part, my attention was directed toward problems in external reality, as it appeared to me. I was extraverted, not introverted, in spite of what might have been appearances to the contrary.

In order to carry through the task which had been imposed upon me, and to defend myself against the terrifying and bewildering dangers of my external situation, I was endowed in my imagination with truly cosmic powers. The sense of power was not always purely defensive but was also connected with a strong sense of valid inspiration. I felt that I had power to determine the weather which responded to my inner moods, and even to control the movement of the sun in relation to other astronomical bodies. None of these powers gave me feelings of competence or satisfaction. They had been given to me to cope with an emergency. I did not know how I obtained them and I derived no feeling of special importance from them. Whatever "magical" powers I did have were directed solely to the control of nonhuman forces, and I did not feel that I had any control over people. I was, on the contrary, acutely aware that in relation to the nursing staff, doctors, etc., I was singularly helpless and unable to make my wants known. Sometimes I did feel that I was able to acquire added power or psychic forces which I was able to use in a defensive way to keep other people from getting control of me. I was also afraid that other people had power to read my mind, and thought I must develop ways of blocking my thoughts from other people.

I was carrying through a predominantly maternal role when I was not preoccupied with the more neutral role of world citizen. I was the one who must protect other people, and I was doing so to the best of my ability. I had never been more conscious of being a woman and a mother. Every once in a while an "inner voice" would say to me "Think of the children first and you will be all right." I clung desperately to this advice, even though it was far from sufficient to ward off fear.

I actually thought very little about my own children. I was convinced that my two older children were safe and well taken care of by relatives and had no wish to see them, but from time to time I did have a strong desire to take my youngest child in my arms. I was also convinced, most of the time, that he was dead. . . . Occasionally I had an intense longing for another baby, a longing so great that it amounted to a physical ache in the breasts. . . .[2]

CONFLICT ABOUT LIFE SACRIFICE. I felt serious anxiety about my capacity to surrender my life voluntarily in any and all circumstances when required in the interests of another individual. Included in the notes which I had written during the initial phase of panic, I found the following statement:

The instinct of the individual to survive is the strongest instinct of all, and we know very well that this is so. Our first impulse is to save ourselves. Any other reaction to a personal danger situation is routed through devious channels. The race can survive only through the individual. Thus though we appear to be working against our own interests, we are not. This is the basic riddle of the universe on a feeling level. Inability to solve it has created a racial neurosis on the subject.

It would have been more correct to say that I had a long-standing personal neurosis on the subject. When I was about twelve or thirteen years old, I had heard that persons (both men and women) were sometimes decorated for bravery because of heroic actions in which the life of another person was saved. I wondered at the time whether I would have the courage to act in this way. I was afraid I would be paralyzed by fear, that I would stop too long to calculate risks, and that I would not act to help the other person if there were a serious chance that I might lose my own life. I pictured myself as totally alone and unobserved with the unknown person who was in danger. I shoved aside the question and forgot about it during adult life, although I think it did cross my mind occasionally when I read about heroic rescues in the newspaper.

It was this long-buried fear of failure in such a type of "cold" isolated situation that was for me one of the sources of greatest anxiety in the early catatonic state of disorganization. This fear was not conscious during acute disturbance. I was, however, being accused of treachery by the entire social group. For a brief time (just before the world catastrophe described above) I felt I was being ostracized by all my friends and relatives. No such person as

---

[2] In an omitted section, Anonymous goes on to describe intense and overwhelming feelings of anger, aggression, fear, and sympathy directed toward individuals (fellow patients, nurses, her children, etc.) in her environment. She also reports on a set of religious confusions.

myself had ever existed. I alone knew that I existed, but could convince no one of this fact.

The fear about my own cowardice and my excessively strong self-protective impulses did not become conscious until a good while after recovery from the second episode, when self-confidence about other types of performance had been restored, and I felt myself to be a normally adequate mother. I had a great resistance to bringing the matter into full awareness, but when I was finally able to do so I realized that I would never dare to say that I would not have failed in a situation of this type. If there had been real danger, perhaps I would have thought, "Why lose two lives rather than one?" while actually there might have been some chance of successful action. Perhaps, on the other hand, I would have become so immediately identified with the person who needed help that I would have been able to act impulsively. There was also the not too pleasant thought that I might have acted differently if under observation by others than if I had been alone. I would never know what I would have done.

In finally thinking through the issue, I recognized that I would never feel justified in risking my life in this way as long as I had children dependent on me, but that if I no longer had such responsibilities, the rule would apply. I also felt that a man who failed to act in this way toward a neighbor or member of his fraternal in-group would be considered a weakling by others, and would consider himself a weakling provided he accepted the standard as morally valid or socially necessary. A childless woman might not have been so strongly condemned in the past in this respect, but new mores are being evolved because of the emancipation of women. Girls are taught first-aid and life-saving techniques along with boys. Just before the second period of hospitalization I planned to join a volunteer rescue and fire-fighting squad in my local community and was upset when I learned that women were not eligible for membership.

Rules regarding life sacrifice are enforced by group opinion as well as by individual acquiescence in their validity. The penalty for violation is loss of "social face" if caught by others, and loss of self-respect if caught by the self. I certainly had not been born with an instinct to act in this way, yet bravery of this type was a vital component of my ego ideal. . . .

CHIEF PERSONALITY CHANGES. The chief personality changes which I consider took place in myself during the period of six or seven years which included the psychosis can be summarized as follows: (1) I lost a chronic, diffused anxiety which I had long carried around in adult life; (2) I grew more capable of self-assertion without anxiety; I acquired a more secure sense of adult authority in my relation with my children. These changes also included a shift from the masochistic to a nonmasochistic emotional orientation; (3) I lost a sense of excessive dependency on other adults; a sense of personal separateness and isolation replaced a former capacity for identification with other individuals and with groups; (4) My relations with people generally became easier and more relaxed; I acquired a greater capacity for warmth and outgoing interest in all sorts of people; (5) I acquired a deeper sense of human equality and of the potential dignity of every human being; (6) My interest in competitive evaluations of myself and others was decreased to a marked degree; (7) There were changes in psychosexual adjustment, including a change from a chronic state of semifrigidity to a state of sexual adequacy; (8) My intellectual capacities functioned more freely and more efficiently than before; (9) I changed from a nonreligious to a religious type of orientation, acquiring a sense of religious dependency and capacity for religious communication.

IMPLICATIONS

To what extent do you see here an apparently normal, active person with a family, who develops a psychosis in adulthood? In what manner do you see better the link between normality and abnormality? What normal activities persisted during the psychotic break? In what ways does this woman's description of the most distressing aspects of her psychotic episode remind you of the "bad" dream of a normal individual? Give some of the specific examples of the *hallucinations* (false perceptions), *delusions* (false thinking), and *motor disturbances* she experienced. What do you think helped her to recover?

REFERENCES

See Jackson (1960) and Arieti (1955) for discussions of two general groups of patients who develop schizophrenia: the *process group* with slow onset, no obvious precipitative factors, and chronically poor achievement in school and work; the *reactive group* in which onset is acute, symptoms floridly psychotic, and identifiable events common. See also Herron (1962) and Garmezy and Rodnick (1959).

[51] MENTAL ILLNESS IN A SIMPLE SOCIETY

Would you expect a simpler life, one free of some of the tensions of the highly complex culture surrounding it in North America, to produce fewer psychoses and neuroses and possibly result in more uniform personalities? The following selection discusses how a small German religious sect of the western United States and Canada was studied to determine whether its unique cultural background influenced the occurrence of neuroses and psychoses among its people. We see a group with different basic values and social organization. In addition to a perspective on mental disorders and antisocial behavior, we gain insight into our own predominant culture in America.

The authors refer to various disturbances that we might define. (The functional psychoses and schizophrenia are described in Section 50.) *Manic-depressive psychosis* is a functional disorder characterized by deviation from normal mood fluctuations, resulting either in exaggerated activity or in depression and despondency. *Neurosis* is an emotional disorder characterized by anxiety and various physical and mental complaints without organic cause. No severe personality derangement occurs in the neuroses.

Joseph W. Eaton and Robert J. Weil

From "The Mental Health of Hutterites," *Scientific American*, December, 1953. Reprinted with permission. Copyright © 1953 in the U.S. and Berne Convention countries by Scientific American, Inc. All rights reserved. Available separately @ 20¢ as offprint No. 440 from W. H. Freeman and Company, 660 Market Street, San Francisco, California.

Is modern life driving many people insane? Would insanity diminish or disappear if mankind could return to a simpler life? From Virgil to Thoreau the philosophers have had little doubt about the answer to these questions, and some modern anthropologists have offered data which seem to bear them out. They say they have found mental disorders rare among technologically primitive peoples. For instance, recent cursory studies of the people in Okinawa and of the natives of Kenya have suggested that these groups are virtually free of some psychoses. Contrasted with this picture is the civilized United States, where some authorities have estimated that one person in ten suffers an incapacitating mental illness at one time or another during his life.

Whether a culture can cause psychoses is not easy to discover, but one way to get at the question is to examine the mental health of a secure, stable society. The Hutterites, an isolated Anabaptist religious sect who inhabit a section of the North American Middle West, provide an ideal social laboratory of this kind. These people live a simple, rural life, have a harmonious social order, and provide every member with a high level of economic security from the womb to the tomb. They are a homogeneous group, free from many of the tensions of the American melting-pot culture. And they have long been considered almost immune to mental disorders. In a study during the 1930's, Lee Emerson Deets said that psychoses were almost non-existent among them. The Manitoba Provincial Legislature received in 1947 a report which said that the Hutterites "do not contribute to the overcrowding of mental hospitals, since the mental security derived from their system results in a complete absence of mental illness."

Three years ago a research team consisting of the writers of this article—a sociologist and a psychiatrist—and the Harvard University clinical psychologists Bert Kaplan and Thomas Plant undertook a more intensive study of the Hutterites' mental health. The investigation was administered by Wayne University and financed largely by the National Institute for Mental Health. The Hutterite people cooperated generously. In the interest of science they opened their "family closets" and helped us to obtain a census of every person in their community who was then or had ever been mentally ill.

The Hutterites, whose origin as a sect goes back to 1528, are a closely knit group of German stock who had lived together in neighboring villages in Europe for a long time before they migrated to the United States from southern Russia between 1874 and 1877. The immigrants—101 married couples and their children—settled in eastern South Dakota. Their descendants have now spread over a wide area in the Dakotas, Montana, and the prairie provinces of Canada. They live in 98 hamlets, which they call colonies. But they remain a remarkably cohesive group; each grownup is intimately acquainted with hundreds of other members in the settlements. The Hutterites believe it sinful to marry outside the sect, and all of the present descendants (8,542 in 1950) stem from the original 101 couples.

Cardinal principles of the Hutterites are pacifism, adult baptism, the communal ownership of all property, and simple living. Jewelry, art, and over-stuffed chairs are regarded as sinful luxuries. Radio sets and the movies are taboo. Children are the only possessions to which there is no limit: the average completed family has more than ten. The Hutterites cling to their own customs and are considered "different" by their neighbors. But they are not primitive in the ethnographic sense. They get a grammar-school education and speak English fluently. They read daily newspapers, have a telephone in most colonies, and own trucks. Since their own members are not encouraged to seek formal education beyond the primary grades, there are no doctors or lawyers

FIGURE 1. Young members of the Hutterite community. (Photo from the *Post-Gazette*, Pittsburgh.)

among them, but they utilize such professional services from outside. Each hamlet engages in a highly mechanized form of agriculture. Their business with the "outside world," as Hutterites are apt to refer to their neighbors, usually exceeds $100,000 per year per colony.

On the surface it seemed that the Hutterites did indeed enjoy extraordinary freedom from mental illness. We did not find a single Hutterite in a mental hospital. The 55 outside doctors patronized by these people said they showed fewer psychosomatic and nervous symptoms than their neighbors of other faiths. But this appearance of unusual mental health did not stand the test of an intensive screening of the inhabitants, carried out colony by colony. Among the 8,542 Hutterites, we discovered a total of 199 (one in 43) who either had active symptoms of a mental disorder or had recovered from such an illness. Of these illnesses, 53 were diagnosed as psychoses, all but five of them of a functional (nonorganic) character.

In short, *the Hutterite culture provides no immunity to mental disorders.** The existence of these illnesses in so secure and stable a social order *suggests that there may be genetic, organic, or constitutional predispositions to psychosis * which will cause breakdowns among individuals in any society, no matter how protective and well integrated.

The distribution of symptoms among the Hutterites was quite unusual. There were *few cases diagnosed as schizophrenia, although elsewhere this is the most common psychosis.** Only nine Hutterites had ever manifested the pattern of delusions, hallucinations, and other recognized symptoms of schizophrenia; the group lifetime rate was 2–1 per 1,500 persons aged fifteen and over. On the other hand, the *proportion of manic-depressive reactions among those with mental disorders was unusual;** this disorder accounted for 39 of the 53 psychoses, and the rate was 9.3 per 1,000 aged fifteen and over. The name of the disorder is misleading; manic-depressives often are not dangerous to other persons, and none of the Hutterite patients was. Their symptoms were predominantly depressive. There was much evidence of irrational guilt feelings, self-blame, withdrawal from normal social relations, and marked slowing of mental and motor activities. Five of the patients had suicidal impulses. Two Hutterites had actually killed themselves.

The fact that in the Hutterite society manic-depression is more common than schizophrenia, reversing the situation in all other populations for whom comparable data have been obtained, *suggests that cultural factors do have some influence on the manifestation of psychoses.** A Johns Hopkins University team of researchers who recently made an extensive analysis of mental hospital statistics concluded that schizophrenic symptoms are most common among unskilled laborers, farmers, urban residents in rooming-house sections, and other persons who are relatively isolated socially, while manic-depressive reactions are more prevalent among professional, socially prominent and *religious persons, who have a stronger need to live up to social expectations.** Our data fit this theory well. Religion is the focus of the Hutterite way of life. Their whole educational system, beginning with nursery school, orients the people to look for blame and guilt within themselves rather than in others. Physical aggression is taboo. Like the Catholic orders, Hutterites own everything in the name of their church. They eat in a common dining room, pay medical bills from the communal treasury, and work at jobs assigned to them

* Editor's italics.

by managers elected by the males of the colony. The group, rather than the individual, comes first.

In projective psychological tests, the Hutterites, like other groups, *show antisocial and aggressive impulses, but in their daily lives they repress these effectively.** Their history showed no case of murder, arson, severe physical assault, or sex crime. No individual warranted the diagnosis of psychopath. Divorce, desertion, separation, or chronic marital discord were rare. Only five marriages were known to have gone on the rocks since 1875. Personal violence and childish or amoral forms of behavior among adults were uncommon, even in persons with psychotic episodes. There were no psychoses stemming from drug addiction, alcoholism, or syphilis, although these disorders account for approximately 10 per cent of all first admissions to state mental hospitals in the United States. In general, our study tends to confirm the theory of many social scientists and public health officials that a favorable cultural setting can largely prevent these forms of social maladjustment.

All this does not entirely rule out the possibility that genetic factors play some part in the unusual proportions of manic-depression and schizophrenia symptoms among the Hutterites. There is some evidence that these disorders tend to run in families. The Hutterites are biologically inbred. Three surnames—Hofer, Waldner, and Wipt—accounted for nearly half of all families in 1950. It is possible that the Hutterite group has a disproportionate number of persons genetically prone to becoming depressed—if there is such a predisposition. A team of Harvard University workers is planning to make a follow-up genetic study of the Hutterites.

The question of the relation of mental disorders to culture is difficult to investigate quantitatively. No country has a really complete record of mental disorders among its population. Censuses of patients in mental hospitals are almost worthless for this purpose; they leave out patients who have recovered and mentally ill persons who have never come to the attention of doctors.

The Hutterite study attempted to track down every case of a mental disorder, past or present, hospitalized or not, in the whole living population. It probably succeeded in finding virtually all the cases of psychosis. Similar studies have been made of seven other communities in various parts of the world, and the results are shown in the tables on page 445. They give the comparative rates of psychosis as standardized by the Hutterite lifetime rate and corrected for variations in age and sex distribution. (The Hutterite population is predominantly youthful—50 per cent under fifteen years of age.)

On this basis the Hutterites apparently rank second highest among the eight populations in the rate of psychosis, being exceeded only by an area in the north of Sweden. But there is considerable evidence that the count of mental disorders was less complete in the other seven groups; that is, in those studies many cases were missed because their illness was not a matter of public record,

* Editor's italics.

while the Hutterite population was thoroughly screened. It is probable that the psychosis rate among the Hutterites is actually low compared with that in other populations. It seems to be only one third as high as the rate in New York State, for instance, taking into consideration the common estimate that even in that state (where mental hospital facilities are among the most extensive) there is at least one undetected psychotic person for every one in an institution.

The statistical comparison of mental disorder rates has many limitations, but it does offer several promising leads to the puzzle that the problem of functional psychoses presents to modern science. Among the Hutterites, as in all the other populations, the frequency of psychoses increases rapidly with age. Among those who showed manic-depressive reactions, females predominated. The social biology of the aging process and of sex probably holds worth-while clues to some of the problems of cause and treatment.

*Neuroses were more common than psychoses among the Hutterites, as elsewhere.** Four fifths of the 69 discovered neurotics were female. Melancholy moods were regarded by teachers as the number one emotional problem of Hutterite school children. Hutterite neurotics showed the same tendency as psychotics to take out mental stress on themselves instead of on others. Self-blame and remorse were common, as were psychosomatic headaches, backaches, and hysteric paralysis of a limb. There was little scapegoating or projection of hostile feelings by imputing them to others.

There is no evidence of any unusual concentration of hereditary mental defects in the Hutterite population. A total of 51 persons was diagnosed as mentally deficient, and 20 normal persons had suffered epileptic attacks. These epilepsy and mental deficiency rates are not high in comparison with other groups.

How does the Hutterite culture deal with mental illness? Although it does not prevent mental disorders, it provides a *highly therapeutic atmosphere for their treatment.** The onset of a symptom serves as a signal to the entire community to demonstrate support and love for the patient. Hutterites do not approve of the removal of any member to a "strange" hospital, except for short periods to try shock treatments. All patients are looked after by the immediate family. They are treated as ill rather than "crazy." They are encouraged to participate in the normal life of their family and community, and most are able to do some useful work. Most of the manic-depressive patients get well, but among neurotic patients, recovery is less common. Most of the epileptics were either cured or took drugs which greatly relieved the condition. No permanent stigma is attached to patients after recovery. The traumatic social consequences which a mental disorder usually brings to the patient, his family, and sometimes his community are kept to a minimum by the patience and tolerance with which most Hutterites regard these conditions. This find-

* Editor's italics.

ing supports the theory that at least some of the severely antisocial forms of behavior usually displayed by psychotic and disturbed patients are not an inherent attribute. They may be reflections of the impersonal manner of handling patients in most mental hospitals, of their emotional rejection by the family and of their stigmatization in the community.

FIGURE 2. One of the men in the Hutterite community. The typical hat worn by the men is on the bookcase.

In the Hutterite social order, people are exposed to a large number of common experiences. Their indoctrination begins in infancy and is continued by daily religious instruction and later by daily church-going. Hutterites spend their entire life within a small and stable group. Their homes consist only of bedrooms, all furnished in an almost identical manner. The women take turns cooking and baking for everybody. Everyone wears the same kind of clothes; the women, for example, all let their hair grow without cutting, part it in the middle and cover it with a black kerchief with white polka dots. The Hutterite religion provides definite answers for many of the problems that come up.

Despite this uniformity in the externals of living, Hutterites are not stereotyped personalities. Differences in genetic, organic, and psychological factors seem to be sufficiently powerful to produce an infinite variety of behavior, even in a social order as rigid as this one. It appears that the nightmare of uniformity sketched in George Orwell's *Nineteen Eighty-four* is actually unachievable in a living society. At least our study in depth disclosed no simple standardization of personality structure among Hutterites.

There is considerable objective evidence that the great majority of Hutterites have a high level of psychological adjustment. Their misfortunes and accidents are alleviated greatly by the group's system of mutual aid. The sick, the aged, the widows, and orphans are well taken care of. In the last three decades, only about one hundred persons (most of them male) have left the community permanently. During World War II, about one third of the men between the ages of twenty and forty served in camps for conscientious objectors; more than 98 per cent of them ultimately returned to their colonies.

There has not, however, been any rush of applicants from outside to join the Hutterite sect. Mental health involves value judgments and depends on what people want from life. Only nineteen adults have joined the sect in America during the last few decades. The austere and puritanical customs of the sect impose restrictions which even the members, who learn to accept them, regard as a "narrow path." Their culture is therapeutic only for conformists. There are occasional rebels; the more able ones find a means of expressing themselves by becoming leaders, the less brilliant have difficulties.

The survival of this sixteenth-century peasant culture in the heart of the

Per Cent of Cases Diagnosed

Study	Number of Cases Diagnosed	Schizo-phrenia	Manic depression	All other diagnosis	Total
Ethnic Hutterites	53	17	74	9	100
North Swedish Area	107	87	2	11	100
West Swedish Island of Abo	94	43	27	30	100
Bornholm Island	481	31	25	43	100
Williamson County, Tenn.	156	27	26	47	100
Baltimore Eastern Health District	367	43	11	46	100
Thuringian Villages	200	37	10	53	100
Bavarian Villages, Rosenheim Area	21	38	10	52	100

Eight groups investigated by independent studies, including the one described here, are analyzed for percentage of each major diagnostic category among their psychotics.

Survey	Total Population	Actual Number of Cases Found	Expected Number of Cases by Hutterites Norms	Expectancy Ratio
North Swedish Area	8,651	107	94	1.14
Ethnic Hutterites	8,542	53	53	1.00
Bornholm Island	45,694	481	773	.62
Baltimore Eastern Health District	55,129	507	822	.62
Williamson County, Tenn.	24,804	156	271	.58
West Swedish Island of Abo	8,735	94	186	.51
Bavarian Villages, Rosenheim Area	3,203	21	49	.43
Thuringian Villages	37,546	200	617	.32

One group, the Hutterites, is compared to the other seven by the standard expectancy method. The frequency of *diagnosed* cases of psychosis among Hutterites is relatively high.

most twentieth-century-minded continent is a vivid demonstration of the power of values and beliefs. Although our data on the Hutterites' mental disorders clearly demonstrate the inadequacy of a purely cultural approach to the problem of mental health, they do show that culture has a large influence in shaping personality. Psychiatrists who work exclusively in hospitals or clinics cannot see the whole patient as he functions in his total environment. Our findings lead us to conclude that the social relations of the patient and his culture, including the things in which he believes, deserve more attention from psychiatric researchers and clinicians than is commonly given to them.

IMPLICATIONS

What are the possible implications in the fact that the Hutterite society provides no immunity to mental disorders? What hypothesis about the causes of such antisocial behavior as crime do the findings tend to support? Speculate on the conditions that might tend to make this society therapeutic or nontherapeutic. This atypical society has grown rather than dwindled in America and has maintained its basic character. Why do you think it has not become assimilated into the predominant American culture, particularly since it accepts medical care and modern farm technology? What would you find desirable or undesirable in this culture as compared with the one in which you live? What are the implications for therapy of the following findings: the Hutterites show none of the antisocial behavior usually displayed by psychotics.

REFERENCES
You may be interested in other writings that support the genetic nature of mental disorders (Kallman, 1959). Eaton and Weil refer to favorable social conditions that can prevent social maladjustment. For further discussion of the relationship of *social status* and mental illness, see Hollingshead and Redlick (1958), Kaplan, Reed, and Richardson (1956), and Malzberg (1956).

It appears that occurrence of psychotic illness tends to increase as one goes down the social status scale. For the *cultural influences* in mental abnormality, see Benedict (1946). For a cross-cultural study of child training, see Whiting and Child (1953).

[52] MURDER AS AGGRESSIVE BEHAVIOR

How does the psychologist regard murder after examining the data collected by behavioral scientists? Does murder fit into the formula *frustration leads to aggression?* Destruction of human life is the ultimate in aggressive behavior. Note how Berkowitz organizes and summarizes the findings about killers, and what factors besides strong aggressiveness lead some frustrated personalities to commit homicide.

Leonard Berkowitz

From *Aggression* by Leonard Berkowitz, copyright © 1962 Mc-Graw-Hill Book Company. Used by permission of McGraw-Hill Book Company.

MURDER

Despite the attention given to homicides in fiction and the popular press, such crimes constitute only a tiny fraction of the illegal actions committed in this country. One tenth of 1 per cent of the arrests reported by the police of some 1,500 American cities in 1958 were for homicide, and most of these probably were due to negligence rather than deliberate intent (Sutherland and Cressey, 1960). Too many lives are taken violently, but murder is a relatively rare phenomenon in our complex society. It apparently is a fairly unusual response to unusual circumstances.

Most of the people displaying these extreme reactions, furthermore, probably would never commit murder again if released from jail. With the exception of hired killers, they typically are not hardened criminals. One study of ninety-six convicted murderers found only about half of the men had even been arrested before. Two thirds of the sex offenders and over 90 per cent of the property offenders surveyed, in comparison, had such prior records.[1] Murderers, by and large, are not habitual lawbreakers and once released from prison are relatively good parole risks (Clinard, 1957). They have taken a life, in most cases at least, not because of a persistent urge to kill, but because their emotions flared up out of control in response to an extreme thwarting. "Most murders," says one authority (cited in Clinard, 1957), "are crimes of passion—explosive reactions to a difficult situation."

INDIVIDUAL CHARACTERISTICS. To say that the violence was provoked by frustrating circumstances is not to rule out the importance of personality characteristics. Experts generally are agreed that the killer's life history has made him susceptible to such "explosive reactions." Another person exposed to the same final instigating condition might have exerted better control over his emotions or may not have been as strongly aroused by the thwarting.

Not surprisingly, many murderers have had a history of frequent frustrations. Palmer (1960) interviewed the mothers of fifty-one male murderers in order to determine how the life experiences of these men had differed from those of their nearest-age nonhomicidal brothers. He found the murderers had apparently suffered many more physical and psychological frustrations, such as illnesses, accidents, and harsh treatments. Because of these relatively frequent thwartings (as I suggested earlier), they conceivably developed a fairly great readiness to perceive further frustrations in the world about them, tended to exhibit relatively intense anger in response to these thwartings, and did not learn strong restraints against socially disapproved actions. Any one frustration, then, was likely to provoke an extreme reaction, and so Palmer also reported the murderers had shown more frequent socially unacceptable aggression than their brothers as they matured. The nonhomicidal siblings probably had stronger inhibitions against antisocial behavior, and what aggression they exhibited tended to be of the controlled, socially acceptable variety.

Homicides may be more common in lower socioeconomic groups than in the higher social strata (Henry and Short, 1954; Falk, 1959) partly because of the greater number of deprivations to which the lower-class individual is typically subjected throughout his lifetime. Lower-class existence is relatively

---

[1] According to at least one study (Berg and Fox, 1947), Negro murderers are more likely than white murderers to have prior convictions for assaultive crimes.

frustrating. Research ... has indicated some of the areas in which the lower-class person is often seriously thwarted. For example, he is frequently prevented from satisfying his economic and status wishes, and his parents probably were also somewhat more punitive toward him in childhood than would have been the case if his had been an average middle-class family. Living in such an environment, he is all too likely to show the consequences of these deprivations: a tendency to intense emotional outbursts as well as to psychoses.

Berg and Fox (1947) have made use of the frustration-aggression hypothesis in explaining the relationship between intelligence and homicides. Consistent with other researchers, they observed that a sample of two hundred murderers had reliably lower school achievement and intelligence than did a control group of other prison inmates and suggested that the former's low intelligence level had led to their being frustrated relatively severely by their victims. But if the killers had been thwarted on this one occasion (presumably in an argument with the victim), they probably had also experienced a good many frustrations in other situations throughout their lifetimes. These recurrent frustrations could have led to the final violent outburst when the murder was committed.

Another reason for such an extreme emotional flare-up can be found in the murderers' occasionally weak inhibitions against socially disapproved behavior. Murderers generally violate criminal laws less frequently than do most property offenders or people guilty of nonhomicidal assaults. They can restrain their antisocial inclinations in most situations. These inner controls, however, may not be too strongly rooted and can give way under periods of severe emotional stress. Wood (1961) has published evidence in accord with this analysis in his previously mentioned study of crime in Ceylon. In contrast to robbers and burglars, the murderers in his sample tended not to be regular gamblers or rowdies. They also were less likely to have a police record. But, attesting to their tenuous controls, almost as many murderers as robbers and burglars used alcohol. Their religion and village customs frowned on intoxicating beverages, but they tended to drink more often than most of the non-criminals around them.

SOCIOLOGICAL DETERMINANTS.　Social conditions producing frequent severe frustrations together with comparatively weak inhibitions against socially disapproved behavior should give rise to a disproportionately high incidence of murders if the present reasoning is correct. Such seems to be the case. We already have seen, for example, that there are high homicide rates in poor and deteriorating city areas. The people living in these urban areas usually experience a good many serious thwartings and in many instances, as was pointed out earlier, have not learned strong inhibitions against unlawful behavior. Frustrations and weak inhibitions are particularly characteristic of lower-class Negroes and may explain why the Negro homicide rate is much higher than that of whites (Sutherland and Cressey, 1960; Falk, 1959).

Much the same argument can also account for regional differences in the incidence of homicides. Thus, there were only 1.5 homicides per 100,000 population known to the police in New England in 1958, while this rate rose to 9.5 in the South Atlantic states (Sutherland and Cressey, 1960). Many Southerners, of course, have been seriously thwarted throughout their lives because of the poverty of their part of the country. But in addition, the lower-class Southerner is more likely than his New England counterpart to feel that he must seek personal retribution for any "wrongs" done to him. His social code often justifies striking out on his own against the people harming him.[2]

We must remember, however, that recurrent frustrations and weak inner controls only create a predisposition to extreme aggression. They do not actually impel such behavior. The frequently thwarted person is easily aroused, and not constantly angry. He does not attack just anyone for the sake of releasing some supposed pent-up "hostile energy." But he can become enraged fairly easily in the course of his daily life. This is why killers and their victims generally come from the same groups, why, for example, whites usually kill whites, Negroes kill primarily other Negroes, and the victims often are relatives or acquaintances of their murderers (Clinard, 1957; Falk, 1959). The murder victim probably had frustrated his slayer in some argument or fight, thereby precipitating the violent, uncontrolled emotional reaction leading to his death.

Frustrations also account for changes in homicide rates as business conditions alter. Henry and Short (1954) have demonstrated that murders committed by whites tend to be most frequent when business conditions are bad. Negro homicides, on the other hand, decrease in such times of depression and are most common when the country is relatively prosperous. Along with Henry and Short, I would say the variation in homicide rates stems primarily from differences in frustrations. But contrary to these writers, it seems to me the thwartings arise, at least in part, from comparisons the individual makes with others in his own group.[3] When a low-status white person loses his job in a depression, he finds himself deprived of status and economic goods relative to those of his friends and acquaintances who still have jobs. However,

---

[2] Several authorities have suggested that homicide rates are high in the South because "cultural definitions call for personal violence in some situations" (Clinard, 1957, p. 214). Along similar lines, Wolfgang (1958) has contended after an analysis of almost 600 cases of criminal homicide in Philadelphia, that many murders take place in a "subculture of violence" which gives social approval to "quick resort to physical aggression."

[3] Henry and Short have contended that the individual is most likely to compare his own status with that of people in other social strata. If he is in a high stratum, he supposedly wants to be better off than the low-status group, while the low-status individual presumably wants to be closer to the higher social levels. The present book argues, on the other hand, that such comparisons tend to be primarily with others in one's own social level. The same objection was raised earlier against A. K. Cohen's (1955) conception of the status deprivations presumably felt by lower-class boys.

since Negroes are generally the first to be fired in hard times, poor business conditions act as a leveler in this group. Nearly all lower-class Negroes suffer from economic privations in a depression, and they do not see themselves as being much worse off than their peers. Prosperous times, however, permit some Negroes to get economically well ahead of their peers. Those not doing too well conceivably feel greatly deprived in comparison with wealthier Negroes; they are frustrated, and anger results.

EFFECTS OF DEATH PENALTIES.   Restraints against socially disapproved behavior are most effective . . . when they are based upon relatively stable moral attitudes rather than on the fear of punishment. The person who believes criminal actions are morally wrong will refrain from engaging in such behavior in most situations, whether he anticipates punishment for the criminal activity or not. However . . . inhibitions based primarily upon fear of punishment are likely to be operative only when the individual expects to be caught and punished for carrying out the disapproved activity.[4]

This reasoning explains why the threat of a death penalty does not reduce the incidence of murders (Cressey and Sutherland, 1960). When a person commits a murder, he usually has done so in a fit of violent rage. He certainly does not think of being apprehended by the police at such times. There are few if any cues in the situation to remind him of the police. The only thing that could have restrained his violence in the absence of such external danger stimuli would have been strong internal prohibitions against antisocial aggression. *Stable and strong internal controls are more likely to prevent murders than are death penalties; the latter often are out of sight and out of mind.*

IMPLICATIONS

What do you see as the major conditions leading to homicide besides recurrent frustrations? Are there certain implications about the death penalty in this discussion? What is an effective preventive, if not drastic punishment? To what extent is it possible to lessen some of the frustrations the individual experiences? What are some feasible programs to bring about stronger and more stable internal controls in the potential murderer? What other ideas came to you as you read the Berkowitz discussion of murder?

[4] People undoubtedly differ in the extent to which they expect to succeed in a risky undertaking. One person may characteristically expect not to get caught if he carried out a crime, while another, more pessimistic, individual may anticipate only the worst and thus would be less likely to commit a crime.

REFERENCES

For a vivid, human interest description of the lives of several individual murderers, see Truman Capote's *In Cold Blood* (1965). Consult the Bibliography for further references cited in the article.

[53] SUICIDE: SELF-DIRECTED HOSTILITY

A person takes his own life and shocks us all. Why? What do the data and interviews to date show us about the suicidal personality? Does it fit the hypothesis that frustration leads to aggression? If so, aggression toward whom? The source of frustration—even if oneself? Study Berkowitz's discussion of the individual with self-blame.

Leonard Berkowitz

From *Aggression* by Leonard Berkowitz, Copyright © 1962 Mc-Graw-Hill Book Company. Used by permission of McGraw-Hill Book Company.

SUICIDE

Few human actions seem to be as difficult to understand as suicide. A fifty-year-old industrialist committed suicide supposedly (according to the newspapers) because he recently had sold his firm and was despondent at no longer controlling its destiny. He left an estate of over two million dollars. Did he feel there was nothing left in life for him? Such an explanation probably is much too simple to be true. Suicide is a highly complex phenomenon, and there is relatively little agreement among authorities as to its cause or even how the potential self-killer should be treated.

Some of the confusion in the study of suicidal behavior arises from the multiplicity of reasons for self-destruction. The eminent French sociologist Emile Durkheim (1951) listed three types of suicides: *altruistic, egoistic,* and *anomic.* In the first of these, the person takes his own life in order to benefit other people. A good example of this is seen in the World War II Japanese kamikaze pilots who dived their planes into American warships. The egoistic suicide, on the other hand, is concerned primarily with himself rather than with others. Not bound to other people by close personal ties, he is wrapped up in his own personal problems and kills himself when he cannot attain his individualistic goals. Finally, the anomic type of suicide presumably occurs when social values disintegrate in a crisis situation and the individual feels "lost." The disruption of the collective order stimulates men's appetites, making them "less disciplined precisely when they need more disciplining." Some people are "declassified" as they are thrown into lower social levels by the cultural turmoil. They must restrain their needs, but they cannot do so. The new social conditions forced on them may be regarded as intolerable, and feeling all is hopeless and meaningless in a world bereft of values, they may take their own lives.

Other writers also insist it is wrong to account for suicides in terms of a single type of motivation. Thus, one authority (Jackson in Shneidman and Farberow, 1957) established a continuum ranging from "irrational" suicides— such as the psychotic who kills himself because he believes the world is coming to an end—to "rational" self-destruction as in the case of the cancer victim suffering from extreme pain. An analysis of over seven hundred notes written by white, native-born suicides also points to the desirability of distinguishing among suicide types. Shneidman and Farberow (1957) found a much higher incidence of direct aggression references (either against the self or others) in the notes written by the younger self-killers, while the "wish to die," characterized by hopelessness, fear, and despair, was predominant in the majority of notes written by suicides over sixty years of age. The younger victims apparently were angrier than the older group and probably did not commit suicides for the same reasons.

INDIVIDUAL CONSIDERATIONS. . . . One possible explanation for suicides: the inhibition of outward-directed aggression. Following a line of thought essentially similar to the orthodox Freudian conception . . . , Dollard *et al.* (1939) suggested that aggression against the self was a consequence of the blocking of all other aggressive reactions to frustration. Just as "aggressive energy" supposedly turned inward if not discharged in attacks upon other people (cf. Hartmann et al., 1949), aggressive responses to the frustrater, the Yale psychologists contended, presumably heightened the instigation to self-aggression. Suicide, then, could conceivably be regarded as an extreme manifestation of inhibited aggression.

There is some evidence that suicide victims do have stronger internal controls against unlawful behavior than do murderers. Wood (1961) reported, for example, that Ceylonese who had taken their own lives were less likely to use alcohol, have a police record, or a reputation as a neighborhood bully than the people charged with killing someone else. But whether such strong restraints were primarily responsible for the self-destruction is, of course, open to question. Other factors are also involved in suicides. According to several psychiatrists (cf. Chs. 2 and 3 in Shneidman and Farberow, 1957), suicidal actions often stem from several complex motives, such as:

1. A *wish to punish some frustrater*. Many victims apparently delighted in the belief that a particular person, someone who supposedly had hurt or tormented them, would feel sorry and—more important—guilty when learning of the suicide.

2. *Yearning for self-punishment and rebirth*. Self-destruction often is self-punishment for crimes the suicide victims thought they had committed. (In some cases the "crime" supposedly arose from "death wishes.") Fenichel (1945) has maintained that self-destruction during fits of melancholia is typically instigated by desires for forgiveness. This self-punishment could then lead to a new start by alleviating guilt. Children and schizophrenics are said to feel that if they can kill the "bad me" they could then achieve a rebirth as a less wicked person.

3. Paradoxically, suicide victims may believe their self-destruction will not really mean the end of their existence. Potential suicide victims sometimes develop grandiose fantasies in compensation for the frustrations they have suffered, and according to psychiatric observations, such fantasies often include ideas of immortality and omnipotence (Shneidman and Farberow, 1957). They will punish themselves, and perhaps other people as well, by taking their lives, but they will still exist to enjoy the aftereffects of their action. Consistent with this, Shneidman and Farberow (1957) have reported that suicide notes frequently contain admonitions and instructions perhaps "indicative of unrealistic feelings of omnipotence and omnipresence." The victims presumably "cannot successfully imagine [their] own death and ... complete cessation."

We cannot say how often such beliefs and desires occur in the incipient suicide or, for that matter, how important these feelings are in the instigation of the self-murder. But it is clear that many suicides are extreme attacks upon the self arising from guilt and self-blame. Inhibitions against attacks upon others may be present and may have had an important role in the sequence of events leading to suicide. Self-killers evidently are frequently angry with other people; their strong inhibitions could have interfered with earlier, milder angry outbursts. Nevertheless, they are extremely angry with themselves as well, and this is important. *Hostility is directed toward the self, at least in part, because the self is regarded as a frustrater.*

SOCIOLOGICAL CONSIDERATIONS. Henry and Short (1954) have employed the frustration-aggression hypothesis in explaining social-status differences in suicide rates, assigning the notion of self as frustrater a prominent place in their theorizing. In almost every status hierarchy, and regardless of the basis for the stratification, members of high-status groups tend to kill themselves at a greater rate than do lower-status people. Thus, while suicides are relatively common at both ends of the economic scale, they occur most often among the well-to-do. Similarly, more whites than nonwhites kill themselves, commissioned officers are more prone to take their own lives than are enlisted men of the same race, and men are greater suicide risks than women. (In this last regard it is assumed men have a higher status than women because of their positions in the economic system of our society.)

To account for these differences in self-destruction, the sociologists made use of two sets of empirical findings. First, the inverse correlation between business conditions and suicide rates is generally highest for the higher-status groups. Depressions lead to more suicides in the upper than the lower social strata. The people in the upper strata probably suffer greater deprivations than their lower-status peers as a result of harsh business conditions; there is a greater discrepancy between their predepression and depression conditions, and consequently they are frustrated more severely. But in addition to such greater frustrations in higher-status levels, social relationships also affect the likelihood of committing suicide, as Durkheim stressed (1951). People having close ties with others are a lesser suicide risk than people living in emotional isolation. Married people, for example, are not as prone to kill themselves as single, widowed, or divorced individuals of the same age, and city dwellers, often having only relatively anonymous and impersonal contacts with others, have a higher suicide rate than people living in the more tightly knit rural communities.

Henry and Short used the concept of "external restraints" to integrate these data. The lower-status person typically does not have the freedom possessed by the members of the higher social groups. He has to accede to the demands of his supervisor and/or employer, and he lacks the financial wherewithal even to think of becoming his own master. In general, his actions are subject to relatively great restraints by his social superiors. Similarly, the individual enmeshed in close relationships with other people also experiences restraints. He has obligations to his family and friends. He must conform to their expectations. He often has to comply with their wishes.

These external restraints, as hampering as they might be, serve an important function in times of stress, according to Henry and Short. They "provide immunity from suicide" presumably because they permit the individual to blame others for his troubles. The individual cannot attack himself for the frustrations he suffers if other people must share in the responsibility for his actions.

The Henry and Short argument is an intriguing one. Their reliance on the concept of "external restraints" might appear forced but actually is in complete accord with scientific tradition. Scientists must seek to develop unifying principles capable of showing that apparently diverse phenomena (*e.g.*, the suicidal deaths of a wealthy person and of a lonely city dweller) are special cases of a more general phenomenon (self-blame for a frustration). The present writer does not reject the Henry-Short emphasis upon external restraints altogether but would prefer to add to this argument. High social status in our society produces more than a relative freedom from restraints. (Indeed, in many cases, well-to-do families feel they have a good deal of responsibility and obligations to others. Witness the Rockefellers.) What may be more important is the greater emphasis upon self-reliance and self-accomplishment in the upper social levels. Middle-class parents frequently teach their children that a person is primarily responsible for whatever happens to him (cf. Kohn, 1959). The lower-class individual, on the other hand, tends to see himself as the hapless victim of forces beyond his control. Thus, *since the people from the upper social levels generally regard themselves as masters of their own fate, they also must blame themselves for their social and economic failures.* In extreme cases, such self-blame can lead to suicide.

IMPLICATIONS
You might find in a newspaper a report of a suicide in which certain facts of the individual's life and circumstances are given. How would you classify the suicide—as *altruistic, egoistic,* or *anomic?* Do you have enough information on the suicide victim to know whether his act gives credence to the concept of *"external restraints"?* To the concept of a *self-punishing personality trend?*

REFERENCES
Consult the Bibliography for references cited in the article.

[54] HOMOSEXUALITY—WHY?

Homosexuality is a personal and social problem as well as a psychological phenomenon. There are strong attitudes about it among the general public. The individual himself experiences conscious fears and vague anxieties, and the lack of understanding by those around him adds immensely to the problem. Often he feels he leads a double life.

An important issue, from the psychological standpoint, is the influence of constitutional or genetic predispositions as well as the complex environment surrounding development—especially interactions with parents. Such factors include *fear of the opposite sex, dependence and self-centeredness encouraged by the boy's mother, lack of interest or hostility on the part of the father,* and *feelings of inadequacy and self-contempt.*

Only recently has the topic of homosexuality been discussed openly in popular media. It is not unusual for a baffling and frightening problem to remain in the "unspeakable" category; many diseases considered incurable and not amenable to science some years ago went through a period in which the public referred to them only in whispers. It is not surprising, therefore, to find considerable confusion and ignorance surrounding homosexuality.

Blaine, a psychiatrist, and McArthur, a psychologist, constantly see college students in the university health services at Harvard University. Their article introduces us to the subject of homosexuality and briefly gives the known hypotheses concerning the development, nature, and possible outcome of homosexuality in the college student.

Graham B. Blaine, Jr. and Charles C. McArthur

From *Emotional Problems of the Student,* by Graham B. Blaine, Jr. and C. C. McArthur, copyright © 1961 Appleton-Century-Crofts, Inc. Reprinted by permission of Appleton-Century-Crofts.

According to Kinsey, over 27 per cent of the young men in America between the ages of seventeen and twenty-five, who have reached the college level in education, have had at least one homosexual experience. This represents a significantly smaller number than those of the same age in the total population who have had a similar experience (36.3 per cent) and seems to be generally consistent with what our experience would lead us to believe to be the prevalence of homosexuality at Harvard.

Making a statistical survey of the prevalence of homosexuality, however, is complicated by the vagueness of the concept. Kinsey, in his work, defined a homosexual experience as a relationship between people of the same sex which leads to orgasm. While this would seem to be a relatively sharp distinction, it does not really tell us very much about the amount of homosexuality which is actually present in a community. Many students have strong homosexual inclinations which they are able to keep so completely under control that they do not engage in any homosexual acts. Other students engage in one homosexual act more or less experimentally, and this one isolated experience serves to solidify their feelings against homosexuality and enables them to put it out of their minds for the rest of their lives. These two types of students obviously distort any kind of statistical analysis of the total situation. The former is often preoccupied so much with thoughts about homosexuality that he should be classified in the homosexual category, while the latter is so briefly concerned with the subject that he does not deserve to be included, and yet, because of his one experience, he would be labeled in Kinsey's statistics as homosexual.

We are a long way from a real understanding of homosexuality. We do not have any clear-cut conclusions to offer about the origin or the causes of this type of deviation. Most psychiatrists and psychoanalysts today seem to feel that a combination of constitutional and environmental factors is involved. There seems to be fairly complete acceptance of the fact that everyone has some degree of homosexuality in his make-up and that there is a variation in amount from one person to another. This variation extends from the rare experiencing of a homosexual dream or a homosexual yearning all the way to the living of a homosexual life with heterosexual desire nonexistent. Although we feel that some people are born with a stronger homosexual instinct than others, we also believe that certain factors in the growth and development of an individual are responsible for the reinforcement or the repression of these instincts.

These factors are, for the most part, concerned with parental characteristics and attitudes. Parents who dress and treat a child of one sex as though he had been born another, even during the earliest stages of the child's development, can have an effect on the sexual orientation of the child during later years. This relatively uncommon treatment of a child is not the only environmental factor, however, which is important. In order for a boy to develop into an independently functioning, normally aggressive man, he must be able to identify to a considerable extent with his father, and this can be accomplished only if he is able to enjoy a relationship with his father in which there is a substantial degree of warmth and closeness. If this cannot be achieved during childhood, it often is sought during adolescence, and it is at this time that substitutes for a cold and rejecting father are sought out. Since adolescence is also a time when sexual impulses are most strongly felt, it is not surprising that the seeking out of a close relationship at this age should be contaminated by some sexual needfulness. It is thought that much of the temporary and sporadic quality of the relationship between homosexuals is due to the fact that each is seeking the gratification of impossible needs— the need of a child for a father—and because of this each homosexual partner in turn is bound to be a disappointment.

The mother, too, plays an important role and can influence her son's future sexual orientation adversely in two strikingly different ways. If she is an overly aggressive, frightening kind of woman who depreciates and humiliates the father, she contributes to the growing boy's picture of all womankind as frightening and dangerous. He then often will feel safer with those of his own sex and grow up preferring their company to that of girls who are associated in his own mind with the dominating and destructive qualities of his mother's personality. On the other hand, we have seen many cases where an overly feminine, seductive type of mother seems to have contributed to the development of homosexual inclinations in her son later in life. This seems to be due in large part to the fact that any introduction of sexuality into the mother-son relationship is felt as threatening and dangerous by the son because of his instinctual feelings of revulsion toward incest. Heterosexual relationships then are associated later in life with these same feelings of disgust in such a way that the burgeoning sexual desires of the adolescent are channeled away from the opposite sex and toward individuals of the same sex instead.

Because adolescence is the time when the first strong outwardly directed sexual impulses are experienced, there is a good deal of confusion in the minds of college boys as to what sort of outlet is most healthy and appropriate. Sexual feeling is at its strongest at this period also, so that whatever degree of homosexuality one may have inherently or as a result of environmental influences is felt more powerfully and urgently during these years. Many students feel and do things at this time which they never repeat again during their adult life. Many students believe, and some physicians agree with them, that this is a time when young men pass through a critical period of choice—a time when their actions and behavior may determine in the period of a few weeks or months their sexual orientation for the entire remaining period of their lives. It is our opinion that this is not a voluntary choice but something which has been predetermined many years before and, for the most part, remains uninfluenced by the ordinary occurrences and encounters during college years. We often see students who feel strongly tempted to experiment with a homosexual experience but fear that doing so will bring about the release of powerful forces within them over which they would then have no control. Their feeling is that they are constantly walking on the brink of the pit of homosexuality and that one misstep will plunge them in forever. Often, however, after they have achieved a more enlightened view of homosexuality, they are able to experiment; and after profiting from the experience by learning more about the details of homosexuality and their own disinclination to pursue it, they can proceed to develop a fulfilling heterosexual life for themselves.

Another manifestation of this fear that homosexuality is lurking deep within and waiting to pounce is the kind of acute panic reaction often seen in students who have suddenly experienced a homosexual dream or a transitory homosexual yearning for a classmate. These students often appear at the clinic in states of extreme anxiety and tension, stating that they have never before been aware of any kind of homosexual feeling and, quite the contrary, have been extremely interested in girls and have had many satisfying hetero-sexual experiences. They are at a loss to explain the sudden appearance of these obviously homosexual feelings in themselves and are filled with disgust and terror. They are almost always quickly relieved of this anxiety when it is explained to them that there are elements of homosexuality in everyone, and that while they are more than offset by stronger heterosexual elements in most of us, occasionally the homosexual constituent comes into consciousness undiluted and causes a homosexual dream or impulse to flash across the mind.

Many boys come to the service each year for help with the resolution of problems which do not appear, at first, to be associated with homosexuality. Sometimes these center around difficulty in accepting a mode of behavior which may be protecting the individual against the expression of homo-sexual wishes. This behavior sometimes is not accepted as being appropriate and yet when it is understood that it serves as a replacement for much less socially accepted activities, it can be tolerated by the student without caus-ing him concern.

A student in the Divinity School came to the psychiatric clinic because he was worried about the fact that he preferred to take boy scouts on camping trips to going out on dates with girls. He was disappointed in himself because of this, feeling that it singled him out as different from others. It also made him feel discouraged about the possibility of eventually getting married. In the course of a few interviews, he was able to see that he had never felt any sexual desire for girls, in fact, had no real interest in them at all as individuals, although the gen-eral concept of being married appealed to him. He was naturally a very conserva-tive individual and considered that getting married was one of those things which every normal person does. He recalled having had a number of very close emo-tional relationships with contemporaries during college and told of some homo-sexual fantasies which he remembered having had at that time. His need for un-usually close emotional relationships with men, as well as his fantasies, had been absent since he had been in the Divinity School and taken so much interest in the boy scouts and other youth activities. As a result of therapy he came to under-stand that while he had no sexual interest in the work he was doing with boys, still it was somehow satisfying to him. By associating with members of the male sex in a helpful and altruistic manner, he was utilizing a defense mechanism in an effective way and by means of it, he was gaining a gratification through com-panionship with boys which satisfied him to such an extent that his homosexual fantasies were entirely eliminated. This understanding about what was going on within him relieved this student of his anxiety completely. . . .

There are some students for whom the relative strength of heterosexual and homosexual impulse is so close to being equal that they feel continually pulled in both directions. For them, there does not seem to be any possible, complete commitment either to men or to women and they feel constantly disloyal to one or the other. Such students often profit from a series of interviews over a fairly long period of time which are directed toward the achievement of insight into the causes of the conflicting impulses as well as toward the ways in which the student himself can help to resolve specific conflicts when they arise. . . .

Students of college level who have homosexual inclinations behave almost without exception in a discreet and inoffensive manner. They do not attempt to seduce other students; nor do they blatantly proclaim their difference from the average student. They do not constitute a menace and they often come from the most creative and academically productive contingent. The psychiatrist can often allay the fears of administrative officers in this respect.

IMPLICATIONS

Despite the lack of clarity as to whether there are predisposing genetic factors conducive to the development of homosexual tendencies, there seem to be implications in the opinions and studies quoted for better psychological climates and relationships within the family. What are they? What mother-son and father-son relationships may prevent homosexual tendencies?

Why is there less discussion of homosexuality in women? Are the same interpersonal relationships between girl and parents factors in encouraging girls to become homosexual? Is there anything the heterosexual person can do to help reduce the personal and social problem of individual homosexuals?

To what extent do you feel that articles devoted to the subject will bring about a more tolerant attitude toward the nonpredatory homosexual who lives quietly and possibly creatively and whose private life is lived within a society of those of similar inclination?

REFERENCES

Another concise discussion of homosexuality as a character disorder will be found in Stern (1965). Cory (1960) writes intimately about the homosexual and the society in which he lives.

Homosexuality is essentially an individual problem to which some adjust better than others, and it rarely occurs in a personality vacuum. The individual's "ego strength," discussed in Selection 5, is relevant, as is the social milieu in which the individual lives. Those who are encouraged to make adjustments in a society that accepts their obvious differences and rewards them for the personal contributions seem to make better adjustments. McKinney (1965) presents a case covering approximately twenty years of a homosexual's life.

Chapter XI

COUNSELING AND PSYCHOTHERAPY

[55] IDEAS OF PSYCHOTHERAPY

Every individual has disturbing emotional and mental difficulties. When they become acute, the individual or members of his family seek professional assistance. The patient enters into a counseling or psychotherapy relationship. What does the psychotherapist expect to happen? The client shows change in some way; what is the nature of this change?

Before we look at Selections 56, 57, and 59, dealing with two very different kinds of psychotherapy, let us review, with the help of Sundberg and Tyler, the various *goals* of psychotherapy and examine their *common features.*

Norman D. Sundberg and Leona E. Tyler

From *Clinical Psychologist* by Norman D. Sundberg and Leona E. Tyler. Copyright © 1962 by Meredith Publishing Company. Reprinted by permission of Appleton-Century-Crofts.

It may be that a slightly frivolous historian in a time to come will look back on our twentieth century and label it *The Age of Psychotherapy.* Hundreds of thousands of men, women, and children are seeking help from thousands of "therapists" of one kind or another: psychiatrists, psychologists, marriage counselors, school counselors, social workers, and clergymen—ministers, rabbis, and priests. Dozens of books are written each year presenting the theory and practice of psychotherapy to technical specialists, students, and the general public. Psychotherapy figures prominently in novels, plays, movies, and television programs. What is it that all these participants are attempting to accomplish? In this chapter we will analyze their purposes and some of the ideas about how they are to be achieved, as they have been set forth by the psychotherapists who have written about their profession.

WAYS IN WHICH GOALS OF THERAPY HAVE BEEN FORMULATED

In this field even more than elsewhere in clinical psychology, complex and elaborate theories have arisen. Undoubtedly, Freudian psychoanalysis is the most influential, but the impact of the views of Adler and Jung, Horney and Sullivan, Rogers, Mowrer, and many others has been strongly felt. Instead of discussing these theories one at a time, however, we shall attempt a different kind of classification.

In the theories as they stand, there is considerable confusion, arising from various sources. One source of confusion is that the ideas of every theorist undergo continual modification as he lives and works. The concepts Freud stressed in 1910 are not identical with those upon which he rested his theoretical structure in 1935. Rogers' second book on psychotherapy differs markedly from his first. Thus, it is difficult to write for the beginning student of clinical psychology an account of one of these comprehensive theories that includes *all* the concepts, early and late, actually incorporated in the thinking of some of its adherents.

Another reason for confusion in the theories therapists have produced about therapy is that they overlap. If such theories are taken up one by one, the student is confronted with the task of judging for himself how great this overlapping is. This is especially difficult for an inexperienced person because much of the common ground is found in practice rather than in conceptualization. Psychologists and psychiatrists, when *writing* about their work, are most likely to stress the aspects they consider to be unique or original, while they slight the aspects that fit in with many other theoretical orientations. Thus, the student trying to find a way of approaching his own professional tasks is likely to assume that the differences between theories are sharper than they actually are, and he may conclude that he is required to identify himself with one and only one of the theorists and to repudiate the others. The richness of his own theoretical formulation and the range of his helpfulness to others may be diminished by such a decision.

Therefore, instead of outlining the different complex approaches to therapy connected with the names of Freud, Rogers, Sullivan, and the other founders of systems or schools, we shall discuss first the principal purposes therapy has been thought to accomplish by some influential thinker at some stage of his development. We shall then look for common threads and basic issues and attempt to put the separate pieces together in a new way.

The first of these major purposes basic to some kinds of therapy might be labeled *strengthening the patient's motivation to do the right things*. It is the oldest of the aims we shall discuss. Suggestion in all its forms, ranging from gentle advice to the use of hypnosis to produce tendencies to act in specified ways, is one kind of procedure through which this purpose is carried out. Encouragement and inspiration, whether administered through informal praise and appreciation or through books and sermons, are intended to serve this purpose. Long before there were any professional specialties like psychology, this kind of treatment was constantly attempted. In our own time, therapeutic organizations like Alcoholics Anonymous attribute most of their success to this kind of influence.

A second purpose of therapy that has often been stated is *to reduce emotional pressure by facilitating the expression of feeling,* the process called *catharsis.* When the average layman thinks about therapy, it is probably this meaning he is most likely to connect with it. Dozens of motion pictures have given dramatic portrayals of a sudden relief from neurotic symptoms and anxiety following a flood of emotional 'expression touched off when contact is made with some repressed memory. Like suggestion and inspiration, the use of this process of emotional expression covers a wide range of depth and intensity, from the common "blowing off steam" at work or at home to the use of drugs or hypnosis to enable a patient to relive a traumatic experience.

A third way of formulating the purpose of therapy makes use of concepts from the psychology of development. Therapy aims to *release the potential for growth.* A basic growth tendency in every person is postulated, a tendency toward maturity and integration. Unfortunate circumstances or adverse influences can block or temporarily reverse this process, but cannot destroy it completely. What therapy aims to do is to remove these obstacles, whatever they are, and allow the person to start growing again along the lines of his own unique pattern. The psychotherapist should not be thought of as a mechanic, locating and repairing defects in a piece of equipment, but rather as more like a gardener, removing weeds, providing light, nutrients, and moisture to stimulate a plant intrinsically disposed to grow. Two aspects of developmental theory may be distinguished. One calls for *the analysis of each life stage* in childhood to ascertain what kinds of neurotic symptoms and faulty character structures may have arisen from failure to negotiate it successfully. The discussions by psychoanalysts of symptoms arising through arrested development at the oral, anal, phallic, or latency period have this focus. The emphasis psychoanalysts place on the necessity for *transference,* a term signifying the process of projecting childish attitudes onto the therapist, comes from the conviction that early periods must in some sense be relived emotionally if personality reorganization is to occur. The other aspect of developmental theory, expressed more clearly by Jung and by Rogers than by Freud, places the emphasis on *development as a process that continues throughout life,* whatever the early handicaps have been. A person is so complex that many avenues of growth and creativity are open to him if they can only be recognized and encouraged. Whether the emphasis is on unraveling the tangled strands of childhood or on opening up new vistas for the future, developmental theories have in common the assumption that therapy means discovering ways of facilitating a natural process rather than undertaking the construction of something new.

A fourth way of stating the purpose of therapy is *habit change*. Neurosis or maladjustment are viewed as the end result of a learning process in which undesirable or ineffective habits have been formed. For many reasons these may be difficult to get rid of, once the person is saddled with them. The task of the therapist, then, is to arrange learning situations in which the patient can modify such undesirable habits or replace them by others. There was real excitement among psychologists when J. B. Watson reported in 1920 that an irrational fear for furry animals had been experimentally produced in a child using conditioned response methods, and when M. C. Jones reported a few years later that conditioning could also be used to remove such fears from children's experience. These experiments seemed to point the way to a rational, scientific kind of therapy free from mystery and uncertainty. The years since the 1920's have sobered hopes for simple methods of "emotional re-education," as many irrational fears have proved to be impervious to such treatment. But straightforward conditioned response methods are still used quite widely in the treatment of behavior patterns such as enuresis and alcoholism, and the modification of social habits such as shyness and tactlessness is often attempted through planned learning situations. Probably more important, however, than these specific applications of the psychology of learning to particular kinds of cases is the task some theorists have undertaken of reformulating *all* the principles of psychotherapy in terms of learning. A thriving partnership between psychoanalysis and learning theory has resulted in an attack on some interesting research problems. Most psychologists engaged in therapy would agree in principle that therapy *is* learning. They would agree much less well about just what the faulty habits are that need to be changed, and what sort of learning process it is that therapy sets in motion.

A fifth purpose of therapy, in some ways related to the two preceding ones, is *the modification of the cognitive structure of the person*, by which is meant the interrelated set of concepts and fixed ideas that determine his perceptions of the world around him, of other persons, and of himself. Theorists who approach the problems of therapy from this direction have surmised that the roots of a person's difficulties lie in his basic misconceptions about the nature of things, mistaken ideas he acquired at some former period of his life. He is likely to be quite unaware of these cognitive structures. The conclusions to which they lead him are axioms, taken for granted. A generation ago, Alfred Adler discussed the effects of this phenomenon under the graphic term *life style*. More recently, George Kelly in his *Psychology of Personal Constructs* (1955) has presented not only a coherent theoretical statement of this point of view, but also a number of ingenious methods for identifying the basic cognitive structures in an individual and for helping him to modify them if they need changing. The theoretical formulations of Carl Rogers have emphasized the importance of clear, finely differentiated perceptions of self and the world as a basis for effective living. As many clinical psychologists see their task today, the aim of therapeutic activity is to make a client aware of his basic cognitive structures and enable him to produce some change in the pattern. Change will often come automatically once the person becomes aware that one of his "personal constructs" is inconsistent with other aspects of his personality. Lecky's oft-quoted little book, *Self-Consistency* (1945), stimulated much thinking along these lines.

A sixth stated purpose of therapy is *self-knowledge*, broadly defined. This, like habit change, can be an extremely inclusive concept. It is basic to most counseling and rehabilitation activities. The client is given aptitude and interest tests and helped to examine his own capacities, attitudes, needs, background, and opportunities. Self-knowledge is also prominent among the goals of psychoanalysis. The attempt to bring unconscious material into consciousness where the ego of the person can cope with it is so basic in therapeutic procedure that for many theorists this growth in self-knowledge *is* therapy. The word that has been much used as a label for the process of attaining self-knowledge is *insight*. As a theoretical concept, insight is not being stressed as much at present as it was in previous periods. There has come the recognition that an intellectual awareness of all the recesses of one's personality does not necessarily make for psychological health. There must be some emotional quality to such insight if it is to be effective, and it has proved to be very difficult to state how the word is to be defined in these emotional terms. Furthermore, striking improvements occurring in the absence of any manifestation of insight whatever have seriously challenged those who would use self-knowledge as a central therapeutic concept. In short, it seems that insight is neither a necessary nor a sufficient factor in therapy. Nevertheless, it still has its place as an important organizing concept, and the procedures most commonly used in therapy perhaps serve this purpose better than any other.

The last type of theory to be considered here emphasizes *interpersonal relationships*. According to such a theory, we must look for the sources of all psychological ills in the person's relationships to the "significant others" in his life. Here, too, some therapists place the emphasis on the very earliest periods of life as the time when the patterns for future relationships are laid down. They hope, by understanding what occurred then, to find ways of modifying these patterns so that they will no longer exert unhealthy influences on present relationships. Other workers pay more attention to their client's current relationships to spouse, children, friends, and colleagues. They hope to find relationships which may be changed for better rather than to identify the remote childhood origins of the difficulties. One major resource inherent in all types of therapy for producing change in interpersonal relationships is the fact that the client is at the time experiencing a new relationship, without the defects of those previously formed—his relationship to the therapist. A strong emphasis on *communication* distinguishes the interpersonal theories of therapy. Isolation and estrangement are involved in much psychological disturbance. One way to combat them is to improve communication.

Furthermore, the possibilities for therapeutic intervention are not limited to the things that can happen between just two individuals. The unique advantage of *group therapy* is that it allows the participants to establish new relationships, observe and study them, and modify them in constructive ways. Patients can make emotional contact with others as individuals; they can also practice the different *roles* they must play in dealing with other people —whether children, bosses, co-workers, or strangers. Clinical psychologists join sociologists in the interest they take in the mental health effects of *social systems*. As a natural extension from the interpersonal approach, some psychotherapists have been asking: Should we be attempting to treat this individual at all? Would it not be a sounder procedure to try to improve some particular social system of which he is a part, and thus increase the level of health and soundness of all the persons who are caught in it? Thinking of this sort has stimulated careful scrutiny of the social situation to be found in a mental hospital—the whole institution and the individual ward—in a search for ways to change the relationships of physicians, nurses, aides, and patients to one another. The work that marriage and family counselors do often rests on a consideration of the kind of a complex system the wife, husband, and children together constitute rather than on the psychological characteristics of one member of the family. The therapist sees the importance of understanding, and perhaps changing, the dynamics of the small groups encountered in the course of living—work groups, recreation groups, and classroom, for example. The implications of this therapeutic approach are very far-ranging. It has even been said that our whole modern society is a kind of neurotic organism needing therapeutic reorganization.

In many situations, psychologists join in collaborative efforts with physicians providing *somatic treatment*, such as the use of drugs, shock therapy, physiotherapy, or other forms of medical treatment. Physiological changes can have direct effects on behavior, or they may make a person more amenable to ordinary psychotherapy. Even nonpsychiatric patients, such as persons who must undergo surgery and are anxious and distraught, can be helped by brief psychotherapy or counseling. In all somatic cases, psychological treatment must be coordinated with medical treatment. The psychological goal in such cases will fall under one or more of the purposes of therapy we have discussed.

COMMON FEATURES

It is not possible to distinguish very sharply between the leading schools of psychotherapy on the basis of such aims as we have been outlining. Most writers put stress on more than one of these purposes, selecting different combinations, weighting them differently, and finding different kinds of links between them. Rogers, for instance, stresses the ideas of catharsis, self-knowledge, perceptual shifts, and creative growth. His publications over the years show that he has emphasized catharsis less and creative growth more as time has passed. Freud's early formulations centered on catharsis and self-knowledge, but he later shifted the focal point to development and interpersonal relationships in infancy and childhood. Adlerian therapists devote a good deal of attention to perceptual and cognitive structures and social relationships, but use suggestion and advice to promote self-knowledge and habit change. One of the reasons for the many controversies in the field of psychotherapy may be that there are so many ways in which complex theories can be contrasted with one another!

The procedures actually used show much common ground. In the first place, all methods of personal therapy must concentrate on bringing about *a sufficient lowering of the patient's level of anxiety so that he will be able to permit himself to explore the painful areas of his experience.* An interview where the person is guaranteed privacy, freedom from interruptions, and complete confidentiality has the effect of making him feel at least a little safer than he does at other times in other places. Special group situations may also produce this relaxed attitude. More important is the whole attitude of the therapist and the feeling he communicates to the patient in many subtle ways that he is no longer alone with his troubles. The strength of another person has been added to his own.

Dealing with anxiety is one of the basic skills that a psychotherapist must acquire, and it can never be learned from books or lectures. It is not accomplished by simple kinds of verbal reassurance, no matter how earnest. Furthermore, the goal can never be to eliminate anxiety completely, because anxiety constitutes the principal motivation for undertaking therapy as well as the chief reason for resisting it. Some therapists approach the problem of reducing anxiety by combining tranquilizing drugs with psychotherapy in the treatment of severely disturbed cases. To calm a person enough so that he can face all kinds of potentially threatening inner feelings and outer situations and cope with them may be a valuable treatment maneuver. But to carry this so far that he no longer cares what happens to him or no longer sees the sharp outlines of unyielding facts is not therapy. One of the reasons alcoholics have responded less well to psychotherapy than many other types of neurotic patient is that drinking has become a habitual way of reducing their anxieties—too much.

The second thing that all varieties of therapy attempt to do is to create *a strong personal relationship that can be used as a vehicle for constructive change.* In individual therapy this is a relationship between patient and therapist; in group methods the ties between group members may be the important ones. Research by Fiedler (1950a, 1950b) has suggested that the nature of this relationship may be very similar for kinds of therapy that are differently labeled. It is a significant fact that many theoretical writers, as their experience increases, come to place much more emphasis on this variable. At first, Freud insisted most on the necessity of achieving *insight;* as time passed, *transference* took its place as his central concept, and he turned his attention to the way in which the patient relates himself to his doctor during the different stages of treatment. More recently in psychoanalytic writings there has been a strong emphasis on *countertransference,* or the way in which the doctor relates himself to the patient. Other theorists also talk about the therapeutic *interaction*—what the situation means to the therapist as well as to the client.

The important idea arising from all of this discussion is one that beginning students sometimes miss—that it is necessary for the therapist himself to participate on a deep emotional level in the psychological process that constitutes therapy. Verbal techniques and skills are no substitute for this emotional participation. There are hazards for the doctor as well as for the patient in launching out upon the deep waters the two of them must traverse together. Learning to deal with such hazards is a far more difficult thing than learning to say something appropriate in response to a client's remark. We shall have more to say of this later.

Another common feature in many diverse systems of thinking about psychotherapy is an emphasis on *communication as a way of enabling the patient to establish connections with his own inner and outer worlds.* Obviously, any talking involves communication to some degree. It might be maintained with some plausibility that all psychological disorders *are* essentially communication problems and that treatment consists in repairing or installing lines of communication so that they will connect the patient with the complex human world in which he must function and assist him in articulating his own thoughts and feelings, thus making them more accessible. At any rate, some of the most essential of the therapist's skills are the ways he has of facilitating free expression in the client with whom he is working. This, like the emotional participation discussed above, is not just a matter of knowing what to say. It consists rather in a sensitive awareness of the way the other person feels, a general perceptiveness that makes it possible for him to pick up faint clues and to grasp meanings in confused and halting attempts to say something—or even in silence, for that matter. A sense of being understood acts as a powerful motivating force for a troubled client, encouraging him to try to communicate more of his experience. To provide this understanding requires great effort as well as extreme sensitivity. One must listen to the other person with a kind of concentrated yet relaxed attention that one seldom brings to the other situations of life. It may even be that it is this *interested attention* rather than the understanding itself that promotes further effort on the part of the client, since occasional failure to grasp some particular meaning seems not to impede therapeutic progress. However, needless to say, if the therapist, well-meaning though he may be, never quite understands what the client is trying to say, the therapeutic process is hardly likely to continue for long.

One of the limitations of psychotherapy as commonly practiced today is that it is almost impossible to make it available to troubled persons whose verbal skills are limited. Most of the patients who receive this form of treatment from private practitioners or public clinics are middle- or upper-class persons of above-average intelligence and with better-than-average education. Even in these privileged parts of the population (Hollingshead and Redlich, 1958) many individuals are unable to express themselves very well verbally. It has occurred to many psychologists who are impressed with the enormous need for therapy that greater use must be made of *nonverbal forms of communication*. In clinics for children, the use of toys, finger paints, clay, and many other kinds of equipment and materials as media in which they can express themselves has become standard procedure. Even very young children are able to express in such ways thoughts and feelings which they are quite incapable of putting into words. Child therapists must learn to receive communications coming to them in these forms. Some attention has. been given in recent years to ways of encouraging nonverbal kinds of expression in adults also. One method, Moreno's psychodrama, has been in use for a considerable period of time and a fairly large body of literature concerning it has accumulated. Therapy using music, painting, or the dance has been tried. Group therapy using activities is not uncommon. There have been nonverbal attempts to condition regressed patients in hospitals. All these new ways of dealing with patients remind us that when we say that communication is essential to therapy we must be sure that we do not define communication too narrowly.

One additional feature characterizes all forms of psychotherapy: *some degree of commitment on the part of the patient, his decision to participate, to try.* This, like the other aspects we have been discussing, is not a simple matter and cannot be brought about by the therapist's use of some particular technique. It is often said, for example, that therapy can occur only if the client takes the initiative by seeking out the therapist, if only by calling the clinic for an appointment. Most professional workers try to arrange things so that this will be the way in which therapy begins. If a college teacher is concerned about the state of mind of a student in his class, the counseling psychologist who is consulted will suggest that the student—not the instructor —call the Counseling Center for an appointment. But the principle involved here is far broader and more fundamental than policies with regard to appointment procedures. Even a person who makes his own arrangements for interviews may feel passive and ambivalent about the whole procedure. On the other hand, rebellious clients forced into therapy by relatives, employers, courts, or school administrative officers may shift their attitudes and make the sort of commitment we are talking about. Especially in early interviews, the therapist's skill can contribute to this end. It requires that one carefully avoid any contest of wills, any obvious or subtle attempt to control the client. But one must also avoid what looks like indifference, an attitude that what the client decides to do is immaterial to the therapist. What the therapist's whole attitude (it cannot be communicated by words alone) must say is: "I really want to help you. I hope you'll give this a trial. But I'm not going to force you or trick you into compliance. The decision really does rest with you." The therapist must be able to communicate hope to the client but without promising anything except sincere effort. What he is asking the person to do is to invest something of himself—a great deal, really—in an enterprise for which a successful outcome cannot be assured.

Once this commitment has occurred, therapy becomes a sort of *partnership*. Menninger (1958) has called the arrangement a *contract* in which each participant agrees to do something in exchange for something from the other person, and both agree to follow certain implicit rules. This, too, is something that characterizes all forms, all schools. There are differences in the way the work to be done is distributed—differences from case to case as well as from one theoretical school to another. But therapy is work, and hard work, for both participants. Both will go through periods of elation as well as periods of extreme discouragement. Progress will often be followed by relapses. Therapy is one of the most fascinating and rewarding of human undertakings, but it is never simple, never easy.

It is generally agreed that patients and clients, even children (Allen, 1942), must be willing to accept changes in themselves if therapy is eventually to succeed. However, this does not mean that psychologists should refuse to work with poorly motivated clients such as chronic schizophrenics, resentful juvenile delinquents, and patients with character disorders. Even though the attitudes of such persons make formal psychotherapy impossible, desirable changes can sometimes be produced by means of direct suggestion, environmental influences, or group activities. There is always room for innovation and research in understanding and modifying behavior.

IMPLICATIONS

Try to express specific examples of the seven purposes of psychotherapy which we have summarized as (1) to do the right things, (2) to get expression of feelings, (3) to release potentials for growth, (4) to bring about habit change, (5) to modify the cognitive structure, (6) to increase self-knowledge, and (7) to effect health producing interpersonal relationships. Then you can better understand the common features in these various aims. Can you recall some instances in which someone aided you at a time of crisis by *reducing your anxiety?* How was this brought about? What are some examples of the kind of communication between people that help to establish connection with a client's inner and outer world?

REFERENCES

For further reading on the viewpoints expressed by Sundberg and Tyler (1962), see Hall and Lindzey (1957). In their book, they discuss the views of Freud, Adler, Jung, Horney, Sullivan, and Rogers. A summary of the views of the followers of Freud is found in Selection 60. Some of Jung's views are presented in Selection 64. See also Mowrer (1954).

[56] THE CONDITIONING THERAPIES

One approach to emotional disturbances, particularly the neuroses, is to regard them as learned, persistent, and nonadaptive habits that merely have to be undone by reconditioning. The following selection is a simple discussion of a movement in psychology and psychiatry to do just this.

Anxiety is a feeling of dread, an objectless "fear," a concern over impending doom or a possible unacceptable consequence of events. Phobia, another fear response mentioned by Wolpe, may be defined as excessive fear in the absence of real danger. How are the conditioning techniques that are developed in the animal laboratory applied in the clinical situation? You will note that the clinician uses behavior and its instigation to treat what some psychologists regard as subjective experience. The conditioning therapist uses a kind of therapy known as reciprocal inhibition, in which symptoms or complaints of the patient are decreased when the stimuli are presented under conditions in which the response is inhibited.

Joseph Wolpe

Reprinted from Joseph Wolpe, Andrew Salter, and L. F. Reyna, *The Conditioning Therapies* (New York: Holt, Rinehart and Winston, 1964), pp. 1–15, by permission of the publisher and the author.

Now let us consider the conditioning therapies. These methods stem from the conception that neuroses are persistent unadaptive habits that have been conditioned (that is, learned). If this conception is correct, the fundamental overcoming of a neurosis *can* consist of nothing but deconditioning—or undoing the relevant habit patterns.

The most characteristic and common feature of neurotic habits is anxiety. There is persuasive evidence, both experimental and clinical, that the great majority of neuroses are fundamentally conditioned autonomic responses (Wolpe, 1958). The individual has persistent habits of reacting with anxiety to situations that, objectively, are not dangerous. Typical stimuli to which the response of anxiety may be regarded as neurotic are the sight of a bird, the interior of an elevator, asking a favor, or receiving a compliment. Experimentally it is possible to condition an animal to respond with anxiety to any stimulus one pleases merely by arranging for that stimulus, on a number of occasions, to appear in an appropriate time relation to the evocation of anxiety; and by manipulating various factors one can obtain an emotional habit that is utterly refractory to extinction in the ordinary way (Wolpe, 1948, 1958). In human neuroses one can usually elicit a history of similar kinds of conditioning. Human neuroses, too, are characterized by the same remarkable resistance to extinction. Since neurotic reactions are, as a rule, autonomic reactions first and foremost, this resistance is in keeping with Gantt's observations of the great refractoriness of cardiovascular conditioned responses to extinction.

It is implicit in conditioning theory that recovery from neurosis should be achieved by applying the learning process in a reverse direction: whatever undesirable behavior has been learned may be unlearned. In experiments performed about fourteen years ago, I demonstrated in cats that had been made neurotic experimentally how this unlearning can be brought about (Wolpe, 1948, 1958). Anxiety reactions had been strongly conditioned to a small confining cage and to other stimuli, and could not be made to extinguish despite repeated exposure to the stimuli. The anxiety response habits could, however, be overcome in piecemeal fashion by counterposing feeding to weak anxiety responses. At first, stimuli distantly similar to the conditioned stimuli were used, until anxiety decreased to zero, and then, step by step, stimuli closer in resemblance to the original conditioned stimuli were introduced, until even the strongest eventually lost its power to evoke anxiety. These findings led to the framing of the reciprocal inhibition principle of psychotherapy, which is that *if a response inhibitory of anxiety can be made to occur in the presence of anxiety-evoking stimuli, it will weaken the bond between these stimuli and the anxiety.*

Experience with human neuroses indicates that the principle has quite general validity; in addition to feeding, a good many other kinds of responses,[1] each of which, empirically, appears to inhibit anxiety, have been successfully used to weaken neurotic anxiety-response habits and related neurotic habits. The reciprocal inhibition principle also affords an explanation for the therapeutic effects of interviewing as such (which is seemingly the main basis of the successes of the traditional therapies) and for so-called spontaneous recoveries.

I have described elsewhere (1958) the deliberate therapeutic use of a considerable range of anxiety-inhibiting responses. I shall briefly review those most widely employed—assertive, relaxation, and sexual responses.

Assertive responses are used where there is a need to overcome neurotic anxieties that arise irrationally in the course of interpersonal relationships—such anxieties as prevent a person from expressing his opinions to his friends lest they disagree, or from reprimanding inefficient underlings. The essence of the therapist's role is to encourage appropriate assertiveness, the outward expression, wherever it is reasonable and right to do so, of the feelings and action tendencies that anxiety has in the past inhibited. In other words, the therapist instigates "acting out." Each act of assertion to some extent reciprocally inhibits the anxiety, and in consequence somewhat weakens the anxiety response habit. The assertion required is not necessarily aggressive, and behavior in accordance with affectionate and other feelings may need to be instigated. The maneuvers involved are largely similar to those described by Salter (1949), though the rationale upon which he bases them is different.

Relaxation responses were first used on a scientific basis by Jacobson (1939), who demonstrated that they have autonomic accompaniments opposite to those of anxiety. His method of intensive training in relaxation for use in the life situation, though of great value, is rather cumbersome. More eco-

---

[1] Gellhorn and Loofbourrow (1963) present a number of modern instances of reciprocally inhibitory relationships between reactions in both the somatic and the autonomic nervous systems. (See also Gellhorn, 1961.)

nomical and clearly directed use of relaxation is made in the technique known as *systematic desensitization* (Wolpe, 1958, 1961).

Lang reports its use in the context of snake phobias, but its range of application is very wide indeed.[2] The therapist has to identify the categories of stimuli to which the patient reacts with anxiety, and then rank the stimuli of each category in order of intensity of evoked anxiety. In the course of about six interviews, the patient is given training in relaxation in parallel with this. When the preliminaries have been completed, the patient is made to relax as deeply as possible (in some cases under hypnosis), and then instructed to imagine the weakest of the anxiety-evoking stimuli for a few seconds. The instruction is repeated at short intervals, and if the response to the stimulus has been weak initially, it declines, on repetition, to zero. Under these circumstances, what apparently happens is that on each occasion the relaxation inhibits the anxiety, to some extent, and somewhat weakens the anxiety-evoking potential of the stimulus concerned. With repetition this potential is brought down to zero.

Recent studies have demonstrated:

that the effects of desensitization are due to the procedure itself and not to suggestion or transference (Wolpe, 1962; Lang, pp. 47–48);

that after one or two sessions it can be predicted with virtual certainty whether a patient will respond to this treatment or not; and

that in phobias with independently measurable parameters, such as acrophobia, the numbers of therapeutic operations involved show consistent mathematical relationships to the stages of decrement of the phobia (Wolpe, 1963) that are suggestively similar to the psychophysical law proposed by Stevens (1962).

Sexual responses are used to inhibit anxiety responses conditioned to sexual situations. By manipulating the conditions of sexual approaches so that anxiety is never permitted to be strong, reciprocal inhibition of anxiety by sexual arousal is effected, and the anxiety response habit is progressively weakened. It is usually possible to overcome impotence or premature ejaculation in a few weeks. Sexual responses have generally only a secondary role in the treatment of frigidity (Lazarus, 1963).

The question is, how effective are these and related techniques in procuring the recovery of neurotic patients in terms of Knight's criteria? *

---

* Briefly these are: symptomatic improvement, increased productiveness, improved adjustment to and pleasure in sex, improved interpersonal relationships, and ability to handle ordinary psychological and reality stresses. See Knight (1941).—Ed.

[2] Some people are erroneously under the impression that this method is effective only for classical phobias. The word "phobia" refers to clearly defined stimulus sources of neurotic anxiety. The conditioning therapist differs from his colleagues in that he *seeks out* the precise stimuli to anxiety, and finds himself able to break down almost every neurosis into what are essentially *phobic systems*. Their subject matter extends far beyond the classical phobias, and includes such contents as neurotic fears of incurring obligations, of being watched, or of receiving praise. (See Wolpe, 1964.)

Using the whole range of available methods according to their indications, I have reported between 1952 and 1958 three series of results embracing 210 neurotic patients. Every patient in whom the reciprocal inhibition techniques had been given a fair trial was included in the series. Nearly 90 per cent of these patients were rated on Knight's criteria as either apparently cured or much improved after an average of about thirty therapeutic interviews. The cases were unselected in the sense that no case diagnosed as neurotic was ever refused treatment. Psychotics and psychopaths were not accepted for treatment unless by error of diagnosis.

Until recently, there were no other studies involving considerable numbers of patients, although numerous accounts had been published describing the successful treatment of individuals or small groups. One noteworthy small group comprised eighteen cases of phobias in children treated by Lazarus (1959). All the patients recovered in a mean of 9.5 sessions; follow-up from six months to two and a half years showed no relapses. Lazarus has recently analyzed his results with reciprocal inhibition therapies. His findings [3] have been summarized in a mimeographed paper as follows: In the course of about 4 years the *total* number of patients who consulted him was 408. Of these, 321 (or 78 per cent) derived "definite and constructive benefit according to certain specified criteria which are unusually stringent." Hussain reports 95 per cent of 105 patients whom he treated by a direct approach involving hypnosis apparently recovered or much improved. Recently, I received from the Hospital for Mental and Nervous Diseases at St. John's, Newfoundland, a report by Drs. Alastair Burnett and Edmond Ryan of the treatment of one hundred neurotic patients on learning theory principles. The usual treatment period was five weeks. The evaluation of outcome was on Knight's criteria. Substantial improvement occurred in almost every case (Burnett, 1962). Twenty-five of the patients were followed up over a year or more, and fifteen of these (60 per cent) were then either apparently cured or much improved. Another 32 per cent were rated "moderately improved." As the outcome of five weeks of therapy this is quite noteworthy. Burnett and Ryan express the view that these methods make effective psychotherapy available for the first time to "fairly large numbers of rural, unsophisticated patients who have limited formal education."

In Table 1, the results of the two largest and most characteristic behavior therapy series are compared with those of the two major psychoanalytic series discussed above.

A critical question is, of course, the durability of the results obtained by conditioning methods. The answer appears to be that they are practically always long-lasting. In 1958, I was able to report only one relapse among forty-five patients who had been followed up for periods ranging from two to seven years. Published communication from other conditioning therapists

[3] These have since been published (Lazarus, 1963). See Table 1.

indicates that their experience is essentially the same. Furthermore, whenever resurgence of symptoms has occurred, and could be investigated, it has always been found to be related to specific events that could clearly have reconditioned the neurotic emotional habit. Learning theory predicts that *unless* there are intervening events that directly recondition neurotic reactions, recovery from neurosis that is radical in the sense defined earlier in this paper will be

TABLE 1

COMPARATIVE RESULTS

Series	No. of cases	Apparently cured or much improved (recoveries)	Percentage recoveries
Psychoanalytic Therapy			
Collected series of psychoneuroses			
Knight (1941)			
a. Over 6 months' therapy	383		63.2
		242	
b. Total cases	534		45.3
Psychoanalytic Fact-Gathering Committee			
Brody (1962)	210	126	60
a. Completely analyzed cases	210	126	60
b. Total cases	595	(184)	(31)[a]
Behavior Therapy			
Wolpe (1958)	210	188	89.5[b]
Lazarus (1963)	408	321	78.0[b]

[a] This percentage is calculated from data of the Fact-Gathering Committee of the American Psychoanalytic Association, as follows. It is granted that the whole "completely analyzed" group of 306 would have shown the 60 per cent recovery rate found in the 210 who were followed up, giving 184 recoveries for 306 patients. These would appear to be the sum total of patients claimed as apparently cured or much improved out of the whole group of 595, which includes 289 who discontinued analysis (Brody, 1962; Masserman, 1963).

[b] Lazarus included in his series *every* neurotic patient—even if he had seen him only once. Wolpe counted only those to whom the available techniques had actually been applied. When treatment was ineffective, this was generally established in 15–30 sessions.

lasting, no matter by what maneuvers it has been obtained. There are facts that bear out this prediction. I elsewhere reported (Wolpe, 1961) a survey of follow-up studies on neurotic patients who, with various therapies, other than psychoanalysis, had either recovered or improved markedly. Of 249 patients followed up from two to fifteen years only four had relapsed. This finding is not only in line with conditioning theory, but also directly contrary to the expectations of the psychoanalytic theory of neurosis.

CONCLUSIONS

The comparison I have presented is, of course, not based on data emanating from a controlled study on matched patients. Such a study, which should include an untreated group of patients similarly matched, is obviously desirable. Nevertheless, I submit that the evidence justifies now substituting behavior therapy for psychoanalysis in the training of therapists, and not temporizing until absolute proof has been provided. There are some who favor waiting for a study on matched groups of patients on the ground that the inferior results of psychoanalysis may be attributable to the psychoanalysts having to treat more difficult cases. There are several reasons for thinking this unlikely. In the first place, while conditioning therapists as a rule undertake treatment of all cases of neurosis, psychoanalysts are often very selective, and surely do not refuse those whom they believe they could *easily* help. Second, conditioning therapists frequently overcome neuroses that have been unsuccessfully treated by psychoanalysis, and often for many years. Third, in private practice, the individual medical practitioner tends to send *all* his neurotic cases to a favored psychotherapist, whether analyst or not. Fourth, it is at least tangentially relevant that, as already noted, psychoanalysts often profess a disinterest in symptomatic recovery, claiming that they aim at something "deeper," such as radical personality change. It may, however, be noted parenthetically that the analysts often represent this alleged deep kind of change as being *prerequisite* to durable freedom from symptoms, a proposition that evidence I have quoted flatly contradicts.

The present position is clear. As far as the evidence goes, conditioning therapies appear to produce a higher proportion of lasting recoveries from the distress and disability of neurosis than does psychoanalysis. Even if a controlled study were to show an equal, or even higher, percentage of recovery for psychoanalysis, the time it requires would remain incomparably greater, and conditioning therapy would therefore still deserve preference. The possible public health implications are great. A psychotherapist who uses behavioristic techniques can handle over ten times as many patients per year as the therapist who employs psychoanalysis, and with greater hope of success for each patient. Effective treatment has thus become possible for many more victims of neurotic disturbance—and at much less expense than psychoanalysis requires.

IMPLICATIONS

Can you visualize, by the patient suffering from a psychological illness, what the therapist does? How is this curative? What everyday behavior might be changed by this procedure? How does this kind of therapy differ basically from play therapy, discussed in Selection 57; family therapy, in Selection 59; or any of the other therapies discussed in Selection 55.

REFERENCES

Consult the Bibliography for references cited in the article.

[57] NONDIRECTIVE PLAY THERAPY

How does the therapist discover the basic problems of the child? The parent may have complaints, but he does not necessarily reveal to the therapist the *conflicts and anxieties* that are disturbing the the child. The child certainly cannot verbalize his difficulties, yet his behavior may give us some clues. But how do we observe his unselfconscious behavior without following him around all day? Play is a natural outlet for the child. It can point to some of his needs and struggles, and if simultaneously used in a context of self-development, it is therapeutic.

Axline, a follower of Carl Rogers, the originator of nondirective therapy, has adapted the theory and techniques of nondirective therapy to play. What do these techniques look like in a practical situation? How does the therapist *exhibit permissiveness, accept the child completely,* and *recognize* and *reflect feelings?* When the therapist engages in these activities in a manner that has meaning for the child with problems, what is the effect upon the child? The following selection presents excerpts from Axline's book-length treatment of the subject.

Virginia Mae Axline

Reprinted from Virginia Mae Axline, *Play Therapy* (Boston: Hougton Mifflin Company, 1947), pp. 15–20, 81–83, 88, 90, 94, 96–98, 102–103, 105, 111 by permission of the publisher and the author.

Nondirective therapy is based upon the assumption that the individual has within himself not only the ability to solve his own problems satisfactorily but also this growth impulse that makes mature behavior more satisfying than immature behavior.

PLAY THERAPY

Nondirective play theory may be described as an opportunity that is offered to the child to experience growth under the most favorable conditions. Since play is his natural medium for self-expression, the child is given the opportunity to play out his accumulated feelings of tension, frustration, insecurity, aggression, fear, bewilderment, confusion.

By playing out these feelings, he brings them to the surface, gets them out in the open, faces them, learns to control them, or abandon them. When he has achieved emotional relaxation, he begins to realize the power within himself to be an individual in his own right, to think for himself, to make his own decisions, to become psychologically more mature, and, by so doing, to realize selfhood.

The play-therapy room is good growing ground. In the security of this room where the child is the most important person, where he is in command of the situation and of himself, where no one tells him what to do, no one criticizes what he does, no one nags, or suggests, or goads him on, or pries into his private world, he suddenly feels that here he can unfold his wings; he can look squarely at himself, for he is accepted completely; he can test out his ideas; he can express himself fully; for this is his world, and he no longer has to compete with such other forces as adult authority or rival contemporaries or situations where he is a human pawn in a game between bickering parents, or where he is the butt of someone else's frustrations and aggressions. He is an individual in his own right. He is treated with dignity and respect. He can say anything that he feels like saying—and he is accepted completely. He can play with the toys in any way that he likes to—and he is accepted completely. He can hate and he can love and he can be as indifferent as the Great Stone Face—and he is still accepted completely. He can be as fast as a whirlwind or as slow as molasses in January—and he is neither restrained nor hurried.

Quotations of what children have actually said in describing the play-therapy experience as the remarks came out spontaneously are more indicative of what it means to the child than anything the therapist can say.

Three boys, aged eight, were experiencing group-therapy sessions. During the eighth interview, Herby suddenly asked the therapist, "Do you have to do this? Or do you like to do this?" Then he added, "I wouldn't know how to do this." Ronny asked, "What do you mean? You play. That's all. You just play." And Owen agreed with Ronny. "Why, sure you do," he said. But Herby continued the discussion. "I mean I wouldn't know how to do what she does. I don't even know what she does. She doesn't seem to do anything. Only all of a sudden, I'm free. Inside me, I'm free." (He flings his arms around.) "I'm Herb and Frankenstein and Tojo and a devil." (He laughs and pounds his chest.) "I'm a great giant and a hero. I'm wonderful and I'm terrible. I'm a dope and I'm so smart. I'm two, four, six, eight, ten people, and I fight and I kill!" The therapist said to Herby, "You're all kinds of people rolled up in one." Ronny added, "And you stink, too." Herby glared at Ronny, and replied, "I stink and you stink. Why, I'll mess you up." The therapist continued to speak to Herby—"You're all kinds of people in here. You're wonderful and you're terrible and you're dopey and you're smart." Herby interrupted exultantly, "I'm good and I'm bad and still I'm Herby. I tell you I'm wonderful. I can be anything I want to be!" Apparently Herby felt that during the therapy hour he could express fully all of the attitudes and feelings that were an expression of his personality. He felt the acceptance and permissiveness to be himself. He seemed to recognize the power of self-direction within himself.

Another boy, aged twelve, commented during a first therapy session: "This is all so different and so strange. In here you say I can do what I want to do. You don't tell me what to do. I can mess up a picture if I want to. I can make a clay model of my art teacher and let the crocodile eat her." He laughed. "I can do anything. I can be me!"

Feeling their way, testing themselves, unfolding their personalities, taking the responsibility for themselves—that is what happens during therapy.

Oscar had no sense of security at all. Some of the helpers mistreated him. He became one of the most maladjusted children imaginable. He was aggressive, belligerent, negative, insecure, defiant, dependent. He was a masterpiece of conflicting feelings. His mother, erratic and nervous, brought him to the psychologist. This is an excerpt from the initial contact.

MOTHER. This is Oscar. Heaven only knows what you can do with him! But here he is.

THERAPIST. Would you like to come over to the playroom with me?

OSCAR. No! Shet up! [*Yells.*]

MOTHER [*also yelling*]. Oscar! Now you be polite. Stop that sass!

OSCAR [*louder than ever*]. No! No! No!

MOTHER. Well, you are! What do you think I brought you up here for? The ride?

OSCAR [*whimpering*]. I don't wanta!

The beginning therapist asks herself at this point, "Now what?" Cajole him into the playroom? "We have such nice toys over in the playroom. You're such a nice big boy now. You come with me and I'll show you what there is to play with." That is not accepting Oscar exactly as he is. He doesn't want to come. Or should she say, with a note of regret in her voice, "Your mother brought you all the way up here and you don't want to come into the playroom with me!" That is a reflection of feeling, but it also carries subtle condemnation. There is an implied "My, aren't you an ungrateful little brute!" If the therapist wants to reflect his feeling only, what should she say? "You don't want to come with me." The therapist tries that.

THERAPIST. You don't want to come with me.

OSCAR. No! [*Makes face at therapist and folds up fists.*] Shet up!

MOTHER. If you don't go over there, I'll leave you here forever.

OSCAR [*attaching self to mother, whimpering*]. Don't leave me. Don't leave me. [*Sobs hysterically.*]

THERAPIST. Oscar is scared when Mother threatens to leave him here. [*This is a recognition of Oscar's feeling, but condemnation of Mother, who flares up.*]

MOTHER. Well, I've got to do something. Honest to God, Oscar, if you don't shut up and go with this lady, I will leave you! Or give you away!

OSCAR. You wait for me? [*Pitifully.*] You be here when I come back.

MOTHER. Of course I will—if you behave.

OSCAR [*transferring deathlike grip from Mother's skirt to therapist's skirt*]. You wait?

THERAPIST. You want Mother to promise you that she will wait.

OSCAR. You promise?

MOTHER. I promise!

[*Therapist and Oscar go into the playroom. Therapist starts to close the door.*]

OSCAR [*screaming*]. Don't shet the door! Don't shet the door! [*Tears roll down his cheeks.*]

THERAPIST. You don't want me to shut the door. You're afraid to stay here with me if I shut the door. Very well. We'll leave the door open and you close the door when you feel like it.

[*This leaves the responsibility up to Oscar. It is up to him to make the choice. Oscar looks around the playroom. As he thaws out, he becomes aggressive.*]

OSCAR. I'll bust up everything in here!

What about limitations? Should the therapist say, "You can play with the toys in here any way you want to, but you can't bust them up." Or, "Other children use these toys, too, so you can't bust them up." That is not responding to Oscar's expressed feeling. That is succumbing to the trap of responding to content rather than feeling back of content.

THERAPIST. You're feeling tough now.

OSCAR [*glaring at therapist*]. I'll bust you up, too.

THERAPIST. You're still feeling tough.

OSCAR. I'll—— [*suddenly laughs*] I'll—— [*He wanders around the playroom and picks up the toy telephone.*] What's this?

Accepting the Child Competely

Jean is brought into the clinic by her mother. Jean, aged twelve, is getting completely out of hand. She shows no respect for her mother, quarrels with her younger brother, will not have anything to do with the other children in her class at school. After introductions, Jean goes to the playroom with the therapist. The therapist attempts to structure the situation verbally. "You may play with any of the toys in here any way that you want to, Jean. There are paints, clay, finger paints, puppets." The therapist smiles at Jean, who stares back at the therapist in obvious boredom. The therapist waits for a few moments. Jean sits down and maintains her stony silence. The therapist, anxious to get things moving, speaks again. "Don't you know just what to do first? Oh, and there is a family of dolls over in the doll house. Do you like to play with dolls?"

Jean shakes her head negatively. The therapist pursues her quarry. "You don't like to play with dolls. Don't you see anything in here that you would like to play with? You may play with any of these things in here in any way that you want to." Jean still maintains the icy silence. Then the therapist says, "You don't want to play. You just want to sit here." Jean nods agreement. "Very well," says the therapist. She, too, sits down and silence descends upon both of them. But the therapist is tense. "Would you rather just talk?" she asks hopefully. "No," says Jean. The therapist taps her pencil on her barren notebook. She taps her foot. She looks a little annoyed at Jean. This silence is maddening. There is a silent battle going on between the two, of which Jean is surely aware.

If the girl has been fighting for acceptance outside the clinic, why must she continue here? If it is obvious that she does not want to play or talk, why not be accepting and permissive to the extent of letting her sit there in silence? After explaining the situation clearly enough so that she understands that she might play with any of the things in the playroom, or use the hour any way she desires, the accepting therapist would go along with the child and, if silence was the order of the hour, then silence it would be. It would seem well to include in the preliminary explanation to the girl that it is her privilege either to play or not to play as she desires, to talk or not to talk, and, after the girl has made the decision, the therapist should abide by it. The therapist might busy herself with notes—or with doodling if she feels that she must do something. She should be on the alert to reflect any feeling the girl might express. A deep sigh, a longing glance out the window, might safely be reflected to her——"It is boring to just sit here with me. Perhaps you would rather be outside." At that understanding, Jean might relax a little.

Establishing a Feeling of Permissiveness

During the first hour, the child explores the materials and is very alert to the therapist's attitude. That is why words alone are not enough. Permissiveness is established by the therapist's attitude toward the child, by facial expressions, tone of voice, and actions.

If the child spills water deliberately and the therapist immediately wipes it up, the action more less cancels the verbal expression of permissiveness.

If the therapist, thinking the child's problem is centered around family relationships, pushes the doll family toward the child with, "See the doll family? Wouldn't you like to play with them?" she is not granting permissiveness of choice to the child.

If the child picks up the ball of clay and rolls it idly between indecisive hands, the therapist will do well to refrain from commenting, "You don't know what to make." Such a remark might be taken by the child to indicate that the therapist is not satisfied to have the child roll the clay aimlessly back and forth. Permissiveness implies choice to use or not to use the materials according to the child's wishes.

There should be no attempt made to guide the actions or conversation of the child. That implies that there must be no probing questions directed toward the child.

For example, five-year-old May, who has been referred to the clinic for therapy because of a traumatic hospital experience, is playing with the family of dolls. She picks up the girl doll, places her in the toy wagon and pushes her across the floor. The therapist, thinking to capture the crucial experience says, "Is the little girl going to the hospital?" "Yes," says the child. "Is she afraid?" "Yes." "Then what happens?" asks the therapist. The child gets up, goes over to the window, turns her back on the therapist and doll family. "How much longer?" she asks. "Is the time up yet?" Thus the child wards off the probing. The child is not yet ready to explore the experience that has been so upsetting. She has not yet been accepted as she is. She has not been granted the permissiveness to open that door when she felt adequate to face what was beyond it.

When he feels so securely accepted by the therapist that he can beat up the mother doll, or bury the baby in the sand, or lie down on the floor and drink from a nursing bottle even though he is nine, ten, or eleven years old, and yet can do these things without a feeling of shame or guilt, then the therapist has established a feeling of permissiveness. The child is free to express his feelings. He gives vent to his most aggressive and destructive impulses. He screams, yells, throws the sand all over the place, spits water on the floor. He gets rid of his tensions. He becomes emotionally relaxed. Then, it seems, the groundwork for more constructive behavior has been laid.

Recognition and Reflection of Feelings

One day Jack went home for a visit. He had been planning on this visit for a long time. He wanted to get his toys. He had been coming for play-therapy contacts for five weeks before the home visit. This was his first day back.

JACK. Well, I went home. [*He sat down at the paint table and drew a clean sheet of paper toward him, opened the box of paints, and began to paint, still grinning happily.*] I saw my father and my brother. And do you know why they hadn't come to see me?

THERAPIST. No.

JACK. Because they thought it would make me feel sad to see them and then have them leave me here. That's what my father said. And they took me on a picnic and we had ice cream and candy and a boat ride. I told my father I wanted to bring my toys back. I asked about my gun. And we went out in the country one day, too.

[*All the time Jack was relating the story of his visit back home, he was painting a tiny green spot in the middle of the paper and all round the green spot a growing expanse of black. Finally the paper was covered over with the black paint.*] Yep, I went home all right. But I didn't get my toys. And my brother had broken my gun. And he had lots of his own toys. He has fun all the time. He stays there.

THERAPIST. You went home, but you were disappointed in your visit. [*This statement is interpretation. The therapist is drawing a conclusion from what Jack had said.*] You didn't get the toys you went after and your gun had been broken.

JACK. Yes. [*He got up from the table and went over to the shelf and got the nursing bottle. He brought it back to the table and sat down across from the therapist.*] I told him a thing or two. I told him I wanted my toys. [*He seemed very close to tears. He looked at the therapist.*] Me baby [*sucking on the nursing bottle*].

THERAPIST. Now you are a baby. You don't think they treated you very nice when you went home. [*This, too, is interpretation, going beyond what the child expressed. In reality, it seems to be what the therapist feels about the home situation, but it was close enough to Jack's feelings to be acceptable by him.*]

[*Jack filled his mouth with water. He leaned over and spat it on the floor.*]

JACK. Look I spit on my home.

THERAPIST. You spit on your home.

[*Jack jerked off the nipple and filled his mouth again and once more spat on the floor.*]

JACK. I spit on my brother. I spit on my father. I spit right in their very faces. They wouldn't give me my toys. He broke my gun. I'll show them. I'll spit on them. [*Again and again he filled his mouth with water and spat it on the floor.*]

THERAPIST. You are very angry with your brother and your father. You would like to spit right in their faces because of the way they have treated you.

In this case the boy progresses from a polite verbalization about his trip home to a violent display of his true feelings. It is interesting to note how he releases his feelings with deeper significance as he receives recognition for each feeling that he does express.

IMPLICATIONS

Recall any experience you have had or observed in dealing with a difficult child—one who was hostile, dependent, or withdrawn. To what extent does the atmosphere created by the therapist differ from other situations you have observed? How do the methods of the therapist differ? Can this kind of atmosphere and similar methods be used in other everyday situations, such as dealing with a difficult roommate, employer, or adversary? How might we adapt these methods to adults? What effect does this approach have on the person on whom they are used?

REFERENCES

You may find books by Carl Rogers (1939, 1951) of value. Also, see Axline's entire book (1947), and another book on play therapy by Moustakas (1953).

[58] UNDERSTANDING THE ALCOHOLIC

For a long time, the nondrinker and the moderate drinker viewed the chronic inebriate as a person of defective character; alcoholism was not regarded as a health or psychological problem. Today most professional workers, including the educated clergyman, know that the individual with poor control over alcoholic drinking is in some way allergic to the effects of alcohol as a beverage.

Alcoholism has been called a disease, and some biologists hypothesize that the drinker has a metabolic pattern that results in nutritional deficiencies predisposing him to become addicted to alcohol. The studies in the following selection show characteristics commonly found among alcoholics. In the United States the excessive use of alcohol is a serious health problem, with personal and social dangers, and it is not decreasing in magnitude. Its control will require the intelligence of all professions concerned with the welfare of the human being. Psychological conditions predisposing the individual to addiction are significant; thus rehabilitation of the alcoholic requires psychological as well as medical, clerical, and psychiatric resources.

The following selection is a portion of an address given at one of the many conferences on alcoholism sponsored by the National Institute of Mental Health, U. S. Public Health Service. The author gives special attention to the religious resources because, as he points out, it has been discovered that 42 per cent of the people interviewed in a survey on alcoholism went first to the clergy for help with their problem.

One of the organizations that has been most helpful in keeping the alcoholic sober is Alcoholics Anonymous. It has a nonsectarian religious orientation. The psychologist with his objective orientation may regard this whole-person commitment on the part of the alcoholic as both a social and psychological force which can affect behavior. We have included that portion of the address which describes seven of the twelve steps of Alcoholics Anonymous—the heart of the organization's creed and program and a good example of the lay therapeutic approach. Catanzaro is medical director of the Alcoholic Rehabilitation Program at Avon Park, Florida.

Ronald J. Catanzaro

Reprinted from Ronald J. Catanzaro, publication of Conference on Alcoholism (Lake Windermere Lodge, Roach, Missouri, 1964), by permission of the author.

UNDERSTANDING THE ALCOHOLIC

In the interest of understanding the alcoholic, let us explore together: (1) factors which appear to be important in causing a person to become an alcoholic and (2) factors which prevent him from having his disease arrested.

Factors Causing a Person to Become an Alcoholic

No one knows all the factors involved in causing a person to become an alcoholic. In light of the current literature on alcoholism and my own experience in the field, most theories of etiology of alcoholism fall into three categories: biological, psychological, and sociocultural.

BIOLOGIC THEORIES. Inherited peculiarities of body biology have been indicted as the cause of alcoholism by many. Dr. E. M. Jellinek (1960), one of the most distinguished workers in the field of alcoholism, compiled a number of studies dealing with rates of alcoholism in families. He found an over-all average of 52 per cent of alcoholics had at least one alcoholic parent. Conversely, the expectancy rate of alcoholism in the children of families where at least one parent is an alcoholic is between 20 and 30 per cent. In contrast, the expectancy rate of alcoholism in the general population is only between 2 and 3 per cent. Two additional personal observations have always struck me as very interesting. Firstly, many of my alcoholic patients have stated that they literally lost control of the use of alcohol with their first experience with alcohol as a teenager. As one alcoholic told me: "The first time I remember drinking was when I was fourteen down in my Daddy's wine cellar. I drank until I got so drunk and sick I vomited." Many never touched a drink again until years later, and when they did, they again drank to the point of drunkenness and have continued to do so since. One might postulate that these people have a high degree of genetic biologic determinancy for addiction to alcohol.

The second interesting observation is that some of my patients are overly dependent, immature, emotionally unstable, come from broken or unhappy homes, and in general have most of the characteristics frequently thought to be the basis of alcoholism by those who adhere to psychologic factors as the cause. Several of these people have told me how they actually set out to become alcoholics during a very unhappy period in their lives. They hoped that once they became an alcoholic, they wouldn't care about anything anymore, including their troubles. They reported drinking heavily over many months and finally decided the whole experiment was a failure; they didn't get much of a lift out of drinking and were tired of the hangover effects of alcohol so they quit without any trouble. Some of them stated they take occasional social drinks now and have no desire to drink heavily. One might postulate that these people have a very low degree of genetic biologic determinancy to become addicted to alcohol—"they just don't have what it takes."

Exactly how would such a genetic biologic factor work? R. J. Williams (1949) postulates that alcoholism may be caused by an inherited metabolic pattern which results in nutritional deficiencies and consequently gives rise to a craving for the specific nutrient called alcohol. No such metabolic deficiency has ever been proven. Does the alcoholic suffer from some other type of metabolic abnormality such as an endocrine imbalance which biologically predisposes him to become addicted to alcohol as J. J. Smith postulates? Again, no conclusive evidence of this has yet come to light. Could the alcoholic genetically inherit an emotional make-up which predisposes to alcoholism (Diethelm, 1955)? A fascinating idea, but no convincing evidence has ever been uncovered. Others that hold to biologic etiology of alcoholism state that if the biologic factor was not inherited, it may well be acquired. Through repeated bouts of heavy drinking, a person may develop an unusual sensitivity to alcohol, that is, he may actually become allergic to alcohol as many members of Alcoholics Anonymous believe. Again, no such allergy has ever been demonstrated.

PSYCHOLOGIC THEORIES.   Other workers in the field of alcoholism feel that since no biologic peculiarities of alcoholics have been discovered, in spite of extensive investigation, the most likely cause of alcoholism lies in the psychologic area. Howard Clinebell, a doctor of theology and a Methodist minister, carefully interviewed 77 alcoholics regarding their home life as a child. He found that 57 per cent of the alcoholics came from severely inadequate homes (Clinebell, 1956). The four outstanding parental characteristics of these homes were authoritarianism, success worship, moralism, and overt rejection. The first three of these characteristics are in part subtle forms of rejection also. The growing child needs generous portions of parental love and harmony. He must feel wanted because of what he is, not because of what he can give to the parents. He must be taught self-control, but a control which is flexible and adjustable to life demands. He must be allowed to mature emotionally so that he can release strong emotions in an efficient and harmless way and thus allow his temperament to remain on a relatively even plateau during his life. His parents must enable him to change the focus of his life from a typically self-centered childish pattern to an extroverted pattern. Finally, his parents must instill in him a reason for living, a spiritual sense of values.

In the best of homes, parents fall short of accomplishing this. It has been observed though that children from severely inadequate homes, as were the people in Dr. Clinebell's study, are correspondingly severely stunted in their psychological growth in many of the above areas. It has also been observed that emotionally immature adults meet their problems as would a child. One of the outstanding characteristics of children is their vivid imagination, *i.e.*, their ability to shut out reality. Consider children's fairy tales which invariably end on the theme "And they lived happily ever after." Real life certainly does not always end in happiness. Consider now an adult with the emotional make-up of a child. Is it unreasonable to postulate that this emotionally immature adult, finding that he is unable to meet life's everyday problems because he is emotionally stunted, attempts to solve his problems in a make-believe childish manner, say by drinking a magic potion (alcohol) which will make his problems disappear temporarily? And when the magic potion begins wearing off and he again begins to feel his problems, he simply drinks more potion. Eventually life is unbearable without the potion.

In psychologic tests of alcoholics, the following are the most commonly found characteristics (Clinebell, 1956): (1) high level of anxiety in interpersonal relations; (2) emotional immaturity; (3) ambivalence toward authority; (4) low frustration tolerance; (5) grandiosity; (6) low self-esteem; (7) feelings of isolation; (8) perfectionism; (9) guilt; (10) compulsiveness.

Alcohol's ability to reduce a high level of anxiety in interpersonal relations has caused Dr. Jellinek to dub alcohol "a social lubricant." Many alcoholics early in their disease use alcohol as a drug for calming anxious and insecure feelings which arise at a social gathering. As their disease progresses, they seem to become even less able to relate to people and therefore become even more dependent on alcohol to "get in the mood to relax and have fun." Thus, as their inability to deal with people effectively becomes more pronounced, they need increasing amounts of alcohol to blot out this increasingly unpleasant reality. It has been my personal experience in a follow-up study of alcoholics treated in a military hospital that the ones who have attained the longest period of sobriety are usually the ones who have noted most improvement in ability to get along with their friends. Conversely, the ones who have been able to maintain little sobriety also note little improvement in ability to get along with their friends.

Emotional immaturity includes being excessively moody, demanding that one's desires be met promptly, having a violent temper, expressing one's emotions through acts rather than words, and being self-centered. Certainly many alcoholics can be described thus. It is not certain, though, whether these alcoholics had always been this way or became this way only after their disease of alcoholism had become established.

Ambivalence toward authority as emphasized by Giorgio Lolli is an extremely prevalent symptom of alcoholics. A constant struggle goes on in many alcoholics between the need to be dependent and subservient and the need to be dominant and mighty. The common example is the alcoholic who married a domineering wife because of his need to be dependent on someone, and upon getting drunk beats her up to prove he is really the dominant one.

Low frustration tolerance is part of emotional immaturity and is a common attribute of children as well as alcoholics. It is this limited ability to stand frustration that often causes the alcoholic to resume drinking.

Grandiosity is present in the alcoholic when he is sober as well as drinking. Everyone knows of the alcoholic sitting in a bar who boasts to his drinking chums of the fantastic business deal he is about to close tomorrow. And when the alcoholic sobers up the next morning, he manifests the opposite side of the same coin. He states to his wife: "I'm the worst person in the world, I've failed in everything I've ever done." To be all that bad is no small accomplishment either.

Low self-esteem is one of the important traits that helps alcoholics continue to drink. "When I drink I feel like a champ, a king, and the next morning I realize what a crumb I am," as one alcoholic expressed it to me. This being the case, what a great temptation it is to have "just one more drink" to feel good again.

Feelings of isolation are the natural outgrowth of his inability to get along with people. As the alcoholic continues drinking, his behavior and conversation become less acceptable to those about him, and consequently his family and friends begin isolating him from their social circle.

Perfectionism and compulsiveness are components of grandiosity. All three of these symptoms are largely an outgrowth of intense feelings of guilt, feelings of being unloved and unlovable. The alcoholic must prove that he is better than his fellow man so that he will not have to feel so guilty about his failures whenever he is sober. For the alcoholic, to be successful is to be loved, to fail is to be unloved.

In order to avoid feeling the guilt which facing unpleasant reality would cause, the alcoholic builds up defenses which are founded in unreality. Tiebout calls these defenses an "alcoholic shell," thus indicating the brittle barrier one must traverse before getting the alcoholic to face his problem realistically. The alcoholic in order to feel worthwhile must maintain a self-image which is identical to his ideal self. As his disease progresses his real self becomes farther and farther removed from this ideal self. In order to feel secure, he must therefore blot out his real self, which he does partly with alcohol and partly with his alcoholic shell of excuses. This unrealistic feeling of being secure in one's own make-believe world is quite comparable to the brand of philosophy expounded by Charles M. Schulz's cartoon character, "Peanuts," when he says, "Security is a thumb and a blanket."

Consequently, we must understand that asking a man to admit he is an-alcoholic is asking him to surrender his meticulously constructed shell of unreality, to realize his life has become confused and chaotic and to acknowledge that he has fallen miserably short of the ideal self which he so desperately needs to be. One must note here the parallel between the phenomenon of truly accepting one's self as an alcoholic who must now try to refrain from drinking in order to be at peace with himself and the phenomenon of religious conversion where one truly accepts one's self as a sinner and must now try to refrain from sinning in order to be at peace with himself.

Of all the psychological characteristics involved in making a person addicted to alcohol, it appears that the two most important characteristics are a chronic high-anxiety level and a chronic inability to face unpleasant reality. These two factors combine to make one not only an alcoholic, but also an addictive personality. It is well known by those who work extensively with alcoholics that someone addicted to alcohol can easily become addicted to other drugs, including barbiturates, certain tranquilizers, chloralhydrate, paralydehyde, etc. Thus, other addicting drugs which also reduce anxiety and blot out reality may be readily substituted for alcohol.

A classical experiment helping to elucidate the mechanism of addiction to alcohol was made by Masserman and Yum (1946). They produced a neurosis in cats by creating an internal conflict in them between fear of pain and desire for food. They taught the cats to push a lever which released a pellet of food to them. Then they placed an electric charge on the lever which shocked the cats whenever they touched the lever. The cats thus were torn between a desire for food and a fear of being shocked. They began behaving in a characteristically neurotic way, losing all interest in activities which previously occupied them. When the cats were given an injection of alcohol, their anxiety was alleviated, their neurotic conflict was numbed and they resumed pressing the lever, eating and behaving normally. Alcohol, which is classified by physiologists as an anesthetic, had made the shock they received painless, that is, as long as they had alcohol in their body. Soon they had become addicted to spiked milk which they had previously ignored. In this particular experiment with cats, the addiction was broken only after the original neurosis was extinguished. In human beings it appears that even after successful psychoanalytic treatment of underlying neurosis the addictive tendency does not disappear.

SOCIOCULTURAL THEORIES. Since the importance of sociocultural factors in the causation of alcoholism is the particular area of interest of Dr. Pittman (1962), I will point out only one observation. Alcoholism tends to be extremely common among certain ethnic groups such as the Irish and French. This fact does not appear to be explained simply by observing that most Irishmen and Frenchmen have tasted of spirits at some time in their life. In a recent study of the Jewish culture, it was reported that 91 per cent of the group had first tasted alcoholic beverages while they were between the ages of five and seven years old. Yet alcoholism is very rare among the Jews. Thus, some other factor besides exposure to alcohol must determine whether the person becomes an alcoholic or not.

FACTORS WHICH PREVENT HIM FROM BREAKING HIS ADDICTION

What are the key factors which prevent the alcoholic from successfully breaking his addiction? First of all one must understand the point that Dr. E. M. Jellinek (1960) emphasized so often, that alcoholism is a *progressive disease*, i.e., the alcoholic progressively deteriorates. Initially, then, such personality traits as marked anxiety in interpersonal relations, emotional immaturity, feelings of inadequacy, etc., may be important in causing a person to begin drinking heavily. As he passes from heavy social drinking to early alcoholism, deterioration begins. Thus, personality traits which were originally defective become even more defective and new character defects are added. In addition, realities of life become progressively more grim as the alcoholic begins neglecting his problems rather than solving them.

The nonprofessional community around him regards these events simply as signs of moral weakness and lack of will power. Upon sobering up each morning the alcoholic, who himself holds similar moral convictions as does the community about him, also begins regarding himself condescendingly. The only way he can relieve these agonizing feelings is to drink some more. Even the professional members of the community, including doctors, nurses, clergymen, social workers, etc., often hold the same erroneous views as does the rest of the community. Thus the trap is complete. Everywhere he turns for help—to his own resources, to his family and friends, to his minister and doctor—he meets a condescending stare. How then can this vicious cycle be broken?

TREATMENT RESOURCES

The problem of getting the alcoholic under treatment and keeping him there is certainly one of the major problems in the field of alcoholism today. Often, the alcoholic initially has to be coerced into treatment, partly because of his agonizing memories of being repeatedly rejected and partly because of his fear of squarely facing reality. At other times, the alcoholic himself initiates the plea for help but does not succeed in finding it. Although there is no pat answer for successfully treating the alcoholic, there are available community resources which are of great aid in achieving this goal. Brief mention will now be given of each of these resources.

1. Well-informed and interested clergymen are essential. A study recently published in a booklet entitled *Americans View Their Mental Health* (Gurin, *et al.*, 1960) revealed that 42 per cent of the people interviewed went first to the clergy for help with their personal problems. If the alcoholic or his family who first turns to the clergy for help meets with misinformation or lack of understanding, it may be many years before another try is made at arresting this dreadful disease.

2. Local physicians who understand the problem of alcoholism are invaluable in helping the alcoholic to "dry out" successfully and then in helping him to continue his sobriety (Catanzaro, 1964). Most communities have at least a few such understanding physicians and the clergyman should make it his business to become acquainted with them before their help is needed in treating an alcoholic parishioner.

3. Almost every sizable community has its active chapter of Alcoholics Anonymous. The clergyman should acquaint himself with at least one male and one female member of this group so that he can enlist their aid when a parishioner seeks help. The minister and several members of the parish should attend at least a few meetings of Alcoholics Anonymous so they can better understand and counsel the alcoholic when he comes for help.

4. The alcoholic is often involved with the traffic court and the probate court (Anon., 1963). A judge who has become interested in rehabilitating alcoholics rather than avoiding or punishing them is an invaluable ally for any professional person trying to help the alcoholic.

5. The clergyman should acquaint himself with and support his local Council on Alcoholism. These councils have as their chief goal to replace the community's erroneous and harmful concepts of alcoholism with accurate and constructive information. This makes it much easier for the alcoholic and his family to begin breaking the vicious cycle of addiction.

6. A long list of good books on alcoholism, which will greatly aid the minister in his pastoral counseling of the alcoholic and his family, is available from the National Council on Alcoholism, New York Academy of Medicine Building, 2 East 103rd Street, New York, N.Y. 10029. Ontstanding in this regard are the books by Howard Clinebell and Thomas Shippe, both of whom are ministers, by Marty Mann who is the founder of the National Council on Alcoholism, and by Dr. David Pittman, Director of the Alcoholic Treatment and Research Center in St. Louis.

As soon as an alcoholic has dried out and has begun building up defenses against drinking, he must find a new way of life if he is going to remain sober. True rehabilitation of the alcoholic implies not only abstinence from the use of alcohol, but also a real change in the patient's personality. If an alcoholic stops drinking and remains functioning in a grossly inadequate manner, little has been accomplished. Alcoholics Anonymous epitomizes in one word the personality change which must accompany successful sobriety; they call it "Serenity." What does "Serenity" involve? It involves an inner feeling of being at peace with one's self, one's fellow man, and one's God. The Twelve Steps of Alcoholics Anonymous are specifically pointed at these three areas of one's personality.

If you are now asking "How can the clergy best use its special talents to help the alcoholic?" the answer lies in this word "Serenity." To repeat the definition, Serenity: "an inner feeling of being at peace with one's self, one's fellow man, and one's God." Yes, one's God! Here is where the clergyman must be of help. No other member of the rehabilitation team can so effectively help a man be at peace with God as can a minister. To emphasize the alcoholic's need to be at peace with God, I will quote the second through the seventh steps of the Twelve Steps of Alcoholics Anonymous (Anon., 1955):

Step 2. Came to believe that a power greater than ourselves could restore us to sanity.

Step 3. Made a decision to turn our will and our lives over to the care of God as we understand Him.

Step 4. Made a searching and fearless moral inventory of ourselves.

Step 5. Admitted to God, to ourselves, and to another human being the exact nature of our wrongs.

Step 6. Were entirely ready to have God remove all these defects of character.

Step 7. Humbly asked Him to remove our shortcomings.

Through continued pastoral counseling, the alcoholic can be once more made aware of the Gospel, whereas for years he had thought of God, like one alcoholic put it, as "The Ten Commandments carrying a big stick."

Whether or not it is true that a loss of spiritual values is important in the development of alcoholism, it is felt by many of those who treat alcoholics successfully that a vital part of recovery from alcoholism is finding a new meaning to life, having a spiritual reawakening of one's life. And who can be more effective in this area than a minister? An alcoholic whom I treated, who did not maintain any semblance of sobriety, told me once, "What's there to stay sober for? Life has no meaning for me; there's really nothing to live for. The only time I can forget about how empty my life is, is when my brain is full of alcohol." One wonders what effect a spiritual reawakening would have had on the course of this man's illness.

Finally, where does the psychiatrist fit into the alcoholic rehabilitation team? The psychiatrist due to his specialized training first as a physician and second as one interested in the psychological aspects of illness can help in three principal ways:

1. As an understanding physician, the psychiatrist can help the alcoholic dry out, acquaint him with the various modalities of help in the community and give him supportive psychiatric help while he is trying to firmly establish his sobriety.

2. As a professional member of the community, the psychiatrist can aid the community in understanding the alcoholic and promote the community, to set up adequate treatment facilities for him (Jones, 1962).

3. After the alcoholic has maintained his sobriety for six months or more and has explored at least a few of the community resources available to help him, he may still find himself debilitated by neurotic conflicts. The psychiatrist can at this time employ more classical techniques of psychotherapy to aid him in resolving these residual internal conflicts. Before the alcoholic has been sober for at least six months, his ego structure is not sufficiently stable to withstand the frequently upsetting experience of the usual psychoanalytic techniques used in treatment of neurosis.

In summary, the more we understand about the alcoholic, what causes him to get ill, what prevents him from getting well, and how we in our own special fields can be of particular help to him, the more effective will be our efforts to answer his cry for help.

IMPLICATIONS

After reviewing the biological, psychological, and sociocultural themes, you may want to take a position as to what you think are the most essential conditions leading to alcoholism. You may find it interesting to discuss your position with someone who differs from you, utilizing from this article the data that support your conclusions as well as the significance of these data. Possibly you have concluded that whereas individuals with an alcoholic problem have many factors in common, each individual is complex and unique, and the means of getting him to face the reality of his condition and to accept assistance and treatment will vary among individuals. You may have a specific person in mind, and you might speculate as to which of the resources mentioned in this selection might have the greatest effectiveness.

REFERENCES

Under "Treatment Resources," in the preceding article, Catanzaro calls your attention to books that are helpful in counseling the alcoholic and his family, available from the National Council on Alcoholism.

An example of this kind of assistance is found in a recent publication by Whitney (1965), who has had long experience in getting the alcoholic into the hands of the proper person for treatment. She presents three interesting cases of male alcoholics and a fourth case of a female.

[59] FAMILY THERAPY: UNDERSTANDING AND CHANGING BEHAVIOR

Can it be that what is "wrong" with the mentally ill person does not reside in him alone? Is he better understood in the context of his significant social relationships—his family? How does this viewpoint alter traditional therapy? How does the therapist proceed to study communications among members of the family?

Murney and Schneider, who have been using the family-therapy approach with their mentally ill patients and their families over a period of time, clearly and interestingly describe their professional activities.

Richard G. Murney and Robert N. Schneider

Used with the permission of the authors.

Consider what happens to a family when one of its members has a psychiatric breakdown and must be hospitalized. In therapy with such a family in which the identified patient was a twenty-one-year-old only son in his first hospitalization, for "schizophrenic reaction, paranoid type," it became clear that his breakdown had a profound effect on his parents. Even after one year of hospitalization and marked improvement in their son, the parents were suffering in such a way that it had many of the qualities of grieving or mourning. The son's psychiatrist was sufficiently concerned about the father's depressive tendencies that he recommended private psychiatric treatment. These parents had practically stopped socializing with their friends after their son was hospitalized. In family therapy their inability to live their own lives became especially poignant and obvious when the prospect of the father's vacation arose. The parents wanted their son to be given a leave from the hospital to go with them on a trip. Although this was highly possible, they were asked by the therapist about their vacation plans should their son not be granted a leave. Their response was that, of course, they would go nowhere. As they expressed it, they couldn't go away on a vacation, knowing that their son would have to stay at the hospital. (It should be noted that they were considering a week's trip, to a place within 200 miles of the hospital; as mentioned, their son was showing progressive improvement and was going home every weekend so that the longest the family would be separated would have been one week.) The obvious overinvolvement of these parents in their son's difficulties comprised one of many considerations that resulted in therapeutic intervention with the whole family. Before going into other such considerations, it might be well to discuss what family therapy is and how it arose.

WHAT IS FAMILY THERAPY?

Family therapy can be defined as a *kind of therapy that focuses on the family as a unit,* even though only one of its members is obviously disturbed and is identified in and by the family as "sick, bad, stupid, or crazy" and therefore in need of help. Implied in this definition are a great many ideas, attitudes, and approaches that are relatively new among people who work in the applied areas of the behavioral sciences. In essence, a discussion of family therapy in terms of these newer emphases is the purpose of this paper. It might be well to outline these newer orientations and to briefly describe how they arose, particularly as they relate to the appearance and development of family therapy.

The above definition has three important aspects: (1) an emphasis on the family as a whole, *i.e.*, a focus on family interactions; (2) a new way of looking at the person in the family who is considered to be disturbed, the "identified patient"; and (3) a new way of considering the kinds of human behaviors that people find problematic, for which the term *dysfunctional* will be used. Let us consider each of these aspects.

FAMILY INTERACTIONS. Most simply, it can be supposed that family therapy arose as a practice because it offers some advantages that are not provided by other approaches to solving behavior problems. Since it has long been recognized that family relations play an important role in the development and maintenance of behavior problems, it is somewhat paradoxical that until quite recently families were not seen as units in the therapy situation. It became gradually apparent to therapists who were trying to effect changes in individual behavior that working with the individual alone was not enough—either for an understanding of the problems or to bring about lasting improvements. Seeing families in interaction promised to such therapists a better way to understand problems as well as to find solutions.

THE IDENTIFIED PATIENT. Experiences in observing family interactions have also altered the ways in which the identified patient is understood. Families who come to the attention of a therapist almost always have one member whom they think of as the "sick one," or the "bad one." However, although one person has been identified as a "patient" by the family, the therapist prefers to de-emphasize the focus on this one member and to shift the focus to family interactions. He prefers this approach because current considerations are bringing into question the traditional concepts of mental illness, delinquency, and so on, as reflecting something wrong with the person. The newer view considers that what is wrong does not entirely reside *in* the person, and it can be better understood in the context of the person's significant interpersonal relationships.

DYSFUNCTION. The term *dysfunction* will be used to designate the "what is wrong" mentioned above. Most students of human behavior agree that the family as a social unit has a number of functions to perform and maintain. Briefly, these functions usually include meeting the emotional needs of each family member, transmitting various culturally prescribed values and behaviors to the offspring, and providing an atmosphere for growth and development. The term *dysfunction* refers to the breakdown or distortion of any of these necessary functions. In actuality, the disruption of any one of these functions usually affects the others so that the entire system is disrupted. It is in this sense that a family system can be dysfunctional.

If family interactions are important, and if the identified patient is not the sole locus of difficulty, then it is reasonable to consider the idea that not only *persons* but also *families* can be dysfunctional. Family therapy focuses on family dysfunction, and some of the best clues to dysfunction can be found in the patterns of communications that a family demonstrates. More about communication will be said later.

To *summarize*, family therapy arose as a method of dealing with dysfunctional behavior because (1) traditional viewpoints about individual dysfunction began to appear inadequate in the understanding they provided and (2) traditional therapies began to appear limited with regard to producing changes in dysfunctioning.

WHY FAMILY THERAPY?

With some idea of what family therapy is and how it arose, a series of questions reasonably follows: Under what circumstances is family therapy indicated? What kinds of problems are reasonably and profitably approached via family therapy? Should family therapy be offered rather than any other form of therapy? Should it be offered in combination with other approaches? Each of these questions emphasizes a slightly different aspect of the problem, but the basic question that can be asked is, Why family therapy? To answer this question requires that a number of factors be considered. For convenience, two classes of considerations can be distinguished: (1) theoretical considerations and (2) practical considerations.

THEORETICAL CONSIDERATIONS. Certain guidelines about therapeutic intervention can be derived from the existing body of theory and knowledge concerning human behavior and behavior change. When family therapy is specifically under consideration, answers to such questions as, What do we know about family structure and function? and What do we know about behavior disorder? can be helpful. Along these lines there are at least two major theoretical considerations that would recommend family therapy as a suitable approach.

The *first* of these comes from evidence which indicates that *whatever is happening with one family member is related to, and has its impact on, the whole family group.* Family interrelationships can be thought of as a system: change in one part of the system depends, to some extent, on what is going on in the total system and has its effects, in some ways, on the whole system. In this sense, dysfunctional behavior on the part of one family member can be understood, at least in part, to be related to the total family system, and it can be expected, to a significant degree, to have its effects on the system. Family therapy would be indicated, then, when it is recognized that the entire family's functioning is involved, even though dysfunctioning is most apparent in one family member.

This consideration is illustrated by the case that opened this discussion. The quality of the feelings expressed by the parents in the case had two aspects—first, out of a sense of duty they would have felt neglectful to "go off and leave" their son "stuck at the hospital for a week"; second, they expressed their genuine belief that they couldn't possibly enjoy themselves under those circumstances. Without going into further detail, this incident can be used to exemplify what was happening in this family system as a result of a disruption imposed by psychiatric hospitalization. In the first place, the meaning of the "grieving" observed in the family organization and its implications about this family and its "sick" member were considered. One of the things that has been observed about the families who have a schizophrenic member is the lack of differentiation, or "separateness," of the members of these families. It is as if the family system is a tightly organized whole and that each member relinquishes his own individuality to that whole.

This lack of separateness implies many things about such a family; but the special point being made here is that, when the son in this family had a breakdown, it *directly* and *overwhelmingly* affected the lives of his mother and father—they *had to* suffer as he suffered. They had to grieve, or mourn, his loss from the family unit, almost as if he had been lost to death. The individual functioning of each of the parents, as well as their cooperative functioning as a married couple, was markedly affected by the breakdown in functioning of the son (and these alterations in the parents' functioning, in turn, had their effects on the son). One of the goals of therapy with this family was to help the parents recover their individuality, to help the son develop his own sense of separateness, and to help the family as a unit to participate in the whole, without the necessity of totally subjugating the identity of each to that whole. A great deal could be said about lack of family and individual differentiation and the development of schizophrenia, but it is beyond the scope of this discussion.

To *summarize* the point being made here, family therapy seemed indicated for this family because it was considered that the son's progress could only be continued and maintained, and the mother's and father's equilibrium re-established, if the family relationships were the focus of therapeutic intervention.

A *second* kind of theoretical consideration concerns the *meaning and nature of dysfunctional behaviors.* Traditionally, these behaviors have been considered to be symptoms of mental illness, with the locus of the difficulty seen as within the person. Currently, a new look is being taken at these problems, and there is evidence to support an approach that attempts to understand such difficulties not simply as reflecting deficits of character or personality, but also as reflecting difficulties in important, ongoing, interpersonal relationships. Thus, the focus is shifting from attention to the personality functioning of the "sick" one to the meanings of his "sick" behaviors in the context of his relationships to others, especially his family.

Although the sick member's personality function is by no means ignored in this approach, emphasis shifts from the study of the "intrapsychic" to a more intensive attempt to understand the person's significant relationships as well as the *other* persons in these relationships. Perhaps another way of characterizing this shift in emphasis is to describe it as a move from considering only a dysfunctional *person* to the possibility of considering dysfunctional *relationships*. This places the meaning of "symptoms" in an entirely new context (which will receive further discussion in the next section). But to return to our main point, family therapy would seem indicated when it appears that the identified patient's symptoms are indirect manifestations of problematic family relationships. A general kind of example, without going into specific details, can be cited. It is not uncommon, in child-guidance work, to have a child brought in by his parents for treatment because he is a "behavior problem." In therapy with these families, it has been found that in order to understand the meaning of the child's dysfunctional behavior, it is necessary to explore conflicts between the parents; frequently it has been found that parents who are not able to recognize or deal directly with their own conflicts become focused on the child, who mediates their difficulties. When these marital conflicts become recognized and new ways of coping with them are learned, the behavior problem of the child discontinues. In these situations it is common that the particular nature of the child's problem is directly related to the hidden conflict between the parents. It goes without saying that in therapy all of these details must be explored in order to understand why the parents cannot deal with their conflicts more directly, why they have focused on this particular child (if there are other children), why the child displays his problem. The important point here is that the symptoms of the child are directly related to, and have their meaning in, dysfunctional family relations, and do not simply "reside in" the child.

To *summarize* the theoretical considerations that recommend family therapy, evidence (research and clinical) indicates (1) that families of an identified patient are more often than not intimately involved in the beginnings and maintenance of his difficulty, and (2) that his difficulty is therefore as much reflection of dysfunctional family relationships as it is an expression of dysfunction on his part alone. To try to reach an enduring resolution of dysfunction, then, requires that families of identified patients cannot be excluded from therapeutic intervention.

PRACTICAL CONSIDERATIONS. So-called practical considerations are closely related to the theoretical and proceed from them.

One practical consideration concerns the "closeness" in the family of the identified patient. The more involved the family is with the identified patient, the greater is the likelihood that family therapy is indicated. This is most often true when the identified patient is a child, but it is also true in other instances, as with some identified patients who are hospitalized with psychiatric difficulties. In these instances, in which the family is very involved, the therapist might find himself doing family therapy inadvertently and informally, e.g., on the telephone in response to frequent inquiries about the identified patient and his progress. Even excluding the theoretical considerations which would point to family therapy as the *best* approach, a therapist might find it more productive of his time and energies to formalize his interactions with family members by setting up a definite time to meet and talk with them.

A second practical consideration concerns the progress (or lack of it) with a given identified patient. When there is a reasonable expectation that a patient should be improving and he is not, a search for the reasons behind this failure might lead to the exploration of family relations. With hospitalized psychiatric patients, this possibility can be reflected in a variety of ways: (1) the patient readily improves in the hospital but has a setback every time he goes home; (2) the patient is judged to have gained as much as possible from hospitalization, is ready to return to his family, but the family is, quite honestly, not ready to receive him; and (3) the patient does not or cannot use other therapeutic approaches because he tends to minimize his difficulties and thereby avoid confronting them. The immediacy of dealing with his own family members who usually are very aware of problems makes it more difficult for him to avoid, evade, or minimize difficulties that require his attention.

A final set of practical considerations that can only be touched on here involve the role of the therapist. In the first place, therapists whose previous therapeutic endeavors excluded contacts with their patients' families have characterized their subsequent experiences with family therapy as "eye-opening." In general, they feel that their understanding of the patient (not to mention the family interactions) becomes a great deal more comprehensive than was ever possible in individual therapy. In addition, therapists typically observe that family therapy offers a much wider range of possible kinds of intervention than can be planned in advance. In short, a common observation made by therapists is that family therapy provides new and increasingly varied kinds of participation in psychotherapy both for the patients and for the therapists. From this point of view, family therapy becomes practical when the therapist becomes dissatisfied with the limitations of understanding and therapeutic progress imposed by other forms of therapy.

These, then, are the general kinds of considerations—theoretical and practical—that might indicate family therapy. Having discussed to this point the what and why of family therapy, let us turn now to the how.

How Does Family Therapy Proceed?

There are many different ways to approach therapy with families, and there is a large and growing literature on the subject. In this discussion, one such approach will be described, the *communications* approach. The presentation is divided into two main sections: first, a discussion of what is meant by communication, why it is a point of focus in therapy, and how it is used in therapy; and second, a discussion of communications theory as it underlies the practice of family therapy.

A FOCUS ON COMMUNICATIONS. In this context the word *communications* refers to the interactions or transactions, both *verbal and nonverbal*, that take place necessarily when any two (or more) people get together. In the next section, more will be said about an assumption underlying human relationships, namely, that people cannot *not* communicate. Granting this assumption provides a very helpful focus of procedure in family therapy: since people unavoidably communicate, their communications *in the therapy* session provide a method both for understanding the people and for attempting to alter their relationships. With this focus, the process of therapy, in large part, consists of gaining an understanding of how the family members communicate with each other.

How does each person express his thoughts, feelings, and actions? Are his expressions clear, direct, and relatively consistent? In turn, how are they "received" by the other family members? Are his "messages" *understood* as the "sender" means for them to be? If not, what are the sources of communication breakdown? With these and many other similar questions in mind, the therapist begins to formulate a picture of how the members of a given family communicate. But even more importantly, he tries to make clear to the family the patterns of communication that he observes in order to help the family members reach a better understanding of themselves, each other, and the nature of their interactions. The process of communication, then, serves the dual purpose of helping the therapist to understand and to intervene in the functioning of the family. Additionally, to the extent that he can express himself clearly, directly, and explicitly, his communication can serve as a model for understanding and improving family relationships. Thus the communication process comprises a method of inquiry as well as a vehicle for intervention, and it is primarily to serve these purposes that it provides the basic focus in family therapy.

Another useful purpose served by focusing on communications in therapy resides in the emphasis that is placed on *interaction*. Most typically it is the current, ongoing, here-and-now interactions of the family that receive attention, and this is of value for at least two reasons: (1) there is a reality about immediacy that has an impact on people which is often lacking in more abstract discussions of thoughts, feelings, and actions; (2) focusing on interaction de-emphasizes the placing of "blame" on any particular family member. In connection with the latter, it has been observed that in searching for an undersatnding of the sources of family difficulties, people often tend to distort this search into a placing of blame. In part this stems from the tendency to consider dysfunctioning as a personal trait, residing *in* a person; in part it stems from attempts to seek out cause-and-effect relationships. In any event, the tendency to find someone to blame—even when it is oneself—almost always impedes progress, and in family therapy this tendency can be dealt with by focusing on family interactions: since interaction must involve participation by at least two people, blaming any particular person becomes less meaningful.

It is important to note at this point that the process of family therapy is not only an analysis and explication of the communication process. Typically, a great deal of time is devoted to *specific and concrete family problems*—problems that have a long history in the family, such as how the "rules" are made, and problems that arise from crises that occur. At these times the communications processes are in the background, perhaps always under the watchful eye of the therapist but not providing the content of the discussion. In this way there is a going back and forth between the content of problems and the *process* of understanding and resolving them (*i.e.*, the communication process).

COMMUNICATIONS THEORY. It has been relatively recently that human communication has become the subject of scientific observation and study. Defining human communication broadly as any behavior occurring in a social context, the students of this approach focus upon the ways in which people affect each other by the "message character" of their behavior. The message character of behavior refers to the fact that all behavior contains messages from one person (the sender) to another (the receiver). Current ideas about the nature of these messages will be presented below. The important point to be made here is that within the framework of the communications approach, relationships and interactions between people rather than internal intrapsychic processes in a single person are the focus of investigation. In communication *theory* there have developed three basic premises about the message character of behavior, which are directly and productively applicable to an understanding of the processes of family function and dysfunction. Although these premises can be stated quite simply, their implications can throw light upon a complex array of phenomena which are observed in the arena of family interactions.

Premise 1. One cannot *not* communicate. This follows with logical inevitability from the definition of human communication as any behavior in a social context. People often believe that they are not communicating unless they are intentionally directing a spoken or written message to someone. Yet, silence or the failure to act in a manner appropriate to a given situation are only two of many nonverbal ways of communicating. In most instances these responses are indirect ways of commenting upon the communication of another. As a tactic in human interactions, their indirectness has both a positive and negative value. On the positive side it lends itself to tactful disagreement as preliminary and preparatory to more direct communication.

Where open disagreement can not yet be tolerated, it is potentially possible that this tactic may open the way to mutual understanding. More frequently, however, such indirectness is used to disqualify the communication of another. Disqualification here refers to a kind of communication by which one can disagree with or negate another and yet evade responsibility for taking a stand. For example, your ignoring the greeting of another by silence may disqualify his implication of a friendly relationship. Should he, however, interpret your silence as a snub and call it to your attention, you can easily plead that you didn't hear him, were preoccupied, and so on. This denial is possible because of the ambiguity of the explicit behavior—silence—which may or may not be a means of conveying an implicit disqualification.

Premise 2. The message that the sender intends to convey is not necessarily the message that is received. This premise is obviously closely related to the first premise. In the foregoing example, the silence perceived as a snub may not have been intended as such. Each of us tends to consider his own view of reality as the only possible one and to expect that others share this view. When it becomes obvious that another does not share this view, the disagreement is frequently attributed to deliberate distortion, stupidity, or craziness on the part of the others. Badness, stupidity, and sickness then are the angry accusations frequently heard when two people interpret each other's messages differently or differ in their understanding of the context of the situation in which they are communicating. "Hello, how are you today?" intended by the speaker as a conventional, casual greeting may be responded to by a hypochondriac as a message of deep interest in his physical well-being and an invitation to describe in morbid detail his myriad symptomatology. Suffice it to say, the ensuing interaction may result in either or both parties angrily resenting the stupidity of the other. "Did you like that play the other night?" a question which may be intended as conversation opener in a social gathering may easily be interpreted as a simple request for information. Such an interpretation, made in such a context and followed by a simple yes or no response, may in turn be received as a snub.

Premise 3. "Every communication has not only a content or an information message but also contains within it another message which is *about* this information message." This second message "frames" the content message in that it tells (1) how the sender intends for the information to be received and (2) how the sender conceives of his relationship to the receiver. One aspect of this framing of the content is provided by both general and specific aspects of the context in which the communication occurs. A quiet "Please come over here and sit down" spoken by a mother to her young child may have quite a different meaning when spoken in a formal social gathering with many adults present than when said in a gathering of young children. It is easily seen, further, that many other nonverbal aspects of this communication, such as tone of voice, gestures and facial expression, will serve further to frame the literal words of the information message so that the receiver may understand "what it is about" and how the sender is construing their relationship at this point. The manifold opportunities for conflict between these levels of message, *i.e.*, the level of literal information content and the contextual messages which frame it, are apparent. This conflict may, in the instance cited, lead the child to act other than in accord with the message content, and thus in a "disobedient" way. Conflict then can occur because of incongruity between levels of message within a communication. Conflict in communication may also occur because of discrepancies and incongruities between the message content of two communications separated in time. For example, the parent who first asks a child whether he "would like" to carry out some task, thus implying a free choice, and who later berates the child for not doing as he "was told," conveying that he was *not* free to choose, sets up this type of conflict for the child.

Approaching the treatment of family dysfunction with these three premises in mind, the therapist has an immediate focus upon the ways in which family members undercut and disqualify each other, form coalitions, and develop rules of interaction and relationships. These rules establish role expectancies and functions and maintain without the awareness of the family members the dysfunction of the family system. For example, the wife who makes the apparently justifiable complaint that her husband is too passive and tells him that she wants him to be dominating and assertive, is not usually aware of the implications of her communication. The therapist, however, should see the trap which she has built for herself and her husband. No matter what he does now, the husband cannot please his wife. If he continues to act as he has, she can still complain of his passivity. If he attempts to be assertive and dominating, she will see his efforts as only another example of his passive following of what she tells him and thus as not genuine. As a consequence, the rules of their interaction which require his passivity and her dominance continue in effect. This peculiar situation results from the paradoxical attempt to demand behavior which by its nature can only be spontaneous. "Don't be so obedient" poses the same dilemma for the child. If he continues to do as he is told, he is wrong. If he now refuses to do so, he still is obeying and so is still wrong. Such paradoxical communications occur in all families and appear to be an unavoidable part of human interactions. Their effects appear to be serious, in terms of individual and family dysfunction, only when several conditions exist: (1) there is frequent repetition of the same type of communication conflict; (2) the relationship is such that the freedom to comment upon the resulting dilemma is not allowed; (3) there are an insufficient number of conflict-free areas of interaction.

In the course of family therapy, it is frequently possible to identify, explicate, and alter these conditions. For example, one mother of an adult, male schizophrenic patient protested with great frequency her utter devotion to her son saying, "Everything I do is for you." The son's effort then to object to any of her behavior was automatically a display of ingratitude. Efforts on the patient's part to point up this dilemma were nullified by the mother's development of symptoms of physical illness (most often angina pectoris) which eloquently conveyed to her son the message that his ingratitude was killing her. Without attempting a full description of the therapeutic efforts to alter the pattern of dysfunctional communication, it will be simply pointed out that the therapist was able through his genuine interest to encourage the mother both to do things for her husband, without reference to the son, and to begin to allow herself the satisfaction of legitimate personal indulgence.

To *summarize*, then, three basic premises of communication theory contribute significantly to the understanding of family interaction and provide a basis for therapeutic interventions that can alter dysfunctional family processes. The communication styles and patterns of the individual and of the family can be understood and used for change when the therapist bases his approach upon these premises. Other aspects of communication theory, not considered in this brief paper, are also of value to the family-oriented psychotherapist.

Having viewed what family therapy is, why it has developed, and how it uses communications theory, we ask, "What can be said of its *future prospects?*" Most needed is the development of terms and concepts adequate to the description and communication of the complex phenomena being observed. Much current research effort is being devoted to this problem. As more family therapists are trained, a more widespread use of this approach is inevitable. Further, as a body of common knowledge about the varying characteristics of different types of family systems is developed, variations in technique and method appropriate to these different types can be expected. At this time, family therapy provides both a hope and a promise for more effective ways of dealing with problems of human behavior through attention to their significance in the context of family interrelations.

IMPLICATIONS

Can you see applications here to *any* individual with emotional or adjustment problems? What are the implications of this article for the improvement of such an adjustment? Can you illustrate the various *blocks to effective communication* in everyday experiences?

You and your classmates may find it interesting to illustrate poor and good communication by staging a dialogue. Arrange a conversation on any subject of interest with emotional ramifications—such as the problem of getting a date or trying to make a good impression on a hard-boiled prospective employer. Two students play the roles of the communicating individuals. Set the stage as to where they are talking and what led up to the interaction. Then let the two interact naturally. They may attempt to communicate as much information as possible; or one may try to cut the other party off by giving as little verbally or nonverbally as possible. The class can then take notes on what takes place under two degrees of communication.

REFERENCES

The following are suggested for further reading: Ackerman (1958), Bell (1963), Bowen (1960), Haley (1962), Jackson and Satir (1961), Morris and Wynne (1965), Satir (1964), and Watzlawick (1964).

[60] FREUD: THEME AND VARIATIONS

Most students have read a few introductory paragraphs on Sigmund Freud, his psychoanalysis, and some of the variations from Freud's original systems. Some may have read parts of books by *Freud, Jung, Adler, Horney,* or *Fromm.* It is rare to find a simply written brief presentation of Freud's major concepts and the main variations by some of his followers.

The following selection is a tight, highly simplified presentation. It represents a good review of the major ideas and resembles a set of introductory lecture notes on Freud and some other outstanding psychoanalysts. How much it will mean to you will depend on previous knowledge, supplementary lectures, or further reading in the books that review *psychoanalytic theory.* The editors of *Time* Magazine thought this article was of sufficient interest to present it to their average readers. It is being used here as a sample of the better popular scientific writing that you may want to read during and after your college years.

Staff of Time *Magazine*

Courtesy *Time;* copyright Time, Inc., 1956.

If self-analysis made Freud a relatively adjusted man, it never blunted the sharpness of his search for understanding. He was too restless an explorer to remain content with his theories, worked until his death on amendments and additions. He was far less tolerant toward others' discontent with his theories, bitterly opposed some followers' deviations, but might well have accepted others that have developed since. Some rudiments of the Freudian main theme and principal variations:

Sigmund Freud held that the nature of man is essentially biological; man is born with certain instinctual drives. Most notable: the drive toward self-gratification. Basic mental energy, or *libido,* is equated with sexual energy by making the word "sex" stand for all pleasure.

Infant's first search for gratification is limited to release of hunger tension—*oral* phase. If there is no nipple handy, he puts thumb in mouth. Next comes satisfaction from defecation—*anal* phase. Third, pleasure from sensation in sexual parts—*phallic* phase. (Association of sexual gratification with reproduction—*genital* phase—does not come until sexual maturity.) Beginning about age two, the child's emotional attachment to mother leads to wishes to displace father—*Oedipal feelings* (the older, more rigid concept of an Oedipus complex is now frowned upon).

The psyche is divided horizontally into *conscious* and *unconscious,* vertically into *id, ego* and *superego.* Gradually the child's unconscious fills more or less deliberately with things forgotten (*suppressed*) because they are unpleasant, and, more importantly, with emotions and drives which are too painful ever to be tolerated in consciousness (*repressed*).

The *id,* entirely unconscious, most primitive part of the mind, is concerned only with gratification of drives. The *ego,* almost entirely conscious, develops from experience and reason, deals with perception of the environment, tries to go about governing id. *Superego,* largely unconscious, sits as judge, decides whether or not ego may permit id the gratification it seeks; it is conscience, made up of attitudes absorbed unwittingly in childhood and (to a much less extent) of attitudes consciously learned or adopted later.

Neurosis, to Freud, results from unsuccessful attempt by the personality to achieve harmony among id, ego, and superego, and this failure in turn results from arrest of development at an *immature* stage. Commonest cause of emotional disharmony: failure to resolve *Oedipal feelings.* Example: many girls who profess to seek marriage actually avoid it because the prospect activates the threat of unacceptable emotions which are *fixated* to their fathers.

Among the *mechanisms* used to deal with conflicts: *projection* involves denial of an unacceptable element in the self and projecting it onto others, e.g., man who bangs desk and shouts: "Who's excited? You're excited, not me!" *Reaction formation* covers conversion of unacceptable hostility into cloying solicitousness, seen in many do-gooders and some overprotective mothers who unconsciously *reject* their children.

Another way of using libidinal energy: *sublimation* into constructive and creative work or play.

To *resolve* neuroses, patient on couch tells in *free association* all that comes into his mind, especially about early *trauma* (shock). Since infancy and much of childhood are consciously "forgotten," these experiences must be recaptured with the help of the language of dreams—perhaps the most important single tool of analysis. There is no absolute symbolism (snakes may be phallic to one dreamer but to another merely reminiscent of a trip to the zoo), hence no universal key to the meaning of dreams. Analysis is complete when the patient has developed social responsibility, having dredged up all pertinent childhood traumas, recognized his unconscious Oedipal and other socially unacceptable impulses, and learned at a deep emotional level rather than a superficial intellectual level to live with such id-bits.

Alfred Adler (1870–1937) developed "individual psychology," which denies the overriding importance of infantile sexuality, argues that sexual maladjustments are a symptom, not a cause of neurosis. Adler gave *inferiority complex* to the language, said infants have *inferiority feelings* because they are small, helpless. Lack of parental tenderness, neglect or ridicule may make these feelings neurotic. Natural tendency is to seek *compensation* by becoming superior, hence open struggle for naked power. *Power drives* are often neurotic because directed to impractical goals. Emphasized ego over id.

Carl Gustav Jung of Zurich holds that primal *libido*, or *life force*, is composed of both sexual and nonsexual energy, accepts an individual unconscious similar to Freud's but sees also a *collective unconscious* containing man's "racial memories." Within this are emotional stereotypes (*archetypes*) common to all races of man, e.g., the Jovian figure of the "old, wise man," the earth-mother. In Jungian "analytical psychology," the analyst participates more actively than in Freudian analysis. Jung aims especially at people over forty, largely because he believes they most feel the need of a religious outlook, which he encourages.

Otto Rank (1884–1939) went Freud one better, held that Oedipal feelings came too late to be decisive. Real trouble, said he, was *birth trauma*—the shock of having to leave the warm security of the womb for the harsh reality of separate life. Anxiety caused by this experience formed sort of reservoir which should seep away gradually during maturation. If it persisted, then neurosis set in. Rank hoped to shorten analysis by going back to birth trauma, ignoring most of childhood.

Karen Horney (1885–1952) applied the thinking of anthropologists and sociologists to psychoanalysis, gave great weight to cultural factors in neurosis. Rejected Freud's biological orientation, emphasized importance of *present life situation*. Modified Adler's concept of neurotic goals, adding that these contain their own sources of anxiety. Thus in coping with one difficulty, patient may set up neurotic defenses which bring on new difficulties, and so on. Widely remembered for her unfortunately titled book, *Self-Analysis* (1942), which is no do-it-yourself kit for cracks in the psyche.

Harry Stack Sullivan (1892–1949) held that the human individual is the product of *interpersonal relations*, based an entire analytic theory on this concept. Pattern of child's earliest nonsexual relationships with significant figures largely (but not rigidly) determines the pattern of all later *interpersonal integration*. Man's aims are seen as pursuit of satisfaction (biological) and pursuit of security (cultural). If society denies satisfaction in sexual sphere, neurosis may result, but according to Sullivanians (a numerically small but influential school in the United States), it comes far more often from frustration, for whatever reason, in cultural sphere.

Erich Fromm of Manhattan and Mexico City denies that satisfaction of instinctual drives is focal problem, points out that man has fewer inherited behavior patterns than any other creature. In feudal times, he argues, the stratified, crystallized society wherein every individual knew his place gave security. Renaissance and mercantilism brought *freedom from* antlike existence but conferred (except on a privileged few) no *freedom to* work toward individual self-fulfillment. Thus neurosis today results mainly from frustrations which present trend of society threatens to intensify.

IMPLICATIONS

Try to define in your own words the human processes called id, superego, and ego by Freud. Can you think of someone you know whose behavior Freud would say results from unsuccessful attempts at harmony among ego, superego, and id? * Speculate on some examples of Jung's archetypes or the emotional stereotypes common to all races of men. To what extent does an accurate description of human behavior consist of the insights of all psychoanalysts? You might find it valuable and inter-

* Think but don't act. We are not trying to encourage amateur and untrained psychoanalysts in all of the suggested projects in this book. Use this caution—may your psychological insights help you in your adjustment rather than serve as a means of offending others.

esting to list these insights as you have found them important in your observations of other people.

REFERENCES

All of the ideas presented are basic to psychoanalytic theory, and you may want to read or question further sources on those ideas that are not clear in this summary. Other psychoanalysts referred to in the article are outstanding contributors to the movement. Selection 64 presents some of Jung's ideas. Adler, Horney, Sullivan, and Fromm have all impressed students of personality as well as the better-informed reading public. Rank's writings have influenced two outstanding American personality theorists—Rogers and Murray.

Hall and Lindzey (1957) present an informative discussion of the views of these theorists in a chapter on social psychological theories. Some of Rogers' methods are shown in Selection 57. Another standard reference on *theories of personality* is by Bischof (1964). In it you will find further references to primary sources by Freud and the other psychoanalysts. Hall (1954) has written a book on Freudian psychology. Fromm's books (1947, 1955) have had wide circulation in the United States. The Ansbachers (1956) have edited a book on Adler's ideas.

You will doubtlessly recognize many of the concepts, such as "ego defense mechanisms," "ego," "unconscious," "free association," as standard in most introductions to personality; they can be reviewed in any standard text.

Chapter XII

DREAMS,
HYPNOSIS, ESP

[61] WHAT PEOPLE DREAM ABOUT

People differ in the attitude they take toward dreams, ranging from a dread of dreaming to an eager interest in what sleep will bring. One intelligent, well-traveled, middle-aged man stated that he looked forward each night to a new dream. He usually read each evening before going to sleep, either travel books or fiction, and consequently his dreams were often an extension of his readings or of the characters in the stories. He stated that he has dreamed of places he has never seen. Sometimes these places are a combination of fragments of previous experiences. Once he made the statement that his most creative moments are in his dream life. He said, "I don't paint, play a musical instrument, or write well, yet my dreams are highly original. Parts of them are as good as some of the motion pictures I have seen."

The psychologist Gardner Murphy (1947), has said, "Probably no sphere of personality expression is richer with individuality than dreaming. . . . Most dreams have a lush or lavish quality which unambiguously bespeak greater psychic freedom and creativeness."

Dreams were very important to Freud and Jung in understanding personality. However, few investigators have studied the content of the dream as extensively as has Hall, and he presents in the following article an analysis of thousands of dreams. He includes a discussion of what the dream does and can mean to the individual. To Hall it is a means of solving problems, and it expresses the person's views of himself and the world about him.

Calvin S. Hall

Man's dreams have always interested and perplexed him. From ancient times and from every civilization and culture, we have evidence of man's concern about the meaning of dreams. They have been interpreted variously as divine messages, as the experiences of disembodied souls roaming heaven and earth during sleep, as visitations from the dead, as prophecies of the future, as the sleeping person's perceptions of external stimuli or bodily disturbances (what Thomas Hobbes called "the distemper of inward parts"), as fulfillments or attempted fulfillments of wishes (Freud), as attempts by the dreamer to discern his psychic development in order to plan for the future (Jung), as expressions of one's style of life (Adler), as attempted resolutions of conflicts (Stekel).

Probably all of these theories, however ancient their origin and however nebulous their validity, have their votaries today. Dream books based on the theory that dreams foretell the future are undoubtedly as widely consulted today as they were during the Renaissance, when the dream book compiled by the second-century soothsayer Artemidorus was republished in many languages and editions, and was plagiarized and elaborated by numerous opportunists, who in that day as in this knew a good thing when they saw it.

Even in modern times, speculations about dreams have been long on theory and short on observation. What do people dream about? What is the content and character of their dreams? As far as I know, no one has made an extensive and systematic study of these questions. To be sure, psychoanalysts have given much careful analysis to the dreams of deranged and disturbed persons, but even for this unrepresentative segment of mankind there are no large-scale surveys of the content of their dreams.

The writer has undertaken to make such a survey, for the purpose of obtaining some empirical facts as a foundation for theorizing. He has collected more than 10,000 dreams thus far, not from mental patients but from essentially normal people. They were asked to record their recollection of each dream on a printed form which included questions requesting certain specific information, such as the setting of the dream, the age and sex of the characters appearing in it, the dreamer's emotions and whether the dream was in color. Obviously we cannot know how faithfully the subjects' recollections mirrored their actual dreams, so, strictly speaking, we should call our project a study of what people *say* they dream about. This has ever been the case and probably always will be, for no one has discovered a means of transcribing a dream while it is being dreamed.

We *classified* * the dream material so that it could be studied statistically. From the many possible methods of classification we chose, as a beginning, a simple breakdown into five fundamental categories: (1) the dream setting, (2) its cast of characters, (3) its plot, in terms of actions and interactions, (4) the dreamer's emotions, and (5) color.

What are the most common settings in people's dreams? An analysis of 1,000 dreams reported by a group of educated adults provided 1,328 different settings. These could be classified into ten general categories. The most frequent scene was a part of a dwelling or other building; this accounted for 24 per cent of all dreams. The other settings, in order of frequency, were: a conveyance of some kind, most commonly an automobile, 13 per cent; an entire building, 11 per cent; a place of recreation, 10 per cent; a street or road, 9 per cent; a rural or other outdoor area, 9 per cent; a store or shop, 4 per cent; a classroom, 4 per cent; an office or factory, 1 per cent; miscellaneous (including restaurants, bars, battlefields, hospitals, churches, and so on), 14 per cent. In dreams occurring in part of a dwelling, the most popular room is the living room, with the bedroom, kitchen, stairway, and basement following in order.

The outstanding feature of these dream settings is their commonplaceness. The typical dream occurs in prosaic surroundings—a living room, an automobile, a street, a classroom, a grocery store, a field. The dreamer may not always recognize the details of the place, but usually it is a type of scene with which he is familiar; seldom does he dream of a bizarre or exotic environment. Yet, dream settings apparently are not entirely representative of waking life, as far as frequency is concerned. Considering the amount of time that people spend in places of work, such as offices, factories, and classrooms, these places appear with disproportionately low frequency in dreams. On the other hand, conveyances and recreational places occupy a larger share in dreams than they do in waking life experiences. In other words, in our dreams we tend to show an aversion toward work, study, and commercial transactions and an affinity for recreation, riding, and residences.

For a study of *characters appearing* * in dreams, we divided our subjects into two groups according to age, since it seemed likely that older people might differ from younger ones in the persons they dreamed about. The younger group was aged eighteen to twenty-eight, the older thirty to eighty. Let us consider the younger group first. They furnished a total of 1,819 dreams. In 15 per cent of these, the only character was the dreamer. In the remaining 85 per cent, in which two or more characters appeared, the average number was two persons besides the dreamer.

* Editor's italics.

Who are these characters? Of the persons other than the dreamer, 43 per cent appeared to be strangers, 37 per cent were identified as friends or acquaintances of the dreamer, 19 per cent were family members, relatives, or in-laws, 1 per cent were famous or prominent public figures. The relatively infrequent appearance of prominent persons in dreams supports other evidence possessed by the writer that dreams rarely concern themselves with current events. Among the members of the family, the character that appears in dreams most often is mother (34 per cent); then come father (27 per cent), brother (14 per cent), and sister (12 per cent).

We also classified the characters in dreams by sex and age. It turns out that men dream about males twice as often as they do about females, whereas women dream almost equally about both sexes. In the dreams of both men and women, 21 per cent of the characters are not identified as to sex.

The analysis showed, as is not surprising, that people dream most often about other people of their own age. In the sample of dreams from the subjects in the eighteen-to-twenty-eight age group, 42 per cent of the dream characters were the dreamers' peers in age, 20 per cent were older, 3 per cent were younger, and 35 per cent were of unspecified age.

We found that in general there were no very pronounced differences between the characters in the dreams of the young and older groups. Older people dream more about family and relatives and less about friends and acquaintances, which is not very surprising, since the younger dreamers were for the most part unmarried. Older people also dream more about younger characters and less about older characters and peers than do younger dreamers. We may generalize our findings by saying that while children are dreaming about their parents, their parents are dreaming about them, and while husbands are dreaming about their wives, their wives are dreaming about them.

We come now to *actions or behavior* *: What do people do in their dreams? We classified 2,668 actions in 1,000 dreams. By far the largest proportion (34 per cent) fall into the category of movement—walking, running, riding, or some other gross change in bodily position. We found that contrary to popular belief, falling or floating in dreams is not very common. After movement, the next most common activities were talking (11 per cent), sitting (7 per cent), watching (7 per cent), socializing (6 per cent), playing (5 per cent), manual work (4 per cent), thinking (4 per cent), striving (4 per cent), quarreling or fighting (3 per cent), and acquiring (3 per cent). From this it can be seen that passive or quiet activities occupy a large part of dreams, while manual activities are surprisingly infrequent. Such common waking occupations as typing, sewing, ironing, and fixing things are not represented in these thousand dreams at all; cooking, cleaning house, making beds, and washing dishes occur only once each. But strenuous recreational

* Editor's italics.

activities, such as swimming, diving, playing a game, and dancing are fairly frequent. In short, dreamers go places more than they do things; they play more than they work; their activities are more passive than active.

What of the relations between the dreamer and the other characters in his dream? We classified the interactions in a sample of 1,320 dreams in various categories according to degrees of friendliness or hostility. In general, hostile acts (by or against the dreamer) outnumbered friendly ones 448 to 188. In the hostile sphere, the acts of aggression ranged from murder (2 per cent) and physical attack (28 per cent) to denunciation (27 per cent) and mere feelings of hostility (8 per cent). The friendly acts ranged from an expressed feeling of friendliness to the giving of an expensive gift.

The *emotions felt* * by dreamers during their dreams were recorded in five classes: (1) apprehension, including fear, anxiety, and perplexity; (2) anger, including frustration; (3) sadness; (4) happiness; and (5) excitement, including surprise. Apprehension predominated, accounting for 40 per cent of all dream emotions; anger, happiness, and excitement were tied with 18 per cent each, and sadness was the least frequent, 6 per cent. Thus 64 per cent of all dream emotions were negative or unpleasant (apprehension, anger, sadness) and only 18 per cent (happiness) were positively pleasant.

Yet, paradoxically in the judgment of the dreamers themselves, the dreams as a whole were rated pleasant much more often than unpleasant. They found 41 per cent of the dreams pleasant, 25 per cent unpleasant, 11 per cent mixed, and 23 per cent without feeling tone. Older dreamers reported more unpleasant dreams than younger ones, but the difference was not great.

A question that has puzzled many students of dreams is why some of them are seen wholly or partly in natural *colors* * ("technicolor"). I am afraid I have little to contribute to the solution of this puzzle beyond a few figures and a few negative conclusions. In a survey of over 3,000 dreams, 29 per cent were colored or had some color in them and the rest were completely colorless. Women report color in dreams more often (31 per cent) than do men (24 per cent). There is a slight tendency for people over fifty to have fewer colored dreams than those under that age. Many people never experience color in dreams; on the other hand, a few have all their dreams in color.

What is the psychological significance of technicolored dreams? We have compared the dreams of people who dream entirely in color with those of people who never dream in color and have found no difference in any aspect of their dreams. We have compared the colored with the colorless dreams of the same person without discovering any way in which they differed. Nor can we find any single specific symbolic meaning in a particular color. We are forced to conclude on the basis of our present evidence that color in dreams is merely an embellishment, signifying nothing in itself.

What do all these facts on the content of dreams mean? I shall present my

* Editor's italics.

general theory of dreams * and show how some of the foregoing findings fit into this theory.

Dreaming is thinking that occurs during sleep. It is a peculiar form of thinking in which the conceptions or ideas are expressed not in the form of words or drawings, as in waking life, but in the form of images, usually visual images. In other words, the abstract and invisible ideas are converted into concrete and visible images. By an odd process which we do not understand, the sleeping person can see his own thoughts embodied in the form of pictures. When he communicates his dream to another person, he is communicating his thoughts, whether he knows it or not.

During sleep we think about our problems and predicaments, our fears and hopes. The dreamer thinks about himself: what kind of person he is and how well fitted he is to deal with his conflicts and anxieties. He thinks about other people who touch his life intimately. His conceptions are purely egocentric; there appears to be no place in dreams for impersonal, detached thoughts. Accordingly the interpretation of dreams—the translation of the dreamer's images into his ideas—gives us an inner view of him, as though we were looking out and seeing the world as he sees it. We see how he looks to himself, how others look to him, and how he conceives of life. This is the heart of the matter, and the reason why dreams are important data for the psychologist.

How a person sees himself is expressed in dreams by the parts the dreamer plays. He may play the part of a victim or an aggressor or both; he may conceive of himself as winning in spite of adverse circumstances, or losing because of these same adversities. He may assume the role of a saint or a sinner, a dependent person or an independent one, a miser or a philanthropist. As Emerson said, "A skillful man reads his dreams for his self-knowledge."

Although the characters in his dreams are many and varied, they probably all have one thing in common—they are all emotionally involved in the dreamer's life. If this is so, one may well ask, why do we dream so often about strangers? The answer is that they are not really strangers but personifications of our conceptions of people we know. A person who conceives of his father as stern and autocratic, for example, may in his dreams turn his father into an army officer or a policeman or a schoolteacher or some other symbol of strict discipline. Very likely he will also have other conceptions of his father, and for each conception he finds an appropriate older figure who personifies the particular father conception uppermost in his mind at the time of the dream. Many of these father figures will be strangers to the dreamer, although the qualities expressed will be familiar enough to him.

Similarly, the dream setting may portray *the ways in which the dreamer looks at the world*.* If he feels that the world is closing in on him, he dreams of cramped places; if the world appears bleak, the dream setting is bleak.

* Editor's italics.

Tumultuous and tempestuous scenery—raging seas, milling crowds, exploding bombs, thunderstorms—betokens and outlook of insecurity and chaos. In one series of dreams studied by the writer, there was a plethora of dirty, dank, and dismal settings—a visible projection of the dreamer's conception of a world decaying.

Dreams are filled with the *gratification* * or attempted gratification of impulses, particularly sexual and aggressive impulses. They tell us how the dreamer regards these impulses. If he thinks of sex or aggression as wicked, the expression of these impulses in his dreams will be followed by some form of punishment or misfortune. If he conceives of sex as a mechanical matter, he may have a dream like that of one young man who reported a nocturnal emission dream in which a lady plumber turned on a faucet for the dreamer. We study dreams, therefore, not to discover the wish motivating the dream, as Freud did, but rather to determine how the dreamer conceives of his wishes.

Dreams also provide a vista of the *dreamer's conceptions of his conflicts.** The dramatic quality of a dream—its plot, tensions, and resolutions—is derived from an underlying conflict in whose grip the dreamer feels himself to be. In a series of dreams from the same individual, we can see his conflict running like Ariadne's thread through the labyrinth of his dreams. The conflict may hang on with surprising tenacity over a period of years. Apparently, the conflicts that motivate dreams are basic ones which rarely become resolved. We suspect that these internal wars have their origins early in life and are not easily, if ever, brought to a satisfactory conclusion.

In our studies of many dream series, a few conflicts stand out as being shared by many people. One such inner tug-of-war is that between the progressive pull of maturity, growth, and independence and the regressive pull of infantile security, passivity, and dependence. This conflict is particularly acute during adolescence and the late teens and early twenties, but in a large proportion of people it persists through later ages and returns to prominence in old age.

Another ubiquitous inner conflict is that between conceptions of good and evil—the moral conflict. The opposing forces are those of impulse and conscience. The dreamer impulsively kills a dream character and is then punished for his crime. Or he is driven to express sexuality for which he suffers some misfortune.

A third conflict arises out of the tug between the opposing tendencies toward integration and disintegration. By integration is meant all of the life-maintaining and love-encompassing aims of man; by disintegration, the forces of death, hate, fear, and anxiety which produce disunity and dissolution. One pole affirms life and love, the other affirms death and hate. Anxiety dreams and nightmares express the conception of personal disintegration.

* Editor's italics.

We study dreams in order to enlarge our understanding of man. They yield information that is not readily obtained from other sources. This information consists of man's most personal and intimate conceptions, conceptions of which not even the person himself is aware. It is important to know these conceptions, for they are the foundation of man's conduct. How we view ourselves and the world around us determines in large measure how we will behave.

IMPLICATIONS

What impressed you most about Hall's findings? How do your dreams duplicate or vary from the kinds of dream content and processes related here? Have you gained any ideas as to what your dreams can mean to you? Possibly, you may find it interesting to discuss the implications of these findings with your fellow students. Include a discussion of the conflicts shared by many people which are dramatized in dreams.

REFERENCES

See "References" following the next selection for reading suggestions. See also Rapaport (1951) and Hall and Van de Castle (1966).

[62] NEW LIGHT ON DREAMING

Now for a discussion of dreams as related to sleep and the brain's electrical activity. When, during our sleep, do we dream most? How long is a dream? Does everyone dream? On what factual bases can an answer to this question be given? Do dreams have a health function? These are some of the questions that can be answered as the result of modern experimentation. Oswald presents the answers and the evidence for them in this article.

Ian Oswald

Reprinted from Ian Oswald, "New Light on Dreaming," *New Scientist*, Vol. 13, No. 272 (London: New Scientist, 1962), pp. 251–253, by permission of the author.

About ten years ago, a number of firms in the United States marketed equipment to enable the common man to transform himself into an encyclopaedia. Tape recorders played information endlessly through the night to an allegedly receptive, though sleeping, brain. There is, however, not a shred of evidence to show that we can learn unless we are conscious. Experiments have been conducted in which the electrical brain waves were used to indicate when volunteers were asleep; they revealed that only when the brain waves were currently indicative of mere drowsiness, or the lightest sleep, was it possible for new memories to be formed. It follows that, even if we were to dream in deeper sleep, we should never afterward succeed in recalling such dreams. Even in drowsiness or very light sleep our efficiency is grossly impaired, and we will quickly drift away from reality to a fantasy life or dreamworld of our own.

It used to be thought that sleep grew steadily deeper for the first two to three hours of the night and then gradually lightened so that we should not have expected people to be able to recall having just dreamed if wakened in the middle of the night. We now know, however, that dreaming occurs cyclically during the night in association with cyclical changes of sleep. The "clever" or "thinking" part of the brain essential for conscious awareness, whether of reality or of dreams, is the gray matter or cerebral cortex. It cannot work properly—that is to say, we are not conscious—unless it receives a constant spray of "energizing" impulses from a lower and central area of the brain called the reticular formation.... While we are awake, the reticular formation is in a state of effervescent excitement. When that effervescence declines and few energizing impulses are sprayed up at the cortex as we fall asleep, we lose consciousness. It appears that the reticular formation has a natural cyclical variation of its degree of upgoing effervescent excitement, and that every one and a half hours or so during nocturnal sleep, it peps up the cerebral cortex sufficiently to permit crude consciousness—namely, dreaming.

IT ALL BEGAN WITH BABIES.   A few years ago, Kleitman and his colleague, Aserinsky, in Chicago studied the sleep of babies in the first months of life. They found that the infants did not sleep uniformly between feeds, but grew restless after an hour, then slept again, to grow restless once more an hour later, and so on. Babies fed on demand would yell for food after an interval which was some multiple of the hourly cycle. They went on to discover a similar cycle present in sleeping adults at a rather slower frequency. About every one and a half hours, for ten to thirty minutes or more, the brain electrical activity, picked up through the scalp, changed to that of light sleep, and from time to time the sleeper's eyes would twist hither and thither in a rapid, jerky fashion.

Kleitman, Dement, and others next woke up sleeping volunteers several times each night. When aroused from those periods of the night in which the rapid eye movements and the brain electrical signs of light sleep were present, on about three quarters of all occasions the volunteers said they had just been dreaming. When aroused from periods when the eyes were quiescent and the brain electrical signs were those of deep sleep, only occasionally were dreams described, and the descriptions themselves lacked detail and were thought probably to be memories of dreams earlier in the night.

The length of each dream description, and the duration which such events might have occupied had they taken place in real life, were found to be closely matched by the length of time the sleeper had been allowed to continue in the period of rapid eye movements and light sleep signs just before being wakened. Research workers in many centers throughout the world have confirmed these results, and it is clear that about five times each night our sleep changes and we dream. As the night progresses, the duration of the dream periods lengthens so that toward the end of the night we may dream for as much as three quarters of an hour at a stretch. There is no evidence to support the old idea that apparently lengthy dream experiences may occur in the space of a few seconds.

You NEVER DREAM? What about people who say they almost never dream? The answer seems to be that they forget. When volunteers are awakened a few minutes after one of their cyclically recurring periods of rapid eye movements and light sleep signs, the amount of dream recall decreases very sharply as the number of minutes increases. Goodenough and his colleagues at New York used two groups of volunteers, one of persons who said they often dreamed, the other of those who said they practically never dreamed. Members of both groups showed the same cyclical changes during the night and, when awakened from the rapid eye-movement periods, they all recalled dreams. The interesting difference between the two groups was that the erstwhile nondreamers showed brain electrical signs of rather lighter sleep and often said, when wakened, that they had not really been asleep and dreaming, but that they had been "thinking." A man might say he had been "thinking" he was riding down the street in an automobile, though actually in bed, and would not call it a dream unless the fantasy had crazy features which were inconsistent with one another.

What is the significance of the rapid, jerky eye movements during dreams? Kleitman and his colleagues proposed that these were like the jerky, scanning eye movements made during waking life when one looks around the world, and that the dreamer was looking around his dreamworld. Attempts were made to compare the direction of the last recorded eye movement of the dream with the last dream event described by the wakened subject. Very close correlations were claimed. Dream descriptions of very active fantasy events followed periods of very active eye movements, whereas periods of few eye movements were followed by a dream description involving little action (for example, of just sitting and watching television). Various arguments can be advanced against the theory, but in its favor, we have found at Edinburgh that men blind all their lives do not have these rapid eye movements during their dreams. They describe how they dreamed they went with their friends to certain places and had certain adventures, without, of course, "seeing" anything. Men blind for only a few years still had the dream eye movements, but men blind for over thirty years, who had lost the ability to "picture" things, no longer had eye movements in their dreams.

TWO KINDS OF SLEEP. Cats also show cyclical changes in their sleep and have been seen apparently dreaming (twitching their whiskers and tails) in their periods of rapid eye movements. Recent French work makes it seem that there are, in fact, two sorts of feline sleep. Electrical activity was recorded from electrodes placed deeply within the brain. When the cats went to sleep, the cerebral cortex showed the usual type of sleep electrical activity, but certain lower areas of the brain still showed wakefulness-type activity. In the dream periods there was a sense of reversal, the cortex having electrical activity not much different from that of wakefulness and consistent with the notion that consciousness was present, whereas the lower brain now showed sleep-type

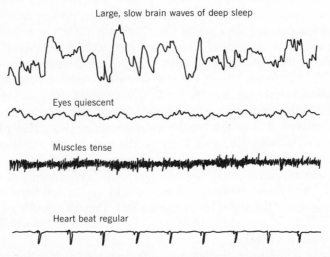

Large, slow brain waves of deep sleep

Eyes quiescent

Muscles tense

Heart beat regular

FIGURE 1(A). Traditional type of sleep with high voltage, slow brain waves, quiescent eyes, and a regular heart beat. Innumerable little electrical impulses from the tense neck muscles produce the thick, spiky muscle trace.

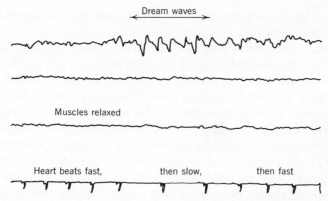

Dream waves

Muscles relaxed

Heart beats fast,   then slow,   then fast

FIGURE 1(B). Paradoxical or dream sleep. The brain waves are now of low voltage, but suddenly the unique "saw-toothed" dream waves appear. The muscle trace is no longer thick and spiky, for the muscles are profoundly relaxed and the heart now beats irregularly. (In this particular section, the eyes are quiescent, although sometimes they do move while the dream waves are actually occurring.)

electrical activity. The term "paradoxical" has been applied to this second kind of sleep. It is accompanied in the cat by a very much greater relaxation of some of the muscles of the body trunk than occurs in the traditional type of sleep, and the heart rate becomes irregular.

It looks as if the comparable cyclical changes in human sleep also involve two different kinds of sleep. On the one hand, cerebral cortex inactivity and unconsciousness (traditional type sleep) and, on the other, cerebral cortex activity with dreaming but with a much greater degree of bodily relaxation (paradoxical sleep). Profound relaxation of some of the trunk muscles is present during the human dream periods, together with irregularity of the heart rate (see Figures 1B and 1C). In addition, in many people there are inter-

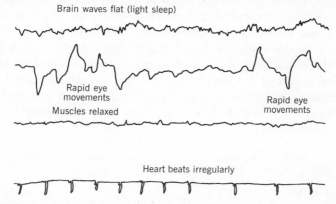

Brain waves flat (light sleep)

Rapid eye movements
Muscles relaxed

Rapid eye movements

Heart beats irregularly

FIGURE 1(C). Suddenly during the dream the eyes twist rapidly hither and thither.

mittent electrical brain waves having an appearance quite unique to the dream periods, generally just before the eyes move (Figure 1B).

The "sleep" of the lower brain with profound body relaxation, despite consciousness "in" the cerebral cortex, helps to explain two old puzzles. In many nightmares, people feel that some catastrophe, like being carried helplessly into a car crash, is about to overtake them. They feel terrified, they struggle to shout and escape, yet find themselves unable to breathe or move—their bodies are in a state of temporary limp paralysis forced from their conscious efforts. There are also people troubled by *narcolepsy* or a recurrent, abnormal drowsiness by day. They frequently fall asleep in trains or buses and often while walking or eating. If they are suddenly startled, made angry or made to laugh, their body muscles suddenly go quite limp (really "helpless with laughter") for several seconds, their jaws sag and they may flop to the ground. I had a patient to whom this would happen just when, in a moment of sudden anger, he was about to clout his son. In a train, the narcoleptic falls into traditional type sleep but, when startled, angry or aroused, he probably falls into paradoxical sleep—he is conscious, but his lower brain is "asleep" and his trunk muscles go limp.

The paradoxical type of sleep may have a special importance in our wellbeing. Dement and others in the United States watched recordings of electrical brain and eye activity during the night and, whenever the sleeper had just entered a dream period, woke him up. They aimed to prevent him dreaming. The procedure was repeated night after night. The volunteers began to enter the paradoxical or dream type of sleep more and more often and went on doing so for several nights after the wakenings ceased. They also grew very unhappy. In another series of nights, they were woken only from traditional type sleep, without any notable consequences. It seemed as if they really needed that dream sleep and, if prevented from getting it, they grew unhappy and tried to make up for it later. In Edinburgh, Ralph Berger decided to deprive volunteers of the dream sleep by preventing them from having any sleep at all, so we kept them awake for 108 hours. Subsequently, they had especially deep, traditional sleep in their first night's sleep, but after that they dreamed much more than normal. Perhaps they were catching up on their dream-sleep lack.

The actual events of our dream life, and the way we incorporate, for instance, outside noises, often seem bizarre, yet certain rules can be discerned. Modern dream researchers do not forget these fascinating puzzles, but they form, alas, another story.

IMPLICATIONS

To what extent do the facts cited in the article change your view of sleep and dreams? What evidence can you use with the person who says he never dreams to show him that he does? Do you recognize paradoxical sleep in your own experience?

REFERENCES
See Dement and Kleitman (1957) and Dement (1960).

[63] A PREFACE TO THE THEORY OF HYPNOTISM

Most people have heard of hypnosis, and some have even seen an individual hypnotized. Hypnosis has almost universal human interest because the trancelike state seems so abnormal and rare to common experience. Hypnosis has had a long association with the magical, mystical, theatrical, and sensational. It also has had a history of association with medicine and science, beginning in the eighteenth century with the Viennese physician Mesmer. In addition, it has some status at present in psychological research and training.

How do we know *what hypnosis is, how it is brought about,* and *who can be hypnotized?* Hypnosis is a temporary state, trancelike in nature, induced by a hypnotic operator. It is a condition of altered attention. The subject appears to have for the time relinquished his normal self-management to the hypnotist. He is hypersuggestible and seems to be compelled to obey the instructions of the hypnotist if he is motivated to cooperate with the hypnotist.

Hypnosis is usually *produced* by having the subject relax and fix his gaze on some point or object while the operator monotonously verbalizes suggestions of relaxation and drowsiness. In a short time the subject will appear to go to sleep and will pass into a sleeplike, lethargic condition. If the procedure is successful, he will exhibit the behavior commanded by the hypnotist. Some of the events that may occur during hypnosis are described in the following excerpt. The events can range widely, including alterations in memory and perceptions, paralysis, changes in vasomotor activity, and muscular rigidity.

The question of who can be hypnotized cannot be answered briefly.

People vary from complete nonsusceptibility to hypnosis to high susceptibility. The factor of depth of hypnosis from light to deep also must be considered. In a situation of security and confidence, it has been stated, willing subjects can undergo some degree of hypnosis by a responsible hypnotist. The best method of determining susceptibility is the actual attempt at hypnosis.

Psychologists, being primarily investigators and scientists, are interested mainly in the facts and theories of hypnosis—the *what* and the *why*. In the excerpt, White also discusses some facts of hypnosis, many of which are found under laboratory conditions. He advances the theory that hypnosis is *goal-directed striving*, a concept found useful in psychology. We see how a psychologist marshals the data about a process and then builds a theory to explain it.

Robert W. White

Reprinted from Robert W. White, "A Preface to the Theory of Hypnosis," *Journal of Abnormal and Social Psychology*, Vol. 4, No. 36 (Washington, D.C.: American Psychological Association, 1941), pp. 479–484, by permission of the publisher and the author.

FACTS WHICH REQUIRE EXPLANATION

To begin with, we shall review briefly the facts that any theory of hypnosis is called upon to explain. What are the characteristics which make hypnosis a perennial object of wonder and amazement? Three things appear to create surprise. One of these is that the hypnotized person can effectuate suggestions lying outside the realm of ordinary volitional control; he can do things that he could not possibly do in the normal state. No less surprising, however, is the way a hypnotized person carries out those suggestions lying within the realm of volition. Stiffening the arm or clasping the hands are actions that anyone could perform volitionally, but in hypnosis they occur without benefit of volition, unaccompanied by the experience of intention, yet at times so strongly that the subject seems unable to arrest them when he tries. Furthermore, hypnotic actions are carried out with a curious lack of humor and self-consciousness, often with an air of abstraction and drowsiness, and they do not seem to have the claim over subsequent memory to which their recency and importance entitle them. Finally, it is a constant source of amazement that these rather drastic effects can be brought about simply by talking. If a person suffered a head injury, took a drug, or was worked into a state of violent emotion, radical changes in the control of behavior would be expected as a matter of course, but no one can believe that mere words entering the ears of a relaxed and drowsy subject can be sufficient cause for the changes which actually take place. It will repay us to consider each of these items in a little more detail.

1. *Hypnotic transcendence of voluntary capacity* is strikingly illustrated by insensitivity to pain. One of the most dramatic chapters in the history of hypnotism is its use by James Esdaile about 1845 as an anaesthetic in major surgical operations. There is still no more convincing way to persuade a skeptic that hypnosis is "real" than by showing that ordinarily painful stimuli can be endured without signs of pain. Carefully controlled experiments designed to exclude every possibility of error have reaffirmed the reality of this phenomenon and have shown that the inhibition extends to such nonvoluntary processes as pulse rate and the galvanic skin reaction (Dynes, 1932; Sears, 1932). Along somewhat different lines, recent experiments show that muscular strength and resistance to fatigue are at least somewhat increased (Williams, 1929) and that recall is substantially improved in consequence of hypnotic suggestions (Stalnaker and Riddle, 1932; White, Fox, and Harris, 1940). There is still some reason to believe that older claims concerning the production of blisters, cold sores, and digestive reactions are not without foundation, although the investigation of these topics has suffered from a lack of control experiments (Frick, Scantlebury, and Patterson, 1935; Hull, 1933; Pattie, 1941). Whatever the ultimate decision upon one or another of the latter claims, there is no danger of concluding that hypnotic suggestion can produce a number of effects beyond the realm of volition, and that among these effects is an increased control over autonomic functions. The implication of these facts for a theory of hypnotism will be considered in a later section.

2. It is not necessary, however, to depend upon these facts of transcendence in order to demonstrate that hypnotic behavior differs from voluntary. If we confine ourselves to actions which could perfectly well be performed intentionally, there is still a *distinct difference in the way they are performed* in response to hypnotic suggestion. When retrospection is possible, as often happens after relatively light hypnosis, a crucial difference in the accompanying experience can be recognized. Janet (1925) reports that a patient, ordinarily suggestible, one day declared that the suggestion "did not take." "I am quite ready to obey you," she said, "and I will do it if you choose: only I tell you beforehand that the thing did not take." This patient clearly recognized the difference between obedience, when one intentionally carries out another person's command, and suggestion, when the action executes itself without the experience of intention, even in defiance of it.

Bleuler, describing his experiences when hypnotized, said, "I felt my biceps contracting against my will as soon as I attempted to move my arm by means of the extensor muscles; once, on making a stronger effort to carry out my intention, the contraction of the flexors became so energetic that the arm, instead of moving outward as I had intended, moved backward on the upper arm." "At other times," he said again, "I felt that the movement was made without any active taking part by my ego, this being especially marked with unimportant commands" (Forel, 1907).

One of the writer's subjects reported himself as "quite marveling at the way my arm stayed up, apparently without volition on my part. I was still aware of myself off in a corner looking on." Observations such as these could be multiplied indefinitely, but further emphasis is scarcely necessary. It is sufficient to remember that subjects after light trances can almost always give evidence concerning their susceptibility, and that their own spontaneous criterion is whether or not they had the feeling of collaborating in the production of the suggested actions. Though there is a hazy borderland between intentional and automatic acts, in the majority of cases, subjects can readily discriminate between the two. Hypnotic suggestion not only transcends the limits of volitional control but also dispenses with volition when bringing about actions which normally lie within those limits.

Subsequent report is frequently impossible because of post-hypnotic amnesia. Even so there is an appreciable difference between hypnotic behavior and the everyday intentional performance of like actions. For one thing, the subject's manner differs from the ordinary: he seems literal and humorless, he shows no surprise and makes no apology for bizarre behavior, he appears entirely unself-conscious, and very often he acts abstracted, inattentive, almost as if he were insulated against his surroundings. Braid's notion of monoideism serves very well to describe the impression a hypnotized person makes on an outside observer. For another thing, hypnotic behavior does not seem to occupy a proper place in the subject's memory. He disclaims recollection of recent and often very complicated actions which in the ordinary way he seems to have every reason to remember. Thus, whether we choose an introspective criterion or whether we prefer external observation, we are entitled to be surprised at the difference between hypnotically suggested actions and similar actions intentionally performed.

3. *The procedure by which hypnosis is made to occur does not seem adequate to produce such an effect.* So great is this discrepancy that for many years it was customary to assume a magnetic force, an invisible fluid, or some similar powerful agent, passing from the operator into the subject. With the decline of such theories, there has been a tendency to argue that the phenomena of hypnosis are after all not unique, that under suitable conditions they can all be duplicated without resort to a hypnotic procedure. It is known, for example, that under stress of excitement and violent emotion, people surpass by a wide margin their usual levels of muscular strength and endurance. In like circumstances there is often a considerable degree of anesthesia for the pain of fairly serious injuries. Hyperamnesia occurs during free association, in drowsy states, and in dreams. Many actions which cannot be initiated by themselves without the experience of intention take place quite involuntarily when embedded in a context of other actions, as in playing a

game. Perhaps these claims are justified; perhaps there is no phenomenon in the repertory of hypnotic suggestion which cannot be produced in some other way. But, even if this be true, we are not exempt from explaining why the hypnotic procedure, which does not create excitement and violent emotion, which does not put one to sleep, which makes no use of free association, which virtually excludes a context of other actions, and which especially with practice requires very little time, brings about so momentous an effect. It is legitimate to be surprised at the power of hypnotic suggestion.

The task which confronts a theory of hypnosis is roughly defined by the three foregoing peculiarities. Any such theory must explain how (1) the hypnotic procedure brings about (2) the nonvolitional performance of acts that ordinarily require volitional assistance and (3) the performance of acts outside the normal range of volition.

HYPNOTIC BEHAVIOR AS GOAL-DIRECTED STRIVING

When Charcot discovered that it was possible to reproduce the symptoms of hysteria by means of hypnosis, he surmised that the two phenomena were closely related, indeed, that they were aspects of the same underlying condition. This dubious bond, however, was not sufficient to keep hypnosis and hysteria long on an equal footing of medical interest. Thus it happened that the theory of hypnotism lingered at the Salpêtrière stage, while the theory of hysteria advanced steadily from Charcot's time to the present, becoming at last the basis for a new understanding of all neurotic conditions and the starting point for modern dynamic psychology. The central insight which transformed the theory of hysteria was the idea that symptoms spring from strivings, that neurosis is an outcome of conflict among fundamental impulses rather than a damaged state of the nervous system. Such a view would have been impossible without the still more basic insight that large parts of a person's striving may take place unconsciously, forming no part of his organized picture of himself and his intentions. In psychopathology these once radical notions have gradually worked their way to acceptance.

The benefits of this progress have been largely withheld from the theory of hypnotism. Two concepts, *automatism* and *dissociation*, once useful in understanding hysteria but long since modified, reshaped, and animated with dynamic ideas, have persisted in a peculiarly literal and lifeless form in hypnotic theory. Automatism, invoked to explain the nonvolitional character of hypnotic behavior, implies that hypnotized persons are helpless executants of the operator's will as this is expressed in verbal suggestion. Dissociation, called upon to account for amnesia, post-hypnotic phenomena, and those instances when impressions seem to be excluded from awareness or when intentions fail to govern motor processes, implies the subject to be in a state of temporary fragmentation such that different parts of his behavior take place independently without their usual communication. These ideas deserve the respect which is due to first approximations, but their prolonged survival keeps the theory of hypnotism in swaddling clothes when it should be grown to adult stature.

The concept of striving, so useful in other parts of psychology, needs to be applied in thorough-going fashion to the behavior of the hypnotized person. This application may be embodied in the following statement: *hypnotic behavior is meaningful, goal-directed striving, its most general goal being to behave like a hypnotized person as this is continuously defined by the operator and understood by the subject.* This point of view is not original with the present writer, having been previously maintained by Rosenow (1928), Lundholm (1928), Pattie (1935, 1937), and Dorcus (1937), who have found it more satisfactory in explaining the facts subsumed under both automatism and dissociation. The hypnotized person is seen not as an almost inanimate object, upon which strange effects can be wrought by touching the right levers or tapping the right lines of cleavage, but as a human being who hears and understands and who tries to behave in the different ways which are proposed to him. The adoption of such a hypothesis should not, of course, depend upon one's general preferences in psychological theory. It is the argument of the present paper that hypnotic behavior, on the face of it, can be adequately described and adequately understood in no other way than as goal-directed striving.

IMPLICATIONS

To what extent are you able now, after reading these facts and the theory proposed, to see hypnosis as compatible with waking behavior? What other behavior less rare than the hypnotic trance can you recall that is somewhat related to hypnosis? What about its relationship to somnambulistic behavior or *sleepwalking, absent-mindedness,* behavior while being highly absorbed in another activity such as an athletic game? Can you think of any other phenomena related to hypnosis?

REFERENCES

In an interestingly written book, Moss (1965) points out that in thirty-one years ending in 1959, 971 entries dealt with hypnosis in the *Psychological Abstracts,* a journal of abstracts of the articles and books of a psychological nature. There is currently a reawakened interest among psychologists, but this was preceded by a period of skepticism and negativism. Moss, in addition to a history of the phenomenon, discusses the power of hypnosis, theories about it, and its current status.

[64] MAN'S UNCONSCIOUS PROCESSES

Man is rational, but he also has an *irrational* side of which he is unconscious or only vaguely conscious. We are indebted first to Sigmund Freud for systematizing this idea that has appeared again and again in literature. Freud emphasized the dynamic nature of these unconscious processes. Unacceptable urges and wishes that cannot be reviewed consciously are repressed but retain their drive nature, appearing in dreams, slips of speech, unconscious mannerisms, and creative ventures of the individual. He maintained that much of man's conflictory and contradictory nature can be understood in terms of the operation of unconscious processes.

Jung saw the unconscious aspects of man as involving *more than repressed sexual and aggressive impulses*. Unconscious processes also contain complements of our conscious strivings: the predominantly extroverted individual has introverted unconscious tendencies; the male has a hidden feminine side; the idealistic, well-behaved person has baser, more hostile repressed impulses. Jung went further, prompted by his interests in many different cultures widely separated by space and even by time—mythology, ancient symbols, and rituals in primitive cultures. He saw all men as possessing *common racial origins* in their personalities. The civilized individual has predispositions that are a heritage from his very distant ancestors. Jung hypothesizes that these predispositions influence man's behavior.

Here we will look at a selection from Jung's writings as he discusses unconscious influences in the extroverted person. He illustrates these influences with a case and discusses generally what can happen when infantile and primitive dispositions are ruthlessly suppressed rather than understood and guided. Then we shall deviate from our usual format and in an Editor's Comment summarize some of Jung's ideas that would require many pages from Jung's books to cover.

Carl G. Jung

Reprinted from Carl G. Jung, *Psychological Types* (London: Routledge & Kegan Paul, 1923), pp. 422–426, by permission of the publisher.

It may perhaps seem odd that I should speak of an "attitude of the unconscious." . . . I regard the relation of the unconscious to the conscious as compensatory. The unconscious, according to this view, has as good a claim to an "attitude" as the conscious. . . .

The attitude of the unconscious as an effective complement to the conscious extraverted attitude has a definitely introverting character. It focusses libido upon the subjective factor, *i.e.*, all those needs and claims which are stifled or repressed by a too extraverted conscious attitude. . . . A purely objective orientation does violence to a multitude of subjective emotions, intensions, needs, and desires, since it robs them of the energy which is their natural right. Man is not a machine that one can reconstruct, as occasion demands, upon other lines and for quite other ends, in the hope that it will then proceed to function, in a totally different way, just as normally as before. Man bears his age-long history with him; in his very structure is written the history of mankind.

The historical factor represents a vital need, to which a wise economy must respond. Somehow the past must become vocal, and participate in the present. Complete assimilation to the object, therefore, encounters the protest of the suppressed minority, elements belonging to the past and existing from the beginning. From this quite general consideration it may be understood why it is that the unconscious claims of the extraverted type have an essentially primitive, infantile, and egoistical character. . . .

I remember the case of a printer who, starting as a mere employee, worked his way up through two decades of hard struggle, till at last he was the independent possessor of a very extensive business. The more the business extended, the more it increased its hold upon him, until gradually every other interest was allowed to become merged in it. At length he was completely enmeshed in its toils, and, as we shall soon see, this surrender eventually proved his ruin. As a sort of compensation to his exclusive interest in the business, certain memories of his childhood came to life. As a child he had taken great delight in painting and drawing. But, instead of renewing this capacity for its own sake as a balancing side interest, he canalized it into his business and began to conceive "artistic" elaborations of his products. His phantasies unfortunately materialized: he actually began to produce after his own primitive and infantile taste, with the result that after a very few years his business went to pieces. He acted in obedience to one of our "civilized ideals," which enjoins the energetic man to concentrate everything upon the one end in view. But he went too far, and merely fell a victim to the power of his subjective infantile claims.

But the catastrophic solution may also be subjective, *i.e.*, in the form of a nervous collapse. Such a solution always comes about as a result of the unconscious counterinfluence, which can ultimately paralyze conscious action. In which case the claims of the unconscious force themselves categorically upon consciousness, thus creating a calamitous cleavage which generally reveals itself in two ways: either the subject no longer knows what he really wants and nothing any longer interests him, or he wants too much at once and has too keen an interest—but in impossible things. The suppression of infantile and primitive claims, which is often necessary on "civilized" grounds, easily leads to neurosis, or to the misuse of narcotics such as alcohol, morphine, cocaine, etc. In more extreme cases the cleavage ends in suicide.

It is a salient peculiarity of unconscious tendencies that, just insofar as they are deprived of their energy by a *lack of conscious recognition*, they assume a correspondingly destructive character, and as soon as this happens their compensatory function ceases. They cease to have a compensatory effect as soon as they reach a depth or stratum that corresponds with a level of culture absolutely incompatible with our own. From this moment the unconscious tendencies form a block, which is opposed to the conscious attitude in every respect; such a block inevitably leads to open conflict.

EDITOR'S COMMENT

The preceding excerpt is from one of Jung's early books in which he introduces introversion and extroversion—the tendency to withdraw into oneself and be concerned with inner experience on the one hand and the tendency to be preoccupied with social life and the external world on the other hand. In these few paragraphs he shows the human need for *balance* between conscious materialistic goals and less conscious impulses from earlier life, serving *creative* needs.

Jung suggests that ignoring unconscious and nonrational forces in oneself may be in part the cause of extreme behavior, neuroses, loss of zest for life, the use of drugs, and even suicide. Contrariwise, he has told his patients that when their conscious minds no longer see any possible road ahead and are blocked, their unconscious processes react to the unbearable standstill. He is telling his patients in therapy to explore the latent possibilities in themselves, their *deep creative tendencies*, to find out what kind of persons they are, and to live accordingly.

His supportive relationship with his patients bolsters the patients' courage to do this.

Here are summarized a few more of Jung's observations from his psychoanalytic practice and his study of man's present and past—his dreams, myths, rituals, and neurotic and psychotic symptoms. Jung regards the *realization of selfhood* and the development of unique potentialities as life's goal, which tends to be reached as the person is able to *unite the many conflicting tendencies* within himself, especially conscious and unconscious processes, into an integrated, whole, balanced personality.

The middle age of man is crucial. It is a time when the individual becomes more introverted and less impulsive; physical and mental vigor are supplanted by social, religious, civic, and philosophic interests. Coping with the environment and with sexual and aggressive urges becomes less predominant; conversely, a search for *personal meaning, wholeness, and self-identity* in a universal context are in the forefront. Religion at this time of life becomes more important. Jung is frank in stating that man possesses a natural religious function and that his mental health and stability depend on the proper expression of this function in addition to the satisfaction of his basic physical drives. Jung defines religion broadly, referring to all attitudes of mind that give careful consideration to the dynamic factors man has always conceived as powers, spirits, demons, gods, laws, or ideals.

IMPLICATIONS

Which of Jung's ideas given here have the greatest meaning to you? Attempt to state them in your own words. What were the unconscious processes in the case of the printer? What are the unique potentials in your life that may be developed? How do you react to Jung's idea that man possesses natural religious functions? Try to state some example of unconscious processes in some individual you know.

REFERENCES

Some scholars regard Jung as one of the greatest thinkers of this century, since his writings have stimulated scholars in so many areas and his many ideas are so provocative. Whereas the intellectual world has great respect for him, psychologists for a long time regarded him critically despite the influence of his broader concepts. His findings were grounded on clinical and less easily verified findings rather than on experimental studies. His writings, say Hall and Lindzey (1957), who devote an excellent chapter to his ideas and influence, "stand as one of the most remarkable achievements in modern thought." They attribute this to his original and audacious thinking, which has few parallels.

Jung is sometimes difficult to read and at other times very expressive. Two of his many works often cited are *Modern Man in Search of a Soul* (1933) and *Psychology and Religion* (1960). Fordham (1961) has written a readable book on Jung's works. William Douglass (1959) has contributed an excellent review of several of Jung's volumes.

[65] E S P AND MENTAL TELEPATHY: AN EVALUATION

In almost every introductory class, students raise questions about the validity of *mental telepathy, clairvoyance, supernaturalism, mediums,* and other occult effects. These phenomena are sometimes called parapsychology. Certain of these effects have been studied under laboratory conditions, and psychologists do have definite opinions about the possible existence of the basic phenomenon known as ESP (extrasensory perception). We are referring here to perception that requires no sense organ stimulation. Psychologists vary in opinion about ESP, from the majority who say "an unlikely possibility" to other less frequently voiced opinions of "an impossibility" or "an unknown." You will note in the selection that Hilgard thinks we should reserve judgment as to its validity.

Ever so often a student will relate the experience of having a catastrophic dream "at the very same time" that a good friend or relative is in a serious accident. He may indicate belief that the dream communicated the accident to him and that this communication was a direct one between the "mind" of the victim and himself at the time of the disaster. Invariably, upon questioning, the student does not have data on the exact time of the dream or the accident, nor does he have any other validating evidence. When further questioned, the student will admit that he has dreamed of accidents before when no accidents have occurred.

The discussion of extrasensory perception by Hilgard is one of the most thorough, clear, and concise presentations of this phenomenon from the standpoint of contemporary psychology.

Most of the experiments that have been done on extrasensory perception have used a deck of twenty-five cards, containing five different kinds of cards with these simple symbols on them: a circle, a plus sign, a rectangle, a star, and parallel wavy lines (see Figure 1). The cards are shuffled, and one subject acts as a sender. The sender remains in one room, picks up a card and studies it carefully while the other subject, the receiver, tries at the same time "to read the mind" of the sender. He does this by calling out either "star," "square," "circle," "plus," or "parallel lines." His judgment can then be recorded as a hit or a miss.

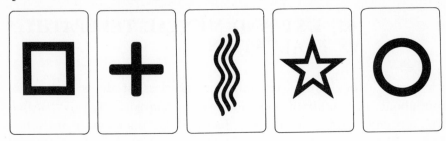

FIGURE 1. ESP cards, 25 in a pack.

With this brief introduction you are ready to read the description of extrasensory perception experiments and those on psychokinesis. You will observe that Hilgard's critical discussion of these phenomena offers us an understanding of why psychologists are dubious about the existence of these and similar "supernatural" phenomena.

Ernest R. Hilgard

From *Introduction to Psychology*, 3rd Edition, by Ernest R. Hilgard, copyright, 1953, © 1957, 1962, by Harcourt, Brace & World, Inc. and reproduced with their permission; published in England by Methuen & Co., London.

EXTRASENSORY PERCEPTION

If there are so many influences upon perception other than those coming from the presented stimuli, are there perhaps perceptions that require no sense-organ stimulation whatsoever? The answer to this question is the source of a major controversy within contemporary psychology over the status of *extrasensory perception* (ESP). A minority of psychologists believe that the evidence for the existence of certain forms of ESP is now incontrovertible (*e.g.*, Murphy, 1949; Rhine and Pratt, 1957; Soal and Bateman, 1954; Thouless, 1950). Despite these contentions, most psychologists remain unconvinced.

The phenomena under discussion are of four main kinds:

I. Extrasensory perception (ESP)
  1. Telepathy, or thought transference from one person to another.
  2. Clairvoyance, or the perception of objects or events not influencing the senses.
  3. Precognition, or the perception of a future event.
II. Psychokinesis (PK), whereby a mental operation affects a material body or an energy system (*e.g.*, wishing for a number affects what number comes up in the throw of dice).

The experimenters go at their work in accordance with the usual rules of science and generally disavow the connection between this work and spiritualism, supernaturalism, mediumistic phenomena, and other occult effects. Yet the phenomena with which they deal are so extraordinary, and so similar to the superstitious beliefs of nonliterate people, that many scientists disavow even the legitimacy of their inquiries. Such *a priori* judgments are out of place in science, however, and the real question is whether or not the empirical evidence is acceptable by ordinary scientific standards. Many psychologists who are not convinced would find it congenial to accept evidence that they found satisfactory. For example, the possibility of some sort of influence from one brain to another, other than by way of the sense organs, would not be inconceivable within the present framework of science were the facts of telepathy to be established in some orderly fashion. Some of the other phenomena are more difficult to find believable (precognition, for example), but if the evidence were firm, previous thought patterns would have to yield to the facts.

The case for ESP is based largely on experiments in card-guessing, in which, under various conditions, the subject attempts to guess the symbols on cards randomly arranged in packs. The usual pack consists of 25 cards with five symbols, so that a chance performance would be 5 hits per pack. Even very successful subjects seldom reach as high a level as 7 hits, but they may score above 5 often enough to meet acceptable standards of statistical significance. If the experimenter or "sender" thinks of the symbol at the time the subject makes his record, the experiment is one on telepathy; if the experimenter does not perceive the card at all (it may be face down on the table before him or sealed in an envelope), then the experiment is one on clairvoyance. The kind of evidence used in support of the nonchance nature of the findings can be illustrated by the successive runs of one "sensitive" subject, Mrs. Gloria Stewart, studied in England over a long period (Table 1). If the evidence is viewed in the same spirit as that from any other experiment, it is clear that Mrs. Stewart responded above chance on the telepathy trials, but not on the clairvoyance ones. This fact also meets certain objections about card arrangements sometimes used against such experiments, for her chance performance on the clairvoyance trials shows that

TABLE 1

RESULTS OF INTERSPERSED TELEPATHY AND
CLAIRVOYANCE TRIALS WITH ONE SUBJECT *

Chronological order of successive groups of 200 trials	Hits per 200 trials (Expected = 40)	
	Telepathy Trials	Clairvoyance Trials
1945	65	51
	58	42
	62	29
	58	47
	60	38
1947	54	35
	55	36
	65	31
1948	39	38
	56	43
1949	49	40
	51	37
	33	42
Total hits	707	509
Expected hits	520	520
Difference	+187	−11
Hits per 25 trials	6.8	4.9

SOURCE: Soal and Bateman (1945), p. 352.
* Each group of 200 trials consisted of alternating blocks of 50 telepathy and 50 clairvoyance trials.

above-chance scores are not an inevitable result of something having to do with the shuffling of the cards. The telepathy results are above the expected level in 11 of the 13 runs of 200, and the average scoring level of 6.8 hits (instead of 5) per pack of 25 is well above chance.

The complaint has been voiced that ESP results are not subject to systematic variation through ordinary experimental control. This also is not entirely fair to the findings. For example, there are some order effects reported, in which early trials are more successful than later ones (Rhine and Humphrey, 1944; McConnell, Snowdon, and Powell, 1955), and there is reported evidence that an attitude favorable to ESP, noted in advance, leads to positive results, while an unfavorable attitude leads to scoring below chance levels (Schmeidler and McConnell, 1958).

Thus, empirical findings are offered in support of ESP and PK, which meet ordinary statistical standards. Why, then, do not the results become a part of established psychological science? Many arguments have been used against the work, but they usually boil down to a few such as the following: (1) the fact that many claims of extraordinary phenomena in the past have turned out to be false when investigated; (2) certain problems in statistical inference that arise when very large numbers of trials are used to establish the significance of small differences; (3) the failure of improved methods to yield better results than crude methods; and (4) general lack of orderliness in the phenomena, without which rational theorizing cannot replace the highly irrational theories now used to account for what occurs.

These arguments are not, in fact, decisive, and it is desirable to keep an open mind about issues that permit empirical demonstration, as the ESP phenomena do. At the same time it should be clear that the reservations of the majority of psychologists are based on more than stubborn prejudice.

The following critical discussion is provided for those who might care to look a little further into these issues.

CRITICAL DISCUSSION

Why Many Psychologists Find ESP Experiments Unconvincing

We may expand a little upon the objections that psychologists have to the ESP and PK experiments and to *psi,* the special ability attributed to the "sensitive" subject.

1. *General scepticism about extraordinary phenomena.* Throughout history there have always been reports of strange happenings, of ghosts, little men, poltergeists (noisy spirits who engage in throwing things about), dreams foretelling the future. The continuing appearance of these stories does not make them true, any more than reported flying saucers establish the visits of men from Mars. Painstaking investigation by the U.S. Air Force yields no "flying saucers"; nobody ever traps the Loch Ness monster. A famous mediumistic case (still mentioned favorably by Soal and Bateman, 1954) is a case in point. Eusapia Palladino was a medium who was able to make a table move and produce other effects, such as tapping sounds, by the aid of a "spirit" called John King. Investigated repeatedly between 1893 and 1910, she convinced many distinguished scientists of her powers, including the distinguished Italian criminologist Lombroso and the British physicist Sir Oliver Lodge. She was caught in deceptive trickery as early as 1895, and the results were published. Yet believers continued to support her genuineness, as some do today, even though in an American investigation in 1910, her trickery was abundantly exposed (Jastrow, 1935; Rawcliffe, 1959). Two investi-

gators, dressed in black, crawled under the table unobserved and were able to see exactly how she used her foot to create the "supernatural" phenomena. When, therefore, those most convinced about ESP are also convinced about already disproven phenomena, their testimony carries less weight than if they were more critical. A similar case in point is Rhine's belief in an ESP interpretation of "water-witching" or "dowsing," in which water is discovered by means of a divining rod (Rhine and Pratt, 1957). Careful study of this bit of primitive magic shows that success in water-witching requires no such explanation (Vogt and Hyman, 1959).[1] While attacking ESP experiments on the basis of the belief systems of the investigators is a kind of *argumentum ad hominem*, and hence somewhat unfair, it is understandable that one is less likely to trust the observations of a person known to be gullible than one known to be critical.

2. *Problems of statistical inference with large numbers and small effects.* One of the major contributions of ESP research to scientific psychology may turn out to be the attention it has drawn to the circumstances that make a scientific finding believable. It is commonly supposed that tests of statistical significance are sufficient guarantees of objectivity, and hence a satisfactory statistical outcome should lead to acceptance of a hypothesis as plausible. This turns out not to be the case in ESP experiments, and it is probably not the case in other experiments either. Statistical tests merely tell us how well measurement seems to establish something that is already plausible; if it is not plausible, we search for some source of error that has produced the non-chance result. For example, in a major attempt to produce random digits by an electronic roulette wheel (The RAND Corporation, 1955), it proved very difficult to eliminate bias; in fact, a sample of 125,000 digits tested after the machine had been running a month departed from a random distribution by an amount that was statistically significant. One does not argue that some devilish scientist was using PK to foul the machine; one assumes that the machine somehow ran down with continuous use.

Let us compare this example with an experiment performed in Rhine's Duke University laboratory (Rhine, 1942). He was trying to detect whether or not a subject might, through some combination of ESP and PK, influence the positions of cards in a mechanical shuffler. In all, 51 persons wrote down their predictions of the orders in which cards would come out of a mechanical shuffler two to ten days later, the order of cards emerging from the shuffler being further complicated by having the cards cut by hand at a random trial. The experiment was carefully performed, and in a total of 57,550 trials the results were at chance level—just 11 hits in excess of expectation. But was this plausible result accepted? No; further statistical analyses were made. Two more of these, based on the division of the trials into segments, failed to yield non-chance results. Finally, a fourth analysis, based on a complex effect called a "covariance of salience ratio," gave a non-chance effect, with odds of 625 to 1 in its favor. When belief in bizarre effects is carried this far, it is no wonder that the unconvinced begins to suspect the statistics, even though the rules are followed and all computations are accurate.

There is a scientific problem here. A phenomenon may be rare and still important; hence large numbers of subjects or experiments may be needed if its existence is to be established. But the "good" or "sensitive" ESP subjects are rare. Soal and Bateman (1954), state that no such subject has turned up in America since 1938, despite the continuing research in the field, and in England

---

[1] It may come as something of a surprise that there are estimated to be some 25,000 waterwitchers in America—more than all the psychologists who are members of the American Psychological Association (Vogt and Hyman, 1959).

they have but three who maintained the ESP ability for a considerable time. These unusually sensitive subjects tend to reach a level of about 7 of 25 hits, instead of the 5 expected; such an ability is not very significant from a social point of view, no matter how established it may be statistically. The possibility of some undetected bias, as was found in the electronic roulette wheel, is real enough to temper belief.

3. *Failure of improved methods to increase the yield.* In most scientific fields, the assay from the ore becomes richer as the methods become more refined. But the reverse trend is found in ESP experiments; it is almost a truism in research in the field of telepathy and clairvoyance that the poorer the conditions the better the results. In the early days of the Duke experiments, subjects yielding high ESP scores were rather common, one virtuoso averaging, in the course of 650 trials, 10.7 hits in 25 instead of the 5 expected. As the experiments have become better controlled, however, these high-scoring subjects have disappeared.

4. *Lack of systematic consistency in the phenomena.* Sensitive subjects in the Rhine laboratory appear to be about equally successful at clairvoyance and telepathy; but the English subjects appear to be good at telepathy and not at clairvoyance. Other peculiarities emerge. In a famous series of experiments in England, Mr. Basil Shackleton (one of the three good subjects mentioned above) gave no evidence of either telepathy or clairvoyance when scored in the usual way against the target card. Instead, he was shown to be successful in *precognition telepathy*, that is, in guessing what was *going to be* on the experimenter's mind in the next trial. He was unsuccessful in clairvoyance, no matter how scored (Soal and Bateman, 1954). Why, the skeptic asks, does the direct telepathy fail with Mr. Shackleton in favor of something far more mysterious than the telepathic success of Mrs. Stewart? [2]

Because the *psi* ability does not follow the ordinary rules, explanations of its operation can be produced with the greatest of freedom. It need not be affected in any ordinary way by space or time, so that success over great distances is accepted as a sign of its extraordinary power rather than something to cause a search for artifacts. Similarly, the precognition experiments are merely evidence that it is as easy to read what is *about* to be on someone else's mind as what is on it now. The PK effects, which require the sorting of cards or the rolling of dice by mental effort ("mind over matter"), are nevertheless said to occur without any transfer of physical energy, thus presumably violating the usual belief in the conservation of energy. But in any experimental work *some* aspects of time and space have to be respected, such as spatial form and color and order of succession in time. Unless some restraint is shown, one might invent such hypotheses as that the subject was sometimes perceiving the cards in reverse order, sometimes in a place-skipping order, and so on; any significance test that depends upon coincidences requires some respect for order.

The believer in *psi* is impatient with this kind of criticism. He says that we ask more of him than we do of other experimenters. In fact, we do ask more. To demonstrate something highly implausible requires better evidence than to demonstrate something plausible. The reason is that supporting evidence for the plausible finding comes from many directions, while the implausible one must hang upon the slender thread of nonrandomness until certain systematic relationships are found that tie it firmly to what is known.

---

[2] Mrs. Stewart, who failed in clairvoyance also, was above chance in hits on the target card, but *also* on the preceding card and the following card.

IMPLICATIONS

To what extent are you convinced, as are many psychologists, that extrasensory perception, psychokinesis, and similar "supernatural" phenomena are an improbability? If not, are you able to state arguments and supply data that will withstand the general skepticism of the scientist? One way to test your understanding of the scientist's criticism of these phenomena is to review them, preparatory to a critical discussion, with someone who is a staunch believer in ESP and related occult effects. You might find an interesting means of integrating the criticism of ESP offered by psychologists. Why do you think so many people want to believe in ESP? Is it the same motivation found in those who patronize fortune tellers, or is there a different motivation in their case?

REFERENCES

Consult the Bibliography for references cited in the article.

BIBLIOGRAPHY*

Ackerman, N. W. *The Psychodynamics of Family Life.* New York: Basic Books, 1958.
Adorno, T. W., E. Frenkel-Brunswik, D. J. Levinson, and R. N. Sanford. *The Authoritarian Personality.* New York: Harper, 1950.
Adrian, E. D. *The Physcial Background of Perception.* Chapter 5. Oxford: Clarendon, 1947.
Alcoholics Anonymous. p. 59. New York: Alcoholics Anonymous, 1955.
"The A1-4-48 in Use: A Selection Study." Hartford, Conn.: Life Insurance Agency Management Association, 1951.
Allen, F. H. *Psychotherapy with Children.* New York: Norton, 1942.
Allen, R. M. *Personality Assessment Procedures.* New York: Harper, 1958.
Allport, G. W. *Becoming: Basic Considerations for the Psychology of Personality.* New Haven, Conn.: Yale University, 1955.
————. *The Individual and His Religion.* New York: Macmillan, 1950.
————. *The Nature of Prejudice.* Cambridge, Mass.: Addison-Wesley, 1954.
————. *Personality: A Psychological Interpretation.* New York: Holt, 1937.
————. "Religion and Prejudice." In Gordon W. Allport (ed.), *Personality and the Social Encounter,* Chapter 16. Cambridge, Mass.: Addison-Wesley, 1954.
Amatora, M. Free expression of adolescents' interests. *Genet. Psychol. Monogr.* 55:173–219. 1957.
An Analysis of the influence of alcohol on experimental neurosis in cats. *Psychosom. Med.* 6:36–52. 1946.
Anastasi, A. *Differential Psychology.* New York: Macmillan, 1958.
————. *Fields of Applied Psychology.* New York: Macmillan, 1964.
Anderson, S. *Seeds* ("The Triumph of an Egg"). New York: Viking, 1921.
Andrews, T. G. A factorial analysis of responses to the comic as a study in personality. *J. Gen. Psychol.* 28:209–224. 1943.
Andrieux, C. Contribution to a study of differences in men and women in spatial perception. *Amer. Psychologist.* 55:41–60. 1955.
Ansbacher, H. L. and R. R. Ansbacher (eds.). *The Individual Psychology of Alfred Adler.* New York: Basic Books, 1956.
Anson, B. J. *Atlas of Human Anatomy.* Philadelphia: Saunders, 1951.
Arieti, S. *Interpretation of Schizophrenia.* New York: Brunner, 1955.
Asch, S. E. Studies of independence and conformity: I. A minority of one against a unanimous majority. *Psychol. Monogr.* 70: No. 416. 1956.
Atkinson, J. W. (ed.). *Motives in Fantasy, Action and Society.* Princeton: Van Nostrand, 1958.
Axline, Virginia M. *Play Therapy.* Boston: Hougton Mifflin, 1947.
Bain, R. Sociology and psychoanalysis. *Amer. Sociol. Rev.* I. 2:203–216. 1936.
Barkin, S. Psychology as seen by a trade unionist. *Pers. Psychol.* 14:259–270. 1961.
Barron, F. The disposition toward originality. *J. Abnorm. Soc. Psychol.* 51:478–485. 1955.
Bartlet, J. E. A. A case of organized visual hallucinations in an old man with cataract and their relation to the phenomena of the phantom limb. *Brain.* 74:363–373. 1951.
Bass, B. M. *Organizational Psychology.* Boston: Allyn & Bacon, 1965.
Bavelas, A. Role-playing and management training. *Sociatry.* 1:183–191. 1947.
Beadle, G. W. and E. L. Tatum. *Proc. Natl. Acad. Sci.* 27:499–506. 1941.

* Standard reference procedures were used except in those cases in which the usual information was not furnished in an author's original bibliography.

Bell, J. E. "Recent Advances in Family Group Therapy." In M. Rosenbaum and M. Berger (eds.), *Group Psychotherapy and Group Function.* New York: Basic Books, 1963.

Bender, I. E. Changing patterns of religious interest. *The Humanist.* 18:139–144. 1958.

Benedict, R. *Patterns of Culture.* Boston: Hougton Mifflin, 1946.

————. "Continuities and Discontinuities in Cultural Conditioning." In C. Kluckhohn and H. Murray (eds.), *Personality in Nature, Society and Culture.* New York: Knopf, 1955.

Bennett, C. C. and C. R. Rogers. Predicting the outcomes of treatment. *Amer. J. Orthopsychiat.* 11:210–221. 1941.

————. The clinical significance of problem syndromes. *Amer. J. Orthospsychiat.* 11:222–229. 1941.

Berelson, B. and G. A. Steiner. *Human Behavior: An Inventory of Scientific Findings.* New York: Harcourt, Brace, 1964.

Berg, I. and V. Fox. Factors in homicides committed by 200 males. *J. Soc. Psychol.* 26:109–119. 1947.

Bergeijk, W. A. and E. E. David, Jr. *Percept. and Motor Skills.* 9:347. 1959.

Bernard, J. Parties and issues in conflict. *Conflict Resol.* 1:111–121. 1957.

Bischof, L. J. *Interpreting Personality Theories.* New York: Harper, 1964.

Blakeslee, A. F. J. *Heredity.* 23:106. 1932.

————. *Proc. Natl. Acad. Sci.* 48:298–299. 1918.

Bowen, M. "A Family Concept of Schizophrenia." In D. D. Jackson (ed.), *The Etiology of Schizophrenia.* New York: Basic Books, 1960.

Bradford, L. P. and R. Lippitt. Building a democratic work group. *Personnel.* 22:2–13. 1945.

Breckinridge, E. L. *Effective Use of Older Workers.* Chicago: Wilcox & Follett, 1953.

Bremer, F. and C. Terzuolo. Nouvelles recherches sur le processus physiologique de réveil. *Arch. Internat. de Physiol.* 61:86–90. 1953.

Bristol, L. (ed.). *Developing the Corporate Image: A Management Guide to Public Relations.* New York: Scribner, 1960.

Brody, M. W. "Prognosis and Results of Psychoanalysis." In J. H. Nodine and J. H. Moyer (eds.), *Psychosomatic Medicine.* Philadelphia: Lea & Febiger, 1962.

Bronfenbrenner, U. The changing American child: a speculative analysis. *Merrill-Palmer O. Beh. Develop.* 7:73–84. 1963.

————. The mirror image in Soviet-American relations. *J. Soc. Issues.* 17:45–46. 1961.

Brown, D. G. Sex-role development in a changing culture. *Psychol. Bull.* 55:232–242. 1958.

Brown, J. H. Acceleration and motor performance. *Human Factors.* 2:175–180. 1960.

Brunswik, E. "The Conceptual Framework of Modern Psychology." In *International Encyclopedia of United Science.* Chicago: University of Chicago, 1952.

Bulletin of Women's Bureau. No. 208: "Women's Wartime Hours of Work." Washington, D.C.: Government Printing Office, 1947.

————. No. 225: "Handbook of Facts on Women Workers." Washington, D.C.: Government Printing Office, 1948.

Burgess, E. W. *Personality and the Social Group.* Chicago: University of Chicago, 1929.

———— and L. S. Cottrell. *Predicting Success and Failure in Marriage.* Englewood Cliffs, N.J.: Prentice-Hall, 1939.

———— and P. Wallin. *Engagement and Marriage.* New York: Lippincott, 1953.

Burnett, A. and E. Ryan. "The Outpatient Treatment of Neurosis by Reciprocal Inhibition Methods." In mimeograph. New Foundland: St. John's Hospital, 1962.

Burt, C. (Review.) Critical notice: *Creativity and Intelligence* by J. W. Getzels and P. W. Jackson. *Brit. J. Educ. Psychol.* 32:292–298. 1962.

Burtt, H. E. *Legal Psychology.* Englewood Cliffs, N.J.: Prentice-Hall, 1931.

Carlson, R. O. How can the social sciences meet the needs of advertisers? *Printer's Ink.* 242:44–56. 1931.

Cartwright, D. and A. Zander. *Group Dynamics: Research and Theory,* 2 ed. Evanston, Ill.: Row Peterson, 1960.

Catanzaro, R. J. Treatment of the alcoholic. *Southwestern Med.* 45:115–117. 1964.

Chapanis, A. *Research Techniques in Human Engineering.* Baltimore: Johns Hopkins University, 1959.
Chaplin, J. P. Sex differences in the perception of autokinetic movement. *J. Genet. Psychol.* 52:149–155. 1955.
Chase, R. A., S. Harvey, S. Standfast, I. Rapin, and S. Sutton. *Science.* 129:903. 1959.
Christie, R. and M. Jahoda (eds.). *Studies in the Scope and Method of "The Authoritarian Personality."* New York: Free Press, 1954.
Clark, K. B. *Dark Ghetto.* New York: Harper, 1965.
Clark, W. H. A study of some of the factors leading to achievement and creativity, with special reference to religious skepticism and belief. *J. Soc. Psychol.* 41:57–69. 1955.
Clinard, M. B. *Sociology of Deviant Behavior.* New York: Holt, Rinehart & Winston. 1957.
Clinebell, H. R., Jr. *Understanding and Counseling the Alcoholic.* Nashville, Tenn.: Abingdon, 1956.
Coch, L. and J. R. P. French, Jr. Overcoming resistance to change. *Hum. Relations.* 1:512–532. 1948.
Cohen, A. K. *Delinquent Boys: The Culture of the Gang.* New York: Free Press, 1955.
Corsini, R. J. and G. A. Miller. Psychology in prisons. *Amer. Psychologist.* 9:184–185. 1954.
Cory, D. W. *The Homosexual in America.* New York: Greenberg, 1951.
Cox, C. M. *Genetic Studies of Genius. II: The Early Mental Traits of Three Hundred Geniuses.* Stanford: Stanford University, 1926.
Crawford, J. W. *Advertising: Communications from Management.* Boston: Allyn & Bacon. 1960.
David, P. R. and L. H. Snyder. *Social Psychology at the Crossroads.* New York: Harper, 1951.
Davis, K. B. *Factors in the Sex Life of Twenty-Two Hundred Women.* New York: Harper, 1929.
Dement, W. The effect of dream deprivation. *Science.* 131:705–707. 1960.
———— and N. Kleitman. The relation of eye movements during sleep to dream activity; an objective method for the study of dreaming. *J. Exp. Psychol.* 53:339–46. 1957.
Deutsch, M. The effect of motivational orientation upon trust and suspicion. *Hum. Relations.* 13:123–140. 1960a.
————. The face of bargaining. *Operation Res.* 9:866–897. 1961.
————. A theory of cooperation and competition. *Hum. Relations.* 2:129–152. 1949.
————. Trust and suspicion. *Conflict Resol.* 2:265–279. 1958.
————. Trust, trustworthiness, and the F scale. *J. Abnorm. Soc. Psychol.* 61:138–140. 1960b.
———— and R. M. Kraus. The effect of threat upon interpersonal bargaining. *J. Abnorm. Soc. Psychol.* 61:181–189. 1960.
Dichter, E. Psychology in market research. *Harvard Bus. Rev.* 25:156–158, 432–433. 1947.
Dickinson, R. L. and L. Beam. *The Single Woman: A Medical Study in Sex Education.* Baltimore: Williams & Wilkins, 1934.
Diethelm, O. *Etiology of Chronic Alcoholism.* Chapter 3. Springfield, Ill.: Thomas, 1955.
Doane, B. K., W. Mahatoo, W. Heron, and T. H. Scott. Changes in perceptual function after solution. *Canad. J. Psych.* 13:210–219. 1959.
Dollard, J. Hostility and fear in social life. *Soc. Forces.* 17:15–25. 1939.
Dorcus, R. M. Modification by suggestion of some vestibular and visual responses. *Amer. J. Psychol.* 49:82–87. 1937.
Douglass, W. A wise man and a young science. *Contemp. Psychol* 4:72–75. 1959.
Downey, J. *Creative Imagination.* London: Routledge & Kegan Paul, 1929.
Drucker, P. F. The promise of automation—America's next twenty years. *Harper's Mag.* 210:41–47. 1955.
Dudycha. G. J. *et al. Psychology for Law Enforcement Officers.* Springfield, Ill.: Thomas, 1955.
Dunbar, H. F. *Emotions and Bodily Changes.* New York: Columbia University, 1935.

Dunnette, M. D. Use of the sugar pill by industrial psychologists. *Amer. Psychologist.* 12:223–225. 1957.

Dunnette, M. D. and Kirchner, W. K. The role of the psychologist. In *Psychology Applied to Industry.* New York: Appleton-Century-Crofts, 1965.

Durkheim, E. *Suicide.* New York: Free Press, 1951.

Dynes, J. B. An experimental study in hypnotic anesthesia. *J. Abnorm. Soc. Psychol.* 27:79–88. 1932.

Ellis, A. *The American Sexual Tragedy.* New York: Twayne, 1959.

Empey, L. T. Role expectations of young women regarding marriage and a career. *Marr. Fam. Liv.* 20:152–155. 1958.

Engstrom, W. C. and M. E. Powers. A revision of the study of values for use in magazine readership research. *J. Appl. Psychol.* 43:74–78. 1959.

Etzioni, A. "International Prestige, Competition and Coexistence." In Q. Wright, W. M. Evan, and M. Deutsch (eds.), *Preventing World War III: Some Proposals.* New York: Simon & Schuster, 1962.

Eysenck. H. J. *Behaviour Therapy and the Neuroses.* Oxford: Pergamon, 1960.

————, M. Tarrant, M. Woolf, and L. England. Smoking and personality. *Brit. Med. J.* 1:(5184) 1456–1460. 1960.

Fairbanks, G. and N. Guttman. *J. Speech and Hearing Research.* 1:12, 1958.

Falk, G. J. Status differences and the frustration-aggression hypothesis. *Int. J. Soc. Psychiat.* 5:214–222. 1959.

Farber, I. E., H. F. Harlow, and L. J. West. Brainwashing, conditioning, and DDD. *Sociometry.* 20:271–285. 1957.

Farmer, E. and E. G. Chambers. A study of personal qualities in accident proneness and proficiency. *Ind. Health Res. Bd. Reports.* 55. 1929.

Fauls, L. B. and W. D. Smith. Sex-role learning of five-year olds. *J. Genet. Psychol.* 89:105–117. 1956.

Feinberg, M. R. Introduction to a symposium on implications of psychology in labor-management relations. *Pars. Psychol.* 14:239–241. 1961.

Fenichel, O. *The Psychoanalytic Theory of Neurosis.* New York: Norton, 1945.

Fiedler, F. E. The concept of an ideal therapeutic relationship in psychoanalytic, non-directive, and Adlerian therapy. *J. Consult. Psychol.* 14:436–445. 1950*a*.

————. The concept of an ideal therapeutic relationship. *J. Consult. Psychol.* 14:239–245. 1950*b*.

Flaherty, B. E. (ed.). *Psychophysiological Aspects of a Space Flight.* New York: Columbia University, 1961.

Flaubert, G. *Sentimental Education.* 2 v. p. 105. London, 1926.

Fleishman, E. A. *Studies in Personnel and Industrial Psychology.* Homewood, Ill.: Dorsey, 1961.

Flichinger, D. Planning by human factor teams. *J. Aviat. Med.* 26:2–12. 1955.

Forbes, T. W. The normal automobile driver as a traffic problem. *J. Gen. Psychol.* 20:471–474. 1939.

Fordham, F. *An Introduction to Jung's Psychology.* Baltimore: Penguin, 1961.

Forel, A. *Hypnotism and Psychotherapy.* New York: Rebman, 1907.

Forer, B. R. The fallacy of personal validations: a classroom demonstration of gullibility. *J. Abnorm. Soc. Psychol.* 44:118–123. 1949.

Frank, J. "The Motivational Basis of a World Without War." In Q. Wright, W. M. Evan, and M. Deutsch (eds.), *Preventing World War III: Some Proposals.* New York: Simon & Schuster, 1962.

Frank, L. K. *Adolescence.* The adolescent and the family. Forty-Third Yearbook, Natl. Soc. Stud. Educ., Part I. Chicago: University of Chicago, 1944.

————. The emancipation of economics. *Amer. Econ. Rev.* 14: No. 1. 1924.

————. Physiological tensions of social structure. *Public. of the Amer. Sociol. Society.* 22. 1928.

————. The principle of disorder and incongruity in economic affairs. *Political Science Quart.* 47: Dec. 1932.

————. Social planning and individual ideas. *J. Ethics.* 45: No. 1. 1934.

————. Social problems. *Amer. J. Sociol.* 4. 1925.

Frankl, V. E. *Man's Search for Meaning.* Boston: Beacon, 1963.

Freud, S. *Collected Papers,* IV. The relation of the poet to daydreaming. Encyclopedia article on psychoanalysis written in 1922. London: Hogarth, 1922.

Frick, H. L., R. E. Scantlebury, and T. L. Patterson. The control of gastric hunger contractions in men by hypnotic suggestion. *Amer. J. Physiol. 113:*471. 1935.

Fromm, E. The case for unilateral disarmament. *Daedelus.* 89:1015–1028. 1960.

————. *Escape from Freedom.* New York: Rinehart, 1941.

————. *Man for Himself.* New York: Rinehart, 1947.

————. *The Sane Society.* New York: Holt, Rinehart & Winston, 1955.

Galbraith, J. K. *The Affluent Society.* Boston: Houghton Mifflin, 1958.

Garmezy, N. and E. Rodnick. Premorbid adjustment and performance in schizophrenia: Implication for interpreting heterogeneity in schizophrenia. *J. Nerv. Ment. Dis.* 129:450–466. 1959.

Gebhard, P. H., J. H. Gagnon, W. B. Pomeroy, and C. V. Christenson. *Sex Offenders.* New York: Harper & Row, 1965.

Gellhorn, E. Prolegomena to a theory of emotions. *Perspec. Biol. Med.* 4:403–436. 1961.

———— and G. N. Loofbourrow. *Emotions and Emotional Disorders.* New York: Harper, 1963.

Gerathewohl, S. J., H. Strughold, and H. D. Stallings. Senso-motor performance during weightlessness, eye-hand coordination. *J. Aviat. Med.* 28:7–12. 1957.

Getzels, J. W. and P. W. Jackson. *Creativity and Intelligence.* New York: Wiley, 1962.

Ghiselli, E. E. and C. W. Brown. *Personnel and Industrial Psychology.* New York: McGraw-Hill, 1948.

Glueck, S. (ed.). *The Problem of Delinquency.* Boston: Houghton Mifflin, 1959.

Golann, S. W. Psychological study of creativity. *Psychol. Bull.* 60:548–565. 1963.

Goldzieher, M. A. *The Endocrine Glands.* New York: Appleton-Century, 1939.

Goodenough, E. W. Interest in persons as an aspect of sex differences in the early years. *Genet. Psychol. Monogr.* 55:287–323. 1957.

Greenwood, M. and H. M. Woods. *Report No. 4. Indust. Fatigue Res. Rep.* London: Her Majesty's Stationery Office, 1919.

Griffith, J. W. "The Time Factor in a Psychological Analysis of Accidents." Master's thesis, Illinois Institute of Technology, 1950.

Grollman, A. *Essentials of Endrocrinology,* 2 ed. Philadelphia: Lippincott, 1947.

Grziwok, R. and A. Scodel. Some psychological correlates of humor preferences. *J. Consult. Psychol.* 20:42. 1956.

Guilford, J. P. *Personality.* New York: McGraw-Hill, 1959.

————. Structure of human intellect. *Science.* 122:875. 1955.

———— et al. *University of Southern California Psychology Laboratory Reports:* 4, 1951; 8, 1952; 11, 1954; 16, 1956.

Gurin, G., J. Veroff, and S. Feld. *Americans View Their Mental Health.* New York: Basic Books, 1960.

Hacker, M. M. New burdens of masculinity. *Marr. Fam. Liv.* 19:227–232. 1957.

————. Women as a minority group. *Soc. Forces.* 30:60–69. 1952.

Haley, J. Whither family therapy? *Fam. Proc.,* 1:69–100. 1962.

Hall, C. S. *A Primer of Freudian Psychology.* Cleveland: World, 1954.

———— and G. Lindzey. *Theories of Personality.* New York: Wiley, 1957.

———— and R. L. Van de Castle. *The Content Analysis of Dreams.* New York: Appleton-Century-Crofts, 1966.

Hamachek, D. E. (ed.). *The Self in Growth: Teaching and Learning, Selected Readings.* Englewood Cliffs, N.J.: Prentice-Hall, 1965.

Hammer, E. F. (ed.). *The Clinical Application of Projective Drawing.* Springfield, Ill.: Thomas, 1958.

Harding, E. *The Way of All Women.* New York: Longmans, Green, 1933.

Harlow, H. F. The heterosexual affectional system in monkeys. *Amer. Psychologist.* 19:1–9. 1962.

——— and C. N. Woolsey (eds.). *Biological and Biochemical Bases of Behavior*. Madison: University of Wisconsin, 1958.
Harris, F. J. A comparison of the personality characteristics of accident and non-accident industrial populations. *Amer. Psychologist*. 4:279. 1949.
Hartmann, H., E. Kris, and R. M. Lowenstein. Notes on the theory of aggression. *Psychoanalytic Study of the Child*, v. 3–4. New York: International Universities, 1949.
Hatch, T. F. Proposed program in ergonomics. *Mech. Engng*. 77:394–395. 1955.
Havemann, E. and P. S. West. *They Went to College*. New York: Harcourt, Brace, 1952.
Heath, C. W. *et al. What People Are*. Cambridge, Mass.: Harvard University, 1945.
Henry, A. F. and J. F. Short, Jr. *Suicide and Homicide*. New York: Free Press, 1954.
Henry, W. E. The thematic apperception technique in the study of culture-personality relations. *Genet. Psychol. Mongr*. 35:3–138. 1947.
Heron, W., P. K. Doane, and T. H. Scott. Visual disturbance after prolonged perception isolation. *Canad. J. Psychol*. 10:13–16. 1956.
Herron, W. G. The process-reactive classification of schizophrenia. *Psychol. Bull*. 59:329–343. 1962.
Hersey, R. B. Emotional factors in accidents. *Person. J*. 15:59–65. 1936.
Herzog, H. "What Do We Really Know About Daytime Serial Listeners?" In P. F. Lazarsfeld and F. N. Stanton (eds.), *Radio Research*. New York: Duell, Sloan & Pearce, 1944.
Hilgard, E. R. *Introduction to Psychology*, 3 ed. New York: Harcourt, Brace & World, 1962.
Hinkle, L. E. and H. C. Wolff. Communist interrogation and indoctrination of "enemies of the State." *Arch. Neurol. Psychiat*. 76:115–174. 1956.
Hoch, E. L. and J. G. Darley. A case at law. *Amer. Psychologist*. 17:623. 1962.
Hollingshead, A. B. and C. F. Redlick. Social satisfaction and psychiatric disorders. *Amer. Sociol. Rev*. 18:163–169. 1958.
Horney, K. Culture and neurosis. *Amer. Sociol. Rev*. I, 2:221–230. 1936.
Hsu, F. L. K. (ed.). *Psychological Anthropology: Approaches to Culture and Personality*. Homewood, Ill: Dorsey, 1961.
Hull, C. L. *Hypnosis and Suggestibility*. New York: Appleton-Century-Crofts, 1933.
Hunt, W. A., C. L. Wittson, and H. W. Burton. Further validation of naval neuropsychiatric screening. *J. Consult. Psychol*. 14:485–488. 1950.
Hunter, I. M. L. The development of problem-solving ability. *Discovery*. 22:344–349. 1961.
Hurlock, E. *Developmental Psychology*, 2 ed. New York: McGraw-Hill, 1953.
Hutton, L. *The Single Woman and Her Emotional Problems*. London: Bailere, Tindall & Cox, 1935.
Icheiser, G. Misunderstandings in human relations. *Amer. J. Sociol*. 55 (part 2): 1–70. 1949.
Institute for Applied Experimental Psychology. *Handbook of Human Engineering Data*. Medford, Mass.: Tufts College, 1952.
Jackson, D. D. *The Etiology of Schizophrenia*. New York: Basic Books, 1960.
——— and V. M. Satir. "Historical Antecedents of Family Therapy." In N. W. Ackerman, F. L. Beatman, and S. N. Sherman (eds.), *Exploring the Base for Family Therapy*. New York: Family Service Association of America, 1961.
——— and J. H. Weakland. Conjoint family therapy. *Psychiat*. 24:30–45. 1961.
Jacob, P. *Changing Values in College*. New York: Harper & Row, 1957.
Jacobson, E. *Progressive Relaxation*. Chicago: University of Chicago, 1939.
Jacobson, E. H. and S. Schachter (eds.). Cross-national research: a case study. *J. Soc. Issues*. 10: No. 4. 1954.
Jahoda, M. *Current Concepts of Positive Mental Health*. New York: Basic Books, 1958.
——— and J. Havel. Psychological problems of women in different social roles. *Educ. Records*. 36:325–335. 1955.
James, W. *Varieties of Religious Experience*. New York: Longmans, Green, 1911.
———. *Memories and Studies*. "The Moral Equivalent of War." New York: Longmans, Green, 1911.

Janet, P. *Psychological Healing*, 2 v., trans. E. & C. Paul. London: Allen & Unwin, 1925.
Janis, I. L. and D. Katz. The reduction of intergroup hostility: Research problems and hypotheses. *J. Conflict Resolut.* 3:85–100. 1959.
Jastrow, J. *Wish and Wisdom*. New York: Appleton-Century, 1935.
Jellinek, E. M. *Disease Concept of Alcoholism*. New Haven: United Printing Service, 1960.
Jessor, R. and K. Hammond. "Construct Validity and the Taylor Anxiety Scale." In M. T. Mednick and S. A. Mednick (eds.), *Research in Personality*. New York: Holt, Rinehart & Winston, 1963.
Johnson, D. M. Psychology versus literature. *Harper Books and Authors.* 12:1–4. 1961.
Johnson, H. M. The detection and treatment of accident-prone drivers. *Psychol. Bull.* 43:489–532. 1946.
Jones, M. *Social Psychiatry*. Chapter I: "Social Psychiatry and the Changing Community." Springfield, Ill.: Thomas, 1962.
Jung, C. G. *Modern Man in Search of a Soul*. New York: Harcourt Brace, 1933.
———. *Psychology and Religion*. New Haven: Yale University, 1960.
Kallman, F. J. "The Genetics of Mental Illness." In S. Arieti (ed.), *American Handbook of Psychiatry*. New York: Basic Books, 1959.
Kalmus, H., P. Denes, and D. B. Fry. Effect of delayed acoustic feedback on some nonvocal activities. *Nature. 175*:1078. 1955.
Kantor, J. R. *An Outline of Social Psychology*. Chicago: Follett, 1929.
Kaplan, B., R. B. Reed, and N. Richardson. A comparison of the incidence of hospitalized cases of psychoses in two communities. *Amer. Sociol. Rev. 21*:572–579. 1956.
Katz, D. (ed.). Attitude change. *Pub. Opin. Quart. 24*:163–365. 1960.
———. Current and needed psychological research in international relations. *J. Soc. Issues.* 17:69–78. 1961.
——— and F. H. Allport. *Students' Attitudes*. Syracuse: Craftsmen, 1931.
Keenan, V., W. A. Kerr, and W. E. Sherman. Psychological climate and accidents in an automotive plant. *J. Appl. Psychol.* 35:108–111. 1951.
Kell, B. L. "The Predictive Possibilities of the Component-Factor Method of Diagnosis as Applied to Children with Behavior Problems." Master's thesis, Ohio State, 1942.
Kellogg, W. N. and L. H. Kellogg. *The Ape and the Child*. New York: McGraw-Hill, 1933.
Kelly, E. L. Concerning the validity of Terman's weights for predicting marital happiness. *Psychol. Bull.* 306:202–203. 1939.
———. Consistency of the adult personality. *Amer. Psychologist.* 10:659–681. 1955.
Kelly, G. A. *The Psychology of Personal Constructs*. v. 1. New York: Norton, 1955.
Kelman, H. C. "A Proposal for Internationalizing Military Force." In Q. Wright, W. M. Evan, and M. Deutsch (eds.), *Preventing World War III: Some Proposals*. New York: Simon & Schuster, 1962.
Kerr, W. A. "Psychological Climate and Safety." Address, Midwest Safety Show, National Safety Council, Chicago, May 4, 1950*a*.
———. Accident proneness of factory departments. *J. Appl. Psychol.* 34:167–170. 1950*b*.
Keys, A. *Biology of Mental Health and Disease*. "Experimental Induction of Neuropsychoses by Starvation." New York: Hoeber, 1952.
Kimber, J. A. M. An introduction to the marriage counselor and his work. *Psychol. Rep.* 8:71–75. 1961.
Kinsey, A. C., W. B. Pomeroy, and C. E. Martin. *Sexual Behavior in the Human Male*. Philadelphia: Saunders, 1948.
Kinsey, A. C., W. B. Pomeroy, C. E. Martin, and P. H. Gebhard. *Sexual Behavior in the Human Female*. Philadelphia: Saunders, 1953.
Kirchner, W. K. and M. D. Dunnette. Applying the weighted application blank technique to a variety of office jobs. *J. Appl. Psychol.* 41:206–208. 1957.
Kirk, R. L. and N. S. Stenhouse. Ability to smell solutions of potassium cyanide. *Nature. 171*:400–409. 1953.
Kirkpatrick, C. A Comparison of generations in regard to attitude toward feminism. *J. Genet. Psychol.* 49:343–361. 1936.

Kitson, H. D. A critical age as a factor in labor turnover. *J. Indust. Hygiene.* 4:199–203. 1922.

Klebanoff, S. G. "Psychologists in Institutions." In W. B. Webb (ed.), *The Profession of Psychology.* New York: Holt, Rinehart & Winston, 1962.

Kleemeier, R. W. (ed.). *Aging and Leisure: A Research Perspective into Meaningful Use of Time.* New York: Oxford, 1961.

Kleitman, N. *Sleep and Wakefulness,* Chicago: University of Chicago, 1939.

Klineberg, O. *Race Differences.* New York: Harper, 1933.

Kluckhohn, F. R. "American Women and American Values." In L. Bryson *et al.* (eds.), *Facing the Future's Risks.* New York: Harper, 1953.

Knight, R. P. Evaluation of the results of psychoanalytic therapy. *Amer. J. Psychiat.* 98:434–446. 1941.

Knopf, O. *The Art of Being a Woman.* Boston: Little, Brown, 1932.

Kohn, M. L. Social class and the exercise of parental authority. *Amer. Sociol. Rev.* 24:352–366. 1959.

Komarovsky, M. *Women in the Modern World.* Boston: Little, Brown, 1953.

Koponen, A. Personality characteristics of purchasers. *J. Advert. Res.* 1:6–11. 1960.

———. *Personality Profile Projects.* New York: Thompson, 1958.

Kotkov, B. and B. Murawski. A Rorschach study of the personality structure of obese women. *J. Clin. Psychol.* 8:391–396. 1952.

Kreidt, P. H. and M. S. Gadel. Prediction of turnover among clerical workers. *J. Appl. Psychol.* 37:338–340. 1953.

La Follette, C. T. A study of the problems of 652 gainfully employed married women homemakers. *Columbia Teachers College Contributions to Education.* 619. 1934.

Landis, C. and J. W. H. Ross. Humor and its relation to other personality traits. *J. Soc. Psychol.* 4:156–175. 1933.

Larson A. "The Role of Law in Building Peace." In Q. Wright, W. M. Evan, and M. Deutsch (eds.), *Preventing World War III: Some Proposals.* New York: Simon & Schuster, 1962.

Lashley, K. S. *Psychol. Rev.* 54:333–334. 1947.

Lazarus, A. A. The elimination of children's phobias by deconditioning. *Med. Proc.* 5:261–265. 1959.

———. The results of therapy in 126 cases of severe neurosis. *Behav. Res. Ther.* 1:69–80. 1963*a.*

———. The treatment of chronic frigidity by systematic desensitization. *J. Nerv. Ment. Dis.* 136:272–278. 1963*b.*

Lecky, P. *Self-Consistency: A Theory of Personality.* New York: Island, 1945.

Lee, B. S. Effects of delayed speech feedback. *J. Acoust. Soc. Am.* 22:824. 1950.

Leuba, C. Laughter: two genetic studies. *J. Genet. Psychol.* 58:201–209, 1941.

Levenstein, A. The psychologist joins the labor conflict. *Pers. Psychol.* 14:250–258. 1961.

Levitas, G. B. *The World of Psychology.* v. I & II. New York: Braziller, 1963.

Lewin, K. "Group Decision and Social Change." In T. M. Newcomb and E. L. Hartley (eds.), *Readings in Social Psychology.* New York: Holt, 1947.

———. *Principles of Topological Psychology.* New York: McGraw-Hill, 1936.

———, R. Lippitt, and R. K. White. Patterns of aggressive behavior in experimentally created social climates. *J. Soc. Psychol.* 11:271–299. 1939.

Lifton, R. L. "Thought reform" of western civilians in Chinese communist prisons. *Psychiatry.* 19:173–198. 1957.

Likert, R. *New Patterns of Management.* New York: McGraw-Hill, 1961.

Linton, R. "Women in the Family." In J. E. Fairchild (ed.), *The Way of Women.* New York: Fawcett, 1956.

Lippman, C. Certain hallucinations peculiar to migraine. *J. Nerv. Ment. Dis.* 116:346–351. 1952.

Lippitt, R., L. P. Bradford, and K. D. Benne. Socio-dramatic clarification of leader and group roles. *Sociatry.* 1:82–91. 1947.

Loftus, J. P. and L. R. Hammer. Weightlessness and performance: a review of the literature. *USAF Aeronaut. Sys. Div. Tech. Rep.* 1961.

Lundberg, F. and M. F. Farnham. *Modern Woman: The Lost Sex.* New York: Harper & Row, 1947.
Lundholm, H. An experimental study of functional anesthesias as induced by suggestion in hypnosis. *J. Anal. Psychol. 23*:337–355. 1928.
Lynn, D. B. A note on sex preferences in the development of masculine and feminine identification. *Psychol. Rev. 66*:125–235. 1959.
Machover, K. *Personality Projection in the Drawing of the Human Figure.* Springfield, Ill.: Thomas, 1962.
MacKinnon, D. W. Personality and the realization of creative potential. *Amer. Psychologist. 20*:273–281. 1965.
Mackworth, N. H. Researches on the measurement of human performance. *Med. Res. Council, Spec. Rep. Ser.,* London. 268. 1950.
Maier, N. R. F. A human relations program for supervision. *Indust. and Lab. Relat. Rev. 1*:443–464. 1948.
———. "Improving Supervision Through Training." In A. Kornhauser (ed.), *Psychology of Labor Management Relations.* Champaign, Ill.: Industrial Relations Research Assn., 1949.
Malzberg, B. and E. S. Lee. *Migration and Mental Disease.* New York: Social Science Research Council, 1956.
Maritz, J. S. On the validity of inferences drawn from the fitting of Poisson and negative binomial distributions to observed accident data. *Psychol. Bull. 471*:434–443. 1950.
Maslow, A. H. "Self Actualizing People: A Study of Psychological Health." In W. Wolff (ed.), *Values in Personality Research.* New York: Grune & Stratton, 1950.
———. *Toward a Psychology of Being.* Princeton: Van Nostrand, 1962.
Masserman, J. H. "Ethology, Comparative Biodynamics, and Psychoanalytic Research." In J. Scher (ed.), *Theories of the Mind.* New York: Free Press, 1963.
——— and K. S. Yum. An analysis of the influence of alcohol on experimental neurosis in cats. *Psychosom. Med. 6*:36–52. 1946.
Mauriac, F. *Thérèse.* Trans. Gerard Hopkins. London: Eyre & Spottiswoode.
May, R. *Existential Psychology.* New York: Random House, 1961.
McCary, J. L. A psychologist testifies in court. *Amer. Psychologist. 15*:53–57. 1960.
McClelland, D. C. *The Achieving Society.* Princeton: Van Nostrand, 1961.
McConnell, R. A., R. J. Snowdon, and K. F. Powell. Wishing with dice. *J. Exp. Psychol. 50*:269–275. 1955.
McCormick, E. J. *Human Engineering.* New York: McGraw-Hill, 1957.
McGill, W. J. *Behavior Genetics and Differential Psychology.* Symposium. American Psychological Association: New York, 1957.
McGuire, F. L. A psychological comparison of accident-violation-free and accident-incurring automobile drivers. *Camp Lejeune Naval Medical Field Research Lab.* February, 1955.
McKinney, F. *Psychology of Personal Adjustment.* New York: Wiley, 1960.
———. *Understanding Personality: Cases in Counseling.* Boston: Houghton Mifflin, 1965.
McNeil, H. "Factors Significantly Related to the Later Adjustment of Children Presenting Problem and Delinquent Behavior." Master's thesis. Ohio State, 1944.
McNemar, Q. Lost: Our intelligence. *Amer. Psychologist. 19*:871–882. 1964.
Mead, M. Cultural aspects of women's vocational problems in post-World War. II. *J. Consult. Psychol. 10*:24. 1946.
———. *Male and Female.* New York: Morrow, 1949.
———. *Sex and Temperament.* New York: Morrow, 1935.
Mednick, M. and S. A. Mednick. *Research in Personality.* New York: Holt, Rinehart & Winston, 1963.
Meltzer, H. Sex differences in children's attitudes to parents. *J. Genet. Psychol. 62*:311–326. 1943.
Melzack, R. and T. H. Scott. The effects of early experience on the response to pain. *J. Comp. Physiol. Psychol. 50*:155–161. 1957.
Menninger, K. *Theory of Psychoanalytic Technique.* New York: Basic Books, 1958.

————. What the girls told. *Saturday Rev.* 36. 1953.

Merton, R. K. *Social Theory and Social Structure: The Self-Fulfilling Prophecy.* Rev. ed. New York: Free Press, 1957.

Minturn, L. and W. W. Lambert. *Mothers of Six Cultures.* New York: Wiley, 1964.

Mintz, A. and M. L. Blum. A re-examination of the accident proneness concept. *J. Appl. Psychol.* 33:195–211. 1949.

Morris, G. O. and L. C. Wynne. Schizophrenic offspring and parental styles of communication. *Psychiatry.* 28:19–44. 1965.

Moss, C. S. "Brief Crisis-Oriented Hypnotherapy." In J. Gordon (ed.), *Handbook of Hynotherapy.* New York: McGraw-Hill, 1953.

Moustakas, C. E. *Children in Play Therapy.* New York: McGraw-Hill, 1953.

Mowrer, O. H. *Psychotherapy: Theory and Research.* New York: Ronald, 1953.

————. "What Is Normal Behavior?" In L. A. Pennington and I. A. Berg (eds.), *An Introduction to Clinical Psychology.* 2 ed. New York: Ronald, 1954.

Mueller, K. H. "The Cultural Pressures on Women." In C. D. David (ed.), *The Education of Women: Signs for the Future.* Washington, D.C.: American Council on Education, 1959.

Munroe, R. *Schools of Psychoanalytic Thought.* New York: Holt, Rinehart & Winston, 1955.

Munsterberg, H. *On the Witness Stand.* New York: McClure, 1908.

Murphy, G. *Human Nature and Enduring Peace.* Boston: Houghton Mifflin, 1945.

————. *In the Minds of Men.* New York: Basic Books, 1953.

————. *Personality: A Biosocial Approach to Origin and Structure.* New York: Harper, 1947.

————. The place of parapsychology among the sciences. *J. Parapsychol.* 13:62–71. 1949.

National Planning Association. *Causes of Industrial Peace.* Washington, D.C., 1953.

Nawas, M. M. "From Adolescence to Adulthood Through the TAT." Ph.D. dissertation. Committee on Human Development, University of Chicago, 1961.

————. "Some Impediments to Growth and Adjustment in the Young Adult Years." Unpublished paper, University of Missouri, 1965.

Nelson, E. N. P. Patterns of religious attitude from college to fourteen years later. *Psychol. Monogr.* No. 424. 1956.

Newbold, E. M. A contribution to the study of the human factor in the causation of accidents. *Indust. Fatigue Res. Bd. Rep.* 34. London: Her Majesty's Stationery Office, 1919.

Newcomb, T. M. Autistic hostility and social reality. *Hum. Relations.* 1:69–86. 1947.

Nielson, G. S. *Psychology and International Affairs: Can We Contribute?* Copenhagen: Munksgard, 1962.

Nissen, A. W., K. L. Chow, and J. Semmes. Effects of restricted opportunity for tactile kinesthetic and manipulative experience on the behavior of a chimpanzee. *Amer. J. Psychol.* 64:485–507. 1951.

Noger, J. The diplomacy of disarmament. *Internat. Conciliation.* 526. Carnegie Endowment for International Peace, 1960.

Ortega y Gasset, J. *The Modern Theme.* New York: Norton, 1933.

Osgood, C. E. An analysis of the cold war mentality. *J. Soc. Issues.* 17:12–19. 1961.

Osterberg, A. E., F. R. Vanzant, W. C. Alvarez, and A. B. Rivers. Studies of pepsin in human gastric juice. III. Physiological aspects. *Am. J. Digestive Dis.* 35:35–41. 1936.

Pabban, M. Sex-role identification in young children in two diverse groups. *Genet. Psychol. Monogr.* 42:81–158. 1950.

Pace, C. R. *They Went to College.* Minneapolis: University of Minnesota, 1941.

Palmer, S. Frustration, aggression, and murder. *J. Abnorm. Soc. Psychol.* 60:430–432. 1960.

Parsons, T. *Essays in Sociological Theory Pure and Applied.* New York: Free Press, 1949.

————. "Polarization and the Problem of World Order." In Q. Wright, W. M. Evan, and M. Deutsch (eds.), *Preventing World War III: Some Proposals.* New York: Simon & Schuster, 1962.

———— and R. F. Bales. *Family Socialization and Interaction Process.* New York: Free Press, 1955.

Pattie, F. A. The genuineness of hypnotically produced anesthesia of the skin. *Amer. J. Psychol. 49:435-443.* 1937.

————. The production of blisters by hypnotic suggestion. *J. Abnorm. Soc. Psychol. 36:62-72.* 1941.

————. A report of attempts to produce uniocular blindness by hypnotic suggestion. *Brit. J. Psychol. 25:230-241.* 1935.

Pavlov, I. P. *Conditioned Reflexes and Psychiatry.* Trans. W. H. Gantt. New York: International, 1941.

Phillips, J. D. Report on discussion 66. *Adult Educ. J. 7:181-182.* 1948.

Pierce, C. S. Logical machines. *Amer. J. Psychol. 1:165-170.* 1887.

Pincus, G. and K. V. Thimann. *The Hormones.* New York: Academic, 1948.

Pittman, D. J. and C. R. Snyder. *Society, Culture, and Drinking Patterns.* See pp. 157-188. New York: Wiley, 1962.

Premack, D. and A. Schwartz. "Preparations for Discussing Behaviorism with Chimpanzees." In F. Smith and C. A. Miller (eds.), *The Genesis of Language in Children and Other Animals.* Cambridge, Mass.: M.I.T., 1966.

Pyle, N. E. *The Psychology of Learning.* p. 73. Baltimore: Warwick & York, 1921.

Raimy, V. E. *Training in Clinical Psychology.* Englewood Cliffs, N. J.: Prentice-Hall, 1950.

RAND Corporation. *A Million Random Digits.* New York: Free Press, 1955.

Rank, O. Psychology and social change. *Newsletter of Amer. Assn. of Psych. Soc. Workers. 4:3.* 1935.

Rapoport, A. "Aggressiveness, Gamesmanship and Persuasion." In Q. Wright, W. M. Evan, and M. Deutsch (eds.), *Preventing World War III: Some Proposals.* New York: Simon & Schuster, 1962.

Rapaport, D. *Organization and Pathology of Thought.* New York: Columbia University, 1951.

Rasmussen, A. T. The morphology of pars intermedia of the human hypophysis. *Endocrinology. 12:129-150.* 1928.

————. A quantitative study of the human hypophysis cerebri, or pituitary body. *Endocrinology. 8:509-524.*

————. The weight of the principal components of the normal male adult human hypophysis cerebri. *Am. J. Anat. 42:27.* 1928.

Rawcliffe, D. H. *Illusions and Delusions of the Supernatural and Occult.* New York: Dover, 1959.

Rees, E. W. and N. K. Copeland. Discrimination of differences in mass of weightless objects. *USAF WADD Tech. Rep. 60:601.* 1960.

Rhine, J. B. Evidence of precognition in the covariation of salience ratios. *J. Parapsychol. 6:111-143.* 1942.

———— and B. M. Humphrey. The PK effect: special evidence from hit patterns. I. Quarter distributions of the page. *J. Parapsychol. 8:18-60.* 1944.

———— and J. G. Pratt. *Parapsychology, Frontier Science of the Mind.* Springfield, Ill.: Thomas, 1957.

Riesman, D. *The Lonely Crowd.* New Haven: Yale University, 1950.

Ring, G. C. *et al.* Estimation of heart output from electrokymographic measurements in human subjects. *J. Appl. Physiol. 5:99-110.* 1952.

Robinson, E. S. *Law and Lawyers.* New York: Macmillan, 1935.

Roe, A. *The Making of a Scientist.* New York: Dodd-Mead, 1952.

————. *The Psychology of Occupation.* New York: Wiley, 1956.

————, J. W. Gustad, B. V. Moore, S. Ross, and M. Skodak. *Graduate Education in Psychology.* Washington, D.C.: American Psychological Association, 1959.

Rogers, C. R. *The Clinical Treatment of the Problem Child.* Boston: Houghton Mifflin, 1939.

————. *Counseling and Psychotherapy.* Boston: Houghton Mifflin, 1951.

————. Some observations on the organization of personality. *Amer. Psychologist.* 2:358–368. 1947.

Rokeach, M. *The Open and Closed Mind.* New York: Basic Books, 1960.

Rose, A. M. The adequacy of women's expectations for adult roles. *Soc. Forces.* 30:69. 1952.

Rosenow, C. Meaningful behavior in hypnosis. *Amer. J. Psychol.* 40:204–235. 1928.

Russell, B. "Psychology and East-West Tension." In Q. Wright, W. M. Evan, and M. Deutsch (eds.), *Preventing World War III: Some Proposals.* New York: Simon & Schuster, 1962.

Russell, R .W. Roles for psychologists in the "maintenance of peace." *Amer. Psychologist.* 15:95–109. 1960.

Rustad, W. H. *J. Clin. Endocrinol. Metabolism.* 14:87–96. 1954.

Ryan, T. A. *Work and Effort.* New York: Ronald, 1947.

Salter, A. *Conditioned Reflex Therapy.* New York: Farrar, Straus, 1949; and Putnam, 1961.

Sanford, E. C. Personal equation. *Amer. J. Psychol.* 1:165–170. 1889.

Sanford, N. (ed.). *College and Character.* New York: Wiley, 1964.

————. Personality development during the college years. *J. Sociol. Issues.* 12. 1956.

Sapir, C. The emergence of the concept of personality in a study of culture. *J. Soc. Psychol.* 5:408–415. 1934.

Satir, V. M. *Conjoint Family Therapy.* Palo Alto, Calif.: Science and Behavior, 1964.

Schattenbrand, G. and P. Bailey. *Introduction to Sterotaxis, with an Atlas of the Human Brain.* 3 v. New York: Grune & Stratton, 1959.

Schmeidler, G. R. and R. A. McConnell. *ESP and Personality Patterns.* New Haven: Yale University, 1958.

Schofield, W. Psychology, law, and the object witness. *Amer. Psychologist.* 11:1–7. 1956.

Scott, E. M. Personality and movie preference. *Psychol. Rep.* 3:17–18. 1957.

Sears, R. R. An experimental study of hypnotic anesthesia. *J. Exp. Psychol.* 15:1–22. 1932.

Sells, H. B. and C. A. Berry. *Human Factors in Jet and Space Travel: A Medical-Psychological Analysis.* New York: Ronald, 1961.

Selye, Hans. *The Stress of Life.* New York: McGraw-Hill, 1956.

Severin, F. T. (ed.). *Humanistic Viewpoints in Psychology.* New York: McGraw-Hill, 1965.

Seward, G. H. *Sex and the Social Order.* New York: McGraw-Hill, 1946.

Shein, H. The Chinese indocrination program for prisoners of war. *Psychiatry.* 19:149–172. 1956.

Sheldon, W. H. *Varieties of Human Temperament.* New York: Harper, 1942.

Shepard, A. B. Pilot's flight report, including in-flight time films. *Results of the First U.S. Manned Suborbital Space Flight,* No. 10, U.S. National Aeronautics and Space Administration, National Institute of Health, and National Academy of Sciences, 1961.

Shepard, H. A. The psychologist's role in union-management relations. *Pers. Psychol.* 14:270–278. 1961.

Sheperd, C. R. *Small Groups: Some Sociological Perspectives.* San Francisco: Chandler, 1964.

Shneidman, E. S. and N. L. Farberow. *Clues to Suicide.* New York: McGraw-Hill, 1957.

Shoben, E. J. Toward a concept of the normal personality. *Amer. Psychologist.* 12:183–189. 1957.

Simons, J. C. Walking under zero-gravity conditions. *USAF WADC Tech. Note.* 59:327, 1959.

———— and M. S. Gardner. Self-maneuvering for the orbital worker. *USAF WADD Tech. Rep.* 60:748. 1960.

Skelley, E. L. Psychological services in state schools for delinquent boys. *Amer. Psychologist.* 9:186–187. 1954.

Skinner, B. F. The experimental analysis of behavior. *Am. Scientist.* 45:4. 1957.

————. The science of learning and the art of teaching. *Harvard Educ. Rev.* 24:86–97. 1954.

Smith, G. H. *Motivation Research in Advertising and Marketing.* New York: McGraw-Hill, 1954.

Smith, K. U. and R. Bloom. The electronic handwriting analyzer and motion study of writing. *J. Appl. Psychol.* 40:302. 1956.

Soal, S. G. and Bateman, F. *Modern Experiments in Telepathy.* New Haven: Yale University, 1954.

Sohn, L. B. "Neo-neutralism and the Neutralization of the United Nations." In Q. Wright, W. M. Evan, and M. Deutsch (eds.), *Preventing World War III: Some Proposals.* New York: Simon & Schuster, 1962.

Stagner, R. The psychologist's function in union-management relations. *Pers. Administration.* 26:24–29. 1963.

——— and M. H. Krout. The study of personality development and structure. *J. Abnorm. Soc. Psychol.* 35:340–355. 1940.

Stalnaker, J. M. and E. L. Riddle. The effects of hypnosis on long-delayed recall. *J. Gen. Psychol.* 6:429–440. 1932.

Stead, W. H. and C. L. Shartle. *Occupational Counseling Techniques.* New York: American, 1940.

Steinmann, A. Lack of communication between men and women. *Marr. Fam. Liv.* 20:350–352. 1958.

Stern, P. J. *The Abnormal Person and His World.* Princeton: Van Nostrand, 1965.

Stevens, S. S. The surprising simplicity of sensory metrics. *Amer. Psychologist.* 17:29–39. 1962.

Strassman, H. D., M. Thaler, and E. H. Shein. A prisoner of war syndrome apathy as a reaction to severe stress. *Amer. J. Psychiat.* 112:998–1003. 1956.

Sultan, E. E. A factorial study in the domain of creative thinking. *Brit. J. Educ. Psychol.* 32:78–82. 1962.

Sundberg, N. D. The acceptability of "fake" versus "bona fide" personality test interpretations. *J. Abnorm. Soc. Psychol.* 50:145–147. 1955.

——— and L. E. Tyler. *Clinical Psychology.* New York: Appleton-Century-Crofts, 1962.

Sutherland, E. H. and D. R. Creasey. *Principles of Criminology.* 6 ed. Philadelphia: Lippincott, 1960.

Symonds, P. M. *The Ego and the Self.* New York: Appleton-Century-Crofts, 1951.

Taylor, C. W. and J. L. Holland. Development and application of tests of creativity. *Rev. Educ. Res.* 32:91–102. 1962.

Taylor, H. "Education for Women." In J. E. Fairchild (ed.), *The Way of Women.* New York: Fawcett, 1956.

Terman, L. M. Kinsey's "Sexual Behavior in the Human Male": Some comments and criticisms. *Psychol. Bull.* 45:443–454. 1948.

———. *Psychological Factors in Marital Happiness.* New York: McGraw-Hill, 1938.

——— and M. Oden. *Genetic Studies of Genius. IV: The Gifted Child Grows Up.* Stanford: Stanford University, 1947.

Thorndike, E. L. *The Psychology of Learning,* v. 2 of *Educational Psychology.* New York: New York Bureau of Publications. Teachers College, Columbia University, 1913.

Thorndike, R. L. Some methodological issues in the study of creativity. *Proceedings of the Invitational Conference on Testing Problems.* Princeton: Educational Testing Service, 1962.

———. The human factor in accidents. *USAF School of Aviation Med. Rep.* Randolph Field, Tex., 1951.

Thouless, R. H. Thought transference and related phenomena. *Proc. Roy. Institution of Great Britain.* 1950.

Tiedman, D. V. "Career Development of Women: Some Propositions." In O. D. David (ed.), *The Education of Women: Signs for the Future.* Washington, D.C.: American Council on Education, 1959.

Tindall, G. T. and E. C. Kunkle. Pain-spots densities in human skin. An experimental study. *A.M.A. Arch. Neurol. Psychiat.* 77:605–610. 1957.

Toch, H. *Legal and Criminal Psychology.* New York: Holt, Rinehart & Winston, 1961.

Torrance, E. P. Measurement and development of the creative thinking abilities. *Yearbook of Education: The Gifted Child.* London: Evans, pp. 125–142. 1962.

Tucker, W. T. and J. J. Painter. Personality and product use. *J. Appl. Psychol.* 45:325–329. 1961.

Tuckman, J. and I. Lorge. *Retirement and the Industrial Worker: Prospect and Reality.* New York: Teachers College, Columbia University, 1953.

Van Zelst, R. H. The effect of age and experience on accident rate. *J. App. Psychol.* 38:313–317. 1954.

Vernon, H. M. *Accidents and Their Prevention.* New York: Macmillan, 1937.

———, T. Bedford, and C. G. Warner. A study of absenteeism in certain Scottish collieries. *Indust. Health Res. Bd. Rep. 62.* London: Her Majesty's Stationery Office, 1931.

Voas, R. B., J. J. Van Bockel, R. G. Zedkar, and P. S. Backer. Results of in-flight pilot performance. *Results of the First U.S. Manned Suborbital Space Flight,* No. 9. U.S. National Aeronautics and Space Administration, National Institution of Health, and National Academy of Science, 1961.

Vogt, E. Z. and R. Hyman. *Water Witching U.S.A.* Chicago: University of Chicago, 1959.

Walter, W. G. *The Living Brain.* New York: Norton, 1953.

Wapner, S. and H. A. Witkin. The role of visual factors in the maintenance of body balance. *Amer. J. Psychol.* 63:385–408. 1950.

Warren, N. D. *Frontiers of Man-Controlled Flight.* "Nontransferable Functions." Los Angeles: Institute of Transportation and Traffic Engineering, University of California, 1953.

Watzlawick, P. *An Anthology of Human Communication.* Text and two-hour tape. Palo Alto, Calif.: Science and Behavior, 1964.

Webb, W. B. The *Profession of Psychology.* New York: Holt, Rinehart & Winston, 1962.

Weitz, J. Selecting supervisors with peer ratings. *Pers. Psychol.* 11:25–35. 1958.

White, R. W. *Lives in Progress.* New York: Dryden, 1952.

———, G. F. Fox, and W. W. Harris. Hypnotic hypermnesia for recently learned material. *J. Abnorm. Psychol.* 35:88–103. 1940.

Whiting, J. W. and I. L. Child. *Child Training and Personality: A Cross Cultural Study.* New Haven: Yale University, 1953.

Whitlock, J. B. and C. W. Crannell. An analysis of certain factors in serious accidents in a large steel plant. *J. Appl. Psychol.* 33:404–408. 1949.

Whitney, E. D. *The Lonely Sickness.* Boston: Beacon, 1965.

Whyte, W. H. *The Organization Man.* New York: Simon & Schuster, 1956.

Wilder, J. Facts and figures on psychotherapy. *J. Clin. Psychopath.* 7:311–347. 1945.

Wilder, R. M. "Experimental Induction of Psychoneuroses through Restriction of Intake of Thiamine," In *Biology of Mental Health and Diseases.* New York: Hoeber, 1952.

Williams, C. D. College student's family problems. *J. Home Econ.* 14:17–23. 1950.

Williams, R. J. *Biochemical Individuality.* New York: Wiley, 1956.

———. The effect of hypnosis on muscular fatigue. *J. Abnorm. Psychol.* 24:318–324. 1929.

———. A medical approach to the problem drinker. *Quart. J. Stud. Alcohol. 4.* 1949.

———. *J. Heredity.* 51:91–98. 1960.

Winch, R. F. *The Modern Family.* New York: Holt, 1952.

Witkin, H. A. Sex differences in perception. *Trans. N.Y. Acad. Sci.* 12:22–26, 1949.

Wolfgang, M. E. *Patterns in Criminal Homicide.* Philadelphia: University of Pennsylvania, 1958.

Wolpe, J. "An Approach to the Problem of Neurosis Based on the Conditioned Response." M.D. thesis, University of the Witwatersrand, Union of South Africa, 1948.

———. Isolation of a conditioning procedure as the crucial psychotherapeutic factor. *J. Nerv. Ment. Dis.* 134:316–329. 1962.

———. Quantitative relation in the systematic desensitization treatment of phobias. *Amer. J. Psychiat.* 119:1062–1068. 1963.

———. The prognosis in unpsychoanalyzed recovery from neurosis. *Amer. J. Psychiat.* 117:35–39. 1961.

————. *Psychotherapy by Reciprocal Inhibition.* Stanford: Stanford University, 1958.
————. The systematic desensitization treatment of neurosis. *J. Nerv. Ment. Dis.* 132:189–203. 1961.
Wood, W. F. A new method for reading the employment questionnaire. *J. Appl. Psychol.* 31:9–15. 1947.
Wood, A. L. A socio-structural analysis of murder, suicide, and economic crime in Ceylon. *Amer. Sociol. Rev.* 26:744–753. 1961.
Wright, B. *Psychology and Rehabilitation.* Washington, D.C.: American Psychological Association, 1959.
Young, P. T. Laughing and weeping, cheerfulness and depression: A study of moods among college students. *J. Soc. Psychol.* 8:311–334, 1937.
Zweig, S. *Romain Rolland.* Trans. E. and C. Paul. See p. 153. London: Allen & Unwin, 1921.

USE OF THE SELECTIONS

Too often, anthologies for introductory psychology have been collections of readings that are highly meaningful mainly for the instructor. Such readings are intended to be routinely assigned to the student for later testing by objective examination, and the student reads to pass the examination rather than *to react and think through the ideas presented*. This book is designed to offset the routine aspects and to attain the goal concerned with reacting to ideas.

The instructor may want to use the material as a stimulus to develop his own approach. He may want to add to the "Implications" given after each article. He may perceive other implications in terms of a critique of methodology or theory.

This common reading core will enable students to compare their comprehension of and reactions to the selections by forming groups within the large lecture room. (For example, three or four students in the first row may form a group with three or four students immediately behind them, and so on throughout the room.) Twenty minutes or so of free or preguided discussion can produce valuable ideational interaction and possibly some pertinent insights. One student may act as a recorder for each group, and the remainder of the hour can be used to raise the puzzling questions discussed by the group or to report significant reactions.

Some articles can be used as a basis for a brief critical written reaction. The reports can be read by a grader or by a fellow student assigned by the instructor to evaluate his peers' critiques. Alternately, several articles, together with appended bibliographies, can be the basis of longer papers to be read by the instructor or a grader. The instructor might find it expedient to schedule either an oral (group) or a written report integrating several selections.

Greater meaningfulness to the ideas and concepts presented in the articles can be fostered by having the students divide into small peer groups to discuss class projects, such as those suggested in the "Implications" sections. (For example, see Selection 18 on human relations, Selection 25 on conferences, Selection 35 on alternatives to war, Selection 39 on communication, and Selection 59 on family therapy.)

The following list contains the topics usually covered in an introductory course, with the corresponding number and title of each selection in this book. This list will enable the instructors to assign readings relevant to text material.

558

INTRODUCTION

MATURATION AND DEVELOPMENT

DRIVES AND MOTIVATION

FEELING AND EMOTION

FRUSTRATION AND CONFLICT

MENTAL HEALTH AND PSYCHOTHERAPY

HUMAN LEARNING AND FORGETTING

LANGUAGE AND THINKING

INDEX OF
CONCEPTS